SOC 2016

FOURTH EDITION

Jon Witt
Central College

McGraw Hill Education

WITT: SOC 2016, FOURTH EDITION

Published by McGraw-Hill Education, 2 Penn Plaza, New York, NY 10121. Copyright © 2016 by McGraw-Hill Education. All rights reserved. Printed in the United States of America. Previous editions © 2015, 2013, and 2011. No part of this publication may be reproduced or distributed in any form or by any means, or stored in a database or retrieval system, without the prior written consent of McGraw-Hill Education, including, but not limited to, in any network or other electronic storage or transmission, or broadcast for distance learning.

Some ancillaries, including electronic and print components, may not be available to customers outside the United States.

This book is printed on acid-free paper.

3 4 5 6 7 8 9 0   RMN   21 20 19 18 17 16

ISBN 978-0-07-813075-5
MHID 0-07-813075-1

Senior Vice President, Products & Markets: *Kurt L.Strand*
Vice President, General Manager, Products & Markets: *Michael Ryan*
Vice President, Content Design & Delivery: *Kimberly Meriwether David*
Managing Director: *Gina Boedeker*
Author: *Jon Witt*
Field Correspondent: *Richard T. Schaefer*
Brand Manager: *Courtney Austermehle*
Director, Product Development: *Meghan Campbell*
Lead Product Developer: *Rhona Robbin*
Product Developer: *Sara Gordus*
Marketing Manager: *Kimberli Brownlee*
Product Coordinator: *Diane Grayson*
Director, Content Design & Delivery: *Terri Schiesl*
Program Manager: *Marianne Musni*
Content Project Managers: *Susan Trentacosti, Katie Klochan, Karen Jozefowicz*
Buyer: *Laura M. Fuller*
Design: *Matt Backhaus*
Content Licensing Specialists: *Shawntel Schmitt, Ann Marie Jannette*
Cover Image: *© Paul Bradbury/GettyImages*
Compositor: *SPi Global*
Typeface: *10/12 Stix MathJax*
Printer: *R. R. Donnelley*

All credits appearing on page or at the end of the book are considered to be an extension of the copyright page.
Photo Credits: *Popcorn box: © D. Hurst/Alamy RF; Earth: © BLOOMimage/Getty Images RF; Hands: © Jeff DeWeerd/Imagezoo/ Getty Images RF*

ISSN: 2164-0696

The Internet addresses listed in the text were accurate at the time of publication. The inclusion of a website does not indicate an endorsement by the authors or McGraw-Hill Education, and McGraw-Hill Education does not guarantee the accuracy of the information presented at these sites.

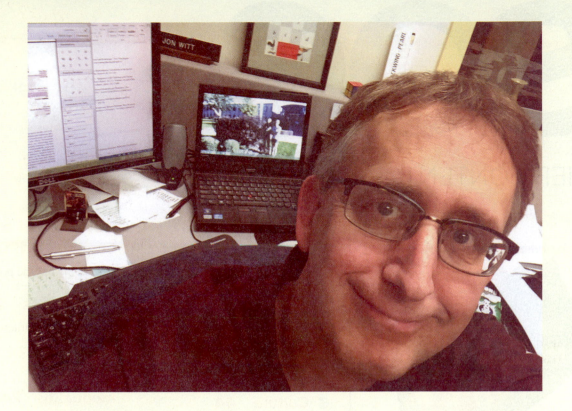

Name: Jon Witt (though my mom calls me Jonathan)

Education: I got my BA from Trinity College in Deerfield, IL, and earned my PhD from Loyola University in Chicago.

Occupations: Sociologist, father, and dog-walker

Hobbies: I like reading, writing, and messing around on computers—and I'm addicted to my iPhone and iPad.

Childhood ambition: To be a printer like my dad until I decided to become a teacher like my mom.

Family: Lori and I have been married for 31 years, and we have two daughters, Emily, 21, and Eleanor, 19.

Last book read: Oryx and Crake by Margaret Atwood.

Favorite film: My most recent favorite is Departures—a Japanese film about a young undertaker.

Favorite soundtrack: Complicated Game by James McMurtry

Latest accomplishment: This book!

Quote: There may be fields of sociological science quite beyond the average mind, and rightly left to the learned specialist; but that is no reason why we should not learn enough of the nature and habits of society to insure a more profitable and pleasant life.
—Charlotte Perkins Gilman, Human Work, 1904

My blog: www.soc101.com or follow SOC on Twitter @soc101

SOC

2016 Edition

BRIEF CONTENTS

© Duncan Walker/Getty Images RF

© Oliver Lantzendorffer/Getty Images RF

WHAT'S NEW IN SOC

> A new opening vignette in Chapter 2 covers Alice Goffman's participant observation research on young, African American males and their community in Philadelphia. Another new vignette in Chapter 4 explores Duncan Watts's experiment on song popularity and the significance of social influence. In Chapter 8, a new vignette compares facilities, programs, and experiences between different high schools. Finally, in Chapter 13, a new vignette addresses cases of police killings of African American males including Michael Brown in Ferguson, Missouri.

> New topics such as the significance of place, the process of language acquisition by babies, multigenerational families, economic sectors, the glass ceiling, and Jamestown and the early treatment of both Native Americans and African Americans are woven into the chapter narratives.

> New Did You Know? features on consumer spending by quintile, an exploratory experiment investigating whether a professor's presumed gender influenced student evaluation scores, and the length of time since a below-average month for global temperature.

> New PopSOC feature contrasting gender representation of occupations in films compared to actual gender representation in the U.S. workforce.

> New graphs showing peer group perception versus practice differences when it comes to alcohol, marijuana, sexual intercourse, and studying; rising labor force participation rates among older adults showing past growth and projections into the future; changes in attitudes regarding same-sex marriage by age; the relationship between religious faith and economic well-being; political party identification in the United States over time; the recorded history of average global temperature per year; U.S. environmental attitudes about global warming over time; and CO_2 emissions per capita for select nations.

> Statistics and data have been updated throughout the book to reflect 2015 research.

> New and revised definitions for key terms to reflect current scholarship.

Left photo: © Kim Kim Foster/The State/MCT/Getty Images

Right photo: © Paul Miles/Axiom Photographic Agency/Getty Images

Reviewers

© Digital Vision/Getty Images RF

Table of Contents

© PhotoDisc/Getty Images RF

© Elmer Martinez/AFP/Getty Images

© Jeff Greenberg/Alamy

© Photodisc/PunchStock RF

© 2009 Jupiterimages RF

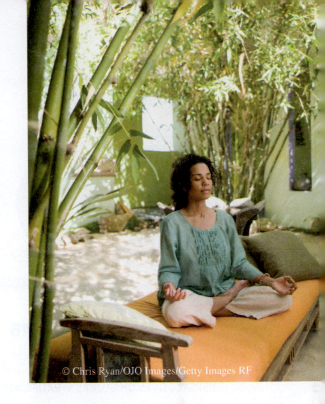

© Chris Ryan/OJO Images/Getty Images RF

© Goodshoot/Alamy RF

© Pavel Filatov/Alamy RF

© Michael Steele/Getty Images

© Gavriel Jecan/The Image Bank/Getty Images

© Blend Images/Getty Images RF

© Bill Kearney

The Sociological Imagination

WHAT'S TO COME

SELF AND SOCIETY

As children, our imaginations often run wild. When someone asks, "What do you want to be when you grow up?," almost anything seems possible—superhero, author, jet pilot, ballet dancer, movie star, secret agent, Olympic athlete, or maybe even president. As we get older, reality hits, and we usually end up narrowing our choices to something a bit more realistic. But not always.

When Sheryl Sandberg was young, her mom encouraged her to work hard so that she could be whatever she wanted to be. She took her mom's advice, and it paid off. She earned an economics degree at Harvard, served as chief of staff at the U.S. Department of the Treasury, and worked as the vice president of global online sales and operations at Google. Now Sandberg is second in command at Facebook, a position she accepted when she was 38 years old. Hers is a classic tale of the American dream.

Yet when she reached the top, she found that very few women had successfully made the journey with her. It didn't start out that way. In college and in her entry-level jobs, Sandberg's peers included equal numbers of men and women. As she climbed each rung of the career ladder, men increasingly outnumbered women. One of the most staggering examples of inequity is the disparity at the very top, among corporate leaders. In fact, only 4 percent of CEOs at Fortune 500 firms are women. In her book, *Lean In: Women, Work, and the Will to Lead,* Sandberg (2013) explores this seemingly systematic reduction in the number of women in positions of power.

With research assistance from sociologist Marianne Cooper, Sandberg cites numerous studies to highlight two key factors that have hindered women's performance in the workplace. First, women experience consistent patterns of discrimination. Studies repeatedly confirm that women's contributions are not recognized or rewarded according to the same standards as are men's. Second, Sandberg claims that women create and accept internal barriers to their success. She writes, "We hold ourselves back in ways both big and small, by lacking self-confidence,

by not raising our hands, and by pulling back when we should be leaning in" (p. 8). Whether the barriers are external or internal, being a woman makes success in business and politics more challenging.

As children, anything may seem possible. But the truth is that the choices we make are shaped by the positions we occupy in society. As we will see in this chapter and throughout this book, sociology enables us to better understand how this works and what we can do about it.

As You READ >>

- What is sociology?
- How do sociologists look at the world?
- How might someone practice sociology?

>> What Is Sociology?

We need one another. We may like to think that we can make it on our own, but our individualism is made possible by our interdependence. We praise the Olympic gold medalist for her impressive skill, dedicated training, and single-minded determination. Yet, if it hadn't been for her mom driving her to the pool every day, for the building manager waking up at 4:00 a.m. to make sure the pool is open, for the women working overnight to make sure the locker room is clean and safe, and so many others who fade into the background in such moments of glory, she would never have had that chance to shine.

The people upon whom we depend are often unknown and invisible to us. Even though we may never meet them, we rely on farmers, truck drivers, secretaries, store clerks, custodians, software engineers, scientists, assembly-line workers, teachers, police officers, inventors, politicians, CEOs, and a whole host of others. Yet we mostly take their contributions for granted without fully appreciating the degree to which they make our lives possible. Sociologists seek to reveal the full extent of our interdependence. **Sociology** is defined as the systematic study of the relationship between the individual and society and of the consequences of difference. We will examine the various components of that definition in detail below, but at its heart is the intimate connection between self and society.

sociology The systematic study of the relationship between the individual and society and of the consequences of difference.

THE SOCIOLOGICAL IMAGINATION

At its core, sociology is about understanding the dynamic relationship between individuals who make choices and the social contexts that shape those choices. American sociologist C. Wright Mills ([1959] 2009) defined the

12 Years a Slave
An 1840s African American man is kidnapped and sold into slavery.

Children of Men
A dystopian vision of society where humans can no longer reproduce.

The Hunger Games
May the odds be ever in your favor.

Philomena
A mother's search for the child she gave up for adoption.

The Pursuit of Happyness
An unemployed father who becomes homeless seeks to do right by his son.

5 Movies on THE SOCIOLOGICAL IMAGINATION

sociological imagination as our recognition of the interdependent relationship between who we are as individuals and the social forces that shape our lives. For example, if we choose to go to college, what factors might influence that decision? What role might age, family background, income, gender, race, ethnicity, or other social factors play in whether we go or what school we choose? Mills argued that we can use the sociological imagination as a tool to make more informed decisions about where we want to go and how we might get there. The sociological imagination, according to Mills, enables us to better understand the intersection between history and biography. When explaining why people think and act the way they do, our tendency is to turn toward individualistic explanations: he or she is wise or foolish, generous or selfish, careful or careless, and so on.

The sociological imagination calls us to also consider the role larger social forces may play. Take unemployment as an example. A person might lose his job for a variety of reasons. A worker who is foolish, selfish, and careless may get fired because he makes a lousy employee. But it's also possible for a worker to lose his job due to factors beyond his control, regardless of how effective he may be as a worker. Unemployment levels rise and fall depending on what is happening in the larger economy. For example, when the economy nosedived in the late 2000s, unemployment rose from 4.8 percent in February 2008 to a peak of 10.1 percent in October 2010. Many wise, generous, and careful workers lost their jobs in the process. Sociology helps us consider the big picture.

To assist us in understanding the role social forces can play, Mills distinguished between private troubles and public issues. **Private troubles** are problems we face in our immediate relationships with particular individuals in our personal lives. Explanations for such troubles are particular to the individuals involved. For example, you lose your job because you failed to show up for work, disobeyed direct orders from your boss, took money from the cash register, and so forth. **Public issues** are problems we face as a consequence of the positions we occupy within the larger social structure. Private troubles are personal problems, but public issues are social problems. If lots of people in similar positions are experiencing the same result, it likely says more about the position than the person. We can better see such patterns by analyzing rates—unemployment, divorce, poverty—which is one of the reasons using statistics is so important in sociology. Analyzing data allows us to see patterns we might otherwise miss.

THE SIGNIFICANCE OF PLACE

To put it simply, place matters. Our position relative to others shapes our access to resources and influences the options available to us. As individuals, we do have the power to make our own choices, but we cannot separate our individual preferences from the influence of parents, teachers, friends, coworkers, politicians, the media, and even total strangers whose decisions enable or constrain opportunities for us. Where and when we were born; our parents' educational attainment, occupation, and income; our nationality; and other such factors all play major roles in shaping who we become.

Social class, gender, and race are positional categories of particular interest to sociologists due to the significance each has in our lives. Our social class position, for example, shapes our access to material resources. Researchers asked people how much they thought a chief executive officer (CEO) and an unskilled factory worker *should* earn and how much they thought they *actually* earned and then compared these numbers. In the United States, respondents said CEOs should earn about 7 times more than an unskilled worker, but they guessed that the real gap was 30 to 1. It turns out that the average yearly compensation for a CEO at a Standard & Poor's (S&P) 500 company was $12 million, approximately 354 times the $35,000 an average worker receives (Kiatpongsan and Norton 2014). This suggests that social class differences, such as that between a CEO and an unskilled worker, are even greater than we think.

Turning to gender, sociologists find a persistent wage gap between men and women. For example, when hackers attacked Sony Pictures and posted thousands of company documents and emails, it turned out that both Jennifer Lawrence (who had already won an Academy Award for her role in *Silver Linings Playbook* and had just starred in the blockbuster film *The Hunger Games: Catching Fire*)

> **sociological imagination** Our recognition of the interdependent relationship between who we are as individuals and the social forces that shape our lives.
>
> **private troubles** Problems we face in our immediate relationships with particular individuals in our personal lives.
>
> **public issues** Problems we face as a consequence of the positions we occupy within the larger social structure.

© Lionsgate/courtesy Everett Collection

and Amy Adams (who had previously been nominated for four Academy Awards) were being paid significantly less for their roles in *American Hustle* than their three male counterparts Christian Bale, Jeremy Renner, and Bradley Cooper, whose record of accomplishment was not as great (Kohn 2014). This pattern of unequal pay mirrors the overall wage gap in the United States. When comparing average earnings for full-time, year-round workers, women earn 78¢ for every $1 men earn (DeNavas-Walt and Proctor 2014:6). Race and ethnicity also shape likely outcomes. Being born into a White family in the United States significantly increases your odds of having access to money. In a study on the distribution of wealth, researchers found that median wealth for White households was 13 times greater than that for African American households and 10 times greater than Hispanic households (Kochhar and Fry 2014).

Place is important because it shapes how we think, act, and even feel. For example, when computer giant Hewlett-Packard was trying to figure out ways to get more women into upper-level management positions, it found that women applied for promotion only when they thought they met 100 percent of the qualifications for the position while men applied when they believed they met 60 percent (Kay and Shipman 2014). In a 2014 national survey, when asked how they would rate Barack Obama's presidency, 81 percent of African Americans and 61 percent of Hispanics said he was a success, compared to 29 percent of Whites (*The Washington Post* 2014). When it comes to analyzing such patterns our tendency is to take sides, but the interesting sociological question is why such significant differences form in the first place.

THE IRONY OF MODERN SOCIETY

Because the positions we occupy relative to each other are so important, understanding the relationships between them is a central task for sociologists. In our everyday lives, we take for granted the structure that these relationships provide for us. We tend not to realize how dependent we are on others. But suppose you had to do something as seemingly simple as making a hamburger and had to do so without relying on any knowledge, skills, tools, or resources obtained from anyone else. Without an interdependent network of people performing myriad small tasks that we take for granted, we would be hard-pressed to provide for our most basic needs. A hamburger can serve as a symbol of our society's shared knowledge and skills.

How hard can it be to make a hamburger from scratch? Considering the ingredients, which seem fairly simple, there are any number of ways to proceed. Let's begin with the burger itself. First, you need to find a cow. How difficult can that be? Well, you can't buy one from a farmer because doing so means relying on resources from others. You can't go out to the country (getting there itself might

present something of a challenge) and steal one from a farm (which implies a farmer, which means dependence on another person). So you need to find a wild cow.

Assuming you do find a wild cow, you then have to kill it. Perhaps you might bash it with a large rock or stampede it off a cliff. Next, you need to butcher it, but cowhide is tough. Imagine what it takes to produce a metal knife (finding ore, smelting, forging, tempering, and so on). Perhaps a sharp rock will do. Assuming you came up with a cutting tool, you now have a chunk of raw cow meat. Given that it's hamburger we're after (though you might be ready to settle for steak at this point), next you need to grind the meat. You might use a couple of those rocks to pulverize the meat into something of a meat mash, although a meat grinder would work better if only it weren't so hard to make one. In any event, at last you have a raw hamburger patty.

Now you need to cook it. Where will you get the fire? Perhaps you could strike two rocks together in hopes of creating a spark, or maybe rub two sticks together. Perhaps it would be easiest to wait around for lightning to strike a nearby tree. However you might accomplish it, after you get fire, you still have to cook the meat. No frying pans are available, so either you make one or perhaps cook it on that handy rock you used to kill the cow. Or you could

© PhotoDisc/Getty RF

just put the meat on a stick that you cut down and whittled with the knife you made (or was that a "sharp" stone?) and roast it over the fire.

Assuming you are successful, you now have a cooked hamburger patty. But, of course, you aren't done yet. There are still many other steps that need to be completed. You need to bake a bun, which involves figuring out how to come up with flour, water, salt, oil, sugar, yeast, and an oven. What about condiments such as ketchup, mustard, pickles, and onions? What if at the end of all that you decide to make it a cheeseburger? Did you remember to milk the cow first?

Making something that seems so simple, that we take for granted, that we can get for a dollar at McDonald's, turns out to be quite complicated. The knowledge and skill to acquire and prepare all the ingredients in a hamburger are beyond the capacity of most individuals. Yet if we eat a burger, we think nothing of it. When you think about it—when you apply the sociological imagination—a hamburger is a miracle. It's miraculous, not in a supernatural sense but as a symbol pointing to the astonishing complexity and taken-for-grantedness of our human interdependence and to the knowledge we share collectively without even realizing it. Of course, this is true not just for hamburgers but for virtually any product we use. It could be a veggieburger, a book, a desk, a shirt, a car, a house, or a computer. The irony of modern society is that we depend on one another now more than ever, but we realize it less. We embrace individualism, yet we lack the basic skills for self-sufficiency. Sociology provides us with the tools necessary to more fully understand and appreciate our interdependence.

DEFINING SOCIOLOGY

Sociologists are committed to investigating, describing, and explaining such interrelationships. A more detailed breakdown of the four components of the definition of sociology helps reveal how they go about doing so.

Systematic Study Sociologists are engaged with the world, collecting empirical data through systematic research. Relying on such data means that sociologists draw their conclusions about society based on experiences or observations rather than beliefs or the authority of others. If they want to understand why the average age for first marriage keeps rising or why people commit crimes, they must gather data from those involved in these activities and base their conclusions upon that information.

Sociological research historically has involved both quantitative and qualitative approaches to data collection.

> The function of sociology, as of every science, is to reveal that which is hidden.
>
> ———
>
> Pierre Bourdieu

Quantitative approaches emphasize counting things and analyzing them mathematically or statistically in order to uncover relationships between variables. The most common way to collect this type of data is through surveys. In contrast, qualitative approaches focus on listening to and observing people and allowing them to interpret what is happening in their own lives. The most common way to collect this type of data is through participant observation, in which the researcher interacts with those she or he studies. In practice, sociologists often draw on both techniques in conducting their research. We will investigate these research techniques, along with others, in more detail in Chapter 2.

The Individual Although sociology is most commonly associated with the study of groups, there is no such thing as a group apart from the individuals who compose it. As individuals we are constantly choosing what to do next. Most of the time, we follow guidelines for behavior we have learned from others, but we have the ability to reject those guidelines at any time. A term sociologists use to describe this capacity is **agency,** meaning the freedom individuals have to choose and to act. In professional sports, for example, we use the term *free agent* to describe a player who has the power to negotiate with whatever team he or she wishes. We, too, have such freedom. We could choose not to go to class, not to go to work, not to get out of bed in the morning, not to obey traffic signals, not to respond when spoken to, not to read the next sentence in this book, and on and on.

> **agency** The freedom individuals have to choose and to act.

As we saw with the significance of place, the positions we occupy relative to others shape the choices we make. In the NBA, LeBron James chose to go from the Miami Heat to the Cleveland Cavaliers. Signing with the NFL's Green Bay Packers or Major League Baseball's Chicago Cubs was not really an option. Having access to varieties of resources, we choose among an array of options with knowledge of various possible outcomes. We usually follow "paths of least resistance"—the accepted and expected actions and beliefs—but the choice of whether to continue to follow them is ours each and every second of our lives (A. Johnson 1997).

Society The study of society is at the heart of sociology. Although we will spend most of this book describing various aspects of society, we can begin by thinking of it as our social environment. Society consists of persistent patterns of relationships and social networks within which we operate. The social structure it provides is analogous

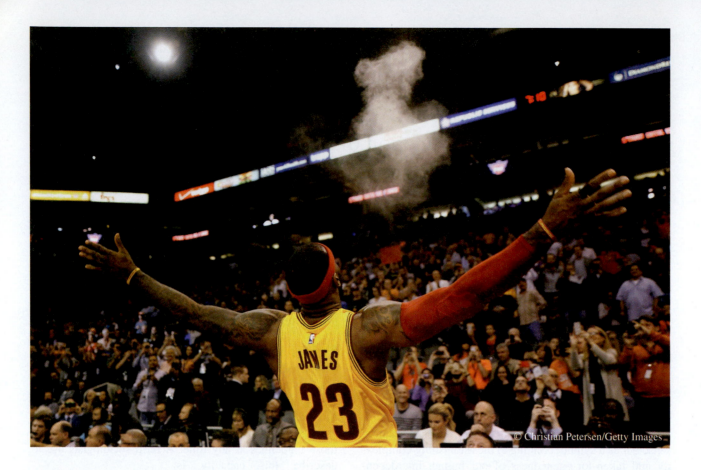

© Christian Petersen/Getty Images

to a building: The layout of a building both encourages and discourages different activities in different rooms (such as kitchens, bedrooms, and bathrooms), and many of the most essential operations of a building (such as heating and air conditioning) are mostly invisible to us. In the same way, the structure of our *institutions*—a term sociologists use to describe some of the major components of social structure, including economy, family, education, government, and religion—shapes what is expected of us. For example, the choices that are available to us in the context of the modern family, such as to go off and pursue our own education and career, are much different from the obligations we would face in more traditional family contexts. Nested within institutions are the groups, subgroups, and statuses that we occupy. We will look at the details of these institutions in coming chapters, but it is helpful to remember that, in order to provide clear pathways for action, we construct culture and create structure.

social inequality A condition in which members of society have differing amounts of wealth, prestige, or power.

The Consequences of Difference The final part of the definition of sociology involves the consequences of difference. Sociology does more than just describe our structure, culture, and interaction; it also looks at how economic, social, and cultural resources are distributed and at the implications of these patterns in terms of the opportunities and obstacles they create for individuals and groups.

Since the founding of sociology, sociologists have been concerned with the impact our social location has on our opportunities or lack thereof. As noted earlier, differential outcomes that result from class, gender, and race have been of particular interest to sociologists.

The analysis of social power deserves particular attention because it shapes how and why we think and act as we do. The simple fact is that those who have access to and control over valued material, social, and cultural resources have different options available to them than do those without such access and control. One of the main tasks of sociology is to investigate and reveal levels of **social inequality**—a condition in which members of society have differing amounts of wealth, prestige, or power. That is why the definition of sociology draws particular attention to the consequences of difference.

In combination, these four aspects of sociology help us understand the things that influence our beliefs and actions. Coming to terms with the reality that our choices are constrained by the positions we occupy can seem depressing, but sociology actually empowers us by providing a more complete picture of the worlds within which we live. French sociologist Pierre Bourdieu (1998a) put it this way: "Sociology teaches how groups function and how to make use of the laws governing the way they function so as to try to circumvent them" (p. 57). In other words, understanding the ways in which our thoughts and actions are determined enhances our freedom to make more effective and informed choices.

U.S. Employment Trends

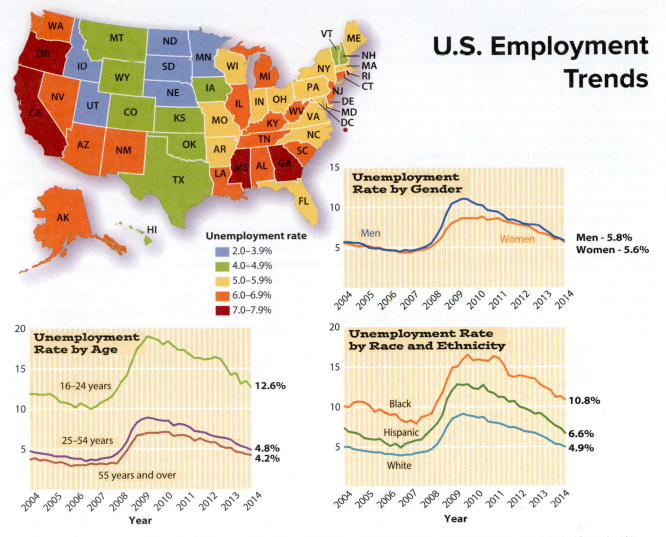

Unemployment rate
- 2.0–3.9%
- 4.0–4.9%
- 5.0–5.9%
- 6.0–6.9%
- 7.0–7.9%

Unemployment Rate by Gender

Men
Women

Men - 5.8%
Women - 5.6%

Unemployment Rate by Age

16–24 years   12.6%
25–54 years   4.8%
55 years and over   4.2%

Year

Unemployment Rate by Race and Ethnicity

Black   10.8%
Hispanic   6.6%
White   4.9%

Year

Note: The unemployment rate includes people 16 years and older who are available for work but do not have a job and who have actively looked for work within the previous four weeks.

Sources: Bureau of Labor Statistics 2015a and 2015b.

SOCIOLOGY AND THE SOCIAL SCIENCES

Is sociology a science? The term **science** refers to the body of knowledge obtained by methods based on systematic observation. Just like other scientific disciplines, sociology involves the organized, systematic study of phenomena (in this case, human behavior) in order to enhance understanding. All scientists, whether studying mushrooms or murderers, attempt to collect precise information through methods of study that are as objective as possible. They rely on the careful recording of observations and the accumulation of data.

Of course, there is a great difference between sociology and physics, and between psychology and astronomy. For this reason, the sciences are commonly divided into natural and social sciences. **Natural science** is the study of the physical features of nature and the ways in which they interact and change. Astronomy, biology, chemistry, geology, and physics are all natural sciences. **Social science** is the study of the social features of humans and the ways in which they interact and change. The social sciences include sociology, anthropology, economics, history, psychology, and political science.

These social science disciplines have a common focus on the social behavior of people, yet each has a particular orientation. Anthropologists usually study past cultures and preindustrial societies that continue today, as well as the origins of humans. Economists explore the ways in which people produce and exchange goods and services. Historians are concerned with the peoples and events of the past and their significance for us today. Psychologists investigate personality and individual behavior. Political scientists study international relations, the workings of government, and the exercise of power and authority. Sociologists, as we have already seen, study the influence that society

science The body of knowledge obtained by methods based on systematic observation.

natural science The study of the physical features of nature and the ways in which they interact and change.

social science The study of the social features of humans and the ways in which they interact and change.

has on people's attitudes and behavior and the ways in which people interact and shape society.

Let's consider how different social sciences might approach the global economic crisis that began in late 2008. Historians would compare recent events to those that occurred in previous crises, such as the Great Depression of the 1930s. Economists would conduct research on the financial impact of the current crisis for individuals, nations, and the world as a whole. Psychologists would study the behavior and reactions of individuals to assess the emotional trauma such crises cause. And political scientists would analyze the stances taken by political leaders and their governments' responses to the crisis.

What approach would sociologists take? Following Mills's lead, they would analyze the economic downturn as a public issue. This necessitates gathering data about how this crisis affected people differently depending upon the social positions they occupied. As the "U.S. Employment Trends" map and graphs demonstrate, a person's geographic location, age, gender, race, and ethnicity all influenced his or her likelihood of experiencing unemployment. Unemployment was more likely in the Southeast and West than in the Midwest. The level for young people was, and continues to be, substantially higher than for those who are older. Men experienced a more significant jump in joblessness than did women. Rates for African Americans and Latinos were, and are, significantly higher than those for Whites. Sociology teaches us that our social location matters. Understanding how different groups are affected helps policy makers decide which actions to take to address the crisis. A singular or universal solution to such a problem is unlikely to be effective in addressing the different needs of the various groups.

theory In sociology a set of statements that seeks to explain problems, actions, or behavior.

Sociologists would take a similar approach when studying episodes of extreme violence. On April 15, 2013, two bombs exploded near the finish line of the Boston Marathon. More than 170 people were injured, and three people were killed, including eight-year-old Martin Richard. Whenever such events occur, our first question is often "why?" And our initial answer is usually that the perpetrator must have been crazy or brainwashed. Sociologists seek to explain these events by analyzing the underlying factors that give rise to such extreme actions.

They explore issues such as the role the media plays in reporting breaking news events, the impact religion has on shaping actions, the politics of immigration or gun control, the consequences of masculinity, and the adequacy of the nation's mental health care system (Force 2011; Glassner 2010; Sharp 2011).

SOCIOLOGY AND COMMON SENSE

At times all of us practice some form of the sociological imagination, weighing the balance between individual and society. So what's the difference between sociology and common sense—the knowledge we get from our experiences and conversations, from what we read, from what we see on television, and so forth? Commonsense knowledge, although sometimes accurate, is not always reliable because it rests on commonly held beliefs rather than on systematic analysis of facts (Watts 2011).

Contrary to the common notion that women tend to be chatty compared to men, for instance, researchers have found little difference between the sexes in terms of their talkativeness. Over a five-year period, they placed unobtrusive microphones on 396 college students in various settings, on campuses in Mexico as well as the United States. They found that both men and women spoke about 16,000 words per day (Mehl et al. 2007).

Similarly, "common sense" tells us that in the United States today, military marriages are more likely to end in separation or divorce than in the past owing to the strain of long deployments in Iraq and Afghanistan. Yet a study released in 2007 shows no significant increase in the divorce rate among U.S. soldiers over the past decade. In fact, the rate of marital dissolution among members of the military is comparable to that of nonmilitary families. Interestingly, this is not the first study to disprove the widely held notion that military service strains the marital bond. Two generations earlier, during the Vietnam War era, researchers came to the same conclusion (Call and Teachman 1991; Karney and Crown 2007).

Like other social scientists, sociologists do not accept something as fact just because "everyone knows it." At times, the findings of sociologists may seem like common sense because they deal with familiar facets of everyday life. The difference is that such findings have been tested by researchers, analyzed in relation to other data, and evaluated in light of what is known by sociologists in the form of sociological theory.

>> What Is Sociological Theory?

Sociology, like all sciences, involves a conversation between theory and research. We gather data through systematic research, and we seek to describe and explain what we find using theories. A **theory** is a set of statements that seeks to explain problems, actions, or behavior.

Theories represent our attempts to make the best possible sense of the world around us. They often start out general and vague, but over time and informed by research, theories provide richer, more complete interpretations of the worlds in which we live. We will look first at theory before turning to methods in Chapter 2.

FORMULATING SOCIOLOGICAL THEORIES

We can better understand how theories develop in sociology by following the logic French sociologist Émile Durkheim employed more than a century ago when sociology was just emerging as a social science. At the time, there were no sociology departments in universities and no academic positions for sociologists. Durkheim wanted to establish sociology's legitimacy as a distinct discipline. His theory was that social forces shape individual action, contradicting the dominant theories that biology, the individual's psyche, or God were the primary causes for our behaviors. In an attempt to create space for sociology as a discipline, he argued that factors above the level of the individual but within the domain of human society shape our actions.

Durkheim set out to prove that social facts exist and affect what we do. He described social facts as consisting of "manners of acting, thinking, and feeling external to the individual, which are invested with a coercive power by virtue of which they exercise control over him" ([1895] 1982:52). In other words, our choices are both enabled and constrained by social facts. But a social fact is kind of like gravity. We can't really see it or measure it directly, but we can observe its effects. Proving the power of social facts depends on demonstrating the impact they have on the choices we make.

To make the strongest case possible, Durkheim chose to study what he saw as the ultimate individual choice: suicide.

© Franky De Meyer/Getty Images RF

He theorized that people commit suicide because they lack the social connections and obligations to prevent them from taking their own life. His hypothesis was as follows: "Suicide varies inversely with the degree of integration of the social groups of which the individual forms a part" ([1897] 1951:209). Durkheim chose religious affiliation as an indicator of social integration, arguing that Protestants are less socially integrated than Roman Catholics. He claimed that Catholicism is a traditional faith with a hierarchical system of authority in which variation in belief (on such topics as birth control, abortion, and women priests) is not up to the individual. Protestantism, in contrast, gives individual believers more power to interpret the Bible for themselves. As a result, when disagreement arises, Protestants feel freer to form new churches. Whereas there is only one Roman Catholic Church, Protestantism includes Baptist, Methodist, Reformed, Episcopalian, Presbyterian, and many other denominations. Protestants' increased individual autonomy reflects reduced levels of social integration, leading Durkheim to predict that Protestants would be more likely to commit suicide than Catholics.

TESTING SOCIOLOGICAL THEORIES

To test his theory, Durkheim gathered data from different countries to see if suicide rates varied. Looking at France, England, and Denmark, he found that England had 67 reported suicides per million inhabitants, France had 135 per million, and Denmark had 277 per million. Durkheim concluded that Denmark's comparatively high suicide rate was due to the fact that Denmark was a more Protestant nation than either France or England. In other words, it was the social makeup of these nations that shaped their suicide rates. More recent research focusing on individual rather than national rates continues to find this same relationship.

In extending his analysis to look at other indicators of social integration, Durkheim continued to obtain results that confirmed his underlying theory: the unmarried had much higher rates of suicide than married people; and people without children were more likely to take their lives than people with children. In addition, there were higher rates in times of economic instability and recession than in times of prosperity. Durkheim concluded that his theory was correct: the suicide rate of a society reflects the extent to which people are or are not integrated into the group life of the society. Durkheim presented his results in his landmark work *Suicide,* published in 1897.

APPLYING SOCIOLOGICAL THEORIES

Built into Durkheim's theory is the presupposition that we find meaning in life through our relationships with others. The more interconnected and interdependent we are, the less likely we are to kill ourselves. Attempting to summarize the significance of our attachment to society, Durkheim put it this way: "The individual alone is not a sufficient end for his activity. He is too little. . . . When, therefore, we

© Rafael Elias/Getty Images RF

Going GLOBAL

What Makes a Country Happy?

Looking on the bright side of life, happiness rates also vary from country to country. The five nations that score highest according to the World Happiness Report are Denmark, Norway, Switzerland, Netherlands, and Sweden. The bottom five are Rwanda, Burundi, Central African Republic, Benin, and Togo. The United States ranks 17th out of 156 nations (Helliwell, Layard, and Sachs 2013). The index considers indicators of both subjective well-being ("Were you happy yesterday?") and life satisfaction ("Are you happy with your life as a whole?").

have no other object than ourselves we cannot avoid the thought that our efforts will finally end in nothingness. . . . Under these conditions one would lose the courage to live, that is, to act and struggle" ([1897] 1951:210). Human beings are, at their very foundation, social beings. According to Durkheim, we cannot consider what it means to be an individual apart from our position in society. This social dimension of individual behavior is what Durkheim wants sociology to explore, elaborate, and explain.

Durkheim's work on suicide provides a classic case of sociological theory at work. He theorized that social facts

shape individual actions. He tested this theory by investigating suicide as one such individual choice—perhaps the most individual of all choices—and demonstrated that the likelihood of committing suicide varied based on group membership. Analysis of more recent data shows that suicide rates continue to vary based on social position. Durkheim concluded that if social facts are at work in this most extreme example of individual choice, they similarly shape all other individual choices. He argued that if social facts have such power in our lives, there should be a discipline dedicated to their study. As a result, Durkheim established Europe's first department of sociology at the University of Bordeaux in 1895.

>> The Development of Sociology

Given the complexity of human life, sociologists have developed a wide range of theories in which they describe and explain the diversity of social behavior. Sometimes their theories can be grand in scope, seeking to encompass the "big picture"; other times they can be more personal, intimate, and immediate. Although we spend most of the rest of this book investigating the insights sociological theories provide, here we will briefly address just five questions sociologists have frequently asked. These questions represent significant doors sociologists have opened to provide additional tools for the sociological imagination. The questions are these: How is social order maintained? How do power and inequality shape outcomes?

Suicide Rates

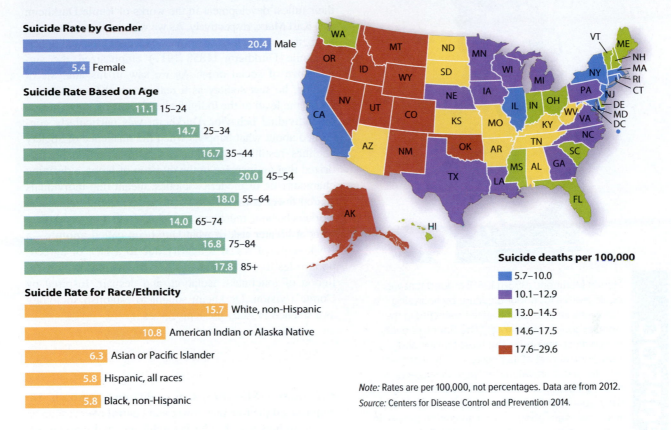

Suicide Rate by Gender

20.4	Male
5.4	Female

Suicide Rate Based on Age

11.1	15–24
14.7	25–34
16.7	35–44
20.0	45–54
18.0	55–64
14.0	65–74
16.8	75–84
17.8	85+

Suicide Rate for Race/Ethnicity

15.7	White, non-Hispanic
10.8	American Indian or Alaska Native
6.3	Asian or Pacific Islander
5.8	Hispanic, all races
5.8	Black, non-Hispanic

Suicide deaths per 100,000

- 5.7–10.0
- 10.1–12.9
- 13.0–14.5
- 14.6–17.5
- 17.6–29.6

Note: Rates are per 100,000, not percentages. Data are from 2012.
Source: Centers for Disease Control and Prevention 2014.

SOC THINK

If Durkheim is correct and the level of social integration influences the likelihood of suicide, why do rates vary for the groups listed in the "Suicide Rates" figure? Why is the rate for men almost four times higher than that for women? Why is the rate for non-Hispanic Whites higher than that for any other racial/ethnic groups? Why is there a midlife suicide peak? Why do rates vary by state and region? What might these patterns suggest about the social integration of people in these categories?

How does interaction shape our worlds? How does group membership (especially class, race, and gender) influence opportunity? How should sociologists respond?

HOW IS SOCIAL ORDER MAINTAINED?

The discipline of sociology grew up in the midst of significant social upheaval. The advent of the Industrial Revolution and urbanization in the early 19th century led to changes in patterns of government, thought, work,

and everyday life. Aristocracy was on the decline while democracy was spreading; people were moving from a primary reliance on religious explanations to more scientific ones; and the world of the village and farm was rapidly giving way to life in the city and factory. It was in this context that French sociologist and philosopher Auguste Comte (1798–1857), in hopes of emulating what natural scientists did for nature, sought to establish a science of society that would reveal the basic "laws of society." Comte believed that knowing these laws would help us understand two key principles that he referred to as "social statics"—the principles by which societies hold together and order is maintained—and "social dynamics"—the factors that bring about change and that shape the nature and direction of that change. Sociologists would then use their knowledge of these laws to help lead us toward the good society, balancing the needs for social order with positive social change. To give this new discipline a name, Comte coined the term *sociology*—which literally means "the study of the processes of companionship" (Abercrombie, Hill, and Turner 2006:367).

English-speaking scholars learned of Comte's works largely through translations by the English sociologist Harriet Martineau (1802–1876). Seeking to systematize the research essential to conducting a science of society, Martineau ([1838] 1989) wrote the first book on sociological methods. She was also a pathbreaking theorist in

Photo: © Kevin Mazur/WireImage/Getty Images

the theoretical and research paths sociologists have pursued since this beginning. In early sociological theory, they find their fullest development in the works of Émile Durkheim and Karl Marx, respectively. As we will see throughout this book, they continue to be primary concerns for sociologists.

Émile Durkheim (1858–1917) emphasized the significance of social order. As we saw in his analysis of suicide, he saw society as a real, external force existing above the level of the individual and exerting its influence on individual behavior. Durkheim was particularly concerned about what happens when the influence of society declines, resulting in weakened social integration. He theorized that an increase in the division of labor, a defining characteristic of modern societies, meant that individuals shared fewer common experiences, ideas, and values. As workers became much more specialized in their tasks, they were at greater risk of what Durkheim called **anomie**—a weak sense of social solidarity due to a lack of agreed-upon rules to guide behavior. Anomie increases the likelihood of loneliness, isolation, and despair. Inspired by Comte's vision, Durkheim sought to establish sociology as a science to study these processes.

HOW DO POWER AND INEQUALITY SHAPE OUTCOMES?

Karl Marx (1818–1883) took a different approach. He emphasized the role that power and control over resources played in how social order is established and maintained. Marx viewed our creative capacity to transform raw materials into products—for example, to take clay and make a pot, or cut down a tree and make a desk—as the key factor distinguishing humans from other animals (whose behavior is ruled by their instincts). For Marx, human history is the progressive unfolding of human creativity in the form of new technology through which we establish our relationship to the natural world and with each other. Unfortunately, for most of human history, we lacked sufficient technology to provide enough material goods (such as food, clothes, and shelter) to meet everyone's needs, so not all people had enough.

Social inequality for Marx, then, is determined by ownership, or lack thereof, of key material resources. The ruling class is defined by its ownership and control of the means of production—the tools and resources necessary for that transformation to happen. Members of the working class, in contrast, own only their capacity to transform raw materials into products, which requires access to the means of production controlled by the ruling class. Whereas Durkheim

anomie A weak sense of social solidarity due to a lack of agreed-upon rules to guide behavior.

her own right, introducing the significance of inequality and power into the discipline. Martineau's book *Society in America* ([1837] 1962) examined religion, politics, child rearing, and immigration in the young nation. It gave special attention to social class distinctions and to such factors as gender and race. In Martineau's ([1837] 1962) view, intellectuals and scholars should not simply offer observations of social conditions; they should act on their convictions in a manner that will benefit society. Martineau spoke out in favor of the rights of women, the emancipation of slaves, and religious tolerance.

These two themes—social order and social inequality—have shaped

Émile Durkheim Photo: Durkheim—© Bettmann/ Corbis; frame—© wrangel/iStock/Getty Images RF.

Karl Marx   Photo: Marx—© Library of Congress Prints and Photographs Division [LC-USZ62-16530]; frame—© Peter Zelei/E+/Getty Images RF.

was concerned with anomie, Marx was concerned with alienation, by which he meant loss of control over our creative human capacity to produce, separation from the products we make, and isolation from our fellow workers. We will consider Marx's work as it relates to capitalism as an economic system in more detail in a later chapter. His influence on sociological theory, however, extends beyond social class to an analysis of additional forms of inequality, such as how gender, race, ethnicity, nationality, and age influence individual opportunity.

Seeking to expand sociological theory further, Max Weber (1864–1920; pronounced "VAY-ber") offered a more general theory of power that was less wedded to capitalism and ownership of the means of production. Weber argued that, although social class and its associated control over material resources may determine who has power in most instances, these are not the only possible foundations for power. Other sources he identified include social status, in which people defer to others out of respect for their social position or prestige, and organizational resources, in which members of a group gain power through their ability to organize to accomplish some specific goal by maximizing their available resources. Weber argued that these social resources draw their power from people's willingness to obey the authority of another person, which in turn is based on their perception of the legitimacy of that person's right to rule.

Max Weber   Photo: Weber—© Hulton Archive/Getty Images; frame—© Visivasnc/Getty Images RF.

have a profound effect on us. Parents, siblings, friends, teachers, classmates, coworkers, and even total strangers influence how we talk, act, think, and feel. Through such interactions we learn what is appropriate and inappropriate, responding accordingly. To describe this process, sociologist W. I. Thomas established what has come to be known in sociology as the Thomas theorem: "If men define situations as real, they are real in their consequences" (Thomas and Thomas 1928:571–572). Or, more simply, how we see the world shapes what we do. We act on the basis of perception, and our perception is a consequence of the interactions we have had with others.

To better understand the processes at work, sociologist Erving Goffman recommended studying everyday interactions as if we are all actors on a stage seeking to successfully put on a performance. In his *dramaturgical approach* (see Chapter 4), we all play roles, follow scripts, use props, work together, and seek to win over our audiences. The parts of ourselves that we project vary based on the roles that we perform. As a student in a class, we may project a serious image; at a party, we may want to look relaxed and friendly. The immediate context of our everyday interactions shapes who we are, what we think, and how we act.

macrosociology Sociological investigation that concentrates on large-scale phenomena or entire civilizations.

microsociology Sociological investigation that stresses the study of small groups and the analysis of our everyday experiences and interactions.

HOW DOES INTERACTION SHAPE OUR WORLDS?

Much of the work of Durkheim, Marx, and Weber involves **macrosociology,** which concentrates on large-scale phenomena or entire civilizations. This top-down approach focuses on society as a whole and how broad social forces shape our lives. A later school of sociologists turned away from this approach in favor of **microsociology,** which stresses the study of small groups and the analysis of our everyday experiences and interactions. Our interactions with others

© Con Tanasiuk/Design Pics RF

HOW DOES GROUP MEMBERSHIP INFLUENCE OPPORTUNITY?

Over time, sociologists came to more fully understand and appreciate the consequences that group membership, especially class, race, and gender, has for opportunity. Black sociologist W. E. B. Du Bois (1868–1963; pronounced "dew BOYS") combined an emphasis on the analysis of the everyday lived experience with a commitment to investigating power and inequality based on race. He was critical of those who relied on common sense or on all-too-brief investigations, arguing that a researcher has to be more than just a "car-window sociologist" because true understanding demands more than "the few leisure hours of a holiday trip to unravel the snarl of centuries" (Du Bois [1903] 1994:94). Through engaged and sustained research on the lives of African Americans, Du Bois documented their relatively low status in Philadelphia and Atlanta. His research revealed the social processes that contributed to the maintenance of racial separation, which extended beyond material differences to include social separation, which he referred to as the "color line."

Similarly, feminist scholarship has broadened our understanding of social behavior by extending the analysis beyond the male point of view that dominated classic sociology. An early example of this perspective can be seen in the life and writings of Ida Wells-Barnett (1862–1931). Carrying on a tradition begun with Martineau, Wells-Barnett argued that societies can be judged based on whether the principles they claim to believe in match their actions. Wells-Barnett found that when it came to the principles of equality and opportunity for women and African Americans, America came up short. Part of the task for the sociologist, then, is to bring to light such inconsistencies that may otherwise go largely unnoticed. This is something Wells-Barnett sought to do in her groundbreaking publications in the 1890s on the practice of lynching African Americans, as well as with her advocacy of women's rights, especially the struggle to win the vote for women. Like feminist theorists who succeeded her, Wells-Barnett used her analysis of society as a means of resisting oppression. In her case, she researched what it meant to be African American, a woman in the United States, and a Black woman in the United States (Wells-Barnett [1928] 1970).

HOW SHOULD SOCIOLOGISTS RESPOND?

Throughout sociology's history, a recurring theme has been the idea that sociological theory and research should contribute to positive social change. In the early 1900s many leading sociologists in the United States saw themselves as social reformers dedicated to systematically studying and then improving a corrupt society. They were genuinely concerned about the lives of immigrants in the nation's growing cities, whether those immigrants came from Europe or from the rural American South. Early female sociologists, in particular, often took active roles in poor urban areas as leaders of community centers known as settlement houses. For example, Jane Addams (1860–1935), an early member of the American Sociological Society, cofounded the famous Chicago settlement, Hull House, which provided social, educational, and cultural programs for recent immigrants. Addams and other pioneering female sociologists commonly combined intellectual inquiry, social service work, and political activism—all with the goal of assisting the underprivileged and creating a more egalitarian society. Working with Ida Wells-Barnett, Addams successfully prevented racial segregation in the Chicago public schools, and her efforts to establish a juvenile court system and a women's trade union reflect the practical focus of her work (Addams 1910, 1930; Lengermann and Niebrugge-Brantley 1998).

This commitment to positive social change was not unique to Addams and her colleagues. From the very beginning to the present, sociologists have recognized an obligation to go beyond explaining how the world works and become actively engaged in making the world a better place. In the words of French sociologist Pierre Bourdieu, "I have come to believe that those who have the good fortune to be able to devote their lives to the study of the social world cannot stand aside, neutral and indifferent, from the struggles in which the future of that world is at stake" (1998a:11). For some this has meant releasing the results of their research to the public so that we might make more informed decisions;

Jane Addams   Photo: Addams–© Hulton Archive/Getty Images; frame–© iStock Getty Images RF.

Did You Know?

. . . First Lady Michelle Obama received a bachelor of arts degree in sociology from Princeton University in 1985. She used that degree as a stepping-stone to law school at Harvard.

Photo: © Mike Segar/Reuters/Corbis.

Personal Sociology

Hooked on Sociology

When I took "Soc101" in college, it took me a long time to understand the sociological imagination. I still remember feeling overwhelmed by all the concepts, facts, and figures. Eventually, as we studied the impact of the media and the power of inheritance, things began to fall into place; I took another course and was hooked. As you begin your study of sociology, my advice is to stay focused on how our individual choices are shaped by our social positions and access to resources. How do our circumstances influence how we understand ourselves and others? I hope that after encountering sociology, you will come away with a new way of seeing, equipped to act in new and more informed ways.

for others it has meant active engagement in establishing social policy or assisting in the lives of others. For example, Durkheim, who considered an educated citizenry essential to democratic success, used his appointment to the Department of Science of Education and Sociology at the Sorbonne in Paris, along with his political connections and appointments, to shape French educational policy and practice. Du Bois cofounded the National Association for the Advancement of Colored People, better known as the NAACP. In fact, one of the dominant reasons students choose to major in sociology is that they want to make a difference, and sociology provides a pathway to do just that.

>> Three Sociological Perspectives

The answers to the five questions that sociologists ask provide us with a glimpse of the mosaic of sociological theories that have developed over time as sociologists consider the complexity of human behavior. Some theorists focus on society as a whole; others concentrate on individual interactions. Some are particularly concerned with inequality; others focus on maintaining social cohesion. Some approaches seem to overlap; others seem at odds with one another. But, regardless of their stance, all theorists share a common commitment to provide us with greater understanding of why we think and act the way we do. Each theory, whether broad or narrow, offers a way of seeing that allows us to perceive things we might have otherwise missed.

Three Sociological Perspectives

	Functionalist	Conflict	Interactionist
View of society	Stable, well integrated	Characterized by tension and struggle between groups	Active in influencing and affecting everyday social interaction
Level of analysis emphasized	Macro	Macro	Micro, as a way of understanding the larger macro phenomena
Key concepts	Social integration Institutions Anomie	Inequality Capitalism Stratification	Symbols Nonverbal communication Face-to-face interaction
View of the individual	People are socialized to perform societal functions	People are shaped by power, coercion, and authority	People manipulate symbols and create their social worlds through interaction
View of the social order	Maintained through cooperation and consensus	Maintained through force and coercion	Maintained by shared understanding of everyday behavior
View of social change	Predictable, reinforcing	Change takes place all the time and may have positive consequences	Reflected in people's social positions and their communications with others
Example	Public punishments reinforce the social order	Laws enforce the positions of those in power	People respect laws or disobey them based on their own past experience
Proponents	Émile Durkheim Talcott Parsons Robert Merton	Karl Marx W. E. B. Du Bois Ida Wells-Barnett	George Herbert Mead Charles Horton Cooley Erving Goffman

To simplify the rich array of sociological theories (especially for someone new to sociology), sociologists have classified various theories into three major theoretical perspectives or paradigms: functionalist, conflict, and interactionist. Each perspective offers a different set of lenses, focusing our attention in slightly different ways. Or, to put it another way, it is like three different people standing on the edge of a circle looking in at the same thing but each seeing it from a different point of view, able to recognize things that others might not even see.

According to the **functionalist perspective,** society is like a living organism with its various parts working together (or functioning) for the good of the whole. Functionalists posit that society and its parts are structured to provide social order and maintain stability. Aspects of society that appear dysfunctional, seemingly contributing to a decrease in social order or integration, will either wither away over time or contribute some hidden benefits that researchers seek to reveal. Durkheim's research into social order and its challenges, especially within modern societies, is a classic example of the functionalist perspective. Durkheim assumed that, over time, society would progress toward greater order as it came to terms with apparent threats or challenges.

Whereas the functionalist perspective emphasizes consensus and cooperation, the **conflict perspective** focuses on power and the allocation of valued resources in society. According to conflict theorists, social order cannot be fully understood apart from an analysis of how the status quo is established and maintained by those who control key resources. Such resources include material resources (such as money, land, and property), social resources (such as family connections, social networks, and prestige), and cultural resources (such as

education, beliefs, knowledge, and taste). The existing social structure helps maintain the privileges of some groups and keep others in inferior positions. Marx's work on inequality, social class, and alienation provides a classic example of the conflict perspective.

Finally, whereas functionalist and conflict theorists both analyze large-scale, society-wide patterns of behavior, theorists who take the **interactionist perspective** generalize about everyday forms of social interaction in order to explain society as a whole. For interactionists, society is the product of our everyday interactions (with parents, friends, teachers, or strangers) through which we establish shared meanings and thus construct order. Because society is dependent on this ongoing construction, society is fluid and subject to change. Goffman's dramaturgical approach is an example of the interactionist perspective.

The three-perspectives model has the advantage of providing us with conceptual hooks that allow us to recall some of the key concerns and issues sociologists have raised. A disadvantage, however, is that it gives the illusion that these three are discrete categories with fundamentally different and incompatible ways of looking at the world. In practice, research rooted in one perspective almost inevitably draws on or addresses insights from the other two.

>> Practicing Sociology

One of the questions that students frequently ask about sociology is "What can I do with it?" This query often comes from students who really like sociology, and might want to pursue it further, but are uncertain about where it leads. The good news is that there are many ways people can practice sociology.

PERSONAL SOCIOLOGY

We don't have to become professional sociologists to practice what we have learned. The sociological imagination can help all of us better understand our beliefs and actions and make more informed choices. We can all practice **personal sociology** by recognizing the impact our individual position has on who we are, and how we think and act. Doing so also calls us to take responsibility for the effects our actions have on others. For example, by drawing on insights gained from sociological theory and research, we might watch the news and ask whose interests are being represented. When we walk through the mall, we might observe how people display their social status and how they are treated accordingly. When we go in for a job interview, we might abide by the largely unspoken norms of conduct that shape interaction and influence our likelihood for success. Personal sociology empowers us by allowing us to see things that were previously invisible and to act on those insights.

functionalist perspective A sociological approach that emphasizes the way in which the parts of a society are structured to maintain its stability.

conflict perspective A sociological approach that assumes social behavior is best understood in terms of tension between groups over power or the allocation of resources, including housing, money, access to services, and political representation.

interactionist perspective A sociological approach that generalizes about everyday forms of social interaction in order to explain society as a whole.

personal sociology The practice of recognizing the impact our individual position has on who we are and how we think and act, and of taking responsibility for the impacts our actions have on others.

SOCTHINK

To what extent was your decision to go to college driven by a desire to fit in and contribute to society? How might access to resources have shaped your decisions about going to college? What specific individuals influenced your decision and how did they do so?

ACADEMIC SOCIOLOGY

Many students opt to take their sociology education further, and the number of U.S. college students who have graduated with a degree in sociology has risen steadily (see figure below). The American Sociological Association (ASA) conducted research on recent sociology graduates and discovered that the top reasons for choosing sociology as a major are because students found the sociological concepts interesting, sociology helped them understand the impact society has on individuals, they particularly enjoyed their first sociology course, sociology helped them understand themselves better, and they wanted to make a difference in the world (Spalter-Roth et al. 2012). As part of their sociology education, sociology majors cultivate a variety of skills, such as developing evidence-based arguments, evaluating research methods, writing a research report understandable to nonsociologists, using computer resources including statistical software to organize and analyze data, and identifying ethical issues in research. Sociology graduates who later use these skills in their jobs express the highest levels of job satisfaction (Spalter-Roth and Van Vooren 2008a, 2008b).

The jobs that sociology majors find shortly after graduation, according to the ASA study, are in a range of fields. The most common occupational category is social services. Examples of jobs include caseworker for abused and neglected children, manager for a not-for-profit organization, case manager for HIV-positive individuals, and child advocate. Researchers also found that graduates were employed in a variety of other positions, including teacher, librarian, paralegal, immigration specialist, office manager, quality assurance manager, crime scene investigator, police officer, probation officer, marketing consultant, research assistant, program evaluator, statistician, and editor (Spalter-Roth and Van Vooren 2008a).

According to the ASA study, of sociology majors who pursued graduate school degrees, only about one-quarter did so in sociology. Instead, most used their sociology major as a stepping-stone to graduate study in social work, education, law, psychology, engineering, and business management (Spalter-Roth and Van Vooren 2009:9). Overall, 51.9 percent of the majors completed a graduate degree within four years of college graduation. Of those who pursued advanced degrees in sociology, the majority enrolled in some form of an applied sociology program (Spalter-Roth and Van Vooren 2010).

SOCTHINK

How much responsibility do individuals have to make things better for society?

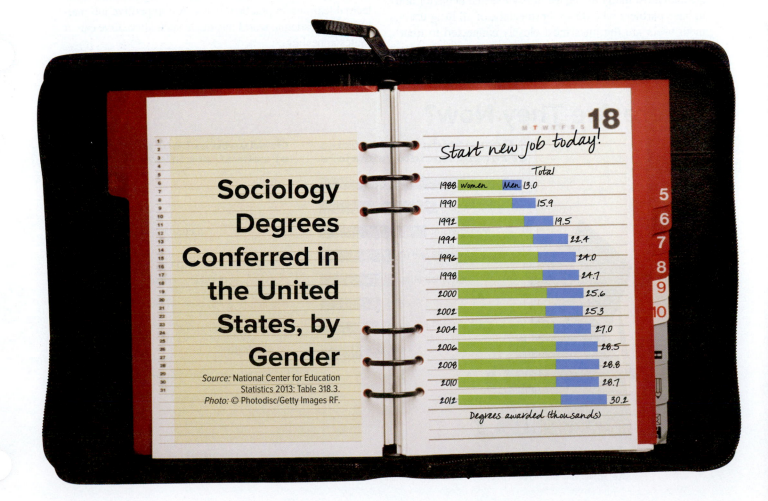

Sociology Degrees Conferred in the United States, by Gender

Source: National Center for Education Statistics 2013: Table 318.3.
Photo: © Photodisc/Getty Images RF.

Start new job today!

	Women	Men	Total
1988			13.0
1990			15.9
1992			19.5
1994			22.4
1996			24.0
1998			24.7
2000			25.6
2002			25.3
2004			27.0
2006			28.5
2008			28.8
2010			28.7
2012			30.2

Degrees awarded (thousands)

APPLIED AND CLINICAL SOCIOLOGY

Applied sociology is the use of the discipline of sociology with the specific intent of yielding practical applications for human behavior and organizations. Often, the goal of such work is to assist in resolving a social problem. For example, in the past 40 years, eight presidents of the United States have established commissions to delve into major societal concerns facing our nation. Sociologists are often asked to apply their expertise to studying such issues as violence, pornography, crime, immigration, and population.

applied sociology The use of the discipline of sociology with the specific intent of yielding practical applications for human behavior and organizations.

clinical sociology The use of the discipline of sociology with the specific intent of altering organizations or restructuring social institutions.

One example of applied sociology involves the growing interest in the ways in which nationally recognized social problems manifest themselves locally. Sociologist Greg Scott and his colleagues sought to better understand the connection between illicit drug use and the spread of HIV/AIDS. By combining a variety of methods, including interviews and observation, with photo and video documentation, researchers found that across all drug users, HIV/AIDS transmission is highest among users of crystal methamphetamine. Meth users are also most likely to engage in risky sexual behavior and to have partners who do so. Fortunately, of all drug users, meth users are the ones most closely connected to treatment programs, which allows them to receive substance abuse education and treatment from their health care providers. Their cases, brought to the forefront by Scott and his team, highlight the need for public health officials to identify other individuals who engage in high-risk sexual behavior and to get them into appropriate treatment programs (G. Scott 2005).

The growing popularity of applied sociology has led to the rise of the specialty of clinical sociology. Whereas applied sociology may involve simply evaluating social issues, **clinical sociology** is dedicated to facilitating change by altering organizations (as in family therapy) or restructuring social institutions (as in the reorganization of a medical center). Louis Wirth (1931) wrote about clinical sociology more than 75 years ago, but the term itself has become popular only in recent years. The Association for Applied and Clinical Sociology was founded in 1978 to promote the application of sociological knowledge in interventions for individual and social change. This professional group has developed a procedure for certifying clinical sociologists—much as physical therapists or psychologists are certified.

Applied sociologists generally leave it to others to act on their evaluations, but clinical sociologists take direct responsibility for implementation and view those with whom they work as their clients. This specialty has become increasingly attractive to graduate students in sociology because it offers an opportunity to apply intellectual learning in practical ways. A competitive job market in the academic world has made such alternative career routes appealing.

Where Are They Now?

Occupational categories of recent sociology majors

- Social services 26.5%
- Administrative, clerical support 15.8%
- Management 14.4%
- Other (includes PR and IT) 10.2%
- Sales, marketing 10.1%
- Services 8.3%
- Education 8.1%
- Research 5.7%

Graduate school programs of recent sociology majors

- 22.4% Sociology
- 16.9% Social work
- 11.4% Education
- 10.5% Law
- 9.4% Other social sciences
- 8.6% Psychology/counseling
- 7.3% Engineering
- 5.1% Other
- 4.5% Business/management
- 3.8% Public policy/affairs

Note: Percentage based on sociology majors attending graduate school 18 months after graduation.

Source: Spalter-Roth and Van Vooren 2009. *Photo:* © Stockbyte/PunchStock RF

© Medioimages/PictureQuest/Jupiter Images RF

SOCTHINK

Consider the obstacles to cross-cultural interaction on college campuses. Why might people be unwilling to interact with others who have alternative cultural practices? How might it perpetuate inequality?

Though the expression has become something of a cliché, it truly is a small world after all. Social, cultural, political, and economic events around the world—including such things as the global financial meltdown or terrorist attacks—have a profound effect on how we think and what we do. The process of **globalization**—the worldwide integration of government policies, cultures, social movements, and financial markets through trade and the exchange of ideas—shows no signs of stopping. The sociological imagination provides us with the tools necessary to more effectively respond to these challenges.

College and university campuses often provide a microcosm of this trend. Students, faculty, staff, and administrators with radically different values, political views, customs, experiences, and expectations are drawn together from around the world into a relatively confined space. If the resulting interactions are to be meaningful, positive, and respectful, we must seek out ways to better understand factors that shape them. Conflicts with roommates, classmates, and professors are often chalked up to personality clashes and other individual attributes, but they cannot be fully understood or dealt with apart from coming to terms with the ways our social backgrounds have shaped how we think, act, and feel. For each of us, the social positions we occupy shape the opportunities and obstacles we face. We must learn to see the implications of this reality both for ourselves and for others. This self-knowledge necessitates a more complete appreciation of the intersection of history and biography in all of our lives.

globalization The worldwide integration of government policies, cultures, social movements, and financial markets through trade and the exchange of ideas.

Using the sociological imagination in our everyday lives enables us to understand others from their perspective and even understand ourselves through their eyes. By opening our eyes to patterns and practices that are often invisible to us, we can make more informed decisions about which pathways we choose to follow. We can also take greater responsibility for the impact that our choices have on others. Sociology provides us with tools to better understand, interpret, and respond to the world around us. Sociology is a verb; it's something you do—it's a way of life.

>> Sociology Is a Verb

Regardless of the level at which it is practiced, sociology is about more than the knowledge gained or career attained. It consists of a body of knowledge along with techniques for gaining more; we will spend much of this book covering those sociological foundations. It can open doors to interesting and challenging careers in a variety of fields. But it is also a way of engaging with the world around us and understanding its complexity and interconnections in new ways. This vantage point can be especially important given the world we live in today.

SOCIOLOGY IS A VERB

The Ties That Bind

Pick an object you own—maybe a pencil, a pair of shoes, or a cell phone—and trace its history. Include a diagram or map of all the people and processes it took for it to come into your possession. What is it made of? Where did all its components come from? Who contributed to its production? After it was made, who was involved in getting it into your hands? What story does it tell?

For
REVIEW

I. **What is sociology?**

- Sociology is a way of seeing that joins theory and research to investigate the relationship between the individual and society and the impact unequal distribution of resources has on opportunity.

II. **How do sociologists look at the world?**

- Sociologists developed theories to provide windows into our lives, including three primary perspectives: functionalist (emphasizing social order), conflict (focusing on inequality), and interactionist (highlighting the significance of our everyday relationships and exchanges).

III. **How might someone practice sociology?**

- Sociology can provide a pathway to a career in a related applied, clinical, or academic context. But more than that, we can practice sociology in our everyday lives by utilizing the sociological imagination to better understand ourselves and others.

SOCVIEWS on the Sociological Imagination

Functionalist View

Society is like a **living organism** with its various parts **working together** for the good of the whole.

The parts of society are structured to maintain **stability and social order**.

Society influences individual behavior and thus helps maintain **social integration through shared experiences**.

INTEGRATION
KEY CONCEPT

Conflict View

Society represents a **struggle over resources**. Those who control valued resources have **greater power** to get their way.

Valued resources include **material** (money, land, property), **social** (status, prestige, authority), and **cultural** (knowledge, beliefs, taste) **resources**.

The existing social structure helps maintain the **privileges** of some groups while keeping others in subservient positions.

KEY CONCEPT
POWER

Interactionist View

Society is the product of our everyday interactions by which we establish **shared meanings** and construct **social order**.

By generalizing from our everyday forms of social interaction (on the **micro level**), we can explain society as a whole.

The **self** exists in **relationship** with others and we come to **perceive** who we are and what our reality is through our interactions.

KEY CONCEPT
CONSTRUCTING SOCIAL REALITY

MAKE THE CONNECTION

After reviewing the chapter, answer the following questions:

1
Why might having multiple theoretical perspectives help us when we practice the sociological imagination?

2
How might each perspective differ in how it looks at what it takes to produce something (such as a hamburger, a house, a book, and so on)?

3
How might each perspective approach the study of unemployment? Of suicide?

4
How does each perspective enable you to see the way you participate in sports, either as a fan or as an athlete, in a different light?

Pop Quiz

1. Sociology is
   a. the analysis of individual motivations and internal struggles.
   b. concerned with predicting what particular individuals do or do not do.
   c. the systematic study of the relationship between the individual and society and of the consequences of difference.
   d. the integration of government policies, cultures, social movements, and financial markets through trade and the exchange of ideas.

2. According to C. Wright Mills, the sociological imagination focuses on the intersection between
   a. natural science and social science.
   b. power and access to resources.
   c. theory and research.
   d. history and biography.

3. What is the primary sociological lesson we learn from the hamburger-as-a-miracle example?
   a. We take our interdependence and the knowledge we collectively share for granted.
   b. An individual could easily survive on his or her own without assistance from others.
   c. Modern technology makes it difficult for us to provide for our individual needs.
   d. Interdependence is no longer necessary because we can provide for our needs through modern technology.

4. In their attempts to describe the relationship between sociology and common sense, sociologists argue that
   a. common sense provides time-tested answers that are reliable most of the time, whereas sociological facts change all the time.
   b. sociology depends on systematic analysis through research, whereas common sense does not.
   c. sociology cannot assess or test the truthfulness of commonsense claims.
   d. there is no significant difference between the two.

5. Émile Durkheim's research on suicide found that
   a. Catholics had much higher suicide rates than Protestants.
   b. the more socially integrated someone is the less likely he or she is to commit suicide.
   c. married people are more likely to take their lives than single people.
   d. suicide is a solitary act, unrelated to group life.

6. Karl Marx argued that in order to understand social order we must include analysis of
   a. anomie.
   b. ownership of the means of production.
   c. the sociological imagination.
   d. microsociology.

7. Which sociologist made a major contribution to society through his in-depth studies of urban life, including both Blacks and Whites?
   a. W. E. B. Du Bois
   b. Émile Durkheim
   c. Auguste Comte
   d. Erving Goffman

8. What is the sociological term for the weak sense of social solidarity that arises due to a lack of agreed-upon rules to guide behavior?
   a. suicide
   b. alienation
   c. anomie
   d. agency

9. Thinking of society as a living organism in which each part of the organism contributes to its survival is a reflection of which theoretical perspective?
   a. the functionalist perspective
   b. the conflict perspective
   c. the Marxist perspective
   d. the interactionist perspective

10. The career path with the specific intent of altering social relationships or restructuring organizations is known as
    a. dramaturgical sociology.
    b. applied sociology.
    c. academic sociology.
    d. clinical sociology.

1. (c), 2. (d), 3. (a), 4. (b), 5. (b), 6. (b), 7. (a), 8. (c), 9. (a), 10. (d)

Sociological Research

ASKING QUESTIONS AND FINDING ANSWERS

As a first-year college student, Alice Goffman got a job at her college cafeteria that changed her life forever. She needed a research site for her ethnography class, a course in which you embed yourself into a social setting to understand it from within, and it seemed perfect. She'd heard her fellow students refer to the cafeteria workers—most of whom were older, African American women—as lazy and rude, and she wondered what the workers thought of her, a young, White, comparatively privileged woman and her similarly privileged peers (Parry 2013). After a year filling plates and scrubbing dishes, Goffman began tutoring the grandchildren of her cafeteria boss, an African American woman in her 60s who lived in a poor Philadelphia neighborhood. Through those grandchildren, Goffman

made contacts with others, and before long, a second research project was born. She moved into the neighborhood during her sophomore year to better observe and understand their social world. She became so committed to the project and connected to the people that she continued her research project through college and graduate school and ultimately published a book telling their stories.

Goffman gained a much deeper understanding of the challenges faced by young African American males living there. As boys, they are told to run from police because, "even if it's not you [they are looking for], nine times out of ten, they'll probably book you" (Goffman 2014a:24). According to Goffman, these young men get taken away for what they see as petty offenses, contributing to suspicions that police are targeting them. Those with legal entanglements—missed court dates, unpaid court fees, parole curfew violations—face the threat of warrants for their arrest. Their fear of capture and confinement leads them to avoid beneficial social connections—visiting family, getting a job, going to the hospital when sick or injured. Such conventional social connections can be used against them, as happens when girlfriends or moms are pressured by police to inform on them. Goffman describes the resulting social fabric as "one woven in suspicion, distrust, and the paranoiac practices of secrecy, evasion, and unpredictability" (2014a:8).

At the same time, Goffman noticed that her fellow college students, who were often White and from financially secure backgrounds, engaged in similar activities—drinking, doing drugs, getting into fights—but no police raided their parties and they walked away from their adolescence with college diplomas and good jobs instead of jail time and permanent police records (Goffman 2014b). As the sociological imagination suggests, if a lot of people in similar positions experience the same result, it likely says more about the position than the person. Through sociological research we can see patterns shaping people's outcomes that might otherwise be invisible to us.

As You READ >>

- What steps do sociologists take when seeking to answer why people think and act the way they do?
- What techniques do sociologists use to collect data?
- What ethical concerns must sociologists consider while conducting research?

>> Steps in the Research Process

Sociology at its core represents a conversation between theory and research. Sociologists seek to describe and explain the patterns and practices of our lives through systematic investigation of what we do and why we do it. If we want to know why people think and act the way they do, we need to know more about what they actually think and do. We need to observe them, ask them questions, participate in their lives, or in other ways come to understand their experiences from their perspective. We cannot sit back and guess.

Sociology inherits this commitment in part from early attempts by some sociologists to emulate the scientific method, used in investigations of the natural world. The **scientific method** is a systematic, organized series of steps that ensure maximum objectivity and consistency in researching a problem. Although not all sociologists today would tie the task of sociology as strongly to the natural science model, the commitment to making sense of the world through engagement with the world remains.

scientific method A systematic, organized series of steps that ensure maximum objectivity and consistency in researching a problem.

Conducting sociological research in the spirit of the scientific method requires adherence to a series of steps designed to ensure the accuracy of the results. Sociologists and other researchers follow five basic steps in the scientific method: (1) defining the problem, (2) reviewing the literature, (3) formulating the hypothesis, (4) selecting

The Scientific Method

Review the literature

Define the problem
Investigate existing theories

Formulate a testable **hypothesis**

Develop the **conclusion**
Ideas for further research

Collect and analyze data
Select a research design
Survey • Observation • Experiment • Existing sources

Photo: © Photodisc/Getty RF.

the research design and then collecting and analyzing data, and (5) developing the conclusion (see "The Scientific Method" figure). To better understand the process, we will follow an example about the relationship between education and income from start to finish.

DEFINING THE PROBLEM

Does it "pay" to go to college? Many people make great sacrifices and work hard to get a college degree. Parents borrow money for their children's tuition. Students take part-time jobs or even work full-time while attending evening or weekend classes. Does it pay off? Are there sufficient monetary returns for getting that degree?

The first step in any research project is to state as clearly as possible what you hope to investigate—that is, to define the problem. Typically, this means explicitly identifying both the concepts we are interested in learning more about and the nature of the relationship we suspect might exist between those concepts. Doing so is necessary for the conversation between theory and research to occur.

Theory plays a central role in our definition of the problem. Theories represent our most informed explanations of what happens and why. When we come up against something we do not yet understand, theories can guide our investigation by suggesting possible research paths. For example, as we saw in Chapter 1, Émile Durkheim theorized that social integration shapes individual action. He set out to test this theory by conducting research on suicide as an example of the most extreme individual choice of all. Through research we

> Without theory we are blind—we cannot see the world.

Michael Burawoy

assess and refine our theories so that our sociological explanations and descriptions of the world are fuller and richer, more accurately reflecting both the simplicity and the complexity of human behavior.

In our current example, we are interested in knowing how education affects a person's economic position. Several competing sociological theories exist concerning this relationship. One approach, growing out of the functionalist paradigm, presumes that, in order to realize its full potential, society needs people to take sufficient time to develop their skills. This leads to the supposition that people who make the sacrifices necessary to develop those skills will be rewarded for doing so (K. Davis and Moore 1945). Another theory, from conflict tradition, suggests that instead of rewarding those with skills, education reinforces the existing system of inequality by providing the illusion of opportunity. In this theory, people more or less end up in the same economic position in which they began their educational journey (Bowles and Gintis 1976). Which theory we start with will shape the kind of data we collect.

© Mike Kemp/Getty RF

We look into both theories in a later chapter, but for the purpose of our example, we will focus on the first.

REVIEWING THE LITERATURE

The next phase of research involves a review of the literature: investigating previous research conducted by sociologists and others regarding the concepts we want to study. Analyzing how others have studied these concepts allows researchers to refine the problem under study, clarify possible techniques for collecting data, and eliminate or reduce avoidable mistakes. An excellent place to start such research is the many sociological journals that regularly publish articles in which sociologists carefully document their findings. (See the "Finding Information" table for more useful tips.)

In our example, we would need to seek out existing research about the relationship between education and income. In that literature we would find significant evidence that the two are linked. We would also learn that other factors besides years of schooling influence earning potential. For example, a person's occupational category (such as plumber, tool-and-die worker, secretary, or professor) might shape her or his income in a way different from educational level alone. We also find that additional background factors such as class, gender, and race affect income. For example, the children of rich parents are more likely to go to college than those from modest backgrounds, so we might consider the possibility that the same parents may later help their children secure better-paying jobs (Walpole 2007). This might lead us to consider adding some concepts to our definition of the problem.

variable A measurable trait or characteristic that is subject to change under different conditions.

FORMULATING THE HYPOTHESIS

After defining the problem in conversation with existing theories and refining the problem by reviewing previous research, we can identify the specific variables we want to study and indicate our expectations about the relationships between them. A **variable** is a measurable trait or characteristic that is subject to change under different conditions. Income, religion, occupation, and gender can all serve as variables in a study. As we move from theory

Finding Information

Begin with material you already have, including this text and others.

Beware of using online sources such as Wikipedia; they can be a helpful place to start, but always double-check claims with a reputable source or organization.

Use books, newspapers, magazines, and journals.

Search using the library catalog and computerized periodical indexes to find related academic journal articles.

Examine government documents (including the U.S. Census).

Contact people, organizations, and agencies related to your topic.

Consult with your instructor, teaching assistant, or reference librarian.

Photo: © Jose Luis Pelaez Inc/Blend Images RF.

toward data collection, we must transform general ideas and abstract concepts into concrete, recognizable variables. Durkheim did this when he used religious affiliation as an indicator of social integration and suicide as representative of individual choice. In our example, education may be a measure of individual ability, initiative, and accomplishment, and income becomes a measure of social inequality. This process, known as creating an **operational definition,** involves the transformation of abstract concepts into indicators that are observable and measurable. The goal in doing so is to show as clearly as possible exactly

what the researcher plans to observe and to justify why observing that variable is appropriate given the theories and concepts being investigated. After the variables have been operationalized, expectations about the relationships between variables can be stated in the form of a hypothesis.

A hypothesis is more than just an educated guess. A **hypothesis** is a testable statement about the relationship between two or more variables. It represents an explicit attempt to indicate what we think is happening and why. It presupposes that **causal logic** is at work, meaning that a relationship exists between variables in which change in one brings about change in the other. Durkheim, for example, hypothesized that a cause-and-effect relationship existed between religious affiliation and suicide rates. In our example, we are hypothesizing that increased education leads to higher income.

In hypotheses, the causal variable that brings about change is called the **independent variable.** The variable that is affected is known as the **dependent variable,** because change in it depends on the influence of the independent variable. In other words, the researcher believes that the independent variable predicts or causes change in the dependent variable. For example, a researcher in sociology might anticipate that the availability of affordable housing (the independent variable; often referred to in equations as x) affects the level of homelessness in a community (the dependent variable; typically represented in equations as y).

We can put these pieces together to generate a generic hypothesis statement: knowledge of the independent

operational definition Transformation of an abstract concept into indicators that are observable and measurable.

hypothesis A testable statement about the relationship between two or more variables.

causal logic A relationship exists between variables in which change in one brings about change in the other.

independent variable The variable in a causal relationship that causes or influences a change in a second variable.

dependent variable The variable in a causal relationship that is subject to the influence of another variable.

Did You Know?

. . . U.S. government agencies regularly release reports on income, education, poverty, and health care. According to the Department of Education, 88.2 percent of people aged 25 and older have received their high school diploma or equivalent, and 31.7 percent have earned at least a bachelor's degree.

Source: National Center for Education Statistics 2014: Table 104.10.   *Photo:* © Fancy Photography/Veer RF

SOC THINK

To what extent do you think each of the independent variables listed in the "Causal Logic" figure would help explain variation in college grade point average? Are there any additional independent variables that you think would help explain GPA performance?

variable (*x*) allows us to better explain or predict the value or position of the dependent variable (*y*). We could then place variables we are interested in studying, such as those in the "Causal Logic" figure, into this statement to clearly present the nature of the relationships we expect to find between variables we wish to study.

In our example, our hypothesis suggests that knowing how many years of schooling a person has completed will allow us to better predict how much money he or she will earn. Our independent variable is the level of education, and the dependent variable is income. Further, we expect the relationship to be positive, meaning the higher a person's educational attainment, the more money she or he will make. In a negative relationship, as the independent variable goes up, the dependent variable goes down, and vice versa.

We should note that just because two variables seem to covary does not mean that change in one causes change in the other. Such covariance is known as a **correlation,** which is a relationship between two variables in which change in one coincides with change in the other. It may well be that the apparent relationship is due to chance or to the influence of some other factors. It is the task of the researcher to demonstrate—drawing on the data, logical reasoning, and theory—that the correlation is also causal. Statistics alone are not enough.

Take, for example, the effect that divorce has on the well-being of children. Studies have shown that the two variables are correlated—children of divorce exhibit long-term adverse effects—but is that relationship causal? Before reaching a conclusion, we should consider other factors. Perhaps negative outcomes for children are due to levels of parental conflict rather than divorce itself, or to the nature of the relationship between the parents and the children, or to contextual factors such as unemployment or geographic mobility (Bhrolcháin 2001; Sun and Li 2008). In the words of sociologist Pierre Bourdieu, "One has explained nothing by establishing the existence of a correlation between an 'independent' variable and a 'dependent' variable" (1984:18). Correlation does not equal causation.

correlation A relationship between two variables in which a change in one coincides with a change in the other.

Causal Logic

Independent variable		Dependent variable
x	→	*y*
Level of educational degree	→	Level of income
Degree of integration into society	→	Likelihood of suicide
Availability of affordable housing	→	Level of homelessness
Parents' church attendance	→	Children's church attendance
Time spent preparing for quiz	→	Performance on quiz
Parents' income	→	Likelihood of children's enrolling in college

Photo: © Image Source/Getty Images RF.

Correlation

DILBERT © 2011 Scott Adams. Used By permission of UNIVERSAL UCLICK.

COLLECTING AND ANALYZING DATA

In science there is a fundamental commitment to using empirical data, meaning data that can be observed and measured, to assess hypotheses. The principle might be summarized this way: Don't tell me, show me. Theory alone is not sufficient. The stories we tell about how the world works must be informed by data gathered from the real world. Sociologists use a variety of research designs to gather data, including surveys, observation, experiments, and the use of existing data. Each is explained later in this chapter. For now we will focus on issues researchers must address regardless of the research design they select.

© U.S. Census Bureau, Public Information Office

sample A selection from a larger population that is statistically representative of that population.

random sample A sample for which every member of an entire population has an equal chance of being selected.

Selecting the Sample

Often, especially in the case of large-scale research projects, sociologists cannot conduct a census, meaning they cannot gather information from everyone in the population they are interested in studying. In such instances, they conduct a **sample**—a selection from a larger population that is statistically representative of that population. To ensure that a sample is representative, sociologists frequently use a **random sample,** in which every member of the entire population being studied has an equal chance of being selected. Thus, if researchers want to examine the opinions of people listed in a city directory (a book that, unlike the telephone directory, lists all households in a community), they might use a computer to randomly select names from the directory. Doing so eliminates the possibility of bias or convenience negatively affecting who gets included.

When conducted properly, such sampling allows researchers to statistically estimate how representative their results are likely to be. The same cannot be said of most online polls, such as on Facebook, BuzzFeed, or news sites, because they usually do not control for who responds, relying instead on whoever logs in and chooses to participate. Though such surveys can be interesting, fun, or provocative, there is no way to tell if they are representative.

To better understand the relationship between education and income, we can draw on research collected by the National Opinion Research Center (NORC) or the U.S. Census Bureau. These two organizations provide invaluable sources of data for sociologists. NORC has administered the General Social Survey regularly since 1972. In this national survey, administered in both English and Spanish, a representative sample of the adult population is interviewed in depth on a variety of topics, including both income and education. They frequently ask the same questions over multiple years, allowing for analysis of how responses change over time.

Did You Know?

. . . A classic case of sampling error occurred when pollsters for *Literary Digest* declared that Alf Landon would defeat President Franklin Roosevelt in 1936. They predicted Landon would win 55 percent of the vote; he received only 37 percent. Although the *Digest* polled 2 million people, it selected names from telephone books and auto registration records. With the country in the midst of the Great Depression, phones and cars were luxuries many people could not afford. As a result, the poll underrepresented poorer people, who were more likely to support Roosevelt (Squire 1988).

Photo: © AP Photo.

Although the Census Bureau is best known for the census it conducts every 10 years of the entire U.S. population (most recently in 2010), researchers there also regularly collect data using representative samples of the U.S. population. Doing so provides them with more frequent updates and allows them to gather more detailed information about more variables than is possible in the decennial census. For example, with regard to our variables of interest, each fall they release an annual report on income, poverty, and health care coverage in the United States (DeNavas-Walt and Proctor 2014).

Ensuring Validity and Reliability To have confidence in their findings, and in keeping with the scientific method, sociologists pursue research results that are both valid and reliable. **Validity** refers to the degree to which a measure or scale truly reflects the phenomenon under study. In our example, a valid measure of income would accurately represent how much money a person earned in a given year. If the question is not written clearly, some respondents might interpret it as asking for earnings from a job, others might add income from other sources, such as investments, and others might report household income, including earnings from children or a spouse. Studies show that, even though income can be a touchy subject, people respond accurately when asked a clear and unambiguous question about how much they have earned.

Reliability refers to the extent to which a measure produces consistent results. Using the same instrument to collect data from the same people in similar circumstances should provide the same results. For example, if you give people the same questionnaire about income and education at two different times, unless something significant has changed between times, the responses should be approximately the same.

DEVELOPING THE CONCLUSION

After having collected the data and analyzed the results, sociologists draw conclusions about what they have learned. They use the information they gathered to better explain why we act and think as we do. The research results inform our theories, which helps generate new questions, and the whole cycle begins again with a new definition of the problem.

Supporting Hypotheses As we can see in the graph at right, data from the U.S. Census support our hypothesis regarding education and income: people with more formal schooling do earn more money than those with less schooling. Looking first at the top two income categories, for those without a college degree, 19 percent earn $60,000 or more, compared to 51 percent of those with a college degree. Contrast this with the bottom two income

categories. Here, 57 percent of those with no more than a high school diploma earn less than $40,000, compared to 24 percent who have received at least an associate's degree. When it comes to income, educational attainment matters.

Of course, this is not true for all individuals. As we see in the graph, having a college degree does not guarantee a high income—4 percent of those with a college degree earn less than $20,000. Exceptions to the rule might include successful entrepreneurs lacking formal schooling or those with a doctorate who choose to work for a low-paying, not-for-profit institution. Sociologically, both of these findings—that education shapes income and that the relationship is not perfect—are interesting. To understand why such variation exists, we would need to consider the possible effects that additional variables have on income.

> **validity** The degree to which a measure or scale truly reflects the phenomenon under study.
>
> **reliability** The extent to which a measure produces consistent results.

Impact of a College Degree on Income

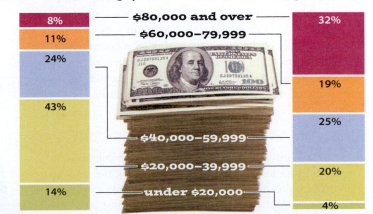

High school diploma or less (includes some college)

Associate's degree or more

	High school diploma or less	Associate's degree or more
$80,000 and over	8%	32%
$60,000–79,999	11%	19%
$40,000–59,999	24%	25%
$20,000–39,999	43%	20%
under $20,000	14%	4%

Note: Data are from 2013 and include those aged 25–64 working full-time, year-round. High school category includes those with some college but no degree.

Source: U.S. Census Bureau 2014a:Table PINC-03.

Controlling for Other Factors Given the complexity of human behavior, it is seldom sufficient to study only one independent and dependent variable. Although such analyses can provide us with insight, we also need to consider other causal factors that might influence the dependent variable. One way to do this is to introduce a **control variable,** which is a factor that the researcher holds constant to test the relative impact of an independent variable. For example, if researchers wanted to explain neighborhood crime rates as a dependent variable, they might look at the neighborhood's poverty rate as an independent variable. It is likely, however, that additional factors influence crime rates, so they might introduce familiarity—the degree to which neighbors know and regularly interact with each other—as a control variable. They would find that neighborhoods with a high level of familiarity do have lower crime rates than those with low familiarity rates. The introduction of the control variable allows us to see that some of the variation in neighborhood crime rates that was initially assumed to be due to poverty is actually due to the influence of the control variable.

control variable A factor that is held constant to test the relative impact of an independent variable.

research design A detailed plan or method for obtaining data scientifically.

─**SOC**THINK─

Sticking with education as our independent variable, what other dependent variables might we study to see the impact of education on society? What do we hope to get out of education both individually and collectively?

Looking at our variables, we cannot consider only the effect education has on income; we should also investigate the role that other variables might play. One possibility is that "who you know" matters as much as "what you know." To study this relationship, we could look at how a person's family background or social network connections influence income. In later chapters we consider such additional background factors that help explain income differences, including gender, race, ethnicity, and social class.

IN SUMMARY: THE RESEARCH PROCESS

We began with a general question about the relationship between education and income. By following the steps in the research process—defining the problem, reviewing the literature, formulating a hypothesis, collecting and analyzing data, and developing a conclusion—we were able to show that education does pay. One of the ways we can check the validity of our findings is to share them with

sociologists, policy makers, and others in a public forum in the form of a paper at a professional conference or an article in a refereed academic journal. Revealing what we did, how we did it, and what we found enables others to check to make sure we did not miss anything and that we proceeded in an appropriate manner.

Research is cyclical in nature. At the end of the process, researchers almost always find that they have more questions they would like to pursue and ideas for further research, and most research papers include a specific section addressing how they might define the problem and carry out the research next time. Along the way, researchers may have discovered new concepts they should consider, better ways to ask questions to get the information they need, individuals or groups they should include in the study, or a whole host of other possibilities. In the end, the studies researchers produce become part of the literature review for the next project, whether theirs or someone else's.

>> Major Research Designs

As we have seen, sociologists go about gathering and making sense of the stories of our lives in a variety of ways. Sometimes sociologists want to tell our larger collective story; other times they want to tell the stories of individuals and groups who are often left out of such large-scale accounts. Different research designs are available to tell these different types of stories. For example, large national surveys allow us to get a sense of the national mood about issues such as politics or religion, and statistics can give insight into where we stand in relation to each other on such issues. To explore the smaller-scale stories of individuals and groups, researchers may employ methods, such as observation, that emphasize more direct and personal interaction with their subjects.

Sociologists draw on four major types of research designs when considering how to collect their data. A **research design** is a detailed plan or method for obtaining data scientifically. Often a selection of research designs is based on the theories and hypotheses the researcher starts with (Denzin 2009; Merton 1948). The choice requires creativity and ingenuity, because it directly influences both the cost of the project and the time needed to collect the data (Vogt, Gardner, and Haeffele 2012). As noted previously, research designs that sociologists regularly use to generate data include surveys, observation, experiments, and existing sources.

© Hill street studios/Getty RF

President Obama's Approval Ratings

Percent approval

Note: Each point represents a single poll conducted by a major polling organization regarding President Obama's handling of the economy.

Source: www.pollster.com.

SURVEYS

Almost all of us have responded to surveys of one kind or another. We may have been asked what kind of detergent we use, which presidential candidate we intend to vote for, or what our favorite television program is. A **survey** is a study, generally in the form of an interview or questionnaire, that provides researchers with information about how people think and act. Surveys become particularly commonplace during election seasons in the form of political polls. Major polling organizations include Gallup, Pew Research, Harris Interactive, ABC/Washington Post, and Rasmussen. All these firms seek to use careful techniques to ensure the accuracy of their results.

Issues in Designing Surveys As indicated earlier, a survey must be based on precise, representative sampling if it is to genuinely reflect a broad range of the population. We might be skeptical that feedback from just a few hundred people can provide an accurate picture of how more than 300 million people think, but properly

Going GLOBAL

Research Abroad

Researchers can gather information even under difficult circumstances. As the Obama administration was escalating the war in Afghanistan against the Taliban in 2009, researchers conducted surveys about people's attitudes in the region. In late 2009 they found that 79 percent of Afghans felt the Taliban had a negative influence, though residents in the south, a Taliban stronghold, were somewhat less negative. At the same time, 45 percent approved of U.S. leadership in Afghanistan, down from 50 percent earlier in the year (Ray and Srinivasan 2010a, 2010b).

run surveys can do just that. When it comes to presidential polling, for example, we can compare the results of such polls against actual election results. In a study of the historical accuracy of presidential polls, political scientist Costas Panagopoulos reports that the polls from 1956 to 2012 were, on average, within 2 percentage points of accurately predicting the final result (Panagopoulos 2009; Panagopoulos and Farrer 2014). We can also get a sense of the accuracy of polls by looking at "polls of polls" that combine various results into a single report or graph to better see the pattern that the polls collectively demonstrate (see the "President Obama's Approval

> **survey** A study, generally in the form of an interview or questionnaire, that provides researchers with information about how people think and act.

© Bettmann/Corbis

interview A face-to-face or telephone questioning of a respondent to obtain desired information.

questionnaire A printed, written, or computerized form used to obtain information from a respondent.

quantitative research Research that collects and reports data primarily in numerical form.

Rating" figure). Examples of current polls for presidential and congressional approval ratings are available at sites such as pollster.com and pollingreport.com. Although the pollsters sometimes fail to "get it right" (for example, predicting that Dewey would defeat Truman in the 1948 presidential election), most often they do, and with amazing precision.

In addition to developing representative samples, sociologists must exercise great care in the wording of questions. An effective survey question must be simple and clear enough for people to understand. It must also be specific enough that researchers have no problems interpreting the results. Open-ended questions ("What do you think of the programming on educational television?") must be carefully phrased to solicit the type of information desired. Surveys can be indispensable sources of information, but only if the sampling is done properly and the questions are worded accurately and without bias.

Studies have also shown that the characteristics of the interviewer influence survey data. For example, female interviewers tend to receive more feminist responses from female subjects than do male researchers, and African American interviewers tend to receive more detailed responses about race-related issues from Black subjects than do White interviewers. The possible impact of gender and race indicates again how much care social research requires (Chun et al. 2011; D. Davis and Silver 2003).

Immigration Rates: Perception vs. Reality

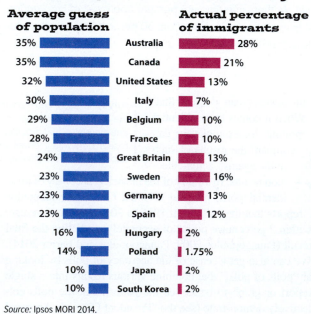

Average guess of population		Actual percentage of immigrants
35%	Australia	28%
35%	Canada	21%
32%	United States	13%
30%	Italy	7%
29%	Belgium	10%
28%	France	10%
24%	Great Britain	13%
23%	Sweden	16%
23%	Germany	13%
23%	Spain	12%
16%	Hungary	2%
14%	Poland	1.75%
10%	Japan	2%
10%	South Korea	2%

Source: Ipsos MORI 2014.

Types of Surveys There are two main forms of the survey: the **interview,** in which a researcher obtains information through face-to-face or telephone questioning, and the **questionnaire,** in which a researcher uses a printed, written, or computerized form to obtain information from a respondent. Each of these has its advantages. An interviewer can obtain a higher response rate because people find it more difficult to turn down a personal request for an interview than to throw away a written questionnaire. In addition, a skillful interviewer can go beyond written questions and probe for a subject's underlying feelings and reasons. For their part, questionnaires have the advantage of being cheaper, especially in large samples. Either way, what we can learn from surveys can be amazing.

To better understand how perceptions vary between countries, for example, researchers conducted a survey. They administered it to a representative sample of 11,527 people in 14 nations, asking questions about a variety of topics (Ipsos MORI 2014). For example, regarding teenage pregnancy they asked, "In your opinion, what percentage of girls aged between 15 and 19 years in [name of country] give birth each year?" In the United States, the average answer was 24 percent, whereas in Great Britain people guessed 16 percent and in Sweden it was 7. Regarding immigration they asked, "What percentage of the [name of country] population do you think are immigrants to this country?" In the United States, the average was 32 percent compared to guesses of 24 percent in Great Britain and 23 percent in Sweden. In addition, they asked about religion, elderly people, voting rates, unemployment rates, homicide rates, and life expectancy. The answers varied significantly from country to country.

Researchers then compared the perceptions to the actual rates for each question asked (Ipsos MORI 2014). They wondered if the degree of difference between the two varied by country. On the question of teenage pregnancy, the actual U.S. rate is 3 percent, a 21-point difference from the perceived rate. People in all 14 countries overestimated their teenage pregnancy rates. The actual percentage of immigrants in the United States is 13 percent, a 19-point difference from the perceived rate. Again, people in all 14 countries overestimated the percentage of their immigrant population. They then ranked each country based on how close their perception was to the actual data. The country that came out on top as the most accurate was Sweden. The country in last place was Italy. The United States finished in 13th place. Understanding perception is important because, as we learned from the Thomas theorem (see Chapter 1), we act on the basis of what we *think* is true, rather than what *is* true. And if our perceptions are inaccurate, our corresponding actions may prove less effective.

Quantitative and Qualitative Research Surveys most often represent an example of **quantitative research,** which collects and reports data primarily in numerical form. Analysis of these data depends on statistics, from the simple

© Sally and Richard Greenhill/Alamy

Research is formalized curiosity. It is poking and prying with a purpose.

Zora Neale Hurston

to the complex, which provide basic summaries describing what variables look like and how they are related. Basic descriptive statistics, such as percentages, are likely familiar. The **mean,** or average, is a number calculated by adding a series of values and then dividing by the number of values. The **median,** or midpoint, is the number that divides a series of values into two groups of equal numbers of values. The median is most often used when there are extreme scores that would distort the mean. The **mode** is the single most common value in a series of scores and is seldom used in sociological research. The mean, median, and mode all seek to provide a single score that is representative of or provides a summary for the whole distribution of scores. When it comes to analyzing relationships between variables, researchers usually rely on computer programs to deal with more complex analysis of quantitative data.

Although quantitative research can make use of large samples, it can't offer great depth on a topic. That is why researchers also make use of **qualitative research,** which relies on what they see in field and naturalistic settings, often focusing on small groups and communities rather than on large groups or whole nations. Here, too, sociologists rely on computers to assist their analysis. Numerous software programs allow researchers not only to record observations but also to identify common themes, concepts, or concerns expressed in interviews. The most common form of qualitative research is observation.

OBSERVATION

Investigators who collect information by participating directly and/or by closely watching a group or community are engaged in **observation.** This method allows sociologists to examine behaviors and communities in greater depth than is possible using other methods. Though observation may seem a relatively informal method compared to surveys, researchers are careful to take detailed notes while observing their subjects.

An increasingly popular form of qualitative research in sociology today is **ethnography**—the study of an entire social setting through extended systematic observation.

mean A number calculated by adding a series of values and then dividing by the number of values.

median The midpoint, or number that divides a series of values into two groups of equal numbers of values.

mode The single most common value in a series of scores.

qualitative research Research that relies on what is seen in field or naturalistic settings more than on statistical data.

observation A research technique in which an investigator collects information through direct participation and/or by closely watching a group or community.

ethnography The study of an entire social setting through extended systematic observation.

Typically, the emphasis is on how the subjects themselves view their social life in some setting. In some cases, the sociologist actually joins the group for a period to get an accurate sense of how it operates. This approach is called *participant observation.*

This is the approach Alice Goffman (2014a) took in her study in Philadelphia. As a result of embedding herself in the community, she was able to portray a fuller description of the lives of the young African American males. In addition, she describes the experience of the women in their lives (their wives, sisters, and girlfriends); the underground marketplace that emerges in which local entrepreneurs provide goods and services, such as clean urine for drug tests, faked documents, and prison guards who provide cell phones to inmates; and the lives of those living in the inner city who keep their distance from illegal activity and those involved in it. Because she used participant observation, her descriptions are deep and rich and she includes many extended quotes from the individuals involved.

Observation research raises questions about the appropriate nature of the relationship between researchers and their subjects. Full participation with study subjects allows for a deeper understanding of life in such social worlds (Adler and Adler 2012), but this depth must be balanced against the need for objectivity. For example, Alice Goffman's decision to become roommates with two of her informants provided her with up-close access to the reality of their everyday experiences, but it also raised questions about her capacity to remain objective. When one of those informants is later murdered, and the other wants to go out looking for the killer, she volunteered to drive. Critics later raised questions about whether or not this act constituted conspiracy to commit murder (Volokh 2015). In addition to the problem of objectivity, a related concern is whether or not closeness to those in one part of a community may result in insufficient detail in describing another. The depth that results from a narrow focus on a specific community, and on particular members within it, comes at the expense of breadth.

experiment An artificially created situation that allows a researcher to manipulate variables.

experimental group The subjects in an experiment who are exposed to an independent variable introduced by a researcher.

control group The subjects in an experiment who are not introduced to the independent variable by the researcher.

Have you ever asked yourself, "What were they thinking?" Maybe it's the music people like, the clothes they wear, the major they choose, the job they get, the person they date, the religion they practice, or the candidate they support. Although sociology cannot provide specific answers for why particular individuals think and act like they do, it does offer insight into the social factors that influence our choices. Imagine that you had the chance to answer some specific question such as those above. Which would you choose? What independent and dependent variables might you identify? What would your hypothesis be? What research design might you select? What makes sociology fun is that we get to ask questions and find answers.

EXPERIMENTS

When scientists want to study a possible cause-and-effect relationship, they conduct an **experiment**—an artificially created situation that allows a researcher to manipulate variables. Researchers carefully control the experimental context in order to measure the degree to which the independent variable causes change in the dependent variable under study. Although experiments can prove insightful, sociologists tend not to use them as frequently as the other research designs, because they are typically more interested in understanding people's natural responses, and there are ethical questions about manipulating people's responses.

In a classic experiment, researchers begin by dividing subjects with similar characteristics into two groups in order to see the impact of one independent variable. The **experimental group** is then exposed to an independent variable; the **control group** is not. Thus, if scientists were testing a new type of antibiotic, they would administer the drug to an experimental group but not to a control group.

SOCTHINK

What social group or setting (such as a religious group, political organization, sorority/fraternity, laboratory, or office) might you want to learn more about through in-depth participant observation? How would you go about making contact? How would you gain members' trust?

SOCTHINK

Imagine you are a researcher interested in the effect playing computer or console games has on a college student's grades. How might you go about setting up an experiment to measure this effect?

One of the disadvantages of experiments, just as in observation research, is that the presence of a social scientist or other observer may affect the behavior of the people being studied. The recognition of this phenomenon grew out of an experiment conducted during the 1920s and 1930s at the Hawthorne plant of the Western Electric Company near Chicago. A group of researchers set out to determine how to improve the productivity of workers at the plant. The investigators manipulated such variables as lighting and working hours to see what impact the changes would have on how much workers produce. To their surprise, they found that every step they took seemed to increase output. Even measures that seemed likely to have the opposite effect, such as reducing the amount of lighting in the plant down to moonlight levels, led to higher productivity (Mayo 1933).

Why did the plant's employees work harder even under less favorable conditions? The researchers initially concluded that the workers modified their behavior because they knew they were being studied. They responded positively to the novelty of being subjects in an experiment and to the fact that researchers were interested in them. Since that time, sociologists have used the term **Hawthorne effect** to describe the unintended influence that observers of experiments can have on their subjects, even though later studies show the situation there was more complex (Brannigan and Zwerman 2001). It highlights the difficulties experiments present in seeking to understand how people behave in their real-world environments.

Sociologists do sometimes try to approximate experimental conditions in the field. Sociologist Devah Pager (2003) devised an experiment to assess the impact of a criminal background on individuals' employment opportunities. She sent four polite, well-dressed young men out to look for an entry-level job in Milwaukee, Wisconsin. All four were 23-year-old college students, but they presented themselves as high school graduates with similar job histories. Two of the men were Black and two were White. One Black applicant and one White applicant claimed to have served 18 months in jail for a felony conviction—possession of cocaine with intent to distribute.

White Privilege in Job Seeking

Percent chance of getting a call back

White — No criminal record: **34%**
17% Criminal record

Black — No criminal record: **14%**
5% Criminal record

Source: Pager 2003:958. Photo: © Dolas/Getty Images RF.

Hawthorne effect The unintended influence that observers of experiments can have on their subjects.

Employees at a Westinghouse Electric and Manufacturing Company in 1925. Photo: © Hulton Archive/Getty Images.

Most Common U.S. Surnames

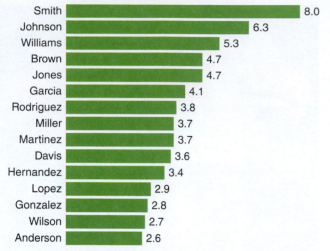

Surname	Value
Smith	8.0
Johnson	6.3
Williams	5.3
Brown	4.7
Jones	4.7
Garcia	4.1
Rodriguez	3.8
Miller	3.7
Martinez	3.7
Davis	3.6
Hernandez	3.4
Lopez	2.9
Gonzalez	2.8
Wilson	2.7
Anderson	2.6

Note: Numbers are per 1,000 people in the population.
Source: Chalabi and Flowers 2014.

The experiences of the four men with 350 potential employers were vastly different. The White applicant with a purported prison record received only half as many callbacks as the other White applicant—17 percent compared to 34 percent (see the "White Privilege in Job Seeking" graphic). But as dramatic as the effect of his criminal record was, the effect of his race was more significant. Despite his prison record, he received slightly more callbacks than the Black applicant with no criminal record (17 percent compared to 14 percent). To assess the validity of her findings, Pager and colleagues later conducted a similar experiment in New York City, and the results were the same (Pager and Western 2012; Pager, Western, and Bonikowski 2009; Pager, Western, and Sugie 2009). This experiment revealed that when it comes to getting a job, race matters.

secondary analysis A variety of research techniques that make use of previously collected and publicly accessible information and data.

USE OF EXISTING SOURCES

Sociologists do not necessarily need to collect new data to conduct research. The term **secondary analysis** refers to a variety of research techniques that make use of previously collected and publicly accessible information and data. As indicated earlier, the U.S. Census Bureau provides a treasure trove of such data.

Every 10 years, as required by the U.S. Constitution, the Bureau attempts to gather information from every household in the United States. In 2010 the initial response rate they received from the Census form they mailed out was 72 percent. After door-to-door contacts were completed, they were ultimately able to gather information from 99.62 percent of the nation's housing units. Gathering data on that scale is very expensive and time-consuming, so the information the Census provides is extremely valuable to researchers. One difficulty, as is the case with all secondary analysis, is that researchers do not have control over the questions that get asked. As such, conclusions they can draw are limited by the available data.

SOC THINK

"NameVoyager" at www.babynamewizard.com is an application that allows you to type in any name to trace its popularity over time. Go there and enter several names to see how they have changed over time. Considering some of the specific names you tried, what factors might have contributed to their rise and fall? How popular is your first name? How and why has its popularity changed over time?

Even though it was not explicitly conducted with the research questions sociologists have in mind, such data analysis can be extremely fruitful. For example, every year the Social Security Administration receives thousands of registrations for newborn babies. Using these

Major Research Designs

Method	Examples	Advantages	Limitations
Survey	Questionnaires Interviews	Yields information about specific issues	Can be expensive and time-consuming
Observation	Ethnography	Yields detailed information about specific groups or organizations	Involves months if not years of labor-intensive data collection
Experiment	Deliberate manipulation of people's social behavior	Yields direct measures of people's behavior	Has ethical limitations on the degree to which subjects' behavior can be manipulated
Existing sources/ Secondary analysis	Analysis of census or health data Analysis of films or TV commercials	Cost-efficiency; nonreactive	Limited to data collected for some other purpose

© Scott Barbour/Getty Images

data, we can recognize shifts in cultural trends in the population. The name John was in the top five for boys from 1900 until 1972 but has since fallen to 27th. The name Mary ranked number one or two from 1900 through 1965 and now ranks 121st. By contrast, the name Juan was ranked 215th in 1900, peaked at 46th in 1999, and now ranks 100th. Maria went from 150th in 1900, peaked at 31st from 1973 to 1975, and now ranks 112th (Social Security Administration 2014b). These shifts reflect the growing influence of the Latino population in the United States.

Existing data from another source, the U.S. Census Bureau, confirm this shift. Analysis of these data revealed that although Smith remained the most common surname in the United States, Garcia and Rodriguez rose into the top 10 starting in 2007. This marked the first time in the nation's history that a non-Anglo name had been counted among the most common names. Such name changes reflect an overall shift in the U.S. population from a nation composed primarily of European descendants to one that is more globally diverse, a trend sociologists expect will continue (Word et al. 2007). In a statistical analysis seeking to combine first and last names, researchers estimate that James Smith is the most common name in the United States. Maria Garcia comes in at 15th (Chalabi and Flowers 2014).

Part of the appeal of secondary analysis to sociologists is that it is nonreactive—that is, doing this type of study does not influence what you find. For example, Émile Durkheim's statistical analysis of existing suicide data neither increased nor decreased human self-destruction. Researchers, then, can avoid the Hawthorne effect by using secondary analysis. However, there is one inherent problem: The researcher who relies on data collected by someone else may not find exactly what he or she needs. Social scientists who are studying family violence can use statistics from police and social service agencies on reported cases of spouse abuse and child abuse, but because not all incidents get reported, government bodies have no precise data on all cases of abuse.

Secondary analysis also allows us to study social contexts, both present and past, through careful analysis of cultural, economic, and political documents, including newspapers, periodicals, radio and television tapes, the Internet, scripts, diaries, songs, folklore, and legal papers. In examining these sources, researchers employ a technique known as **content analysis**—the systematic coding and objective recording of data, guided by a given rationale.

Using content analysis, Erving Goffman (1979) conducted a pioneering exploration of how advertisements portray women. The ads he studied typically showed women as subordinate to or dependent on others, or as taking instruction from men. Women engaged in caressing and touching gestures more than men. Even when presented in leadership roles, women were likely to be shown striking seductive poses or gazing out into space. Jeanne Kilbourne's content analysis of ads demonstrates that women continue to be portrayed as objects. She found that advertisers' primary message is that women should spend their time, energy, and money trying to attain the idealized, airbrushed image of female beauty only achievable with the assistance of Photoshop. She quotes supermodel Cindy Crawford as saying, "I wish I looked like Cindy Crawford" (Kilbourne 2010).

> **content analysis** The systematic coding and objective recording of data, guided by some rationale.

Researchers have also used content analysis to investigate media portrayals of other public health issues. For example, Sargent and Heatherton (2009) analyzed the top-25 films for each year from 1990 to 2007 and found that the average number of smoking occurrences fell from 3.5 to 0.23 per film. They compare this with the declining smoking levels of U.S. eighth-graders, an average of 1.3 percent per year after 1996. Given the complexity of possible factors, they cannot assert a direct causal link between the two, although they point to other research that demonstrates that exposure to smoking in films does affect youth smoking rates (National Cancer Institute 2008).

© Craig Blankenhorn/© AMC/Courtesy: Everett Collection.

Primary Themes in Children's Television Food Commercials

- 47% Fun/happiness
- 18% Taste/flavor/smell
- 12% Product's uniqueness
- 10% Other
- 8% Physical strength
- 5% Popularity of product
- 0% Healthy product

Source: Stitt and Kunkel 2008. *Photo:* © RubberBall Productions RF.

code of ethics The standards of acceptable behavior developed by and for members of a profession.

Concerns about childhood obesity led researchers to analyze commercials aired during Saturday children's television programming on broadcast and cable channels. For example, in an analysis of more than 1,200 ads, Stitt and Kunkel (2008) found that food ads made up almost half of the commercial time, an average of 11 food ads per hour. Of these ads, 9 out of 10 were for high-calorie, low-nutrient food products such as sugared snacks, sugared cereals, and fast food. The researchers also found that the most common strategy used to persuade viewers to try the products was to associate the product with having fun or happiness.

>> Research Ethics

When conducting research involving people, sociologists, like all scientists, are limited in what they can do. They have an ethical responsibility to treat their subjects with respect and not expose them to undue harm. To clarify expectations for researchers, the American Sociological Association (1999) provides guidelines in the form of its **Code of Ethics.** It lays out the following general principles:

- *Professional Competence:* Use appropriate research techniques in proper ways.
- *Integrity:* Be honest, respectful, and fair.
- *Professional and Scientific Responsibility:* Adhere to the highest scientific and professional standards.
- *Respect for People's Rights, Dignity, and Diversity:* Be unbiased and non-discriminatory, respecting the dignity and worth of all people.
- *Social Responsibility:* Contribute to the public good.

Over time, these general principles have given rise to some concrete practices for researchers to follow. For example,

researchers should secure informed consent from subjects, meaning that, if at all possible, the people being studied should be aware of any possible risks of participation and explicitly agree to participate.

CONFIDENTIALITY

One of the most common techniques used to protect subjects is to promise them confidentiality, shielding their identity so that it is impossible to identify those who participated. Ensuring the privacy of subjects helps protect them from potential negative effects of participation. Sometimes participation can be totally anonymous, so that not even the researcher knows who provided which responses. To ensure that these protections are properly secured, researchers typically submit their proposals to an institutional review board that confirms that the research does not place subjects at an unreasonable level of risk.

These basic principles and procedures may seem clear-cut in the abstract but can be difficult to adhere to in practice. For example, should a sociologist who is engaged in participant observation research always protect the confidentiality of subjects? What if the subjects

We often make decisions based on common sense, but doing so can result in errors. Analyzing data reveals underlying patterns that we might otherwise miss, enabling us to make more effective decisions. In the film *Moneyball,* and in the book it's based on, Michael Lewis (2003) tells the story of general manager Billy Beane, whose Oakland A's team lacked the money to afford big-money free agents. Beane goes against baseball's conventional wisdom and uses statistical analyses to make decisions about how best to produce runs; by bringing the nonobvious patterns to the surface, he turns the team into a winner.

POPSOC

Photo: © Columbia Pictures/Courtesy Everett Collection.

are members of a group involved in unethical or illegal activities? What if the sociologist is interviewing political activists and is questioned by government authorities about the research?

Like journalists, sociologists occasionally find themselves facing the ethical dilemma of whether to reveal their sources to law enforcement authorities. In May 1993 sociologist Rik Scarce was jailed for contempt of court because he declined to tell a federal grand jury what he knew—or even whether he knew anything—about a 1991 raid on a university research laboratory by animal rights activists. At the time, Scarce was doing research for a book about environmental protestors and knew at least one suspect in the break-in. Although he was chastised by a federal judge, Scarce won respect from fellow prison inmates, who regarded him as a man who "won't snitch" (Monaghan 2012; Scarce 2005).

The ASA, in defense of the principle of confidentiality, supported Scarce's position when he appealed his sentence. Scarce maintained his silence. Ultimately, the judge ruled that nothing would be gained by further incarceration, and Scarce was released after spending 159 days in jail. The U.S. Supreme Court ultimately declined to hear Scarce's case on appeal. The Court's failure to consider his case led Scarce (1994, 1995, 2005) to argue that federal legislation is needed to clarify the right of scholars and members of the press to preserve the confidentiality of those they interview.

© Siqui Sanchez/The Image Bank/Getty Images.

SOC THINK

Under what circumstances might researchers need to deceive subjects, even if it might result in their emotional harm, in order to get genuine responses?

RESEARCH FUNDING

An additional concern of the ASA's *Code of Ethics* is the possibility that funding sources could influence research findings. Accepting funds from a private organization or even a government agency that stands to benefit from a study's results can clash with the ASA's first principle of maintaining objectivity and integrity in research. As such, all sources of funding should be disclosed.

Another example is ExxonMobil's support for research on jury verdicts. On March 24, 1989, its oil tanker *Exxon Valdez* hit a reef off the coast of Alaska, spilling over 11 million gallons of oil into Prince William Sound. Until the Deepwater Horizon spill in the Gulf of Mexico in 2010, the *Valdez* disaster was regarded as the world's worst oil spill in terms of its environmental impact. In 1994 a federal court ordered ExxonMobil to pay $5.3 billion in damages for the accident. It appealed the verdict and began approaching legal scholars,

sociologists, and psychologists who might be willing to study jury deliberations. The corporation's objective was to develop academic support for its lawyers' contention that the punitive judgments in such cases result from faulty deliberations and do not deter future incidents.

Some scholars have questioned the propriety of accepting funds under these circumstances, even if the source is disclosed. The scholars who accepted ExxonMobil's support deny that it influenced their work or changed their conclusions. To date, the company has spent more than $1 million on the research, and at least one compilation of studies congenial to the corporation's point of view has been published. As ethical considerations require, the academics who conducted the studies disclosed ExxonMobil's role in funding the research. In 2006, drawing on these studies, the corporation's lawyers succeeded in persuading an appeals court to reduce the corporation's legal damages from $5.3 to $2.5 billion (Freudenburg 2005; Liptak 2008a, 2008b). In 2008, the amount was further reduced to $508 million, though in 2009 the Ninth U.S. Circuit Court of Appeals ordered ExxonMobil to pay on additional $500 million in punitive damages, court costs, and interest payments.

> **value neutrality** Max Weber's term for objectivity of sociologists in the interpretation of data.

VALUE NEUTRALITY

The ethical considerations of sociologists lie not only in the methods they use and the funding they accept but also in the way they interpret their results. Max Weber ([1904] 1949) recognized that personal values would influence the topics that sociologists select for research. In his view, that was perfectly acceptable, but he argued that researchers should not allow their personal feelings to influence the interpretation of data. In Weber's phrase, sociologists must practice **value neutrality** in their research.

As part of this neutrality, investigators have an ethical obligation to accept research findings even when the data run counter to their own personal views, to theoretically based explanations, or to widely accepted beliefs. For example, Émile Durkheim challenged popular conceptions when he reported that social (rather than supernatural) forces were an important factor in suicide.

> The greatest obstacle to discovery is not ignorance—it is the illusion of knowledge.
>
> Daniel Boorstin

Some sociologists believe that such neutrality is impossible. They worry that Weber's insistence on value-free sociology may lead the public to accept sociological conclusions without exploring researchers' biases. Others have suggested that sociologists may use objectivity as a justification for remaining uncritical of existing institutions and centers of power (Gouldner 1970). Despite the early work of W. E. B. Du Bois and Jane Addams, for example, sociologists still need to be reminded that the discipline often fails to adequately consider all people's social behavior.

Sociologists should not focus only on those in the majority but must also seek out the stories of those who are often invisible due to their relative lack of power and resources. In fact, sociologists have learned much about society by listening to the voices of those who are excluded from mainstream sources of power and denied access to valuable resources. In her book *The Death of White Sociology* (1973), Joyce Ladner called attention to the tendency of mainstream sociologists to investigate the lives of African Americans only in the context of social problems. Similarly, feminist sociologist Shulamit Reinharz (1992) has argued that sociological research should not only include the research of sociologists who are outside the mainstream but should also be open to drawing on relevant research by nonsociologists who might provide additional depth and understanding of social life. The issue of value neutrality does not mean that sociologists can't have opinions, but it does mean that they must work to overcome any biases, however unintentional, that they may bring to their analysis of research.

FEMINIST METHODOLOGY

Although researchers must be objective, their theoretical orientation necessarily influences the questions they ask—or, just as important, the questions they fail to ask. Because their contributions have opened up so many new lines of inquiry, sociologists using the feminist perspective have had perhaps the greatest impact on the current generation of social researchers. Until the 1960s, for example, researchers frequently studied work and family separately, as if they were two discrete institutions. Feminist theorists, however, reject the notion that these are separate spheres. They were the first sociologists to look at housework as real work and to investigate the struggles people face in balancing the demands of work and family (Hochschild 1989; Lopata 1971).

Feminist theorists have also drawn attention to researchers' tendency to overlook women in sociological studies. For most of the history of sociology, researchers conducted studies of male subjects or male-led groups and organizations, then generalized their findings to all people. For many decades, for example, ethnographic studies of urban life focused on street corners, neighborhood taverns, and bowling alleys—places where men typically congregated. Although researchers gained valuable insights in this way, they did not form a true impression of

5 Movies on SOCIOLOGICAL RESEARCH

Kinsey
The father of modern sexual research employs individual case studies.

Thank You for Smoking
A satire about the tobacco industry, showing how statistics can lie.

Supersize Me
A reporter investigates the American fast-food industry by eating at McDonald's for one month.

56 Up
Documentary following 14 children as their lives progress from age 7 to 56.

Devil's Playground
Amish teens experiment with drinking, drugs, and sex before committing to a lifetime within the Amish community.

city life, because they overlooked the areas where women were likely to gather, such as playgrounds, grocery stores, and front stoops. These are the arenas that the feminist perspective focuses on.

Feminist scholars have also contributed to a greater global awareness within sociology. To feminist theorists, the traditional distinction between industrial nations and developing countries overlooks the close relationship between these two supposedly separate worlds. Feminist theorists have called for more research on the special role that immigrant women play in maintaining their households, on the use of domestic workers from less developed nations by households in industrial countries, and on the global trafficking of sex workers (Cheng 2003; K. Cooper et al. 2007).

Finally, feminist researchers tend to involve and consult their subjects more than other researchers, contributing to a significant increase in more qualitative and participatory research. They are also more oriented toward seeking change, raising the public consciousness, and influencing policy, which represents a return to sociology's roots (Harding 2003; Naples 2003; Sprague 2005).

Sociologists must be engaged with the world. Although there are numerous ways in which they accomplish this, first and foremost this involvement comes through research. As we have seen throughout this chapter, it is not enough for sociologists to stand back and theorize or even hypothesize about why we think and act the way we do. We must go out, collect data, and use it to inform our interpretations and explanations of human behavior. Having done so, we bear a responsibility for that knowledge, whether that means simply sharing it with other sociologists through conference presentations and journal articles or actively working for positive social change.

SOCIOLOGY IS A VERB

People Watching

As a mini-observation project, do some intentional people watching. Pick a public place, such as a mall, where people frequently walk by, and record what you observe. What characteristics stick out? How do people vary by gender, age, race, or ethnicity? To what extent do they travel individually or in groups? Record all your observations and then use your data to write up a summary of what you have learned.

For REVIEW

I. What steps do sociologists take when seeking to answer why people think and act the way they do?
- They need to define the problem, review existing literature, formulate a hypothesis, collect and analyze data, and develop a conclusion.

II. What techniques do sociologists use to collect data?
- Research designs used to collect data include surveys, observation, experiments, and use of existing sources.

III. What ethical concerns must sociologists consider while conducting research?
- They have a responsibility to follow the ASA *Code of Ethics*, particularly respecting confidentiality, revealing research funding, maintaining value neutrality, and overall, treating their subjects with respect.

Functionalist View

Sociological research seeks to better understand how the various parts of society **fit together** to create social order and stability.

Researchers focus on **consensus and cooperation** and on the large-scale (or **macro**) level, looking at society from the top down.

Research can also help determine whether the facets of our society are **functioning** as intended. For example, does more education "pay off" in higher income?

STABILITY, CONSENSUS, COOPERATION
KEY CONCEPTS

Conflict View

Sociological research seeks to better understand how **power** operates and how **resources** are distributed and controlled.

Focus of research tends to be on the large-scale (or **macro**) level, looking at society from the top down.

Key questions behind research include: Who benefits? How does the status quo maintain **privileges** for some and denial of opportunity for others? How does **access** to resources shape outcomes?

KEY CONCEPTS
INEQUALITY, STRATIFICATION, INTERESTS

Interactionist View

Sociological research seeks to better understand how we construct meaning and establish order through **everyday interactions** with others.

Focus of research is on the small-scale (or **micro**) level, looking at the construction of society from the bottom up.

Researchers are most likely to use **participant observation** because it provides a window into people's everyday lived experiences.

KEY CONCEPTS
ROLES, SYMBOLS, LABELING

MAKE THE CONNECTION

After reviewing the chapter, answer the following questions:

1
Which perspective did Alice Goffman use in her research? Why?

2
How might a researcher's perspective influence the research design he or she picks? Give an example for each perspective.

3
How might each perspective interpret Devah Pager's findings in her experiment about race and job seeking?

4
How might each perspective study the relationship between education and income in a slightly different way?

Pop Quiz

1. **The first step in any sociological research project is to**
   a. collect data.
   b. define the problem.
   c. review previous research.
   d. formulate a hypothesis.

2. **An explanation of an abstract concept that is specific enough to allow a researcher to measure the concept is a(n)**
   a. hypothesis.
   b. correlation.
   c. operational definition.
   d. variable.

3. **In sociological and scientific research, a hypothesis**
   a. is an educated guess.
   b. is a testable statement about the relationship between two or more variables.
   c. insists that science can deal only with observable entities known directly to experience.
   d. ensures that the people being studied are representative of the population as a whole.

4. **The variable hypothesized to cause or influence another is called the**
   a. dependent variable.
   b. hypothetical variable.
   c. correlation variable.
   d. independent variable.

5. **The degree to which a measure or scale truly reflects the phenomenon under study is known as**
   a. reliability.
   b. sampling.
   c. validity.
   d. control.

6. **Which research technique do sociologists use to ensure that data are statistically representative of the population being studied?**
   a. sampling
   b. experiments
   c. correlation
   d. control variables

7. **Ethnography is an example of which type of research design?**
   a. surveys
   b. observation
   c. experiments
   d. use of existing resources

8. **When Devah Pager did her studies analyzing the relationship between race, criminal records, and job callbacks, which research technique did she use?**
   a. experiment
   b. survey
   c. secondary analysis
   d. participant observation

9. **The unintended influence that observers of experiments can have on their subjects is known as**
   a. the correlation effect.
   b. confidentiality.
   c. validity.
   d. the Hawthorne effect.

10. **According to Max Weber, researchers should not allow their personal feelings to influence the interpretation of data. He referred to this as**
    a. the code of ethics.
    b. content analysis.
    c. value neutrality.
    d. secondary analysis.

1. (b), 2. (c), 3. (b), 4. (d), 5. (c), 6. (a), 7. (b), 8. (a), 9. (d), 10. (c)

3

Culture

BREAKING RULES AND LOWERING BARRIERS

On January 11, 2015, Charlie Todd took a train ride on the New York City subway. He wasn't wearing any pants. Charlie was not alone. In fact, he was joined by more than 4,000 other pantsless riders in New York City that day. They gathered in seven locations around the city, boarded 11 different subway lines, and headed toward a rendezvous at Union Station. They spaced themselves out across many subway cars, had minimal interaction with one another, and acted as normally as possible. The event was all part of the now-annual No Pants Subway Ride coordinated by Improv Everywhere, a self-described "prank collective that causes scenes of chaos and joy in public places," which Charlie Todd founded in 2001.

Improv Everywhere has sponsored over 100 missions, some of which may be familiar because their videos have often gone viral. The No Pants event started in 2002 with just seven participants and grew larger each year, celebrating its fourteenth anniversary in 2015 with over 10,000 participants worldwide in 60 cities across 25 countries, including London, Tokyo, and Bangalore. In 2008, over 200 participants ("agents") converged on Grand Central Station and simultaneously froze in place for five minutes, after which they resumed what they were doing as if nothing had happened. In 2009, they randomly picked a just-married couple departing the City Clerk's Office and threw them a wedding reception complete with a formally attired wedding party, cake, a toast, gifts, and dancing.

In 2013, agents served as "seeing eye persons" for people who were texting and walking in New York City, clearing a path while the person texting trailed behind, holding on to a leash. In 2014, 40 agents entered New York City's Fifth Avenue Gap store and pretended to be mannequins until 911 was called and police escorted them out. (Videos for these and many other missions are available at ImprovEverywhere.com.)

The scenes that Improv Everywhere creates help reveal our taken-for-granted rules for behavior. In our daily lives we follow routines that are largely invisible to us, and we expect others to do likewise. When people do things differently, we tend to get uncomfortable. It disrupts our sense of order. One of the best parts of their videos is watching how people respond. Initial confusion and nervousness are often followed by smiles as people realize they are seeing a performance. We want and need the actions of others to be predictable, so we create both formal and informal rules to guide our behaviors. Such rules are an important component of culture.

As You READ >>

- **Why do humans create culture?**
- **What does culture consist of?**
- **How does culture both enable and constrain?**

>> Culture and Society

We need culture. As humans, we lack the complex instincts other species are born with that enable them to survive. Unlike birds, for example, our genes do not provide us with the knowledge to build nests (or homes) for ourselves, and we can choose whether to seek out warmer climates for the winter or cooler ones in the summer. Because our actions are not narrowly determined by such instincts, we must construct their equivalent in order to provide food, clothes, shelter, and a host of other human needs. **Culture** consists of everything humans create in establishing our relationships to nature and with each other. It includes language, knowledge, material creations, and rules for behavior. In other words, it encompasses all that we say, know, make, and do in our efforts to survive and thrive.

Culture mediates between individuals and the external world. While we experience the natural world through our senses—hearing, sight, touch, smell, and taste—we depend on culture to interpret those sensations. Our retinas may send visual images to our brains, but recognition of patterns is made possible through culture. For example, we might fail to see an image in an optical illusion until someone nudges us to "look at it this way." Nothing about the physical image changed, but our perspective on it, with the help of others, has. We do not perceive nature directly; we perceive the world around us through the lens of culture.

Through interactions with others, we develop and share perceptions of what the world is like and how we should act within it. The shared culture that results provides us with a tool kit of similar habits, skills, and styles (Swidler 1986). For example, when someone says hello, we know how to respond. When we show up for the first day of class, we know where to sit or stand depending on whether or not we are the student or professor. Culture facilitates social interaction.

Over time, we take shared culture for granted. The ways we think, the rules we follow, the things we have created all seem natural to us. We pass along these expectations to others within the contexts of families, schools, places of worship, and workplaces. As a result, we know what to do, when to do it, and with whom.

culture Everything humans create in establishing our relationships to nature and with each other.

© The McGraw-Hill Companies, Inc./ Jill Braaten, photographer

society The structure of relationships within which culture is created and shared through regularized patterns of social interaction.

cultural universal A common practice or belief shared by all societies.

In so doing, we create society. **Society** consists of the structure of relationships within which culture is created and shared through regularized patterns of social interaction. Society provides the taken-for-granted structure within which we interact. It both enables and constrains the culture we construct. In a given culture, some ways of thinking, acting, and making seem inevitable, whereas other ways may not even be conceivable. For example, the way our society organizes government determines our rights and responsibilities and the way we organize education shapes how and what we learn.

Because cultural preferences are constructed by different people in different times and places, culture varies across societies. People often confront this reality when they travel abroad and find their taken-for-granted ideas and actions to be out of place and inappropriate. Educational methods, marriage ceremonies, and religious doctrines vary significantly. In India, parents are accustomed to arranging marriages for their children, but in the United States, parents typically leave such choices up to their children. Lifelong residents of Cairo consider it natural to speak Arabic, whereas lifelong residents of Buenos Aires feel the same way about Spanish.

>> Creating Culture

Because we are not narrowly determined by our genes, human beings throughout history have demonstrated the innovative capacity to create amazing cultural artifacts. Examples include the cave paintings at Lascaux, France, poems by Langston Hughes, novels by Toni Morrison, and films such as *Schindler's List*. We now take for granted what once seemed impossible, from air travel, to the cloning of cells, to organ transplants, to always-on wireless Internet access. We can peer into the outermost reaches of the universe or analyze our innermost feelings. In all these ways, our cultural creativity sets us apart as remarkably different from other species of the animal kingdom.

CULTURAL UNIVERSALS

Given that we have a certain amount of freedom to construct culture in a multitude of ways, one of the early sociological questions was whether there are any aspects of culture shared by all people. Some sociologists, such as Comte, sought to discover whether there are fundamental laws of society equivalent to the laws of nature. Such patterns were referred to as **cultural universals**—common practices and beliefs shared by all societies. Anthropologist George Murdock (1945) compared results from studies of hundreds of cultures and concluded that, although there are common denominators shared by all cultures, how cultures go about addressing each varies significantly. Included among his list of 70 categories were athletic sports, community organization, dancing, division of labor, folklore, funeral rites, housing, incest taboos, marriage, personal names, property rights, religious ritual, sexual restrictions, and trade. The degree of human variation we see in how we organize such activities suggests that we do not have universal laws determining human behavior that are the equivalent of the laws of nature in science.

The debate about the degree to which our behavior is determined harkens back to philosophical questions regarding nature versus

SOCTHINK

How does social context influence how we relate to others? If you were asked about how school is going, how might you respond differently at home with your parents compared to in a dorm with friends or at work with colleagues?

Going **GLOBAL**

Is success in life determined by forces outside our control?

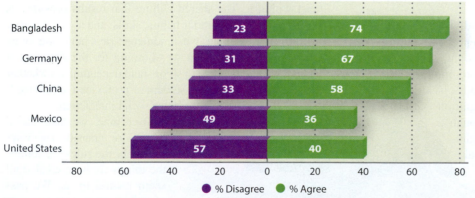

	% Disagree	% Agree
Bangladesh	23	74
Germany	31	67
China	33	58
Mexico	49	36
United States	57	40

Source: Pew Research Center 2014a.

As the graph illustrates, perceptions about the degree to which we control our fates vary by country. In a survey of 44 nations, only Venezuelans (62 percent) were more likely than people in the United States to disagree. The global median was 38 percent.

In Guatemala, Tanzania, and around the world, material culture varies across time and place.

Did You Know?

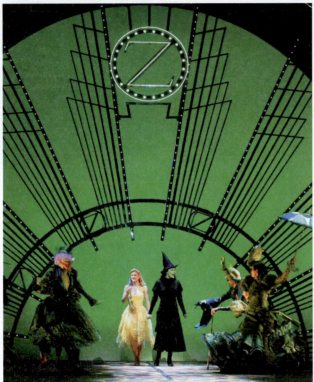

. . . Marc Platt, producer of the Broadway play *Wicked* and numerous movies, including *Legally Blonde*, *Rachel Getting Married*, *Drive*, and *Ricki and the Flash*, was a sociology major.

Photo: © AP Photo/Thomas Kienzle

nurture. According to the "nature" argument, the genes we inherit determine our outcomes, as if our fates were programmed by computer code over which we have limited control. **Sociobiology** is a discipline dedicated to the systematic study of how biology affects human social behavior. On the other side, "nurture" means that our destiny is shaped primarily by the social and psychological influences of others around us (especially parents); human nature is malleable, and we become who we are in the contexts of the societies we create. Over time most researchers have realized that this either-or argument is inadequate or misleading, because the relationship between the two forces is more fluid, better represented by shades of gray.

Sociological research reveals significant cross-cultural and cross-time variation in how we think and act. For example, in the 19th century it was thought that, biologically speaking, women were not capable of success in college because their brains were too small and their reproductive organs made them too emotional. Over time we learned that such presuppositions are false—women now make up almost 60 percent of college graduates—but at one time these assertions were accepted as "natural" and therefore resistant to change. Similar biologically based claims have been used in the past to justify inequality (claims that were later revealed to be scientifically untrue), leading many sociologists to question biological explanations for human behavior (Lucal 2010). One of the lessons we learn about culture throughout human history is that variety and change are the norm.

More recently, researchers in both the natural sciences and sociology have sought a nuanced understanding of the relationship between biology and culture. In the scientific community there has been growing support for gene-culture coevolution, in which each shapes the other through the course of human development. From this perspective, how individuals turn out isn't simply a matter of whether they inherited a set of "bad genes" or "good genes." Instead, researchers argue that an interdependent relationship exists between genes and environment. How genes are expressed (whether or not they are triggered, in other words) can depend on our natural, social, and cultural contexts. From this perspective, genes are responsive to the social context and do not inevitably trigger predetermined responses

sociobiology The systematic study of how biology affects human social behavior.

© Business Wire

innovation The process of introducing a new idea or object to a culture through discovery or invention.

discovery The process of uncovering or revealing an existing aspect of reality.

invention The combination of existing cultural artifacts to create something new.

at predetermined times (Rutter 2010; Rutter, Moffitt, and Caspi 2006; Shenk 2010). In pursuit of a more informed understanding of this interplay, the American Sociological Association established a new section called "Evolution, Biology, and Society" in 2005 (Machalek and Martin 2010).

INNOVATION

Humans have the freedom and ability to create new things. Whereas a robin's nest in the year 2016 looks very much like one in 1916 or 1016 because robins act on a nest-building instinct, human abodes vary widely. We can live in a cave, a castle, a sod house, a pueblo, a high-rise apartment, a McMansion, or a dorm room. Such variation is possible because we are free to innovate. **Innovation**—the process of introducing a new idea or object to a culture—interests sociologists because it can have ripple effects across a society.

There are two main forms of innovation: discovery and invention. **Discovery** involves uncovering or revealing an

─ **SOC**THINK ─

Taking into account the sociological imagination, to what extent do you think innovation is a matter of individual genius versus being in the right place at the right time?

existing aspect of reality. The identification of the DNA molecule and the sighting of a new moon of Saturn are both acts of discovery. A significant factor in the process of discovery is the sharing of newfound knowledge with others. By contrast, an **invention** combines existing cultural artifacts to create something new. The bow and arrow, the automobile, and the television are all examples of inventions, as are abstract concepts such as Protestantism and democracy.

DIFFUSION

More and more cultural expressions and practices are crossing national borders and influencing the traditions and customs of the societies exposed to them. Sociologists

U.S. Wireless Phone Usage

2013 — 335.7 million subscribers

2010 — 302.9

2005 — 207.9

2000 — 109.5

1995 — 33.8

1990 — 5.3

= 7 million subscribers

1985 — 0.3

Technology makes it possible for us to keep in touch with almost anyone anywhere, as these numbers showing the explosion in the number of wireless phone subscribers since 1985 demonstrate.

Source: CTIA 2014.

use the term **diffusion** to refer to the process by which some aspect of culture spreads from group to group or society to society. Historically, diffusion typically occurred through a variety of means, including exploration, war, military conquest, and missionary work. Today, societal boundaries that were once relatively closed owing to the constraints of transportation and communication have become more permeable, with cross-cultural exchange occurring more quickly. Through the mass media, the Internet, immigration, and tourism, we regularly confront the people, beliefs, practices, and artifacts of other cultures.

Cultural innovation has global consequences in today's world. Starbucks, with its familiar green logo, was founded in Seattle, Washington, in 1971 but now has a global presence. Today it is possible to order a decaf latte in the heart of Beijing's Forbidden City, just outside the Palace of Heavenly Purity, the former residence of Chinese emperors. The first Starbucks in mainland China opened in 1999 and by January 2015 there were 1,657 of them. The success of Starbucks in a country in which coffee drinking is still a novelty (where the average person drinks only five cups of coffee per year and tea is the preferred drink) has been striking. In fact, for many, drinking coffee has now become a status symbol of middle-class success (Christian 2009; Halper 2013; Loxcel Geomatics 2015).

The emergence of Starbucks in China demonstrates the cultural impact of globalization. Starbucks' expansion affects not only coffee consumption patterns but also the international trade in coffee beans, which are harvested mainly in developing countries. Our consumption-oriented culture supports a retail price of three to five dollars for a single cup of premium coffee. Even though coffee prices have reached all-time highs, millions of farmers around the world can barely eke out a living. Worldwide, the growing demand for coffee, tea, chocolate, fruit, and other natural resources is straining the environment, as poor farmers in developing countries clear more and more forestland to enlarge their fields (Herman 2010).

Diffusion often comes at a cost. In practice, globalization has led to the cultural domination of developing nations by more affluent nations. In these encounters, people in developed nations often pick and choose the cultural practices they find intriguing or exotic, whereas people in developing nations often lose their traditional values and begin to identify with the culture of the dominant nations. They may discard or neglect their native language and dress, attempting to imitate the icons of mass-market entertainment and fashion. In this way, Western popular culture represents a threat to native cultures. For example, Walt Disney's critics have called his work "perhaps the primary example of America's cultural imperialism, supplanting the myths of native cultures with his own" (Gabler 2006). So something is gained and something is lost through diffusion, and often it is the poorer societies that sacrifice more of their culture.

> **diffusion** The process by which a cultural item spreads from group to group or society to society.

>> Elements of Culture

To better understand what culture consists of we can categorize it into three primary types: material, cognitive, and normative. Each type enables us to interact more effectively with the world around us. We will look at each in turn.

MATERIAL CULTURE

Because we lack complex instincts that determine our behavior, we must establish a relationship to the natural world in order to survive. We do so by constructing **material culture,** our physical modification of the natural environment to suit our purposes. Material culture includes the clothes we wear, the books we read, the chairs we sit in, the carpets we walk on, the lights we use, the buildings we live in, the cars we drive, the roads we drive on, and so much more. When such objects become part of our lives, we often take them for granted, thinking of them as just natural. Take cell phones, for example. Back in 1985 there were only 340,213 total cell phone subscribers in the United States. By the end of 2013, that number exceeded 335 million (CTIA 2014). What was once a luxury item for elites has become something that many of us can't imagine living without. Material culture exists because we as human beings have the innovative capacity to modify our world.

The most common term we use to refer to material culture is *technology*. **Technology** is a form of culture in which humans modify the natural environment to meet particular wants and needs. It includes not only high-tech items such as computers, cars, and cell phones, but low-tech items including spoons, paper, and chalk.

Technology enhances our human abilities, giving us powers we often associate with superheroes, including X-ray vision, healing powers, flight, and more. A pivotal moment in the development of such power was the invention of the steam engine during the Industrial Revolution. It provided us with historically unprecedented strength and stamina—the ability to lift and move extremely heavy objects and to do so over sustained periods of time. It made modern coal mining practical, provided manufacturing machinery with the power needed for early factories, and powered early tractors and locomotives, setting the stage for modern global mobility (Rosen 2010).

© iStock/Getty Images RF

material culture Our physical modification of the natural environment to suit our purposes.

technology A form of culture in which humans modify the natural environment to meet particular wants and needs.

cultural lag A period of adjustment when the nonmaterial culture is still struggling to adapt to new material conditions.

Advances in technology, especially when it comes to the revolutions in communication and transportation, have linked more individuals in a global network than was ever possible in the past. Cell phones, for example, enable us to stay in touch with friends and family from almost anywhere. Planes, trains, and automobiles allow us to travel over long distances in almost no time at all, reducing the historic significance of geographic separation and isolation. And laptops and iPads allow us to bring the workplace with us wherever we go.

Sometimes technological change occurs faster than our capacity to interpret and understand the impact of such changes. Because it goes to the core of our perception of reality, nonmaterial culture, including our values, beliefs, and expectations, is often more resistant to change than is the material culture. Sociologist William F. Ogburn (1922) introduced the term **cultural lag** to refer to the period of adjustment when the nonmaterial culture is struggling to adapt to new conditions of the material culture. For example, the nine-month school calendar was designed with an agricultural economy in mind so that children would be home to help families in the fields during the summer month. Even though only a small percentage of jobs remain agricultural, most schools still adopt it. Or, another example, global climate change has become a pressing concern. Scientists overwhelmingly point to the role carbon

Photo: © Paramount/Courtesy Everett Collection

? Did You Know

. . . The United States Patent and Trademark Office issued 287,831 patents in 2013 and has approved over 8 million since the United States began issuing patents in 1790.

dioxide plays, yet we find it difficult to make the kinds of lifestyle changes that might be called for, such as driving smaller cars, using more public transportation, or reducing consumption.

COGNITIVE CULTURE

The second component of culture, **cognitive culture,** consists of our mental and symbolic representations of reality. It is the part of culture that includes values, beliefs, knowledge, and all other representations constructed to make sense of the world around us. However, its most basic component, and perhaps the most important human cultural creation and the one upon which all others depend, is language.

Language The building block of all communication and cooperation, **language** is a system of shared symbols; it includes speech, written characters, numerals, symbols, and nonverbal gestures and expressions. It provides the foundation of a common culture because it facilitates day-to-day exchanges with others, making collective action possible. According to the Ethnologue, a database of all known languages around the world, there are 7,106 living languages today. Of these, 1,519 (21 percent) are classified as "in trouble" and 915 (13 percent) are "dying." There are 341 languages with fewer than 10 speakers, and 373 languages have become extinct since 1950 (Lewis, Simons, and Fennig 2015).

Language is fundamentally social in nature. There are no inherent meanings in the sounds we make when talking or in the written alphabet we use. Instead, words get their meaning from us. We come together to agree that certain sounds or shapes mean certain things, and then we act based on those shared meanings. What matters most is our shared perception rather than the actual sound or image we use. We could, for example, teach a dog the wrong meanings of commands (*fetch* means stay, *roll over* means shake, and so on). The dog would never know the difference, but we would laugh because its responses would clash with our expectations. In fact,

Personal Sociology

Inventing New Words

I was reminded of our ability to create new words while on a family hiking trip in Oregon. Eleanor, who was four at the time, was riding on my shoulders along the trail while her sister, Emily, and my wife, Lori, were falling behind. Eleanor turned and yelled as loud as she could, "Stop chickenjagging!" We knew immediately what she meant and have used this word ever since. Anyone can create words, but they become meaningful only when they are shared with others. For Eleanor's new word to become part of the common language, the chickenjagging network must extend beyond our immediate family into the wider world. Have you ever done something similar with friends or family?

when we start to learn a new language, we are at the mercy of those who teach us. We rely on their authority, and the only way to test our fluency is through interactions with other speakers. Because language is socially constructed, it allows change. We create new words and modify existing ones—especially in our modern global culture where innovation is never-ending. Dictionaries are regularly modified in an effort to try to keep up. In 2015, the *Merriam-Webster Collegiate Dictionary* added over 1,700 new words including *photobomb, emoji, meme, twerk, jegging,* and *sriracha.*

Some linguists, including amateurs, have seized on the socially constructed nature of language in hopes of creating whole new languages from scratch, with varying motivations (Okrent 2009). Some, inspired by the scientific revolution, were appalled by the inefficiencies and irregularities of existing languages. They invented new languages in the 17th and 18th centuries (such as Francis Lodwick's *Common Writing* or John Wilkins's *Philosophical Language*) in hopes of providing us with a logical system of communication in which the relationships between concepts were rational and everything fit together into a coherent whole. They didn't want words to be arbitrary sounds we attach to things, hoping instead to map the essence of things through language. Even though they succeeded in creating coherent systems, the languages they created were difficult to use and failed to attract widespread acceptance.

cognitive culture Our mental and symbolic representations of reality.

language A system of shared symbols; it includes speech, written characters, numerals, symbols, and nonverbal gestures and expressions.

During the 20th century, other language inventors, driven in part by a desire to come to terms with globalization and increased contact across cultures, combined various aspects of existing languages. Their goal was to create a universally accepted language that would transcend national and ethnic differences. Rather than focus on purity of representation, such inventors emphasized pragmatic communication. The most successful language of this type was Esperanto, which continues to be used today. It was originally created by Ludwik Zamenhof in 1887 and literally means "one who hopes." It was Zamenhof's hope that his hybrid language would not only facilitate international commerce and communication but also contribute to world peace by reducing the cultural differences that separate us.

In spite of the relative success of Esperanto, none of these invented languages has achieved widespread adoption. Part of what such attempts seem to miss is that language is a community endeavor built up over generations of shared experiences that lead to common understandings of how the world works. Though it is technically possible to create a language from scratch, doing so undercuts the importance that such experiences have in shaping who we are. As linguist Arika Okrent put it in her history of invented languages, "[Languages] are the repositories of our very identities. . . . [Esperanto, along with other invented languages,] asks us to turn away from what makes our languages personal and unique and choose one that is generic and universal. It asks us to give up what distinguishes us from the rest of the world for something that makes everyone in the world the same" (Okrent 2009:112). To the extent that Esperanto has succeeded, it has done so by creating a community of shared participants who are committed to keeping the language alive.

A more recent wave of constructed languages comes mostly from hobbyists, known as "conlangers," who view the construction of a complete, functioning language as a challenge. The inspiration for these attempts often traces back to J. R. R. Tolkien's creation of Elvish for the *Lord of the Rings* book trilogy. Tolkien was a philologist—one who studies the history, structure, and criticism of language—and he used this knowledge to ensure that his constructed languages followed common linguistic patterns and practices. Due to the level of technical detail required, many recent conlangers are often similarly trained, such as Marc Okrand who created Klingon for the *Star Trek* movie franchise (see www.kli.org) and Paul Frommer who created the Na'vi language used in the film *Avatar* (see www.LearnNavi.org).

Sapir-Whorf hypothesis The structure and vocabulary of language shapes our perception of reality and therefore also our actions.

POPSOC

The Dothraki language used in the HBO series *Game of Thrones* was created by linguist David J. Peterson, one of the founders of the Language Creation Society. Using just a handful of words and names coined by George R. R. Martin, the author of the book series the show is based on, Peterson built a complete language system (including grammar, syntax, and vocabulary). According to the Social Security Administration, in 2013, 241 parents named their daughters Khaleesi, the Dothraki word for "queen." An introduction to the language is available at www.livinglanguage.com /dothraki. Athchomarchomakann!

Photo: © HBO/courtesy Everett Collection

Even though it is possible to construct languages for fun, throughout human history the most basic purpose of language has been to enable us to make sense of the world around us in communication with others. Once we internalize and use a language, its structure and vocabulary shapes our perception of reality and therefore also our actions. This insight is known as the **Sapir-Whorf hypothesis** (after linguists Edward Sapir and Benjamin Whorf) or the linguistic relativity hypothesis. It implies that our understanding of reality is not strictly determined by nature, but more so by the tools available to us in the languages we use.

In a literal sense, language may color how we see the world. Anthropologist Brent Berlin and linguist Paul Kay (1991) noted that humans possess the physical ability to make millions of color distinctions, yet languages differ in the number of colors they recognize. For example, the English language distinguishes between yellow and orange, but some other languages do not. In the Dugum Dani language of New Guinea's West Highlands, there are only two basic color terms—*modla* for "white" and *mili* for "black." (Roberson, Davies, and Davidoff 2000; Wierzbicka 2008).

© Photo by Kevin Mazur/WireImage/Getty Images

In Japan, what people in the United States would call a green light is often called a blue light, even though it is the same color there as it is here. This practice derives from an earlier time in Japan when there was only one word, *ao* (青), to describe both green and blue (Backhaus 2013). The more recent practice of making a clear distinction between the two colors in Japan has been tied to the importation of crayons into Japan starting in 1917, which distinguished between *midori* (緑) for green and *ao* for blue. The Allied occupation of Japan after World War II reinforced this distinction in educational materials distributed throughout the country (Bhatia 2012). And yet remnants of the earlier linguistic pattern remain in the form not only of "blue" traffic lights, but also of "blue" vegetables, "blue" apples, and "blue" leaves.

Feminists have noted that gender-related language can reinforce the stereotype that some jobs are more appropriate for men than women. Each time we use a term such as *mailman, policeman,* or *fireman,* we are implying (especially to young children) that these occupations can be filled only by males. Yet many women work as *letter carriers, police officers,* and *firefighters*—a fact that is being increasingly recognized and legitimized through the use of such nonsexist language (Eckert and McConnell-Ginet 2003; McConnell-Ginet 2011).

Linguist Suzette Haden Elgin went so far as to invent a new language that gives voice to women's experience (Elgin 1984). She argued that "existing human languages are inadequate to express the perceptions of women," which leads to inadequate perception of critical issues in the lives of women (Elgin 1988). Drawing on her expertise in the Navajo language (*Diné bizaad*), she created Láadan as a test of the Sapir-Whorf hypothesis. She argued that using Láadan would open up new dimensions of reality that are not easily accessible using such languages as English. Láadan lessons for beginners are available at www.LáadanLanguage.org.

Language can also transmit stereotypes related to race. Look up the meanings of the adjective *black* in dictionaries published in the United States, and you will find "dismal, gloomy or forbidding, destitute of moral light or goodness, atrocious, evil, threatening, clouded with anger." By contrast, dictionaries list "pure" and "innocent" among the meanings of the adjective *white*. Through such patterns of language, our culture reinforces positive associations with the term (and skin color) *white* and negative associations with *black*. Is it surprising, then, that a list meant to prevent people from working in a profession is called a "blacklist," and a fib that we think of as somewhat acceptable is called a "white lie"? Such examples demonstrate that language can shape how we see, taste, smell, feel, and hear (Henderson 2003; Moore 1976; Reitman 2006).

Of course, we communicate using more than just words. If you do not like the way a meeting is going, you might suddenly sit back, fold your arms, and turn down the corners of your mouth. When you see a friend in tears, you

may give her a quick hug. After winning a big game, you may high-five your teammates. These are all examples of **nonverbal communication**— the use of gestures, facial expressions, and other visual images to communicate. We are not born with these expressions. We learn them, just as we learn other forms of language, from people who share our culture. We learn how to show—and to recognize— happiness, sadness, pleasure, shame, distress, and other emotional states (Burgoon, Guerrero, and Floyd 2010).

nonverbal communication The use of gestures, facial expressions, and other visual images to communicate.

values Collective conceptions of what is considered good, desirable, and proper—or bad, undesirable, and improper—in a culture.

Like other forms of language, nonverbal communication is not the same in all cultures. For example, people from various cultures differ in the degree to which they touch others during the course of normal social interactions. Even experienced travelers are sometimes caught off guard by these differences. In Saudi Arabia a middle-aged man may want to hold hands with a male partner after closing a business deal. The gesture, which would surprise most Americans, is considered a compliment in that culture. The meaning of hand signals is another form of nonverbal communication that can differ from one culture to the next. For instance, in both Australia and Iraq the thumbs-up sign is considered rude (Koerner 2003; Lefevre 2011).

Values In addition to creating a shared language as part of our cognitive culture, we also jointly agree that some principles are at the core of who we are and what we believe. **Values** are the collective conceptions of what is considered good, desirable, and proper—or bad, undesirable, and improper—in a culture. They are typically expressed as general principles that then shape what we see as appropriate actions. Examples include family, love, opportunity, community, and freedom. Even individualism

© Jupiter Images/ BananaStock/Alamy RF

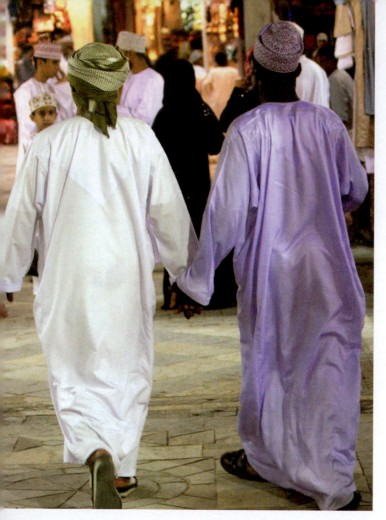

In Arab cultures, men sometimes hold hands as a sign of affection and friendship.   Photo: © dbimages/Alamy.

Life Goals of First-Year College Students in the United States

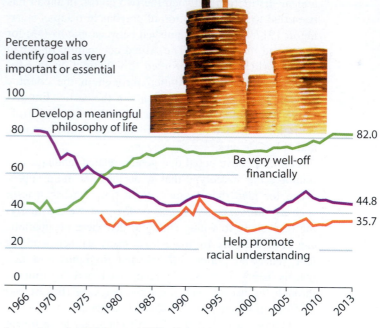

Percentage who identify goal as very important or essential

Develop a meaningful philosophy of life

Be very well-off financially

82.0

44.8

35.7

Help promote racial understanding

100
80
60
40
20
0

1966 1970 1975 1980 1985 1990 1995 2000 2005 2010 2013

Sources: Eagan et al. 2013; Pryor et al. 2007.   *Photo:* © Design Pics/Carson Ganci RF

represents a collective value. As American essayist Richard Rodriguez points out, "American individualism is a communally derived value, not truly an expression of individuality. The teenager persists in rebelling against her parents, against tradition or custom, because she is shielded . . . by American culture from the knowledge that she inherited her rebellion from dead ancestors and living parents" (2002:130). Of course, all members of a society do not uniformly agree on its values. Angry political debates and billboards promoting conflicting causes tell us that much.

The values of a culture may change, but most remain relatively stable during any one person's lifetime. Socially shared, intensely felt values are a fundamental part of our lives in the United States. Sociologist Robin Williams (1970) has offered a list of U.S. basic values. These include freedom, equality, democracy, morality, conformity, progress, humanitarianism, and material comfort. Obviously, not all 320 million people in the United States agree on all these values, but such

SOC THINK

Consider Williams's list of basic values. Do you think most people value these things? How might some values, such as freedom and conformity, conflict? How do we resolve such conflicts?

a list serves as a starting point in defining America's national character.

Each year more than 200,000 first-year college students at approximately 270 of the nation's four-year colleges fill out a questionnaire asking them which values are most important to them. Because of its coverage, content, and scope, this survey provides a kind of barometer of the nation's values. The top value of the first-year class of 1966, the year the survey was first conducted, was "developing a meaningful philosophy of life," with 80 percent of the new students identifying it as either essential or very important. By contrast, only 44 percent chose "being very well-off financially." Since that time, the relative position of these two values has flipped (see graph). Among the first-year class

© Ballyscanlon/PhotoDisc/Getty RF

of 2013, for example, a record high 82 percent identified "being very well-off financially" as a significant value compared to 44.8 percent who selected "developing a meaningful philosophy" (Eagan et al. 2013).

Researchers have also studied other family and community values among first-year students. The second-highest-rated value identified by the 2013 class was "raising a family," at 73.3 percent. This value has remained at approximately the same level for nearly 50 years (Eagan et al. 2013). Students in 2013 were also committed to "helping others who were in difficulty" (72 percent), although only 30 percent selected "participating in a community action program" as either essential or very important. The proportion that identified "helping to promote racial understanding" rose over the previous year to 35.7 percent. As these numbers demonstrate, a nation's values are not necessarily set in stone.

Because it challenges honesty as a shared value, cheating is a significant concern on college campuses. Professors who take advantage of computerized services that can identify plagiarism, such as the search engine Google or TurnItIn.com, have found that many of the papers their students hand in are plagiarized, in whole or in part. When high school students were asked about academic honesty, 32 percent admitted to copying an Internet document for a classroom assignment, 51 percent said they'd cheated during a test at school, and 74 percent had copied someone's homework, all within the past year. At the same time, 86 percent agreed that "it's not worth it to lie or cheat because it hurts your character" (Josephson Institute of Ethics 2012).

Perhaps cheating has become a normal part of student culture even if it is at odds with dominant school values.

Sometimes values shift in response to historic events. Americans have always valued their right to privacy and resented government intrusions into their personal lives. In the aftermath of the terrorist attacks of September 11, 2001, however, many citizens called for greater protection against the threat of terrorism. In response, the federal government broadened its surveillance powers and increased its ability to monitor people's behavior without court approval. In 2001, shortly after the attacks, Congress passed the USA PATRIOT Act, which empowers the FBI to access individuals' medical, library, student, and phone records without informing them or obtaining a search warrant.

normative culture Consists of the ways we establish, abide by, and enforce principles of conduct.

norm An established standard of behavior maintained by a society.

folkways Norms governing everyday behavior, whose violation raises comparatively little concern.

mores Norms deemed highly necessary to the welfare of a society.

NORMATIVE CULTURE

Whereas cognitive culture highlights what we think or believe, normative culture, the third element of culture, focuses on how we act. **Normative culture** consists of the ways we establish, abide by, and enforce principles of conduct. In our everyday lives, we typically abide by **norms**—the established standards of behavior maintained by a society—both big and small, from "Thou shalt not kill" to "Chew with your mouth closed." Most of the time, we do so without thinking much about it.

For a norm to become significant, it must be widely shared and understood. For example, in movie theaters in the United States, we typically expect that people will be quiet while the film is shown. Of course, context matters, and the application of this norm can vary, depending on the particular film and type of audience. People who are viewing a serious artistic film will be more likely to insist on the norm of silence than those who are watching a slapstick comedy or a horror movie.

Types of Norms Sociologists distinguish between norms in two ways. First, norms are classified by their relative importance to society. When presented this way, they are known as *folkways* and *mores*. **Folkways** are norms governing everyday behavior. They play an important role in providing general guidelines for how to act within a culture. Such norms are less rigid in their application, and their violation raises comparatively little concern. **Mores** (pronounced "MOR-ays") are norms deemed highly necessary to the welfare

5 Movies on U.S. CULTURE

Revolutionary Road
A look at the social isolation and gender roles of 1950s America.

The Invention of Lying
What would society be like if we never told a lie?

Dawn of the Planet of the Apes
When human culture collapses and intelligent apes arise.

The Greatest Movie Ever Sold
Morgan Spurlock attempts to finance a movie completely with product placement.

Good Hair
Chris Rock's documentary about the culture of hair in the Black community.

of a society, often because they embody core values. Each society demands obedience to its mores; violation can lead to severe penalties. Thus, the United States has strong mores against murder, treason, and child abuse, which have been institutionalized into formal norms.

Clothing provides an example of the difference between the two. For example, fashion is a folkway, and there is wide latitude in what we might wear. But what about not wearing any clothes in public? For most of us, most of the time (except perhaps on No Pants Subway Ride days) that would be crossing the line into the territory of mores, and we might expect a strong and swift response if we did so.

Norms are also classified as either formal or informal. **Formal norms** generally have been written down and specify strict punishments for violators. In the United States we often formalize norms into laws, which are very precise in defining proper and improper behavior. Sociologist Donald Black (1995) defined *law* as "governmental social control"; that is, **laws** are formal norms enforced by the state. But laws are just one example of formal norms. The requirements for a college major and the rules of a card game are also considered formal norms.

By contrast, **informal norms** are generally understood but not precisely recorded. We follow largely unspoken rules for all kinds of everyday interactions, such as how to ride on an elevator, how to pass someone on a sidewalk, and how to behave in a college classroom. Knowledge of such norms is often taken for granted.

SOCTHINK

Improv Everywhere's No Pants Subway Ride calls people to do something outside their comfort zone. What factors might influence someone's decision to participate? What would it take to get you to participate?

In many societies around the world, norms reinforce patterns of male dominance. For example, various folkways reveal men's hierarchical position above women within the traditional Buddhist areas of Southeast Asia. In the sleeping cars of trains, women do not sleep in upper berths, above men. Hospitals that house men on the first floor do not place female patients on the second

> The past is never dead.
> It's not even past.
>
> ———
>
> William Faulkner

floor. Even on clotheslines, folkways in Southeast Asia dictate male dominance: women's attire is hung lower than that of men (Bulle 1987).

Breaking Norms Although norms provide us with guidelines on how to act, we can choose not to abide by them. Sometimes we violate the mainstream norms because we are actually following alternative norms from a subgroup within society. Teenage drinkers are often conforming to the standards of their peer group when they violate norms that condemn underage drinking. Similarly, business executives who use shady accounting techniques may be responding to a corporate culture that demands the maximization of profits at any cost, including the deception of investors and government regulatory agencies.

Norms are violated in some instances because one norm conflicts with another. For example, suppose you live in an apartment building and one night hear the screams of the woman next door, who is being beaten by her husband. If you decide to intervene by knocking on their door or calling

Break-a-Norm Day

- Wearing formal clothes in an informal setting
- Eating with the wrong utensil or none at all
- Responding to friends or family the same as to a boss or teacher
- Having long gaps in speech when talking with someone
- Standing just a little too close to or far from someone when talking with him or her
- Facing the back of an elevator instead of getting in and turning around

Norms provide us with rules that guide our everyday behavior. All we need to do is step outside the lines even a little bit to see the influence they have over our lives. These are some examples of how people violate norms. How would you feel about violating any of these norms? How might others respond to you? Photo: Dress—© Gordana Sermek/Getty Images RF; jeans—© C Squared Studios/Getty Images RF.

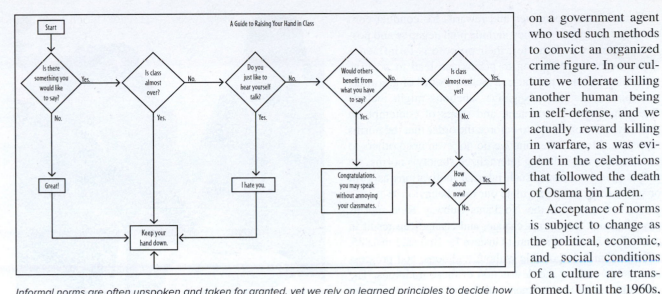

A Guide to Raising Your Hand in Class

Start → Is there something you would like to say? — Yes. → Is class almost over? — No. → Do you just like to hear yourself talk? — No. → Would others benefit from what you have to say? — No. → Is class almost over yet? — Yes. → ...

No. → Great!

Is class almost over? — Yes. → Keep your hand down.

Do you just like to hear yourself talk? — Yes. → I hate you.

Would others benefit from what you have to say? — Yes. → Congratulations. you may speak without annoying your classmates.

Is class almost over yet? — No. → How about now? — Yes. / No.

Informal norms are often unspoken and taken for granted, yet we rely on learned principles to decide how we (and we hope others) should proceed, as this cartoon humorously demonstrates.

the police, you are violating the norm of minding your own business while at the same time following the norm of assisting a victim of domestic violence.

Even if norms do not conflict, there are exceptions to any norm. The same action, under different circumstances, can cause one to be viewed as either a hero or a villain. For instance, secretly taping telephone conversations is normally considered not just intrusive but illegal. However, it can be done with a court order to obtain valid evidence for a criminal trial. We would heap praise on a government agent who used such methods to convict an organized crime figure. In our culture we tolerate killing another human being in self-defense, and we actually reward killing in warfare, as was evident in the celebrations that followed the death of Osama bin Laden.

Acceptance of norms is subject to change as the political, economic, and social conditions of a culture are transformed. Until the 1960s, for example, formal norms throughout much of the United States prohibited the marriage of people from different racial groups. Over the past half century, however, such legal prohibitions have been cast aside. The process of change can be seen today in the increasing acceptance of single parents and the growing support for the legalization of marriage for same-sex couples.

When circumstances require the sudden violation of long-standing cultural norms, the change can upset an entire population. In Iraq, where Muslim custom strictly forbids touching by strangers for men and especially for women, the war that began in 2003 has brought numerous daily violations of the norm. Outside mosques, government offices, and other facilities likely to be targeted by terrorists, visitors must now be patted down and have their bags searched by Iraqi security forces. To reduce the discomfort caused by the procedure, women are searched by female guards and men by male guards. Despite that concession, and the fact that many Iraqis admit to or even insist on the need for such measures, people still wince at the invasion of their personal privacy. In reaction to the searches, Iraqi women have begun to limit the contents of the bags they carry or simply to leave them at home (Rubin 2003).

Sanctions When norms are violated, we can usually expect a response designed to bring our behavior back into line. If a basketball coach sends a sixth player into the game, we count on the referee to call a foul. If a job seeker shows up for a formal interview in shorts and a T-shirt, we predict that no job offer will follow. If we park without putting money into the meter, we should expect a ticket. In each of these cases, some form of negative repercussion results from our failure to abide by expected norms.

5 Movies on CULTURES OUTSIDE THE U.S.

Leviathan
A Russian man struggles for justice against an oppressive system.

Ajami
A collection of stories taking place in a Muslim–Christian neighborhood in Tel Aviv.

Caramel
A comedy following the lives of five women working in a Beirut beauty salon.

Persepolis
An animated coming-of-age film set during the Iranian Revolution.

Departures
An unemployed man violates Japanese norms by becoming an undertaker.

Sanctions are penalties and rewards for conduct concerning a social norm. They include both negative and positive responses to behavior; their purpose is to influence future behavior. Adhering to norms can lead to positive sanctions such as a pay raise, a medal, a word of gratitude, or a pat on the back. Negative sanctions might include fines, threats, imprisonment, and stares of contempt. In this way sanctions work to enforce the order that the norms represent. Most of the time we do not even need others to sanction our acts. Having internalized society's norms, we police ourselves, using such internal motivations as guilt or self-satisfaction to regulate our own behavior.

As we saw with the No Pants Subway Ride, norms provide order, but norms change, and change can result in confusion. As social scientist Gustave Le Bon said in 1895, "Civilization is impossible without traditions, and progress impossible without the destruction of those traditions. The difficulty, and it is an immense difficulty, is to find a proper equilibrium between stability and variability." In a world of norms, we constantly face this tension: to obey or not to obey.

>> Cultural Variation

Together the elements of culture provide us with social coherence and order. Culture clarifies for us what we think is good and bad, and right and wrong, giving us a sense of direction. That is not to say, however, that there is universal agreement on values and norms or that culture works on behalf of all for the greater good. Culture helps unify and provide meaning, but it also serves the interests of some individuals and groups to the detriment of others. As such, in addition to analyzing ways in which norms and values unite us, sociologists seek out and study cultural variation within society and investigate how culture can be used to secure and enhance power.

DOMINANT IDEOLOGY

One of the ways culture can function to maintain the privileges of certain groups is through the establishment of a **dominant ideology**—the set of cultural beliefs and practices that legitimate existing powerful social, economic, and political interests. The dominant ideology helps explain and justify who gets what and why in a way that supports and maintains the status quo. Dominant ideas can even squelch alternative expressions of what might be, casting such alternatives as threats to the existing order. Karl Marx argued that the dominant ideas in society help maintain the interests of the ruling class. This idea was picked up and developed by sociologists Georg Lukács (1923) and Antonio Gramsci (1929), who argued that the dominant ideology can be used as an instrument of power.

sanction A penalty or reward for conduct concerning a social norm.

dominant ideology A set of cultural beliefs and practices that legitimates existing powerful social, economic, and political interests.

Agricultural strikes and boycotts in the 1960s and 1970s alerted the nation to the harsh economic plight of migrant workers. Photo: © Rob Crandall/The Image Works.

A society's most powerful groups and institutions control wealth and property. Armed with a dominant ideology, they can also shape beliefs about reality through religion, education, and the media. In so doing, they can influence what we come to accept as true. Feminists would argue that if all of society's most important institutions send the message that women should be subservient to men, this dominant ideology will help control and subordinate women. Images of boys and girls in toy ads typically reinforce gender stereotypes with girls playing with pink and pastel kitchen toys while boys play with pretend power tools and video games. Similarly, images of women in magazine ads reinforce unrealistic (and usually Photoshopped) images of feminine beauty that have consequences for how women see themselves and how men see and treat women.

ASPECTS OF CULTURAL VARIATION

To more fully understand cultural variation, sociologists pay particular attention to differences that exist both within and between societies. Inuit tribes in northern Canada, clad in furs and dieting on whale blubber, have little in common with farmers in Southeast Asia, who dress for the heat and subsist mainly on the rice they grow in their paddies. Cultures adapt to meet specific sets of circumstances, such as climate, level of technology, population, and geography. This adaptation to different conditions shows up in differences in all elements of culture, including language, values, norms, and sanctions. Thus, despite the presence

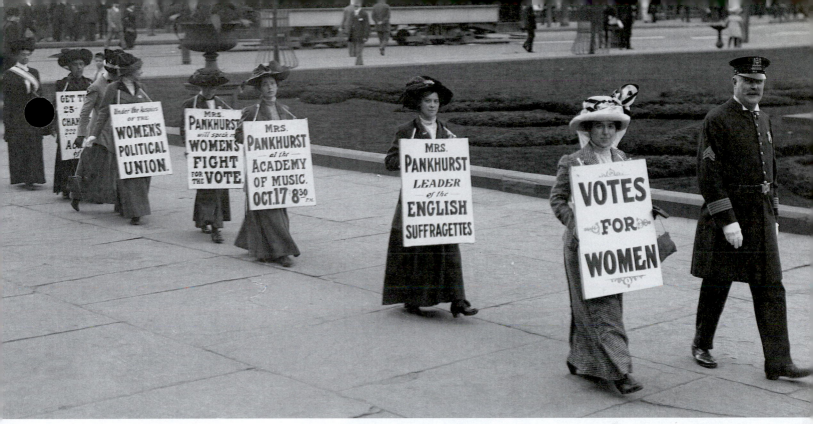

of cultural universals such as courtship and religion, great diversity exists among the world's many cultures. Moreover, even within a single nation, certain segments of the populace develop cultural patterns that differ from the patterns of the dominant society. Cultural variation, as described by sociologists, takes a number of forms.

Subcultures Rodeo riders, residents of a retirement community, workers on an offshore oil rig—all are examples of what sociologists refer to as subcultures. A **subculture** is a segment of society that shares a distinctive pattern of mores, folkways, and values that differs from the pattern of the larger society. In a sense, a subculture can be thought of as a culture existing within a larger, dominant culture. The existence of many subcultures is characteristic of complex societies such as the United States.

SOCTHINK

What subcultures are common on college and university campuses? What indicators make them recognizable? Why might such subcultures be more likely to form there?

Members of a subculture participate in the dominant culture while engaging in unique and distinctive forms of behavior. Frequently, a subculture will develop its own slang, known as **argot**—specialized language that distinguishes it from the wider society. Such argot allows insiders—the members of the subculture—to understand words with special meanings and establishes patterns of communication that outsiders cannot understand. In so doing, it clarifies the boundary between "us" and "them" and reinforces a shared identity. We see something like this in the taken-for-granted words and acronyms in the instant-messaging and text-messaging world. There, abbreviations come fast and furious, from the well known, such as *lol* (laughing out loud), *brb* (be right back), and *g2g* (got to go), to the more obscure, such as *1337* (meaning "elite" and referring to symbolic language or "leet-speak") or *pwned* (leet term meaning "defeated").

In India a new subculture has developed among employees at the international call centers established by multinational corporations. To serve customers in the United States and Europe, the young men and women who work there must be fluent speakers of English. But the corporations that employ them demand more than proficiency in a foreign language; they expect their Indian employees to adopt Western values and work habits, including the grueling pace that U.S. workers take for granted. In return, the corporations offer perks such as Western-style dinners and dances and coveted consumer goods. Ironically, they allow employees to take the day off only on such American

subculture A segment of society that shares a distinctive pattern of mores, folkways, and values that differs from the pattern of the larger society.

argot Specialized language used by members of a group or subculture.

Subculture Slang

Anime and Manga Fans

chibi eyes: the characteristic, big childlike eyes used in anime

majoko: a girl anime character with magical powers who must save the world

Con Artists & Scammers

grifter: a person who steals through deception

phishing: seeking personal information by sending out emails that appear to be from legitimate companies

Graffiti Writers

bite: to copy another graffiti writer's work

burner: a stylistically impressive, brilliantly colored piece of graffiti, usually written in a complex pattern of interlocking letters and other visual elements

toy: an inexperienced or unskilled graffiti writer

kill: to saturate an area with one's graffiti

Bikers (Motorcyclists)

brain bucket: a helmet

ink slinger: a tattoo artist

pucker factor: the degree of panic felt during a near-accident

yard shark: a dog that races out to attack passing motorcyclists

Skateboarders

deck: a skateboard platform

face plant: a face-first crash

sketchy: in reference to a trick, poorly done

Subcultures often produce their own unique jargon. The words may be appropriate in those subcultures, but they have the effect of drawing a line between insiders and the rest of us.

Source: Reid 2006.   Photo: © RubberBall Productions RF

holidays as Labor Day and Thanksgiving—not on Indian holidays such as Diwali, the Hindu festival of lights. While most Indian families are home celebrating, call center employees see mostly one another. When they have the day off, no one else is free to socialize with them. As a result, these employees have formed a tight-knit subculture based on hard work and a taste for Western luxury goods and leisure-time pursuits. Increasingly, they are the object of criticism from Indians who live a more conventional Indian lifestyle centered on family and holiday traditions (Kalita 2006).

counterculture A subculture that deliberately opposes certain aspects of the larger culture.

Countercultures Sometimes a subculture can develop that seeks to set itself up as an alternative to the dominant culture. When a subculture conspicuously and deliberately opposes certain aspects of the larger culture, it is known as a **counterculture.** Countercultures typically thrive among the young, who have the least investment in the existing culture.

The 1960s, now often characterized by the phrase "sex and drugs and rock 'n' roll," provide a classic case of an extensive counterculture. Largely composed of young people, members of this counterculture were turned off by a society they believed was too materialistic and technological. It included many political radicals and "hippies" who had "dropped out" of mainstream social institutions, but its membership was extensive and diverse. The young people expressed in their writings, speeches, and songs their visions, hopes, and dreams for a new society. As was reflected in the 1966 survey of first-year college students, these young women and men rejected the pressure to accumulate more expensive cars, larger homes, and an endless array of material goods. Instead, they expressed a desire to live in a culture based on more humanistic values, such as sharing, love, and coexistence with the environment. As a political force, they worked for peace—opposing U.S. involvement in the war in Vietnam and encouraging draft resistance—as well as racial and gender equality (T. Anderson 2007; Gitlin 1993).

In the wake of the attacks of September 11, 2001, people around the United States learned of the existence of terrorist groups operating as a counterculture within their own country. Many nations have had to deal with internal counterculture groups—often rooted in long-standing national, ethnic, or political differences—whose members strongly disagree with the values and norms of the dominant culture. In most cases this does not result in violence, but in some cases, as in Northern Ireland and Israel, groups have used attacks, including suicide bombings, to make a statement, both symbolic and real, seeking to bring attention to their situation and an end to their repression (Juergensmeyer 2003). In Northern Ireland, Israel, the Palestinian territory, and other parts of the world, many generations have lived in such circumstances. But terrorist cells are not necessarily fueled only by outsiders. Frequently, people become disenchanted with the policies of their own country, and a few take very violent steps (Juergensmeyer 2003).

Culture Shock Today we are more and more likely to come into contact with and even immerse ourselves in cultures unlike our own. For example, it has become increasingly common for students to study abroad. Though they may well have predeparture orientation sessions, when they get in-country, they often have a difficult time adjusting because so many of the little things that they took for granted, things they barely noticed before, no longer apply. Anyone who feels disoriented, uncertain, out of place, or even fearful when they encounter unfamiliar cultural practices

© Marvy! Advertising Photography

may be experiencing **culture shock.** For example, a resident of the United States who visits certain areas in Cambodia and wants meat for dinner may be stunned to learn that a local specialty is rat meat. Similarly, someone from a strict Islamic culture may be shocked upon first seeing the comparatively provocative dress styles and open displays of affection that are common in the United States and other Western cultures.

Interestingly, after students who study abroad return home, they may experience a kind of reverse culture shock. Their time away has changed them, often in ways they were unaware of, and they find that they cannot so easily slip back into the old routines that those who remained at home expect of them. Culture shock reveals to us both the power and the taken-for-granted nature of culture. The rules we follow are so ingrained that we barely notice that we were following them until they are no longer there to provide the structure and order we assume as a given.

All of us, to some extent, take for granted the cultural practices of our society. As a result, it can be surprising and even disturbing to realize that other cultures do not follow our way of life. The fact is, customs that seem strange to us are considered normal and proper in other cultures, which may view our own mores and folkways as odd.

ATTITUDES TOWARD CULTURAL VARIATION

Ethnocentrism Living in the modern world, especially as a result of the revolutions in transportation and communication, makes it far more likely that we will encounter people from a whole range of cultural backgrounds than we were in the past. As a result, we are also more likely to struggle with what we think about the beliefs, values, and practices of others. When we hear people talking about "our" culture versus "their" culture, we are often confronted with statements that reflect the attitude that "our" culture is best. Terms such as *underdeveloped, backward,* and *primitive* may be used to refer to other societies. What "we" believe is a religion; what "they" believe is superstition and mythology.

It is tempting to evaluate the practices of other cultures on the basis of our own perspectives. Sociologist William Graham Sumner (1906) coined the term **ethnocentrism** to refer to the tendency to assume that one's own culture and way of life represent what's normal or are superior to all others. The ethnocentric person sees his or her own group as the center or defining point of culture and views all other cultures as deviations from what is "normal." Thus, Westerners who see cattle as a

culture shock The feelings of disorientation, uncertainty, and even fear that people experience when they encounter unfamiliar cultural practices.

ethnocentrism The tendency to assume that one's own culture and way of life represent what's normal or are superior to all others.

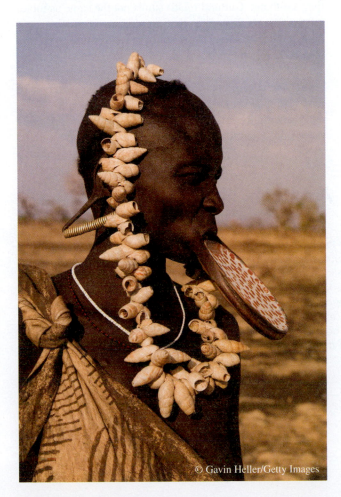

© Gavin Heller/Getty Images

food source might look down on the Hindu religion and culture, which view the cow as sacred. People in one culture may dismiss as unthinkable the mate selection or child-rearing practices of another culture.

Ethnocentric value judgments complicated U.S. efforts at democratic reform of the Iraqi government. Before the 2003 war in Iraq, U.S. planners had assumed that Iraqis would adapt to a new form of government in the same way the Germans and Japanese did following World War II. But in the Iraqi culture, unlike the German and Japanese cultures, loyalty to the family and the extended clan comes before patriotism and the common good. In a country in which almost half of all people, even those in the cities, marry a first or second cousin, citizens are predisposed to favor their own kin in government and business dealings. Why trust a stranger from outside the family? What Westerners would criticize as nepotism, then, is actually an acceptable, even admirable, practice to Iraqis (J. Tierney 2003).

One of the reasons ethnocentrism develops is that it contributes to a sense of solidarity by promoting group pride. Denigrating other nations and cultures can enhance our own patriotic feelings and belief in our way of life. Yet this type of social stability is established at the expense of other peoples. One of the negative consequences of ethnocentric value judgments is that they serve to devalue groups and to deny equal opportunities.

Of course, ethnocentrism is hardly limited to citizens of the United States. Visitors from many African cultures are surprised at the disrespect that children in the United States show their parents. People from India may be repelled by our practice of living in the same household with dogs and cats. Many Islamic fundamentalists in the Arab world and Asia view the United States as corrupt, decadent, and doomed to destruction. All these people may feel comforted by membership in cultures that in their view are superior to ours (Juergensmeyer 2003).

Cultural Relativism Whereas ethnocentrism means evaluating foreign cultures using the familiar culture of the observer as a standard of correct behavior, **cultural relativism** means viewing people's behavior from the perspective of their own culture. It places a priority on understanding other cultures, rather than dismissing them as "strange" or "exotic." Unlike ethnocentrists, cultural relativists seek to employ the kind of value neutrality that Max Weber saw as so important.

Cultural relativism stresses that different social contexts give rise to different norms and values. Thus, we must examine practices such as polygamy, bullfighting, and monarchy within the particular contexts of the cultures in which they are found. Cultural relativism is not the same as moral relativism, which implies that no ultimate normative standards exist. Sociologists do not have to abandon their own morals and unquestionably accept every cultural variation. But cultural relativism does require a serious and unbiased effort to evaluate norms, values, and customs in light of their distinctive culture.

Practicing the sociological imagination calls for us to be more fully aware of the culture we as humans have created for ourselves and to be better attuned to the varieties of culture other people have established for themselves. Culture shapes our everyday behaviors all the time, and we select from the tools it provides. For the most part, we are not aware of the degree to which we are immersed in a world of our own making. Whether that includes the capacity to read a book, make a meal, or hug a stranger on the street, it is through culture that we establish our relationship to the external world and with one another.

> You never really understand a person until you consider things from his point of view . . . until you climb into his skin and walk around in it.
>
> Harper Lee, *To Kill a Mockingbird*

SOCIOLOGY IS A VERB

Break a Norm

Choose some minor norm of face-to-face interaction (rather than disrupting a group) and violate it. Avoid anything that would harm another person, violate policies, or break the law. Be sure to give the impression that what you are doing is perfectly normal, and record how others respond to you. In what ways do they seek to make sense of your behavior or to restore order? How did breaking the norm affect you? What lessons did you learn about our everyday actions?

For REVIEW

I. Why do humans create culture?

   - Humans lack the complex instincts present in other animals, and as such they must construct a relationship to nature and with each other. We do this through the construction of shared culture.

II. What does culture consist of?

   - There are three primary elements of culture. Material culture consists of our modification of the physical environment. Cognitive culture is the thinking part of culture, including language, values, beliefs, and knowledge. Normative culture provides rules for behavior.

III. How does culture both enable and constrain?

   - Although culture provides us with the knowledge, rules, and artifacts we need to survive, it also limits our options. Words enable us to see, and tools enable us to make things, but both are designed for particular purposes and shield us from alternative possibilities. Further, with ethnocentrism, we cut ourselves off from new possibilities from different cultures.

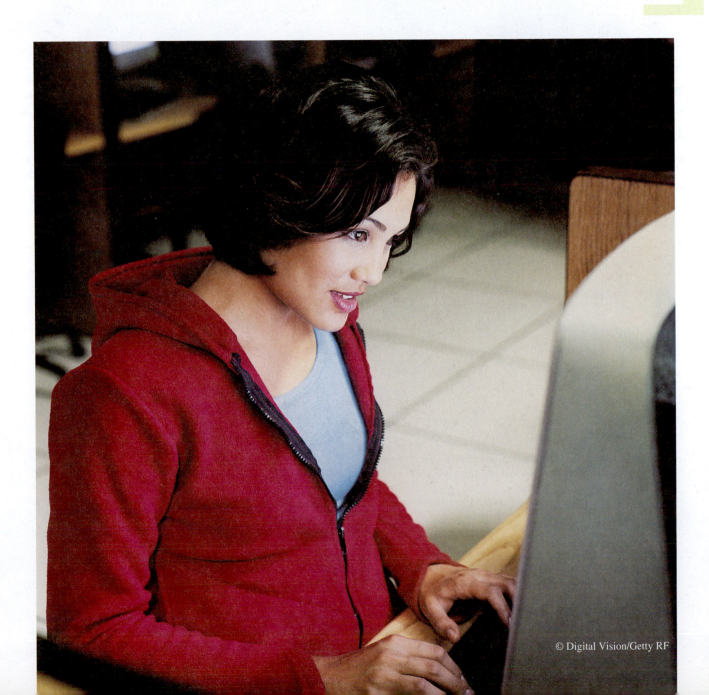

Functionalist View

Sharing a culture helps define the society to which one belongs, establishing **social order**.

Society **preserves** its culture by transmitting shared language, norms, and values from one generation to the next, thus providing social **stability**.

The interests of **subgroups** within a culture are served by formation of **subcultures**.

PRESERVATION, FACILITATION, COMMUNICATION
KEY CONCEPTS

Conflict View

While a common culture helps unify a society, it also **privileges** some to the detriment of others.

The **dominant ideology** reinforces the power of the ruling class.

The existence of subcultures reflects **unequal social arrangements**, as brought to light by the civil rights and feminist movements.

Language in a culture can be a source of conflict, as in the case of **sexist** language or language that transmits **racial stereotypes**.

KEY CONCEPTS
PRIVILEGE, DOMINANCE, INEQUALITY

Interactionist View

Without social interaction, people would not be able to **construct their culture** or transmit it to others. In turn, having a common culture simplifies everyday transactions.

Cultural diffusion is enhanced by interactions involved in immigration, tourism, the Internet, and the mass media.

Both a culture's **language** and **nonverbal communication** facilitate day-to-day exchanges between people.

KEY CONCEPTS
SOCIAL CONSTRUCTION, NONVERBAL COMMUNICATION

MAKE THE CONNECTION

After reviewing the chapter, answer the following questions:

1
How would each of the three perspectives describe the lessons learned from the No Pants Subway Ride?

2
How would each perspective explain the existence of ethnocentrism?

3
How would each perspective approach the role that dominant ideology performs in a culture?

4
How would you use the perspectives to describe one of the subcultures at your school?

Pop Quiz

1. _____ consists of everything humans create in establishing our relationships to nature and with each other.
   a. Innovation
   b. Society
   c. Ethnocentrism
   d. Culture

2. People's need for food, shelter, and clothing is an example of what George Murdock referred to as
   a. norms.
   b. folkways.
   c. cultural universals.
   d. cultural practices.

3. What is an invention?
   a. introducing a new idea or object to a culture
   b. combining existing cultural artifacts to create something new
   c. making known or sharing the existence of an aspect of reality
   d. the physical or technological aspects of our daily lives

4. What term do sociologists use to refer to the process by which a cultural item spreads from group to group or society to society?
   a. diffusion
   b. globalization
   c. innovation
   d. cultural relativism

5. Which of the following statements is true according to the Sapir-Whorf hypothesis?
   a. Language simply describes reality.
   b. Language legitimates existing social, economic, and political interests.
   c. Language shapes our perception of reality.
   d. Language formation is constrained by cultural universals.

6. What do norms provide for us that we need?
   a. shared beliefs that unite us as one
   b. established standards of behavior
   c. a system of shared symbols enabling us to communicate with each other
   d. justification of existing inequality through shared beliefs and practices

7. What type of norms is deemed highly necessary to the welfare of a society, often because these norms embody the most cherished principles of a people?
   a. formal norms
   b. informal norms
   c. mores
   d. folkways

8. Which of the following terms describes the set of cultural beliefs and practices that help maintain powerful social, economic, and political interests?
   a. mores
   b. dominant ideology
   c. consensus
   d. values

9. Terrorist groups are examples of
   a. cultural universals.
   b. subcultures.
   c. countercultures.
   d. dominant ideologies.

10. What is the term used when one seeks to understand another culture from its perspective, rather than dismissing it as "strange" or "exotic"?
    a. ethnocentrism
    b. culture shock
    c. cultural relativism
    d. cultural value

1. (d), 2. (c), 3. (b), 4. (a), 5. (c), 6. (c), 7. (c), 8. (b), 9. (c), 10. (c)

Socialization

© Gareth Cattermole/Getty Images

SUCCESS AND SOCIAL INFLUENCE

As an unknown author just starting out, Jo Rowling experienced repeated rejection. Her first book, *Harry Potter and the Philosopher's Stone* (as it's known in England), was turned down by a dozen publishers. Her big break came when Nigel Newton, chair of the board for Bloomsbury Publishing, gave his eight-year-old daughter, Alice, a copy of the first chapter. She loved it. Alice insisted that her father read it and "nagged and nagged" him over the next several months, "wanting to see what came next" (Lawless 2005).

Rowling's story of initial rejection followed by award-winning success and massive sales is hardly unique. Herman Melville's *Moby Dick*, George Orwell's *Animal Farm*, Anne Frank's *The Diary of a Young Girl*, Madeleine L'Engle's *A Wrinkle in Time*, Sylvia Plath's *The Bell Jar*, Ursula K. Le Guin's *The Left Hand of Darkness*, and Meg Cabot's *The Princess Diaries* were all initially rejected by publishers. How is it possible that the widespread appeal of such works was not obvious to experts in the field who are paid to recognize such things?

Sociologist Duncan Watts, along with two colleagues, conducted an online experiment to measure the power of inherent quality versus social influence in determining artistic success (Salganik, Dodds, and Watts 2006). They presented each of their 14,341 online participants with a list of 48 new songs by unknown artists, asking them to listen to the songs, rate them, and then, if they wanted, download them for free. To test their variables, the researchers divided the participants into nine groups. One of the groups, the control group, was presented only with the name of the artist and title of the song. Participants of the eight other groups, the experimental groups, saw not only the artist and title, but also how many times each song had been downloaded by people within their group. If quality alone mattered, then the same songs should rise to the top or sink to the bottom in all nine groups. But that's not what happened. Knowing how often songs had been downloaded by others affected which songs participants in the experimental groups favored. Songs that were preferred early varied significantly between experimental groups. As a result, the songs that rose to the top also varied (D. Watts 2007, 2011). These results suggest that the popularity of songs, novels, and works of art is not determined by inherent quality alone. Social influence plays a substantial role in determining artistic success. Change that influence, especially early on, and a different outcome is likely.

As You READ >>

- **How do we become ourselves?**
- **Who shapes our socialization?**
- **How does our development change over time?**

>> The Role of Socialization

Whether in the form of novels, songs, or steam engines, humans create culture to establish a relationship to nature and with each other (see Chapter 3). The good news is that we don't have to start from scratch. We can rely on the culture created by others who came before us. We start internalizing that culture at birth, and we need to do so because, as babies, we are extremely vulnerable. Imagine what the world must look like through a newborn's eyes. Without language to give names to things, without beliefs to give things meaning, without norms to know what to do, without skills to use tools or utensils,

SOC THINK

What skills that you learned before age two do you now take for granted? From whom did you learn them? In what contexts?

how could we possibly survive? At birth, we are almost totally dependent on the assistance of others.

INTERNALIZING CULTURE

Through interactions with others, we internalize what we need to know. Perhaps the most basic element of culture is language, and we begin teaching it to infants right away. We start doing so using baby talk with its higher and more varied pitch, longer vowel sounds, and slower speech. Infants prefer baby talk, also known as infant directed speech, until they are about eight months old. Such speech provides important building blocks for what will later become a child's native language (Soderstrom 2007).

Even though baby talk is a near cultural universal, the frequency of sounds, including both vowels and consonants, and the relationships between them vary from culture to culture. An infant in an English-speaking environment hears different combinations than one in a Swedish- or Japanese-speaking context. Such variation provides the foundation for children learning the particulars of their native tongue. For example, English has 10 vowel sounds, whereas Swedish

© iStock/Getty Images RF

has 16 and Japanese has 5. Baby talk in these different contexts varies accordingly, opening some linguistic pathways while closing others (Kuhl 2004).

We can see this process at work when babies begin experimenting with sounds, mimicking what they hear even before they know any words. This was evident when a video of bantering twins went viral. In the video, available at TwinMamaRama.com, the two 17-month-olds "talked" back and forth, saying little more than "da da da." But they did so with expression, hand gestures, turn taking, and laughter in what seemed like all the right places. They knew what language sounded like—they'd learned that through interactions with family, friends, and others—and it was only a matter of time until they also learned the words that go with it.

Sociologists refer to this practice of internalizing culture as **socialization,** the lifelong process through which people learn the attitudes, values, and behaviors appropriate for members of a particular culture. We absorb culture through interactions with parents, teachers, friends, coworkers, and many others. We are exposed to it in formal contexts, such as schools and workshops, and informal contexts, such as on the playground or through Instagram. We become who we are through our encounters with others.

Genie at age 13.   Photo: © Bettmann/Corbis.

Extreme Childhood Isolation Children who have been isolated or severely neglected (sometimes called *feral children* to suggest that they have reverted to a wild or untamed state) typically have a difficult time recovering from the lack of early childhood socialization. One famous case was Genie, a 13-year-old girl discovered by California authorities in 1970. Genie had been kept in extreme isolation since she was 20 months old. During the

socialization The lifelong process through which people learn the attitudes, values, and behaviors appropriate for members of a particular culture.

THE IMPACT OF ISOLATION

Because socialization at a young age plays a major role in shaping who we become, missing out on such exposure can have a devastating impact on our development. We get a sense for the consequences of such deprivation through studies of children who have experienced extreme childhood isolation and research on primates who are denied care.

Ten Modern Cases of Feral Children

Shamdeo, the Sultanpur Wolf Boy	He was about 4 years old when discovered playing with wolves in 1974.
Memmie LeBlanc, the Wild Girl of Champagne	About 18 to 20 years old when found, she had learned language before having been abandoned.
John Ssebunya, the Ugandan Monkey Boy	Found living with a pack of monkeys in 1991 at age 6, he now gives talks about his experience.
Ng Chhaidy of India	She disappeared in the jungle when she was 4 and, after persistent local rumors about a jungle girl, was found 38 years later in 2012.
Oxana Malaya, the Ukrainian Dog Girl	She was found living in the dog pen in her family's back yard in 1991 at the age of 8.
Vanya Yudin, the Russian Bird Boy	Found in February 2008, he was cared for by his mother but never spoken to and chirps like a bird.
The Leopard Boy of Dihungi	He was found among leopards at age 5 in 1915 after having been in the wild three years.
Kamala and Amala, the Wolf Girls of Midnapore	These two girls were found living among wolves at about the ages of 8 and 2 in 1920.
The Russian Cow Girl	This 5-year-old girl, found living with cows in 2012, communicated using mooing sounds.
Natasha, the Siberian Dog Girl	This 5-year-old Russian girl, discovered in 2009, was raised like a pet in a room full of dogs and cats.

Source: www.feralchildren.com.   *Photo:* © Mary Evans Picture Library/Image Works.

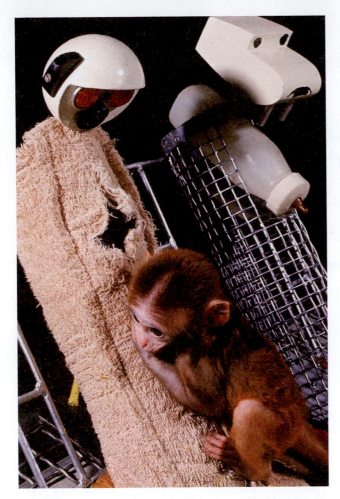

A cloth-covered "artificial mother" of the type used by Harry Harlow. Photo: © Nina Leen/Time & Life Pictures/Getty Images.

body. She was in a room piled high with her dirty diapers. Her name was Danielle. She was almost seven years old and weighed only 46 pounds. She couldn't eat solid food. She wouldn't make eye contact. She didn't react to pain. She couldn't talk. In terms of her social, psychological, and intellectual development, she was no further along than a six-month-old baby.

The long-term consequences of extreme isolation can be substantial. Danielle was adopted in 2007 and eventually learned basic self-care skills, including how to go to the bathroom and how to feed herself using a fork and spoon, but she barely speaks and cannot read. Her family continues to work with her in hopes that she will learn to dress herself, brush her own teeth, make a sandwich, and recognize classmates. After running several medical tests, doctors determined that nothing was wrong with her physically that would explain her condition. Instead, they attributed it to extreme neglect (DeGregory 2008, 2011; Lierow 2011). Her family provides videos and updates about Dani's progress at www.danisstory.org.

Cases of extreme isolation demonstrate the importance of the earliest socialization experiences for children. We now know that it is not enough to attend only to an infant's physical needs; parents must also concern themselves with children's social development. If parents severely limit their children's interaction with family, friends, and others, including strangers—even as infants and toddlers—those children miss out on social interactions with people that are critical for their social, psychological, and emotional development.

day she was strapped to a potty chair and unable to move about. At night she was bound and placed in a crib. If she made sounds, her father would growl at her, scratch her, and beat her. She was fed baby food instead of solid foods. Family members were prohibited from speaking to her. Because there was no television or radio in her home, she had never heard the sounds of normal human speech. After a year of extensive therapy, Genie's grammar resembled that of a typical 18-month-old. Though she made further advances with continued therapy, she never achieved full language ability. Today Genie, now in her late 50s, lives in a home for adults with developmental disabilities in California (Curtiss 1977; James 2008; Rymer 1993).

In a similar, more recent case, police were called to investigate a child abuse claim in Plant City, Florida, in 2005. In a trash-filled house overrun with roaches and reeking of urine and feces, they discovered an emaciated girl whose hair was crawling with lice and who had rashes and sores all over her

Primate Studies Our need for early socialization is reinforced by studies of animals raised in isolation. Although we would never conduct such experiments on human babies, psychologist Harry Harlow (1971) conducted tests with rhesus monkeys that had been raised away from their mothers and away from contact with other monkeys. As was the case with Genie and Dani, the rhesus monkeys raised in isolation were fearful and easily frightened. They did not mate, and the females, who were artificially inseminated, became abusive mothers. Early isolation had long-term damaging effects on the monkeys.

A creative aspect of Harlow's experimentation was his use of "artificial mothers." In one such experiment, Harlow presented monkeys raised in isolation with two substitute mothers—one a cloth-covered replica and one a wire-covered model that had the capacity to offer milk. Monkey after monkey went to the wire mother for the life-giving milk, yet spent much more time clinging to the more motherlike cloth model. Apparently, the infant monkeys developed greater social

© Glow Images RF attachments based on their

need for warmth, comfort, and intimacy than their need for food.

What we learn from cases of extreme childhood isolation and research on primates is that we lack complex instincts that will ensure our survival. Instead, we rely on the care and concern provided by others, especially when we are young. Without that early childhood socialization, we would struggle to establish working relationships with the outside world. Biology alone is not enough. The culture we create provides us with the tools we need. And through socialization, we share those tools with others.

> It matters not what someone is born, but what they grow to be.
>
> J. K. Rowling

>> The Self and Socialization

Even though we must learn from others what we need to survive, we are not simply robots who are programmed to do what others say, whether they be parents, teachers, bosses, politicians, or religious leaders. As individuals we are engaged in an ongoing dance with the world around us. We choose what to think and how to act, but we do so within the confines of the cultural resources to which we have access.

self Our sense of who we are, distinct from others, and shaped by the unique combination of our social interactions.

looking-glass self A theory that we become who we are based on how we think others see us.

I The acting self that exists in relation to the Me.

Me The socialized self that plans actions and judges performances based on the standards we have learned from others.

SOCIOLOGICAL APPROACHES TO THE SELF

We come to be who we are in the context of our relationships with others. The **self** is our sense of who we are, distinct from others and shaped by the unique combination of our social interactions. It is not a static entity; instead, it develops and changes as we seek to make sense of our life experiences. Sociologists and psychologists alike have expressed interest in how the individual develops and modifies his or her sense of self as a result of social interaction.

Cooley: The Looking-Glass Self According to American sociologist Charles Horton Cooley (1864–1929), we become our self through our interactions with others. We use their responses to what we say and do as a mirror that shapes our understanding of our self. Cooley used the expression the **looking-glass self** to describe his theory that we become who we are based on how we think others see us.

Our understanding of our self, according to Cooley, involves a complex calculation in which we constantly read and react. This process of self-development has three phases. First, we imagine how others see us—relatives, friends, even strangers on the street. Second, we imagine how others evaluate what we think they see—as intelligent, attractive, shy, or strange. Finally, we define our self as a result of these assumptions—"I am smart" or "I am beautiful" (Cooley 1902). This process is ongoing; it happens during each and every one of our interactions. According to Cooley, we become who we are based not on how others actually see us, and not on how they judge us, but on how we think they will judge us based on what we think they perceive.

In Cooley's model, our sense of self results from our "imagination" of how others view us. Because we never truly know what others think, we can develop self-identities based on often *incorrect* perceptions of how others see us. Imagine you are on a first date or a job interview. All the cues you receive throughout the interaction are positive—your date or interviewer smiles, laughs, and nods at all the right times. You go home feeling happy, confident that things went really well. But your date never returns your call, or the expected job offer never comes. You go from a feeling of elation and confidence to a sense of disappointment, doubt, and recrimination, asking yourself, "What's wrong with me?" without ever really knowing what the date or interviewer truly thought about you. In Cooley's world, who we are is very much dependent on our interpretations of the interactions we have with others.

Mead: Stages of the Self George Herbert Mead (1863–1931), another American sociologist, sought to expand on Cooley's theory. Mead especially sought to clarify the relationship between our self and our environment. He argued that there are two core components of the self: "I" and "Me." The **I** is our acting self. It is the part of us that walks, reads, sings, smiles, speaks, and performs any other action we might undertake. The **Me** is our socialized self. It draws on all our previous training and experience to plan our actions and then uses these standards to judge our performance afterward.

For Mead the self represents an ongoing interaction between our socialized self and our acting self. The Me

SOCTHINK

What cues do you rely on to know if things are going well on a first date? How about on a job interview? To what extent do you think it is possible to fake such cues?

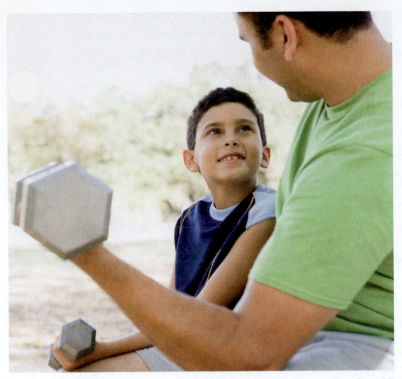

© Somos/Veer/Getty RF

individuals we interact with who are most important in the development of our self. Over time, however, we begin to see that the positions these significant others occupy are part of a larger social network. Mead (1934, 1964a, 1964b) described that realization as a three-stage process of self-development: preparatory stage, play stage, and game stage.

Preparatory Stage During the *preparatory stage,* which lasts until about age three, children merely imitate the people around them, especially family members with whom they continually interact. That can take the form of babbling babies who internalize language before they even know the words or a small child who bangs on a piece of wood while a parent is engaged in carpentry work or tries to throw a ball if an older sibling is doing so nearby. This imitation is largely mindless—simple parroting of the actions of others.

significant other An individual who is most important in the development of the self, such as a parent, friend, or teacher.

symbol A gesture, object, or word that forms the basis of human communication.

role taking The process of mentally assuming the perspective of another and responding from that imagined viewpoint.

As they grow older, children begin to realize that we attach meanings to our actions, and they become more adept at using symbols to communicate with others. **Symbols** are the gestures, objects, and words that form the basis of human communication. By interacting with family and friends, as well as by watching cartoons on television and looking at picture books, children in the preparatory stage begin to develop interaction skills they will use throughout their lives. They learn that they can use symbols to get their way, such as saying please and thank you, or perhaps throwing a tantrum in the candy aisle of the local supermarket.

plans. The I acts. The Me judges. For example, in a classroom discussion, our Me may have something to say but fears that the words won't come out quite right, which could lead to embarrassment. So our I stays silent. Our Me then kicks our self afterward when someone else says exactly what we planned to say and receives praise from the professor for having said it.

In all our interactions, we rely on a feedback loop in which we gather information, process it, and use it to guide our reaction. In some respects, this relationship is not unlike the technique math teachers turn to when using the "guess and check" problem-solving strategy for certain types of story problems. In this approach, you try a solution to see if it works out, and if it doesn't, you try again. With each successive attempt, you use the information you've gained to make more informed guesses and in so doing find the appropriate pathway to the correct solution. Similarly, in our interactions with others, pathways of appropriate action emerge over time. We become more confident that certain responses are appropriate, making our decisions about how to act in the future easier and providing us with greater self-confidence.

In developing our sense of who we are and what is appropriate, we rely on the interactions we have with our parents, friends, coworkers, coaches, and teachers. Mead used the expression **significant others** to describe the particular

Self and others do not exist as mutually exclusive facts.

Charles Horton Cooley

Play Stage As children develop skill in communicating through symbols, they gradually become more aware of social relationships out of which those symbols grow. During the *play stage,* from about ages three through five, they begin to pretend to be other people: a doctor, parent, superhero, or teacher. Such play need not make a lot of sense or be particularly coherent to adults, and children, especially when they are young, are able to move in and out of various characters with ease. For Mead, playing make-believe is more than just fun; it is a critical part of our self-development.

Mead, in fact, noted that an important aspect of the play stage is role playing. **Role taking** is the process of mentally assuming the perspective of another and responding from that imagined viewpoint. Through this process a young child imagines how others might respond in particular situations and gradually learns, for example, when it is best to ask a parent for favors. If the parent usually comes home from work in a bad mood, the child might wait until after dinner, when the parent is more relaxed and approachable.

Game Stage In Mead's third stage, the *game stage,* the child of about six to nine years of age learns to more fully appreciate that he or she is involved in interconnected and interdependent relationships. Success depends upon each person playing his or her appropriate part, and each individual must often submit to the expectations of the group. The transition from play to game is evident when teaching kids to play team sports such as T-ball or soccer. When they are little, you will often see a clump of kids chasing after a ball or moving up the field together. They have yet to learn that different people play different positions and that they will be more successful as a team if everyone plays the position to which they are assigned. When they do, they can take for granted that someone will be covering a base so they can throw a runner out or that a goalie will be there to make a save if the ball gets behind them. Visualizing the map of who should be where and who should do what enables us to see a kind of blueprint for society, and internalizing it represents the final stage of development in Mead's model.

generalized other The attitudes, viewpoints, and expectations of society as a whole that a child takes into account in his or her behavior.

dramaturgical approach A view of social interaction in which people are seen as actors on a stage attempting to put on a successful performance.

impression management The altering of the presentation of the self in order to create distinctive appearances and satisfy particular audiences.

Mead uses the term **generalized other** to refer to the attitudes, viewpoints, and expectations of society as a whole that a child takes into account in his or her behavior. Simply put, this concept suggests that when an individual acts, he or she takes into account the relative positions, contributions, and expectations for an entire group of people. For example, a child comes to see that acting courteously is important not just because his or her parent says so; rather, it is a widespread norm expected in a variety of contexts, whether at home, school, religious services, or the grocery store.

© Laurie Swope/Getty RF

At this stage, children begin to see that there really is something like a game going on with an underlying logic and shared rules and expectations for its various players. They may know their principal, Ms. Sanchez, as a significant other, but also see that the position of principal exists independent of Ms. Sanchez and that it carries with it certain expectations that make sense in the context of a school in which other positions include teacher, custodian, aide, and student. And if the individuals who come to occupy the various positions in the game fail to act accordingly, the whole thing falls apart.

Goffman: Presentation of the Self This idea that we must all play our roles as part of something larger led Erving Goffman, a Canadian sociologist, to study our everyday social interactions using the **dramaturgical approach,** which studies interaction as if we were all actors on a stage seeking to put on a successful performance. He was inspired, in part, by the William Shakespeare quote "All the world's a stage, And all the men and women merely players: They have their exits and their entrances; And one man in his time plays many parts." As we perform our roles, according to Goffman, each of us seeks to convey impressions of who we are to others, even as those others are doing the same with us.

Building on this analogy, Goffman draws our attention to various *aspects of performance,* analysis of which allows us to better understand what makes a show a success. Performances take place on a stage. *Front stage* is where we perform for our audience and includes appropriate sets and props and may involve other cast members with whom we work as a *team.* We largely follow *scripts* and, although some improvisation is permissible, too much may threaten the credibility of the character we are trying to portray. *Backstage* is where we prepare, including getting into costumes and gathering together appropriate *props* to make our

SOCTHINK

Imagine that going to class is like performing in a play. Who are the key players? What are some of their most-used lines? What props do people use to be convincing? How might the performance break down, and what steps might be taken to save the show?

performance believable. Ultimately, the *audience* judges how well we did. Whether in our role as students, restaurant servers, or even lovers, we all know that we have a part to play and that if we don't say the right lines or use the correct props, the show will collapse, undermining our sense of self.

Early in life, we learn to slant our presentation of our self to create distinctive appearances and satisfy particular audiences. Goffman (1959) referred to this altering of the presentation of the self as **impression management.** To maintain a proper image and avoid public embarrassment,

© Robbie Jack/Robbie Jack/Corbis

we engage in **face-work.** We often initiate some kind of face-saving behavior when we are feeling flustered or rejected. In response to a rejection at a singles bar, a person may engage in face-work by saying, "This place is full of losers. I'm out of here." Or, if we do poorly on an exam, we may say to a friend who did likewise, "This professor sucks." We feel the need to maintain a positive self-image if we are to continue social interaction.

In some cultures, people engage in elaborate deceptions to avoid losing face. In Japan, for example, where lifetime employment has until recently been the norm, "company men" thrown out of work during a severe economic recession may feign employment, rising as usual in the morning, donning suit and tie, and heading for the business district. But instead of going to the office, they congregate at places such as Tokyo's Hibiya Library, where they pass the time by reading before returning home at the usual hour. Many of these men are trying to protect family members, who would be shamed if neighbors discovered that the family breadwinner was unemployed. Others are deceiving their wives and families as well (French 2000).

> **face-work** The efforts people make to maintain a proper image and avoid public embarrassment.

For Goffman, Mead, and Cooley, our self is fundamentally social. Each encounter we have provides opportunities for self-assessment. Even though our sense of self may seem relatively fixed over time, it is always subject to revision as we move into and out of relationships with others. A novel interaction or experience is often all it takes to get us to question things we have taken for granted, leading to new understandings of who we really are.

SOCIAL-PSYCHOLOGICAL APPROACHES TO THE SELF

Psychologists have shared the interest of Cooley, Mead, and other sociologists in the development of the self. Early work in psychology, such as that of Sigmund Freud (1856–1939), stressed the role of inborn drives—among them the drive for sexual gratification—in channeling human behavior. Later psychologists such as Jean Piaget emphasized the stages through which human beings progress as the self develops.

Like Cooley and Mead, Freud believed that the self is a social product and that aspects of one's personality are influenced by other people (especially one's parents). However, unlike Cooley and Mead, Freud suggested that the self has components that work in opposition. According to Freud, we have a natural instinct that seeks limitless

© Brand X Pictures/PunchStock RF

© Mark Wilson/Getty Images

pleasure, but this is at odds with our societal needs for order and constraint. By interacting with others, we learn the expectations of society and then select behavior most appropriate to our own culture.

Through his research on children, including newborns, the Swiss child psychologist Jean Piaget (1896–1980) underscored the importance of social interactions in developing a sense of self. In his well-known **cognitive theory of development,** Piaget (1954) identified four stages in the development of children's thought processes. In the first, or *sensorimotor,* stage young children use their senses to make discoveries. For example, through touching they discover that their hands are actually a part of themselves. During the second, or *preoperational,* stage children begin to use words and symbols to distinguish objects and ideas. The milestone in the third, or *concrete operational,* stage is that children engage in more logical thinking. For example, they learn that even when a formless lump of clay is shaped into a snake, it is still the same clay. Finally, in the fourth, or *formal operational,* stage adolescents become capable of sophisticated abstract thought and can deal with ideas and values in a logical manner.

cognitive theory of development
The theory that children's thought progresses through four stages of development.

Piaget suggested that moral development becomes an important part of socialization as children develop the ability to think more abstractly. When children learn the rules of a game such as hopscotch or Candy Land, they are learning to obey societal norms. Those under eight years of age display a rather basic level of morality: rules are rules, and there is no concept of "extenuating circumstances." As they mature, children become capable of greater autonomy, and they begin to experience moral dilemmas and doubts as to what constitutes proper behavior.

According to Piaget, social interaction is the key to development. As children grow older, they pay increasing attention to how other people think and why they act in particular ways. To develop a distinct personality, each of us needs opportunities to interact with others. As we saw earlier, Genie and Dani were deprived of the chance for normal social interactions, and the consequences were severe (Kitchener 1991).

>> Agents of Socialization

Because our sense of self develops through interactions we have with others, sociologists pay particular attention to the commonplace contexts within which such interaction occurs. Family, friends, schools, peers, the mass media, the workplace, religion, and the state are among the agents of socialization that play the most powerful roles in shaping who we become. In keeping with the sociological imagination, we cannot understand our biography without taking into account the influence of our social environment.

FAMILY

Our families are our most important agent of socialization. Research shows that the role of the family in socializing a child cannot be overestimated (McDowell and Parke 2009). As we saw with baby talk and language, the lifelong process of learning begins shortly after birth. Because newborns can hear, see, smell, and taste, and can feel heat, cold, and pain, they are constantly orienting themselves to the surrounding world. Human beings, especially family members, constitute an important part of their social environment. People minister to the baby's needs by feeding, cleaning, carrying, and comforting her or him. In the context of families, we learn to talk, walk, feed ourselves, go to the bathroom, and so on—basic skills that we take for granted as natural but that we learned thanks to our families. As children grow up, they observe their parents expressing affection, taking care of finances, quarreling, dealing with work stress, and so forth, which prepares them for what family life might be like in their future.

Children do not play a passive role in their socialization. As Mead's I implies, they choose, sometimes to the disappointment of their parents. In so doing, they are active participants in their self-creation. We can see the power of family socialization among the Amish. Children in Amish communities are raised in a highly structured and disciplined manner, but they are not immune to the temptations posed by their peers in the non-Amish world. Around the time they turn 16, Amish teens begin dating, or courtship. They refer to this phase of their lives as *rumspringa,* a word meaning "running around," which lasts until they get married, usually by their early 20s. During this transitional time between childhood and adulthood they have greater freedom and can experiment with activities that would otherwise be forbidden, ranging from wearing non-Amish clothes, owning a cell phone, buying a TV and DVD player, driving cars, smoking, drinking, even doing drugs (though most don't go that far). During this time, they must also decide whether to commit to being Amish for the rest of their lives by taking a vow and getting baptized or to pursue life outside the Amish community. Parents often react by looking the other way, sometimes literally, pretending not to notice. They remain secure in the knowledge that, after a lifetime of Amish socialization, their children almost always return to the traditional Amish lifestyle. Research shows that only about 20 percent of Amish youths leave the fold, and most of them join one of the only somewhat more modern Mennonite groups. Rarely does a baptized adult leave (Kraybill, Johnson-Weiner, and Nolt 2013; Schachtman 2006).

Cross-Cultural Variation How children are socialized varies significantly around the world. In Vietnam, potty training starts by the time babies are six months old. Mothers whistle to remind their children to go and children are effectively potty trained by the time they are nine months old (Duong, Jansson, and Hellström 2013). In Sweden, parents routinely leave babies asleep in strollers outside shops, even on the coldest days, while the parents go in to buy something or get something to eat, to expose their children to more fresh air. They believe that doing so makes the babies healthier and less likely to get sick (Lee 2013). In Japan, parents push their children to commute to school on their own from an early age. In cities like Tokyo, first-graders must learn to negotiate buses, subways, and long walks. To ensure their safety, parents carefully lay out rules: never talk to strangers; check with a station attendant if you get off at the wrong stop; stay on to the end of the line, then call, if you miss your stop; take stairs, not escalators; don't fall asleep. One parent acknowledges that she worries, "but after they are 6, children are supposed to start being independent from the mother. If you're still taking your child to school after the first month, everyone looks at you funny" (Tolbert 2000:17).

In the United States, whether out of fear for their child's safety or concern about being charged with child endangerment, few parents would consider giving their young child this much independence. Parenting norms in the United States have shifted in recent decades, resulting in greater oversight and involvement in children's lives. Reflecting on the question of whether or not parents have become overprotective, journalist Hanna Rosin (2014) points out, "Actions that would have been considered paranoid in the 70s—walking third-graders to school, forbidding your kid to play ball in the street, going down the slide with your child in your lap—are now routine." The variety of parenting practices across cultures and

© blue jean images/Getty RF

© Bill Pugliano/Getty Images

across time reinforces the idea that our actions are not narrowly determined by our genes.

The Influence of Race and Gender In the United States, social development includes exposure to cultural assumptions regarding gender and race. African American parents, for example, have learned that children as young as two years old can absorb negative messages about Blacks in children's books, toys, and television shows—the vast majority of which are designed primarily for White consumers. At the same time, African American children are exposed more often than others to the inner-city youth gang culture. Because most Blacks, even those who are middle class, live near very poor neighborhoods, their children are susceptible to these influences, despite their parents' strong family values (Benhorin and McMahon 2008; Friend, Hunter, and Fletcher 2011; Kliewar and Sullivan 2009).

The term **gender roles** refers to expectations regarding the proper behavior, attitudes, and activities of males and females. For example, we traditionally think of "toughness" as masculine—and desirable only in men—while we view "tenderness" as feminine. As we will see in Chapter 12, other cultures do not necessarily assign these qualities to each gender in the way that our culture does. As the primary agents of childhood socialization, parents play a critical role in guiding children into those gender roles deemed appropriate in a society.

Other adults, older siblings, the mass media, and religious and educational institutions also have a noticeable influence on a child's socialization into feminine and masculine norms. A culture or subculture may require that one sex or the other take primary responsibility for the socialization of children, economic support of the family, or religious or intellectual leadership. In some societies girls are socialized mainly by their mothers and boys by their fathers—an arrangement that may prevent girls from learning critical survival skills. In South Asia, for example, fathers teach their sons to swim to prepare them for a life as fishermen; girls typically do not learn to swim. When the deadly tsunami hit the coast of South Asia in 2004, many more men than women survived.

gender roles Expectations regarding the proper behavior, attitudes, and activities of males and females.

SCHOOL

In school we typically move beyond the more sheltered confines of our family and learn to become members of the larger social groups to which we belong. Schools teach us the taken-for-granted knowledge of the broader society—not only basic skills such as reading, writing, and 'rithmatic but also shared cultural knowledge, such as the national anthem, the heroes of the American Revolution, and the pillars of good character. Like the family, schools have an explicit mandate to socialize people in the United States—and especially children—into the norms and values of U.S. culture.

Schools teach children the values and customs of the larger society because that shared culture provides the glue that holds us together as a society. If we did not transmit our knowledge and skills from one generation to the next, society would collapse. The knowledge we gain there, however, goes beyond the official curriculum to include the more informal lessons we learn on the playground. We do learn the facts and figures of history, science, reading, math, and more, but we also learn how to stand up for ourselves when our parents or teachers are not there to hover over us or to bail us out.

In addition to reinforcing social order, schools open doors for us as individuals. We are exposed to new ways of thinking and acting that allow us to make new choices about our future. Although this can include training for careers that allow us to "get ahead," it also involves exposure to new cultures, ideas, practices, and possibilities. It might even lead us to an unexpected future such as a career in sociology!

Although schools provide both social order and individual opportunity, they can also reinforce existing inequality through the ways students are socialized. As economists Samuel Bowles and Herbert Gintis (1976) have observed, schools produce teachable students who become manageable workers. They argue that schools have less to do with transmitting academic content than with socializing students into the proper attitudes and behaviors of the workplace. Schools teach students how to work for rewards, how to work in teams, how to meet deadlines, how to take responsibility for a task or work product, how to comply with instructions, and so on. The students who internalize these skills best are rewarded with opportunities in the workplace while others are left behind.

© Jose Luis Pelaez Inc/Blend Images RF

These differential outcomes are compounded by the fact that the positions we occupy when we enter school shape where we end up. For example, higher education in the United States is costly despite the existence of public colleges and universities and financial aid programs. Students from affluent backgrounds, therefore, have an advantage in gaining access to universities and professional training. At the same time, less affluent young people may never receive the preparation that would qualify them for the best-paying and most prestigious jobs.

PEER GROUPS

As we grow older, and especially in our adolescent years, our friends, schoolmates, and other peers become increasingly important in shaping how we think and act. To understand the role peers play at a relatively young age, sociologists Patricia and Peter Adler conducted participant observation research at elementary schools with fourth- through sixth-grade students. They found that, even this early, a pecking order is established ranging from the "popular clique" at the top that includes the "cool kids" on down to what they call the "social isolates" at the bottom, whom other kids sometimes call "dweebs" or "nerds" (Adler and Adler 1996). Children get the message about where they fit and how they should behave. In another study of elementary schoolchildren, the Adlers found that popularity reinforces gender stereotypes. To be popular as a boy is to be athletic, tough, and not too academic. To be popular as a girl is to be attractive, to be able to manipulate others using social skills, and to come from a family wealthy enough to permit shopping for the latest cool stuff (Adler, Kless, and Adler 1992).

The impact of peer groups among high schoolers has become a pop culture staple, perhaps best captured in the classic film *The Breakfast Club,* in which "a brain, an athlete, a basket case, a princess, and a criminal" were forced together during Saturday morning detention. In the end, the five students got past their stereotypical perceptions of each other to find common ground. To better understand peer group culture in the real world, researchers from the University of North Carolina explored how high school peer groups were perceived by outsiders and contrasted those perceptions with the actual, self-reported behaviors of members within each group. Based on interviews with high school students, they focused on four groups: populars, jocks, brains, and burnouts. They found a whole series of misperceptions, such as:

- Non-populars overestimated populars' number of sexual partners.
- Non-jocks overestimated jocks' amount of alcohol consumption.
- Non-brains overestimated brains' time spent studying.
- Non-burnouts overestimated burnouts' frequency of property damage.

Overall, researchers concluded that students especially tend to overestimate the degree to which students in the two most popular groups engage in sex, drugs, and property damage. In a follow-up study, the researchers found that,

High School Behavior: Perception versus Reality

Note: Actual represents the average of self-reported practices for students within that peer group; Perceived represents responses from students outside the group.

Source: Helms et al. 2014.

when analyzed over time, those students who perceived the popular kids as being more likely to engage in risky behaviors were themselves more likely to engage in those behaviors. As we have learned already from the Thomas theorem (see Chapter 1), perception shapes action.

MASS MEDIA AND TECHNOLOGY

In the past 100 or so years, media innovations—radio, motion pictures, recorded music, television, and the Internet—have become important agents of socialization. In the United States, 78 percent of teens own a cell phone and 47 percent of them have smartphones. Among teens, 95 percent use the Internet compared to 52 percent of those aged 65 and older. Overall, 71 percent of Internet users use Facebook including 87 percent of those aged 18–29 and 56 percent of people aged 65 and older (Duggan et al. 2015; Madden et al. 2013). We are spending more and more of our time interacting with technology, which has an inevitable impact on our interactions with each other. For example, 70 percent of Facebook users visit the site daily (Duggan et al. 2015). Adding up totals from television, radio, print media, phones, computers, movies, and music—and taking multitasking (doing more than one task at a time) into account—Americans consume the equivalent of 13.6 hours of information per day outside of work (Short 2013).

New technologies are changing how we interact with family, friends, and even strangers. Through email, cell phones, texting, and instant messaging, we can maintain close, almost constant, connections with family and friends both near and far. Services such as Facebook and Twitter can expand our worlds, enabling us to establish and extend networks with "friends" both known and unknown (Hampton et al. 2009). Using social media makes us more aware of stressful events in the lives of people we know, such as hospitalization, marriage, divorce, or purchase of a new home

Did You Know?

. . . The average person in the United States watches 32 hours and 15 minutes of television per week. Viewing varies substantially by age, with those aged 2–11 watching 25 h, 6 min to those 65+ at 40 h, 39 min.

Source: Nielsen 2013a.   *Photo:* © Datacraft Co Ltd/Getty RF.

How Young People Use the Media

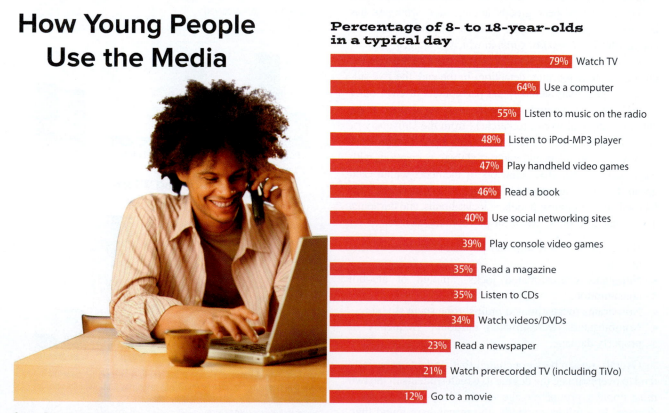

Percentage of 8- to 18-year-olds in a typical day

79%	Watch TV
64%	Use a computer
55%	Listen to music on the radio
48%	Listen to iPod-MP3 player
47%	Play handheld video games
46%	Read a book
40%	Use social networking sites
39%	Play console video games
35%	Read a magazine
35%	Listen to CDs
34%	Watch videos/DVDs
23%	Read a newspaper
21%	Watch prerecorded TV (including TiVo)
12%	Go to a movie

Source: Rideout et al. 2010:44–45.   *Photo:* © Creatas/PictureQuest RF.

© Purestock/SuperStock RF

Video game designer Mike Mika's three-year-old daughter enjoys playing the classic arcade game Donkey Kong. In it, a King Kong–like ape kidnaps Pauline, and Mario's task is to save her. One day Mika's daughter asked, "How can I play as the girl? I want to save Mario!" After days spent hacking the Donkey Kong ROM, Mika (2013) fulfilled his daughter's wish to make the princess the hero. According to Anita Sarkeesian (2013), "Damsel in Distress" plot devices are exceedingly common in video games. She concludes, "Distilled down to its essence, the plot device works by trading the disempowerment of female characters for the empowerment of male characters." With the help of more than 6,000 Kickstarter backers, she has produced a series of online videos investigating the portrayal of women in video games.

Photo: © Mike Mika.

SOCTHINK

Among tablet and smartphone owners, 57 percent check email while watching TV and 44 percent visit social network sites. They also download applications, check sports scores, look up information related to the program they are watching, and more (Nielsen 2012). What are possible effects, both positive and negative, of such multitasking?

(Hampton et al. 2015). But new technologies can also lead to narrowcasting, in which we interact mainly with people who are most like ourselves. Social scientist Sherry Turkle (2011) argues that such technologies detract from even our more intimate relationships, which require concentrated time together to flourish. In a similar vein, Nicholas Carr (2010) suggests that the Internet is making us shallow, arguing that even though we have access to more information, we are not sufficiently attentive to ideas or to one another.

Around the world, including Africa and other developing areas, people have been socialized into relying on new communications technologies. For instance, not

Telephones and Cell Phones by Country (rates per 100 people)

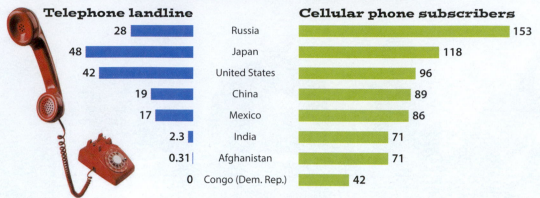

	Telephone landline	Country	Cellular phone subscribers	
	28	Russia	153	
	48	Japan	118	
	42	United States	96	
	19	China	89	
	17	Mexico	86	
	2.3	India	71	
	0.31	Afghanistan	71	
	0	Congo (Dem. Rep.)	42	

Source: International Telecommunications Union 2015.   *Photo:* © Getty Images RF.

long ago, if Zadhe Iyombe wanted to talk to his mother, he had to make an eight-day trip from the capital city of Kinshasa (in the Democratic Republic of the Congo) up the Congo River by boat to the rural town where he was born. Now both he and his mother have access to a cell phone, and they send text messages to each other daily. And Iyombe and his mother are not atypical. A substantial percentage of people own a cell phone in such nations. For example, Tunisia: 88 percent; Kenya:

82 percent; Senegal: 81 percent; El Salvador: 79 percent; Ghana: 79 percent; Nigeria: 78 percent; and Pakistan: 53 percent. Many developing nations have essentially skipped over the use of landlines, along with the infrastructure costs they would entail, and have gone directly to cell technology (Pew Research Center 2014b; K. Sullivan 2006).

Access to media can also increase social cohesion by presenting a common, more or less standardized view of culture through mass communication. Sociologist Robert Park (1922) studied how newspapers helped immigrants to the United States adjust to their environment by changing their customary habits and teaching them the values and views of people in their new home country. Unquestionably, the mass media play a significant role in providing a collective experience for members of society. Think about how the mass media bring together members of a community or even a nation by broadcasting important events and ceremonies (such as inaugurations, press conferences, parades, state funerals, and the Olympics) and by covering disasters.

The sources we rely on to learn about the transformative events of our time have shifted. People learned about the murder of Abraham Lincoln via newspapers, the death of Franklin D. Roosevelt over the radio, and the assassination of John

Did You Know?

. . . The National Day of Unplugging occurs on the first Friday of each March. Organizers encourage us to take a 24-hour break from the "relentless deluge of technology and information" by shutting down our computers and turning off our cell phones. Participants are urged to use the time they gain to connect with loved ones, get outside, nurture their health, find silence, and give back.

Photo: © Ariel Skelley/Blend Images/Corbis RF

Child Care Arrangements for Preschoolers

Relative care	Grandparent/other relative	31.1%
	Parent(s)	21.3%
	Sibling 2.6%	
Nonrelative care	Organized care facility (including day care)	23.5%
	Other nonrelative	11.2%

Note: Organized care includes day care, Head Start, preschool, and school.

Source: Laughlin 2013:Table 1.   *Photo:* © Glow Images RF.

F. Kennedy on television. Nowadays, the Internet plays a more prominent role, and Twitter and Facebook lead the way in breaking news, as was the case with the Boston Marathon bombings in 2013. On any given day, according to national surveys, 55 percent of people watch news on TV, 33 percent listen to radio news, and 29 percent read a newspaper. That compares to 50 percent who get their news from one or more digital platforms, including online news sites, mobile devices, social networks such as Facebook or Twitter, email, and podcasts. Age clearly matters, with 60 percent of 18- to 24-year-olds getting their news from digital platforms compared to 28 percent of those aged 65 and older (Pew Research Center 2012e).

THE WORKPLACE

Learning to behave appropriately in an occupation is a fundamental aspect of human socialization. In the United States, working full-time confirms adult status; it indicates that one has passed out of adolescence. In a sense, socialization into an occupation can represent both a harsh reality ("I have to work in order to buy food and pay the rent") and the realization of an ambition ("I've always wanted to be an airline pilot") (W. Moore 1968:862; Simmons 2009).

It used to be that our work life began with the end of our formal schooling, but that is no longer necessarily the case, at least not in the United States. More and more young people work today, and not just for a parent or relative. Adolescents generally seek jobs to earn spending money; 80 percent of high school seniors say that little or none of what they earn goes to family expenses. These teens rarely look on their employment as a means of exploring vocational interests or getting on-the-job training (Hirschman and Voloshin 2007).

Some observers believe that the increasing number of teenagers who are working earlier in life and for longer hours are finding the workplace to be almost as important an agent of socialization as school. In fact, a number of educators complain that time spent at work is adversely affecting students' schoolwork. The level of teenage employment in the United States is the highest among industrial countries, which may provide one explanation for why U.S. high school students lag behind those in other countries on international achievement tests (Cavanagh 2012).

Socialization in the workplace changes when it involves a more permanent shift from an after-school job to full-time employment. Occupational socialization can be most intense during the transition from school to job, but it continues throughout one's work history. Technological advances and corporate reorganization may alter the requirements of the position and necessitate new training. According to the Bureau of Labor Statistics (2012d), between the ages of 18 and 46 alone, the typical person holds 11.3 different jobs. We can no longer assume that we will have a job-for-life, so whether by choice or by necessity, we must be open to ongoing occupational socialization.

RELIGION AND THE STATE

Increasingly, social scientists are recognizing the growing importance of government ("the state") and the continued significance of religion as agents of socialization. Traditionally, family members served as the primary caregivers in U.S. culture, but in the 20th century, the family's protective function was steadily transferred to outside agencies such as public schools, hospitals, mental health clinics, and child care centers, many of which are run by the state. Historically, religious groups also provided such care and protection. Despite early sociological predictions

Leh Village, India, schoolchildren.   Photo: © Nevada Wier/Getty Images.

Although many 18-year-olds choose not to vote, voter turnout in the 2008 presidential election was the highest it had been in decades, causing long lines at some polling stations. Rates among young people declined a bit in 2012.   Photo: © Autumn Payne/Sacramento Bee/MCT via Getty Images.

passage—most 18-year-olds choose not to vote, and most people choose their age of retirement without reference to government dictates—they do symbolize the fact that we have moved on to a different stage of our life, with different expectations regarding our behavior.

>> Socialization Throughout the Life Course

Adolescents among the Kota people of the Congo in Africa paint themselves blue. Cuban American girls go on a day-long religious retreat before dancing the night away. These are both **rites of passage**—rituals that mark the symbolic transition from one social position to another, dramatizing and validating changes in a person's status.

In the Kota rite the color blue—the color of death—symbolizes the death of childhood and the passage to adulthood. For adolescent girls in Miami's Cuban American community, the *quinceañera* ceremony celebrating the

Body painting is a ritual marking the passage to puberty in some cultures.   Photo: © Thomas S. England/Science Source.

rite of passage A ritual marking the symbolic transition from one social position to another dramatizing and validating changes in a person's status.

that religion would cease to play a substantial role in modern society, these groups continue to play a significant role in identity formation and collective life (Warner 2005).

Preschool children in particular are often cared for by someone other than a parent. More than 90 percent of employed mothers depend on others to care for their children, and almost 40 percent of mothers who aren't employed have regular care arrangements. Approximately one-third of children under age five are cared for by nonrelatives in nursery schools, Head Start programs, day care centers, family day care, and other providers. Children this age are also more likely to be cared for on a daily basis by grandparents than by their parents (Laughlin 2013).

Both government and organized religion act to provide markers representing significant life course transitions. For example, religious organizations continue to celebrate meaningful ritual events—such as baptism, bismillah, or bar/bat mitzvah—that often bring together all the members of an extended family, even if they never meet for any other reason. Government regulations stipulate the ages at which a person may drive a car, drink alcohol, vote in elections, marry without parental permission, work overtime, and retire. Although these regulations do not constitute strict rites of

SOCTHINK

Should government play a larger role in socializing children by funding public education for all children starting at age two?

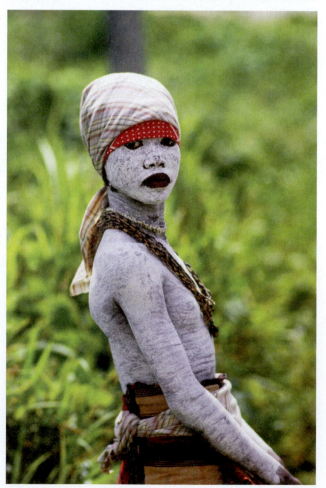

Milestones in the Transition to Adulthood

Expected age	Life event	Percentage who view event as extremely/quite important
20.9	Financial independence from parents/guardians	80.9%
21.1	Separate residence from parents	57.2%
21.2	Full-time employment	83.8%
22.3	Completion of formal schooling	90.2%
24.5	Capability of supporting family	82.3%
25.7	Marriage	33.2%
26.2	Parenthood	29.0%

Source: T. Smith 2004.

attainment of womanhood at age 15 supports a network of party planners, caterers, dress designers, and the Miss Quinceañera Latina pageant. For thousands of years, Egyptian mothers have welcomed their newborns to the world in the Soboa ceremony by stepping over the seven-day-old infant seven times. And Naval Academy seniors celebrate their graduation from college by hurling their hats skyward.

THE LIFE COURSE

Such specific ceremonies mark stages of development in the life course. They indicate that the process of socialization continues through all stages of the life cycle. In fact, some researchers have chosen to concentrate on socialization as a lifelong process. Sociologists and other social scientists who take such a **life course approach** look closely at the social factors, including gender and income, that influence people throughout their lives, from birth to death. They recognize that biological changes help mold but do not dictate human behavior.

In the transition from childhood to adulthood, we can identify certain markers that signify the passage from one life stage to the next. These milestones vary from one society and even one generation to the next. In the United States, according to one national survey, completion of formal schooling has risen to the top, with 90 percent of people identifying it as an important rite of passage. On average, Americans expect this milestone to be attained by a person's 23rd birthday. Other major events in the life course, such as getting married or becoming a parent, are expected to follow three or four years later. Interestingly, the significance of these markers has declined, with only about one-third of survey respondents identifying marriage and less than one-third identifying parenthood as important milestones representing adulthood (Furstenberg 2010; T. Smith 2004).

One result of these staggered steps to independence is that in the United States, unlike some other societies, no clear dividing line exists between adolescence and adulthood. Nowadays, the number of years between childhood and adulthood has grown, and few young people finish school, get married, and leave home at about the same age, clearly establishing their transition to adulthood. The term *youthhood* has been coined to describe the prolonged ambiguous status that young people in their 20s experience (Côté 2000; Roberts and Côté 2014).

life course approach A research orientation in which sociologists and other social scientists look closely at the social factors that influence people throughout their lives, from birth to death.

anticipatory socialization Processes of socialization in which a person "rehearses" for future positions, occupations, and social relationships.

SOCTHINK

What are some of the markers of youthhood? When does it begin? When does it end? To what extent do you feel like an adult (regardless of your age)? What characteristics of our society contribute to ambiguity in our passage into adulthood?

ANTICIPATORY SOCIALIZATION AND RESOCIALIZATION

In our journey through our lives, we seek to prepare ourselves for what is coming and to adapt to change as necessary. To prepare, we undergo **anticipatory socialization,** which refers to processes of socialization in which a person "rehearses" for future positions, occupations, and social relationships. A culture can function more efficiently and smoothly if members become acquainted with the norms, values, and behavior associated with a social position before actually assuming that status. Preparation for many aspects of adult life begins with anticipatory socialization during childhood and adolescence and continues throughout our lives as we prepare for new responsibilities (Levine and Hoffner 2006).

High school students experience a bit of anticipatory socialization when they prepare for college. They begin to imagine what college life will be like and what kind of person they will be when they get there. They may seek out information from friends and family to get a better sense of what to expect, but increasingly, they also rely on campus websites and Facebook entries. To assist in this process and to attract more students, colleges are investing more time and money in websites through which students can take "virtual" campus tours, listen to podcasts, and stream videos of everything from the school song to a sample zoology lecture.

Occasionally, assuming a new social or occupational position requires that we *unlearn* an established orientation. **Resocialization** refers to the process of discarding old behavior patterns and accepting new ones as part of a life transition. Often resocialization results from explicit efforts to transform an individual, as happens in reform schools, therapy groups, prisons, religious conversion settings, and political indoctrination camps. The process of resocialization typically involves considerable stress for the individual—much more so than socialization in general, or even anticipatory socialization (Hart, Miller, and Johnson 2003).

resocialization The process of discarding former behavior patterns and accepting new ones as part of a transition in one's life.

total institution An institution that regulates all aspects of a person's life under a single authority, such as a prison, the military, a mental hospital, or a convent.

Resocialization is particularly effective when it occurs within a total institution. Erving Goffman (1961) coined the term **total institution** to refer to an institution that regulates all aspects of a person's life under a single authority. Examples can be more or less extreme, from summer camp or boarding school to prison, the military, a mental hospital, or a convent. Because the total institution is generally cut off from the rest of society, it provides for all the needs of its members. In its extreme form, so elaborate are its requirements, and so all-encompassing its activities, that the total institution represents a miniature society.

Goffman (1961) identified several common traits of total institutions:

- All aspects of life are conducted in the same place under the control of a single authority.
- Any activities within the institution are conducted in the company of others in the same circumstances—for example, army recruits or novices in a convent.
- The authorities devise rules and schedule activities without consulting the participants.
- All aspects of life within a total institution are designed to fulfill the purpose of the organization. Thus, all activities in a monastery might be centered on prayer and communion with God (Malacrida 2005; Mapel 2007; K. Williams and Warren 2009).

Life in prison is highly regulated—even recreation time.   Photo: © Justin Sullivan/Getty Images.

© Paula Bronstein/Getty Images

People often lose their individuality within total institutions. For example, a person entering prison may experience the humiliation of a **degradation ceremony** as he or she is stripped of clothing, jewelry, and other personal possessions. From that point on, scheduled daily routines allow for little or no personal initiative. The individual becomes secondary and rather invisible in the overbearing social environment (Garfinkel 1956).

ROLE TRANSITIONS DURING THE LIFE COURSE

As we have seen, one of the key transitional stages we pass through occurs as we enter the adult world, perhaps by moving out of the parental home, beginning a career, or entering a marriage. As we age we move into the midlife transition, which typically begins at about age 40. Men and women often experience a stressful period of self-evaluation, commonly known as the **midlife crisis,** in which they realize that they have not achieved basic goals and ambitions and may feel they have little time left to do so. This conflict between their hopes and their outcomes causes strain. Compounding such stresses that are often associated with one's career or partner is the growing

responsibility for caring for two generations at once (Mortimer and Shanahan 2006; Wethington 2000).

During the late 1990s, social scientists began focusing on the **sandwich generation**—adults who simultaneously try to meet the competing needs of their parents and their children. Their caregiving goes in two directions: to children, who even as young adults may still require significant support and direction; and to aging parents, whose health and economic problems may demand intervention by their adult children. Among adults aged 40–59, 47 percent report having both a parent 65 years old or older and a minor child or are supporting a grown child (Parker and Patten 2013).

degradation ceremony An aspect of the socialization process within some total institutions, in which people are subjected to humiliating rituals.

midlife crisis A stressful period of self-evaluation that begins at about age 40.

sandwich generation The generation of adults who simultaneously try to meet the competing needs of their parents and their children.

Like the role of caring for children, that of caring for aging parents falls disproportionately on women. Overall, women provide 60 percent of the care their parents receive, and even more as the demands of the role grow more intense and time-consuming. Increasingly, middle-aged women and younger are finding themselves on the "daughter track," as their time and attention are diverted by the needs of their aging mothers and fathers (Dotinga 2014; Gross 2005; P. Taylor et al. 2009).

>> Aging and Society

Due to advances in areas such as health care, nutrition, and working conditions, life expectancy has risen significantly both in the United States and around the world. Someone born in 1900 in the United States had an average life expectancy of 47 years, but babies born in the U.S. in 2011 can anticipate living to 76.3 if they're boys and 81.1 if they're girls (National Center for Health Statistics 2014:Table 18). Globally, life expectancy in more developed nations is 79 years compared to 61 years in least developed nations (Population Reference Bureau 2014:13).

5 Movies on SOCIALIZATION

Boyhood
Growing up, through the eyes of a child.

Bully
The true story of the tragic costs of peer group intimidation.

Children Underground
Documentary about children surviving in the subway systems of Romania.

Mama
In this supernatural thriller, a family adopts two girls who were abandoned in the woods.

Training Day
A day in the life of a rookie narcotics officer in the LAPD.

Going GLOBAL

Aging Around the World

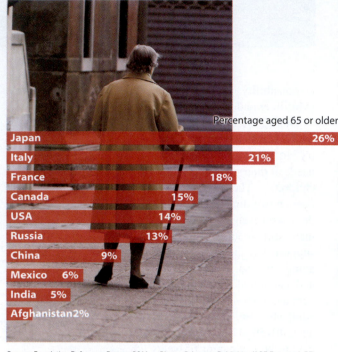

Percentage aged 65 or older

Country	Percentage
Japan	26%
Italy	21%
France	18%
Canada	15%
USA	14%
Russia	13%
China	9%
Mexico	6%
India	5%
Afghanistan	2%

Source: Population Reference Bureau 2014. *Photo:* © Ingram Publishing/AGE Fotostock RF.

How societies deal with their elderly population varies significantly across cultures. One society may treat older people with reverence, whereas another sees them as unproductive and "difficult." The Sherpas—a Tibetan-speaking Buddhist people in Nepal—live in a culture that idealizes old age. Almost all elderly members of the Sherpa culture (see photo) own their homes, and most are in relatively good physical condition. Typically, older Sherpas value their independence and prefer not to live with their children. Among the Fulani of Africa, however, older men and women move to the edge of the family homestead. Since that is where people are buried, the elderly sleep over their own graves, for they are viewed socially as already dead (Goldstein and Beall 1981; Stenning 1958; Tonkinson 1978).

Understandably, all societies have some system of age stratification that associates certain social roles with distinct periods in life. Some of this age differentiation seems inevitable; it would make little sense to send young children off to war or to expect older citizens to handle physically demanding tasks, such as loading freight at shipyards.

In the United States, the proportion of the population that was 65 and older grew from 4.1 percent in 1900 to 13.7 percent in 2012; it is expected to rise to 20.9 percent by 2050. These rates vary by race and ethnicity. As of 2012, non-Hispanic Whites over age 65 made up 17.3 percent of the U.S. population compared to 9.2 percent for older African Americans, and 5.9 percent for elderly Hispanics. By 2050, it is anticipated that non-Hispanic Whites over 65 will make up 27.4 percent, while African Americans comprise 17.9 percent and Hispanics make up 13.8 percent (Oilman, Velkoff, and Hogan 2014).

ADJUSTING TO RETIREMENT

Making the role transition into retirement can be a difficult process. Retirement is a rite of passage that typically marks a transition out of active participation in the full-time labor market. Symbolic events are associated with this rite of passage, such as retirement gifts, a retirement party, and special moments on the last day on the job. The preretirement period itself can be emotionally charged, especially if the retiree is expected to train his or her successor (Reitzes and Mutran 2004).

Actual and Projected Growth of the Elderly Population of the United States

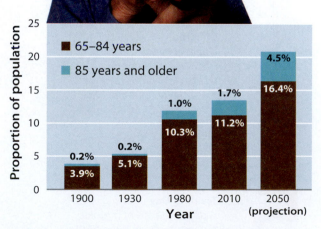

Proportion of population / Year

Legend:
- 65–84 years
- 85 years and older

Year	65–84 years	85 years and older
1900	3.9%	0.2%
1930	5.1%	0.2%
1980	10.3%	1.0%
2010	11.2%	1.7%
2050 (projection)	16.4%	4.5%

Sources: He et al. 2005:9; Ortman et al. 2014; Werner 2011. *Photo:* © Darren Greenwood/Design Pics RF.

Gerontologist Robert Atchley (1976) has identified several phases of the retirement experience:

- *Preretirement,* a period of anticipatory socialization as the person prepares for retirement.
- *The near phase,* when the person establishes a specific departure date from his or her job.
- *The honeymoon phase,* an often euphoric period in which the person pursues activities that he or she never had time for before.
- *The disenchantment phase,* in which retirees feel a sense of letdown or even depression as they cope with their new lives, which may include illness or poverty.
- *The reorientation phase,* which involves the development of a more realistic view of retirement alternatives.
- *The stability phase,* in which the person has learned to deal with life after retirement in a reasonable and comfortable fashion.
- *The termination phase,* which begins when the person can no longer engage in basic, day-to-day activities such as self-care and housework.

Retirement is not a single transition, then, but a series of adjustments that varies from one person to another. The length and timing of each phase will differ for each individual, depending on such factors as financial and health status. In fact, a person will not necessarily go through all the phases identified by Atchley. For example, people who are forced to retire or who face financial difficulties may never experience a honeymoon phase. And many retirees continue to be part of the paid labor force of the United States, often taking part-time jobs to supplement their pensions, either because they want to or because they need to.

>> Perspectives on Aging

Aging is an important aspect of socialization throughout the life course. The particular problems of older adults have become the focus of a specialized field of research and inquiry known as **gerontology**—the study of the sociological and psychological aspects of aging and the problems of aging adults. It originated in the 1930s, as an increasing number of social scientists became aware of the plight of this population.

Gerontologists rely heavily on sociological principles and theories to explain the effects of aging on the individual and society. They also draw on psychology, anthropology, physical education, counseling, and medicine in their study of the aging process. Three perspectives on aging—disengagement theory, activity theory, and age discrimination—arise out of these studies.

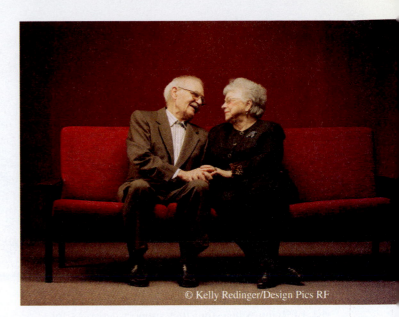
© Kelly Redinger/Design Pics RF

SOCTHINK

What age do you think counts as getting "old"? What factors influence our conception of what counts as old?

DISENGAGEMENT THEORY

After studying elderly people in good health and relatively comfortable economic circumstances, Elaine Cumming and William Henry (1961) introduced their **disengagement theory,** which implicitly suggests that society and the aging individual mutually sever many of their relationships. Highlighting the significance of social order in society, disengagement theory emphasizes that passing social roles on from one generation to another ensures social stability.

According to this theory, the approach of death forces people to drop most of their social roles—including those of worker, volunteer, spouse, hobby enthusiast, and even reader. Younger members of society then take on these functions. The aging person, it is held, withdraws into an increasing state of inactivity while preparing for death. At the same time, society withdraws from aging adults by segregating them residentially (in retirement homes and communities), educationally (in programs designed solely for senior citizens), and recreationally (in senior citizens' centers). Implicit in disengagement theory is the view that society should help older people withdraw from their accustomed social roles.

Since it was first outlined more than five decades ago, disengagement theory has generated considerable controversy. Some gerontologists have objected to the implication that older people want to be ignored and put away—and even more to the idea that they should be encouraged to withdraw from meaningful social roles. Critics of disengagement theory insist that society forces elderly people into an involuntary and painful withdrawal from the paid labor force and from meaningful social relationships.

> **gerontology** The study of the sociological and psychological aspects of aging and the problems of aging adults.
>
> **disengagement theory** A theory of aging that suggests that society and the aging individual mutually sever many of their relationships.

Rather than voluntarily seeking to disengage, older employees find themselves pushed out of their jobs—in many instances, even before they are entitled to maximum retirement benefits (Boaz 1987).

ACTIVITY THEORY

How important is it for older people to stay actively involved, whether at a job or in other pursuits? A tragic disaster in Chicago in 1995 showed that it can be a matter of life and death. An intense heat wave lasting more than a week—with a heat index exceeding 115 degrees on two consecutive days—resulted in 733 heat-related deaths. About three-fourths of the deceased were 65 or older. Subsequent analysis showed that older people who lived alone had the highest risk of dying, suggesting that support networks for older adults literally help save lives. Older Hispanics and Asian Americans had lower death rates from the heat wave than other racial and ethnic groups. Their stronger social networks probably resulted in more regular contact with family members and friends (Klinenberg 2002; Schaefer 1998a).

Often seen as the opposite of disengagement theory, **activity theory** suggests that those elderly people who remain active and socially involved will have an improved quality of life. Proponents of this perspective acknowledge that a 70-year-old person may not have the ability or desire to perform various social roles that he or she had at age 40. Yet they contend that older people have essentially the same need for social interaction as any other group.

activity theory A theory of aging that suggests that those elderly people who remain active and socially involved will have an improved quality of life.

The improved health of older people—sometimes overlooked by social scientists—has strengthened the arguments of activity theorists. Illness and chronic disease are no longer quite the scourge of aging adults that they once were. The recent emphasis on fitness, the availability of better medical care, greater control of infectious diseases, and the reduction in the number of fatal strokes and heart attacks have combined to reduce the traumas of growing older.

Accumulating medical research also points to the importance of remaining socially involved. Among those who decline in their mental capacities later in life, deterioration is most rapid in those who withdraw from social relationships and activities. Fortunately, aging adults are finding new ways to remain socially engaged, as evidenced by their

Movies on AGING

5

Gran Torino
A widowed veteran confronts gang violence in his neighborhood.

Up
A cranky old man and a young boy embark on an unusual adventure.

Nebraska
An aging father and his estranged son hit the road to claim their lottery grand prize.

Crazy Heart
Life takes a country music singer down paths he never saw coming.

The Bucket List
Two men confront death by ticking off items on their to-do list.

POPSOC

In 2002, the Senate Special Committee on Aging convened a panel on the media's portrayal of older people and sharply criticized media and marketing executives for bombarding audiences with negative images of aging adults. How many characters on top TV shows today can you think of who are over 65? How does that compare to the number of characters you can think of who are under 30?

© AP Photo/The Billings Gazette, Larry Mayer

Photo: © Ronnie Kaufman/Blend Images RF.

Rising Labor Force Participation Rates Among Older Adults

	1992	2002	2012	2022
65–69 years	20.6%	26.1%	32.1%	38.3%
70–74 years	11.1%	14%	19.5%	24%
75–79 years	6.3%	7.4%	11.4%	14.9%
75 years and older	4.5%	5.1%	7.6%	10.5%

Source: Toossi 2013.   *Photos:* © Lisa F. Young/Getty Images RF.

increasing use of the Internet, especially to keep in touch with family and friends (P. Taylor et al. 2009; A. Williams et al. 2010).

Admittedly, many activities open to older individuals involve unpaid labor, for which younger adults may receive salaries. Unpaid elderly workers include hospital volunteers (versus aides and orderlies), drivers for charities such as the Red Cross (versus chauffeurs), tutors (in contrast to teachers), and craftspeople for charity bazaars (in contrast to carpenters and dressmakers). However, some companies have recently begun programs to hire retirees for full- or part-time work.

Continued engagement in the workforce has been a growing trend. In 2012, 31.8 percent of those aged 65–74 worked full- or part-time. Of those who consider themselves retired but who continue to work, almost 70 percent say they do so primarily because they want to, not because they need to for financial reasons. In fact, the percentage of those who choose to work after what we conventionally think of as retirement age continues to rise, even among the oldest in the population (P. Taylor et al. 2009:91; Toossi 2013). Though many continue to work for social engagement, those who must do so for financial reasons often find their workforce experience to be a challenge.

AGEISM AND DISCRIMINATION

Physician Robert Butler (1990) became concerned nearly 40 years ago when he learned that a housing development near his home in metropolitan Washington, D.C., barred elderly people. Butler coined the term **ageism** to refer to prejudice and discrimination based on a person's age. For example, we may choose to assume that someone cannot handle a rigorous job because he is "too old," or we may refuse to give someone a job with authority because she is "too young."

To more fully understand issues regarding aging, we must also consider the impact of social structure on patterns of aging. Critics argue that neither disengagement nor activity theory answers the question of *why* social interaction must change or decrease for aging adults. The low status of older people is seen in prejudice and discrimination against them, in age segregation, and in unfair job practices—none of which are directly addressed by either disengagement or activity theory.

Although firing people simply because they are old violates federal law, courts have upheld the right to lay off older workers for economic reasons. Critics contend that, later, the same firms hire young, cheaper workers to replace experienced older workers. When economic growth slows and companies cut back on their workforces, the number of complaints of age bias rises sharply as older workers begin to suspect they were bearing a disproportionate share of the layoffs. For example, between 2006 and 2008, during which the U.S. economy entered into a deep economic recession, complaints of age discrimination filed with the Equal Employment Opportunity Commission rose by 49 percent (EEOC 2014).

ageism Prejudice and discrimination based on a person's age.

As a group, elderly people in the United States enjoy a standard of living that is much higher now than at any point in the nation's past. To some extent, older people owe their overall improved standard of living to a greater accumulation of wealth—in the form of home ownership, private pensions, and other financial assets. But much of the improvement is due to more generous Social Security benefits. Although modest when compared with other countries' pension programs, Social Security nevertheless provides 35 percent of all income received by older people in the United States. Still, in 2013, 9.5 percent of people aged 65 or older lived below the poverty line (DeNavas-Walt and Proctor 2014; Social Security Administration 2014a).

Members of groups who face a greater likelihood of income inequality earlier in their lives, including women and members of racial and ethnic minorities, continue to do so when they are older. For women aged 65 or older, the poverty rate is 11.6 percent compared to the rate for elderly men of 6.8 percent. Considering race and ethnicity, in 2013, the 17.6 percent poverty rates for African Americans and 19.8 percent for Hispanics aged 65 or older was more than twice the 7.4 percent rate for non-Hispanic Whites of the same age (DeNavas-Walt and Proctor 2014; U.S. Census Bureau 2014b:Table Pov01).

DEATH AND DYING

In the film *The Bucket List,* Morgan Freeman and Jack Nicholson play the two main characters who are diagnosed with terminal cancer and have less than one year to live. They make a list of all the things they would like to do before they "kick the bucket." On the list are things they had never dared to do, such as traveling the world and skydiving, but it also includes reconciling broken relationships.

Until recently, death was a taboo topic in the United States. Death represents a fundamental disruption that cannot be undone, so we often find it easier to live with a sense of denial about our mortality. In the words of sociologist Peter Berger, "Death presents society with a formidable problem . . . because it threatens the basic assumptions of order on which society rests" (1969:23). However, psychologist Elisabeth Kübler-Ross (1969), through her pioneering book *On Death and Dying,* greatly encouraged open discussion of the process of dying. Drawing on her work with 200 cancer patients, Kübler-Ross identified five stages of the experience: denial, anger, bargaining, depression, and finally acceptance.

hospice care Treatment of the terminally ill in their own homes, or in special hospital units or other facilities, with the goal of helping them die comfortably, without pain.

Although we may still be uncomfortable with the topic, *The Bucket List*'s portrayal of a "good death" represents one of the ways we have become more open about it. Gerontologist Richard Kalish (1985) laid out some of the issues people must face to prepare for a "good death." These included completing unfinished business, such as settling insurance and inheritance matters; restoring harmony to social relationships and saying farewell to friends and family; dealing with medical needs; and making funeral plans and other arrangements for survivors. In accomplishing these tasks, the dying person actively contributes to smooth intergenerational transitions, role continuity, compliance with medical procedures, and minimal disruption of the social system, despite the loss of a loved one.

We have also begun to create institutions to facilitate our wishes for a good death. The practice of **hospice care,** introduced in England in the 1960s, is devoted to easing this final transition. Hospice workers seek to improve the quality of a dying person's last days by offering comfort and by helping the person remain at home, or in a homelike setting at a hospital or other special facility, until the end. Currently, more than 5,800 hospice programs serve almost 1.54 million people a year (NHPCO 2014).

Recent changes in the United States suggest additional ways in which people have broken through the historical taboos about death. For example, bereavement practices—once highly structured—are becoming increasingly varied and therapeutic. More and more people are actively addressing the inevitability of death by making wills, establishing "living wills" (health care proxies that explain their feelings about the use of life support equipment), donating organs, and providing instructions for family members about funerals, cremations, and burials. Given medical and technological advances and increasingly open discussion and negotiation regarding death and dying, it is possible that good deaths may become a social norm in the United States (Pew Research Center 2006).

We encounter some of the most difficult socialization challenges (and rites of passage) in these later years of life. Retirement undermines the sense of self we had that was based in our occupation, a particularly significant source of identity in the United States. Similarly, taking stock of our accomplishments and disappointments, coping with declining physical abilities, and recognizing the inevitability of death may lead to painful adjustments. Part of the difficulty is that potential answers to the "Now what?" question that we might have asked in previous life stages are dwindling, and we begin to face the end of our days.

And yet, as we reflect on the story of our lives, we can look back to see all the people who shaped us into becoming who we are. Such relationships play a crucial role in our overall self-concept and self-satisfaction. As we have already seen, we are interdependent. And, though the influences of others on our life can be both a blessing and a curse, we wouldn't be who we are without them.

> ## First you are young; then you are middle-aged; then you are old; then you are wonderful.
>
> Lady Diana Cooper

SOCIOLOGY IS A VERB

Technology Fast

To learn more about how much we take technology and its impact for granted, go on a "technology fast." In other words, give up your cell phone, computer, television, Internet access, and so on for some preset period of time, such as a day, several days, or a week. Keep a journal. What do you miss most? What do you find yourself doing instead? How difficult was it? Did it get any easier over time? What lessons did you learn?

For REVIEW

I. How do we become ourselves?

- We are vulnerable at birth and depend on the socializing influences of others with whom we interact to provide us with the cultural tools necessary for our survival.

II. Who shapes our socialization?

- Although almost anyone with whom we interact can have a significant influence on us, particularly important to our development are the family, school, peer group, mass media, religion, and the state.

III. How does our development change over time?

- We learn new things at various stages of our life course, experiencing significant transitions as we pass from childhood to adulthood and again from adulthood into retirement. At each stage, the kinds of things expected of us by others shift significantly.

SOCVIEWS on Socialization

Functionalist View

Socialization is a **lifelong process** that enables us to **learn the attitudes, values, and behaviors** appropriate for our culture.

Socialization promotes **integration** and **intimacy** with others and keeps us from being isolated.

The institutions of the family, school, mass media, workplace, government, and religion act as **agents of socialization** from childhood through adulthood.

INTEGRATION, AGENTS OF SOCIALIZATION
KEY CONCEPTS

Conflict View

We learn to accept a culture's dominant ideology as natural, which **reinforces existing inequalities.**

Alternative perspectives and experiences are often underrepresented and devalued.

Schools help reproduce the status quo in the way they socialize students into the proper attitudes and behaviors of the workplace.

KEY CONCEPTS
GENDER AND RACE, INEQUALITY

Interactionist View

Our **concept of the self**, who we are, emerges from our interactions with others.

Parents, friends, coworkers, coaches, teachers are among the **significant others** who play a major role in socialization and shaping a person's self.

Role taking, impression management, and face-work are concepts that convey the idea of social interactions as **performances.**

KEY CONCEPTS
CONCEPT OF SELF, PERFORMANCE

MAKE THE CONNECTION

After reviewing the chapter, answer the following questions:

1
How would each perspective describe the impact that extreme isolation has on people?

2
How would each perspective explain the role socialization performs among children?

3
How would a functionalist look at anticipatory socialization? How might this view differ from a conflict approach?

4
Which agents of socialization have been most influential in your life? How does each perspective help shed light on those influences?

Pop Quiz

1. Babies learn to imitate the sounds of the language they hear even before they know the words. What term do sociologists use to describe the process of internalizing culture?
   a. socialization
   b. culturalization
   c. symbolization
   d. degradation

2. According to Charles Horton Cooley, the process of developing a self-identity by imagining how others see us is known as
   a. socialization.
   b. the looking-glass self.
   c. the Me.
   d. the generalized other.

3. In George Herbert Mead's *play stage* of socialization, people mentally assume the perspectives of others, thereby enabling them to respond from that imagined viewpoint. This process is referred to as
   a. symbolization.
   b. the significant other.
   c. impression management.
   d. role taking.

4. Suppose a clerk tries to appear busier than he or she actually is when a supervisor happens to be watching. Erving Goffman would say this is a form of what?
   a. degradation ceremony
   b. impression management
   c. resocialization
   d. looking-glass self

5. Which social institution is considered to be the most important agent of socialization in the United States, especially for children?
   a. family
   b. school
   c. peer group
   d. mass media

6. The term *gender role* refers to
   a. the biological fact that we are male or female.
   b. a role that is given to us by a teacher.
   c. a role that is given to us in a play.
   d. expectations regarding the proper behavior, attitudes, and activities of males and females.

7. On the first day of basic training in the army, a male recruit has his civilian clothes replaced with army "greens," has his hair shaved off, loses his privacy, and finds that he must use a communal bathroom. All these humiliating activities are part of
   a. becoming a significant other.
   b. impression management.
   c. a degradation ceremony.
   d. face-work.

8. What do sociologists call the symbolic representations of major change in a person's status throughout his or her life course?
   a. rites of passage
   b. anticipatory socialization
   c. impression management
   d. role taking

9. The process of discarding former behavior patterns and taking on new ones is known as
   a. resocialization.
   b. impression management.
   c. anticipatory socialization.
   d. the I.

10. Which theory argues that elderly people have essentially the same need for social interaction as any other group and that those who remain active and socially involved will be best adjusted?
    a. disengagement theory
    b. institutional discrimination theory
    c. activity theory
    d. ageism theory

1. (a), 2. (b), 3. (d), 4. (b), 5. (a), 6. (d), 7. (c), 8. (a), 9. (a), 10. (c)

© B2M Productions/Getty Images

WINNING AND LOSING

Life is like a game. Saying so has become something of a cliché, the kind of thing that appears on greeting cards and motivational posters, usually followed by some inspirational comments about how one should play. And yet, sociologically speaking, paying attention to how games operate can help us better understand what happens in our lives and why.

In the United States, players in most games start with the same basic chances—equal numbers of cards, identical amounts of cash, or the same space on the board. Card shuffling and dice throwing introduce randomness that could tilt the odds, but the presupposition is that winners and losers are determined more by skill than by anything else. In some games, however, the structure of the game itself shapes likely outcomes. One example is the traditional Chinese card game Zheng Shangyou (争上游), meaning "struggling upstream." Many variations of this game exist, including Dai Hin Min (大貧民) in Japan and Tiên Lên in Vietnam. In the United States, adaptations include Kings and Servants, the Great Dalmuti, President, and Scum.

What makes such games distinctive is that the position each player occupies conveys advantages or disadvantages. In one six-player version, positions include king, queen, jack, merchant, peasant, and servant. After all the cards have been dealt, the servant gives the king his or her best three cards, receiving the king's three worst cards in return. The peasant and queen similarly exchange two cards and the merchant and jack exchange one. Play then commences with people seeking to get rid of their cards by playing higher cards than those played by the person with the lead. At the end of each hand, after all the cards have been played, players change seats: the first person to go out, having played all his or her cards, becomes the new king, continuing until the last one out becomes the new servant. Because of the card exchanges, people at the top tend to stay at the top and those at the bottom stay at the bottom.

As a player at the top, you can easily feel good about yourself and chalk your success up to skill. As a player at the bottom, you can get discouraged, doubt your skill, and resent the unfair advantages of those at the top. There's nothing like having to give up two aces and a king only to receive worthless cards in return to make transparent the consequences of the game's unequal structure.

The choices we make do not occur in a vacuum. What these games suggest for those at the bottom is that, even if you play your cards right, you can still lose. In these games, as in life, our structural positions shape the options and opportunities available to us.

As You READ >>

- What makes up society?
- How does social structure shape individual action?
- How do sociologists describe traditional versus modern societies?

>> Social Interaction

Whether we are working together to construct culture or learning from each other through socialization, we do so via **social interaction,** a reciprocal exchange in which two or more people read, react, and respond to each other. Through this process we come to know what is expected of us. When parents discipline us or teachers praise us, we use those punishments and rewards to better inform how we might act in the future. The choices we make create patterns of behavior over time; thus our everyday interactions form the building blocks of society.

SELF AND SOCIETY

We come to be who we are through the daily interactions we have with others—whether going to class, working on the job, or driving in traffic. We seek to make sense of our interactions as they occur and then respond accordingly. Our self, as we saw in Chapter 4, must be understood as an ongoing project constantly created through our interactions with others rather than as an isolated, singular unchanging object. Society provides the context within which that dynamic process of self-creation occurs. In the words of George Herbert Mead, "Selves can only exist in definite relationships to other selves. No hard-and-fast line can be drawn between our own selves and the selves of others" (1934:164). This social or relational conception of the self runs counter to the dominant sense of the self in the United States expressed in phrases such as "rugged individualism" or "I did it my way." But even these phrases are collective sentiments learned in the context of U.S. culture.

Over time we develop routine patterns of behavior that we take for granted—sitting at the same desk, having lunch with the same coworkers, traveling the same route. We do the same things and think many of the same thoughts, day after day. And so do others. Eventually such repeated practices can solidify into formal and informal norms, or become institutionalized in the form of laws. The resulting predictability allows us to know what to do most of the time.

In time, the positions we occupy relative to others (such as student, boss, or traffic cop) also solidify, and we develop mutual expectations of how people in such positions should act. As these perceptions are shared with others beyond our immediate sphere of experience, it becomes possible to talk about the positions themselves—and the various relationships between them—apart from the individuals who occupy them. The end result is society—the structure of relationships within which culture is created and shared through regularized patterns of social interaction.

> **social interaction** A reciprocal exchange in which two or more people read, react, and respond to each other.

SOCIAL CONSTRUCTION OF REALITY

In working out the relationship between our self and society, we are engaged in the "social construction of reality." Sociologists Peter Berger and Thomas Luckmann (1966) use this phrase to describe the interdependent relationship in which we as individuals create society through our actions and, at the same time, become products of the society we construct. They present their argument in their three-part model of world construction. The three parts include

- *Constructing culture.* Our actions are not strictly determined by biological instincts. To survive, we must establish a relationship to nature and with one another. We do so by creating tools, language, ideas, beliefs, rules for behavior, and so on to establish order and meaning. Culture enables us to make sense of our experiences and to pattern our actions. (See Chapter 3 on culture.)

- *Constructing the self.* We become products of the worlds we create. Anytime we enter into a new social world (for example, at birth, going away to college, the first day at a new job, marriage), we do not begin from scratch. We are shaped by the tools, ideas, and rules for action that have been constructed by others who have gone before us. We learn how we should think and act through our interactions with others, sharing ideas and experiences. Through socialization, we are constrained by the very culture we construct. (See Chapter 4 on socialization.)

- *Constructing society.* Between these first two steps is an intervening stage in which we share the culture we create with others. After it is shared, we lose control over it as individuals. It is no longer something "I" control; it is now in "our" hands. As a result of our shared acceptance, it comes to feel solid, real, or natural, even though we created it in the first place. One way to think of it is as an environment, a social world, or a structure within which we live. We come to take for granted that it simply "is."

In short, the social construction of reality is an ongoing process of constructing the material, cognitive, and normative culture that we come to share collectively. These creations then shape or limit the ideas and actions that are available to us. We then use them to create new culture. The result is predictability and order that are necessary for social interaction and collective action. Through social interaction, we are always creating and being created, producers and products.

social structure The underlying framework of society consisting of the positions people occupy and the relationships between them.

The more we share culture with others, the more resistant it becomes to change. The ability to define social reality often reflects a group's power within a society. In fact, one of the crucial aspects of the relationship between dominant and subordinate groups is the ability of the former to set values and norms. Those who wield power and influence in a society are often reluctant to relinquish their positions of control. As a result, it is a struggle to change the meanings attached to the positions people occupy. Since the mid-1900s—starting with the civil rights movement of the 1950s and 1960s and continuing among women, older adults, gays and lesbians, and people with disabilities—an important aspect of the process of social change has involved redefining or reconstructing social reality.

When members of subordinate groups challenge traditional social assumptions, they can raise our collective awareness about the consequences of group membership or social position and help us perceive and experience reality in a new way. For example, when Olympic gold medalist Muhammad Ali began his professional boxing career in the early 1960s, he was much like any other young Black fighter. He was managed and sponsored by a White boxing syndicate and went by his given name, Cassius Clay. Soon, however, the young boxer rebelled against the stereotypes of the self-effacing Black athlete and began to define his own social role. He converted to Islam, becoming a member of the U.S.-based Nation of Islam, and abandoned his "slave name" to take the name Muhammad Ali. He insisted on expressing his own political views, including refusing to fight in the Vietnam War. Ali changed the terms of social interaction for Black athletes by rebelling against racist thinking and terminology. In redefining culture, he helped open up structural opportunities for himself and for other African Americans in the world of sports and beyond.

>> Elements of Social Structure

Although not all sociologists accept the idea that society is a real, external, objective thing, the concepts of society and social structure provide tools useful when trying to make sense of why we act and think the way we do. **Social structure** represents the underlying framework of society consisting of the positions people occupy and the relationships between them. Structure provides order. Its existence appears to transcend the particular individuals who populate it. We take its reality as a given and learn to move into social positions that already exist. Thinking of structure as something like a skeleton that holds us together—or as analogous to the framework of a building—helps us better understand ourselves and others. We can identify the following elements that make up social structure: statuses, social roles, groups, social networks, virtual worlds, and social institutions.

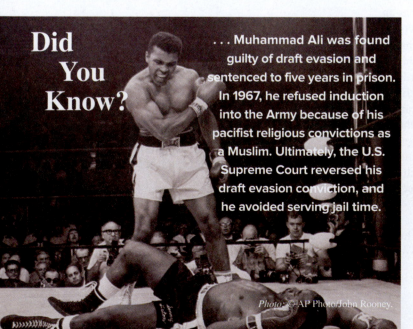

Did You Know?

. . . Muhammad Ali was found guilty of draft evasion and sentenced to five years in prison. In 1967, he refused induction into the Army because of his pacifist religious convictions as a Muslim. Ultimately, the U.S. Supreme Court reversed his draft evasion conviction, and he avoided serving jail time.

Photo: ©AP Photo/John Rooney.

Social Statuses

Daughter

20 years old

Latina

Female

Sister

Me

Classmate

Student

Roommate

Teammate

Employee

Friend

Achieved statuses

Photo: © Amos Morgan/Photodisc/Getty Images RF.

STATUSES

Status is perhaps the most basic component of social structure. It refers to the social positions we occupy relative to others. Such positions exist independent of the individuals who occupy them. Within our society, a person can occupy the status of student, fruit picker, son or daughter, violinist, teenager, resident of St. Louis, dental technician, or neighbor. A person can also occupy a number of different statuses at the same time.

Ascribed and Achieved Status

Sociologists categorize statuses as either ascribed or achieved. An **ascribed status** is assigned to a person by society without regard for the person's unique talents or characteristics. Generally, the assignment takes place at birth; thus a person's age, race/ethnicity, and sex are all considered ascribed statuses. Though such characteristics are biological in origin, the key is the social meaning we attach to such categories. Ascribed statuses are often used to justify privileges or reflect a person's membership in a subordinate group, and we will analyze the impacts of race, ethnicity, and gender as ascribed statuses in Chapters 12 and 13.

The meanings attached to ascribed statuses can vary cross-culturally. In China, for example, respect for elderly people, known as filial piety, is an important norm. There, in many cases, the adjective *old* is used respectfully: calling someone "old teacher" or "old person" is like calling a judge in the United States "your honor." In countries such as the United States or Britain, which put a premium on youth, the term *old man* is often more of an insult than a celebration of seniority and wisdom (Huang 1988; Kline and Zhang 2009; Laidlaw et al. 2010).

The categories we use for ascribed statuses can shift. Currently, we see that happening to definitions of sex, gender, and sexuality. For a long time in the United States, people assumed that our sex was determined at birth, that there are only two distinct sexes, and that the one you belong to is patently obvious. Furthermore, they assumed that how you think and act was largely determined by which category you are in, and that there was nothing you could do about it. Increasingly, people have come to understand that biology is not destiny. People can make choices about pursuing a career, having and raising children, exhibiting emotions, choosing what to wear, or expressing their sexuality. For example, in a national Gallup poll, 3.4 percent of Americans identified themselves as lesbian, gay, bisexual, or transgender (LGBT), which

status The social positions we occupy relative to others.

ascribed status A social position assigned to a person by society without regard for the person's unique talents or characteristics.

© Jim Arbogast/Getty Images RF

© Jim West/The Image Works

Chapter 5 / Social Structure and Interaction • **97**

works out to millions of people. The percentage varied by age, with 6.4 percent of those aged 18–29 and 1.9 percent of people 65+ identifying as LGBT (Gates and Newport 2012). In addition, perceptions regarding sexuality and its expression also vary across generations. Among 18- to 29-year-olds, 69 percent favor allowing gays and lesbians to legally marry compared to 40 percent of those aged 65 and up (Kiley 2014). As we learned with the Thomas theorem (see Chapter 1), perception shapes action and, in cases such as this, our perception is subject to change.

achieved status A social position that is within our power to change.

master status A status that dominates others and thereby determines a person's general position in society.

social role A set of expected behaviors for people who occupy a given social status.

Unlike ascribed statuses, an **achieved status** is a social position we have earned as a consequence of something we have done. Those accomplishments can be either positive or negative. For example, pianist, college student, sorority member, and lawyer are all achieved statuses. Each is attained by taking actions necessary for their accomplishment—practicing, going to school, pledging, and getting a law degree. But becoming a prisoner is also an achieved status, a consequence of committing a crime.

The line between ascribed and achieved statuses can become fuzzy as happens when someone is given the benefit of the doubt, or denied it, because of inheritance rather than effort. For example, when a CEO hires his daughter to be the company's new executive vice president, it may well be that her achieved status as an MBA graduate from the Harvard Business School mattered. But it's also possible that her ascribed status as a daughter whose father was able to finance her degree, along with having a say in who gets hired, played a role, too.

Master Status Each of us holds many different and sometimes conflicting statuses; some may signify a higher social position, and others a lower position. How, then, do others view our overall social position? According to sociologist Everett Hughes (1945), societies deal with inconsistencies by agreeing that certain statuses are more important than others. A **master status** is a status that dominates others and thereby determines a person's general position in society.

People with disabilities frequently observe that non-disabled individuals see them only as blind, or only as wheelchair users, and so on, rather than as complex human beings with individual strengths and weaknesses whose disability is merely one aspect of their lives. Often people with disabilities find that their status as "disabled" receives undue weight, overshadowing their actual ability to hold meaningful employment and contributing to widespread prejudice, discrimination, and segregation (Banks and Lawrence 2006). For example, most voting places are inaccessible to wheelchair users and fail to provide ballots that can be used by the blind. Activists argue that such unnecessary and discriminatory barriers restrict people with disabilities more than do any biological limitations.

Ascribed statuses frequently influence our achieved status. The African American activist Malcolm X (1925–1965), an eloquent and controversial advocate of Black power and Black pride in the 1960s, recalled that his feelings and perspectives changed dramatically while in eighth grade. When his English teacher, a White man, advised him that his goal of becoming a lawyer was ridiculous and suggested he become a carpenter instead, Malcolm X (1964:37) found that his position as a Black man (ascribed status) was an obstacle to his dream of becoming a lawyer (achieved status). In the United States, the ascribed statuses of race and gender can function as master statuses that play an important part in one's efforts to achieve a desired professional and social status (Brownfield, Sorenson, and Thompson 2001).

SOCIAL ROLES

The statuses we occupy carry with them expectations and obligations regarding how we should act. If you are a parent, you are expected to provide food, clothes, and shelter for your child. If you are a student, you are expected to study. If you are a custodian, you are expected to mop the floors. Sociologists use the term **social role** to describe the set of expected behaviors for people who occupy a given social status. While we occupy a status, we play a role.

Roles are a significant component of social structure. Roles contribute to a society's stability by enabling members to anticipate the behavior of others and to pattern

Throughout his life, Malcolm X worked to redefine the significance of race as master status. Photo: © Burt Shavitz/Pic Inc/The LIFE Images Collection/Getty Images.

their own actions accordingly. Yet social roles also restrict people's interactions and relationships. Young children, for example, often have a difficult time seeing their teachers as persons who might play other roles, and can be surprised when they see them in settings outside school, such as at the grocery store. If we view a person *only* as a teacher, police officer, or supervisor, it can be difficult to relate to him or her as a friend or neighbor.

Role Conflict Sometimes the statuses we occupy can clash. **Role conflict** occurs when incompatible expectations arise from two or more social statuses held by the same person. Fulfillment of the roles associated with one position may directly violate the roles linked to a second status.

SOC THINK

List the social statuses you occupy. Which ones are ascribed, and which are achieved? What roles are you expected to play as a consequence of the positions you occupy? How do you resolve possible role conflicts?

Imagine the delicate situation of a woman who has worked for a decade on an assembly line in an electrical plant and has recently been named supervisor of her unit. She now must balance her status as a friend with her status as the boss. How should she treat her long-time friends and coworkers? Should she still have lunch with them? Should she recommend the firing of an old friend who cannot keep up with the demands of the assembly line? She will most likely experience a sharp conflict between her friendship and supervisory roles. Such role conflicts involve difficult ethical choices. The new supervisor will have to make a difficult decision about how much allegiance she owes her friend and how much she owes her employers, who have given her supervisory responsibilities.

SOC THINK

Is there no such thing as our true self? Are we only actors performing roles based on the positions we occupy?

Another type of role conflict occurs when individuals move into occupations that are not common among people with their ascribed status. Male preschool teachers and female police officers experience this type of role conflict. In the latter case, the women must strive to reconcile their workplace status in law enforcement with the societal view of the status of women, which historically has not embraced many skills associated with police work. And even as female police officers encounter sexual harassment, as women do throughout the labor force, they must also deal with the "code of silence," an informal norm that precludes their implicating fellow officers in wrongdoing (Maher 2008; Pershing 2003).

> **role conflict** The situation that occurs when incompatible expectations arise from two or more social statuses held by the same person.
>
> **role strain** The difficulty that arises when the same social status imposes conflicting demands and expectations.

Role Strain Role conflict describes the situation of a person dealing with the challenge of occupying two social statuses simultaneously. However, even a single status can cause problems. Sociologists use the term **role strain** to describe the difficulty that arises when the same social status imposes conflicting demands and expectations.

Sociologist Krista Marie Clark Cline wondered how role strain might differ for persons whose status was single versus married (Cline 2010). As a test, she studied how the additional role responsibility of dog ownership affected each. She argued that married persons, as a consequence of being in a relationship, need to juggle more social role obligations than do single persons. Examples include working out expectations regarding housework, balancing work–home roles with their partner, maintaining relationships with in-laws, engaging in the emotional work expected in a relationship, along with other such normative obligations. As a result, Cline hypothesized, married persons would not receive the same benefits of dog ownership as would single persons, and the data she collected supported her hypothesis. She theorized that the responsibilities of dog ownership—taking her out for walks, cleaning up after her, taking her to the vet—constituted yet another role obligation among the many others that married persons

© ImageDJ/Alamy RF

Transsexuals, such as Jenna Talackova (pictured here), often have to negotiate the four stages of role exit. Photo: © Photo by Kevork Djansezian/Getty Images.

Although I love teaching, I hate grading. When I mention that to students, they say I have no one to blame but myself; if I didn't assign things, I wouldn't have to grade them. But I don't teach in a vacuum. If I didn't assign papers and tests, students would focus their time and energy on their looming chemistry test or their literature paper instead of reading for, participating in, or even attending my course. It is not that students aren't interested or sincere; it's that they are forced to budget their time for which professors compete using assignments. Because we exist in social systems, the expectations of those systems limit the amount of innovation we might desire. In what ways might the structures we are embedded within—school, work, recreation—inhibit us from making changes even if we would like to do so?

accustomed status and the roles associated with that social position. The second stage involves a search for alternatives. An individual who is unhappy with his or her career may take a leave of absence; an unhappily married couple may begin what they see as a trial separation.

SOCTHINK

Whether from a sports team, a religious group, the military, or some other close-knit group, what experience, if any, have you had with role exiting? To what extent does your experience match the four stages Ebaugh describes?

The third stage of role exit is the action stage, or departure. Ebaugh found that the vast majority of her respondents could identify a clear turning point when it became essential to take final action and leave their jobs, end their marriages, or engage in some other type of role exit. Only 20 percent of respondents saw their role exit as a gradual, evolutionary process that had no single turning point.

The last stage of role exit involves the creation of a new identity. Traditionally, students experience a form of role exit when they make the transition from high school to college. They may leave behind the role of a child living at home and take on the role of a somewhat independent college student living with peers in a dorm. Sociologist Ira Silver (1996) has studied the central role that material

were expected to fulfill. As a consequence, dog ownership created greater role strain for married persons than for those who were single.

Role Exit In addition to having to learn the social roles expected of us as we enter into new statuses, there are also steps we go through when we are leaving a status. Sociologist Helen Rose Fuchs Ebaugh (1988) used the term **role exit** to describe the process of disengagement from a role that is central to one's self-identity in order to establish a new role and identity. Drawing on interviews—with, among others, ex-convicts, divorced men and women, recovering alcoholics, ex-nuns, former doctors, retirees, and transsexuals—Ebaugh (herself a former nun) studied the process of voluntarily exiting from significant social roles.

role exit The process of disengagement from a role that is central to one's self-identity in order to establish a new role and identity.

Ebaugh has offered a four-stage model of role exit. The first stage begins with doubt. The person experiences frustration, burnout, or simply unhappiness with an objects play in this transition. The objects students choose to leave at home (like stuffed animals and dolls) are associated with their prior identities. They may remain deeply attached to those objects but not want them to be seen as part of their new identities at college. The objects they bring with them symbolize how they now see themselves and how they wish to be perceived. iPads and wall posters, for example, are calculated to say, "This is who I am."

GROUPS

The statuses we occupy, along with their corresponding social role expectations, are linked together with other statuses to form groups. In sociological terms, a **group** consists of two or more people, united by a shared sense of identity or purpose, who interact with each other over time in ways that distinguish them from outsiders. The members of a women's softball team, a hospital's business office, a synagogue, or a symphony orchestra constitute a group. A group can be distinguished from an aggregate, which consists of a collection of people who happen to be in the same place at the same time but who do not interact regularly or have a shared sense of purpose or common practices. Examples of aggregates include people waiting to cross the street at a busy intersection or riding together in an elevator.

We spend much of our time interacting in group settings. The type of group we are in influences our level of commitment and participation. Some groups demand our almost undivided attention and shape our core identity; others allow us to more easily accomplish specific goals.

Primary and Secondary Groups Charles Horton Cooley (1902) coined the term **primary group** to refer to a small group characterized by intimate, face-to-face association and cooperation. Such groups often entail long-term commitment and involve more of what we think of as our whole self. Families constitute primary groups for many, although people also build close-knit, in-depth relationships with teammates, like-minded religious believers, coworkers, and fellow street gang members. In sports, for example, commitment to the cliché that there is "no 'I' in 'team'" often leads to a sense that teammates are "like family." Their level of trust and interdependence grows. Teammates come to know that the pitcher, outfielder, or catcher on the team not only will be there for them on the field, but will also have their backs when they need it in other circumstances.

We also participate in many groups that are not characterized by close bonds of friendship, such as large college

> **group** Two or more people, united by a shared sense of identity or purpose, who interact with each other over time in ways that distinguish them from outsiders.
>
> **primary group** A small group characterized by intimate, face-to-face association and cooperation.

© Courtesy of Central College, photographer Dan Vander Beek

Comparison of Primary and Secondary Groups

Primary group	Secondary group
Generally small	Usually large
Relatively long period of interaction	Relatively short duration, often temporary
Intimate, face-to-face association	Little social intimacy or mutual understanding
Some emotional depth to relationships	Relationships generally superficial
Cooperative, friendly	More formal and impersonal

© Keith Srakocic/AP Images

SOCTHINK

How do in-groups and out-groups function in a typical U.S. high school? What groups are common? How are boundaries separating insiders and outsiders maintained?

secondary group A formal, impersonal group in which there is little social intimacy or mutual understanding.

in-group A category of people who share a common identity and sense of belonging.

out-group A category of people who do not belong or do not fit in.

reference group Any group that individuals use as a standard for evaluating themselves and their own behavior.

classes and business associations. The term **secondary group** refers to a formal, impersonal group in which there is little social intimacy or mutual understanding. Participation in such groups is typically more instrumental or goal-directed, often involving only what we think of as one part of our self. Given these characteristics, we are more likely to move into and out of such groups as suits our needs.

The distinction between primary and secondary groups is not always clear-cut, however. Some social clubs may become so large and impersonal that they no longer function as primary groups; similarly, some work groups can become so close-knit that they are experienced as primary groups (Hochschild 1989; Sennett 2012). The "Comparison of Primary and Secondary Groups" table demonstrates some significant differences between primary and secondary groups.

In-Groups and Out-Groups The shared norms, values, and goals of group members, along with their common experiences, create a boundary distinguishing insiders and outsiders. The resulting us–them divide can lead to a strong sense of group identity, but it often does so at the expense of others, frequently serving as a basis for exclusion, especially if "they" are perceived as different either culturally or racially. Sociologists use the terms in-group and out-group to identify these two classifications.

An **in-group** consists of a category of people who share a common identity and sense of belonging. Members differentiate between themselves and everybody else (Sumner 1906). The in-group may be as narrow as a teenage clique or as broad as an entire nation. An **out-group** is defined, relative to the in-group, as a category of people who do not belong or do not fit in. Among an in-group of high school "populars" or "jocks," for example, a science "brain" might be considered an out-group member, and vice versa.

In-group members typically feel distinct and superior, seeing themselves as better than people in the out-group. Proper behavior for the in-group can be simultaneously viewed as unacceptable behavior for the out-group. This double standard enhances the sense of superiority. Sociologist Robert Merton (1968) described this process as the conversion of "in-group virtues" into "out-group vices." We can see this differential standard operating in the context of terrorism. When a group or a nation takes aggressive actions, it usually justifies them as necessary even if civilians are hurt or killed. Opponents are quick to assign the emotion-laden label of *terrorist* to such actions and to appeal to the world community for condemnation. Yet these same people may themselves retaliate with actions that hurt civilians, which the first group will then condemn as terrorist acts (Juergensmeyer 2003).

Reference Groups Both in-groups and primary groups can dramatically influence the way an individual thinks and behaves. Sociologists call any group that individuals use as a standard for evaluating themselves and their own behavior a **reference group.** For example, a high school student who aspires to join a social circle of hip-hop music devotees will pattern his or her behavior after that of the group. The student will begin dressing like these peers, listening to the same music, sharing "tags" on Instagram, and hanging out at the same stores and clubs.

Reference groups have two basic purposes. They serve a normative function by setting and enforcing standards of conduct and belief. The high school student who wants the approval of the hip-hop crowd will have to follow the group's dictates, at least to some extent. Reference groups also perform a comparison function by serving as a standard against which people can measure themselves and others. An actor will evaluate himself or herself against a

I belong, therefore I am.

—An old Māori proverb

© Reza Estakhrian/Reportage/Getty Images

reference group composed of others in the acting profession (Merton and Kitt 1950).

Often, two or more reference groups influence us at the same time. Our family members, neighbors, and coworkers all shape different aspects of our self-evaluation. In addition, reference group attachments change during the life cycle. A corporate executive who quits the rat race at age 45 to become a social worker will find new reference groups to use as standards for evaluation. We shift reference groups as we take on different statuses during our lives.

Coalitions As groups grow larger, coalitions begin to develop. A **coalition** is an alliance, whether temporary or permanent, geared toward a common goal. Coalitions can be broad-based or narrow and can take on many different objectives. Sociologist William Julius Wilson (1999) has reported on community-based organizations in Texas that include Whites and Latinos, working-class and affluent, who banded together to work for improved sidewalks, better drainage systems, and comprehensive street paving. Out of this type of coalition building, Wilson hopes, will emerge better interracial understanding.

SOCIAL NETWORKS

These days, the term *social network* is primarily associated with our online connections through Instagram, Twitter, and the like, but it has always been possible to map the links that connect us with others. A **social network** is a web of relationships through which people interact both directly and indirectly to accomplish formal and informal

goals. Networks consist of two principal elements: nodes and relationships. In a social network, nodes consist of individuals and relationships are the connections between them. The most basic building block of a social network is a **dyad** which consists of two connected nodes, for example, a tutor and a student or a boss and a worker. A **triad** consists of the relationships between three nodes including both direct relationships (relationships between each of the possible pairs in the group) and indirect relationships (relationships connecting two people through the link provided by the third person). For example, a friend of a friend would constitute an indirect relationship. Beyond triads, the addition of each additional node to the network compounds the complexity of the network's interrelationships, multiplying the number of possible indirect relationships and increasing the possible distance between any two individuals to friend of a friend of a friend status and beyond. Centrality measures the degree to which any particular individual has more direct and indirect relationships than do others (Fowler and Christakis 2009). As networks become larger, centrality becomes an important additional dimension.

Sometimes social network connections are intentional and public; other times networks can develop that link us in ways that are not intentional or apparent. Sociologists Peter Bearman, James Moody, and Katherine Stovel (2004) investigated one such network, asking themselves this question: If you drew a chart of the romantic relationship network at a typical American high school, what would it look like? Using careful data-collection techniques to enhance the validity of their findings, they found that 573 of the 832 students they surveyed had been either romantically or sexually involved in the previous 18 months. Of these, 63 couples represented dyads, connected only with each other as pairs with no other partners. Other students connected directly or indirectly with a handful of partners. One larger group, however, connected 288 students directly or indirectly into a single extended network (see the figure "Adolescent Sexual Networks"). Such an example points to the fact that the choices we make often link us with others both known and unknown.

Research on how social networks function has produced some surprising results. For example, sociologist Scott Feld (1991) discovered that, on average, "most people have fewer friends than their friends have." This claim, which has come to be known as the friendship paradox, is somewhat counterintuitive; most people believe that the opposite is the case (Zuckerman and Jost 2001). When taking an objective look at the composition of social networks, however,

coalition A temporary or permanent alliance geared toward a common goal.

social network A web of relationships through which people interact both directly and indirectly to accomplish formal and informal goals.

dyad The most basic building block of a social network, it consists of two nodes and the relationship between them.

triad Within a social network, it consists of three nodes and the direct and indirect relationships between them.

Adolescent Sexual Networks

Each dot represents a boy or a girl at "Jefferson High." The lines that link them represent romantic and sexual relationships that occurred over an 18-month period. Though most of the teenagers had had just one or two partners, 288 of the 832 students interviewed were linked in a giant sexual network. Another 90 students were involved in relationships outside the school (not shown on this chart).

- Boys
- Girls

Other relationships. (If a pattern was observed more than once, numeral indicates frequency.)

2   2   9   12   63

Source: Bearman, Moody, and Stovel 2004:58.   *Photo:* © Stockbyte/Getty Images RF.

it turns out that the average number of friends our friends have is elevated by the fact that, even though the number of people with many friends is relatively small, those individuals appear repeatedly in our friend's networks, driving up their averages. In other words, popular friends have a disproportionate effect because they are named as friends over and over again. Researchers at Facebook decided to put the friendship paradox to the test. They found that 93 percent of active Facebook users had fewer friends than their friends had. On average, users had 190 friends while their friends averaged 635 friends (Strogatz 2012). Overall, as mathematician Steven Strogatz (2012) put it, "Our friends are typically more popular than we are."

Social network researchers, inspired by the friendship paradox, have explored a number of related phenomena. For example, in an analysis of Twitter users, and in an effort to control for the effect that outliers with high numbers of friends can have on the average, it turns out that, when analyzing the median instead of the mean, it's not just that the average number of our friend's friends is higher, it's also true that the majority of our friends have more friends than we do. This holds true for 98 percent of Twitter users (Kooti, Hodas, and Lerman 2014). Another study found that, if you are a scientist who has published a journal article, your coauthors will have more coauthors, more publications, and more citations than you (Eom and Jo 2014). It is hypothesized that the paradox is likely also true when it comes to wealth and number of sexual partners (Mullins 2014). One of the possible applications of the friendship paradox is that it can help with alerts for, and treatments of, infectious diseases by targeting friends of friends rather than simply using random samples by getting us closer to those who are most socially connected (Christakis and Fowler 2010).

Even our levels of happiness are influenced by the social networks to which we belong. Social network researchers found that our probability of being happy goes up 15 percent if someone with whom we have a direct link is happy (Fowler and Christakis 2008). The nature of the link affects the degree to which our happiness rises or falls. When considering mutual friends, those who would count each other as friends, our probability for happiness increases by 63 percent. Contrast that with the happiness of a spouse with whom we live, which increases our probability for happiness by 8 percent. Nearby siblings increase the probability of happiness by 14 percent while neighbors living on the same block increase it by 34 percent. The happiness of coworkers had no significant effect. Centrality also matters. People who are more central to local networks tend to be happier than those who are at the periphery, and it is their centrality that leads to their happiness, not vice versa. In addition, happiness is more likely to spread between members of the same sex than the opposite sex. The researchers conclude, "Human happiness is not merely the province of isolated individuals" (Fowler and Christakis 2008). Once again this demonstrates the significance of place. If we are to understand how we think, act, and even feel, we must take into account the social context within which we live.

It turns out that the networks we participate in can play a major role in our lives. In fact, though our closest ties to family and friends represent our strongest relationships, some of the most valuable connections can come through weaker links we have with others. Sociologist Mark Granovetter (1973) argued that we can categorize our network relationships as more or less strong using measures such as time spent together, emotional intensity, mutual confidences, and a shared sense of reciprocal obligation. In denser parts of a network, clusters of people are drawn together by strong ties that exist between them. The connections between such individuals are typically characterized by **homophily,** which literally means love of the same, a term sociologists use to describe our tendency to establish close social network relationships with others who share our same knowledge, beliefs, practices, and characteristics (McPherson, Smith-Lovin, and Cook 2001). For example, people tend to associate with others who have the same jobs, interests, education, race, ethnicity, and more. These dense clusters within a social network can be linked together through ties between individuals within two different clusters who have direct ties between each other. In an argument that came to be known as "the strength of weak

ties," Granovetter (1973) maintained that weaker ties can be extremely important because they can connect us with whole new networks of people with whom we have no direct relationships. For example, when it comes to getting a job, he reported that most jobs were found not through contacts with close friends, but through people who job seekers saw occasionally or rarely. Such people, with whom we have weak ties, serve as a bridge between social networks, providing us access to valuable resources and information.

Further support for the strength of weak ties principle emerged when Facebook researchers explored how relationships formed. They discovered that the most effective way to meet someone and start a relationship was through friends of friends. Mutual friends, in effect, serve as matchmakers. Those who played this matchmaking role have 73 percent more friends than do the people they set up. Their friendship networks are also less dense, meaning the matchmaker's friends are less likely to know each other, presenting people a potential pool of possible partners. The matchmakers serve as bridges between people who might otherwise never connect (Burke, Diuk, and Friggeri 2015).

ONLINE SOCIAL NETWORKS

Historically, the size and scope of our social networks were constrained by geography. Over time, revolutions in transportation and communication expanded our pool of possible contacts. Now, online social networks

> **homophily** Our tendency to establish close social network relationships with others who share our same knowledge, beliefs, practices, and characteristics.

TOLES © 2000 The Washington Post. Reprinted with permission of UNIVERSAL UCLICK. All rights reserved.

Going GLOBAL

Social Networking

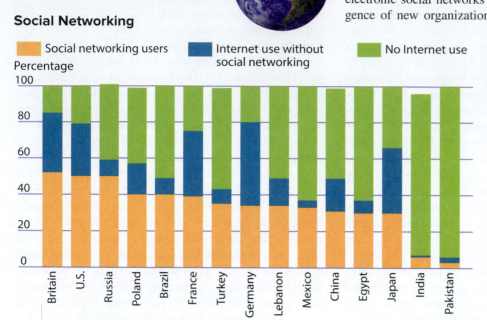

Legend:
- Social networking users (orange)
- Internet use without social networking (blue)
- No Internet use (green)

Percentage axis: 0, 20, 40, 60, 80, 100

Countries (x-axis): Britain, U.S., Russia, Poland, Brazil, France, Turkey, Germany, Lebanon, Mexico, China, Egypt, Japan, India, Pakistan

Note: Don't know/Refused responses are not shown. Samples in China, India, and Pakistan are disproportionately urban.
Source: Pew Research Center 2012g.

expand our possible connections beyond the limitations of geographic space. Participation levels in social network sites continues to grow. In a survey of U.S. Internet users, researchers found that 71 percent use Facebook, 28 percent use LinkedIn, 28 percent use Pinterest, 26 percent use Instagram, and 23 percent use Twitter. A person's status affects his or her usage. For example, women are more likely than men to use social networking sites (77 percent versus 66 percent). Usage of particular sites also varies. For example, 42 percent of women use Pinterest compared to 13 percent of men. Similarly, African Americans are more likely to use Instagram than are non-Hispanic Whites, 38 percent to 21 percent respectively (Duggan et al. 2015).

Teens are especially active social network users. Eighty-one percent of 12–17-year-olds use social networking sites, and of these, 67 percent do so daily. Their median number of Facebook friends is 300. When deciding who to "friend," 98 percent have friended school friends, but only 70 percent have friended parents—with teachers and coaches even further behind at 30 percent. When it comes to sharing personal information, only 9 percent are "very concerned" about third-party access to their data, although 60 percent keep their profiles private. Only 19 percent of teens regret something they posted. They view Facebook as a valuable tool for extending their social

social institution An integrated and persistent social network dedicated to ensuring that society's core needs are met.

networks, and 39 percent have met someone online who became a good friend (Madden et al. 2013).

Sociologist Manuel Castells (1997, 1998, 2000) views electronic social networks as important tools in the emergence of new organizations, businesses, and movements. They provide opportunities for people to establish connections, share information, and mobilize for action. In the United States, for example, 39 percent of all adults took part in some form of political activity through social networking sites. Those who are civically engaged online are also more likely than the average citizen to be politically engaged offline as well (A. Smith 2013). In a survey of 21 nations, researchers found that 34 percent of people use social networking sites. What people share online can vary across cultures. Social network users in the Arab world—in this case, users from Lebanon, Tunisia, Egypt, and Jordan—are substantially more likely to share views online about politics, community issues, and religion than are those in other nations (Pew Research Center 2012f).

Social media theorist Clay Shirky (2008) maintains that the Internet has radically transformed the possibilities for collective action. He argues that previous technologies inhibited collective behavior because those that allowed two-way communication (for example, the telephone) were largely limited to one-to-one conversations, and those that facilitated large-scale group formation through broadcasting were mostly limited to one-way communication (for example, television news viewers). With the Internet, he suggests, "group action just got easier" because it supports interactive, large-scale group formation. People can talk back and forth with each other and coordinate action, as occurred during the "Arab Spring" protests in countries including Egypt, Tunisia, and Libya in 2011.

SOCIAL INSTITUTIONS

Combinations of statuses, groups, and networks can coalesce to address the needs of a particular sector of society, forming what sociologists refer to as institutions. **Social institutions** are integrated and persistent social networks dedicated to ensuring that society's core needs are met. Sociologists have tended to focus on five major institutions that serve as key elements of the larger social structure: family, education, religion, economy, and government. Though these institutions frequently overlap and interact, considering each institution individually

© Pixtal/AGE Fotostock RF

provides us with a perspective within which we can analyze the larger social system. We look in depth at all five in future chapters, but we begin here by considering the contributions each makes to the social structure.

If a society is to survive, certain functions must be performed, and focusing on these institutions allows us to see how different societies fulfill these needs (Aberle et al. 1950). It is within the context of *families,* for example, that we ensure the society's continued existence by producing the next generation. Families carry out both biological reproduction (having children) and social reproduction (teaching them the culture they need for survival). Families also provide care and protection for members. Through *education* we teach the more formal and public culture necessary to be members of the larger society. This includes the formal curriculum (history, math, science, and so on) but also includes learning to interact with others outside our immediate families. We rely on *religion* to be the glue that holds society together by establishing a clear identity with shared beliefs and practices, answering basic questions about meaning, and enforcing both individual and collective discipline. *Government* helps maintain internal order through laws, policing, and punishment and seeks to establish stable relations with other societies through diplomacy. Finally, the *economy* regulates the production, distribution, and consumption of goods and services.

How societies choose to fulfill these functions can vary significantly, as can the degree to which these institutions overlap. For example, one society may protect itself from external attack by amassing a large arsenal of weaponry; another may make determined efforts to

remain neutral in world politics and to promote cooperative relationships with its neighbors. No matter what its particular strategy, any society or relatively permanent group must address all these functional prerequisites for survival.

Focusing on the functions institutions fulfill can help us better understand social order, but it often implies that the way things are is the way things should be. Sociologists using the conflict paradigm focus more on power, the consequences of difference, and resource distribution. They suggest that we must also look at the ways our construction of these institutions reinforces

In February 2010, an Austin, Texas, man flew his plane into the city's IRS building. Photo: © Bob Pearson/epa/Corbis.

© Image Source/Getty RF

SOCTHINK

How is it possible for education to represent both a path for opportunity and an instrument for maintaining inequality? Where in your experience have you seen both at work?

inequality. We can meet these functional needs in a variety of ways, so we should consider why some groups might seek to maintain the status quo.

Major institutions, such as education, help perpetuate the privileges of the most powerful individuals and groups within a society while contributing to the powerlessness of others. To give one example, public schools in the United States are financed largely through property taxes. This arrangement allows more-affluent areas to provide their children with better-equipped schools and better-paid teachers than low-income areas can afford. As a result, children from prosperous communities are better prepared to compete academically than children from impoverished communities. The structure of the nation's educational system permits and even promotes such unequal treatment of schoolchildren (Kozol 2005).

Using the interactionist paradigm to study what goes on within these institutions provides additional insight into why we think and act the way we do. Focusing on the economy, sociologist Mitchell Duneier (1994a, 1994b) studied the social behavior of the word processors, all women, who worked in the service center of a large Chicago law firm. Duneier was interested in the informal social norms that emerged in this work environment and the rich social network these female employees created.

Duneier learned that, despite working in a large office, these women found private moments to talk (often in the halls or outside the washroom) and shared a critical view of the firm's attorneys and day-shift secretaries. Expressing their frustration about their relative lack of power and respect, the word processors routinely suggested that their assignments represented work that the "lazy" secretaries should have completed during the normal workday. One word processor, seeking to reclaim a sense of personal power, reacted to the lawyers' superior attitude and pointedly refused to recognize or speak with any attorney who would not address her by name (Duneier 1994b).

Such approaches to viewing life in the contexts of social institutions allow us to better understand what it means to live in the world as it is structured today. Looking at society through the lens of social structure gives us a sense of what is going on with regard to both the "big picture" and the intimate details of our daily interactions.

>> Bureaucracy

Maintaining and managing social order has become more complex since the Industrial Revolution. In response, traditional norms, designed for smaller and more local social networks, gave way to more systematic approaches to governance. According to Max Weber ([1913–1922]

Characteristics of a Bureaucracy

	Positive consequences	Negative consequences	
		For the individual	For the organization
Division of labor	Produces efficiency in a large-scale corporation	Limits knowledge	Creates communication barriers
Hierarchy of authority	Clarifies who is in command	Deprives employees of a voice in decision making	Permits concealment of mistakes
Written rules and regulations	Let workers know what is expected of them	Stifle initiative and imagination	Lead to goal displacement
Impersonality	Reduces bias	Contributes to feelings of alienation	Discourages loyalty to company
Employment based on technical qualifications	Discourages favoritism and reduces petty rivalries	Discourages ambition to improve oneself elsewhere	Inhibits innovative thinking

Photo: © Mark Evans/Getty Images RF.

A chief executive officer typically rests atop the pyramid structure of bureaucratic hierarchy. Don Thompson, pictured here, became the CEO for McDonald's in 2012.   Photo: © AP Photo/Yves Logghe.

1947), the most rational form of management, suitable to the demands of the modern age, is bureaucracy. A **bureaucracy** is a formal organization built upon the principle of maximum efficiency.

CHARACTERISTICS OF A BUREAUCRACY

Bureaucratic success depends upon the establishment of rational principles of organization throughout the firm. Weber identified five core characteristics of bureaucracies

each area to carry out those tasks. In traditional societies, a furniture maker might carry out every step of the production process, from cutting down the tree to finishing the table, herself. On top of that, she might have to do everything else that running a small business entails, including bookkeeping, marketing, and sales. In a modern bureaucracy, that table will likely be produced on an assembly line where each worker has responsibility for only one part of the process. In addition, workers in other parts of the company would make their contributions including the engineers who design the product line, marketing experts who create advertising campaigns, salespersons who entice customers to buy, accountants who do the bookkeeping, mechanics who maintain the machines, custodians to clean up afterward, and a whole host of others. The justification for such complexity is that, in the context of a large firm, it would be impossible for one individual to have sufficient expertise to carry out all those tasks well. The combined expertise that each specialized worker contributes produces greater efficiency than would exist if all workers were trained in every skill.

bureaucracy A formal organization built upon the principle of maximum efficiency.

ideal type An abstract model of the essential characteristics of a phenomenon.

alienation Loss of control over our creative human capacity to produce, separation from the products we make, and isolation from our fellow workers.

© Ingram Publishing/ SuperStock RF

© Muntz/Taxi/Getty Images

© Adam Crowley/ Getty Images RF

© Creatas/PunchStock RF

(see "Characteristics of a Bureaucracy" table for a summary). He did so by constructing what he called an **ideal type,** an abstract model of the essential characteristics of a phenomenon. In actuality, perfect bureaucracies do not exist. Nonetheless, Weber's model provided a useful tool for comparing and contrasting functioning bureaucracies.

Division of Labor The goal of a bureaucracy is to accomplish some specific goal in the most efficient manner possible. The most effective way to do so is to identify all of the tasks necessary for success and assign specialists in

Dividing up labor in this way does have potential disadvantages. Workers who do routine tasks over and over again can feel like little more than a cog in the machine. This can produce a sense of **alienation** in which we experience loss of control over our creative human capacity to produce, separation from the products we make, and isolation from our fellow workers. It also can subject workers to greater job insecurity when jobs are deskilled through simplification and mechanization, making it easier to find and train a replacement worker. In addition, bureaucracy can produce what business executives refer to as "silos" in which there are limited connections between the various parts of a firm, inhibiting possible information exchange and collaboration between departments thus resulting in greater inefficiencies (Lencioni 2006). Further, the frustration we can experience when dealing with bureaucratic red tape—whether in the workplace, at a university, or with the government—frequently results from having to deal with different segments of a bureaucratic machine.

Hierarchy of Authority Bureaucracies follow the principle of hierarchy; that is, each position is under the supervision of a higher authority. A president heads a college bureaucracy; he or she selects members of the administration, who in turn hire their own staff. In the Roman Catholic Church, the pope is the supreme authority; under him are cardinals, bishops, and so forth. In businesses, the most basic relation is between boss and worker, but in large corporations there are various levels of authority. To track relationships, such companies map those connections using organizational charts that identify all the links of who answers to whom, ultimately leading up to the president or CEO at the top.

goal displacement Overzealous conformity to official regulations of a bureaucracy.

Written Rules and Regulations Through written rules and regulations, bureaucracies generally offer employees clear statements of their rights and responsibilities in the

Did You Know?

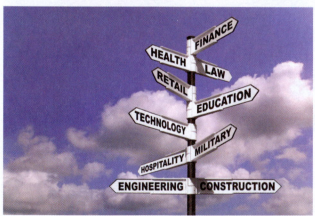

. . . In the 2010 Census, the U.S. Census Bureau identified 539 distinct occupational categories including Chief Executive, Aerospace Engineer, Phlebotomist, Crossing Guard, and Sociologist. They organized these occupations into six major categories.

Photo: © Rtimages/Alamy RF.

> # Bureaucracy is . . . the most rational known means of exercising authority over human beings.
>
> **Max Weber**

form of detailed job descriptions and comprehensive employee handbooks. If situations arise that are not covered by the rules, bureaucracies are self-correcting. They have rules in place to ensure that new rules are established that make work expectations as clear and exhaustive as possible. Because bureaucracies are hierarchical systems of interrelated positions, such procedures provide a valuable sense of continuity for the organization. Individual workers may come and go, but the structure and past records of the organization give it a life of its own that outlives the services of any one particular person.

SOCTHINK

Why do we tend to associate bureaucracies with red tape and inefficiency when they are explicitly organized to be the opposite? To what extent is our desire to be treated as an individual at odds with the principles of bureaucracies?

Of course, rules and regulations can overshadow the larger goals of an organization to the point that they become dysfunctional. What if a hospital emergency room physician failed to treat a seriously injured person because he or she had no valid proof of U.S. citizenship? If blindly applied, rules no longer serve as a means to achieving an objective but instead become important (perhaps too important) in their own right. Robert Merton (1968) used the term **goal displacement** to refer to overzealous conformity to official regulations of a bureaucracy in which we lose sight of the larger principle from which the rule was created.

Impersonality Bureaucratic norms dictate that officials judge people based on performance rather than personality. So long as everyone follows the rules as written, without regard for emotion or personal preference, the greatest good will result. The intent is to ensure equal treatment for each person. But it can also contribute to the cold, uncaring feeling often associated with modern organizations. Whether registering for college classes or getting tech support for a malfunctioning computer, most of us have had some experience of feeling like a number and longing for some personal attention. The larger the organization or society, however, the less possible such personal care becomes because attending to individual wants and needs is inefficient.

Employment Based on Technical Qualifications Within the ideal bureaucracy, hiring is based on technical qualifications rather than on favoritism, and performance is measured against specific standards. Written personnel policies dictate who gets promoted, and people often have a right to appeal if they believe that particular rules have been violated. In combination with the principle of impersonality, the driving personnel principle is supposed to be that it is "what you know, not who you know" that counts. Such procedures protect workers against arbitrary dismissal, provide a measure of security, and encourage loyalty to the organization.

Weber developed his five indicators of bureaucracy almost 100 years ago, and they continue to describe the ideal type. Not every formal organization will fully realize all of Weber's characteristics. The underlying logic they represent, however, points toward a way of doing things that is typical of life in modern societies.

BUREAUCRATIZATION AS A WAY OF LIFE

Bureaucracy for Weber was an indicator of a larger trend in modern society toward rational calculation of all decision making using efficiency and productivity as the primary standards of success. We recognize this pattern first at the level of businesses and organizations. More companies seek greater efficiency through **bureaucratization**—the process by which a group, organization, or social movement increasingly relies on technical-rational decision making in the pursuit of efficiency. Over time, however, the technical-rational approach pervades more and more areas of our lives.

The Spread of Bureaucratization

One example of the expansion of bureaucratization is found in the spread of what sociologist George Ritzer (2008) calls **McDonaldization**—the process by which the principles of efficiency, calculability, predictability, and control shape organization and decision making, in the United States and around the world. Ritzer argues that these principles, which are at the heart of the McDonald's fast-food chain's success, have been emulated by many organizations, ranging from medical care to wedding planning to education. Even

sporting events reflect the influence of McDonaldization. Around the world, stadiums are becoming increasingly similar, both physically and in the way

www.buttersafe.com © 2011 Alex Culang and Raynato Castro Buttersafe.

they present the sport to spectators. Swipe cards, "sports city" garages and parking lots, and automated ticket sales maximize efficiency. All seats offer spectators an unrestricted view, and a big screen guarantees them access to instant replays. Scores, player statistics, and attendance figures are updated by computer and displayed on an automated scoreboard. Spectator enthusiasm is manufactured through video displays urging applause or rhythmic chanting. At food counters, refreshments include well-known brands whose customer loyalty has been nourished by advertisers for decades. And, of course, the merchandising of teams' and even players' names and images is highly controlled.

Weber predicted that eventually even the private sphere would become rationalized. That is, we would turn to rational techniques in an effort to manage our self in order to handle the many challenges of modern life. A trip to any bookstore would seem to prove his point: we find countless self-help books, each with its own system of steps to help us solve life's problems and reach our goals.

Weber was concerned about the depersonalizing consequences of such rationalization, but he saw no way out. Because it is guided by the principle of maximum efficiency, the only way to beat bureaucratization, he thought, was to be more bureaucratic. He argued that, unfortunately, something human gets lost in the process. Culture critic Mike Daisey describes something like this through his experience working at Amazon.com. His job performance was measured based on five factors: time spent on each call, number of phone contacts per hour, time spent on each customer email, number of email contacts per hour, and the sum total of phone and email contacts per hour. Of these calculations,

bureaucratization The process by which a group, organization, or social movement increasingly relies on technical-rational decision making in the pursuit of efficiency.

McDonaldization The process by which the principles of efficiency, calculability, predictability, and control shape organization and decision making, in the United States and around the world.

iron law of oligarchy The principle that all organizations, even democratic ones, tend to develop into a bureaucracy ruled by an elite few.

scientific management Theory of management that measures all aspects of the work process to eliminate any inefficiencies.

he writes, "Those five numbers are who you are. They are, in fact, all you are. . . . Metrics will do exactly what it claims to do: It will track everything your employees do, say, and breathe, and consequently create a measurable increase in their productivity" (Daisey 2002:114). Metrics do work, but they do so by dehumanizing the worker. "The sad thing," Daisey continues, "is that metrics work so well precisely because it strips away dignity—it's that absence that makes it possible to see precisely who is pulling his weight and who is not" (p. 114). When workers' performance is measured only in numbers, the only part of the self that counts is that part that produces those numbers. Weber predicted that those parts of the self deemed not necessary to the job, such as emotional needs and family responsibilities, would be dismissed as irrelevant.

From Bureaucracy to Oligarchy One of the dangers, then, is that bureaucratization overwhelms other values and principles, including the goal of greater efficiency. Sociologist Robert Michels ([1915] 1949) studied socialist parties and labor unions in Europe prior to World War I and found that such organizations were becoming increasingly bureaucratic. The emerging leaders of the organizations—even some of the most egalitarian—had a vested interest in clinging to power. If they lost their leadership posts, they would have to return to full-time work as manual laborers.

Through his research, Michels originated the idea of the **iron law of oligarchy,** the principle that all organizations,

even democratic ones, tend to develop into a bureaucracy ruled by an elite few (called an oligarchy). Why do oligarchies emerge? People who achieve leadership roles usually have the skills, knowledge, or charisma to direct, if not control, others. Michels argued that the rank and file of a movement or organization look to leaders for direction and thereby reinforce the process of rule by a few. In addition, members of an oligarchy are strongly motivated to maintain their leadership roles, privileges, and power.

Concerns about oligarchy are often raised when ideologically driven social and political movements become institutionalized. In U.S. politics, ideologically committed followers, who often represent their party's base, frequently complain that elected leaders become "Washington insiders" who look out only for their self-interests. For example, during debates about the federal budget deficit in the summer of 2011, Tea Party conservatives, who are ideologically committed to small government and fiscal restraint, challenged Republican leaders to be true to their ideals and not raise taxes regardless of the electoral consequences. Similarly, progressive Democrats, ideologically committed to equality and opportunity, argued that Democratic leaders should not agree to cuts in funding for education, Social Security, Medicare, Medicaid, and other social support programs. In both cases, questions were raised about whether the craving to stay in office trumped the desire to do the right thing (Clemons 2011; D. Jones 2011).

BUREAUCRACY AND ORGANIZATIONAL CULTURE

One of the impressions Weber's model can leave is that there is only one right, most efficient way to organize a firm. Over time, however, managers have adopted a variety of strategies in their efforts to maximize productivity. For example, according to **scientific management,** established by Frederick Winslow Taylor in the late 1800s, managers should seek to measure all aspects of the work process in an effort to eliminate any inefficiencies. One of the primary tools they used was time-motion studies in which they measured each movement a worker would make using a stopwatch. They then sought ways to minimize the amount of time each task took. In this system, workers were treated as objects to be managed rather than as subjects whose cares and concerns were of any relevance to the manager (Taylor 1911).

Not until workers organized unions—and forced management to recognize that they were not objects—did theorists of formal organizations begin to revise the scientific management model. Along with management and administrators, social scientists became aware that informal groups of workers have an important impact on organizations

(Perrow 1986). An alternative management philosophy, the **human relations approach,** emphasizes the role of people, communication, and participation in a bureaucracy. This type of analysis reflects the significance of interaction and small-group behavior. Unlike planning under the scientific management approach, planning based on the human relations perspective focuses on workers' feelings, frustrations, and emotional need for job satisfaction (Mayo 1933). Today, many workplaces—primarily for those in higher-status occupations—have been transformed to family-friendly environments (Hochschild 1997). To the extent that managers are convinced that helping workers meet all their needs increases productivity, care and concern are instituted as a result of rational calculation.

>> Social Structure in Global Perspective

Principles of bureaucratization may influence more and more spheres of our lives today, but it has not always been thus. In fact, sociology arose as a discipline in order to better understand and direct the transition from traditional to modern society. Early sociologists sought to develop models that described the basic differences between the two. They hoped that by better understanding how traditional societies operate, we might more effectively identify the underlying factors that shape core concerns in modern society, such as social order, inequality, and interaction.

GEMEINSCHAFT AND GESELLSCHAFT

Ferdinand Tönnies (1855–1936) was appalled by the rise of industrial cities in his native Germany during the late 1800s. In his view, the city marked a dramatic change from the ideal of a close-knit community, which Tönnies termed a *Gemeinschaft,* to that of an impersonal mass society, or *Gesellschaft* (Tönnies [1887] 1988).

The *Gemeinschaft* (pronounced "guh-MINE-shahft") is typical of rural life. It is a small community in which people have similar backgrounds and life experiences. Virtually everyone knows one another, and social interactions are intimate and familiar, almost like an extended family. In this community there is a sense of commitment to the larger social group and a sense of togetherness among members. People relate to others in a personal way, not just as, say, clerk or manager. However, with such personal interaction comes little privacy and high expectations of individual sacrifice.

Social control in the *Gemeinschaft* is maintained through informal means, such as moral persuasion, gossip, and even gestures. These techniques work effectively because people genuinely care how others feel about them. Social change is relatively limited in the *Gemeinschaft;*

the lives of members of one generation may be quite similar to those of their parents, grandparents, and so on.

In contrast, the *Gesellschaft* (pronounced "guh-ZELL-shahft") is characteristic of modern urban life. In modern societies, most people are strangers who feel little in common with other residents. Relationships are governed by social roles that grow out of immediate tasks, such as purchasing a product or arranging a business meeting. Self-interest dominates, and there is little consensus concerning values or commitment to the group. As a result, social control must rest on formal techniques, such as laws and legally defined sanctions. Social change is a normal part of life in the *Gesellschaft,* with substantial shifts evident even within a single generation.

human relations approach An approach to the study of formal organizations that emphasizes the role of people, communication, and participation in a bureaucracy and tends to focus on the informal structure of the organization.

Gemeinschaft A close-knit community, often found in rural areas, in which strong personal bonds unite members.

Gesellschaft A community, often urban, that is large and impersonal, with little commitment to the group or consensus on values.

Sociologists have used these two terms to compare social structures that stress close relationships with those that feature less personal ties. It is easy to view the *Gemeinschaft* with nostalgia, as a far better way of life than the rat race of contemporary existence. However, the more intimate relationships of the *Gemeinschaft* come at a price. The prejudice and discrimination found there can be quite confining; ascribed statuses such as family background often outweigh a person's unique talents and achievements. In addition, the *Gemeinschaft* tends to distrust individuals who are creative or simply different (Garrett 2003).

SOCTHINK

What might be appealing about living in a community characterized by *Gemeinschaft?* What are possible drawbacks?

MECHANICAL AND ORGANIC SOLIDARITY

While Tönnies looked nostalgically back on the *Gemeinschaft,* Émile Durkheim was more interested in the transition to modern society, which he felt represented the birth of a new form of social order. Durkheim hoped to use sociology as a science to better understand this transition. In his book *The Division of Labor in Society* ([1893] 1933), Durkheim highlighted the seemingly inverse relationship between the division of labor and the collective conscience. As jobs became more specialized, the shared sentiments that united communities grew weaker.

In societies in which there is minimal division of labor, a sense of group solidarity develops because people do the same things together over time. Such societies are characterized by what Durkheim calls **mechanical solidarity,** a type of social cohesion based on shared experiences, knowledge, and skill in which social relations function more or less the way they always have. Societies with strong mechanical solidarity operate like a machine with limited change over time. Most individuals perform the same basic tasks—as did their parents and grandparents before them—and they do so together. These shared experiences—whether hunting, farming, preparing meals, making clothes, or building homes—result in shared perspectives and common values. Each individual acts, thinks, and believes very much like the next. Among the Amish, for example, what you will be when you grow up is virtually set at birth. There is limited opportunity for individual variation, because deviation from expected pathways represents a threat to social solidarity (Kraybill 2001; Kraybill et al. 2013).

As societies become more advanced technologically, their division of labor expands, and jobs become increasingly specialized. The person who cuts down timber is no longer the same person who builds your house. In most cases, it now takes many people with diverse sets of skills to produce even a single item, such as a chair or a cell phone. As a result, the solidarity that arose through common experience breaks down as differences emerge in how the members of the society view the world and their place in it. While Tönnies saw this and despaired, Durkheim suggested that a new form of solidarity would develop in its place.

As we saw in the "hamburger as miracle" example in Chapter 1, specialization breeds interdependence. The irony of modern society is that we combine extreme interdependence with a strong sense of individualism. We couldn't be self-sufficient because of our extreme division of labor, but we have a strong desire to be independent. We need one another more than ever,

but we realize it less. Durkheim argued that society would evolve to address this tension and ensure social order. He maintained that mechanical solidarity would give way to **organic solidarity**—a type of social cohesion based on our mutual interdependence in the context of extreme division of labor. The various components of society would recognize how much they need one another and work together in the same way as do organs of the human body, each performing a vital function, but none capable of surviving alone.

TECHNOLOGY AND SOCIETY

Some sociologists focus more explicitly on technology than on social organization, expressed as division of labor, to understand distinctions between traditional and modern societies. In sociologist Gerhard Lenski's view, a society's level of technology is critical to the way it is organized. Lenski defines technology as "cultural information about how to use the material resources of the environment to satisfy human needs and desires" (Nolan and Lenski 2006:361). As technology changes, new social forms arise, from preindustrial, to industrial, to postindustrial. The available technology does not completely define the form that a particular society and its social structure will take. Nevertheless, a low level of technology may limit the degree to which a society can depend on such things as irrigation or complex machinery.

Preindustrial Societies Perhaps the earliest form of preindustrial society to emerge in human history was the **hunting-and-gathering society,** in which people simply rely on whatever foods and fibers are readily available.

mechanical solidarity Social cohesion based on shared experiences, knowledge, and skills in which things function more or less the way they always have.

organic solidarity Social cohesion based on mutual interdependence in the context of extreme division of labor.

hunting-and-gathering society A preindustrial society in which people rely on whatever foods and fibers are readily available in order to survive.

© PhotoDisc/Getty Images RF

Such groups are typically small and widely dispersed, and technology in such societies is minimal. Organized into groups, people move constantly in search of food. There is little division of labor into specialized tasks because everyone is engaged in the same basic activities. Because resources are scarce, there is relatively little inequality in terms of material goods.

In **horticultural societies,** people plant seeds and crops rather than merely subsist on available foods. Members of horticultural societies are much less nomadic than hunter-gatherers. They place greater emphasis on the production of tools and household objects. Yet technology remains rather limited in these societies, whose members cultivate crops with the aid of digging sticks or hoes (Wilford 1997).

The third type of preindustrial development is the **agrarian society.** As in horticultural societies, members of agrarian societies are engaged primarily in the production of food, but technological innovations such as the plow allow farmers to dramatically increase their crop yields and cultivate the same fields over generations. As a result, it becomes possible for larger, more permanent settlements to develop.

Agrarian societies continue to rely on the physical power of humans and animals (in contrast to mechanical power). Division of labor increases because technological advances free up some people from food production to focus on specialized tasks, such as the repair of fishing nets or blacksmithing. As human settlements become stabler and more established, social institutions become more elaborate and property rights more important. The comparative permanence and greater surpluses of an agrarian society allow members to specialize in creating artifacts such as statues, public monuments, and art objects and to pass them on from one generation to the next.

Industrial Societies The Industrial Revolution transformed social life in England during the late 1700s, and within a century its impact on society had extended around the world. An **industrial society** is one that depends on mechanization to produce its goods and services. The strength and stamina humans gained from new inventions such as the steam engine opened up a new world of possibilities by applying nonanimal (mechanical) sources of power to most labor tasks. As such, industrialization significantly altered the way people lived and worked, and it undercut taken-for-granted norms and values.

During the Industrial Revolution, many societies underwent an irrevocable shift from an agrarian-oriented economy to an industrial base. Specialization of tasks and manufacture of goods increasingly replaced the practice of individuals or families making an entire product in a home workshop. Workers, generally men but also women and even children, left their family homesteads to work in central locations such as urban factories.

The process of industrialization had distinctive social consequences. Families and communities could not continue to function as self-sufficient units. Individuals,

villages, and regions began to exchange goods and services and to become interdependent. As people came to rely on the labor of members of other communities, the family lost its unique position as the main source of power and authority. The need for specialized knowledge led to formalized schooling, and education emerged as a social institution distinct from the family.

Postindustrial Societies

Mechanized production continues to play a substantial role in shaping social order, relationships, and opportunities, but technological innovation once again has reshaped social structure by freeing up some people from the demands of material production. This has led to the rise of the service sector of the economy in many technologically advanced countries. In the 1970s sociologist Daniel Bell wrote about the technologically advanced **postindustrial society,** whose economic system is engaged primarily in the processing and control of information. The main output of a postindustrial society is services rather than manufactured

horticultural society A preindustrial society in which people plant seeds and crops rather than merely subsist on available foods.

agrarian society The most technologically advanced form of preindustrial society. Members are engaged primarily in the production of food, but they increase their crop yields through technological innovations such as the plow.

industrial society A society that depends on mechanization to produce its goods and services.

postindustrial society A society whose economic system is engaged primarily in the processing and control of information.

Did You Know?

. . . TV talk-show host Regis Philbin was a sociology major. He graduated from the University of Notre Dame with a BA in sociology in 1953. Sociology, he says, "gave me a great insight into human nature."

Photo: © Frederick M. Brown/Getty Images.

goods. Large numbers of people become involved in occupations devoted to the teaching, generation, or dissemination of ideas. Jobs in fields such as advertising, public relations, human resources, and computer information systems are typical of a postindustrial society (Bell 1999).

Some sociologists, including Bell, view this transition from industrial to postindustrial society as largely a positive development. Others, however, point to the often hidden consequences that result from differential access to resources in postindustrial society. For example, Michael Harrington (1980), who alerted the nation to the problems of the poor in his book *The Other America,* questions the significance that Bell attaches to the growing class of white-collar workers. Harrington concedes that scientists, engineers, and economists are involved in important political and economic decisions, but he disagrees with Bell's claim that they have a free hand in decision making, independent of the interests of the rich. Harrington follows in the tradition of Marx by arguing that conflict between social classes will continue in the postindustrial society.

postmodern society
A technologically sophisticated, pluralistic, interconnected, globalized society.

Going GLOBAL

International Favorability Ratings for the United States

Bottom seven nations		Top seven nations	
Greece	34%	Philippines	92%
Palestinian Territories	30%	Israel	84%
Russia	23%	South Korea	82%
Turkey	19%	Kenya	80%
Pakistan	14%	El Salvador	80%
Jordan	12%	Italy	78%
Egypt	10%	Ghana	77%

Note: Data are for 2014.
Source: Pew Research Center 2014c.

Because we exist in an interdependent global network, the consequences of our actions, both large and small, reverberate throughout the world. In a global survey of 43 other nations conducted in 2014, the Pew Research Center looked at international favorability ratings for the United States. How favorably do other nations view the United States? The global median was 65 percent, with regional variation from 74 percent in Africa to 30 percent in the Middle East.

POSTMODERN LIFE

Sociologists recently have gone beyond discussion of the postindustrial society to contemplate the emergence of postmodern society. A **postmodern society** is a technologically sophisticated, pluralistic, interconnected, globalized society. Although it is difficult to summarize what a whole range of thinkers have said about postmodern life, four elements provide a sense of the key characteristics of such societies today: stories, images, choices, and networks.

Stories Because postmodern societies are pluralistic and individualistic, people hold many different, often competing, sets of norms and values. Fewer people assume that a single, all-inclusive story—whether a particular religious tradition, or an all-encompassing scientific theory of everything, or even the faith many early sociologists had in the inevitability of modern progress—can unite us all under a common umbrella. Instead, we embrace the various individual and group stories that help us make sense of the world and our place in it. We do so in the full knowledge that others out there are doing exactly the same thing and often coming to dramatically different conclusions. This multiplicity of stories undercuts the authority that singular accounts of reality have had in the past.

Images Postmodern society is also characterized by the explosion of the mass media, which emphasizes the importance of images. The average person in the United States watches almost 5 hours and 15 minutes of television per day (Short 2013). This works out to the equivalent of almost 80 full days per year. We are bombarded by images everywhere we turn, but in postmodern theory, the significance of the image goes much deeper than television and advertisements; it impacts our taken-for-granted notion of material reality itself. Theorists argue that we do not confront or interact with the material world directly. Just as language shapes our perception of reality according to the Sapir-Whorf hypothesis, our experience of "reality" is always mediated through representations of reality in the form of signs, symbols, and words. According to postmodernists, our images or models of reality come before reality itself. Postmodern theorists use a geography metaphor to illuminate this concept: "The map precedes the territory" (Baudrillard [1981] 1994). In other words, the images we construct draw our attention to certain features that we might not otherwise single out. A road map, for example, highlights different features, and for different purposes, than does a topographical map or political map. In so doing, it shapes what we see. We cannot step around or look through such cultural constructs to approach the thing itself, and so our knowledge of what is real is always constrained by the images we construct.

Choices In a postmodern world, reality is not simply given; it is negotiated. We pick and choose our reality from the buffet of images and experiences presented to us. In fact, we *must* choose. In contrast to societies characterized by mechanical solidarity, where one's life path is virtually set at birth, members of postmodern societies must make life choices all the time. Assuming we have access to sufficient resources, we choose what to eat, what to wear, and what to drive. Shopping, which in the past would have been viewed primarily as an instrumental necessity to provide for our basic needs, becomes an act of self-creation. As advertising professor James B. Twitchell (2000) put it, "We don't buy things, we buy meanings" (p. 47). An iPhone, a Coach purse, and a MINI Cooper are more than just a phone, a handbag, and a car. They are statements about the kind of person we are or want to be. The significance of choice goes much deeper than just consumer products. We also choose our partners, our schools, our jobs, our faith, and even our identities. As individuals, we may choose to affirm traditions, language, diet, and values we inherited from our family through socialization, but we can also choose to pursue our own path.

Networks Members of postmodern societies live in a globally interconnected world. The food we eat, the clothes we wear, the books we read, and the products we choose often come to us from the other side of the world. The computer technician we talk to for assistance in the United States may be located in India. McDonald's has even experimented with centralized drive-through attendants—who might even be located in another state—who take your order and transmit it to the restaurant you are ordering from (Richtel 2006). Increasingly, all corners of the globe are linked into a vast, interrelated social, cultural, political, and economic system. A rural Iowa farmer, for example, must be concerned with more than just the local weather and community concerns; he or she must know about international innovations in farming technology, including biotech, as well as the current and future state of international markets.

Whether in the form of traditional, modern, or postmodern society, social structure provides order, shaping the options that are available to us. It provides the context within which we interact with others. The statuses we occupy shape the roles we perform. What we think and do is influenced by the relationships we have with others in the contexts of groups, networks, and institutions. Sociology as a discipline is committed to making sense of our structural context and the impact it has on our lives.

Still, society and social structure are not singular things. Though we are, in many respects, products of society, socialized to think and act in appropriate ways, we always have the option to think and act in new ways and to construct new culture. The possibility for such change may be more apparent in our pluralistic world. Ours is a world not of "the" structure, "the" family, and "the" religion, but of structures, families, and religions. We have the possibility for more contact with more people who have more ways of thinking and acting than at any time in the past. As such, we can become aware of more alternatives for how we might think and act that might lead us to change our worlds.

SOCIOLOGY IS A VERB

The Significance of Place

We occupy many statuses over the course of our lives, and they can both open and close doors for us. Ask five people in various positions— whether as parents, professors, child care providers, custodians, managers, religious leaders, or so on—how they came to be in those positions. How have the positions they occupy enabled them to accomplish their personal and collective goals? How have they been constrained by their positions?

For REVIEW

I. What makes up society?
- Society provides a structure that is built from the statuses we occupy; the roles we perform; and the groups, networks, and institutions that connect us.

II. How does social structure shape individual action?
- The positions we occupy shape our perceptions, the resources to which we have access, and the options that are available. For example, in the context of bureaucracies, our social position, connections, and performance expectations are clearly defined.

III. How do sociologists describe traditional versus modern societies?
- Sociologists highlight the impact that division of labor and technological development have on the organization of community, work, and social interaction in traditional and modern societies.

© Veer/Getty Images RF

Functionalist View

The **elements of social structure**—statuses, groups, social networks, and social institutions—provide order, shape our options, and give context to our lives.

Social roles create a **stable society** by allowing people to anticipate the behavior of others and to act accordingly.

Institutions contribute to **social order** by performing **vital functions**, whether it is producing children (family), teaching them (schools), establishing order (government), or distributing goods and services (economy).

STRUCTURE, ORDER
KEY CONCEPTS

Conflict View

The elements of the social structure justify and reinforce existing systems of inequality and unequal distributions of resources.

Ascribed statuses, often conferred at birth, can be used to justify **privileges** for some while limiting opportunities for others by consigning them to a **subordinate group.**

In-groups and out-groups serve to highlight **differences** between people and can foster antagonism.

SUBORDINATION, INEQUALITY, PRIVILEGE
KEY CONCEPTS

Interactionist View

It is through social interaction—the **shared experiences** through which we relate to others—that the elements of social structure are constructed.

Our social roles are governed by a set of expectations, but how we actually **perform** those roles can vary from individual to individual.

A **micro, bottom-up perspective** of social structure reinforces the significance of our actions, and helping us appreciate how we can think and act in new ways to bring about social change.

SHARED EXPERIENCES, MICRO PERSPECTIVE
KEY CONCEPTS

MAKE THE CONNECTION

After reviewing the chapter, answer the following questions:

1
How does Berger and Luckmann's social construction of reality model integrate elements of functionalist, conflict, and interactionist perspectives?

2
Briefly describe how a functionalist, a conflict theorist, and an interactionist would view social institutions.

3
Sociologists Daniel Bell and Michael Harrington have differing views of postindustrial society. Which perspectives do you think their views reflect?

4
Have you ever been part of an in- or out-group? If so, how might each perspective shed light on your experience?

Pop Quiz

1. The three stages of Berger and Luckmann's model describing the interdependent relationship between the individual and society are
   a. statuses, groups, and institutions.
   b. telling stories, making choices, and establishing networks.
   c. constructing culture, constructing the self, and constructing society.
   d. role conflict, role strain, and role exit.

2. In the United States, we expect that cab drivers know how to get around a city. This expectation is an example of which of the following?
   a. role conflict
   b. role strain
   c. social role
   d. master status

3. What occurs when incompatible expectations arise from two or more social positions held by the same person?
   a. role conflict
   b. role strain
   c. role exit
   d. role playing

4. In sociological terms, what do we call any two or more people, united by a shared sense of identity or purpose, who interact with each other over time in ways that distinguish them from outsiders?
   a. a category
   b. a group
   c. an aggregate
   d. a society

5. Primary groups are characterized by
   a. a series of relationships that link individuals directly to others and, through them, indirectly to still more people.
   b. formal, impersonal relationships with minimal social intimacy or mutual understanding.
   c. social positions that are within our power to change.
   d. intimate, face-to-face association and cooperation.

6. What is the definition of a social institution?
   a. A series of social relationships that link individuals directly to others, and through them indirectly to still more people.
   b. An alliance, whether temporary or permanent, geared toward a common goal.
   c. An integrated and persistent social network dedicated to ensuring that society's core needs are met.
   d. A component of a formal organization that uses rules and hierarchical ranking to achieve efficiency.

7. Which characteristic of bureaucracy is carried out on the basis of performance rather than personality?
   a. impersonality
   b. hierarchy of authority
   c. written rules and regulations
   d. division of labor

8. What type of society did Ferdinand Tönnies describe as a close-knit community in which members have strong personal bonds?
   a. *Gesellschaft*
   b. mechanical
   c. *Gemeinschaft*
   d. organic

9. According to Émile Durkheim, which type of solidarity is characterized by extensive division of labor?
   a. postindustrial
   b. mechanical
   c. horticultural
   d. organic

10. What characteristic of postmodern life emphasizes the importance of consumption on identity creation?
    a. stories
    b. images
    c. choices
    d. networks

1. (c), 2. (c), 3. (a), 4. (b), 5. (d), 6. (c), 7. (a), 8. (c), 9. (d), 10. (c)

© Photo by Robert Nicklesberg/Getty Images

Deviance

6

MURDER AND MAYHEM

On the morning of December 14, 2012, a gunman forced his way into Sandy Hook Elementary School in Newtown, CT, and started shooting. Principal Dawn Hochsprung and school psychologist Mary Sherlach confronted him; both were immediately killed. Teachers and staff members throughout the school scrambled to try to protect their students. The gunman entered Lauren Rousseau's classroom, killing her and all her students. He then entered Victoria Soto's classroom, killing her and six of her students. In as few as 10 minutes, 26 people were dead, including 20 first-graders and 6 staff members.

The massacre at Sandy Hook was the second deadliest mass shooting in U.S. history. The deadliest occurred at Virginia Tech in 2007, when 32 people were killed and 17 were wounded, but there have been many others. In December 2013, 12 people were killed and three injured by a lone gunman at the Naval Sea Systems Command in Washington, D.C. In August 2012, 6 people were killed and 4 were wounded at a Sikh temple in Wisconsin. Less than a month earlier, 12 were killed and 58 were wounded in Aurora, Colorado, at the midnight debut of *The Dark Knight Rises*. In January 2011, Congresswoman Gabrielle Giffords was shot in the head near Tucson, Arizona, at a planned public gathering. She survived, but 6 others did not and 13 were wounded. According to the FBI, there were 160 active shooter incidents in the United States between 2000 and 2013, killing 486 and wounding 557. In 96 percent of the incidents, the shooter was male. The average number of incidents per year has been rising (Blair and Schweit 2014).

After each incident, questions arise about guns and violence. The United States has the highest rate of gun ownership of any nation. Of all the civilian-owned firearms in the world, 41.5 percent are owned in the United States (India is second at 7.1 percent). In 2013, guns were used

121

in 70 percent of all U.S. homicides, resulting in 11,208 deaths. The good news is that homicide rates have dropped by nearly half since the early 1990s. Yet these mass shootings are a reminder that gun violence persists, and that as a nation, we're deeply conflicted on how to respond to it. On the one hand, 92 percent of Americans support requiring background checks for all gun buyers, but only 37 percent rate gun control as a top priority for lawmakers, ranking it 18th out of 21 policy goals (Centers for Disease Control and Prevention 2014; Pew Research Center 2013a, 2013b; Quinnipiac 2014; Small Arms Survey 2011; Smith and Cooper 2013).

Why do mass shootings occur? Are they due to unchecked mental illness? Gun ownership rates? A culture of violence? Ineffective socialization? Economic inequality? Or something else entirely? Through research, sociologists help us better understand crime by asking these questions, and we, in turn, can better understand how to prevent it.

As You READ >>

- **How do groups maintain social control?**
- **What is the difference between deviance and crime?**
- **How do sociologists explain deviance and crime?**

>> Social Control

At some point in our lives, all of us have likely asked ourselves, "Should I do what *they* want or should I do what *I* want?" Perhaps it happened when we were little and our parents asked us to put away our toys or maybe at college when a professor assigned a lot of reading or at a job when the boss requested that we work an extra shift. We may not want to give in to the demands of others, yet we know that there are consequences for not doing so. To better understand the power that others wield over us, and how we respond to it, sociologists study social control, deviance, and crime.

social control The techniques and strategies for preventing deviant human behavior in any society.

conformity Abiding by the norms of our peers even though they have no direct authority over us.

As a species, we need the social order that norms provide. Knowing that others will follow shared rules for behavior makes coordinated action possible, thus enabling us to meet our individual and collective needs. To ensure sufficient obedience regarding norms, we use **social control**— the techniques and strategies for preventing deviant human behavior in any society.

One of the primary tools for achieving social control is the use of sanctions (see Chapter 3). We take for granted that people in positions of authority have both the right and responsibility to impose

sanctions in order to encourage compliance with norms. We assume that parents will discipline their children for disobeying, teachers will reward outstanding performance with good grades, police officers will write tickets for speeders, and bosses will reward a job well done with raises and promotions. There are consequences, both positive and negative, for our actions. Sanctions point to the power that the societies, institutions, and groups to which we belong have over our lives. As the old saying goes, don't do the crime if you can't do the time.

Although social control contributes to social order, such power can be oppressive, limiting individual freedom and advancing the interests of some at the expense of others. Entrenched interests often seek to maintain the status quo and use their control over sanctions, including the power to hand out rewards and impose punishments, to do so. In fact, positive social change often comes through active resistance to the status quo, with individuals and groups rejecting existing norms and following new paths. Such attempts may meet with significant opposition, as was evident in the struggle to end slavery, the fight for women's right to vote, the civil rights movement, and the protests to end the war in Vietnam.

CONFORMITY AND OBEDIENCE

We experience social control in a variety of forms. The people around us who are most like ourselves shape how we think and act. **Conformity** is a more horizontal form of social control that involves abiding by the norms of our

© Scott Garfield/© American Movie Classics/ Courtesy Everett Collection

peers even though they have no direct authority over us. Going along with the crowd, whether that means attending a basketball game, studying abroad, or going to a party all because your friends do, is a form of conformity. **Obedience,** on the other hand, is a vertical form of social control that involves doing what a person in a position of authority over you says you should. In this form of social control, the social status of a person whose authority we respect, whether as a teacher, religious leader, or coach, gives them power over us. We are inclined to do what they ask because we trust them and defer to their presumed knowledge and wisdom.

© Comstock/Jupiter Images RF

Social psychologist Stanley Milgram (1963, 1974a) wondered how far people would go when asked to do something by a trusted authority figure. He was motivated to do so, in part, because he wanted to better understand the involvement of the German people in the murder of 6 million Jews and millions of others during World War II. One of the rationalizations given after the war was that they were "just following orders." Milgram conceived of a test to demonstrate people's willingness to obey.

Milgram set up a scenario in which a volunteer, recruited from the local community, was told that researchers were investigating the effects of punishment on learning. The volunteer was then brought into a lab setting and asked to serve as a "teacher" who would ask questions of a "learner." If the learner got the question wrong, the teacher was instructed by a scientist, dressed in a lab coat, to administer an electric shock to the learner. For each additional question the learner got wrong, the teacher was instructed to increase the shock's voltage. Unbeknownst to the volunteer, however, no actual shock was administered. The real purpose of the study was to see how far the teacher/volunteer would go before refusing to obey the scientist.

> **obedience** Doing what a person in a position of authority over you says you should.

In a prearranged script, the learner deliberately gave incorrect answers and pretended to be in pain when "shocked." For example, at 150 volts the learner would cry out, "Get me out of here!" At 270 volts the learner would scream in agony. When the shock reached 350 volts, the learner would fall silent. If the teacher wanted to stop the experiment, the experimenter would insist that the teacher continue, using such statements as "The experiment requires that you continue" and "You have no other choice; you must go on." Milgram repeated this experiment numerous times, altering 23 different experimental conditions, such as the gender of the scientist, the number of scientists, and the presence of the scientist in the room, to see what effects they might have. In Experiment 5, the variation for which Milgram is best known, 65 percent of the volunteers continued all the way up to the 450-volt maximum (Blass 1999; Haslam, Loughnan, and Perry 2014; Milgram 1974a).

Researchers since Milgram have conducted similar demonstrations seeking

POPSOC

The zombie apocalypse has become a pop culture staple. Examples include George Romero's *Living Dead* films, Max Brooks's *World War Z* book and film, and *The Walking Dead* graphic novel and TV series. Such accounts often say more about humans and the breakdown of social order than they do about zombies. In the event of a zombie apocalypse, how quickly do you think social order would break down? What factors might minimize social chaos? What steps should people take?

Photo: © Everett Collection

SOCTHINK

According to the American Sociological Association *Code of Ethics,* researchers must "protect subjects from personal harm." To what extent might Milgram's subjects have experienced emotional harm? How and why might a researcher seek to justify such a risk?

to replicate his findings and have produced comparable results. The average obedience rate for 17 similar studies was 65 percent, though rates for these studies varied significantly from 28 to 91 percent (Blass 1999). Due to the potentially harmful psychological side effects on the volunteers, studies such as these ceased. In a more recent attempt, social psychologist Jerry Burger (2009) attempted to minimize the ethical concerns by, among other things, assuring volunteers they could stop at any time, guaranteeing they could keep the money they were paid for volunteering even if they stopped, and ending the experiment immediately after the 150-volt level when the "learner" asked for the experiment to stop, at which point the true nature of the experiment was revealed and the learner was shown to be unharmed. Burger found that 65 percent of his subjects continued to administer what they thought were shocks until the end.

informal social control Social control that is carried out casually by ordinary people through such means as laughter, smiles, and ridicule.

Milgram concluded that we are willing to do things we would otherwise not do, including inflicting pain, when a person in a position of authority tells us to do so. He pointed out that, in modern society, we are accustomed to submitting to impersonal authority figures whose status is indicated by a title (professor, president, doctor) or by a uniform (police officer, army lieutenant, scientist). Because we defer to authority, we shift responsibility for our behavior to the authority figure

without fully appreciating what we are doing. Under similar circumstances, otherwise normal people can and do treat one another inhumanely, as demonstrated by the revealing photos taken at Iraq's Abu Ghraib prison in 2004 which showed U.S. military guards humiliating, if not torturing, Iraqi prisoners (Hayden 2004; Zimbardo 2007). Reflecting on his research, Milgram wrote, "It may be that we are puppets—puppets controlled by the strings of society. But at least we are puppets with perception, with awareness. And perhaps our awareness is the first step to our liberation" (1974b: 568). We do not make choices in a vacuum and sociology enables us to better recognize the social forces that shape our actions so that we can make more informed choices.

SOCTHINK

Do you think a person's background factors would influence how far he or she would go in Milgram's experiment? How might age, gender, religion, or education make a difference?

INFORMAL AND FORMAL SOCIAL CONTROL

In addition to being horizontal and vertical, social control can be formal and informal. As the term implies, people use **informal social control** casually to enforce norms. Examples include smiles, laughter, a raised eyebrow, and ridicule. We seek to read such cues in new situations such as a first date or a job interview so that we might adjust our behavior accordingly.

A participant in the Milgram experiment. Photo: © From the film *OBEDIENCE* © 1968 by ALexandra Milgram, © renewed 1993 by Alexandra Milgram. Reprinted by permission of Alexandra Milgram.

Formal social control is carried out by authorized agents, such as police officers, judges, school administrators, employers, military officers, and managers. It can serve as a last resort when socialization and informal sanctions do not bring about desired behavior. An increasingly significant means of formal social control in the United States is imprisonment. In 2013, 6.9 million adults underwent some form of correctional supervision—jail, prison, probation, or parole. Put another way, 35 percent, or 1 out of every 35 adult Americans, was subject to this very formal type of social control (Glaze and Kaeble 2014).

In the wake of mass campus shootings, such as those at Virginia Tech in 2007 and Oikos University in Oakland, California, in 2012, many college officials reviewed security measures on their campuses. Administrators were reluctant to end or even limit the relative freedom of movement students on their campuses enjoyed. Instead, they concentrated on improving emergency communications between campus police and students, faculty, and staff. Reflecting a reliance on technology to maintain social control, college leaders called for replacement of the "old" technology of email with instant alerts that could be sent to people's cell phones via text messaging.

Similarly, in the aftermath of the terrorist attacks of September 11, 2001, new measures of social control became the norm in the United States. Some of them, such as stepped-up security at airports and high-rise buildings, were highly visible to the public. The federal government also publicly urged citizens to engage in informal social control by watching for and reporting people whose actions seem suspicious. But many other measures taken by the government have increased the covert surveillance of private records and communications.

Only a month and a half after September 11, and with virtually no debate, Congress passed the USA PATRIOT Act of 2001. It was reauthorized in 2005 and 2006, and extended by the Obama administration in 2011. Sections of this sweeping legislation revoked legal checks on the power of law enforcement agencies. Without a warrant or probable cause, the FBI can now secretly access most private records, including medical histories, library accounts, and student registrations. In 2002, for example, the FBI searched the records of hundreds of dive shops and scuba organizations. Agents had been directed to identify every person who had taken diving lessons in the past three years because of speculation that terrorists might try to approach their targets underwater (Moss and Fessenden 2002).

Many people think that this kind of social control goes too far. Civil rights advocates also worry that the government's request for information on suspicious activities may encourage negative stereotyping of Muslims and Arab Americans. Clearly, there is a trade-off between the benefits of surveillance and violation of the right to privacy.

The interplay between formal and informal social control can be complicated, because we sometimes have to balance one source of control against another. College students, for example, receive conflicting messages about the acceptability of binge drinking. On the one hand, it represents deviance from the standards of conduct expected of those in an academic context. On the other hand, binge drinking shows conformity to the peer culture, especially in the context of sororities and fraternities (see the figure "Binge Drinking on Campus"). Increasingly, colleges and universities are taking steps to exert greater social control by instituting rules banning kegs, closing fraternities and sororities that violate

> **formal social control** Social control that is carried out by authorized agents, such as police officers, judges, school administrators, and employers.

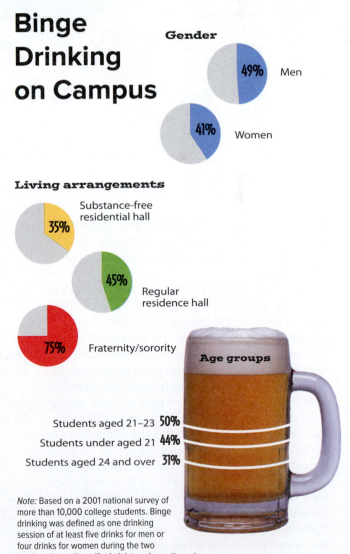

Binge Drinking on Campus

Gender

49% Men

41% Women

Living arrangements

35% Substance-free residential hall

45% Regular residence hall

75% Fraternity/sorority

Age groups

Students aged 21–23 **50%**

Students under aged 21 **44%**

Students aged 24 and over **31%**

Note: Based on a 2001 national survey of more than 10,000 college students. Binge drinking was defined as one drinking session of at least five drinks for men or four drinks for women during the two weeks prior to the self-administered questionnaire.

Source: Wechsler et al. 2002:208; Wechsler and Nelson 2008. *Photo:* © Comstock/Jupiter Images RF.

standards of conduct, expelling students after multiple alcohol-related violations, and working with local liquor retailers to discourage high-volume sales to students (Wechsler and Nelson 2008).

LAW AND SOCIETY

Some norms are so important to a society that they are formalized into laws limiting people's behavior. Laws—formal norms enforced by the state—are a form of governmental social control. Some laws, such as the prohibition against murder, are directed at all members of society. Others, such as fishing and hunting regulations, primarily affect particular categories of people. Still others govern the behavior of social institutions (for instance, corporate law and laws regarding the taxing of nonprofit enterprises).

Sociologists see the creation of laws as a social process. Because laws are passed in response to a perceived need for formal social control, sociologists have sought to explain how and why such a perception arises. In their view, law is not merely a static body of rules handed down from generation to generation. Rather, it reflects continually changing standards of what is right and wrong, of how violations are to be determined, and of what sanctions are to be applied (Deflem 2008).

In diverse societies the establishment of laws inevitably generates conflicts over whose values should prevail, and so the creation of civil and criminal laws can be controversial. For example, should it be against the law to employ illegal immigrants? To have an abortion? To allow prayer in public schools? To smoke on an airplane? Such issues have been bitterly debated because they require a choice among competing values. Not surprisingly, unpopular laws—such as the 18th Amendment, which prohibited the manufacture and sale of alcohol (ratified in 1919), or the nationwide 55-mile-per-hour speed limit that was imposed in 1974—become difficult to enforce when there is no consensus supporting the norms. In both cases the public commonly violated the stated government policy, and the laws proved unenforceable; the states repealed Prohibition in 1933, and Congress overturned the national speed-limit policy in 1987.

The current debate over the legalization of marijuana illustrates the difficulty in crafting public laws governing private behavior. In a country where federal law prohibits the use of marijuana, 48 percent of U.S. adults admit to having tried it, a 10-percentage-point increase over the previous decade. Twenty-three states have responded by legalizing its use for medical purposes. Four states—Washington, Colorado, Oregon, and Alaska—took the

Marijuana Laws by State

■ Washington, DC

■ 23 states have legalized the possession and use of marijuana for medical purposes.

■ 4 states and the District of Columbia have legalized marijuana for personal recreational use.

Source: National Conference of State Legislatures 2015.   *Photo:* © Brand X Pictures/PunchStock RF.

Views of Legalizing Marijuana: 1969–2014

Percentage saying marijuana should be . . .

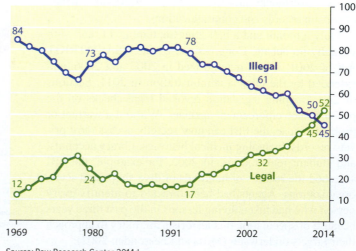

Source: Pew Research Center 2014d.

additional step of legalizing marijuana for personal recreational use. This move is consistent with the trend in U.S. public opinion. The percentage of people supporting outright legalization rose from 12 percent in 1969 to 52 percent in 2014 (Pew Research Center 2013c, 2014d).

Socialization is the primary vehicle for instilling conforming and obedient behavior, including obedience to law. Generally, it is not external pressure from a peer group or authority figure that makes us go along with social norms. Rather, we have internalized such norms as valid and desirable and are self-policing. In a profound sense, we want to see ourselves (and to be seen) as loyal, cooperative, responsible, and respectful of others. In the United States and other societies around the world, people are socialized both to want to belong and to fear being viewed as different or deviant.

Oscar-winning director Alejandro González Iñárritu's Birdman *was downloaded 7,967,697 times leading up to the Academy Awards.* Photo: © Steve Granitz/WireImage/Getty Images.

Control theory suggests that our connection to other members of society leads us to conform systematically to society's norms. According to sociologist Travis Hirschi and other control theorists, our bonds to family members, friends, and peers induce us to follow the mores and folkways of our society. We give little conscious thought to whether we will be sanctioned if we fail to conform. Socialization develops our self-control so well that we don't need further pressure to obey social norms. Although control theory does not explain the rationale for every conforming act, it nevertheless reminds us that although the media may focus on crime and disorder, most members of most societies conform to and obey basic norms most of the time (Gottfredson and Hirschi 1990; Hirschi 1969).

> **control theory** A view of conformity and deviance that suggests our connection to members of society leads us to systematically conform to society's norms.
>
> **deviance** Behavior that violates the standards of conduct or expectations of a group or society.

>> Deviance

The flip side of social control is deviance. **Deviance** is behavior that violates the standards of conduct or expectations of a group or society (Wickman 1991:85). In the United States, most people classify those who are alcoholics, compulsive gamblers, or mentally ill as deviant. Being late for class is categorized as a deviant act, as is wearing jeans to a formal wedding. On the basis of the sociological definition, we are all deviant from time to time. Each of us violates common social norms in certain situations.

WHAT BEHAVIOR IS DEVIANT?

Because deviance involves violation of some group's norms, defining an act as deviant depends on the context. File sharing on the Internet—including MP3s, movies, computer games, books, and almost anything else that can be digitized—provides an example of how deviance can be in the eye of the beholder. Whenever a new film is released, online piracy groups compete with each other to see who can be the first to upload a high-definition copy. Competition to upload films nominated for an Academy

International Gun Homicide Rates

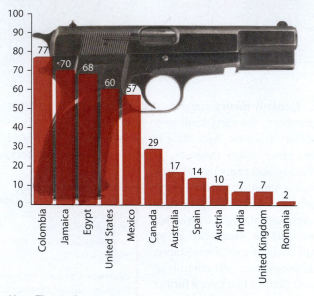

Note: The number represents the percentage of homicides committed using firearms.
Source: UNODC 2014.   *Photo:* © Stockbyte/PunchStock RF.

Award is even more intense. On average, more than 90 percent of Academy Award–nominated films are available for illegal download before Oscar night. And because Academy Award voters typically receive DVDs in order to screen the films, online film pirates actually watch higher-quality versions of the films than voters do (Baio 2015). In the week after the 2015 Oscar nominees were announced, the nominated films saw a 385 percent increase in illegal downloads, with *Selma* experiencing the biggest jump at a 1,033 percent increase. During the four weeks that followed the nominations, *American Sniper* led the pack with 1,389,819 downloads (Irdeto 2015a, 2015b).

stigma Labeling individuals or members of a group as less than whole persons due to some attribute that marks them as different in the eyes of others.

Because the "property" these movie, music, and game files represent is not physical, it can be copied over and over again for virtually no cost. Anyone with a computer and an Internet connection can grab the files from people willing to share and pass them along to others who want them. People find it easy to justify doing so, thinking it does little harm to anyone. The entertainment companies that produce these products take a different view. In 2015, the estimated revenue lost to just the six Oscar-nominated films that had not yet been released on DVD or Blu-ray was over $40 million in the month between nominations

and awards (Irdeto 2015b). These companies have actively pursued lawsuits against those who share files in part to scare those who might think of doing it. However, the widespread availability of these files suggests that many people do not view this practice as particularly deviant. Some even view it as an act of protest against what they consider unfair prices charged by big corporations.

An important dimension of deviance to remember is that social change occurs when people choose to act differently. Our tendency is to go with the flow, thus reproducing the status quo. As a result, we frequently fail to see the ways in which our existing practices may violate our core principles. At times such as these, people who stand up for what they believe is right are often punished. The civil rights movement provided numerous examples of this, such as when nonviolent protestors at sit-ins and marches were met with attack dogs, fire hoses, beatings, and jail time. In the end, however, these protests led to greater political, legal, and economic opportunity for African Americans and others. Part of what makes such change difficult is that those with the greatest status have the capacity to define what is acceptable and what is deviant. It often takes a concerted effort, and the mobilization of substantial resources, to counteract such power.

DEVIANCE AND SOCIAL STIGMA

People who deviate from the norm in terms of how they think, believe, act, or look are frequently categorized as different, strange, unusual, or abnormal by people in social positions of power. Whole groups of people—whether on the basis of hair color, skin color, height, weight, clothing, nationality, physical ability, or other attributes—can be denied respect due to their presumed shortcomings. Sociologist Erving Goffman (1963) coined the term **stigma** to describe the process of labeling individuals or members of a group as less than whole persons due to some attribute that marks them as different in the eyes of others. Because our perception of others shapes how we treat them, such labels have consequences, as we learned from the Thomas theorem (see Chapter 1). As a result, stigmatizing represents a form of social control. First we label people as different using stereotypes to characterize them as "other." Then the distinction between "us" and "them" is used to justify discrimination against those in the stigmatized group, denying them access to valued material, social, and cultural resources (Link and Phelan 2001).

The pressure to conform to the norm, and thus avoid stigma, can have powerful effects. People try not to deviate too far from cultural expectations. Women, for example, can feel pressured to approximate what Naomi Wolf (1992) refers to as the "beauty myth," an exaggerated ideal of beauty, beyond the reach of all but a few females. In an effort to attain this ideal, many women undergo plastic surgery. In 2013, 290,000 women received breast augmentations, 120,000 had a facelift, 164,000 received rhinoplasty, and 176,000 underwent liposuction. When it comes to less invasive procedures,

5.9 million opted for Botox and 1.1 million received chemical peels. Overall, women received 13.1 million cosmetic procedures in 2013 alone. But it wasn't only women. Men, too, are opting for plastic surgery and accounted for 9 percent of all cosmetic procedures in 2013 (American Society of Plastic Surgeons 2014). The desire to avoid stigma reinforces the standards of the status quo.

Often people are stigmatized for deviant behaviors that they may no longer practice. The labels "former gambler," "ex-convict," and "ex–mental patient" can stick to a person for life. Goffman draws a useful distinction between a prestige symbol that calls attention to a positive aspect of one's identity, such as a wedding band or a badge, and a stigma symbol that discredits or debases one's identity, such as a conviction for child molestation. Although stigma symbols may not always be obvious, they can become a matter of public knowledge. Starting in 1994, many states required convicted sex offenders to register with local police departments. Some communities publish the names and addresses, and in some instances even the pictures, of convicted sex offenders on the web.

Being stigmatized can limit a person's opportunities. For example, people who are homeless often have trouble getting a job because employers are wary of applicants who cannot provide a home address. Though many hiring agencies use a telephone for contacts, cell phones are expensive, and owning one while homeless is often looked at with suspicion by others. If a homeless person has access to a telephone at a shelter, the staff generally answers by announcing the name of the institution, which discourages prospective employers from hiring the applicant. And, even if the person is hired, the stigma attached to homelessness, should the employee's past or present situation become known, can negatively impact opportunities, even in the face of positive work performance.

>> Crime

If deviance means breaking group norms, **crime** is a violation of criminal law for which some governmental authority applies formal penalties. It is a type of deviance representing a violation of social norms administered by the state. Laws divide crimes into various categories, depending on the severity of the offense, the age of the offender, the potential punishment, and the court that holds jurisdiction over the case.

crime A violation of criminal law for which some governmental authority applies formal penalties.

OFFICIAL CRIME REPORTS

When we think of crime, the categories most likely to come to mind involve what we might think of as street crimes. The FBI breaks such crimes into two major categories: violent

National Crime Rates and Percentage Change

Offenses in 2013	Number reported	Rate per 100,000 inhabitants	Percentage change in rate since 2004
Murder	14,196	4.5	−18.3
Violent crimes Forcible rape	79,770	25.2	−22.1
Robbery	345,031	109	−20.2
Aggravated assault	724,149	229	−20.6
Total	1,163,146	368	−20.6
Burglary	1,928,465	610	−16.5
Property crimes Larceny-theft	6,004,453	1,899	−19.6
Motor vehicle theft	699,594	221	−47.5
Total	8,632,512	2,731	−22.3

= 10,000 Offenses

Note: Insufficient data are available on arson to estimate accurate totals. Because of rounding, the offenses may not add to totals.

Source: U.S. Department of Justice 2014a: Tables 1, 1A.
Photo: © D. Hurst/Alamy.

Crimes Reported to Police

Percentage reported to police

- 46% Total violent crime
- 64% Aggravated assault
- 68% Robbery
- 35% Rape/sexual assault
- 39% Simple assault
- 36% Total property crime
- 76% Motor vehicle theft
- 57% Burglary
- 29% Larceny-theft

Note: Percentages based on the National Crime Victimization Survey for 2013.
Source: Truman and Langton 2014: Table 6.   *Photo:* © McGraw-Hill Companies.

crimes and property crimes. They do not include all types of crime in these reports, focusing only on four major types within each category. Violent crimes include murder, forcible rape, robbery, and aggravated assault; property crimes include burglary, larceny-theft, motor vehicle theft, and arson. The FBI provides an annual account of the number of these crimes in its *Uniform Crime Reports* (UCR), which is available online. Because they

index crimes The eight types of crime reported annually by the FBI in the *Uniform Crime Reports:* murder, forcible rape, robbery, aggravated assault, burglary, larceny-theft, motor vehicle theft, and arson.

victimization survey A questionnaire or interview given to a sample of the population to determine whether people have been victims of crime.

are tracked so closely by the FBI and have been for a long time, these crimes have come to be known as **index crimes.**

As we can see in the "National Crime Rates and Percentage Change" table, property crimes occur at a much higher rate than do violent crimes. In fact, according to the "crime clock" that the FBI provides as part of its report, a property crime occurs on average every 3.7 seconds. The most frequent property crime is larceny-theft, which includes incidents such as shoplifting and stealing items from cars. By contrast, a violent crime occurs every 27.1 seconds. Robbery, which involves the use or threat of force, is the most frequent violent crime, with one occurring every 1.5 minutes. Murder is the least frequent of the index crimes, with one occurring every 37 minutes (U.S. Department of Justice 2014b).

Trends in Crime Crime rates vary over time, and sociologists seek to explain factors that contribute to these changes. In the past ten years, as indicated in the "National Crime Rates and Percentage Changes" figure, crime rates have fallen in every major category. Murder rates, for example, have declined 18.3 percent since 2004 (U.S. Department of Justice 2014a:Table 1a). To explain these trends, sociologists would seek to identify possible causal factors, including the potential effects of

- The overall aging of the population, because people are more likely to commit crimes when they are young;
- Changes in the economy, including the economic downturn starting in 2008;
- The expansion of community-oriented policing and crime prevention programs;
- Increased incarceration rates, removing potential offenders from the streets;
- New prison education programs designed to reduce the number of repeat offenders.

Knowledge of the impact of these and other possible factors would help us establish more effective policies designed to further reduce the crime rate in the future.

Victimization Surveys Because not all crimes that are committed are reported to the police, the UCR underestimates the actual number of crimes. In the case of larceny-theft, for example, people may conclude that, because there is little chance of getting stolen items back, it simply isn't worth the hassle. More significantly, members of racial and ethnic minority groups often distrust law enforcement

SOC THINK

The Clery Act, passed in 1990, requires schools to provide students with timely reports of campus crimes. How much do you trust official campus crime reports? Why might reports of crime on college campuses underestimate the actual number of incidents?

agencies and may not contact the police when they are victimized. Further, many women do not report rape or spousal abuse out of fear they will be blamed for the crime.

To address such deficiencies in official statistics, the U.S. Department of Justice conducts its annual National Crime Victimization Survey. **Victimization surveys** are questionnaires or interviews given to a sample of the population to determine whether people have been victims of crime. In their yearly report, Department of Justice officials draw on interviews with more than 70,000 people in over 40,000 households in the United States. They interview each household in their sample twice during the given year. Over 90 percent of selected households agree to participate (Truman and Langton 2014).

Results from the National Crime Victimization Survey demonstrate significant variability in which types of crimes are reported to police. As shown in the "Crimes Reported to Police" graph, motor vehicle theft is the most likely to be reported, with 76 percent of victims contacting the authorities. Larceny-theft is the least likely at 29 percent. When it comes to violent crimes, only about one-half of victims contact the police (Truman and Langton 2014:Table 6). What these numbers suggest is that a substantial amount of crime goes unreported and, as such, many offenses never see justice served within the U.S. legal system.

5 Movies on CRIME

Dallas Buyers Club
A cowboy turned drug dealer saves lives.

The House I Live In
The war on drugs and the price we pay.

The Town
Bank robbery as a way of life in South Boston.

American Hustle
Power, politics, and corruption.

Girl with the Dragon Tattoo
A journalist and a young computer hacker search for a woman who has been missing for 40 years.

Another limitation of the UCR official statistics is that they exclude many offenses that we would count as criminal. In so doing, they minimize the degree to which we see perpetrators of other types of crime as criminal in the same way as violators of the index crimes. We turn next to several such categories, including white-collar crime, victimless crimes, and organized crime.

WHITE-COLLAR CRIME

Income tax evasion, stock manipulation, consumer fraud, bribery and extraction of kickbacks, embezzlement, and misrepresentation in advertising—these are all examples of **white-collar crime,** or illegal acts committed in the course of business activities, often by affluent, "respectable" people. Historically, we have viewed such crimes

SOCTHINK

Should gambling, prostitution, and recreational drugs be legalized? What are the potential consequences, both positive and negative, of doing so?

differently because they are often perpetrated through respected occupational roles (Sutherland 1949, 1983).

Sociologist Edwin Sutherland (1940) coined the term *white-collar crime* to refer to acts by individuals, but the term is now used more broadly to include offenses by businesses and corporations as well. Corporate crime, or any act by a corporation that is punishable by the government, takes many forms and includes individuals, organizations, and institutions among its victims. Corporations may engage in anticompetitive behavior, environmental pollution, medical fraud, tax fraud, stock fraud and manipulation, accounting fraud, the production of unsafe goods, bribery and corruption, and health and safety violations (Coleman 2006).

The downfall of Bernie Madoff represents the largest case of white-collar crime of its type in history. Madoff, an American businessman who managed people's financial investments, promised investors annual returns of 15 to 20 percent and delivered on that promise for years. This enabled him to attract extremely wealthy clients from around the world, even charitable organizations. In the end, he was just running a scam. Madoff had provided investors with false statements showing nonexistent trades and profits. Estimates are that he defrauded his clients out of $65 billion in purported assets. Life savings and family fortunes were gone in an instant (Gaviria and Smith 2009).

The scheme collapsed in December 2008, after Madoff confessed to his sons that his investment company was a "giant Ponzi scheme." After consulting an attorney, they reported their father to the FBI. Madoff was arrested the next day. In a Ponzi scheme, the fraudulent investor uses money from new investors to pay off old ones rather than investing the money. The payoff is at higher-than-average rates of return, which encourages new investors who are attracted by the profits. The whole system topples if current investors want to pull their money out, or if there aren't enough new investors to cover profits and payouts to existing investors. Both happened with the economic collapse in late 2008. On March 12, 2009, Madoff pled guilty to 11 felony counts, including securities fraud, mail fraud, money laundering, and perjury. He was sent directly to jail and was sentenced to the maximum of 150 years in prison (Henriques and Healy 2009).

What is particularly interesting about the Madoff case is that officials at the Securities and Exchange Commission (SEC) were tipped off numerous times to the possibility that Madoff's investments were a scam. Finally, after receiving documented accusations that he was running a Ponzi scheme, the SEC launched an official investigation in 2006. Two years later they concluded that there was "no evidence of fraud." The SEC failed to see what analysts now say should have

white-collar crime Illegal acts committed by affluent, "respectable" individuals in the course of business activities.

victimless crime Acts involving the willing exchange among adults of widely desired, but illegal, goods and services.

organized crime The work of a group that regulates relations among criminal enterprises involved in illegal activities, including prostitution, gambling, and the smuggling and sale of illegal drugs.

been obvious. Red flags were ignored, but why? Sociologists suggest that white-collar criminals are often given the benefit of the doubt. In fact, during each previous investigation, Madoff deliberately and successfully used his status as a respected businessman as evidence of his innocence. He might have avoided detection had it not been for his own confession (Berenson and Henriques 2008).

VICTIMLESS CRIMES

Another category of crimes that raises questions about how we define deviance consists of so-called victimless crimes. **Victimless crime** refers to the willing exchange among adults of widely desired, but illegal, goods and services, such as drugs or prostitution (Schur 1965, 1985). The fact that the parties involved are willing participants has led some people to suggest that such transactions should not constitute crimes.

> You come at the king, you best not miss.

Omar Little, *The Wire*

Some activists are working to decriminalize many of these illegal practices. Supporters of decriminalization are troubled by the attempt to legislate a moral code for adults. In their view, prostitution, drug use, gambling, and other victimless crimes are expensive to enforce and impossible to prevent. The already overburdened criminal justice system should instead devote its resources to "street crimes" and other offenses with obvious victims.

Despite widespread use of the term *victimless crime*, however, many people object to the notion that there is no victim other than the offender in such crimes. Excessive drinking, compulsive gambling, and illegal drug use contribute to an enormous amount of personal and property damage. A person with a drinking problem can become abusive to a spouse or children; a compulsive gambler or drug user may steal to pursue his or her obsession. Feminist sociologists contend that prostitution, as well as the more disturbing aspects of pornography, reinforce the misconception that women are "toys" who can be treated as objects rather than people. According to critics of decriminalization, society must not give tacit approval to conduct that has such harmful consequences (Farley and Malarek 2008; Meier and Geis 1997).

POPSOC

The HBO series *The Wire* has been widely praised for its realistic portrayal of urban life in Baltimore including its coverage of drugs, gangs, and law enforcement. A growing number of sociologists teach courses based on the show to demonstrate lessons about community, crime, poverty, and corruption. Sociologist William Julius Wilson, who teaches such a course at Harvard, maintains, "Although *The Wire* is fiction, not a documentary, its depiction of [the] systemic urban inequality that constrains the lives of the urban poor is more poignant and compelling [than] that of any published study, including my own" (D. Bennett 2010).

Photo: © HBO/Courtesy Everett Collection.

ORGANIZED CRIME

When it comes to organized crime, the name Tony Soprano is the first that comes to mind for many people. He was the fictional boss of the DiMeo crime family on HBO's classic series *The Sopranos*. In real life, examples of organized crime groups go beyond the Mafia to include the Japanese Yakuza, the Russian Organization, Colombian drug cartels, and many other international crime syndicates. **Organized crime** is the work of a group that regulates relations among criminal enterprises involved in illegal activities, including prostitution, gambling, and the smuggling and sale of illegal drugs (National Institute of Justice 2007).

Organized crime dominates the world of illegal business, just as large corporations dominate the conventional business world. It allocates territory, sets prices for goods and services, and acts as an arbiter in internal disputes. A secret, conspiratorial activity, organized crime generally evades law enforcement. It takes over legitimate businesses, gains influence over labor unions, corrupts public officials, intimidates witnesses in criminal trials, and even "taxes" merchants in exchange for "protection" (Federal Bureau of Investigation 2012).

Historically, organized crime has provided a means of upward mobility for groups of people struggling to escape poverty. Sociologist Daniel Bell (1953) used the term *ethnic succession* to describe the sequential passage of leadership from Irish Americans in the early 1900s to Jewish Americans in the 1920s and then to Italian Americans in the early 1930s. Recently, ethnic succession has become

Going GLOBAL

International Incarceration Rates

Rank
out of 222 nations

International incarceration rates
(prison population rates per 100,000 of the national population)

Rank	Nation	Rate
1	Seychelles	868
2	United States	707
10	Russian Federation	467
34	South Africa	290
51	Israel	240
62	Mexico	214
98	England and Wales	148
123	China	124
124	Kenya	121
128	Canada	118
190	Sweden	57
198	Japan	50
212	India	33

Source: International Centre for Prison Studies 2015.   *Photo:* © Trista Weibell/Getty Images RF.

governments did not regard slavery as a crime but merely regulated it as they would trade in any other good. In the 20th century, transnational crime grew to include trafficking in endangered species, drugs, and stolen art and antiquities.

Transnational crime is not exclusive of some of the other types of crime we have discussed. For example, organized criminal networks are increasingly global. Technology definitely facilitates their illegal activities, such as trafficking in child pornography. The United Nations tracks a variety of transnational crimes, such as trafficking in persons, smuggling migrants, drug trafficking, counterfeiting, and cybercrime (UNODC 2010).

One way to fight such crime has been through multilateral cooperation in which countries cooperate to pursue border-crossing crime. The first global effort to control international crime was the International Criminal Police Organization (Interpol), a cooperative network of European police forces founded to stem the movement of political revolutionaries across borders. Although such efforts to fight transnational crime may seem lofty—an activity with which any government would want to cooperate—they are complicated by sensitive legal and security issues. Most nations that have signed protocols issued by the United Nations, including the United States, have expressed concern over potential encroachments on their national judicial systems, as well as concern over their national security. Thus, they have been reluctant to share certain types of intelligence data. The terrorist attacks of September 11, 2001, increased both the interest in combating transnational crime and sensitivity to the risks of sharing intelligence data (Deflem 2005; Felson and Kalaitzidis 2005).

transnational crime Crime that occurs across multiple national borders.

International Crime Rates Taking an international perspective on crime reinforces one of the key sociological lessons about crime and deviance: place matters. Although cross-national data comparison can be difficult, we can offer insight about how crime rates differ around the world.

Violent crimes tend to be much more common in the United States than in the nations of western Europe. Murders, rapes, and robberies were reported to the police at much higher rates in the United States. Yet the incidence of certain other types of crime appears to be higher elsewhere. For example, England, Italy, Australia, and New Zealand all have higher rates of car theft than the United States. Developing nations have significant rates of reported homicide due to civil unrest and political conflict among civilians (van Dijk, van Kesteren, and Smit 2007; World Bank 2003). But when it comes to putting offenders in jail, the United States tops them all. On a typical day, the United States imprisons 707 of every 100,000 adults, compared to 467

more complex, reflecting the diversity of the nation's latest immigrants. Colombian, Mexican, Russian, Chinese, Pakistani, and Nigerian immigrants are among those who have begun to play a significant role in organized crime activities (Friman 2004; Kleinknecht 1996).

There has always been a global element in organized crime. However, law enforcement officials and policy makers now acknowledge the emergence of a new form of organized crime that takes advantage of advances in electronic communications. International organized crime includes drug and arms smuggling, money laundering, and trafficking in illegal immigrants and stolen goods (Lumpe 2003; National Institute of Justice 2007).

INTERNATIONAL CRIME

In the past, international crime was often limited to the clandestine shipment of goods across the border between two countries. Increasingly, however, crime is no more restricted by such borders than is legal commerce. Rather than concentrating on specific countries, international crime now spans the globe.

Transnational Crime More and more, scholars and law enforcement officials are turning their attention to **transnational crime,** or crime that occurs across multiple national borders. Historically, probably the most dreaded example of transnational crime has been slavery. At first, in Russia, 214 in Mexico, and 118 in Canada (International Centre for Prison Studies 2015).

Why are rates of violent crime so much higher in the United States than in western Europe? Sociologist Elliot Currie (1985, 1998) has suggested that U.S. society places greater emphasis on individual economic achievement than other societies. At the same time, many observers have noted that the culture of the United States has long tolerated, if not condoned, many forms of violence. Coupled with sharp disparities between poor and affluent citizens, significant unemployment, and substantial alcohol and drug abuse, these factors combine to produce a climate conducive to crime.

Violent crime remains a serious problem in nations around the world. In Mexico, for example, approximately 60 percent of the 18,146 homicides in 2013 were attributed to drug trafficking and organized crime (Heinle, Ferreira, and Shirk 2014). Attacks have been especially concentrated in the Mexican states of Chihuahua, Sinaloa, Guerrero, and Jalisco. The violence is a consequence, in part, of governmental attempts to crack down on the illegal drug trade. After his election in 2006, President Felipe Calderón sent in tens of thousands of troops to enforce the law. As a result, drug cartels fought both the authorities and one another in a struggle to maintain their local power (Camp 2010a, 2010b).

>> Sociological Perspectives on Deviance and Crime

Why do people violate social norms? We have seen that deviant acts are subject to both informal and formal social control. The nonconforming or disobedient person may face disapproval, loss of friends, fines, or even imprisonment. Why, then, does deviance occur?

Sociologists have been interested in crime and deviance from the very beginning and have generated numerous theories of deviance and crime. Though we might wish otherwise, there is no one, simple, universal theory that explains all such acts. Here we look to just a few of the theories that sociologists have offered in order to identify significant factors that we must consider in our attempt to understand deviance and crime more fully.

FUNCTIONS OF DEVIANCE

Émile Durkheim's ([1895] 1964) emphasis on the importance of social order led him to investigate the nature and causes of deviance and crime. He wondered why deviance, which would seem to undermine order, is found in all societies. For Durkheim the answer rested with how such actions were perceived by others.

Durkheim's Theory of Deviance Durkheim argued that there is nothing inherently deviant or criminal in any act; the key is how society responds to the act. He put it this way: "We must not say that an action shocks the common consciousness because it is criminal, but rather that it is criminal because it shocks that consciousness" ([1895] 1964:123–24). In other words, nothing is criminal or worthy of condemnation unless we decide it is. For example, we do not regard killing in self-defense or in combat in the same way we view killing in cold blood. At least, that is the case until we change our minds about how we view wartime killing, as has happened at various times in our past. When it comes to war, for example, our attitudes about what is appropriate can shift. In both Vietnam and Iraq, strong public support gave way to serious misgivings about U.S. involvement in these nations. In both cases, this was driven in part by images from the conflict, including, for example, the killing of civilians at My Lai and the treatment of prisoners at Abu Ghraib. In this way, our understanding of what constitutes deviance and crime is tied to issues of social solidarity.

In fact, Durkheim concluded that deviance and crime actually can have a positive impact on society in a variety of ways. For example, identifying acts as deviant clarifies our shared beliefs and values and thus brings us closer together. We say, in effect, "This is who we are, and if you want to be one of us you cannot cross this line. Some things we might let go, but if you push the limits too far you will face sanctions." Punishment, too, can draw a group together, uniting members in their opposition to the offender. Sanctions also discourage others from similar violations, thus increasing conformity. When we see a driver receiving a speeding ticket, a department store cashier being fired for yelling at a customer, or a college

Movies on DEVIANCE

5

Trainspotting
Scottish youths struggle with unemployment, dissatisfying relationships, and addiction.

Girl, Interrupted
A young girl enters a mental institution during the 1960s.

Compliance
When it comes to obedience, how far would you go?

The Dark Knight Rises
The Dark Knight resurfaces after eight years of hiding to protect the city of Gotham from a brutal terrorist, Bane.

Ghost World
A prank by two outcast teenagers takes an unexpected turn.

student getting a failing grade for plagiarizing a term paper, we are reminded of our collective norms and values and of the consequences of their violation. Finally, Durkheim did recognize that deviant acts might also force us to recognize the limits of our existing beliefs and practices, opening up new doors and leading to cultural innovation.

Based on Durkheim's analysis, it is possible to conclude that all societies identify criminals for the sake of social order. No matter how much unity a society might appear to have, there will always be some who push the limits. Regardless of how "good" such people may appear to be to outsiders, they may face sanction within the group for the good of the whole.

Durkheim did, however, also recognize that some social circumstances increase the likelihood of turning toward deviance and crime. As we have already seen, Durkheim ([1897] 1951) introduced the term *anomie* into the sociological literature to describe the loss of direction felt in a society when social control of individual behavior has become ineffective. Anomie is a state of normlessness that typically occurs during a period of profound social change and disorder, such as a time

> ## Law and justice are not always the same.
>
> Gloria Steinem

SOCTHINK

Durkheim argues that increased division of labor results in fewer shared experiences and thus a weakened sense of community. What impact might a strong commitment to individualism have on our likelihood of committing crime?

---

of economic collapse, political or social revolution, or even sudden prosperity. The power of society to constrain deviant action at such times is limited because there is no clear consensus on shared norms and values. Just as we saw with Durkheim's analysis of suicide, at times when social integration is weak, people are freer to pursue their own deviant paths.

Merton's Theory of Deviance

Sociologist Robert Merton (1968) took Durkheim's theory a step further. He suggested that a disconnect can exist between a society's goals and the means people have to attain them. By *goals* he meant the dominant

values that most members of a society share, and by *means* he meant the material, social, and cultural resources necessary for success. He did not assume that all people in a society would be equally committed to those values. He also did not assume that everyone would have the same opportunity to attain those goals. Putting these together, he developed the **strain theory of deviance,** which views deviance as an adaptation of socially prescribed goals or of the means governing their attainment, or both.

> **strain theory of deviance**
> Merton's theory of deviance as an adaptation of socially prescribed goals or of the means governing their attainment, or both.

We can better understand Merton's model by looking at economic success as an important goal in the United States. Socially agreed upon pathways exist in order to attain that goal—go to school, work hard, do not quit, take advantage of opportunities, and so forth. Merton wondered what happened when someone who shared the goal of economic success lacked the means to attain that end. For example, a mugger and a merchant may share a common goal of making money, but their means of attaining it are radically different. Merton put together various combinations of goals and means and developed a model with five possible adaptations.

Conformity to social norms, the most common adaptation in Merton's typology, is the opposite of deviance. The "conformist" accepts both the overall societal goal (for example, to become wealthy) and the approved means (hard work). In Merton's view, there must be some consensus regarding accepted cultural goals and the legitimate means for attaining them. Without such a consensus, societies could exist only as collectives of people rather than as unified cultures, and they might experience continual chaos.

The other four types of behavior all involve some departure from conformity. The "innovator" accepts the goals of society but pursues them with means that are regarded as improper. For instance, a safecracker may steal money to buy consumer goods and take expensive vacations.

In Merton's typology, the "ritualist" has abandoned the goal of material success and become compulsively committed to the institutional means. Work becomes simply a way of life rather than a means to the goal of success. An example would be the bureaucratic official who blindly applies rules

Merton's Typology of Deviance

	Institutionalized Means	
	Accept	Reject
Cultural Goals Accept	Conformist	Innovator
Cultural Goals Reject	Ritualist	Retreatist
New Goals		Rebel (New Means)

Source: Merton, 1968. *Photo:* © Kobal Foundation/Getty Images.

and regulations without remembering the larger goals of the organization. Certainly, that would be true of a welfare caseworker who refuses to assist a homeless family because their last apartment was in another district.

The "retreatist," as described by Merton, has basically withdrawn (or retreated) from both the goals and the means of society. In the United States, drug addicts and vagrants are typically portrayed as retreatists. Concern has been growing that adolescents who are addicted to alcohol will become retreatists at an early age.

The final adaptation identified by Merton reflects people's attempts to create a *new* social structure. The "rebel" feels alienated from the dominant means and goals and may seek a dramatically different social order. Members of a revolutionary political organization, such as a militia group, can be categorized as rebels according to Merton's model.

Merton's theory, though popular, does not fully account for patterns of deviance and crime. Although it is useful in explaining certain types of behavior, such as illegal gambling by disadvantaged "innovators," it fails to explain key differences in crime rates. Why, for example, do some disadvantaged groups have lower rates of reported crime than others? Why do many people in adverse circumstances reject criminal activity as a viable alternative? Merton's theory does not easily answer such questions (Clinard and Miller 1998). To more fully appreciate such nuances, we must add to what we can learn from Merton by turning to additional theories that seek to better understand deviance and crime at an interpersonal level.

cultural transmission A school of criminology that argues criminal behavior is learned through social interactions.

differential association A theory of deviance that holds violation of rules results from exposure to attitudes favorable to criminal acts.

INTERPERSONAL INTERACTION AND DEFINING DEVIANCE

Perhaps the likelihood of committing deviant acts is not solely shaped by social integration or the acceptance of society's larger goals and means to attain them. Maybe parents around the world were right all along that it really does depend on who your friends are. If we are to understand and explain such acts, we must also consider the importance of social interaction and the local context.

Cultural Transmission As humans, we learn how to behave in social situations, whether properly or improperly. Sociologist Edwin Sutherland (1883–1950) proposed that, just as individuals are socialized to conform to society's basic norms and values, so also are they socialized to learn deviant acts. It's not that we are born to be wild; we learn to be wild.

Sutherland drew on the **cultural transmission** school, which emphasizes that individuals learn criminal behavior by interacting with others. Such learning includes not only the techniques of lawbreaking (for example, how to break into a car quickly and quietly), but also the motives, drives, and rationalizations of the criminal. The cultural transmission approach can also be used to explain the behavior of those who habitually abuse alcohol or drugs.

Sutherland maintained that through interactions with a primary group and significant others, people acquire definitions of proper and improper behavior. He used the term **differential association** to describe the process through which exposure to attitudes favorable to criminal acts leads to the violation of rules. Research suggests that this view of differential association also applies to noncriminal deviant acts, such as smoking, binge drinking, and cheating (Higgins, Tewksbury, and Mustaine, 2007; Nofziger and Hye-Ryeon 2006; Vowell and Chen 2004).

To what extent will a given person engage in an activity that is regarded as proper or improper? For each individual, it will depend on the frequency, duration, and importance of two types of social interaction—those experiences that endorse deviant behavior and those that promote acceptance of social norms. People are more likely to engage in norm-defying behavior if they are part of a group or subculture that stresses deviant values, such as a street gang.

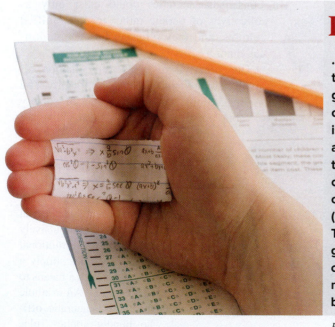

Did You Know?

... In a 2006 survey of more than 5,000 students at 32 graduate schools, 56 percent of master of business administration (MBA) students admitted to cheating within the past academic year. This contrasted with 47 percent of nonbusiness students (D. McCabe, Butterfield, and Treviño 2006). Considering goals and means, into which category of Merton's model might those MBA students belong?

Photo: © 2009 Jupiterimages RF.

Sutherland offers the example of a boy who is sociable, outgoing, and athletic and who lives in an area with a high rate of delinquency. The youth is very likely to come into contact with peers who commit acts of vandalism, fail to attend school, and so forth, and he may come to adopt such behavior. However, an introverted boy who lives in the same neighborhood may stay away from his peers and avoid delinquency. In another community, an outgoing and athletic boy may join a Little League baseball team or a scout troop because of his interactions with peers. Thus, Sutherland views improper behavior as the result of the types of groups to which one belongs and the kinds of friendships one has (Sutherland, Cressey, and Luckenbill 1992).

Although the cultural transmission approach may not explain the conduct of the first-time, impulsive shoplifter or the impoverished person who steals out of necessity, it does help explain the deviant behavior of juvenile delinquents or graffiti artists. It directs our attention to the paramount role of social interaction and context in increasing a person's motivation to engage in deviant behavior (Morselli, Tremblay, and McCarthy 2006; Sutherland et al. 1992).

Social Disorganization Theory The relative strength of social relationships in a community or neighborhood influences the behavior of its members. Social psychologist Philip Zimbardo (2007) studied the effect of these communal relationships by conducting the following experiment. He abandoned a car in each of two different neighborhoods, leaving its hood up and removing its hubcaps. In one neighborhood, people started to strip the car for parts even before Zimbardo had finished setting up a remote video camera to record their behavior. In the other neighborhood, weeks passed without the car being touched, except for a pedestrian who stopped to close the hood during a rainstorm.

Social disorganization theory attributes increases in crime and deviance to the absence or breakdown of communal relationships and social institutions, such as the family, school, church, and local government. The lack of such local community connections, with their associated

© Janine Wiedel Photography/Alamy

cross-age relationships, makes it difficult to exert informal control within the community, especially of children. Without community supervision and controls, playing outside becomes an opportunity for deviance and for older violators to socialize children into inappropriate paths. Crime becomes a normal response to a local context.

This theory was developed at the University of Chicago in the early 1900s to describe the apparent disorganization that occurred as cities expanded with immigrants from abroad and migrants from rural areas. Using precise survey techniques, Clifford Shaw and Henry McKay (1969) literally mapped the distribution of social problems in Chicago. They found high rates of social problems in neighborhoods where buildings had deteriorated and the population had declined. Interestingly, the patterns persisted over time, despite changes in the neighborhoods' ethnic and racial composition.

> **social disorganization theory** The theory that attributes increases in crime and deviance to the absence or breakdown of communal relationships and social institutions, such as the family, school, church, and local government.

Labeling Theory Sometimes when it comes to deviance, what you see determines what you get. The Saints and Roughnecks were two groups of high school males who were continually engaged in excessive drinking, reckless driving, truancy, petty theft, and vandalism. There the similarity ended. None of the Saints was ever arrested, but every Roughneck was frequently in trouble with police and townspeople. Why the disparity in their treatment? On the basis of observation research in their high school, sociologist William Chambliss (1973) concluded that how they were seen, as rooted in their social class positions, played an important role in the varying fortunes of the two groups.

The Saints hid behind a facade of respectability. They came from "good families," were active in school organizations, planned on attending college, and received good grades. People generally viewed their delinquent acts as a few isolated cases of sowing wild oats. The Roughnecks had no such aura of respectability. They drove around town in beat-up cars, were generally unsuccessful in school, and aroused suspicion no matter what they did.

We can understand such discrepancies by using an approach to deviance known as **labeling theory,** which emphasizes how a person comes to be labeled as deviant or to accept that label. Unlike Sutherland's work, labeling theory does not focus on why some individuals come to commit deviant acts. Instead, it attempts to explain why society views certain people (such as the Roughnecks) as deviants, delinquents, bad kids, losers, and criminals, while it sees others whose behavior is similar (such as the Saints) in less harsh terms. Sociologist Howard Becker (1963:9; 1964), who popularized this approach, summed up labeling theory with this statement: "Deviant behavior is behavior that people so label."

Labeling theory is also called the **societal-reaction approach,** reminding us that it is the response to an act, not the act itself, that determines deviance. Traditionally, research on deviance has focused on people who violate social norms. In contrast, labeling theory focuses on police, probation officers, psychiatrists, judges, teachers, employers, school officials, and other regulators of social control. These agents, it is argued, play a significant role in creating the deviant identity by designating certain people (and not others) as deviant (Bernburg, Krohn, and Rivera 2006). An important aspect of labeling theory is the recognition that some individuals or groups have the power to define

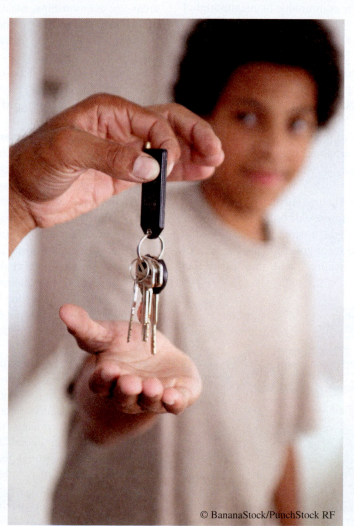

© BananaStock/PunchStock RF

labels and apply them to others. This view ties into the conflict perspective's emphasis on the social significance of power.

In recent years, the practice of racial profiling, in which people are identified as criminal suspects purely on the basis of their race, has come under public scrutiny. Studies confirm the public's suspicion that in some jurisdictions, police officers are much more likely to stop African American males than White males for routine traffic violations, in the expectation of finding drugs or guns in their cars. Civil rights activists refer to these cases sarcastically as DWB (Driving While Black) violations (Warren et al. 2006). The deaths of three young African American men—Trayvon Martin in Sanford, Florida; Michael Brown in Ferguson, Missouri; and Eric Garner in New York City—raised substantial concerns about the life-and-death consequences of labeling young African American males as threats.

Although the labeling approach does not fully explain why certain people accept a label and others manage to reject it, labeling theorists do suggest that the power an individual has relative to others is important in determining his or her ability to resist an undesirable label. It opens the door to additional emphasis on the undeniably important actions of people with power who can shape what counts as deviance.

CONFLICT, POWER, AND CRIMINALITY

In addition to its significance for labeling theory, the story of the Saints and Roughnecks points toward the role that power and control over valued resources can play in defining deviance. Sociologist Richard Quinney (1974, 1979, 1980) is a leading proponent of the view that the criminal justice system serves the interests of the powerful; people with power protect their own interests and define deviance to suit their own needs. Crime, according to Quinney (1970), is defined as such by legislators who may be influenced by the economic elites to advance their interests.

Executions by State Since 1976

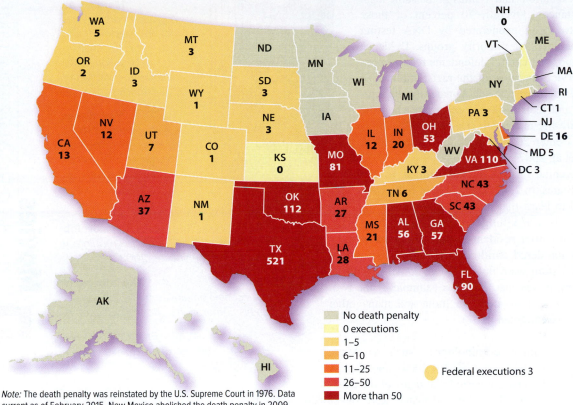

No death penalty	
0 executions	
1–5	
6–10	
11–25	
26–50	Federal executions 3
More than 50	

Note: The death penalty was reinstated by the U.S. Supreme Court in 1976. Data current as of February 2015. New Mexico abolished the death penalty in 2009.

Source: Death Penalty Information Center 2015.

Race and Class Looking at crime from this perspective draws our attention to the effects that power and position might have throughout the criminal justice system in the United States. Researchers have found that the system treats suspects differently based on their racial, ethnic, or social class background. In many cases, officials using their own discretion make biased decisions about whether to press charges or drop them, whether to set bail and how much, and whether to offer parole or deny it. Researchers have found that this kind of **differential justice**—differences in the way social control is exercised over different groups—puts African Americans and Latinos at a disadvantage in the justice system, both as juveniles and as adults. On average, White offenders receive shorter sentences than comparable Latino and African American offenders, even when prior arrest records and the relative severity of the crime are taken into consideration (Brewer and Heitzeg 2008; Quinney 1974).

We see this pattern of differential justice at work with death penalty cases. Simply put, poor people cannot afford to hire the best lawyer and often must rely on court-appointed attorneys, who typically are overworked and underpaid. With capital punishment in place, these unequal resources may mean the difference between life and death for poor defendants. Indeed, the American Bar Association (2009) has repeatedly expressed concern about the limited defense most defendants facing the death penalty receive. Through mid-2015, DNA analysis and other new technologies had exonerated 20 death row inmates and 325 inmates total with an average of 13.5 years served in prison. Thirty-one of the exonerees pleaded guilty to crimes they did not commit. Overall, 63 percent of those found innocent were African American (Innocence Project 2015).

Various studies show that defendants are more likely to be sentenced to death if their victims were White rather than Black. Approximately 76 percent of the victims in death penalty cases are White, even though about half of *all* murder victims are White. There is some evidence that

> **differential justice** Differences in the way social control is exercised over different groups.

> ### Whenever you find yourself on the side of the majority, it is time to pause and reflect.
>
> Mark Twain

Black defendants, who constituted 42 percent of all death row inmates in 2014, are more likely to face execution than Whites in the same legal circumstances. Overall, 70 percent of those who have been exonerated by DNA testing were members of minority groups. Evidence exists, too, that capital defendants receive poor legal services because of the racist attitudes of their own defense counsel. Apparently, discrimination and racism do not end even when the stakes are life and death (Death Penalty Information Center 2015; Innocence Project 2015; Jacobs et al. 2007).

Differential justice is not limited to the United States. In 2007, the people of India were alarmed to learn that police had never investigated a series of killings in the slums of New Delhi. Only after residents found 17 bodies of recently murdered children in a sewer drain on the edge of a slum were police moved to act. For many onlookers, it was just the latest example of the two-tier justice system found in India and many other countries (Gentleman 2007).

Gender Feminist criminologists such as Meda Chesney-Lind (with Lisa Pasko 2004) and Gillian Balfour (2006) have suggested that many of the existing approaches to deviance and crime were developed with only men in mind. For example, in the United States, for many years any husband who forced his wife to have sexual intercourse—without her consent and against her will—was not legally considered to have committed rape. The law defined rape as pertaining only to sexual relations between people who were not married to each other, reflecting the overwhelmingly male composition of state legislatures at the time.

It took repeated protests by feminist organizations to get changes in the criminal law defining rape. It was not until 1993 that husbands in all 50 states could be prosecuted under most circumstances for the rape of their wives. However, significant exceptions remain in no fewer than 30 states. For example, the husband is exempt when

5 Movies on ORGANIZED CRIME/CORPORATE CRIME

Margin Call
A group of employees at an investment firm react to sensitive information in the immediate wake of the 2008 financial collapse.

Wall Street
A young stockbroker gets swept away with greed and insider trading on his ruthless climb to the top of the corporate ladder.

Inside Job
A documentary detailing the lax regulatory environment behind the 2008 recession.

The Informant!
An eccentric employee blows the whistle on his corporation's price-fixing scheme.

Eastern Promises
The inner workings of the Russian mafia.

he does not need to use force because his wife is asleep, unconscious, or mentally or physically impaired. In such cases, the presupposition is that the husband has a right to nonconsensual sex with his wife (Bergen 2006).

When it comes to crime and to deviance in general, society tends to treat women in a stereotypical fashion. For example, consider how women who have many and frequent sexual partners are more likely to be viewed with scorn than men who are promiscuous. Cultural views and attitudes toward women influence how they are perceived and labeled. The feminist perspective also emphasizes that deviance, including crime, tends to flow from economic relationships. Traditionally, men have had greater earning power than their wives. As a result, wives may be reluctant to report acts of abuse to the authorities and thereby lose what may be their primary or even sole source of income. In the workplace, men have exercised greater power than women in pricing, accounting, and product control, giving them greater opportunity to engage in such crimes as embezzlement and fraud. But as women have taken more active and powerful roles both in the household and in business, these gender differences in deviance and crime have narrowed (Bisi 2002; Chesney-Lind 1989; Kruttschnitt and Carbone-Lopez 2006).

SOCIOLOGY IS A VERB

Observing Justice

Visit a local courthouse to observe a trial in action. If possible, stay for several cases in different courts. What do you observe about the key players, including the defendants, attorneys, judge, and witnesses? Drawing on Goffman's dramaturgical analysis, in what ways are the performances staged? What scripts and props are used? How does the trial you observed compare to trials portrayed in television dramas or on cable news channels?

Together, sociological perspectives on crime and deviance help us better understand and explain such acts. No single explanation is sufficient. We must consider multiple factors from a variety of perspectives, including the extent to which deviance exists for the sake of social order; the degree of opportunity to attain both means and ends; the role of socialization in deviance; the strength of local community networks; the power to administer labels and make them stick; and differential access to valuable resources based on class, race, and gender. If we are to fully understand crime and deviance, we need to dig deep enough and consider what is going on from enough angles and with sufficient care, concern, and curiosity.

For REVIEW

I. How do groups maintain social control?
- They use positive and negative sanctions in both formal and informal ways to bring about conformity and obedience.

II. What is the difference between deviance and crime?
- Deviance involves violating a group's expected norms, which may lead the offender to be stigmatized. Crime is a form of deviance that involves violating the formal norms administered by the state for which the offender may receive formal sanctions.

III. How do sociologists explain deviance and crime?
- Sociologists offer a number of theories of crime, each of which provides additional factors to be considered—such as the need for social order, the significance of interpersonal relationships and local context, and the importance of power and access to resources—that help us better understand why deviance and crime occur.

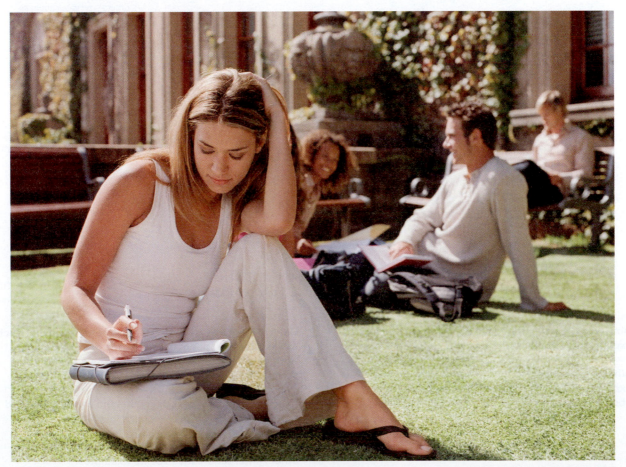

© BananaStock/JupiterImages RF

SOCVIEWS on Deviance

Functionalist View

Agents of **social control** aim to limit deviant social behavior by enforcing norms and providing negative sanctions for disobedience. Government exerts formal social control through its **laws**.

Deviance can actually contribute to social stability by defining the limits of proper behavior and encouraging **conformity** to laws and rules.

Social **integration** constrains deviant acts because it provides a clear **consensus** on shared norms and values.

CONFORMITY, OBEDIENCE, LAW, ORDER
KEY CONCEPTS

Conflict View

In diverse societies, the process of making laws generates conflicts over whose values should prevail.

Individuals and groups with the greatest **status and power** generally define who or what is deviant in a society.

The criminal justice system **treats suspects differently** based on their racial, ethnic, or class background, which leads to distrust in the criminal system.

KEY CONCEPTS
POWER, DIFFERENTIAL JUSTICE

Interactionist View

People learn what is proper and improper behavior through their interactions with others—an idea known as **cultural transmission.**

Informal social control is achieved through casual interactions—a smile, a raised eyebrow, ridicule—that prompt us to adjust our behavior.

A breakdown in interpersonal social relationships in a local community can lead to increases in crime and deviance.

KEY CONCEPTS
LABELING, CULTURAL TRANSMISSION

MAKE THE CONNECTION

After reviewing the chapter, answer the following questions:

1

How would each perspective approach, explore, and explain mass public shootings in the United States?

2

What perspective do you think provides the best explanation for the results of Milgram's experiment on obedience? Why?

3

Describe victimless crime from the point of view of each of the three perspectives, using one of the following examples in your response: drug use, gambling, or prostitution.

4

Which perspective best describes the way you learned proper social behavior? Were social norms socialized and internalized (functionalist), imposed by powerful authority figures (conflict), or learned from observing others (interactionist)? Provide examples.

Pop Quiz

1. **Society brings about acceptance of basic norms through techniques and strategies for preventing deviant human behavior. This process is termed**
   a. stigmatization.
   b. labeling.
   c. law.
   d. social control.

2. **The penalties and rewards we face for conduct concerning a social norm are known as**
   a. informal social controls.
   b. stigmas.
   c. sanctions.
   d. conformities.

3. **Stanley Milgram used the word *conformity* to mean**
   a. going along with peers even though they have no direct authority over us.
   b. compliance with higher authorities in a hierarchical structure.
   c. techniques and strategies for preventing deviant behavior in any society.
   d. penalties and rewards for conduct concerning a social norm.

4. **According to Hirschi's control theory,**
   a. deviance involves acceptance and/or rejection of society's goals and means.
   b. our connection to members of society leads us to systematically conform to society's norms.
   c. we come to view ourselves as deviant based on how others view us.
   d. power and access to resources shape whose norms and values determine individual action.

5. **Which of the following statements is true of deviance?**
   a. Deviance is always criminal behavior.
   b. Deviance is behavior that violates the standards of conduct or expectations of a group or society.
   c. Deviance is perverse behavior.
   d. Deviance is inappropriate behavior that cuts across all cultures and social orders.

6. **The FBI reports which two major categories of crime in its annual *Uniform Crime Reports*?**
   a. violent crime and property crime
   b. organized crime and white-collar crime
   c. victimless crime and transnational crime
   d. transnational crime and victimization crime

7. **Which type of crime involves the willing exchange among adults of widely desired, but illegal, goods and services?**
   a. index crimes
   b. white-collar crime
   c. victimless crime
   d. organized crime

8. **Which of the following is *not* one of the basic forms of adaptation specified in Robert Merton's strain theory of deviance?**
   a. conformity
   b. innovation
   c. ritualism
   d. hostility

9. **Which of the following theories contends that criminal victimization increases when communal relationships and social institutions break down?**
   a. labeling theory
   b. conflict theory
   c. social disorganization theory
   d. differential association theory

10. **Even though they committed the same deviant acts, the Saints and the Roughnecks did not receive the same treatment from authorities. Sociologist William Chambliss suggests this was due to the fact that authorities viewed members of the groups differently. Which theory supports that conclusion?**
    a. Merton's strain theory
    b. culture transmission theory
    c. differential association theory
    d. labeling theory

1. (d), 2. (c), 3. (a), 4. (b), 5. (b), 6. (a), 7. (c), 8. (d), 9. (c), 10. (d)

7

Families

© AFP/Getty Images

LOVE AND MARRIAGE

On April 29, 2011, Prince William married Catherine ("Kate") Middleton at Westminster Abbey in London. Though William's status as second-in-line to the British throne ensured much pomp and circumstance, as royal weddings go, it included both something old and even more of something new. Although William and Kate respected traditions, including the kiss on the Buckingham Palace balcony after the ceremony, their marriage was in a variety of ways unconventional. Instead of a fancy sit-down wedding feast, they opted for a buffet-style lunch. In lieu of wedding presents, they requested that people contribute to the Royal Wedding Charity Fund. Prince William is the first king-to-be to have openly lived with his future bride before marriage. Kate is the first royal bride with a university education to marry an heir to the throne. At age 29 she is the oldest not-previously-married bride to marry a king-in-waiting. And, on top of all that, she is the first commoner to marry someone in the direct line of

succession to the throne since the year 1660 (Chu 2011; Pearson 2011; Rayner 2011).

Although such innovations may have been shocking in the past, now they are in keeping with broader cultural shifts regarding the norms of partner selection and marriage. Even among other royals, traditional norms have become much less binding. Since 1945, a majority (71 percent) of European princes have married commoners. Often these relationships began, like William and Kate's, at a university, where love trumped lineage (Badoo 2011).

On July 22, 2013, Kate gave birth to their first baby, George Alexander Louis. She and William continued to break with tradition in how they approached parenthood. In preparation for his arrival, they shopped for their own baby clothes and furniture rather than having it done for them. When they brought George home from the hospital, rather than hiring a full-time nanny, they decided to care for Prince George themselves along with help from Kate's mom. When it was time

144

for his christening, they chose close friends to be George's godfather rather than selecting elderly royals (Bryant 2013; Tucker 2013; Winter 2013). On May 2, 2015, George gained a baby sister when Charlotte Elizabeth Diana was born.

In many ways, rather than breaking new ground, Prince William and Kate simply conformed to emerging norms influencing who, when, and whether to marry and how to parent. Throughout this chapter we investigate these and other shifts in current marriage and family practices.

As You READ >>

- What is the family?
- How do people pick partners?
- How do families vary?

>> Global View of the Family

Families around the world come in many shapes and sizes. Among Tibetans, a woman may be married simultaneously to more than one man, usually brothers. This system allows sons to share the limited amount of good land. Among the Betsileo of Madagascar, a man has multiple wives, each one living in a different village where he cultivates rice. Wherever he has the best rice field, that woman is considered his first or senior wife. Among the Yanomami of Brazil and Venezuela, it is considered proper to have sexual relations with one's opposite-sex cousins if they are the children of one's mother's brother or father's sister. But if one's opposite-sex cousins are the children of one's mother's sister or father's brother, the same practice is considered to be incest (Haviland et al. 2005; Kottak 2004).

In the United States, families of today often look different than they did a century or even a generation ago. New roles, new gender distinctions, and new child-rearing patterns have all combined to create new forms of family life. These days, for example, more and more women are taking the breadwinner's role, whether as a spouse or as a single parent. Blended families—the result of divorce and remarriage—are common. Same-sex marriages have become legal in more and more states. And many people are seeking intimate relationships outside marriage (Fry and Cohn 2010; Patten and Parker 2012).

Because families as we experience them are varied in structure and style, we need a sociological approach that is sufficiently broad to encompass all those relationships we experience as family. Two definitional approaches are helpful. The first is a substantive definition that focuses on what a family *is*, and the second is a functional definition that focuses on what families *do*.

substantive definition of the family A definition of the family based on blood, meaning shared genetic heritage, and law, meaning social recognition and affirmation of the bond including both marriage and adoption.

SUBSTANCE: WHAT A FAMILY IS

Perhaps the most conventional approach to defining family is the **substantive definition,** which focuses on blood and law. Blood, in this case, means that people are related because they share a biological heritage passed on directly from parent to child,

Did You Know?

. . . More than 2.1 million couples get married in the United States every year. In 2012, Nevada had the highest marriage rate at 35.1 marriages per 1,000 people, followed by Hawaii at 17.5 and Arkansas with 10.9. Perhaps not everything that happens in Vegas stays in Vegas.

Source: Centers for Disease Control and Prevention 2014b.   *Photo:* © Brand X Pictures RF.

TV families in the 1950s showed very little diversity in terms of family structure, race, and ethnicity.
Photo: © NBC Television/Courtesy Getty Images.

in-laws, and so forth. In a society such as the United States, the kinship group may come together only rarely, for a wedding or funeral. However, kinship ties frequently involve obligations and responsibilities. We may feel compelled to assist our kin, and we feel free to call on them for many types of aid, including loans and babysitting (O'Brien 2012; Rossi Del Corso and Lanz 2013).

How do we identify kinship groups? The principle of descent assigns people to kinship groups according to their relationship to a mother or father. There are three primary ways of determining descent. The United States follows the system of **bilateral descent,** which means that both sides of a person's family are regarded as equally important. For example, no higher value is given to the brothers of one's father than to the brothers of one's mother.

linking people indirectly to grandparents, aunts and uncles, and other biological relatives. Law means the formal social recognition and affirmation of a bond as family, particularly in the form of marriage and adoption.

The primary advantage of this definitional approach is that boundaries are clear; we can tell who is in and who is out. This makes it easier to count such families, so perhaps it is no surprise that the U.S. Census relies on a substantive approach: "A family is a group of two people or more (one of whom is the householder) related by birth, marriage, or adoption and residing together" (U.S. Census Bureau 2012a). It also allows us to track who is related to whom over time.

kinship The state of being related to others.

bilateral descent A kinship system in which both sides of a person's family are regarded as equally important.

patrilineal descent A kinship system in which only the father's relatives are significant.

matrilineal descent A kinship system in which only the mother's relatives are significant.

Kinship Patterns Many of us can trace our roots by looking at a family tree or by listening to elderly family members talk about their lives—and about ancestors who lived and died long before we were born. Yet a person's lineage is more than simply a personal history; it also reflects societal traditions that govern descent. In every culture, children encounter relatives to whom they are expected to show an emotional attachment. The state of being related to others is called **kinship.** Kinship is culturally learned, however, and is not totally determined by biological or marital ties. For example, adoption creates a kinship tie that is legally acknowledged and socially accepted.

The family and the kin group are not necessarily one and the same. Whereas the family is a household unit, kin do not always live together or function as a collective body on a daily basis. Kin groups include aunts, uncles, cousins,

— **SOC**THINK —
How important are intergenerational kinship networks and extended family members in your family? How has this changed since your parents' and grandparents' generations?

However, most societies—according to anthropologist George Murdock, 64 percent of societies—give preference to one side of the family or the other in tracing descent. In **patrilineal** (from the Latin *pater,* "father") **descent,** only the father's relatives are significant in terms of property, inheritance, and emotional ties. Conversely, in societies that favor **matrilineal** (from the Latin *mater,* "mother") **descent,** only the mother's relatives are significant.

Family Types The substantive approach also shapes what we traditionally view as common family types. If we assume that we are connected through blood and law, we can analyze how we structure those relationships. Families might place greater emphasis on immediate family members or on extended family networks. They also are shaped by the number of partners deemed appropriate.

Historically, family connections served as a valuable resource, providing us with access to material, social, and cultural resources. We depended on relatives for food, shelter, opportunities, and knowledge. In fact, historian Stephanie Coontz (2005) argues that, historically, the primary reason to get married was to obtain not a partner but in-laws, thus extending one's network of cooperative relationships. This was the logic of the matchmaker tradition in which resource distribution mattered more than romantic love. The matchmaker, as a member of the community, sought to maximize social network connections for the good of the whole.

A family in which relatives—such as grandparents, aunts, or uncles—live in the same household as parents and their children is known as an **extended family.** Historically, the extended family, along with relatives living in close proximity to each other, was the norm. In an era before cotton gins, spinning jennies, tractors, and combines, each additional family member, whether in the form of children or in-laws, represented another producer. As the old saying goes, many hands make light work. Extending the family network provided a material advantage. The Amish, because they value the multigenerational extended family, and gain solidarity by working together, intentionally limit the use of technology that would otherwise make their work easier and more efficient (Kraybill et al. 2013). In addition to economic advantages, the extended family network has also proven to be a source of strength in times of crisis such as death, disaster, or illness.

With the advent of the Industrial Revolution, the economy shifted away from agricultural production and its corresponding small-town life and toward industrial production in urban areas. A large family went from being an asset to something of a debit. Rather than serving as producers, children primarily became consumers whom parents had to feed, clothe, and shelter, which represented a significant expense. In addition, jobs were less place specific, so the capacity to be mobile was an advantage if the company wanted to transfer you to another location. As a result, families became smaller. The **nuclear family** includes a married couple and their unmarried children living together. The concept of nuclear family builds on the essence or nucleus of the substantive definition of blood and law, including as it does both the parent-to-child and the marriage relationship.

Types of Marriage In considering these different family types, we have limited ourselves to the form of marriage that is characteristic of the United States—monogamy. The term **monogamy** describes a form of marriage in which one woman and one man are married only to each other. Individuals in the United States are more likely to move into and out of a number of serious romantic relationships, what sociologist Andrew Cherlin (2009) refers to as the "marriage-go-round." Termed **serial monogamy,** a person may have several spouses in his or her lifetime, but only one spouse at a time.

Some cultures allow an individual to have several husbands or wives simultaneously. This form of marriage is known as **polygamy.** In fact, most societies throughout the world, past and present, have preferred polygamy to monogamy. Anthropologist George Murdock (1949, 1957) sampled 565 societies and found that in more than 80 percent, some type of polygamy was the preferred form. While polygamy declined steadily through most of the 20th century, in 28 sub-Saharan African countries, at least 10 percent of men still have polygamous marriages (Tertilt 2005).

© 2009 Jupiterimages RF

There are two basic types of polygamy. The more common is **polygyny,** which refers to the marriage of a man to more than one woman at the same time. Less common is **polyandry,** in which a woman may have more than one husband at the same time. Such is the case, for example, in the Nyinba culture of Nepal and Tibet, in which brothers share a common wife. This arrangement provides a sufficient number of physical laborers in the difficult farming environment yet minimizes the number of offspring (Zeitzen 2008).

The primary advantage of the substantive approach to defining families is that it provides clear boundaries separating who counts as family and who does not. It makes it easy, in theory at least, to trace our family tree. Just track parent-to-child relationships between generations, and track socially sanctioned relationships (such as marriage and adoption) within generations. In practice, however, people who attempt to do so find it is more difficult than it might seem. In the case of adoption, for example, do you count

extended family A family in which relatives—such as grandparents, aunts, or uncles—live in the same household as parents and their children.

nuclear family A married couple and their unmarried children living together.

monogamy A form of marriage in which one woman and one man are married only to each other.

serial monogamy A form of marriage in which a person may have several spouses in his or her lifetime but only one spouse at a time.

polygamy A form of marriage in which an individual may have several husbands or wives simultaneously.

polygyny A form of polygamy in which a man may have more than one wife at the same time.

polyandry A form of polygamy in which a woman may have more than one husband at the same time.

U.S. Households by Family Type

1940 76% · 5% · 5% · 10% · 4%

1960 74% · 10% · 5% · 8% · 2%

1980 61% · 15% · 11% · 11% · 2%

2000 53% · 17% · 14% · 12% · 4%

2014 48% · 18% · 16% · 13% · 5%

● Married-couple families ● Female householders ● Male householders ● Female-headed families ● Male-headed families

Note: Male and female householders include women and men living alone or exclusively with people to whom they are not related, including those in a college dormitory, homeless shelter, or military base.

Source: U.S. Census Bureau 2015b:Table HH-1.   *Photo:* © S. Greg Panosian/Getty Images RF.

SOCstudies

SOC THINK

Why do you think that polygamy was the most common form of marriage historically? Why has it given way to monogamy in modern societies?

the child's biological ancestors as part of the family tree? What about the ancestors of a stepfather or stepmother? And what happens when a parent and stepparent divorce? Is that stepparent, who might have played a vital role in child rearing, no longer related? What about close friends who are very much part of the family? Does Dad's college friend "Uncle" Bob count? New forms of reproductive technology, involving donated sperm and eggs and surrogate parents, also challenge conventional thinking. Any substantive definition we might come up with runs the risk of excluding those whom we think of as family members. In response, sociologists turn toward the more inclusive functionalist definition of families to address such limitations.

FUNCTIONS: WHAT FAMILIES DO

People in the United States seem to agree that traditional definitions of family are too restrictive. When they are asked how they would define family, their conception is much more inclusive than the substantive definition

© Brand X Pictures/Jupiterimages RF

implies. In one survey, only 22 percent of the respondents defined family in the same way as the U.S. Census Bureau. Instead, 74 percent considered a family to be "any group whose members love and care for one another" (Coontz 1992:21).

We need a definition of family that is inclusive enough to encompass the broad range of intimate groups that people form, such as extended families, nuclear families, single-parent families, blended or reconstituted or step-families, gay and lesbian families, child-free families, racially and ethnically mixed families, commuter marriage families, surrogate or chosen families, and more. One way to avoid getting trapped into overly narrow conceptions of families and to embrace their diversity is to shift the emphasis away from what families *are,* which a substantive approach highlights, toward what families *do.* A **functionalist definition of families** focuses on how families provide for the physical, social, and emotional needs of individuals and of society as a whole.

Sociologist William F. Ogburn (Ogburn and Tibbits 1934) identified six primary functions that families perform for us:

- *Reproduction.* For a society to maintain itself, it must replace dying members. Families provide the context within which biological reproduction takes place.
- *Socialization.* Parents and other family members monitor a child's behavior and transmit the norms, values, and language of their culture to the child.
- *Protection.* Unlike the young of other animal species, human infants need constant care and economic security. In all cultures, the family assumes the ultimate responsibility for the protection and upbringing of children.
- *Regulation of sexual behavior.* Sexual norms are subject to change both over time (for instance, in the customs for dating) and across cultures (compare strict Saudi Arabia to the more permissive Denmark). However, whatever the time period or cultural values of a society, standards of sexual behavior are most clearly defined within the family circle.
- *Affection and companionship.* Ideally, families provide members with warm and intimate relationships, helping them to feel satisfied and secure. Of course, a family member may find such rewards outside the family—from peers, in school, at work—and may even perceive the home as an unpleasant or abusive setting. Nevertheless, we expect our relatives to understand us, to care for us, and to be there for us when we need them.
- *Provision of social status.* We inherit a social position because of the family background and reputation of our parents and siblings. For example, the race, ethnicity, social class, education level, occupation, and religion of our parents all shape the material, social, and cultural resources to which we have access and therefore the options we might have.

No matter how it is composed, any group that fulfills these functions is family to us. Many of us have had close-knit

relationships like this. Members of a sports team can be this way, as can a group of college friends who remain close for life. They are people we can count on in times of trouble; people who will have our backs. We turn to them for all kinds of support, including care and affection, guidance in how to think and act, dating advice, and sometimes even material support, whether borrowing a car or just some money for pizza. Increasingly, people even count pets as family members, especially when it comes to providing affection and companionship. Some couples go so far as to include dogs as participants in their wedding ceremonies (Peters 2009; Slater 2012; Stoeckel et al. 2014; Walsh 2009a, 2009b). We may use the expression

functionalist definition of families A definition of families that focuses on how families provide for the physical, social, and emotional needs of individuals and of society as a whole.

© 3bugsmom/Getty Images RF

that such groups are "like family" to convey that sense, or we may even refer to the significant people in our lives as our sister, brother, mom, or dad. For many people, it is already the case that a family *is* what a family *does*.

CONFLICT: WHO RULES?

Regardless of which definition we choose, it is inevitably the case that people living in relationship with each other will have to address the issue of power. Couples, for example, must decide where to live; how to furnish their home; who will shop, cook, and clean; which side of the family to visit on holidays; and a whole host of other decisions both big and small. Siblings may have to decide difficult end-of-life care questions regarding their parents. A society's social norms inform which family members have more or less power over such decisions, and these norms vary cross-culturally and across time.

Historically, decision-making power has largely been shaped by gender. A society that expects males to dominate in all family decision making is termed a **patriarchy.** In patriarchal societies, such as Iran, the eldest male often wields the greatest power, although wives are expected to be treated with respect and kindness. An Iranian woman's status is typically defined by her relationship to a male relative, usually as a wife or daughter. In many patriarchal societies, women find it more difficult to obtain a divorce than a man does (Farr 1999). In contrast, in a **matriarchy,** women have greater authority than men. Formal matriarchies, which are uncommon, emerged among Native American tribal societies and in nations in which men were absent for long periods because of warfare or food-gathering expeditions.

patriarchy A society in which men dominate in family decision making.

matriarchy A society in which women dominate in family decision making.

egalitarian family An authority pattern in which spouses are regarded as equals.

More than a century ago, Friedrich Engels ([1884] 1959), a colleague of Karl Marx, went so far as to say that the family is the ultimate source of social inequality because of its role in the transfer of power, property, and privilege. Historically, he argues, the family has legitimized and perpetuated male dominance. It has contributed to societal injustice, denied women opportunities that are extended to men, and limited freedom in sexual expression and mate selection. In the United States, it was not until the first wave of contemporary feminism, in the mid-1800s, that there was a substantial challenge to the historical status of wives and children as the legal property of husbands and fathers.

Partly because of the efforts of women and men in similar movements over the years, we have seen the rise of a third type of authority pattern. In the **egalitarian family,** spouses are regarded as equals. This shift has been driven at least in part by occupational and financial opportunities for women that previously had been denied them (Wills and Risman 2006). That does not mean, however, that all decisions are shared in such families. Wives may hold authority in some spheres, and husbands in others. For example, sociologists have found that, in terms of paid and unpaid labor in two-parent families, the total hours worked by mothers and fathers is roughly equal at about 65 hours per week, though the distribution of tasks varies (Bianchi, Robinson, and Milkie 2006).

Historian Stephanie Coontz (2008) suggests that, when it works, marriage today is better than ever. She writes that it "delivers more benefits to its members—adults and children—than ever before. A good marriage is fairer and more fulfilling for both men and women than couples of the past could ever have imagined." She points to shared decision making and housework, increases in time spent with children, and declines in violence and sexual coercion and in the likelihood of adultery.

Although the egalitarian family has become a more common pattern in the United States in recent decades, male dominance over the family has hardly disappeared. Sociologists have found that although married men are increasing their involvement in child care, their wives still perform a disproportionate amount of it. Furthermore, with 5.2 million stay-at-home moms versus 211,000 stay-at-home dads, a ratio of 25 to 1, the dominant practice reinforces normative expectations (U.S. Census Bureau 2015: Table SHP-1).

Families also provide a foundation for power within the larger society. Family serves as the basis for transferring power, property, and privilege from one generation to the next. Although the United States is widely viewed as a land of opportunity, access to valued resources is not evenly distributed to all. Children inherit the privileged or less-than-privileged social and economic status of their parents (and in some cases, of earlier generations as well). The social class of parents significantly influences the material, social, and cultural resources to which their children have access. Thus, the socioeconomic status of a child's family will have a marked influence on his or her nutrition, health care, housing, educational opportunities, and in many respects, life chances as an adult. In many ways the family helps to maintain inequality (Lareau 2011; Shipler 2004).

>> Marriage and Family

Despite concerns about power and inequality in the family sphere, people's faith in marriage persists. Currently, almost 80 percent of adults aged 25 and older are, or have been, married, and about half of those who have not yet married say they would like to eventually (Wang and Parker 2014). In spite of this high level of commitment to marriage, the likelihood of marriage varies over time, and the marriage rate in the United States is actually at or near a record low. In the United States, the median age of first marriage in 2014 was 27.0 for women and 29.3 for men. Contrast that with the medians in 1960, which were 20.3 for women and 22.8 for men (Cherlin 2009; Sterbenz

2014; U.S. Census Bureau 2015a:Table MS-2). Rates also vary based on a variety of factors including income, education, race, ethnicity, and nationality.

The increased likelihood of delaying marriage is shaped by our perception of where marriage fits as a milestone in the transition to adulthood (see Chapter 4). One approach, more common in the 1950s, viewed marriage as a *cornerstone*, something that happens relatively early in adulthood providing us with the foundation upon which other adult relationships and responsibilities are built. An alternative perspective arose as more people in the United States waited to marry until after they had completed their educational degrees and established themselves in careers. Sociologist Andrew Cherlin (2009) argues that the symbolic significance of marriage shifted as a result.

Median Age at First Marriage, United States

Source: U.S. Census Bureau 2015a: Table MS-2.   Photo: © Janis Christie/Getty Images RF.

Ten Questions Couples Should Ask (or Wish They Had) Before Marrying

Do you want to have children?

Who will do what when it comes to housework?

What are your expectations regarding sex?

What do you think about having a television in the bedroom?

What do you expect regarding religious training for our children?

How much money do you owe?

Do you like and respect my friends?

What do you really think about my parents?

What does my family do that annoys you?

Are there some things you are not willing to give up in the marriage?

Signature

Source: The New York Times 2006.   Photo: © Image Source, all rights reserved RF.

We are now more likely to view marriage as a *capstone*, something we do as a sign we have our act together and are ready to settle down and into adulthood. There are people who still adhere to the cornerstone model (Prior 2013), but as the graph "Median Age at First Marriage" demonstrates, more and more people are opting to wait.

COURTSHIP AND MATE SELECTION

There are many ways that we might go about finding someone to marry. Historically, it was not uncommon for marriages to be arranged by families or matchmakers. This is a practice that continues in many cultures today. In the Asian nation of Uzbekistan, for example, courtship is largely orchestrated by the couple's parents. A young Uzbekistani woman is socialized to eagerly anticipate her marriage to a man whom she has met only once, at the final inspection of her dowry (Kamp 2008; Rand 2006).

When it comes to marriage in the United States, most of us assume that true love will guide the way. We can't imagine allowing others, including parents and matchmakers, to select partners for us through arranged marriages. Many are surprised to hear that this practice continues today in some subcultures in the United States. We tend to take for granted that we are best suited to make this personal and intimate selection. We may look to advice from family and friends, but the deciding factor is how we feel about the other person.

SOCTHINK

Why might people turn to matchmaking services today? What are the disadvantages of relying on our own contacts and judgment when it comes to finding a romantic partner?

Going GLOBAL

Percentage of People Aged 20–24 Ever Married, Selected Countries

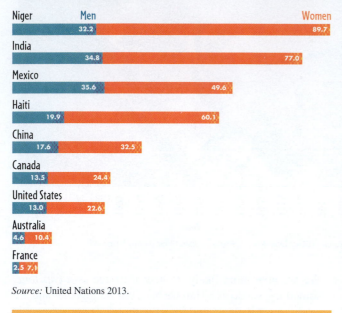

Country	Men	Women
Niger	32.2	89.7
India	34.8	77.0
Mexico	35.6	49.6
Haiti	19.9	60.1
China	17.6	32.5
Canada	13.5	24.4
United States	13.0	22.6
Australia	4.6	10.4
France	2.5	7.1

Source: United Nations 2013.

In practice, however, our pool of potential partners is substantially reduced by our social location. We are sometimes blind to the basic social rules that inevitably narrow our choices (Kalmijn 1998):

- We are limited to those who are available and with whom we have contact.
- We are heavily influenced by opinions of family, friends, and the organizations to which we belong (including religious groups and the workplace).
- We are most attracted to people like ourselves.

In the first case, our position in the social structure influences the degree to which we have the opportunity to establish a relationship with someone. Second, partner selection involves more than just the happy couple; those close to us play a significant role in shaping which characteristics we perceive as acceptable. Finally, as the saying goes, like attracts like (or at least it tends to).

When sociologists analyze social factors that shape our selection of partners, they pay particular attention to the balance between endogamy and exogamy. **Endogamy** (from the Greek *endon,* "within") specifies the groups within which a spouse must be found and prohibits marriage with outsiders. For example, in the United States, many people are expected to marry within their own racial, ethnic, or religious group and are strongly discouraged or even prohibited from

endogamy The restriction of mate selection to people within the same group.

exogamy The requirement that people select a mate outside certain groups.

incest taboo The prohibition of sexual relationships between certain culturally specified relatives.

marrying outside the group. Endogamy is intended to reinforce the cohesiveness of the group by suggesting that we should marry someone "of our own kind."

In contrast, **exogamy** (from the Greek *exo,* "outside") requires mate selection outside certain groups, usually one's own family or certain kinfolk. The **incest taboo,** a social norm common to virtually all societies, prohibits sexual relationships between certain culturally specified relatives. In the United States, this taboo means that we must marry outside the nuclear family. We cannot marry our siblings, and in most states, we cannot marry our first cousins.

Endogamy influences a number of social location variables. We tend to pick partners who are the same age, race, ethnicity, education, and religion. Though the degree of influence of these variables has shifted over time, each continues to play a significant role. When it comes to age, for example, one-third of all married couples in the United States are within one year of each other and 76 percent are within five years. Only 1.5 percent of couples have an age difference of 20 or more years (U.S. Census Bureau 2015d:Table FG3). Age is one of the factors for which third-party pressure can exert significant influence; people tend to look suspiciously at relationships in which the age difference is perceived to be too large.

The role of race in selecting partners demonstrates how social norms can both change and remain the same. For a long time, interracial marriage was illegal in the United States. This was still the case in some states until a 1967 Supreme Court ruling overturned these laws. Since then,

© Erica Simone Leeds

© Don Tremain/Getty Images RF

Patterns of Interracial Marriage

	White wife	Black wife	Asian wife
White husband	50,314	202	730
Black husband	400	4,305	47
Asian husband	231	18	3,487

Number in thousands

Percentage of husbands with same-race wife

97.0%	White
88.7%	Black
92.9%	Asian

Percentage of wives with same-race husband

97.7%	White
94.5%	Black
80.7%	Asian

Note: Numbers in thousands. Table does not show data for other-race husbands and wives.

Source: Based on U.S. Census Bureau 2015d:Table FG3.   *Photo:* © Burke/Triolo Productions/Getty Images RF.

interracial marriages in the United States have become more common. Now, 3 million married couples, or just under 5 percent of the total, include partners from different racial groups (U.S. Census Bureau 2015d:Table FG3).

Despite the overall increase in the acceptance and practice of interracial marriage, most married people continue to select a partner of the same race. As we can see from the accompanying table, however, there is some variation both by race and by gender. Those who are White are the most likely to practice racial endogamy; 97 percent of both men and women select a marital partner of the same race. Among African Americans, men are more likely than women to be involved in interracial marriages. For those who are Asian, however, there is an even larger gender difference; women are much more likely to be in an interracial marriage than men. Still, more than 80 percent of Asian women select a partner of the same race. Such patterns demonstrate the continued significance endogamy plays in partner selection (U.S. Census Bureau 2015d:Table FG3; Wang 2012).

Even within these broader endogamous social categories, we tend to pick people like ourselves. This is known as **homogamy**—the conscious or unconscious tendency to select a mate with personal characteristics and interests similar to one's own. Internet dating services depend upon this principle to help find matches. Sociologist Pepper Schwartz (2006), who worked as a consultant for PerfectMatch.com, has developed a 48-question survey that covers everything from decision-making style to degree of impulsivity. Internet dating site eHarmony claims that an average of 438 clients marry each day as a result of matches made through its site. Overall, researchers claim that between a quarter and a third of couples meet online. The rate is even higher for those whose immediate pool of potential partners is smaller, including gays, lesbians, and middle-aged heterosexuals. And there is some evidence that couples who first meet online experience greater marital satisfaction and are slightly less likely to divorce (Cacioppo et al. 2013; eHarmony 2014; Rosenfeld and Thomas 2012).

In theory, Cupid's arrow could strike anyone on our behalf. But love is not blind. Love is a product of the social and cultural forces that shape the choices we make. Of course, knowledge of the ways our choices are patterned can free us up to follow different paths.

homogamy The conscious or unconscious tendency to select a mate with personal characteristics and interests similar to one's own.

SOCTHINK

How important are factors such as age, education, race, ethnicity, social class, gender, and religion in your choice of someone for a serious relationship? To what extent are (were) you conscious of such influences when you pick (picked) someone to date?

5 Movies on MARRIAGE AND FAMILIES

The Loving Story
A couple's true love conquers all, even the Supreme Court.

Monsoon Wedding
An Indian wedding celebration.

The Princess Bride
True love conquers all.

This Is 40
When romance confronts middle age.

Amour
An elderly couple faces the end of the road.

PARENTING PATTERNS AND PRACTICES

Caring for children is a universal function of the family, yet the ways in which different societies assign this function to family members can vary significantly. The Nayars of southern India acknowledge the biological role of fathers, but the mother's eldest brother is responsible for her children. In contrast, uncles play only a peripheral role in child care in the United States. Even within the United States, child-rearing patterns are varied. Just as our conception of families has changed, so also has our practice of child rearing.

Parenthood The socialization of children is essential to the maintenance of any culture. Consequently, parenthood is one of the most important (and most demanding) social

> The goal in marriage is not to think alike, but to think together.
>
> Robert C. Dodds

roles in the United States. Sociologist Alice Rossi (1968, 1984) has identified four factors that complicate the transition to parenthood and the role of socialization. First, there is little anticipatory socialization for the social role of caregiver. The normal school curriculum gives scant attention to the subjects most relevant to successful family life, such as child care and home maintenance. Second, only limited learning occurs during the period of pregnancy itself. Third, the transition to parenthood is quite abrupt. Unlike adolescence, it is not prolonged; unlike the transition to work, the duties of caregiving cannot be taken on gradually. Finally, in Rossi's view, our society lacks clear and helpful guidelines for successful parenthood. There is little agreement on how parents can produce happy and well-adjusted offspring—or even on what it means to be well adjusted. For these reasons, socialization for parenthood involves difficult challenges for most men and women in the United States.

How we choose to parent varies by a variety of social factors. Sociologist Annette Lareau (2003), for example, conducted an in-depth study of parenting and found significant social class differences. She found that middle- and upper-middle-class parents tend to see their children as a project. For them, parenting involves active engagement with their children in order to foster their growth and development. Using a gardening analogy, she labeled this parenting style *concerted cultivation,* arguing that such children are like flowers grown in a greenhouse that receive oversight, care, and protection. These children are encouraged to participate in varieties of activities, including organized sports and summer camps. They are taught to engage with adults, including physicians and teachers, and ask them questions. As a result, they often grow up with a sense of entitlement.

The upper- and middle-class parenting approach differed from that found in working-class and poor families. These parents see their primary responsibility as ensuring that their children's material needs are met and then granting their children greater freedom to navigate the world on their own. These parents presume that children will spontaneously grow and thrive. Their instructions to children are more directive—do this, don't do that—rather than viewing encounters as teachable moments. These children are more like seeds that have been thrown to the wind and grow to be wildflowers. As a result, Lareau labels this style of parenting the *accomplishment of natural growth.* The assumption is that children will learn more responsibility if they face challenges on their own rather than having a hovering helicopter parent there to bail them out. These children, much like their parents, were less likely to engage with authority figures such as teachers or doctors. Because children are taught interpersonal skills that

POPSOC

Romantic comedies are a dime a dozen, and it's easy to see why. There's the thrill of the chase and the hoped-for, and almost inevitable, happy ending. But how will the contented couple come to terms with the mundane reality of everyday life together? Film historian Jeanine Basinger (2012) argues that films about marriage are a tougher sell, because marriage is more like a merry-go-round than a roller-coaster ride. To make films about marriage viable, filmmakers use a predictable plot: begin by showing the happy couple facing the promise of eternal bliss, disrupt the relationship using one of seven common threats (money, infidelity, in-laws/children, incompatibility, class, addiction, and murder), and finally, restore order by overcoming the threat and recommitting to living happily ever after.

Photo: © Metro-Goldwyn-Meyer/Getty Images.

grow out of their social class positions, the social class of their childhood is a strong predictor of their social class as adults. Lareau (2011) confirmed as much when she checked back with the children and their families 10 years after her initial research.

Parenting also differs by race and ethnicity. Among Mexican American families, for example, placing the interests of the family before those of the individual, also known as **familism,** is a core value. The importance of the extended family is manifested through the maintenance of close ties and strong obligations to kinfolk outside the immediate family. Within African American families, strong kinship networks, especially through mothers, grandmothers, and aunts, serve as valuable conduits for sharing material, social, and cultural resources (Goffman 2014a; Stack 1974). Among Chinese American families, the "tiger mom" phenomenon received a significant amount of attention after Amy Chua (2011) published a book describing her parenting style. This strict style of extremely demanding parenting worries less about developing the self-esteem of the child and focuses more on achievement, especially academic achievement. For Chua, that meant denying her daughters things other children might take for granted, such as attending sleepovers, being in school plays, watching television or playing computer games, playing any instrument other than piano or violin, or getting any grade less than an A. Research among Chinese American families, however, finds significant variation in parenting styles and suggests that the tiger mom approach is neither the most typical nor the most effective. The more common supportive parenting profile produced children with better GPAs, higher educational attainment, less depressive symptoms, and a stronger sense of family obligation (Kim et al. 2013).

In some homes, child-rearing responsibilities fall to grandparents. In 2014, 7.4 million children in the United States, 10.1 percent overall, lived in a household with a grandparent. Of these, 1.6 million (2.2 percent) had no parent present to assist in child rearing (U.S. Census Bureau 2015e: Table C4). Special difficulties are inherent in such relationships, including legal custodial concerns, financial issues, and emotional problems for adults and youths alike. Perhaps not surprisingly, support groups such as Grandparents as Parents have emerged to provide assistance.

Adoption Adoption involves the socially recognized and affirmed transfer of the legal rights, responsibilities, and privileges of parenthood. It fits with the "law" part of the substantive definition of the family. In most cases, parental rights are transferred from the biological or birth parents to the adoptive parents. Approximately 1.7 percent of U.S. children live with at least one adoptive parent (U.S. Census Bureau 2015e:Table C9).

There are two legal methods of adopting an unrelated person: (1) the adoption may be arranged through a licensed agency, or (2) in some states it may be arranged through a

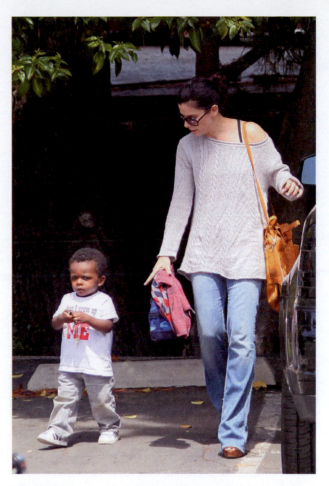

Hollywood star Sandra Bullock and her son, the result of a domestic adoption. Photo: © Splash News/Corbis.

private agreement sanctioned by the courts. Adopted children may come from the United States or from abroad. In 2013, 7,094 children entered the United States as the adopted children of U.S. citizens. The top three nations of origin for U.S. adoptions were China with 2,306, Ethiopia with 993, and Ukraine with 438. The median fee for adopting a child from China was $15,675 (U.S. Department of State 2014). Although the number of international adoptions remains substantial, it has declined in recent years, down from 23,000 in 2004.

In the United States, one of the limitations historically was that only married couples could adopt. In 1995 an important court decision in New York held that a couple does not have to be married to adopt a child. Under this ruling, unmarried heterosexual couples, lesbian couples, and gay couples can all legally adopt children in New York. Writing for the majority, Chief Justice Judith Kaye argued that by expanding the boundaries of who can be legally recognized as parents, the state may be able to assist more children in securing "the best possible home." At the time, New York became the third state

familism Placing the interests of the family before those of the individual.

adoption The socially recognized and affirmed transfer of the legal rights, responsibilities, and privileges of parenthood.

(after Vermont and Massachusetts) to recognize the right of unmarried couples to adopt children. Now adoption by unmarried persons is legal in all 50 states (Dao 1995; Human Rights Campaign 2009).

For every child who is adopted, many more remain the wards of state-sponsored child protective services. In 2013, 402,378 children in the United States were living in foster care. Of these children, 101,840 were waiting for adoption (U.S. Department of Health and Human Services 2014).

Dual-Income Families The classic image of the 1950s family, idealized in TV shows such as *Father Knows Best,* portrays a breadwinner father and a homemaker wife. His job was to provide for the family's material needs by earning money, and her job was to nurture and care for her husband and their children. At the time, that image was more myth than fact for millions of American families (Coontz 1992), and today even fewer families conform to it.

SOCTHINK

What are the advantages and disadvantages of the dual-income model for women, for men, for children, and for society as a whole?

For example, among married couples with children under 6, 54.1 percent have both a husband and a wife in the labor force and among those with children aged 6–17, it is 62.9 percent. Among all married couples, with or without children, 20 percent of wives make $5,000-plus more than their husbands (Bureau of Labor Statistics 2014a:Table 4; U.S. Census Bureau 2015d:Table FG3).

Both opportunity and need have driven the rise in the number of dual-income couples. Women now have the chance to pursue opportunities in a way that previously had been closed due to cultural expectations regarding gender.

single-parent family A family in which only one parent is present to care for the children.

This has resulted in increased education levels for women and increased participation in occupational fields that had been largely closed. At the same time, however, couples find it harder to make it on a single income. Evidence of this trend can be found in the rise of married couples living apart for reasons other than marital discord. The 3.6 million couples who now live apart represent 1 out of every 33 marriages. More than half live farther than 100 miles apart, and half of those live 1,000 or more miles apart. Of course, couples living apart are nothing

new; men have worked at transient jobs for generations as soldiers, truck drivers, or traveling salesmen. The existence of such household arrangements reflects an acceptance of the egalitarian family type (Cullen 2007; Holmes 2006; Stafford 2010).

Single-Parent Families Over time, **single-parent families,** those in which only one parent is present, have become more common and more accepted in the United States. In 2014, 27.5 percent of all children lived with only one parent. This varied by race and ethnicity with 19.8 percent of White, non-Hispanic children, 54.9 percent of African American children, 11.2 percent of Asian children, and 30.7 percent of Hispanic children living with one parent (U.S. Census Bureau 2015e:Table C9).

The life of single parents and their children is not inevitably more difficult than that of a traditional nuclear family. It is as inaccurate to assume that a single-parent family is necessarily deprived as it is to assume that a two-parent family is always secure and happy. Nevertheless, to the extent that such families have to rely on a single income or a sole caregiver, life in the single-parent family can be extremely stressful. A family headed by a single mother faces especially difficult problems when the mother is a teenager, especially when she lacks access to significant social and economic resources (Sawhill 2006).

Why might low-income teenage women wish to have

> What greater thing is there for human souls than to feel that they are joined for life—to be with each other in silent unspeakable memories.

George Eliot

children and face the obvious financial difficulties of motherhood? Some theorists argue that these women tend to have low self-esteem and limited options; a child may provide a sense of motivation and purpose for the teenager whose economic worth in our society is limited at best. Given the barriers that many young women face because of their gender, race, ethnicity, and class, many teenagers may believe they have little to lose and much to gain by having a child (Edin and Kefalas 2005).

Although 86 percent of single parents in the United States are mothers, the number of households headed by single fathers nearly quadrupled between 1970 and 2014. Single mothers often develop social networks, but single fathers are typically more isolated. In addition, they must deal with schools and social service agencies that are more accustomed to women as custodial parents (U.S. Census Bureau 2015f:Table CH1).

Stepfamilies As a result of single parents who marry or divorced parents who remarry, approximately 5.7 percent of children under 18 live with at least one stepparent (U.S. Census Bureau 2015e:Table C9). But stepfamilies can involve more than just young children in these relationships. Sociologist Susan Stewart (2007) recommends expanding our definition of stepfamilies to include cohabiting couples with children from previous relationships, families whose stepchildren do not live with them full-time, gay or lesbian couples with children from former heterosexual relationships, and stepfamilies with adult children. The expanded definition highlights the fact that stepfamily membership extends throughout the life course. The exact nature of blended families has social significance for adults and children alike.

Family members in stepfamilies must deal with resocialization issues when an adult becomes a stepparent or a child becomes a stepchild and stepsibling. In evaluating these stepfamilies, some observers have assumed that children would benefit from remarriage, because they would be gaining a second custodial parent and would potentially enjoy greater economic security. However, after reviewing many studies of stepfamilies, sociologist Andrew J. Cherlin (2008b:800) concluded that "the well-being of children in stepfamilies is no better, on average, than the well-being of children in divorced, single-parent households."

Stepparents can and do play valuable and unique roles in their stepchildren's lives, but their involvement does not guarantee an improvement in family life. In fact, standards may decline. Studies suggest that children raised in families with stepmothers are likely to have less health care, education, and money spent on their food than children raised by biological mothers. The measures are also negative for children raised by stepfathers, but only half as negative as in the case of stepmothers. This may be due to the stepmother holding back out of concern for seeming too intrusive or relying on the biological father to carry out parental duties (Schmeeckle 2007; Schmeeckle et al. 2006).

Multigenerational Families With the rise of the Industrial Revolution and the corresponding spread of the

© Universal/Courtesy Everett Collection

Living Arrangements of Children

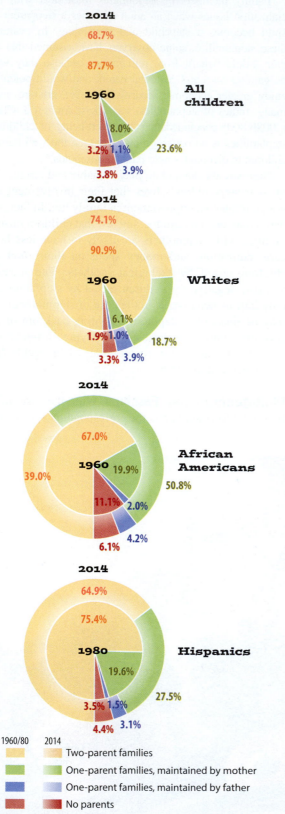

2014
68.7%

1960
87.7%

All children

8.0%
3.2% 1.1%
3.8% 3.9%
23.6%

2014
74.1%

1960
90.9%

Whites

6.1%
1.9% 1.0%
3.3% 3.9%
18.7%

2014
67.0%

1960
39.0%

African Americans

19.9%
11.1% 2.0%
6.1%
4.2%
50.8%

2014
64.9%

1980
75.4%

Hispanics

19.6%
3.5% 1.5%
4.4% 3.1%
27.5%

1960/80   2014

- Two-parent families
- One-parent families, maintained by mother
- One-parent families, maintained by father
- No parents

Note: The "No parents" category includes children living with either other relatives or nonrelatives. Persons of Hispanic origin can be of any race.

Source: Based on U.S. Census Bureau 2015f: Tables Ch-1, Ch-2, Ch-3, Ch-4.

nuclear family model, the era of multiple generations of families living in the same household seemed largely to be over. Throughout much of the 20th century that appeared correct. The percentage of U.S. households that includes adults from at least two generations (and, if living with parents, aged 25 and older) dropped from 23.7 in 1900 to 12.1 percent in 1980. Since that time, however, the percentage of such households rose to 18.1 percent including a marked increase since 2006 (Fry and Passel 2014; Pew Research Center 2010g:Table 1).

Much of that change can be attributed to the rise in the percentage of younger adults who either continue to live with, or move back in with, their parents. This represents a change from what had been the much more common multigenerational pattern of elderly parents living with their middle-aged adult children. In 1940, 62.7 percent of adults aged 85 and older lived in a multigenerational household compared to 22.7 in 2012. Among young adults aged 25–34, the numbers were 27.7 percent in 1940 and 23.6 percent in 2012. Currently, nearly one-half of all multigenerational families include three or more generations (Fry and Passel 2014).

One of the factors influencing the recent rise was the economic downturn that started in 2007 which significantly limited job opportunities for young people (Pew Research Center 2014e). In addition, as we have already seen, the average age of first marriage has gone up, and, for some percentage of young adults, opting to live with family represents a rational choice to minimize expenses. Focusing on the slightly younger 18–24 age demographic, some percentage of which includes college graduates who return home, 54.9 percent now live with their parents compared to 43 percent in 1960 (U.S. Census Bureau 2015g:Table AD-1). Living at home helps recent graduates face the challenge of managing college debt with trying to get established in their career while earning a starting salary (Davidson 2014). Just as changes in the economy helped drive the rise of the isolated nuclear family, these more recent economic events may well be contributing to the emergence of a new form of the extended family whose members leverage the material, social, and cultural resource advantages that such an arrangement provides.

>> Diverse Lifestyles

Though getting married and having children was the normative expectation for most adults throughout much of American history, significant variation existed in practice and a wider array of options is now available.

COHABITATION

In the United States, testing the relationship waters by living together without being married is an increasingly

Unmarried-Couple Households by State

Percentage of couples who are unmarried, 2010
- 0%–9%
- 10%–12%
- 13%–14%
- 15%–17%
- 18%–34%

Source: El Nasser and Overberg 2011.

maybe." In Iceland, 62 percent of all children are born to single mothers; in France, Great Britain, and Norway, the proportion is about 40 percent. Government policies in these countries make few legal distinctions between married and unmarried couples or households (Lyall 2002; M. Moore 2006; Thomson and Bernhardt 2010).

People commonly associate cohabitation only with younger, child-free couples who are testing the waters before marriage. Census data show that 47 percent of the 15.3 million cohabiting heterosexual individuals in the United States are aged 35 and older. Overall, 41 percent of cohabiting couples have children living with them. These cohabitants are more like spouses than dating partners. Moreover, in contrast to the common perception that people who cohabit have never been married, researchers report that about half of all people involved in cohabitation in the United States have been previously married. Cohabitation serves as a temporary or permanent alternative to matrimony for many (Jayson 2012a, 2012b).

common practice. **Cohabitation** is conventionally defined as the practice of a man and a woman living together in a sexual relationship without being married. The percentage of currently cohabiting adults aged 30–44 rose from 3 percent in 1995 to 7 percent in 2010 (Fry and Cohn 2011).

About half of all currently married couples in the United States say that they lived together before marriage. And this percentage is likely to increase. The number of unmarried-couple households in the United States rose sixfold in the 1960s and increased another 72 percent between 1990 and 2000. Adults aged 30–44 without a college education are more likely to cohabit than those with a college degree. Cohabitation is more common among African Americans and American Indians than among other racial and ethnic groups; it is least common among Asian Americans. The "Unmarried-Couple Households by State" map shows how cohabitation varies by region (Goodwin et al. 2010; Kreider 2010; T. Simmons and O'Connell 2003).

In much of Europe, cohabitation is so common that the general sentiment seems to be "Love, yes; marriage,

> Call it a clan, call it a network, call it a tribe, call it a family. Whatever you call it, whoever you are, you need one.
>
> Jane Howard

cohabitation The practice of a man and a woman living together in a sexual relationship without being married.

REMAINING SINGLE

Increasingly, people are opting to remain single. In 1960, 9 percent of adults aged 25 and older had never married. It has since more than doubled to approximately 20 percent (Wang and Parker 2014). A variety of factors help explain this trend, including rising cohabitation rates and, as we saw earlier, the fact that those who do marry are waiting longer to do so. Of those who have never married, 13 percent do not want to marry compared to 45 percent of those who have been married before (Wang and Parker 2014).

There are many reasons a person may choose not to marry. Some singles do not want to limit their sexual intimacy to one lifetime partner. Some men and women do not want to become highly dependent on any one person—and do not want anyone depending heavily on them. In a society that values individuality and self-fulfillment, the single lifestyle can offer certain freedoms that marriage may not.

Remaining single represents a clear departure from societal expectations and singles can feel targeted in a society that presumes marriage. A single adult must confront the inaccurate view that he or she is always lonely, is a workaholic, or is immature. These stereotypes help support the traditional assumption in the United States and most other societies that to be truly happy and fulfilled, a person must get married and raise a family. To counter these societal expectations, singles have formed numerous support groups (Hertz 2006; Lundquist 2006).

REMAINING CHILD-FREE

There has also been a significant increase in childlessness in the United States. According to census data, 16.1 percent of women aged 40–50 have never had children. Those with at least a college degree are more likely to opt out of parenthood than those who have less education. At 22.7 percent, the childless rate for women aged 40–50 who have graduate or professional degrees is nearly twice the 11.6 percent rate for those who have not completed high school (Monte and Ellis 2014).

Childlessness within marriage has generally been viewed as a problem that can be solved through such means as adoption and artificial insemination. More and more couples today, however, choose not to have children and regard themselves as child-free rather than childless. They do not believe that having children automatically follows from marriage, nor do they feel that reproduction is the duty of all married couples. Child-free couples have formed support groups (with names like No Kidding and Childless by Choice) and set up websites (K. Park 2005; Terry 2000).

Economic considerations have contributed to this shift in attitudes; having children has become quite expensive. Estimates are that middle-income parents of children born in 2013 can anticipate spending $304,480 to feed, clothe, and shelter a child from birth to age 18. If the child attends college, that amount could double, depending on the college chosen. Aware of the financial pressures, some couples are having fewer children than they otherwise might, and others are weighing the advantages of a child-free marriage (Lino 2014).

LESBIAN AND GAY RELATIONSHIPS

One of the more active political debates about how we define family has involved

marriage of same-sex couples. If we stick with a narrow, substantive definition that marriage necessarily involves one man and one woman, such relationships do not count as families. When we define families in terms of what functions they perform, we find growing support that such relationships do count. In 2004, 31 percent of Americans favored allowing gays and lesbians to marry. By 2015, that number rose to 57 percent who supported legalizing marriage between same-sex couples. As the "Approval of Same-Sex Marriage by Age" graph demonstrates, younger people are more supportive. Attitudes also vary by religious affiliation, political party, race, and gender (Pew Research Center 2015c; Silver 2013).

The movement to legalize same-sex marriage in the United States crossed its first major legal hurdle in 2003 when the Massachusetts Supreme Judicial Court ruled 4–3 that, under the state's constitution, gay couples have the right to marry. In 2008 the Connecticut Supreme Court reached the same conclusion, as did Iowa's in 2009. Vermont, also in 2009, became the first state to pass a law that legalized same-sex marriage. By June 2015, 37 states

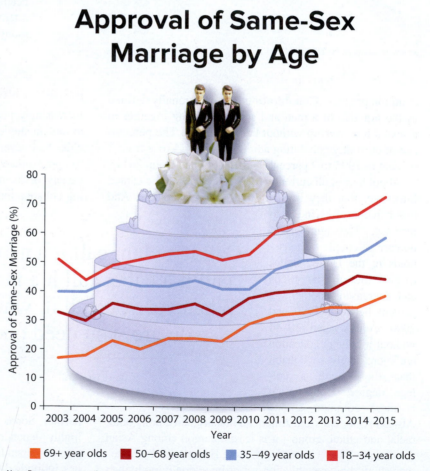

Approval of Same-Sex Marriage by Age

Note: Responses are to the question, "Do you favor allowing gays or lesbians to marry legally?"
Source: Pew Research Center 2015c.   Photo: © Angela Wyant/Stone/Getty Images.

James Obergefell was the lead plaintiff in the Supreme Court case that affirmed same-sex couples' constitutional right to marry. Photo: © Drew Angerer/Bloomberg via Getty Images.

Census estimates, there are 726,600 same-sex households in the United States, 35 percent of which include married couples. Sixteen percent of same-sex couples have their own children—biological, adopted, or step—in their households (U.S. Census Bureau 2014c). On average, gay and lesbian couples have more education, a greater likelihood of both members being employed, and higher incomes than married opposite-sex couples (C. Johnson 2012; Lofquist et al. 2012). Research finds that same-sex families score above average on measures of general health and family cohesion, and the children of these families have psychosocial development comparable to that of others (Crouch et al. 2014; Tasker 2005).

and the District of Columbia provided gay and lesbian couples the same right to marry as guaranteed to heterosexual couples.

On June 26, 2015, same-sex marriage became legal in all 50 states as a result of a decision by the United States Supreme Court. In the ruling, Justice Anthony Kennedy, writing for the majority, declared:

> "the right to marry is a fundamental right inherent in the liberty of the person, and under the Due Process and Equal Protection Clauses of the Fourteenth Amendment couples of the same-sex may not be deprived of that right and that liberty. The Court now holds that same-sex couples may exercise the fundamental right to marry."

The decision set off a celebration by same-sex marriage advocates across the land. Many got married that same day, including Jack Evans, 85, and George Harris, 82, of Dallas County, Texas, who tied the knot after having been together for 54 years.

Getting an accurate count of the prevalence of lesbian and gay families has been difficult because, up until recently, no official agencies attempted to do so. According to the best

Same-sex couples throughout the United States took advantage of the opportunity to marry as soon as their legal right to do so was recognized. Photo: © George Frey/ Getty Images.

>> Divorce

"Do you promise to love, honor, and cherish . . . until death do you part?" Every year, people of all social classes and racial and ethnic groups make this legally binding agreement. Yet a significant number of these promises shatter before divorce.

STATISTICAL TRENDS IN DIVORCE

Just how common is divorce? Surprisingly, this is not a simple question to answer; divorce statistics are difficult to interpret. The media frequently report that one out of every two marriages ends in divorce. But that figure is misleading in that many marriages last for decades. It is based on a comparison of all divorces that occur in a single year (regardless of when the couples were married) with the number of new marriages in that same year. We get a somewhat more complete picture by looking at marital milestones people reach based on the year they first married (as shown in the "Percentage of Marriages to Reach Milestones" table). These data include marriages that end owing to the death of the partner; given that life expectancy has increased, the data do provide a sense of shifting patterns. Following

Percentage of Marriages to Reach Milestones*

Men, year of first marriage	Anniversary (percentage still married)*								Women, year of first marriage	Anniversary (percentage still married)*							
	5th	10th	15th	20th	25th	30th	35th	40th		5th	10th	15th	20th	25th	30th	35th	40th
1960–64	94.6	83.4	74.7	70.2	66.9	64.5	62.1	60.1	1960–64	93.0	82.8	73.5	67.0	60.8	57.2	53.6	49.7
1965–69	91.7	88.0	69.9	65.8	62.7	60.5	57.9		1965–69	90.7	79.3	69.6	64.0	59.1	55.8	52.1	
1970–74	88.0	75.0	65.7	60.2	56.8	53.8			1970–74	89.2	74.5	66.1	61.3	56.2	52.6		
1975–79	88.2	73.4	63.7	58.7	54.4				1975–79	86.9	72.8	63.2	57.4	53.2			
1980–84	90.6	74.3	65.2	60.0					1980–84	87.8	71.1	62.9	56.6				
1985–89	87.7	75.4	66.6						1985–89	87.9	74.5	66.4					
1990–94	89.7	77.3							1990–94	87.1	74.5						
1995–99	89.6								1995–99	89.5							

*Counts marriages ended by divorce, separation, and death.

Source: Kreider and Ellis 2011:Table 4.

either the rows or the columns provides insight into both the generational effect and the effects of changing attitudes and practices over time.

Of first marriages that ended in divorce, the median duration is 8 years. Overall, in the United States, 20.5 percent of men and 22.4 percent of women aged 15 and older have been divorced. Among adults aged 50–59, 35.7 percent of men and 37.3 percent of women divorced at some point in their lives (Kreider and Ellis 2011).

In the United States, overall divorce rates increased significantly in the 1960s but then leveled off; since the late 1980s the divorce rate has declined by 30 percent. This trend is due partly to the aging of the baby boomer generation and the corresponding decline in the proportion of people of marriageable age. But it also indicates an increase in marital stability in recent years (Coontz 2006; Kreider and Ellis 2011).

Getting divorced does not necessarily sour people on marriage. About 63 percent of all divorced people in the United States have remarried. The median time between their divorce and second marriage is four years. Women are less likely than men to remarry, because many retain custody of their children after a divorce, which complicates a new adult relationship (Kreider and Ellis 2011; Saad 2004).

FACTORS ASSOCIATED WITH DIVORCE

One of the major factors shaping the increase in divorce over the past 100 years has been the greater social acceptance of divorce. It is no longer considered necessary to endure an unhappy marriage. Even major religious groups have relaxed what were often negative attitudes toward divorce, commonly having treated it as a sin in the past.

In the United States, a variety of factors have contributed to the growing social acceptance of divorce. For instance, most states have adopted less restrictive divorce laws in the past three decades. No-fault divorce laws, which allow a couple to end their marriage without assigning blame (by specifying adultery, for instance), accounted for an initial surge in the divorce rate after they were introduced in the 1970s, though these laws appear to have had little effect beyond that. Additionally, a general increase in family incomes, coupled with the availability of free legal aid to some poor people, has meant that more couples can afford costly divorce

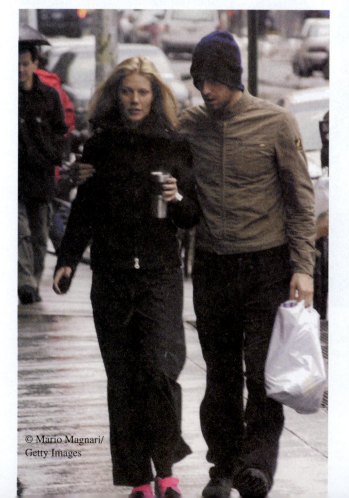

© Mario Magnari/
Getty Images

Trends in Marriage and Divorce in the United States

Rate per 1,000 total population

```
16
14
12
10
 8
 6
 4
 2
 0
   1920  1930  1940  1950  1960  1970  1980  1990  2000  2012
```

Marriage

Divorce

Sources: Centers for Disease Control and Prevention 2012; Tejada-Vera and Sutton 2010; U.S. Census Bureau 1975:64.
Photo: © TriggerPhoto/Getty Images RF.

SOCstudies

researchers recommended that parents should stay together in a "good enough" marriage for the sake of the children. One of the limitations of this research is the relatively small sample size, raising questions about the degree to which the results can be generalized.

Other sociologists have concluded that, for many children, divorce signals the welcome end to a highly dysfunctional relationship. A national study conducted by sociologists Paul R. Amato and Alan Booth (1997) showed that in about a third of divorces, the children actually benefited from parental separation because it lessened their exposure to conflict. Additional researchers, also using larger samples, have concluded that the long-term harmful effects of divorce affect only a minority of children (Booth and Amato 2001; Cherlin 2009; Hetherington and Kelly 2002; Sun and Li 2008).

The debates surrounding issues such as divorce, cohabitation, and same-sex families highlight many of the issues sociologists seek to address in their investigation of family life. What families are, what they do, how they do it, and what obstacles they face are issues relevant for all families. In our modern, pluralistic world, the singular traditions of the past can no longer be taken for granted. People come from many different cultures with multiple taken-for-granted assumptions. Sociology investigates such complexity, providing us with tools so that we might better understand how we think and act in the context of families.

proceedings. Also, as society provides greater opportunities for women, more and more wives are becoming less dependent on their husbands, both economically and emotionally. They may feel more able to leave a marriage if it seems hopeless (Coontz 2011).

IMPACT OF DIVORCE ON CHILDREN

Divorce is traumatic for all involved, but it has special meaning for the more than 1 million children whose parents divorce each year. There is significant sociological debate on the effects divorce has on children. One major study tracked 131 children of divorce over a 25-year period. It concluded that the impacts of divorce are substantial and long-lasting, including higher rates of drug and alcohol abuse, limited resources for college, and fear of intimacy in adulthood (Wallerstein, Lewis, and Blakeslee 2000). These

SOCIOLOGY IS A VERB

Family Counts

Interview 5 to 10 people (such as classmates) about families. Ask them questions such as: How do they define family? Does family include only those related by blood and law or does it include others? Do pets count as family? How many siblings do they have? How many siblings did their parents have? What role should parents and friends play in partner selection? Take notes on their responses. Do any patterns emerge? What conclusions can you draw from such a sample?

For REVIEW

I. **What is the family?**

    - Sociologists define the family in terms of both what a family is, with an emphasis on blood and law, and what families do or what functions they perform, including reproduction, socialization, protection, regulation of sexual behavior, affection and companionship, and provision of social status.

II. **How do people pick partners?**

    - Social factors shape the pool of potential partners from which individuals select. People balance selection, favoring someone who is from within their group (endogamy) but not too close (exogamy). People tend to pick partners with similar social characteristics (homogamy), including age, education, class, race, and ethnicity.

III. **How do families vary?**

    - There is significant variation in terms of proximity (extended versus nuclear), authority (patriarchal, matriarchal, and egalitarian), duration (divorce), and structure (dual-income, single-parent, stepfamilies, cohabitation, singlehood, child-free, and same-sex).

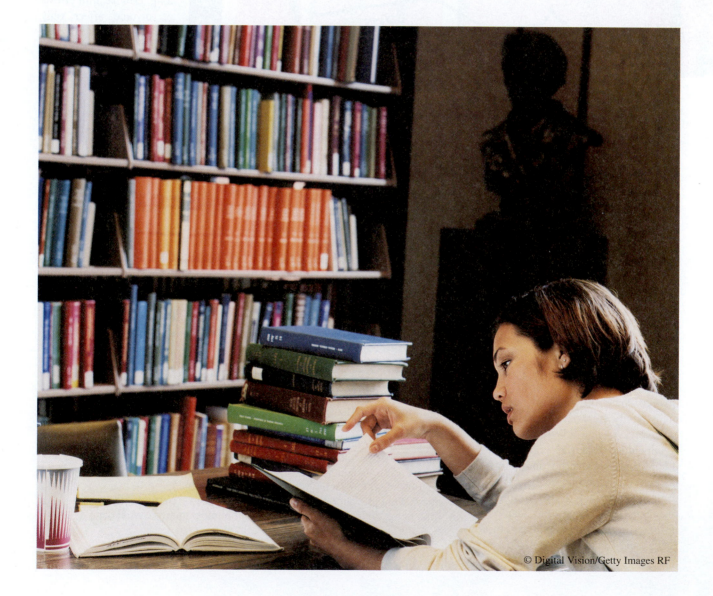

© Digital Vision/Getty Images RF

SOCVIEWS on Families

Functionalist View

The family contributes to **social stability** by performing important functions: reproduction, protection, socialization, regulation of sexual behavior, affection and companionship, and providing social status.

Kinship ties involve both obligations and responsibilities, but also serve as a source of aid in time of trouble.

Parenthood is a crucial **social role** because one of its tasks is the **socialization** of children, which is essential to maintain any culture.

STABILITY, SOCIAL ROLES, SOCIALIZATION
KEY CONCEPTS

Conflict View

A family's social position helps determine a child's opportunities in life as a result of **power, property, and privilege** that is passed from one generation to the next.

Endogamous restrictions on marriage perpetuate existing inequality and may raise **racial barriers**.

Discrimination against gay and lesbian partners is seen in bans on same-sex marriage, denial of legal rights that married couples enjoy, and restrictions on adoption of children.

POWER, DISCRIMINATION
KEY CONCEPTS

Interactionist View

Families provide the context within which we are born, **socialized**, and establish our basic identities.

We construct new family patterns—whether dual-career, single-parent, blended, or gay or lesbian—in response to social and historical changes we both experience and cause.

In egalitarian marriages, couples **interact as equals**, sharing decision making, housework, and child care.

MICRO LEVEL, INTIMATE RELATIONSHIPS
KEY CONCEPTS

MAKE THE CONNECTION

After reviewing the chapter, answer the following questions:

1
How would each perspective shed light on shifts represented by William and Kate's wedding?

2
Take a look at the pie charts of family types. What factors would each perspective focus on to explain the changes over the years?

3
Why does a functionalist definition of what the family *does* provide more insight into families today than trying to define what it *is*?

4
Who rules in your family? Would a functionalist, conflict, or interactionist perspective best describe your family dynamics?

Pop Quiz

1. **Which definition of the family focuses on the importance of blood and law?**
   a. functionalist
   b. matrilineal
   c. substantive
   d. extended

2. **Which system of descent is followed in the United States?**
   a. matrilineal
   b. patrilineal
   c. bilateral
   d. unilateral

3. **Alice, age seven, lives at home with her parents, her grandmother, and her aunt. Alice's family is an example of a(n)**
   a. nuclear family.
   b. patrilineal family.
   c. extended family.
   d. polygynous family.

4. **In which form of marriage may a person have several spouses in his or her lifetime but only one spouse at a time?**
   a. serial monogamy
   b. monogamy
   c. polygamy
   d. polyandry

5. **The marriage of a woman to more than one man at the same time is referred to as**
   a. polygyny.
   b. monogamy.
   c. serial monogamy.
   d. polyandry.

6. **In what type of societies do women dominate in family decision making?**
   a. polygyny
   b. egalitarian
   c. patriarchy
   d. matriarchy

7. **Which norm requires mate selection outside certain groups, usually one's own family or certain kinfolk?**
   a. exogamy
   b. endogamy
   c. matriarchy
   d. patriarchy

8. **The principle that prohibits sexual relationships between certain culturally specified relatives is known as**
   a. monogamy.
   b. the incest taboo.
   c. polygamy.
   d. endogamy.

9. **What is the projected cost of raising a child born in 2013 until she or he is 18 years old?**
   a. $107,011
   b. $304,480
   c. $408,425
   d. $646,464

10. **Overall, how has the divorce rate in the United States changed since the late 1980s?"**
    a. The divorce rate rose dramatically.
    b. The divorce rate rose slowly, but steadily.
    c. The divorce rate declined after having risen significantly in the 1960s and 1970s.
    d. Change in the divorce rate shows no clear pattern.

1. (c), 2. (c), 3. (c), 4. (a), 5. (d), 6. (d), 7. (a), 8. (b), 9. (b), 10. (c)

© Barry Brecheisen/WireImage/Getty Images

8

Education and Religion

WHAT'S TO COME

168 Education in Society / **169** Sociological Perspectives on Education / **176** Schools as Formal Organizations / **180** Defining Religion / **182** Components of Religion / **186** World Religions / **188** Sociological Perspectives on Religion

TRADING PLACES

Over the past decade, thanks to a program called Classroom Connections, students from two very different New York City high schools have exchanged letters and periodically met and worked together. The schools include University Heights, located in a poor South Bronx neighborhood, and Fieldston School, an elite, private school with a tuition of over $43,000 per year. Building on the bridge that those years of exchanges established, Narrative 4, an organization whose mission is "Fearless Hope through Radical Empathy," gathered together students from both schools, paired them up, and assigned each person the responsibility of telling his or her partner's story (Narrative 4 2015). Juliet, a Fieldston student, gave voice to

the spirit of the project, saying, "When you tell someone's story, that's something precious, and you have to take care of it, you have to take care of them." Students from each school came away with a deeper appreciation of the experiences, perspectives, and challenges faced by students at the other school (Lovell and Pfluger 2014).

Years ago, Oprah Winfrey took a slightly different approach. She had students from Chicago's Harper High School and suburban Naperville's Neuqua Valley High School visit each other's schools. The contrast was striking. At Harper, the suburban school students were surprised by the metal detectors, the leaky pool that hadn't been filled in 10 years, a music program lacking instruments, and more. At Neuqua Valley, the city school students encountered a state-of-the-art facility with an Olympic-sized pool, a well-equipped fitness center, a Grammy Award–winning music program, an up-to-date computer lab, and a wide selection of

AP course offerings. As one Harper student put it, "I feel like I've been cheated" (*The Oprah Winfrey Show* 2006).

In spite of investments and upgrades at Harper since then, substantial differences remain today. Harper offers only two AP courses and two languages, Spanish and American Sign Language. Neuqua Valley offers over 20 AP courses and the school's language options include Chinese, French, German, and Spanish. At Harper, 7.3 percent of students pass the state achievement standards exam compared to 87.2 percent at Neuqua Valley. The ACT average at Harper is 14.3 compared to 25.0 at Neuqua Valley. At Harper, 95.8 percent of students are from low-income households compared to 9.4 percent at Neuqua Valley (Illinois State Board of Education 2015b). In the United States, education is seen as a pathway to opportunity for all, but what happens when substantial differences exist in facilities, staffing, and programming?

As You READ >>

- How does education help maintain social order?
- How does education support the existing system of inequality?
- How do sociologists define religion?

>> Education in Society

We need schools. They are so important, in fact, that we often take their existence and necessity for granted. Historically, families had the primary responsibility for teaching us the knowledge and skills we needed to survive and thrive in society. With the advent of the Industrial Revolution and the rise of globalization, however, schools became essential agents of socialization. As a society, we now invest a substantial amount of time and money in **education,** a social institution dedicated to the formal process of transmitting culture from teachers to students. We do so because we believe the individual and collective benefits are worth it.

Schools provide a place where we are exposed to the knowledge of those who have gone before us, enabling us to build on their wisdom as we carve out our pathways into the future. They expose us to beauty and help us investigate the deeper meanings of life. As sociologist W. E. B. Du Bois ([1903] 1994) put it, "The true college will ever have one goal—not to earn meat, but to know the end and aim of that life which meat nourishes" (p. 51). But schools also provide us with the practical

education A social institution dedicated to the formal process of transmitting culture from teachers to students.

Did You Know?

. . . Among high school graduates from the class of 2014, 68.4 percent enrolled in college the following fall. Of these, 64 percent enrolled in 4-year programs, and 36 percent enrolled in 2-year schools.

Source: Bureau of Labor Statistics 2015f. Photo: © Corbis RF.

knowledge and skills we need as members of society, enabling us to get good jobs, become better parents, exercise our citizenship responsibilities, and more.

In the United States this commitment to education is built on a belief that our outcomes should not be determined by birth but by ability and effort. According to this value, being born to wealthy parents should not ensure economic and social privilege any more than being born into meager circumstances should consign one to a life of poverty. Early American political leaders such as Benjamin Franklin and Thomas Jefferson advocated public education as an essential component of democratic societies because it provides individuals with opportunities and society with informed citizens. Horace Mann, often called the "father of American public education," wrote in 1848, "Education, beyond all other devices of human origin, is the great equalizer of the conditions of men" ([1848] 1957). Mann hoped that public education would ensure that children without means would share the same classrooms, curriculum, and

---

SOCTHINK

Who most influenced you to go to college? Considering people you know who did not go to college, what influenced them to make that choice? How powerful are socialization and social networks in making such decisions?

Going GLOBAL

Percentage of Young Adults with University Degrees

Iceland	Poland	Denmark	Ireland	Japan	Czech Republic	United States	OECD Average	Germany	Turkey	Italy	Mexico
60%	53%	49%	46%	45%	40%	39%	38%	31%	27%	26%	22%

Note: Young adult typically means age 22–25, but different countries report data for slightly different ranges. University degree is the equivalent of a BA or BS. The Organisation for Economic Co-operation and Development (OECD) is an international organization composed of 30 democratic nations.

Source: OECD 2014a:Table A3,2a.   *Photo:* © McGraw-Hill Education.

experiences with children of the well-off, thus providing everyone a chance for success.

Over time, education as an institution in the United States became more inclusive and expansive. Initially, public schools were open only to White males. In the 19th century, education was for the most part racially segregated, a practice that was affirmed by the 1896 Supreme Court decision in *Plessy v. Ferguson,* which reinforced the principle of "separate, but equal." Through education reform efforts and legal decisions over two centuries, public education eventually opened up to include everyone regardless of race, ethnicity, sex, or national origin. Examples of education reformers include Emma Hart Willard, who opened the first college-level school for women in 1821, and sociologists such as Du Bois and Jane Addams, both of whom fought for racial and gender equality in the late 19th century. Legal decisions, such as *Brown v. Board of Education* in 1954, found that separate facilities are inherently unequal, and laws such as Title IX in 1972 required equal educational opportunities for both males and females as a requisite for receiving federal funding. Its expansion is reflected in higher levels of educational attainment. From 1940 to 2014, the proportion of people with a high school diploma increased from 24.5 to 88.3 percent, and the number with a college degree rose from 4.6 to 32.0 percent (U.S. Census Bureau 2015h:Table A-2). In spite of these accomplishments, questions remain about the degree to which the principle of opportunity is fully achieved in practice.

>> Sociological Perspectives on Education

Sociologists have closely examined the degree to which education actually succeeds in providing social order and individual opportunity. They have found that although it does offer opportunity and helps establish social order, it also perpetuates inequality. Fulfilling the hopes of Jefferson, Franklin, Emma Hart Willard, and Mann, it has produced an educated citizenry equipped to take on the challenges of modern life. At the same time, however, it reinforces existing beliefs, values, and norms that justify the status quo and its inequalities. Sociologists seek to understand how education can do both at the same time.

EDUCATION AND SOCIAL ORDER

Society needs people with the knowledge and skills to perform the tasks necessary for its continued existence, and individuals need this know-how to survive and prosper. Schools teach students how to read, speak foreign languages, repair automobiles, and much more. Sociologists have identified five functions that education serves for both individuals and society.

Culture Transmission Each society has a common stock of cultural knowledge deemed important for its members. As a social institution, education preserves and transmits society's norms, values, beliefs, ideas, and skills, thus reinforcing society's dominant culture. This endorsed knowledge is transmitted through the formal curriculum taught in schools including "the three 'Rs" (reading, 'riting, and 'rithmatic), as well as history, science, and much more. As a result, young people of each generation learn what they need to survive and succeed.

In addition to the formal curriculum, schools create social space for children to transmit unofficial culture among their peers and to establish themselves as individuals separate from their families. Parents aren't hovering over their shoulders to ensure their children say the right things or keep their coats on at recess, and they can't protect children from getting hurt. School is the place where children learn to stand on their own and to establish relationships with their peer group (Adler and Adler 1996). As children get older, peer relationships grow stronger, and the distance from the parental world grows greater.

Social Integration Why do we need to know things such as, "in 1492 Columbus sailed the ocean blue" and

$a^2 + b^2 = c^2$? The answer is simple: the culture we share binds us together. Even if no one individual possesses all of it—and even if any single item seems necessary only for contestants on *Jeopardy!*—such knowledge represents who we are and what we believe is important. To put it in Durkheim's terms, it is part of our collective conscience, the social glue that holds us together; or, in Mead's terms, the shared culture we learn in schools contributes to our sense of the generalized other, the map of society we hold in our heads.

SOCTHINK

Why do students often feel like schools teach a lot of useless facts? What might this attitude suggest about social integration in modern society?

In the past the integrative function of education was most obvious in its emphasis on promoting a common language. Immigrant children were expected to learn English. In some instances, they were even forbidden to speak their native language on school grounds. More recently, bilingualism has been defended both for its educational value and as a means of encouraging cultural diversity. However, critics argue that bilingualism undermines the social and political integration that education traditionally has promoted.

In an effort to promote social integration, many colleges and universities have established learning communities within which students share common experiences, or they may require first- and second-year students to live on campus. Such programs become more important when students come from diverse backgrounds with different cultural expectations. The goal is to provide experiences that will unify a population composed of diverse racial, ethnic, and religious groups into a community whose members share—to some extent—a common identity. The social integration fostered by education contributes to societal stability and consensus.

Training and Social Control In schools, students learn general behaviors that are expected of them as members of society and specialized skills they will need in the workforce. In the early grades in particular, significant time and effort are spent getting students to do what the teacher wants them to do, when and how the teacher wants them to do it. Through the exercise of social control, schools teach students various skills essential to their future positions in society. Norms provide us with the order and stability we need to make our individual and collective lives predictable, and schools help us internalize normative expectations. Students learn manners, punctuality, creativity, discipline, and responsibility—skills and abilities we need well beyond the classroom. In effect, schools serve as a transitional agent of social control, bridging the gap between childhood and entry into the labor force and wider society.

In a society with a complex division of labor, we especially count on schools to select and train students so that they can become effective workers in specialized jobs. We expect schools to choose those with the most ability to pursue degrees in fields that demand the greatest skill. For example, we want students with aptitude in math and science to become engineers. We use grades as an indicator of such ability and provide degrees to certify that the graduate has sufficient training to perform the job well. We hold out the promise of higher pay to reward those who make the sacrifices that higher education calls for in terms of time and money.

Education Pays

Education level	Median annual earnings
Some high school, no degree	$25,404
High school graduate (includes GED)	$30,909
Some college, no degree	$35,041
Associate's degree	$37,906
Bachelor's degree	$49,350
Master's degree	$57,392
Professional degree	$69,733
Doctorate degree	$70,853

Note: Includes full-time, full-year wage and salary for workers aged 25–34.

Source: U.S. Census Bureau 2014a:Part 1.3.2.1. *Photo:* © Photodisc/Getty Images RF.

Government policies at the national, state, and local levels all influence what happens within the classroom.   Photo: © Mandel Ngan/AFP/Getty Images.

hosted 886,052 international students. In 2012–2013, 289,408 U.S. students studied abroad. Such exposure provides opportunities for cultural innovation as people from various cultures are exposed to and experiment with new and different cultural norms and values (Institute of International Education 2014).

Child Care Historically, family members had the primary responsibility to teach and care for their children until adulthood. Increasingly, we expect schools and teachers to do more of the job—and at younger and younger ages. The movement toward day care and preschool is driven in part by changes in the economy. Although this shift does provide children with a head start in learning the skills they will need in a globally competitive world, working parents have come to depend on schools to essentially babysit their kids, making sure they are cared for and protected. Because they take responsibility for the children during the school day, schools effectively free up parents to participate in the paid labor force.

EDUCATION AND INEQUALITY

In the United States, faith is strong that schools can and should level the playing field by providing a fair chance for success to all. This belief grows out of a commitment to meritocracy, the principle that our outcomes in life should be determined by ability and effort, and a rejection of aristocracy, a system in which outcomes are determined by inherited position or wealth. But researchers have found that schools can and do reproduce the existing system of inequality. To better understand how that is possible, sociologists explore a variety of possible factors including unequal resource distribution.

Cultural Innovation Although schools do preserve and transmit existing culture, education can also stimulate social change. In response to the soaring pregnancy rate among teenagers, for example, public schools began to offer sex education classes. As a means of countering discrimination based on sex or race, many schools turned to affirmative action in admissions—giving priority to females or minorities. Project Head Start, an early-childhood program that served 1,076,000 children in 2014, has sought to compensate for the disadvantages in school readiness experienced by children from low-income families (Administration for Children and Families 2015). To ensure school readiness, it provides classes for preschool children from families below a certain income level, working with them on letter recognition, vocabulary, nutrition, and other basic skills.

Colleges and universities are particularly committed to cultural innovation. Faculty members, especially at large universities, must pursue research and publish articles and books. In so doing, they produce new technology, techniques, knowledge, and practices. Cultural innovation on campuses goes beyond such concrete results, however, because college provides a context within which we can challenge existing ideas and try out new practices. Such experimentation sometimes leads people to accuse professors, especially those with innovative or unpopular ideas, of being out of touch or out of line, but we need people to experiment with new ideas so that our culture does not stagnate.

Campuses also provide an environment in which students from around the world with widely divergent ideas and experiences can interact. In 2013–2014, U.S. campuses

> Good schools, like good societies and good families, celebrate and cherish diversity.
>
> Deborah Meier

Unequal Resource Distribution As we saw at the beginning of this chapter, schools are not all the same. The facilities and programs available to students vary widely. Jonathan Kozol (1991, 2005, 2012), who has studied educational inequality for decades, argues that wealthier districts have the money to offer opportunities that poor districts cannot hope to match, including more AP (Advanced Placement) classes, high-tech labs, athletic facilities, and elective courses in art, music, and languages. This type of disparity occurs because school funding comes primarily through local property taxes. As a result, schools in wealthier areas have access to more funds than do schools in poor communities. In Chicago, for example, the Chicago public school district spent $13,791 per student in 2012–2013. Compare that to the

Effect of Parents' Education on Students' Test Performance

Parental education

Parental education	Percentage below Basic	Percentage at or above Basic
Did not finish high school	Below Basic 55	At Basic 35, At Proficient 9, 0
Graduated from high school	Below Basic 51	At Basic 37, At Proficient 12, 0
Some education after high school	Below Basic 35	At Basic 46, At Proficient 19, 1
Graduated from college	Below Basic 23	At Basic 39, At Proficient 32, 5

Below Basic • At Basic • At Proficient • At Advanced

Note: Percentage distribution of 12th-grade students across NAEP mathematics achievement levels, by highest level of parental education, 2013.
Source: NAEP 2015.

$23,184 per student spent by the wealthy northern suburban Highland Park/Deerfield district (Illinois State Board of Education 2015a). As a former New York City principal put it, "I'll believe money doesn't count the day the rich stop spending so much on their own children" (quoted in Kozol 2005:59).

Of course, money isn't the only factor shaping outcomes. We must also take into account social and cultural resources. Sociologist Annette Lareau, for example, found that a parent's level of educational attainment is a strong predictor of his or her child's educational outcome (Lareau 2011). This is due, in part, to a cultural divide between children that opens up at a young age. Researchers focusing on early childhood socialization compared language use and exposure among families from different social class positions. They found that children whose parents are professionals hear, on average, 2,153 words per hour compared to 1,251 for working-class kids, and 616 for children in families receiving welfare assistance. By the age of three, children in the professional families have a vocabulary of 1,116 words compared to 749 words in working-class families, and 525 words in families receiving welfare assistance (Hart and Risley 1995).

By the time children enter formal schooling, those with larger vocabularies are more prepared to succeed and receive more positive feedback from their teachers.

In the classic comic strip *Calvin and Hobbes,* Calvin is a first-grader who often struggles with balancing what he wants to do versus doing what is expected of him. That is especially true when it comes to school. He gives voice to the experience many of us have had as we are socialized to accept the institutional expectations of the larger society at the cost of our individual freedom.

Source: CALVIN AND HOBBES © 1988 Watterson. Reprinted with permission of UNIVERSAL UCLICK. All rights reserved.

Such differences carry all the way through high school. For example, as the "Effect of Parents' Education on Students' Test Performance" graph demonstrates, performance on standardized tests, in this case for math, vary based on the educational attainment of parents. Among high school seniors whose parents have graduated from college, 37 percent score at proficient or advanced levels in math. Compare that to 12 percent for those whose parents have only graduated from high school (NAEP 2015). SAT scores are similarly influenced by factors such as race, ethnicity, family income, and school type (National Center for Education Statistics 2014;Tables 226.10, 226.30).

Teacher Expectancy Teacher's perceptions have powerful effects on student outcomes. Psychologist Robert Rosenthal and school principal Lenore Jacobson (1968) documented what they referred to as a **teacher-expectancy effect**—the impact that a teacher's expectations about a student's performance may have on the student's actual achievements. They conducted experiments to document this effect.

Rosenthal and Jacobson informed teachers that they were administering a verbal and reasoning pretest to children in a San Francisco elementary school. After administering the tests, the researchers told the teachers that some of the students were "spurters"—children who showed particular academic potential. However, rather than using the actual test scores to make this determination, the researchers randomly selected the 20 percent of the students they identified as spurters. When the students were later retested, the spurters scored not only significantly higher than they had in previous tests but also significantly higher than their peers. Moreover, teachers evaluated the spurters as more interesting, more curious, and better adjusted than their classmates. These results provide a classic case of a self-fulfilling prophecy at work. Teachers expected some students to do well, and so they did. Such effects are of particular concern given that factors such as race, ethnicity, class, and gender shape teachers' perceptions (McKown and Weinstein 2008; Rubie-Davies 2010; van den Bergh et al. 2010).

Tracking As we saw earlier, one of the functions of education is job training. Ideally, we want to match a person's inherent ability to the position for which he or she is best suited. In principle, schools sort students based on their ability. To put it crudely, we want to match smart students to smart jobs and we expect schools to help us do so. In a classic study, sociologists Kingsley Davis

Personal Sociology

Unearned Advantages

My daughters Emily and Eleanor make me proud. They get good grades, and their scores on the standardized exams are sky high. But as a sociologist, I know that they benefit from the fact that their parents are college graduates. As parents, Lori and I provide Em and El with economic, social, and cultural resources in the form of books, activities, and even vacations to historic locations. Kids from such families tend to do better in school than children who lack such opportunities. It's almost as if Emily and Eleanor are cheating. They did nothing to deserve such advantages, and yet, as a society, we act as if educational outcomes—good or bad—are solely based on merit.

and Wilbert E. Moore (1945) argued that all societies have positions that are more important for society's survival or that require greater skill or knowledge to perform and that not everyone has the ability to fill those jobs. For example, not everyone has what it takes to become a medical doctor, accountant, or lawyer. Because we value such skills, we promise that we will reward those who take the time and effort required to develop those skills with high incomes and social esteem. By implication, high pay and prestige become indicators of the superior inherent ability—what Davis and Moore referred to as human capital—possessed by those at the top.

The problem with that model is that factors other than inherent ability, including social class, race, and ethnicity, shape likely outcomes. One way schools reinforce existing differences is by putting students in different tracks. The term **tracking** refers to the practice of placing students in specific curriculum groups on the basis of their test scores and other criteria. In theory, tracking is beneficial because it allows students to be taught

teacher-expectancy effect The impact that a teacher's expectations about a student's performance may have on the student's actual achievements.

tracking The practice of placing students in specific curriculum groups on the basis of their test scores and other criteria.

Did You Know?

SOCTHINK

What experiences have you had with tracking? To what extent do you believe it was effective for both high-track and low-track students? What are its limitations in terms of equal opportunity?

hidden curriculum Teaching students to submit to authority and accept society's dominant ideology.

correspondence principle Schools' reproduction of the existing class structure through socializing students to embrace their social class position.

credentialism An increase in the lowest level of education required to enter a field.

at a level and pace most consistent with their abilities. In practice, however, tracking often starts at a young age, and student selection for low- versus high-ability groups is often correlated with their social class, race, or ethnicity. In effect, the differences children bring with them on their first day of kindergarten

scored high enough to qualify for college credit—a much higher proportion than in selective programs, in which only 17 percent of students qualified for college credit. When given an opportunity to do so, students who were otherwise excluded were able to succeed (B. Ellison 2008; Sacks 2007).

Issues such as teacher expectancy and tracking raise questions about whose interests schools really serve. Sociologists from the conflict perspective argue that, in addition to schools' formal curriculum, there is also a **hidden curriculum** through which students learn to submit to authority and accept society's dominant ideology. For example, children learn to obey orders, not to not speak until called on, to provide appropriate answers, and to regulate their behavior according to the clock. In ways such as these, schools socialize students to willingly submit to authority figures, including bosses and politicians.

Sociologists Samuel Bowles and Herbert Gintis (1976) claim that the needs of the economy shape the structure of education. Capitalism requires a diverse workforce with varieties of skill levels from the simple to complex. According to what they call the **correspondence principle,** schools reproduce the existing class structure by socializing students to embrace their social class position. Thus, working-class children, assumed to be destined for subordinate positions, are likely to be placed in high school vocational and general tracks, which emphasize close supervision and compliance with authority. In contrast, young people from more affluent families are likely to be directed to college preparatory tracks, which stress leadership and decision making—the skills they are expected to need as adults.

shape their likely long-term educational outcomes (Oakes 2008).

Research on tracking raises questions about its effectiveness, especially for low-ability students. In one study of low-income schools in California, researchers discovered a staggering difference between students who were tracked and those who were not. At one school, all interested students were allowed to enroll in advanced placement (AP) courses, not just those who were selected by the administration. Half the open-enrollment students

Did You Know?

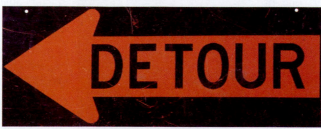

Credentialism When issues of inequality arise, education is often presented as a pathway to opportunity. This may be true at the individual level, but there is a structural problem with that solution. The more people who get degrees, the less valuable those degrees become. If everyone has a high school diploma, it loses its power as a source of distinction. As the supply of graduates exceeds employers' demand, students feel compelled to pursue associate's or bachelor's degrees to stand out from the crowd. This leads to **credentialism,**

5 Movies on EDUCATION

The Class
A year in the life of an inner-city classroom in Paris.

School of Rock
A substitute teacher shakes up a private grade school.

Freedom Writers
Students bond by giving voice to the stories of their lives.

Terri
An assistant principal looks out for an oversized teen misfit.

Precious
An overweight, illiterate pregnant teen finds a different path in life through an alternative school.

they may have to take on significant levels of debt in the form of student loans to do so (Pew Research Center 2014g). At public colleges and universities, 59 percent of graduates who received bachelor's degrees in 2012–2013 took out student loans with an average debt of $25,600. At private colleges and universities, the 64 percent who graduated with loans had an average debt of $31,200. Overall, 45 percent of students from families in the top 25 percent of income earners graduated with no student debt, compared to 21 percent of students in the lowest-income quartile (College Board 2014).

Gender Women and girls in the United States experienced a long history of educational discrimination. It took until 1833 for Oberlin College to become the first institution of higher learning to admit female students—some 200 years after the founding of Harvard, the first men's college in the United States. Even so, Oberlin believed that women should aspire to become wives and mothers, not lawyers and college professors. In addition to attending classes, female students washed men's clothing, cared for their rooms, and served them meals.

In the 20th century, sexism in education showed up in many ways—in textbooks with negative stereotypes of women, in counselors' pressure on female students to prepare for "women's work," and in unequal funding for women's and men's athletic programs. In fact, throughout much of the century, only about one-third of college students were women. During that time they sat in classrooms staffed predominantly by male professors, because few college faculty members were female (U.S. Department of Education 2014:Table 301.20).

the increase in the lowest level of education needed to enter a field. Many students today fear that such credential inflation means that even a college degree is not enough to ensure a good job.

Credentialism can reinforce existing patterns of social inequality. Students from poor, working-class, and middle-class families, including those in minority groups, want to go to college because of the income advantages a degree confers, but, because they lack sufficient resources,

Women in Higher Education

- Percentage of bachelor's degrees earned by women
- Percentage of college faculty who are women
- Percentage of doctorates earned by women

Source: U.S. Department of Education 2013:Table 301.20. *Photo:* © Mike Kemp/Getty Images RF.

Today women have much greater educational opportunity, largely as a result of women's movements that worked for social change. Title IX of the Education Amendments of 1972 played a pivotal role in expanding access. It states, "No person in the United States shall, on the basis of sex, be excluded from participation in, be denied the benefits of, or be subjected to discrimination under any education program or activity receiving Federal financial assistance." While Title IX is most commonly associated with equal opportunity for women in athletics, among other things, it also eliminated sex-segregated classes and prohibited sex discrimination in admissions. And women have made the most of this opportunity. In 1900, women received 19.1 percent of bachelor's degrees conferred. Since the 1950s, the percentage has risen dramatically so that by 2012, 57.3 percent of bachelor's degrees went to women, as the "Women in Higher Education" graph demonstrates. Women students are also more likely to be taught by women professors, who now compose 48.2 percent of total faculty (U.S. Department of Education 2014:Table 301.20).

Inequality and Opportunity The fact that schools can actually reinforce existing patterns of inequality has led some educators to wonder whether schools should discourage members of disadvantaged groups from even attempting college. They fear that the long-term emotional toll of failure would be too great. Sociologists John R. Reynolds and Chardie L. Baird (2010) sought to answer the question "Do students who try but fail to achieve their educational dreams experience long-term frustration and anxiety?" Based on research from two national longitudinal studies, they concluded that the answer to this question is no. Those who fail to fulfill their aspirations develop "adaptive resilience," allowing them to cope with their lack of college success. Reynolds summarizes it this way: "Aiming high and failing is not consequential for mental health, while trying may lead to higher achievements and the mental and material benefits that go along with those achievements" (quoted in Elish 2010). As a result of their research, Reynolds and Baird recommend encouraging students to aim higher because it significantly increases students' chances of getting ahead, as the experience of women in higher education demonstrates. In fact, researchers have found that those with characteristics making them least likely to pursue a college degree—such as coming from low-income families, having parents with less education, or being African American or Latino—are most likely to benefit from obtaining one (Brand and Xie 2010).

Education does establish social order and provide opportunities for individuals to get ahead. At the same time, in preserving the existing order, it reproduces existing patterns of inequality. Sociology allows us to better understand how these seemingly contradictory outcomes can be accomplished through education. As the experience with Title IX demonstrates, positive social change is possible. Having a better appreciation of how education functions enables us to more effectively work toward realizing the initial goal of education: to provide opportunity and a more open society.

Did You Know

. . . In 2012, women earned more than 75 percent of the bachelor's degrees awarded in health professions, education, and psychology, but less than 20 percent in computer and information sciences and engineering.
Source: U.S. Department of Education 2014:Table 318.30.

SOCTHINK

Women's participation in NCAA college athletics has increased more than 500 percent since 1972, from 31,852 then to 205,021 participants in 2013–2014 (NCAA 2014). And high school rates rose from 294,015 in 1972 to 3,267,664 participants in 2013–2014 (NFHS 2014). To what extent would we have seen such an increase had it not been for a law that mandated increased opportunity? How might increased opportunity for women in athletics have an impact on increased opportunity in other areas?

>> Schools as Formal Organizations

The early advocates of public education would be amazed at the scale of the education system in the United States in the 21st century. In many respects, today's schools, when viewed as an example of a formal organization, are similar to factories, hospitals, and business firms. Instead of producing cars, patients, or profits, they pump out millions of students per year. In doing so, schools must be responsive to the various constituencies outside of the student body, including parents, employers, neighborhoods, and politicians. To handle their complex mission, schools have had to become increasingly institutionalized.

THE BUREAUCRATIZATION OF SCHOOLS

It simply is not possible for a single teacher to transmit all the necessary culture and skills to children who will enter many diverse occupations. The growing number of students being served by school systems and the greater

Average Salaries for Teachers

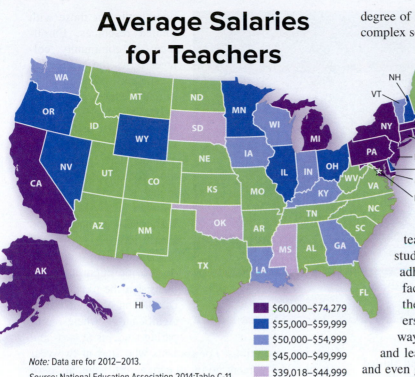

■	$60,000–$74,279
■	$55,000–$59,999
■	$50,000–$54,999
■	$45,000–$49,999
■	$39,018–$44,999

Note: Data are for 2012–2013.
Source: National Education Association 2014:Table C-11.

Teacher Turnover

21%
High-poverty

Leavers

11% 2% 3% 1% 3% 1%

15%
Low-poverty

Leavers

6% 3% 4% 1%
0.5% 0.5%

■ Transferred to another school
■ Retired
■ Took other job
■ Pursued further education
■ Left for family reasons
■ Other

Note: Percentage of public K–12 teachers who did not teach in the same school the following year, by poverty level of school and the reason teachers left.
Source: Planty et al. 2008:51. *Photo:* © Brand X Pictures/PunchStock RF.

---

degree of specialization required within a technologically complex society have combined to bureaucratize schools.

In many respects, schools put into practice all of Max Weber's principles of bureaucracy that we considered in Chapter 5. When it comes to the division of labor, teachers specialize in particular age levels and specific subjects. Schools are hierarchically organized, with teachers reporting to principals, who are themselves answerable to the superintendent of schools and the board of education.

In terms of written rules and regulations, teachers must submit written lesson plans, and students, teachers, and administrators must all adhere to established policies and procedures or face sanctions for not doing so. As schools grow, they become increasingly impersonal, and teachers are expected to treat all students in the same way, regardless of their distinctive personalities and learning needs. Finally, hiring and promotion—and even grading—are based on technical qualifications alone, and standards are established and rubrics created in an effort to ensure this practice (Vanderstraeten 2007).

The trend toward more centralized education particularly affects disadvantaged people, for whom education promises to be a path to opportunity. The standardization of educational curricula, including textbooks, generally reflects the values, interests, and lifestyles of the most powerful groups in our society and may ignore those of racial and ethnic minorities. In addition, in comparison to the affluent, the resource-poor often lack the time, financial resources, and knowledge necessary to sort through complex educational bureaucracies and to organize effective lobbying groups. As a result, low-income and minority parents will have even less influence over citywide and statewide educational administrators than they have over local school officials (Kozol 2005).

TEACHING AS A PROFESSION

As schools become more bureaucratic, teachers increasingly encounter the conflicts inherent in serving as a professional within the context of a bureaucracy. Teachers must work within the system, submitting to its hierarchical structure and abiding by its established rules. At the same time, teachers want to practice their profession with some degree of autonomy and respect for their judgment. Conflicts arise from having to serve simultaneously as instructor, disciplinarian, administrator, and employee of a school district.

As professionals, teachers feel pressure from a number of directions. First, the level of formal schooling required for teaching remains high, and the public has begun to call for new competency examinations. Second, teachers' salaries are significantly lower than those

© Scott Olson/Getty Images

of many comparably educated professionals and skilled workers. Finally, respect for teachers as competent and responsible professionals has been challenged in the political arena. Many teachers, disappointed and frustrated, have left the educational world for careers in other professions. In fact, between a quarter and a third of new teachers quit within their first three years, and as many as half leave poor urban schools within their first five years (Wallis 2008). Even within a single year, teacher turnover is significant; in high-poverty areas, more than 20 percent of teachers did not teach in the same school the following year.

COMMUNITY COLLEGES

Community colleges exist as a testament to the ideals put forth by Jefferson, Franklin, and Mann. The GI bill in the 1940s and Pell Grants in the 1960s provided significant college financial aid for those with limited means, opening wide the doors to college. However, availability of financial aid, especially in the form of grants, has declined. Community colleges continue to give students a chance to prove themselves, however, and their relatively low cost and open enrollment lower the barriers to success. As a result, an increasing number of students have turned to community colleges, including a surge that started in the fall of 2009 because of a weak economy.

In 2013, there were 7.1 million community college students in the United States, making up 39.5 percent of all students. This represents an almost 750 percent increase in students since 1963. These students are more likely to be older, female, Black, Hispanic, low-income, and part-time, compared to their peers at four-year schools. In fact, the more income and education a student's parents have, the less likely she or he is to attend a community college. This highlights the role these schools play in providing

opportunity for those with limited resources. Enrollment at community colleges raises the aspirations of students. Whether they initially expected to take only a few courses or to finish with a two-year degree, almost one-half of these students later aspired to more education, including a four-year degree or beyond (Ginder, Kelly-Reid, and Mann 2014; Provasnik and Planty 2008).

Community colleges do provide opportunity for many, but the likelihood of completing a degree varies significantly when comparing students at two- and four-year institutions. For students who start at two-year schools, 35.1 percent go on to earn a certificate, an associate's degree, or a bachelor's degree. Contrast that with the 64.2 percent of students who start at four-year schools and earn a degree. The likelihood of giving up also differs. Six years after they started, 46.2 percent of students from two-year schools are no longer enrolled and have no degree. Compare that to 23.6 percent of students who started at four-year schools (U.S. Department of Education 2014:Table 326.40).

Some sociologists have suggested that community colleges serve a "cooling out" function in which students blame themselves for their lack of success. According to this theory, there are a limited number of good jobs in society, so not everyone can obtain one. At the level of the individual, such schools appear to provide opportunity for everyone. Because they got the chance, students who give up are more likely to blame themselves for failure than to develop a critique of the social structure that shaped their likely outcomes. In this way, community colleges can help justify the existing system of inequality (Bahr 2008; Clark 1960, 1980).

HOMESCHOOLING

Some parents view formal schooling as a path to opportunity; others have decided to opt out altogether. More than 1.7 million students are now being educated at home—about 3.4 percent of the K–12 school population. Homeschooled families are more likely to be White, have two parents in the household with only one in the labor force, have parents with a bachelor's degree, and have three or more children (Planty et al. 2009; U.S. Department of Education 2014:Table 206:10).

In a sense this represents a return to the pre–public school days of American education, in which the primary

The High School Class of 2023

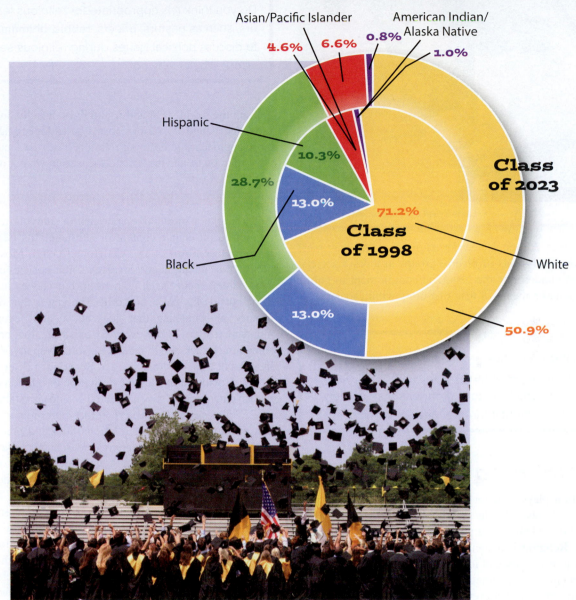

Asian/Pacific Islander
4.6%   6.6%

American Indian/
Alaska Native
0.8%   1.0%

Hispanic
10.3%
28.7%

Black
13.0%
13.0%

Class of 2023

Class of 1998

White
71.2%
50.9%

Note: Projected high school graduating class of 2023 by race and ethnicity.
Source: Hussar and Bailey 2014: Table 13.   *Photo:* © Getty Images RF.

responsibility for teaching rested with parents. When asked to identify the most important reason for choosing this path, 36 percent of parents said they were motivated by a desire to provide religious or moral instruction (the most common response), and 83 percent overall identified that as an important factor. A concern about the environment of schools—safety, drugs, and negative peer pressure—was most important to 21 percent, and 17 percent attributed their decision primarily to dissatisfaction with the school's academic instruction (Planty et al. 2009). In addition, some immigrants choose homeschooling as a way to ease their children's transition to a new society. For example, increasing numbers of the nation's growing Arab American population have joined the movement toward homeschooling (Cooper and Sureau 2007; MacFarquhar 2008). Other parents see it as a good alternative for children who suffer from attention deficit hyperactivity disorder (ADHD) and learning disorders (LDs). A study by the Home School Legal Defense Association (2005), a homeschool advocacy organization, found that homeschooled students score higher than others on standardized exams in every subject and in every grade.

The rise in homeschooling points toward a growing dissatisfaction with the institutionalized practice of education. Early public school advocates argued for the importance of a common curriculum rooted in a shared sense of values. Homeschooling, however, points toward pluralism and the desire to retain the unique subcultural values of a

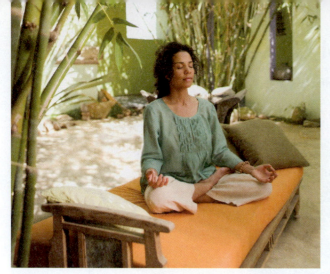
© Chris Ryan/OJO Images/Getty Images RF

community. Although new forms of schooling may meet the individual needs of diverse groups in today's society, they also undermine the historical commitment to public education as a means of fostering unity within society.

SOCTHINK

What do you think are the advantages and disadvantages of being homeschooled? How might it contribute to a stronger sense of identity? How might it threaten the social order?

>> Defining Religion

Education plays a major role in socializing members of society into shared values and norms, and religion helps cement those beliefs and practices into people's hearts and minds. **Religion** is a social institution dedicated to establishing a shared sense of identity, encouraging social integration, and offering believers a sense of meaning and purpose. Though levels of religious participation vary from place to place, religion continues to be a major force

religion A social institution dedicated to establishing a shared sense of identity, encouraging social integration, and offering believers a sense of meaning and purpose.

sacred Elements beyond everyday life that inspire respect, awe, and even fear.

profane The ordinary and commonplace elements of life, as distinguished from the sacred.

© PhotoDisc/Getty Images RF

SOCTHINK

Do you think it is appropriate for religious leaders, such as pastors, priests, rabbis, or imams, to discuss political issues during religious services? Why or why not?

both on the world stage and in the lives of individuals. To fully understand its various forms, sociologists take two basic approaches to defining religion. The first focuses on what religion is, and the second focuses on what it does.

SUBSTANCE: WHAT RELIGION IS

According to a substantive approach to studying religion, religion has a unique content or substance that separates it from other forms of knowledge and belief. Most commonly, this unique focus involves some conception of a supernatural realm, such as heaven, but it does not have to be outside the physical world. The key is that religion centers on something that goes above and beyond the mundane realities of our everyday existence, that points to something larger, and that calls for some response from us in terms of how we think and act. Sociologist Peter Berger (1969) provided a substantive definition of religion as "the human enterprise by which a sacred cosmos is established" (p. 25). The sacred here refers to that extraordinary realm that becomes the focus of religious faith and practice. It provides believers with meaning, order, and coherence. In describing that sacred realm, people might touch on concepts such as gods and goddesses, angels and demons, heaven and hell, nirvana, or other beings or realms. A society with broad agreement about the nature and importance of this sacred realm is, by definition, more religious.

Sociologists who follow a substantive approach focus on the ways in which religious groups rally around what they define to be sacred. The **sacred** encompasses elements beyond everyday life that inspire respect, awe, and even fear. People interact with the sacred realm through ritual practices, such as prayer or sacrifice. Because believers have faith in the sacred, they accept what they cannot understand. The sacred realm exists in contrast to the **profane**, which includes the ordinary and commonplace.

Different religious groups define their understanding of the sacred or profane in different ways. For example, who or what constitutes "god" varies among Muslims, Christians, and Hindus. Even within a group, different believers may treat the same object as sacred or profane, depending on whether it connects them to the sacred realm. Ordinarily, a piece of bread is profane, but it becomes sacred for Christians during their practice of communion because

Personal Sociology

Victory Dance

I confess to being a Green Bay Packers fan. I follow them religiously. Even though I know better, I practice superstitions in the hope that they will help, including wearing a lucky shirt, not talking on the phone during the game, and though I am embarrassed to admit it, doing a "touchdown dance" around the dining-room table after the Packers score, with high-fives for everyone including our dog. My wife Lori is an even bigger fan. We own stock in the Packers and have season tickets. We've made many pilgrimages to the "frozen tundra of Lambeau Field." Each time we go to a game, we follow the same rituals: park in the same spot, eat a pregame meal at the same restaurant, and enter the stadium early so we can soak it all in.

© Goodshoot/Alamy RF

through it believers enter into connection with God. Similarly, a candelabrum becomes sacred to Jews if it is a menorah. For Confucians and Taoists, incense sticks are not mere decorative items, but highly valued offerings to the gods in religious ceremonies that mark the new and full moons.

FUNCTION: WHAT RELIGIONS DO

A functionalist approach focuses less on what religion is than on what religions do, with a particular emphasis on how religions contribute to social order. According to a functionalist approach to studying religion, religion unifies believers into a community through shared practices and a common set of beliefs relative to sacred things. The emphasis is on the unifying dimension of religion rather than on the substance of that which unifies. For functionalists, the supernatural or something like it is not an essential part of religion. Religion need not have gods or goddesses, an afterlife, or other such conventional elements. In fact, any social practices that strongly unite us, such as being a sports fan, can function like religion for the individual and for society.

The functional approach to defining religion has roots in the work of Émile Durkheim. He defined religion as "a unified system of beliefs and practices relative to sacred things, that is to say things set apart and forbidden—beliefs and practices which unite into a single moral community, called a 'church,' all those who adhere to them" ([1887] 1972:224). This definition points to three aspects sociologists focus on when studying religion: a unified system of beliefs and practices, involving sacred things, in the context of community.

The first element of Durkheim's functional approach is the unified system of beliefs and practices. What those beliefs and practices are matters less than the fact that they are shared. Terms historically used to describe religious beliefs include *doctrine, dogma, creeds,* and *scripture,* all representing principles believers share through faith. Practices refer to shared rituals such as attendance at services, prayer, meditation, and fasting. Because beliefs and practices are central to religion, we look at them in more detail below.

Unlike the substantive approach, Durkheim's emphasis on sacred things focuses less on the objects themselves than on the believers' attitude toward those objects. Sacred objects and sacred places convey a sense of awe, and religion calls upon believers to treat them with reverence and care. Roman Catholics, for example, treat the bread and wine of communion with respect because they believe that the sacrament transforms those elements into the body and blood of Christ. For Muslims, the Qur'an is a sacred object, and the Kaaba in Mecca is a sacred place. In the functional approach to religion, however, sacredness is in the eyes of the beholders. Any object can be sacred so long as people define it as such and treat it accordingly.

The most important component of Durkheim's definition is this third part: community. It is not the church, mosque, or temple as a building that matters, but the unification of a body of believers into a shared community. What they believe, what they practice, or what they view as sacred is less important than that they have these beliefs, practices, and shared sacred things in common.

SOC THINK

What other things function like religion for us? How about followers of bands, celebrities, TV shows, or politics? To what extent might consumerism, or even work, function like religion?

As suggested, according to this approach, religion need not look like what we conventionally think of as religion. Anything that does what Durkheim's three elements do can function as religion. Just as our understanding of what families are has expanded to include people who are "like family" to us, so also has the definition of religion expanded to include things that function like religion (Cusack and Digance 2008; Jindra 1994; Mathisen 2006). Sports provides a classic example. When it comes to beliefs and practices, sports fans—short for *fanatics*, a term that historically had religious connotations—share beliefs about the superiority of their team and regularly practice rituals in hopes that it will help their team win. They may wear the same jersey to watch the game, sit in the same chair, or do a touchdown dance after their team scores, all out of superstitious fear that failure to do so will make their team lose. In terms of sacred things, there are autographs, jerseys, balls; and the stadium where the team plays, often referred to by fans as a shrine, represents a sacred space. Finally, fans are united into a community with other fans of the team. Being a fan of the team becomes part of their identity. It provides them with joy, satisfaction, and even a sense of purpose. In a personal essay recounting his obsession with soccer, journalist Michael Elliott (2005) put it this way: "What does being a fan mean? It means you will never walk alone" (p. 76).

Going GLOBAL

How Often Do You Attend Religious Services?

Percentage attending religious services once a week or more

Country	Percentage
Rwanda	70.6%
Poland	50.4%
Mexico	46.2%
Egypt	45.2%
Iraq	38.4%
United States	33.3%
South Korea	29.9%
India	24.5%
Russia	4.9%
Sweden	4.2%
China	1.9%

Source: World Values Survey 2015: V145.

>> Components of Religion

In studying religion, regardless of which definitional approach they take, sociologists investigate components of religion that are common to most groups. Their goal is to gain a more complete picture of the role religion plays for both individuals and groups. Sociologists using both approaches focus on how religious groups organize beliefs, rituals, experience, and community.

BELIEFS

Some people believe in life after death, in supreme beings with unlimited powers, or in supernatural forces. **Religious beliefs** are statements to which members of a particular religion adhere. The focus can vary dramatically from religion to religion.

In the late 1960s a significant shift occurred in the nature of religious belief in the United States. Denominations that held to relatively liberal interpretations of religious scripture (such as the Presbyterians, Methodists, and Lutherans) declined in membership, while those that held to more conservative interpretations and sought a return to the fundamentals of the faith grew in numbers. The term

religious belief A statement to which members of a particular religion adhere.

fundamentalism Rigid adherence to core religious doctrines, often accompanied by a literal application of scripture or historical beliefs to today's world.

fundamentalism refers to a rigid adherence to core religious doctrines. Often, fundamentalism is accompanied by a literal application of scripture or historical beliefs to today's world. Fundamentalism grows out of a sense that the world is falling apart due to a decline in true religious belief and practice. Fundamentalists see themselves as presenting a positive vision for the future through a return to the purity of the original religious message.

The phrase "religious fundamentalism" was first applied to Protestants in the United States who took a literal interpretation of the Bible, but fundamentalism is found worldwide among most major religious groups, including Roman Catholicism, Islam, and Judaism. Fundamentalists vary immensely in their beliefs and behavior. Some stress the need to be strict in their own personal faith but take little interest in broad social issues. Others are watchful of societal actions, such as government policies, that they see as conflicting with fundamentalist doctrine (Emerson et al. 2006).

Christian fundamentalists in the United States have fought against the teaching of evolution in public schools because they believe not only that it represents a threat to their beliefs, but also that it is itself a type of religious faith in naturalism (as opposed to the supernaturalism of God). The first, and most famous, court case over the teaching of evolution in public schools occurred in 1925 and is often referred to as the "Scopes Monkey Trial." In that trial, high school biology teacher John T. Scopes was convicted of violating a Tennessee law that made it a crime to teach the scientific theory of evolution in public schools (Larson

2006). Since that time there have been numerous other court challenges, including *Kitzmiller v. Dover Area School District* in Pennsylvania in 2005. In this major case, those opposed to the teaching of evolution sought to force schools to teach the "science" of intelligent design—the idea that life is so complex that there had to be some form of intelligence behind its creation. The judge ruled that intelligent design was a variation on creationism, the teaching of which in a public school would violate the separation of church and state (Padian 2007).

RITUALS

Religious rituals are practices required or expected of members of a faith. Rituals usually honor the divine power (or powers) worshiped by believers; they also remind adherents of their religious duties and responsibilities. Rituals and beliefs can be interdependent; rituals generally affirm beliefs, as in a public or private statement confessing a sin. Like any social institution, religion develops distinctive norms to structure people's behavior. Moreover, sanctions are attached to religious rituals, in the form of either rewards (such as bar mitzvah gifts) or penalties (such as expulsion from a religious institution for violation of norms).

Rituals may be very simple, such as saying a prayer at a meal, meditating, or observing a moment of silence to commemorate someone's death. Other rituals, such as the *hajj*—the Muslim pilgrimage to the Grand Mosque in Mecca, Saudi Arabia—are quite elaborate. Most religious rituals in the United States focus on services conducted at houses of worship. Attendance at a service, silent and spoken prayers, communion, and the singing of hymns and chants are common forms of ritual behavior that generally take place in group settings. These rituals serve as important face-to-face encounters in which people reinforce their religious beliefs and their commitment to their faith. Religious participation varies widely from country to country.

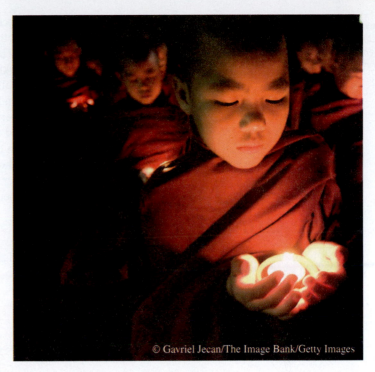
© Gavriel Jecan/The Image Bank/Getty Images

Researchers have found that performing rituals, even apart from religious beliefs, has a significant impact on how we think and feel. For example, upon suffering loss—the death of a loved one, the breakup of a relationship, or even losing the lottery—people who engage in rituals experience lower levels of grief. This is true even for individuals who do not believe that participating in rituals would make a difference. Part of the effectiveness of rituals is the sense of control they provide (Norton and Gino 2013).

EXPERIENCE

In the sociological study of religion, the term **religious experience** refers to the feeling or perception of being in direct contact with the ultimate reality, such as a divine being, or of being overcome with religious emotion. A religious experience may be rather slight, such as the feeling of exaltation a person might receive from hearing a choir sing Handel's "Hallelujah Chorus." Many religious experiences, however, are more profound, such as a Muslim's experience on a *hajj*. In his autobiography, the late African American activist Malcolm X (1964:338) wrote of his *hajj* and how deeply moved he was by the way that Muslims in Mecca came together across racial and color lines. For Malcolm X, the color blindness of the Muslim world "proved to me the power of the One God."

Another profound religious experience for many Christians is being "born again," which involves making a personal commitment to Jesus Christ, marking a major turning point in one's life. According to a 2008 national survey,

religious ritual A practice required or expected of members of a faith.

religious experience The feeling or perception of being in direct contact with the ultimate reality, such as a divine being, or of being overcome with religious emotion.

Did You Know?

. . . Forty-eight percent of Christians in the United States believe Jesus will definitely or probably return to earth within the next 40 years.

Source: Pew Research Center 2013e. *Photo:* © DAJ/Getty Images RF.

ecclesia A religious organization that claims to include most or all members of a society and is recognized as the national or official religion.

34 percent of people in the United States claim they have had a born-again Christian experience at some time in their lives (Kosmin and Keysar 2009). Another survey found that 81 percent of Assembly of God attendees reported having had such experiences, with Baptists coming in at 67 percent. In contrast, only 25 percent of Catholics responded that they had been born again (Barna Group 2001).

The collective nature of religion, as emphasized by Durkheim, is evident in these statistics. The beliefs and rituals of a particular faith can create an atmosphere either friendly toward or less conducive to this type of religious experience. Thus, an Assembly member would be encouraged to "come forward" to make such a commitment and then to share her or his experience with others. A Roman Catholic who claimed to have been born again, on the other hand, would receive much less attention within his or her church (Gallup 2008c).

Major Religious Traditions in the United States

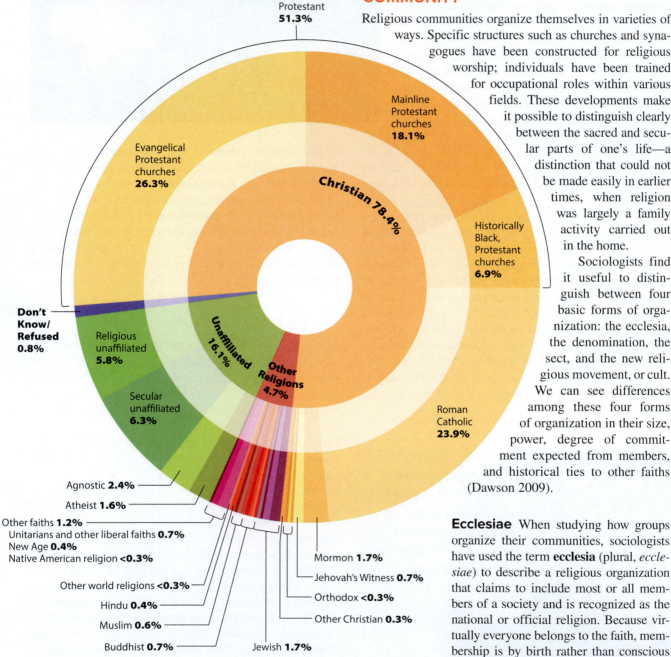

Protestant **51.3%**

Mainline Protestant churches **18.1%**

Evangelical Protestant churches **26.3%**

Christian 78.4%

Historically Black, Protestant churches **6.9%**

Don't Know/ Refused 0.8%

Religious unaffiliated **5.8%**

Unaffiliated 16.1%

Other Religions **4.7%**

Roman Catholic **23.9%**

Secular unaffiliated **6.3%**

Agnostic **2.4%**
Atheist **1.6%**
Other faiths **1.2%**
Unitarians and other liberal faiths **0.7%**
New Age **0.4%**
Native American religion **<0.3%**

Other world religions **<0.3%**
Hindu **0.4%**
Muslim **0.6%**
Buddhist **0.7%**

Mormon **1.7%**
Jehovah's Witness **0.7%**
Orthodox **<0.3%**
Other Christian **0.3%**
Jewish **1.7%**

Note: Due to rounding, figures may not add to 100 and nested figures may not add to the subtotal indicated.
Source: Pew Research Center 2008a.

COMMUNITY

Religious communities organize themselves in varieties of ways. Specific structures such as churches and synagogues have been constructed for religious worship; individuals have been trained for occupational roles within various fields. These developments make it possible to distinguish clearly between the sacred and secular parts of one's life—a distinction that could not be made easily in earlier times, when religion was largely a family activity carried out in the home.

Sociologists find it useful to distinguish between four basic forms of organization: the ecclesia, the denomination, the sect, and the new religious movement, or cult. We can see differences among these four forms of organization in their size, power, degree of commitment expected from members, and historical ties to other faiths (Dawson 2009).

Ecclesiae When studying how groups organize their communities, sociologists have used the term **ecclesia** (plural, *ecclesiae*) to describe a religious organization that claims to include most or all members of a society and is recognized as the national or official religion. Because virtually everyone belongs to the faith, membership is by birth rather than conscious decision. The classic example in sociology was the Roman Catholic Church in medieval Europe. Contemporary examples of ecclesiae include Islam in Saudi Arabia and Buddhism in Thailand. However, significant differences exist within this category. In Saudi Arabia's Islamic regime, leaders of the ecclesia hold vast power over actions of the state. In contrast, the historical state church in Sweden, Lutheranism, holds no such power over the Riksdag (parliament) or the prime minister.

Generally, ecclesiae are conservative in that they do not challenge the leaders of a secular government. In a society with an ecclesia, the political and religious institutions often act in harmony and reinforce each other's power in their relative spheres of influence. In the modern world, ecclesiae are declining in power.

Denominations A **denomination** is a large, organized religion that is not officially linked to the state or government. Like an ecclesia, it tends to have an explicit set of beliefs, a defined system of authority, and a generally respected position in society. Denominations often claim large segments of a population as members. Generally, children accept the denomination of their parents and give little thought to membership in other faiths. Although considered respectable and not viewed as a challenge to the secular government, unlike ecclesia, denominations lack the official recognition and power held by an ecclesia (Doress and Porter 1977).

The United States is home to a large number of denominations. This diversity is largely the result of the nation's immigrant heritage. Many settlers brought with them the religious commitments native to their homelands. Some Christian denominations in the United States, such as the Roman Catholics, Episcopalians, and Lutherans, are the outgrowth of ecclesiae established in Europe. New Christian denominations also emerged, including the Mormons and Christian Scientists. Within the last generation, immigrants have increased the number of Muslims, Hindus, and Buddhists living in the United States.

Although by far the largest single denomination in the United States is Roman Catholicism, at least 24 other Christian faiths have 1 million or more members. Protestants collectively account for about 51.3 percent of the nation's adult population, compared to 23.9 percent for Roman Catholics and 1.7 percent for Jews. Muslims account for approximately 0.6 percent, Buddhists about 0.7 percent, and Hindus about 0.4 percent. Self-described atheists and agnostics make up about 4 percent of the population (Pew Research Center 2008a).

Sects A **sect** can be defined as a relatively small religious group that has broken away from some other religious organization to renew what it considers the original vision of the faith. Many sects, such as that led by Martin Luther during the Reformation in the 1500s, claim to be the "true church" because they seek to cleanse the established faith of what they regard as extraneous beliefs and rituals. Max Weber ([1916] 1958b: 114) termed the sect a "believer's church" because affiliation is based on

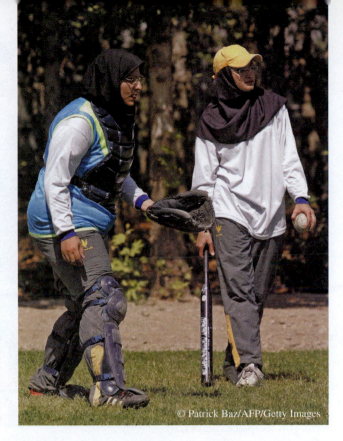

© Patrick Baz/AFP/Getty Images

conscious acceptance of a specific religious dogma.

Sects are at odds with the dominant society and do not seek to become established national religions. Unlike ecclesiae and denominations, they require intensive commitments and demonstrations of belief by members. Partly owing to their outsider status, sects frequently exhibit a higher degree of religious fervor and loyalty than more established religious groups. They actively recruit adults as new members, and acceptance comes through conversion.

Sects are often short-lived. Those that are able to survive may become less antagonistic to society over time and begin to resemble denominations. In a few instances, sects have been able to endure over several generations while remaining fairly separate from society. Sociologist J. Milton Yinger (1970:226–73) uses the term **established sect** to describe a religious group that is the outgrowth of a sect, yet remains isolated from society. The Hutterites, Jehovah's Witnesses, Seventh-Day Adventists, and Amish are contemporary examples of established sects in the United States.

Throughout the world, including the United States, Muslims are divided into a variety of sects, such as Sunni and Shia (or Shiite). The great majority of Muslims in the United States are Sunni Muslims—literally, those who

denomination A large, organized religion that is not officially linked to the state or government.

sect A relatively small religious group that has broken away from some other religious organization to renew what it considers the original vision of the faith.

established sect A religious group that is the outgrowth of a sect, yet remains isolated from society.

follow the *Sunnah,* or way of the Prophet. Compared to other Muslims, Sunnis tend to be more moderate in their religious orthodoxy. The Shia, who come primarily from Iraq and Iran, are the second-largest group. Shia Muslims are more attentive to guidance from accepted Islamic scholars than are Sunnis. About two-thirds of Muslims in the United States are native-born citizens.

Cults or New Religious Movements

Historically, sociologists have used the term *cult* to describe alternative religious groups with unconventional religious beliefs. Partly as a result of the notoriety generated by some of these more extreme groups—such as the Heaven's Gate cult members who committed mass suicide in 1997 so that their spirits might be freed to catch a ride on the spaceship hidden behind the Hale-Bopp comet—many sociologists have abandoned the use of the term. In its place they have adopted the expression "new religious movement."

A **new religious movement (NRM)** or **cult** is generally a small, alternative religious group that represents either a new faith community or a major innovation in an existing faith. NRMs are similar to sects in that they tend to be small and are often viewed as less respectable than more established faiths. Unlike sects, however, NRMs normally do not result from schisms or breaks with established ecclesiae or denominations. Some cults, such as those focused on UFO sightings, may be totally unrelated to existing faiths. Even when a cult does accept certain fundamental tenets of a dominant faith—such as a belief in Jesus as divine or in Muhammad as a messenger of God—it will offer new revelations or insights to justify its claim to being a more advanced religion (Stark and Bainbridge 1979, 1985).

new religious movement (NRM) or cult A small, alternative faith community that represents either a new religion or a major innovation in an existing faith.

secularization Religion's diminishing influence in the public sphere, especially in politics and the economy.

Like sects, NRMs may be transformed over time into other types of religious organization. An example is the Christian Science Church, which began as a new religious movement under the leadership of Mary Baker Eddy. Today, this church exhibits the characteristics of a denomination. In fact, most major religions, including Christianity, began as cults. NRMs may be in the early stages of developing into a denomination or new religion, or they may just as easily fade away through the loss of members or weak leadership (Schaefer and Zellner 2007).

© Pierre-Philippe Marcou/AFP/Getty Images

To summarize, ecclesiae are recognized as national churches. Denominations, although not officially approved by the state, are widely accepted as legitimate. On the other hand, sects are countercultures at odds with society's dominant norms and values. NRMs provide innovative, though not necessarily exclusive, types of faith. The boundaries between these four types are somewhat fluid, and it is helpful to view them as a continuum based on their level of acceptance in the larger society.

>> World Religions

Early sociologists predicted that modern societies would experience widespread **secularization,** which involves religion's diminishing influence in the public sphere, especially in politics and the economy. In the United States, one of the most significant recent trends in religion has been the increase in the number of individuals who, when asked about their religious affiliation, answer "none." Often referred to as "nones," some are agnostic or atheist, but most say they believe in nothing in particular. As a portion of the U.S. population, they have increased from 7 percent in 1972 to 19.6 percent in 2012. The trend is especially pronounced among young adults, with 34 percent of those born from 1990 to 1994 identifying themselves as nones. Globally, 1.1 billion people, 16 percent of the world's population, identify themselves as religiously unaffiliated. This includes atheists and agnostics along with religious believers who do not identify with a particular religious group (Pew Research Center 2012i; Putnam and Campbell 2012). Yet, in the United States and around the world, religion continues to exert a significant influence both individually and collectively.

Christianity is the largest single faith in the world; the second largest is Islam (see the "Major World Religions" figure). Although global news events often suggest an inherent conflict between Christians and Muslims, the two faiths are similar in many ways. Both are monotheistic (that is, based on a single deity), and both include a belief in prophets, an afterlife, and a judgment day. In fact, Islam recognizes Jesus as a prophet, though not as the son of God. Both faiths impose a moral code on believers, which varies from fairly rigid proscriptions for fundamentalists to relatively relaxed guidelines for liberals.

The followers of Islam, called Muslims, believe that the prophet Muhammad received Islam's holy scriptures from Allah (God) nearly 1,400 years ago. They see Muhammad

Going GLOBAL

Religions of the World

Predominant Religions

Christianity (C)*
- Roman Catholic
- Protestant
- Mormon (LDS)
- Eastern Churches
- Mixed Sects

Islam (M)
- Sunni
- Shia

Buddhism (B)
- Hinayanistic
- Lamaistic

Hinduism (H)
Judaism (J)
Sikhism
Animism (Tribal)
Chinese Complex
(Confucianism, Taoism, and Buddhism)

Korean Complex
(Buddhism, Confucianism, Christianity, and Chondogyo)

Japanese Complex
(Shinto and Buddhism)

Vietnamese Complex
(Buddhism, Taoism, Confucianism, and Cao Dai)

Unpopulated Regions

* Capital letters indicate the presence of locally important minority adherents of nonpredominant faiths.

Religious adherence is one of the defining social characteristics of a culture.

Source: Allen 2008.

---

as the last in a long line of prophets, preceded by Adam, Abraham, Moses, and Jesus. Islam is more communal in its expression than Christianity, particularly the more individualistic Protestant denominations. Consequently, in countries that are predominantly Muslim, the separation of religion and the state is not considered necessary or even desirable. In fact, Muslim governments often reinforce Islamic practices through their laws. Muslims do vary sharply in their interpretation of several traditions, some of which—such as the wearing of veils by women—are more cultural than religious in origin.

Like Christianity and Islam, Judaism is monotheistic. Jews believe that God's true nature is revealed in the Torah, which Christians know as the first five books of the Old Testament.

© George Doyle/Stockbyte/Getty Images RF

According to these scriptures, God formed a covenant, or pact, with Abraham and Sarah, the ancestors of the twelve tribes of Israel. Even today, religious Jews believe this covenant holds them accountable to God's will. If they follow both the letter and the spirit of the Torah, a long-awaited Messiah will one day bring paradise to earth. Although Judaism has a relatively small following compared to other major faiths, it forms the historical foundation for both Christianity and Islam. That is why Jews revere many of the same sacred Middle Eastern sites as Christians and Muslims.

Two other major faiths developed in a different part of the world—India. The earliest, Hinduism, originated around 1500 B.C.E. Hinduism differs from Judaism, Christianity, and Islam in that it embraces a number of gods and minor

Major World Religions

Percentage of world population

	Current following, in millions	Primary location of followers today	Founder (and approximate birth date)	Important texts (and holy sites)
Christianity	2,281	Europe, North America, South America	Jesus (6 B.C.E.)	Bible (Jerusalem, Rome)
Islam	1,553	Middle East, Central Asia, North Africa, Indonesia	Muhammad (570 C.E.)	Qur'an, or Koran (Mecca, Medina, Jerusalem)
Hinduism	943	India, Indian communities overseas	No specific founder (1500 B.C.E.)	Sruti and Smrti texts (seven sacred cities, including Vavansi)
Buddhism	463	Southeast Asia, Mongolia, Tibet	Gautama Siddhartha (563 B.C.E.)	Triptaka (areas in Nepal)
Judaism	15	Israel, United States, France, Russia	Abraham (2000 B.C.E.)	Torah, Talmud (Jerusalem)

Sources: Based on Barrett, Johnson, and Crossing 2011; Swatos 2011.

gods, although most worshipers are devoted primarily to a single deity, such as Shiva or Vishnu. Hinduism is also distinguished by a belief in reincarnation, or the perpetual rebirth of the soul after death. Unlike Judaism, Christianity, and Islam, which are based largely on sacred texts, Hindu beliefs have been preserved mostly through oral tradition.

Buddhism developed in the sixth century B.C.E. as a reaction against Hinduism. This faith is founded on the teachings of Siddhartha (later called Buddha, or "The Enlightened One"). Through meditation, followers of Buddhism strive to overcome selfish cravings for physical or material pleasures, with the goal of reaching a state of enlightenment, or nirvana. Buddhists created the first monastic orders, which are thought to be the models for monastic orders in other religions, including Christianity. Though Buddhism emerged in India, its followers were eventually driven out of that country by the Hindus. It is now found primarily in other parts of Asia.

Although the differences among religions are striking, they are exceeded by variations within faiths. Consider the differences within Christianity, from relatively liberal denominations such as Presbyterians or Episcopalians

to the more conservative Mormons and Greek Orthodox Catholics. Similar divisions exist within Hinduism, Islam, and other world religions (Barrett, Johnson, and Crossing 2011; Swatos 1998).

>> Sociological Perspectives on Religion

Sociology emerged as a discipline in the 19th century in the context of significant intellectual, political, and economic upheaval. Intellectuals at the time felt that the religious teachings that had guided society in times of crisis in the past were failing. Auguste Comte and other early sociologists sought to provide a science of society that would tap the ways of knowing built into the scientific method and apply them to the study of society. They recognized the significant role that religion had played in maintaining social order in the past and believed it essential to understand how it had accomplished this, so the study of religion became a significant topic in early sociology. Among classical theorists, for example, Émile Durkheim concluded that religion promoted social order; Max Weber maintained that it helped generate social change; and Karl Marx argued that it reinforced the interests of the powerful.

INTEGRATION

Durkheim was particularly interested in how religion contributed to social integration. He argued that, in traditional societies, religion served as the social glue holding society together. Religion legitimized society's core values and norms in the form of doctrine, statements of faith, sacraments, and rituals. Violating social norms meant more than just disobeying societal, political, or familial leaders. It meant going against the will of gods, goddesses, supernatural beings, or a whole host of other possible forces throughout human history. In this way, religion helped ensure compliance and minimize deviance.

For Durkheim, religious unity grew out of shared experiences. The Amish still provide an example of how living and working in common gives rise to a unified faith (Kraybill et al. 2013). With the transition to modern society, however, especially given the rise of the division of labor, people no longer do all the same things together. We no longer possess the same knowledge and skill. As a result, religion's capacity to provide meaning and a shared sense of purpose is undercut. Yet we still see evidence of its integrating power in shared rituals today, including confessions of faith, bar and bat mitzvahs, public prayers, weddings, and funerals.

The integrative power of religion can be seen, too, in the role that churches, synagogues, and mosques have traditionally played and continue to play for immigrant groups in the United States. For example, Roman Catholic immigrants may settle near a parish church that offers services in their native language, such as Polish or Spanish. Similarly, Korean immigrants may join a Presbyterian church that has many Korean American members and follows religious practices similar to those of churches in Korea. Like other religious organizations, these Roman Catholic and Presbyterian churches help integrate immigrants into their new homeland (Peek 2005; Warner 2007).

Religious integration, while unifying believers, can come at the expense of outsiders. In this sense, religion can contribute to tension and even conflict between groups or nations. During the Second World War, Nazi Germany

© Pavel Filatov/Alamy RF

Religious Faith and Economic Well-Being

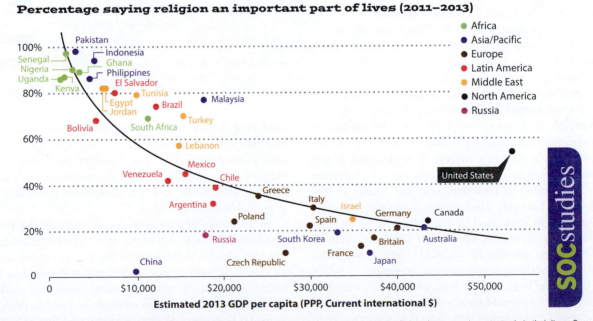

Percentage saying religion an important part of lives (2011–2013)

Legend:
- Africa
- Asia/Pacific
- Europe
- Latin America
- Middle East
- North America
- Russia

Note: The curve represents the logarithmic relationship between GDP per capita and the percentage saving that religion plays a very important role in their lives. Germany, France, Britain % data from spring 2011; U.S., Japan % data from spring 2012.

Source: Gao 2015.

attempted to exterminate the Jewish people; approximately 6 million European Jews were killed. In religious clashes, nations such as Lebanon (Muslims versus Christians), Israel (Jews versus Muslims, as well as Orthodox versus secular Jews), Northern Ireland (Roman Catholics versus Protestants), and India (Hindus versus Muslims and, more recently, Sikhs) have been torn by clashes that are in large part based on religion. Such conflicts often do, however, have the effect of drawing the believers closer together (Juergensmeyer 2003).

SOCIAL CHANGE

Max Weber sought to understand how religion, which so often seems conservative in that it works to maintain order, might also contribute to social change. To do so, he focused on the relationship between religious faith and the rise of capitalism. Weber's findings appeared in his sociology classic, *The Protestant Ethic and the Spirit of Capitalism* ([1904] 2009).

The Weberian Thesis Weber noted that in European nations with both Protestant and Catholic citizens, an overwhelming number of business leaders, owners of capital, and skilled workers were Protestant. In his view, this was no mere coincidence. Weber explained it as a consequence of what he called the **Protestant ethic**— a disciplined commitment to worldly labor driven by a desire to bring glory to God that was shared by followers of Martin Luther and John Calvin. Weber argued that this emphasis on hard work and self-denial provided capitalism with an approach toward labor that was essential to capitalism's development.

To explain the impact of the Protestant ethic on the rise of capitalism, Weber highlights three keys: Luther's concept of a calling, Calvin's concept of predestination, and Protestant believers' resulting experience of "salvation panic." According to Protestant reformer Martin Luther (1483–1546), God called believers to their position in life, and they had to work hard in that calling so as to bring glory to God, regardless of whether they were rich or poor. Protestant reformer John Calvin (1509–1564) added to this the concept of predestination, according to which God, before the beginning of time, picked who would go to heaven and who would go to hell, and there was nothing anyone could do to change their fate. It was impossible to earn salvation through good works; salvation was totally dependent on the grace of God. Complicating this was the fact that no individual could ever know for sure that he or

she was saved because none could presume to know the mind of God. Weber concluded that this created a sense of salvation panic among believers who wanted assurance that they were going to heaven.

Weber theorized that believers would seek to resolve this uncertainty by leading the kinds of lives they thought God would expect godly people to lead. This meant hard work, humility, and self-denial, not for the sake of salvation or individual gain, but for the sake of God. Although doing so would not earn them salvation, to do otherwise would be an almost certain sign that they were not among the chosen. But they could never fully be sure, so they could never let up in their commitment to do God's will. Thus they worked hard not because they had to (either for subsistence or because they were forced) but because they wanted to in response to the salvation they hoped would come from God. It was precisely this kind of worker, internally motivated to

5 Movies on RELIGION

The Master
A charismatic religious leader recruits believers into The Cause.

Jonestown: The Life and Death of Peoples Temple
Documentary about American cult leader Jim Jones.

The Apostle
A Pentecostal preacher in the South.

Everything Is Illuminated
A young man explores his Jewish family's past.

The Tree of Life
An exploration on the meaning of life through the experiences of a 1950s Texas family.

work hard and willing to show up every day even after getting paid, that capitalism needed if it was to engage in rationally planned production. This "spirit of capitalism," to use Weber's phrase, contrasted with the moderate work hours, leisurely work habits, and lack of ambition that Weber saw as typical of traditional labor.

In this way, religion contributed, through the Protestant Reformation, to one of the most significant examples of social change, in the form of the rise of capitalism and its effects, in human history. Weber's argument has been hailed as one of the most important theoretical works in the field and as an excellent example of macrolevel analysis. Like Durkheim, Weber demonstrated that religion is not solely a matter of intimate personal beliefs. He stressed that the collective nature of religion has consequences for society as a whole.

SOC THINK

To what extent do you think religion can be a force for social change? What examples have you seen in your lifetime?

Liberation Theology A more contemporary example of religion serving as a force for social change came through liberation theology, in which the clergy were at the forefront. Many religious activists, especially in the Roman Catholic Church in Latin America, support **liberation theology**—the use of a church in a political effort to eliminate poverty, discrimination, and other forms of injustice from a secular society. Advocates of this religious movement sometimes sympathize with Marxism. Many believe that radical change, rather than economic development in itself, is the only acceptable solution to the desperation of the masses in impoverished developing countries. Activists associated with liberation theology believe that organized religion has a moral responsibility to take a strong public stand against the oppression of the poor, racial and ethnic minorities, and women (Bell 2001; Rowland 2007).

The term *liberation theology* dates back to the publication in 1973 of the English translation of *A Theology of Liberation.* The book was written by a Peruvian priest, Gustavo Gutiérrez, who lived in a slum area of Lima in the early 1960s. After years of exposure to the vast poverty around him, Gutiérrez concluded that "in order to serve the poor, one had to move into political action" (R. M. Brown 1980:23; Gutiérrez 1990). Eventually, politically committed Latin American theologians came under the influence of social scientists who viewed the domination of capitalist multinational corporations as central to the hemisphere's problems. One result was a new approach to theology that built on the cultural and religious traditions of Latin America rather than on models developed in Europe and the United States.

SOCIAL CONTROL

Liberation theology is a relatively recent phenomenon that marks a break with the traditional role of churches. It was this traditional role that Karl Marx opposed. In his view, religion inhibited social change by encouraging oppressed people to focus on otherworldly concerns rather than on their immediate poverty or exploitation.

Marx on Religion Marx described religion as the "opiate of the masses." He felt that religion often, in essence, drugged the believers into submission by offering a consolation for their harsh lives on earth: the hope of salvation in an ideal afterlife. For example, during the period of slavery in the United States, White masters forbade Blacks to practice native African religions. Instead, they encouraged slaves to adopt Christianity, which taught that obedience would lead to salvation and eternal happiness in the hereafter. Viewed from this perspective, Christianity may have pacified certain slaves and blunted the rage that often fuels rebellion.

For Marx, religion plays an important role in propping up the existing social structure. The values of religion, as already noted, tend to reinforce other social institutions and the social order as a whole. From Marx's perspective, however, religion's promotion of social stability only helps perpetuate patterns of social inequality. According to Marx, the dominant religion reinforces the interests of those in power.

From a Marxist perspective, religion keeps people from seeing their lives and societal conditions in

> But the poor person does not exist as an inescapable fact of destiny. . . . The poor are a by-product of the system in which we live and for which we are responsible.
>
> Liberation Theologian Gustavo Gutiérrez

© M. Freeman/PhotoLink/Stockbyte/Getty Images RF

political terms—for example, by obscuring the overriding significance of conflicting economic interests. Marxists suggest that by inducing a "false consciousness" among the disadvantaged, religion lessens the possibility of collective political action that could end capitalist oppression and transform society. Sociological analysis in this tradition seeks to reveal the ways in which religion serves the interests of the powerful at the expense of others.

Gender and Religion Drawing on the feminist approach, researchers and theorists point to the fundamental role women play in religious socialization. Women play a critical role in the functioning of religious organizations, yet when it comes to positions of leadership, women generally take a subordinate role in religious governance. Indeed, most faiths have a long tradition of exclusively male spiritual leadership. Furthermore, because most religions are patriarchal, religious beliefs tend to reinforce men's dominance in secular as well as spiritual matters. Women are more likely than men to say religion is important in their lives, more likely to pray daily, and more likely to attend weekly services. Women play a vital role as volunteers, staff, and religious educators, but even today, religious decision making and leadership typically falls to men. Exceptions to this rule, such as the Shakers and Christian Scientists, as well as Hinduism with its long goddess heritage, are rare (Pew Research Center 2009a; Schaefer and Zellner 2007).

In the United States, women compose 18.6 percent of the clergy, even

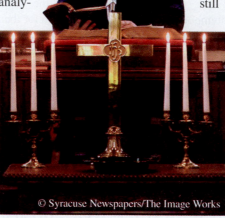

© Syracuse Newspapers/The Image Works

though they account for 33 percent of students enrolled in theological institutions. Female clerics typically have shorter careers than men and are often relegated to fields that do not involve congregational leadership, such as counseling. In faiths that restrict leadership positions to men, women still serve unofficially. For example, about 4 percent of Roman Catholic congregations are led by women who hold nonordained pastoral positions—a necessity in a church that faces a shortage of male priests (J. Adams 2007; Association of Theological Schools 2015; Bureau of Labor Statistics 2015c: Table 11).

In this chapter we have looked at both education and religion. In both cases we find institutions that play a powerful role in shaping how we think and act. Each provides opportunity and reinforces the status quo, including its system of inequality. Sociologists believe that by having a better appreciation for both the opportunities and constraints such institutions present, we can better act both individually and collectively to bring about positive social change.

SOCIOLOGY IS A VERB

Exploring Faith

Pick a local religious group that is significantly different from any you may have experienced in the past. Study their history, beliefs, rituals, expectations, and structure. Interview one of their local religious leaders to gain a better understanding of their beliefs and practices from an insider's point of view. Visit their services at least twice. What were your initial expectations about the group? How, if at all, did your views change?

For REVIEW

I. How does education help maintain social order?
- Education transmits culture, promotes social integration, provides training and social control, stimulates cultural innovation, and provides child care.

II. How does education support the existing system of inequality?
- Education reinforces the status quo, and therefore its existing inequalities, through the hidden curriculum, teacher expectancy, bestowal of status, and credentialism.

III. How do sociologists define religion?
- One approach focuses on the substance of what religion is, defining religion as knowledge and beliefs relating to the sacred realm. The other approach looks at what religions do for society in terms of social order and integration. Both approaches analyze common components including belief, ritual, experience, and community.

SOCVIEWS on Education and Religion

Functionalist View

Education serves five positive functions: transmitting culture, promoting **social integration**, providing training and social control, stimulating cultural innovation, and providing child care.

As societies have become more diverse, education has taken on more of the task of formal **socialization**.

Religion provides **social order**, a sense of **shared identity**, and meaning and purpose in people's lives.

SOCIAL INTEGRATION, SOCIALIZATION, SOCIAL ORDER
KEY CONCEPTS

Conflict View

The education system helps reproduce the existing system of **inequality**.

Unequal funding, **tracking**, the **hidden curriculum**, and **credentialism** serve to reinforce the status quo.

According to Marx, religion can function like a drug that blinds people to their true interests, prompting them instead to accept **submission to authority**, thereby reinforcing the interests of those in power.

INEQUALITY, SUBMISSION TO AUTHORITY
KEY CONCEPTS

Interactionist View

Students from grade school through graduate school learn formal and informal norms, values, and interpersonal skills through classroom interactions.

A teacher's **expectations** about a student impact on student performance and achievement.

Religious rituals generally involve important **face-to-face interactions** with fellow worshipers at services.

EXPECTATIONS, INTERACTIONS
KEY CONCEPTS

MAKE THE CONNECTION

After reviewing the chapter, answer the following questions:

1
The "Education Pays" graph shows one way that "education pays." Using each perspective, how does education pay? Who benefits?

2
How do educational institutions bestow status from both the functionalist and conflict perspectives?

3
Using the conflict perspective, describe how women experience (or have experienced) discrimination in both the educational and religious spheres.

4
Which perspective do you think best describes the dynamics of a typical classroom setting? Explain, including examples.

Pop Quiz

1. Horace Mann, often called the "father of American public education," refers to education as
   a. the great equalizer.
   b. the opiate of the masses.
   c. an instrument for social control.
   d. an opportunity engine.

2. One of the ways education contributes to social order is by providing an environment within which we can challenge existing ideas and experiment with new norms and values. This is known as
   a. transmitting culture.
   b. promoting social integration.
   c. providing training and social control.
   d. stimulating cultural innovation.

3. Samuel Bowles and Herbert Gintis have argued that capitalism requires a skilled, disciplined labor force and that the educational system of the United States is structured with that objective in mind. Citing numerous studies, they offer support for what they call
   a. tracking.
   b. credentialism.
   c. the correspondence principle.
   d. the teacher-expectancy effect.

4. Fifty years ago, a high school diploma was often enough to get a good job. Today it typically takes a college degree or more. This change reflects the process of
   a. tracking.
   b. credentialism.
   c. the hidden curriculum.
   d. the correspondence principle.

5. Which of the following includes this provision, "No person in the United States shall, on the basis of sex, be excluded from participation in, be denied the benefits of, or be subjected to discrimination under any education program or activity receiving Federal financial assistance?"
   a. Title IX of the Education Amendments of 1972
   b. *Brown v. Board of Education of Topeka* (1954)
   c. No Child Left Behind Act of 2001
   d. Higher Education Opportunity Act of 2008

6. The approach to defining religion that emphasizes the significance of the sacred, most often supernatural, realm is known as the
   a. functionalist approach.
   b. conflict approach.
   c. substantive approach.
   d. ecclesia approach.

7. Religious rituals are
   a. statements to which members of a particular religion adhere.
   b. the feelings or perceptions of being in direct contact with the ultimate reality, such as a divine being.
   c. the religious structures through which faith communities organize themselves.
   d. practices required or expected of members of a faith.

8. Of the world religions, the one with the most followers is
   a. Buddhism.
   b. Islam.
   c. Judaism.
   d. Christianity.

9. Sociologist Max Weber pointed out that the followers of John Calvin emphasized a disciplined work ethic, worldly concerns, and a rational orientation to life. Collectively, this point of view has been referred to as
   a. capitalism.
   b. the Protestant ethic.
   c. the sacred.
   d. the profane.

10. The use of a church, primarily Roman Catholic, in a political effort to eliminate poverty, discrimination, and other forms of injustice evident in a secular society is referred to as
    a. creationism.
    b. ritualism.
    c. religious experience.
    d. liberation theology.

1. (a), 2. (d), 3. (c), 4. (b), 5. (a), 6. (c), 7. (d), 8. (d), 9. (b), 10. (d)

© Brendan Smialowski/AFP/Getty Images

Government and Economy

MONEY AND POLITICS

On February 15, 2011, thousands of protestors streamed into Wisconsin's state capitol building to protest Governor Scott Walker's proposed legislation to cut the wages, benefits, and collective bargaining power of most public employees. Protestors came bearing signs, singing songs, and chanting slogans including "Kill the bill" and "This is what democracy looks like." They stayed for weeks. They failed (at least in terms of their immediate goals). Scott Walker was elected governor of Wisconsin in November 2010 as part of a national wave of Republican victories. Dissatisfied with the apparent failure of Democratic leadership to fix the weak economy, voters turned to Republicans. Walker ran on a platform of economic growth via lower taxes and reduced government spending. At his inauguration he declared, "Wisconsin is open for business," and he immediately went into action.

The protests were triggered by Governor Walker's "Budget Repair Bill." He claimed that drastic measures were required to address a projected $3.6 billion budget shortfall. Union representatives for the affected employees agreed to his wage and benefit cuts, but they refused to budge on collective bargaining rights, negotiations between the government and union representatives that deal with wages, benefits, working conditions, and other workplace issues. Walker's bill denied negotiation rights over benefits, including health care, and capped salary increases at no more than the rate of inflation. Critics argued that his real goal was to bust the unions rather than balance the budget. Walker claimed that curtailing collective bargaining was economically necessary.

With Republican majorities in both the state senate and assembly, it was assumed that the bill would quickly become law. But, because it involved spending, the bill required a minimum of 20 voting senators. Senate Democrats left the state denying Republicans that quorum. The standoff, with a boost from the protestors, continued for over three weeks before Republicans stripped all spending provisions from the bill and passed it 18–1. Governor Walker signed the bill on March 11, but a judge struck down the bill, ruling Republican legislators did not provide enough public notice before passing the measure, a ruling that was appealed to the state's supreme court.

In the end, the Republicans wielded their power, yet the unintended consequence was to reenergize Democrats. The conflict is sociologically interesting, because it represents a struggle between institutions (economy vs. government), interests (business vs. labor), and ideologies (conservative vs. liberal). It raises important questions about who rules and why.

As You READ >>

- **How are economic and political power organized?**
- **How does power operate?**
- **How has the economy changed over time?**

>> Economic Change

The upheaval that overtook Wisconsin's capitol building was a manifestation of widespread frustration about the state of the economy and politics in the United States. The protests occurred in the context of a global recession that was triggered by a global financial crisis. That crisis started when a decline in the housing market revealed fault lines in the financial sector which led to the economic collapse of the nation's top investment banks, including Bear Stearns, Lehman Brothers, Merrill Lynch, Goldman Sachs, and Morgan Stanley. Banks around the world, including those in England, Germany, and the Netherlands, faced similar crises and the overall ripple effects resulted in global economic destabilization. Stocks crashed, businesses went bankrupt, unemployment skyrocketed, and governments around the world struggled to figure out how best to respond.

As these negative economic effects lingered, frustration grew. People looked for political solutions. Barack Obama's 2008 campaign for the presidency drew heavily upon the themes of hope and change, and his election turned control of the White House over to Democrats. When the economy remained weak, beleaguered voters in the 2010 midterm elections handed control of the House of Representatives over to Republicans. In 2012, President Obama was reelected while Democrats maintained control of the Senate and Republicans maintained control of the House of Representatives. In the 2014 election, Republicans took control of the Senate and maintained control over the House.

Another group of protestors, frustrated by what they saw as an inability or unwillingness on the part of elected leaders to institute change, staged a sit-in protest in Zuccotti Park in New York City's Wall Street district in September 2011. Known as Occupy Wall Street, the group's primary intent was to call attention to extreme economic inequality in the United States. They argued that the current economic and political system was stacked so that the interests of the top 1 percent of income earners were served at the expense of the bottom 99 percent. They called for systemic economic and political change. The Occupy movement spread to various cities throughout the United States and around the world, The Zuccotti Park sit-in lasted for two months before it was shut down and evacuated by police.

Using the sociological imagination allows us to better understand such economic and political change. Doing so

© AP Photo/Don Ryan

draws our attention to the fact that the economic and political systems we construct influence likely outcomes for individuals. In other words, structures have consequences. Adopting a capitalist economy or a democratic system of government leads us down different paths than we would likely have followed had we adopted alternatives. In this chapter we will look at economic and political systems and their consequences.

ECONOMIC SECTORS

Focusing on the structure of the economy enables us to better see the patterns at work that rise above the level of our individual experiences and that shape the options and opportunities available to us. As we saw in Chapter 1, for example, unemployment must be considered a public issue rather than only as a private trouble. The **economy** is a social institution dedicated to the production, distribution, and consumption of goods and services. The structure of the economy varies across time and place, but we can identify three distinct sectors: primary, secondary, and tertiary.

As a species, we must provide for our subsistence needs. Without food, clothes, and shelter we will die. Throughout human history, we have most frequently done so by taking from nature the things that we need. The *primary sector* of the economy involves activities that extract products directly from the natural environment. The most important manifestation of this for us historically was the rise of agriculture, but extraction also includes activities such as fishing, hunting, forestry, and mining. The economies of the hunting-and-gathering, horticultural, and agrarian societies we encountered in Chapter 5 were characterized primarily by this economic sector.

The Industrial Revolution fundamentally altered our relationship to nature. Advances in technology, including Eli Whitney's cotton gin, Cyrus McCormick's mechanical reaper, and John Deere's steel plow, all contributed to the mass production of agricultural products. As a result, fewer agricultural workers were needed to produce food, freeing them up for work in the new factories that arose as a result of technological innovations in industrial production. The *secondary sector* of the economy consists of activities that transform raw or intermediate materials into finished products. Workers in this sector manufacture products. The mechanization of production contributed to revolutions in transportation and communication, which effectively made the world a much smaller place. It became possible to communicate in real time with whomever we wanted whenever we wanted or to travel to the other side of the globe in a matter of hours. As a result, companies can now obtain raw materials from almost anywhere, transform them into products, and sell those products to customers around the world.

Technological innovation continued to the point where industrial production also became less labor intensive. The mechanization of production meant that fewer workers were needed in manufacturing, once again freeing them up for new jobs that contributed to the expansion of a third economic sector. The *tertiary sector* of the economy consists of activities that provide services rather than produce tangible goods. Put simply, the service sector involves doing things for others rather than offering them a material product. Service-sector occupations include teacher, physician, social worker, food server, hotel housekeeper, truck driver, data processor, financial adviser, investment counselor, insurance agent, real estate broker, custodian, actor, personal trainer, and life coach (U.S. Census Bureau 2013d). Most college students today are pursuing degrees in hopes of obtaining a good job in this sector.

DEINDUSTRIALIZATION

When a society's economic foundation transitions from one economic sector to another, significant upheaval occurs. Moving from a traditional, agriculturally based economy to a modern, industrial economy, as happened during the Industrial Revolution, had traumatic consequences for how people lived and worked. Sociology emerged as a discipline in order to come to terms with its effects. The ongoing transition to an economy built upon the tertiary or service sector has proved no less challenging.

The consequences of this shift became apparent starting in the 1970s when the U.S. economy moved away from its manufacturing base through a process known as **deindustrialization,** which refers to the systematic and widespread reduction of investment in domestic manufacturing and material production. Two key factors play a role in its expansion. The first is the mechanization of labor. Through technological innovation, a single machine can do the job of many workers. The coordination of production in the form of the assembly line multiplied that effect and the advent of robots and computers expanded it even further. Economist John Maynard Keynes (1930a, 1930b) referred to the resulting loss of jobs as "technological

economy A social institution dedicated to the production, distribution, and consumption of goods and services.

deindustrialization The systematic and widespread reduction of investment in domestic manufacturing and material production.

SOCTHINK

If you were the CEO of an American manufacturing company that was facing declining profits because of international competition, what would you do? Would you move your production facilities overseas to reduce labor costs? What other options might exist? To what extent does the system within which companies operate shape the choices that are available to them?

Reprinted with the permission of Mike Thompson and Creators Syndicate.

unemployment." In such a situation, productivity can remain high while the number of secondary-sector jobs, along with their level of wages, declines (Carr 2014; Rotman 2013; A. Smith and Anderson 2014). The second factor is the globalization of labor. In the United States, this began with companies moving their industrial production plants from the nation's central cities to the suburbs, then to the South where

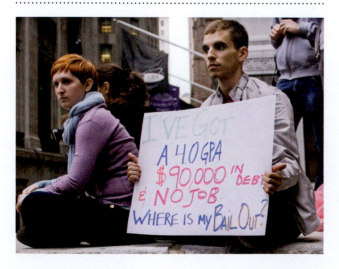

The effects of the economic downturn have been widespread. Recent college graduates have found a difficult job market. Many people have expressed frustration that large corporations have received billions while individual workers struggle. Photo: © Tony Savino/Corbis.

labor laws were weaker, and finally out of the country where wages were lower and health, safety, and environmental regulations were less restrictive. At the same time, many companies sought to become leaner and did so by **downsizing,** organizational restructuring to reduce the size of a company's workforce. The goal of downsizing is to increase efficiency and reduce costs in the face of worldwide competition.

Companies are also able to leverage their economic assets by subcontracting tasks that used to be performed within the firm. Such outsourcing happens domestically, for example, when a company hires an external firm to provide security or janitorial services. Companies can take this a step further by **offshoring,** which involves outsourcing work to foreign contractors. This practice hit the manufacturing sector first, as happened when U.S. television companies contracted with Chinese manufacturing firms to produce their TVs. But it is increasingly affecting service-sector jobs as well due to advanced telecommunications and the growth of skilled, English-speaking workers in developing nations that have relatively inexpensive labor forces. These jobs can require considerable training, such as accounting and financial analysis, computer programming, or radiology. Today, it is increasingly possible that the person reading your CT scan or MRI is located in another country (Clark, Huckman, and Staats 2013; Olofsson et al. 2014).

While this shift has brought jobs and technology to nations such as India, there is a downside to offshoring for foreign workers as well. Although outsourcing is a significant source of employment for India's upper-middle class, hundreds of millions of other Indians have benefited little if at all from the trend. Most households in India do not possess any form of high technology: only about 2.3 percent have land lines and 71 percent have cell phones, and 10 percent are Internet users (International Telecommunications Union 2015). Instead of improving these people's lives, the new business centers have siphoned water and electricity away from those who are most in need. Even the high-tech workers are experiencing negative consequences. Many suffer from stress disorders such as stomach problems and difficulty sleeping; more than half quit their jobs before the end of a year (Waldman 2004a, 2004b, 2004c).

THE GREAT RECESSION

The process of deindustrialization was part of a larger economic shift toward a global economy consisting of complex, worldwide networks of producers and consumers. The resulting interdependent connections increased the possibility that, if one part of the system collapsed, it could have global consequences. That is precisely what happened starting in 2007 when the global financial collapse, described earlier, occurred. The resulting economic crisis, often referred to as the Great Recession, had significant and long-term consequences. People's taken-for-granted assumptions about how their lives would and should proceed—get a good education, work hard in your job, and success will follow—were called into question (Packer 2013).

Unemployment became a widespread problem. Rates more than doubled from February 2008 to October 2010 and remained high for an extended period of time. On top of that, increasing numbers of people experienced long-term unemployment. In the first quarter of 2013, for example, 37.4 percent of the 11.7 million people who were unemployed had been jobless for 27 weeks or more, many of whom had exhausted unemployment benefits (Bureau of Labor Statistics 2013e; Pew Charitable Trusts 2012).

Among those who were working, wages were flat for most and fell for many; young adults were particularly hard hit. The employment rate among 18- to 24-year-olds reached a record low of 54 percent and their wages declined more than those of any other age group since the economic downturn began (Levanon, Chen, and Chang 2012; Pew Research Center 2012b). A record percentage of young adults turned toward higher education, which accounts for part of their decreased employment rate (P. Taylor 2011). The hope for many was that getting a degree would bolster their employability, yet the job prospects for recent college graduates have also dimmed.

Among recent college graduates, 43 percent report they are working in a job that does not require a college degree (Stone, Van Horn, and Zukin 2012). On top of that, most graduates faced the prospect of paying back the substantial student loan debt they incurred in order to get their degrees. For college graduates in the Class of 2013, the average debt among those who took out student loans was $28,400 (Project on Student Debt 2014). Among those who graduated with college debt, 27 percent of borrowers had balances that were past due and 27 percent moved in with parents or family members to save money (Brown et al. 2012; Stone et al. 2012).

SOCTHINK

What impact did the global economic crisis have on you, your friends, and family? How did it figure in to your plans for the future?

For many people, bad news seemed everywhere. There was an increase in the number of people who were working yet not earning enough to get out of poverty (Smiley and West 2012), and the age at which people could expect to retire was going up (Brandon 2012). Yet, for some, things were looking up. In 2010, overall average income rose 2.3 percent, but the benefits of a slowly improving economy were not equally shared. Income for the top 1 percent grew 11.6 percent while the bottom 99 percent saw only a 0.2 percent increase (Saez 2012). Corporations also did well, earning record profits in part because they reduced their costs by cutting their workforce and expecting more productivity from their remaining employees (Tully 2012).

THE CHANGING FACE OF THE WORKFORCE

The workforce in the United States constantly adapts to such economic changes. During World War II, when men were mobilized to fight abroad, women entered the workforce in large numbers. With the coming of the civil rights movement in the 1960s, minorities found numerous job opportunities opening to them. Sociologists and labor specialists foresee a workforce increasingly composed of women and racial and ethnic minorities. In 1970, women made up 38.1 percent of the civilian labor force; there were more women out of the labor force than in it. By 2012, that number rose to 47 percent. Overall, 57.7 percent of women aged 16 and up were in the paid labor force compared to 70.2 percent for men (Bureau of Labor Statistics 2014c). The dynamics for minority group workers are even more dramatic, as the number of Black, Latino, and Asian American workers continues to increase at a faster rate than the number of White workers owing to demographic changes (Burns, Barton, and Kerby 2012).

As the workforce has become more diverse, companies have sought ways to adapt. A sociological study of workplace programs designed to increase managerial diversity found that 39 percent of employers had diversity training programs. Researchers discovered that relying solely on education programs designed to reduce managerial bias was not particularly effective. The most successful approach is to have a point person, task force, or affirmative action plan that holds people responsible for change (Kalev, Dobbin, and Kelly 2006).

>> Power and Authority

Sociologists have always been interested in how power is achieved and maintained. In the midst of major political and economic shifts, early sociologists developed theories of power intended to be sufficiently broad to explain the rise of democracy or the expansion of market-based capitalism yet sufficiently narrow to explain who gets their way within interpersonal relationships.

Workforce Diversity: Past, Present, and Future

Percentage of the workforce

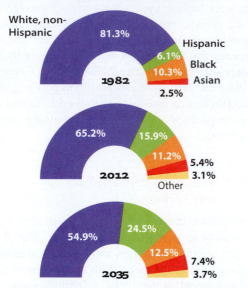

1982
- White, non-Hispanic: 81.3%
- Hispanic: 6.1%
- Black: 10.3%
- Asian: 2.5%

2012
- 65.2%
- 15.9%
- 11.2%
- 5.4%
- 3.1%
- Other

2035
- 54.9%
- 24.5%
- 12.5%
- 7.4%
- 3.7%

Note: "Other" includes American Indian and Alaska Native, Hawaiian and Other Pacific Islander, and People of Two or More Races. Numbers may not add up to 100 owing to categorization of White, non-Hispanic.

Sources: Bureau of Labor Statistics, 2010b, 2014d; Toossi 2004.

Weber conceived of power as a continuum based on the extent to which it is accepted as legitimate by those over whom it is exercised. On one end is **force,** the actual or threatened use of coercion to impose one's will on others. When leaders imprison or execute political dissidents, they are applying force; so, too, are terrorists when they seize or bomb an embassy or assassinate a political leader. Slave-based economies typically rely on force. Such systems are not terribly efficient due to the policing costs necessary to make people do what they do not wish to do.

On the other end of the continuum is what Weber calls **authority,** power that is recognized as legitimate by the people over whom it is exercised. This type of power depends upon people's faith in their leader's right to rule. In a democracy, for example, people who continue to obey the laws even if the candidates they voted for do not win demonstrate an underlying faith in the legitimacy of the system. The presidential election in 2000 took that a step further when Al Gore received 539,947 more votes nationally than did George W. Bush, yet Bush won the election. This outcome was possible because, in the U.S. system, Bush received more electoral votes, and those are the votes that actually determine who wins. Weber views authority as more efficient than force because the motivation to obey comes from inside the follower rather than having to be externally imposed.

POWER

According to Max Weber, **power** is the ability to exercise one's will over others, even if they resist. To put it another way, if you can make people do what you want them to do—whether that is to go to war, coordinate a business meeting, clean their room, or even take an exam—you have power. Power relations can involve large organizations, small groups, or even people in intimate relationships.

power The ability to exercise one's will over others even if they resist.

force The actual or threatened use of coercion to impose one's will on others.

authority Power that is recognized as legitimate by the people over whom it is exercised.

traditional authority Legitimate power conferred by custom and accepted practice.

TYPES OF AUTHORITY

Weber identified three major types of authority: traditional, charismatic, and rational-legal. Oftentimes the legitimacy of leaders depends primarily upon only one, though elements of all three can be present at the same time.

Traditional Authority Until the middle of the 20th century, Japan was ruled for generations by a revered emperor whose absolute authority went largely unquestioned. In a political system based on **traditional authority,** legitimate power is conferred by custom and accepted practice. In other words, past practice justifies our present actions. As Weber put it, such authority rests in the belief that "everyday routine [provides] an inviolable norm of conduct" ([1922] 1958d: 296). We do things the way we do because we have always done them that way. The emperor, queen, or tribal leader may be loved or hated, competent or destructive; in terms of legitimacy, that does not matter. For the traditional

Personal Sociology

Because I Said So

I am astonished at how often my daughters, Emily and Eleanor, do what I ask. When they were little, if they disobeyed, they had to "sit in the green chair." It wasn't much of a punishment. The chair is located in our living room in full view of the television and not isolated from the rest of the family. In time, just the threat of having to sit there was enough. Eventually they simply accepted the traditional authority of "because I said so" as sufficient justification. Of course, as they grew, they began to question the legitimacy of my authority, seeking reasons for why they should obey. And yet, even now, they are usually willing to do as I say simply because I am their dad.

SOCTHINK

Which of these three forms of power do parents, bosses, or professors most rely on? Are there times when each of those groups use each of the three types of power?

leader, authority depends on people's faith in custom, not in the leader's personal appeal, technical competence, or even written law.

Charismatic Authority Joan of Arc was a simple peasant girl in medieval France, yet she was able to rally the French people and lead them into major battles against English invaders despite having no formally recognized position of power. How was this possible? As Weber observed, power can be legitimized by the charisma of an individual. **Charismatic authority** refers to power made legitimate by a leader's exceptional personal or emotional appeal to his or her followers.

Charisma lets a person such as Joan of Arc lead or inspire without relying on set rules or traditions. In fact, charismatic authority is derived more from the beliefs of followers than from the actual

qualities of leaders. So long as people perceive a charismatic leader such as Jesus, Joan of Arc, Gandhi, Malcolm X, or Martin Luther King Jr. as having qualities that set him or her apart from ordinary citizens, that leader's authority will remain secure and often unquestioned (Adair-Toteff 2005; Potts 2009). That unfortunately is also the case with malevolent figures such as Adolf Hitler, whose charismatic appeal turned people toward violent and destructive ends in Nazi Germany.

Political leaders increasingly depend on television, radio, and the Internet to establish and maintain charismatic authority. This practice took hold with President Franklin D. Roosevelt's use of fireside chats over the radio to calm a nation that faced the Great Depression and World War II. Barack Obama had high approval ratings early on in his presidency and news reports frequently mentioned his capacity to charm. Over time, however, these ratings declined as faith in his capacity to deliver waivered (Bligh and Kohles 2009). President George W. Bush learned a similar lesson. His approval ratings reached a high of 85 percent after the 9/11 terrorist attacks, but by the end of his second term they hovered around 25 percent, making it difficult for him to advance his legislative agenda.

Rational-Legal Authority The U.S. Constitution gives Congress and the president the authority to make and enforce laws and policies. Power made legitimate by law is a form of rational-legal authority.

Rational-legal authority involves formally agreed-on and accepted rules, principles, and procedures of conduct that are established in order to accomplish goals in the most efficient manner possible. Such authority extends beyond governments to include any organization. Bureaucracies are the purest form of rational-legal authority (for characteristics of bureaucracies, see Chapter 5). Generally, in societies based on rational-legal authority, leaders are thought to have specific areas of competence and authority, but are not thought to be endowed with divine inspiration, as in certain societies with traditional forms of authority.

Analyzing power using Weber's model focuses our attention in a way that allows us to better understand economic and political relationships. The degree to which we accept the legitimacy of the people that rule over us shapes the kind of power they are likely to use. For example, when police evacuated Occupy Wall Street

charismatic authority Power made legitimate by a leader's exceptional personal or emotional appeal to his or her followers.

rational-legal authority Authority based on formally agreed-upon and accepted rules, principles, and procedures of conduct that are established in order to accomplish goals in the most efficient manner possible.

© Elliot & Fry/Hulton Archive/Getty Images

Did You Know?

capitalism An economic system in which owners of private property compete in the marketplace in pursuit of profit.

laissez-faire The principle that people should be able to compete freely, without government intervention, in the capitalist marketplace.

monopoly Control of a market by a single business firm.

protestors from their encampments, some degree of force was used. Protestors were made to do things that they did not otherwise wish to do, and failure to do so resulted in physical injury and jail time for some of those who questioned the legitimacy of the current system. Yet the presupposition that police and political leaders had the legitimate right to act in this way was widespread. As Weber suggested, when the legitimacy to rule is internalized in the form of authority, most people will simply comply with the wishes of the leader and will expect others to do likewise.

>> Economic Systems

For the most part, we accept the legitimacy of the economic systems within which we operate. We may even find it difficult to accept the viability of alternatives. Yet people throughout history and around the world continue to provide for their needs using varieties of economic principles such as gift exchange, bartering, or shared ownership of goods. Analyzing the characteristics of the dominant economic systems of our time allows us to better understand how and why events happen as they do.

CAPITALISM

Capitalism is an economic system in which owners of private property compete in the marketplace in pursuit of profit. Value under capitalism is determined based on what people are willing and able to pay for available goods and services. The basic principles of capitalism were laid out by Adam Smith in his book *The Wealth of Nations* ([1776], 2003) including four key concepts: pursuit of profit, competition in the market, the law of supply and demand, and laissez-faire.

- *Pursuit of profit.* One of the basic presuppositions of capitalism is that, in our exchanges with others, human beings naturally seek to get the greatest return on their investments. This extends beyond economic exchanges (i.e., making a financial profit) to include social and cultural exchanges (in which even a conversation represents an exchange of symbolic resources such as status or attention). Under capitalism, humans are seen as naturally competitive, looking out for their own interests above all others. Pursuit of profit is presented as both morally acceptable and socially desirable.

- *Competition in the market.* The marketplace is the context in which we exchange goods and services (such as shoes, cell phones, and college degrees); we do so in competition with other producers and consumers. Competition keeps prices in check. The marketplace must be open to whoever has the ability to compete so that no individual or firm controls a disproportionate share of the market.

- *Law of supply and demand.* In a competitive marketplace, a natural balance will be reached between production and consumption at the appropriate price. If the demand for a good or service is high and the supply is low, prices will go up, and vice versa. If a producer charges too much, another producer will step in to provide the good or service at a more reasonable price. Adam Smith described this process as the "invisible hand" of the marketplace through which prices reach their natural level. Companies that don't respond to the prompting of the invisible hand—for example, by charging too much or too little—will ultimately fail.

- *Laissez-faire.* The expression **laissez-faire** means "let them do [as they please]," and in this context it means that outside entities, especially the government, should not intervene in the marketplace. Instead, the market should be allowed to function free from external influence. Ideally, markets self-correct using the invisible hand. The capitalist model presupposes that, though governments may mean well, they cannot bring about a better result for society as a whole than can individuals who are allowed to compete on their own. In capitalism, the greatest social good is attained through the competition of profit-seeking individuals.

In practice, capitalism struggles to stick to these ideals because contradictions inevitably arise. On the one hand, capitalism tends toward the establishment of **monopolies,** in which a single business firm controls the market. Though the system needs competition, capitalists, in their pursuit of profits, seek to dominate the market to the point of monopolizing it. This violates the principle of competition. On the other hand, governments often respond by intervening in the marketplace—through policies such as antitrust legislation—to ensure sufficient competition, thus violating the principle of laissez-faire. In addition, some goods and services (such as police, fire protection, roads, national defense, and public education) are deemed important enough for the public good to be provided for all, even at the expense of government intervention.

> Nowadays people know the price of everything and the value of nothing.
>
> Oscar Wilde

SOCIALISM

Socialism is an economic system in which the means of production and distribution in a society are collectively rather than privately owned. Value under socialism is determined by the amount of work it takes to produce products and the use we get out of those products. The basic principles of socialism were laid out by Karl Marx in the middle to late 1800s in a variety of publications, including *The Communist Manifesto* which he coauthored with Friedrich Engels ([1847] 1955). Marx believed socialism to be inevitable because eventually, as a result of technological innovation, we would be able to produce enough so that everyone could have more than enough. At that point we would welcome socialism as a new system of social relations because the inequality that capitalism presupposes would no longer make sense. The following five presuppositions help clarify how he reached that conclusion.

- *Humans must produce.* Unlike animals, humans lack the complex instincts that direct how we provide for our basic human needs (food, shelter, and clothing) from nature. Therefore, we must fulfill those basic needs through technological innovation and culture creation.
- *Production makes us uniquely human.* Our capacity to produce distinguishes humans from the rest of the natural world. It is this free and creative productive ability, what Marx referred to as labor power, that must

be protected, nourished, and valued because it is at the core of our identity as humans.

- *We pour ourselves into our products.* For Marx, when we make something, we put part of who we are into each product; this is most apparent in craft labor. For example, a handmade bookshelf inspires pride because our labor power is the difference between the original stack of lumber and the finished shelf. To put it in an equation: *Raw materials + Labor power = Products.* According to Marx, we naturally find joy in labor and take pleasure in sharing both the process and products with others.
- *Economy determines society.* Marx argued that, because our capacity and need to produce is at the core of who we are, it serves as the foundation for society. In essence, how we organize the economy determines all other forms of social relations, such as government, family, education, and religion. In most agrarian societies production is rooted in the land, so ownership and control of land becomes the foundation of power. Social institutions may reinforce the privileged position of landowners, for example, by justifying a king's "divine right" to rule using religious authority. Over time, this material foundation shifts as our capacity to produce evolves through technological innovation. Eventually, the systems of social relations that grew out of that particular set of economic relations no longer match the new economic base, and a revolution to a new set of social relations occurs. Marx contended that this shift brought about the transition from feudalism to capitalism—when the agricultural power base that gave rise to royalty gave way to the industrial power base of capitalists and corporations—and he predicted it will shift again from capitalism to communism.
- *Scarcity and distribution are obstacles to the good of society.* For Marx, the ideal society is one in which we as humans have control over, and reap the full benefits of, our labor power. Until this point in history, however, no large-scale society has fully attained this ideal because we lacked the technological capacity to produce enough for everyone. This has resulted in social systems that divide the haves and have-nots: slavery's separation between masters and slaves, feudalism's separation between lords and peasants, capitalism's separation between owners and workers. Thanks to technological innovation—a consequence of our creative capacity to produce—we can eventually solve the problem of inadequate production. In fact, Marx praised capitalism, because it ultimately solves this problem by

socialism An economic system under which the means of production and distribution are collectively owned.

Li Keqiang assumed office as premier of the People's Republic of China in 2013. Photo: © Feng Li - Pool/Getty Images.

mixed economy An economic system that combines elements of both capitalism and socialism.

placing pressure on producers for constant innovation. Once we are technically capable of producing enough for all, any continued poverty, hunger, or extreme inequality is due to how we choose to distribute the products we make, rather than to our inability to produce enough. In other words, it's a social problem, solvable by the establishment of a new set of social relations that ensures equitable distribution. According to Marx, people will eventually decide that it doesn't make sense to maintain such economic extremes in the face of material abundance; thus a revolution in social relations toward socialism is inevitable.

In practice, the socialist ideal of collective ownership has been difficult to attain. The grand experiment in what was known as the Soviet Union—uniting Russia and neighboring countries as one large socialist bloc—ultimately collapsed in 1989. It did so under the weight of bureaucratic inefficiency, political corruption, and insufficient productivity—problems that seem endemic to

socialist states. In addition, crackdowns on dissidents by the totalitarian socialist governments in both the Soviet Union and communist China have led to the murders of millions of their own people, purportedly for the good of the state. Recent surveys show that majorities in almost all of the former Soviet-bloc nations approve of the steady transition from socialism to democracy and free markets (Pew 2009b).

THE MIXED ECONOMY

In practice, national economic systems combine elements of both capitalism and socialism. A **mixed economy** features elements of more than one economic system. Starting from a socialist ideal and moving toward a mixed economy (as China has done in recent years) involves opening up some aspects of the state-controlled economy to competition and the free market. Conversely, moving from a capitalist ideal toward a mixed economy removes some goods and services from the competitive free market and provides them for all or subsidizes them to ensure broader access. In the United States, we are provided with goods and services such as police and fire protection, roads, and public schools. Most agree that we should all have access to such public goods without regard for our ability to pay. There is currently a debate under way about whether health care should be considered a similar public good.

There has long been a debate in the United States about the degree to which the government should be involved

International Economic Growth, 1970–2014

Percentage GDP increases

Ghana	65%
Russia	80%
Mexico	93%
Sweden	104%
Canada	110%
USA	118%
Brazil	140%
Japan	148%
India	354%
China	2840%

Percentage Increase in per Capita GDP Growth, 1970–2014

Source: U.S. Department of Agriculture 2014. *Photo:* © Amanda Rhode/E+/Getty Images RF.

in the economy, but the economic upheaval of the Great Recession challenged people's commitment to laissez-faire principles. Government officials decided that some companies were "too big to fail," meaning that the domino effect of their failure would be greater than the cost of violating the nonintervention ideal. The Bush administration, itself a strong proponent of free-market principles, took the first steps toward government intervention in the economy during this crisis. In September 2008 it pushed the Troubled Assets Relief Program (TARP) through Congress to provide up to $700 billion to buy mortgage-backed securities and to prop up the financial sector. The Obama administration continued along the same lines. For example, in an effort to kick-start the U.S. economy, Congress passed the American Recovery and Reinvestment Act in February 2009, providing almost $800 billion for infrastructure projects, education and health care funding, and tax cuts. And in June 2009 General Motors, which for years was the world's largest company, went bankrupt. The U.S. government became its majority stockholder, owning 60 percent of its shares. These funds helped many firms

SOCTHINK

Should the U.S. government let companies fail regardless of apparent economic consequences?

survive that otherwise would have failed. Now that they are back on their feet, some companies have paid back the loans they received from the government. For example, General Motors paid back its $8.4 billion of government loans in full, with interest, and five years early. In 2013, the U.S. Department of Treasury sold off the last of its remaining shares of GM stock.

Though critics charged that Presidents Bush and Obama were moving the nation toward socialism, most people hoped that their efforts would minimize the negative effects the economic downturn had on their lives. The majority of citizens ultimately accepted these huge government expenditures as a means to save capitalism from its own excesses. Billionaire investor Warren Buffett later reflected on the government intervention and concluded, "Only one counterforce was available, and that was you, Uncle Sam. . . . Well, Uncle Sam, you delivered" (Buffett 2010).

THE INFORMAL ECONOMY

An informal economy operates within the confines of the dominant macroeconomic system in many countries, whether capitalist or socialist. In this **informal economy,** transfers of money, goods, or services take place but are not reported to the government. Examples of the informal economy include bartering, in which people trade goods and services with someone (say, exchanging a haircut for

a computer lesson), selling goods on the street, and engaging in illegal transactions, such as gambling or drug deals. Participants in this type of economy avoid taxes and government regulations.

In the developing world, governments often create burdensome business regulations that overworked bureaucrats must administer. When requests for licenses and permits pile up, delaying business projects, legitimate entrepreneurs find that they need to "go underground" to get anything done. Despite its apparent efficiency, this type of informal economy is dysfunctional for a country's overall political and economic well-being. Because informal firms typically operate in remote locales to avoid detection, they cannot easily expand when they become profitable. And given the limited protection for their property and contractual rights, participants in the informal economy are less likely than others to save and invest their income.

> **informal economy** Transfers of money, goods, or services that are not reported to the government.

SOCTHINK

When doing jobs in the informal economy, such as babysitting, lawn mowing, housecleaning, or construction, it can be nice to get cash under the table without having to pay taxes, Social Security, and so on. What are the long-term disadvantages of doing so for the individual? What about for society? Why might someone opt to do so anyway?

Informal economies can also be dysfunctional for workers. Working conditions in these businesses are often unsafe or dangerous, and the jobs rarely provide any benefits to those who become ill or cannot continue to work. Perhaps more significant, the longer a worker remains in the informal economy, the less likely he or she is to make the transition to the regular economy. No matter how efficient or productive a worker may be, employers expect to see experience in the formal economy on a job application. Experience as a successful street vendor or self-employed cleaning person does not carry much weight with interviewers (Venkatesh 2006).

>> Political Systems

Just as new economic systems developed in response to broader historical changes, political systems also adapted. In all societies, someone or some group—whether it be a tribal chief, a dictator, a council, or a parliament—makes important decisions about how to use resources and allocate goods. Inevitably, the struggle for power and authority involves **politics,** the competition between individuals or groups over the allocation of valued resources. Politics takes place within the context of a **political system,** which is the social institution that is founded on a recognized set of procedures for implementing and achieving society's goals.

Government represents an institutionalized form of authority. Given the responsibilities governments have for establishing and enforcing laws and the scope of international relations and the globalization of national economies, these formal systems of authority make a significant number of critical political decisions. Such systems take a variety of forms, including monarchy, oligarchy, dictatorship, totalitarianism, and democracy.

MONARCHY

A **monarchy** is a form of government headed by a single member of a royal family, usually a king, queen, or some other hereditary ruler. In earlier times, many monarchs claimed that God had granted them a divine right to rule. Typically, they governed on the basis of traditional forms of authority, sometimes accompanied by the use of force. By the beginning of the 21st century, however, relatively few monarchs held genuine governmental power, such as Monaco. Most monarchs, including Queen Elizabeth II in England, now have little practical power; they serve primarily ceremonial roles.

OLIGARCHY

An **oligarchy** is a form of government in which a few individuals rule. A venerable method of governing that flourished in ancient Greece and Egypt, oligarchy now often takes the form of military rule. In developing nations in Africa, Asia, and Latin America, small factions of military officers may forcibly seize power, either from legally elected regimes or from other military cliques (Michels [1915] 1949).

Strictly speaking, the term *oligarchy* is reserved for governments that are run by a few selected individuals. However, the People's Republic of China can be classified as an oligarchy if we stretch the meaning of the term. In China, power rests in the hands of a large but exclusive ruling *group,* the Communist Party. In a similar vein, we might argue that many industrialized nations of the West should be considered oligarchies (rather than democracies), because only a powerful few—leaders of big business, government, and the military—actually rule. Later in this chapter, we will examine the "elite model" of the U.S. political system in greater detail.

DICTATORSHIP AND TOTALITARIANISM

A **dictatorship** is a government in which one person has nearly total power to make and enforce laws. Dictators rule primarily through the use of force, which often includes imprisonment, torture, and executions. Typically, they seize power rather than being freely elected (as in a democracy) or inheriting power (as in a monarchy). Some dictators are quite charismatic and manage to achieve a certain popularity, although their supporters' enthusiasm is almost certainly tinged with fear. Other dictators rely on coercion and are often bitterly hated by their people.

Frequently, dictators develop such overwhelming control over people's lives that their governments are called totalitarian. (Monarchies and oligarchies may also achieve this type of dominance.) **Totalitarianism** involves virtually complete government control and surveillance over all aspects of a society's social and political life. Germany during Hitler's reign, the Soviet Union under Stalin in the 1930s, and North Korea today are classified as totalitarian states.

Did You Know?

. . . **One of Queen Elizabeth's official duties is to appoint the prime minister. Given that political power rests with Parliament, however, this too has become largely a ceremonial duty.**

Photo: © Peter Macdiarmid/Getty Images.

politics The competition between individuals or groups over the allocation of valued resources.

political system The social institution that is founded on a recognized set of procedures for implementing and achieving society's goals.

monarchy A form of government headed by a single member of a royal family, usually a king, queen, or some other hereditary ruler.

oligarchy A form of government in which a few individuals rule.

dictatorship A government in which one person has nearly total power to make and enforce laws.

totalitarianism Virtually complete government control and surveillance over all aspects of a society's social and political life.

Sudan President Omar al-Bashir is widely considered an authoritarian dictator by the international community. Photo: © Ashraf Shazly/ AFP/Getty Images.

The way representatives are chosen can vary, and the system used to select them influences the kind of politics we get. For example, the two-party system that dominates in the United States is a consequence, in part, of how legislators are selected. To select members to

━SOC THINK━

The United States is commonly classified as a representative democracy, because the elected members of Congress and state legislatures make our laws. However, critics have questioned how representative our democracy really is. Do Congress and the state legislatures genuinely represent the masses? Are the people of the United States legitimately self-governing, or has our government become a forum for powerful elites?

━SOC THINK━

In 2001, expressing a sentiment shared by many past presidents, George W. Bush joked that, when it came to working with Congress, "a dictatorship would be a heck of a lot easier." In what ways is the U.S. system of government intentionally inefficient? Why might that be on purpose?

DEMOCRACY

In a literal sense, **democracy** means government by the people. The word comes from two Greek roots—*demos,* meaning "the populace" or "the common people," and *kratia,* meaning "rule." In a democracy, power is not vested in a particular person or position. Individual citizens provide the foundation for political authority, and the underlying principle of power is "one person, one vote." This principle implies that, in theory at least, everyone has equal power when it comes to decision making. Direct democracy, in which all citizens vote on all major decisions and the most votes win, provides perhaps the purest example. In large, populous nations such as the United States, direct democracy is impractical at the national level. All Americans cannot vote on every important issue. Consequently, popular rule occurs in the form of **representative democracy,** a system of government in which citizens elect political leaders to make decisions on behalf of the people.

the House of Representatives, the country is divided into 435 geographically distinct congressional districts. Each district has a single seat. Elections are held within each, and the winner becomes the representative for that district. As a result of this winner-take-all system, candidates have an incentive to appeal to a majority of voters which tends to result in the creation of two parties, each vying to gain that majority. Even though there are plenty of "third parties" in the United States—in the 2012 election, for example, there were candidates on the ballot for the Constitution Party, Green Party, Libertarian Party, Party of Socialism and Liberation, and many others—the winner-take-all system makes it difficult for a minority party to break through to win a majority of votes, especially against the entrenched power and influence of the two major parties.

An alternative system for selecting legislators involves proportional representation, some form of which exists in Brazil, Israel, the Netherlands, and South Africa. In such cases, a single district can be represented by multiple seats, and winners are determined based on the percentage of votes received in that district. For example, if a party receives 15 percent of the vote, that party would receive approximately 15 percent of the legislative seats. In such a

democracy In a literal sense, government by the people.

representative democracy A system of government in which citizens elect political leaders to make decisions on behalf of the people.

© National Archives and Records Administration

© AP Photo/Chris O'Meara

© AP Photo/Steven Senne

system, parties that might never be able to win a majority of votes can still win seats in the legislature. In addition, the likelihood that a single party secures a majority of seats declines. As a result, parties often need to work together to create a ruling coalition, which has the effect of giving those minority parties more power than they might otherwise have.

If citizens in a democracy are unhappy with the current direction of things, they can vote to establish new policies or elect new leaders. Over time, significant changes in policy can occur in response to the changing will of the people. For example, early on in U.S. history, the "self-evident" truth that everyone was created equal and endowed with unalienable rights applied only to White, property-holding men. Over time the definition of who counts as a citizen expanded to include others. Debates about citizenship rights in the United States continue to this day as evidenced, for example, in arguments regarding the rights of children or immigrants.

Citizenship rights involve more than just the right to vote. Sociologist T. H. Marshall (1950) identified three categories of such rights including civil rights, political rights, and social rights:

- *Civil rights.* These citizenship rights protect individual freedoms. We find some of them articulated in the Bill of Rights, the first 10 amendments to the U.S. Constitution. Included are protections such as freedom of speech, freedom of assembly, the right to bear arms, and freedom of religion.
- *Political rights.* These ensure the right to full participation in the political process. In principle, any citizen can be involved in politics, by voting or running for office. But universal political participation wasn't always guaranteed. The 15th Amendment to the U.S.

Constitution extended political rights to African Americans in 1870 and the 19th Amendment secured those rights for women in 1920.

- *Social rights.* These rights provide for our welfare and security. They are based on the presupposition that a minimum standard of living is necessary in order to ensure the ability of all to exercise their civil and political rights. To secure these rights, some goods and services—such as public education or police and fire protection—are taken out of the marketplace, ensuring that everyone has at least a minimum amount of access regardless of their ability to pay. Substantial debates exist over the role government should play in ensuring access to basic material, social, and cultural resources.

Making this distinction between categories of rights allows us to better understand the evolution of rights in the United States. We often take for granted that basic civil and political rights are secured for all, yet ongoing debates about the rights of immigrants or same-sex couples often fall within these two categories. Arguments regarding the extension of social rights to cover more items—for example, the ongoing debate about securing health care coverage for all—are particularly contentious.

Debates over social rights are due, in part, to a basic tension between core values in the United States. On the one hand is the principle of *equality,* a basic presupposition at the heart of democracy. On the other is the principle of *competition,* which is an essential premise of capitalism. A capitalist economy assumes that an economic hierarchy exists and that there will be winners and losers, but in a democracy all are created equal. Economist Arthur Okun (1975) described this tension as "the double standard of a capitalist democracy, professing and pursuing an egalitarian political and social system and simultaneously generating gaping disparities in economic well-being" (p. 1). The simultaneous adherence to these two principles helps explain why social policies regarding the extension

SOCTHINK

To what extent do you think that the principles of political equality and economic competition are at odds with each other in the United States?

Percentage turnout of registered voters at parliamentary elections

Country	Percentage
Rwanda	98.8
Australia	93.2
Sweden	85.8
South Africa	73.5
United States	68.0
India	66.4
Mexico	62.5
Egypt	62.0
Russian Federation	60.1
Lithuania	52.9
Afghanistan	38.9
Nigeria	28.7

Note: Results are for the most recent national election; includes national elections to the legislative body. U.S. results are for the 2012 elections.

Source: International Institute for Democracy and Electoral Assistance 2015.   *Photo:* © Evirgen/E+/Getty Images RF.

---

of social rights go back and forth over time with one or the other becoming dominant in public discourse. Leading up to the 2008 midterm congressional elections, for example, Tea Party conservatives advocated strongly in favor of lower taxes and substantial cuts in federal funding for social welfare programs. Not long thereafter, as we saw earlier, Occupy Wall Street protestors advocated in favor of higher taxes on the wealthy and a stronger social support safety net.

>> The Power Structure in the United States

The issue of power extends beyond just politics and the people who occupy formally recognized offices. Over the years, sociologists repeatedly have sought to discover who really holds power in the United States. Do "we the people" genuinely run the country through our elected representatives? Or does a small elite behind the scenes control both the government and the economic system? In exploring these questions, social scientists have developed two basic models of our nation's power structure: political pluralism versus the power elite.

THE PLURALIST MODEL

According to the pluralist approach, power is widely dispersed throughout society. Though some groups may have more power in certain areas at particular times, there is no core group at the top that is able to consistently advance its interests at the expense of others. According to this **pluralist model,** many competing groups have access to government so that no single group is dominant.

To support their claims, advocates of the pluralist model point to data gathered from intensive case studies of communities gathered using observation research. One of the most famous—an investigation of decision making in New Haven, Connecticut—was reported by Robert Dahl (1961). Dahl found that, although the number of people involved in any important decision was rather small, community power was nonetheless diffuse. Few political actors exercised decision-making power on all issues, and no one group got its way all the time. One individual or group might be influential in a battle over urban renewal but have little effect on educational policy.

Historically, pluralists have stressed ways in which large

> **pluralist model** A view of society in which many competing groups within the community have access to government, so that no single group is dominant.

increases the opportunity for the average citizen to have a voice in politics.

The pluralist model has its critics. Sociologist G. William Domhoff (1978, 2006) reexamined Dahl's study of decision making in New Haven and argued that Dahl and other pluralists had failed to trace how local elites who were prominent in decision making belonged to a larger national ruling class. In addition, studies of community power, such as Dahl's work in New Haven, can examine decision making only on issues that become part of the political agenda. They fail to address the potential power of elites to keep certain matters entirely out of the realm of political debate.

Dianne Pinderhughes (1987) has criticized the pluralist model for failing to account for the exclusion of African Americans from the political process. Drawing on her studies of Chicago politics, Pinderhughes points out that the residential and occupational segregation of Blacks and their long political disenfranchisement violate the logic of pluralism—which would hold that such a substantial minority should always have been influential in community decision making. This critique applies to many cities across the United States, where other large racial and ethnic minorities, among them Asian Americans, Puerto Ricans, and Mexican Americans, are relatively powerless.

numbers of people can participate in or influence governmental decision making. New communications technologies like the Internet are increasing the opportunity to be heard, not just in countries like the United States but in developing countries the world over. The ability to communicate with political leaders via email, for example,

Public Trust in Government

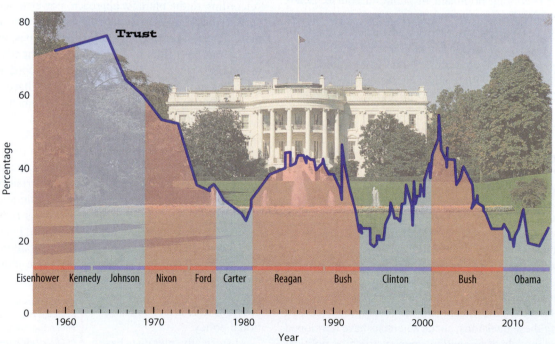

Note: The percentage represents those who say they "can trust the government in Washington to do what is right" either "just about always" or "most of the time."

Source: Pew Research Center 2010c, 2014h.   *Photo:* © Digital Vision/PunchStock RF.

POWER ELITE MODELS

Such criticisms lend support for an alternative model of how power functions. This model traces its roots back to Karl Marx, who believed that 19th-century representative democracy was essentially a sham. He argued that industrial societies were dominated by relatively small numbers of people who owned the factories and controlled natural resources. In Marx's view, government officials and military leaders were essentially servants of this capitalist class and followed their wishes. Therefore, any key decisions made by politicians inevitably reflected the interests of the dominant business owners. Like others who hold an **elite model** of power relations, Marx believed that society is ruled by a small group of individuals who share political and economic interests.

Mills's Model Sociologist C. Wright Mills, who developed the concept of the sociological imagination that we looked at in Chapter 1, put forth a model similar to Marx's in his pioneering work *The Power Elite* ([1956] 2000). Mills described a small group of military, industrial, and government leaders who controlled the fate of the United States—the **power elite.** Power rested in the hands of a few, both inside and outside government.

A pyramid illustrates the power structure of the United States in Mills's model (see SOC Studies feature "Power Elite Models"). The power elite rests at the top and includes the corporate rich, leaders of the executive branch of government, and heads of the military (whom Mills called the "warlords"). Directly below are local opinion leaders, members of the legislative branch of government, and leaders of special-interest groups. Mills contended that these individuals and groups basically follow the wishes of the dominant power elite. At the bottom of the pyramid are the unorganized, exploited masses.

A fundamental element in Mills's thesis is that the power elite not only includes relatively few members but also operates as a self-conscious, cohesive unit. Although not necessarily diabolical or ruthless, the elite comprises similar types of people who interact regularly with one another and have essentially the same political and economic interests. Mills's power elite represents not a conspiracy but rather a community of interest and sentiment among a small number of influential people (Jenness, Smith, and Stepan-Norris 2006).

In analyzing the scandals that have rocked major corporations such as Enron and Lehman Brothers over the past decade, observers have noted that members of the business elite are closely interrelated. In a study of the members of the boards of directors of Fortune 1000 corporations, researchers found that each director can reach *every* other board of directors in just 3.7 steps. That is, by consulting acquaintances of acquaintances, each director can quickly reach someone who sits on each of the other 999 boards. Furthermore, the face-to-face contact directors regularly have in their board meetings makes them a highly cohesive elite. Finally, the corporate elite not only is wealthy, powerful, and cohesive but also is overwhelmingly White and male (G. Davis 2003, 2004; Kentor and Jang 2004; Mizruchi 1996; Strauss 2002).

elite model A view of society as being ruled by a small group of individuals who share a common set of political and economic interests.

power elite A small group of military, industrial, and government leaders who control the fate of the United States.

Domhoff's Model Sociologist G. William Domhoff (2006, 2009) agrees with Mills that a powerful elite runs the United States. Domhoff stresses the role played by elites from within networks of organizations, including the

Power Elite Models

THE POWER ELITE

Corporate rich
Executive branch
Military leaders

Interest group leaders
Legislators
Local opinion leaders

Unorganized, exploited masses

C. Wright Mills's model, 1956

Sources: Left, based on C. W. Mills (1956) 2000; right, Domhoff 2006:105.

Social upper class

THE POWER ELITE

Corporate community

Policy-formation organizations

G. William Domhoff's model, 2006

SOCstudies

corporate community; policy-formation organizations such as think tanks, chambers of commerce, and labor unions; and the social upper class. Membership in these groups overlaps, and members with connections in more than one of these spheres have more power and influence. Domhoff finds that those in this latter group are still largely White, male, and upper class, but he notes the presence of a small number of women and minority men in key positions—groups that were excluded from Mills's top echelon and are still underrepresented today (Zweigenhaft and Domhoff 2006).

> Majority rule only works if you're also considering individual rights. Because you can't have five wolves and one sheep voting on what to have for supper.
>
> Larry Flynt

SOCTHINK

Is it possible for a small and unified group of powerful people in the United States to use their power and influence to, in effect, rule the country?

Although the three groups in Domhoff's power elite model do overlap, they do not necessarily agree on specific policies. Domhoff notes that in politics, two different coalitions have exercised influence. A corporate-conservative coalition has played a large role in both political parties, generating support for particular candidates through direct-mail appeals. A liberal-labor coalition is based in unions, local environmental organizations, a segment of the minority group community, liberal churches, and the university and arts communities (Zweigenhaft and Domhoff 2006). The power this coalition wields suggests that the interests of members of the power elite are not always singular or uniform but that overall they do work together to advance their larger interests.

>> Political Participation in the United States

Citizens of the United States take for granted many aspects of their political system. They are accustomed to living in a nation with a Bill of Rights, two major political parties, voting by secret ballot, an elected president, state and local governments distinct from the national government, and so forth. Because political representatives still must be elected to serve, citizens have substantial potential power to shape the nature and direction of public policy. Yet, if not all participate, because either they choose not to or they are discouraged or even prevented from doing so, some interests might be better served than others. In practice, two particular concerns—voter participation and race and gender representation—raise questions about the degree to which this is happening.

VOTER PARTICIPATION

In a democratic system, voters have the right to select their political leaders. They are free to vote for whom they choose, and political parties seek to persuade voters to support their positions. In March 2015, 31.1 percent of registered voters in the United States saw themselves as Democrats, 24.4 percent as Republicans, and 34.0 percent as independents (Pollster.com 2015).

Historically, voter participation rates in the United States were highest from 1848 to 1896, during which an average of about 80 percent of eligible voters participated in presidential elections. (Of course, that does not count women or African Americans, who were not legally permitted to vote.) The rate declined steadily

Did You Know?

. . . President Obama's reelection in 2012 owed a lot to young people. He received **60 percent** of the vote from those aged **18–29** and **52 percent** among 30- to 40-year-olds. Those who were older preferred Mitt Romney. Obama received **47 percent** from 45- to 64-year-olds and **44 percent** from those 65 and older.

Photo: © AP Photo/Nati Harnik

What's Your Party?

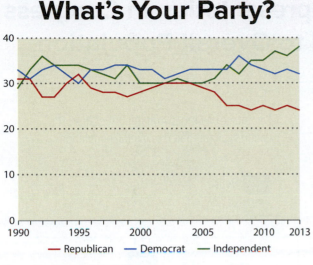

Source: Pew Research Center 2013h.

until it reached 48.9 percent in 1928. It fluctuated throughout the rest of the 20th century, rising to more than 60 percent in 1940 and 1960 and falling to around 50 percent in 1948, 1988, and 1996. Concerns about voter apathy were expressed going into the 21st century, so increases in the new millennium were greeted as a welcome trend (McDonald 2009).

Voter turnout for the past three U.S. presidential elections has been more encouraging. In the 2012 election between incumbent President Barack Obama and Republican challenger former governor Mitt Romney, turnout was down slightly after hitting a 40-year high in 2008. In the 2012 battle, 60 percent of eligible voters participated. Compare this to 61.6 percent in the race between Barack Obama and John McCain in 2008 and 60.1 percent in the 2004 election, which pitted George W. Bush against John Kerry. Yet, compared to other countries with national legislative-body or parliamentary elections, the United States ranks 95th out of 198 countries in voter turnout (International Institute for Democracy and Electoral Assistance 2015).

Political participation makes government accountable to the voters. If participation declines, government operates with less of a sense of accountability to society. This issue is most serious for the least powerful individuals and groups in the United States. Historically, voter turnout has been particularly low among members of racial and ethnic minorities.

Lower voter turnout increases the likelihood that issues of concern to minority communities will not be addressed by politicians. Participation rates for Hispanics and Asians are below 50 percent compared to rates above 60 percent for non-Hispanic Whites. Similarly, young people have the lowest participation rates of any age group. In the 2012 election, for example, only 45 percent of people aged 18–29 voted compared to 72 percent of those aged 65 and older. African Americans have been an exception to this rule. Over the past five presidential election campaigns, their turnout rates have gone up each time. In 1996, 53 percent of African Americans voted. In 2012, rates jumped to 66 percent, overtaking non-Hispanic Whites for the first time (CIRCLE 2013a; File 2013).

Reasons for Not Voting, among Young Adults

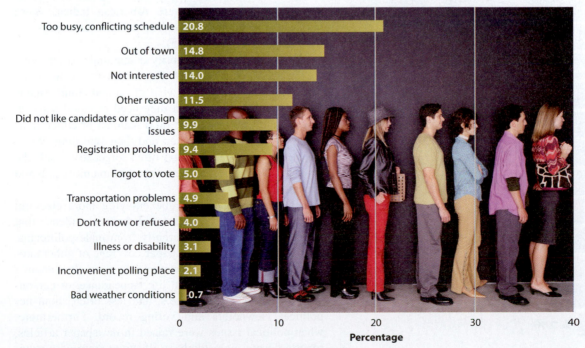

Note: Young adults include 18- to 24-year-olds. Results are for the 2012 presidential election.

Source: U.S. Census Bureau 2012q: Table 10.   *Photo:* © Ryan McVay/Getty Images RF.

Because politics is synonymous with power and authority, we should not be surprised that marginalized groups lack political strength. Nationally, women did not get the vote until 1920. Most Chinese Americans were turned away from the polls until 1926. American Indians did not win the right to vote until 1954. And African Americans were, in practice, largely disenfranchised until 1965, when national voting rights legislation was passed. It has taken these groups some time to develop their political power and begin to exercise it fully.

Progress toward the inclusion of minority groups in government has been slow as well. As of 2015, 20 of 100 U.S. senators were women. Two senators were African American, 4 were Latino,

(Under) Representation in Congress Compared to Overall Population

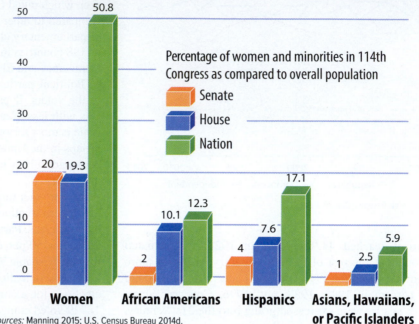

Percentage of women and minorities in 114th Congress as compared to overall population

- Senate
- House
- Nation

Women | African Americans | Hispanics | Asians, Hawaiians, or Pacific Islanders

Sources: Manning 2015; U.S. Census Bureau 2014d.

and 1 was Asian American or Native Hawaiian/Pacific Islander, leaving 74 non-Hispanic White men. Among the 435 members of the U.S. House of Representatives, 294 were non-Hispanic White men. Eighty-four were women, 44 were African Americans (including 18 women), 33 were Latinos (including 9 Latinas), 11 were Asian Americans or Native Hawaiian/Pacific Islanders (including six women), and 2 were American Indian. These numbers, though low, represent a high-water mark for these groups (Manning 2015).

Many critics within minority communities decry what they term "fiesta politics." This refers to the tendency of White power brokers to visit racial and ethnic minority communities only when they need electoral support, making a quick appearance on a national or ethnic holiday to get their picture taken and then vanishing. When the election is over, they too often forget to consult the residents who supported them about community needs and concerns.

Female politicians may be enjoying more electoral success now than in the past, but there is evidence that the media cover them differently from male politicians. A content analysis of newspaper coverage of gubernatorial races showed that reporters wrote more often about a female candidate's personal life, appearance, or personality than a male candidate's, and less often about her political viewpoints and voting record. Furthermore, when political issues were raised in newspaper articles, reporters were more likely to illustrate them with statements made by male candidates than by female candidates (Devitt 1999; Jost 2008; Paxton, Kunovich, and Hughes 2007).

Going GLOBAL

Women in National Legislatures, Selected Countries

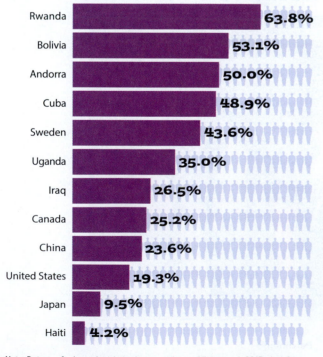

Country	Percentage
Rwanda	63.8%
Bolivia	53.1%
Andorra	50.0%
Cuba	48.9%
Sweden	43.6%
Uganda	35.0%
Iraq	26.5%
Canada	25.2%
China	23.6%
United States	19.3%
Japan	9.5%
Haiti	4.2%

Note: Data are for lower legislative houses only, as of February 1, 2015; data for upper houses, such as the U.S. Senate or the UK. House of Lords, are not included.
Source: Inter-Parliamentary Union 2015.

Women account for at least half the members of the national legislature in only three countries. The African Republic of Rwanda ranks the highest, with 63.8 percent, Bolivia has 53.1 percent, and the European nation Andorra has 50.0. Overall, the United States ranked 95th among 188 nations in the proportion of women serving as national legislators in 2015 (Inter-Parliamentary Union 2015).

To remedy this situation, many countries have adopted quotas for female representatives. In some, the government sets aside a certain percentage of seats for women, usually 10–30 percent. In others, political parties have decided that 20–40 percent of their candidates should be women. Fifty-seven countries now have some kind of quota system (Inter-Parliamentary Union 2011; Quota-Project 2012).

© Blank Archives/Getty Images

>> War and Peace

When it comes to political power, perhaps no decision is as weighty as the decision to go to war. Conflict is a central aspect of social relations. Sociologists Theodore Caplow and Louis Hicks (2002:3) have defined **war** as conflict between organizations that possess trained combat forces equipped with deadly weapons. This meaning is broader than the legal definition, which typically requires a formal declaration of hostilities.

WAR

Sociologists approach war in three different ways. Those who take a global view study how and why two or more nations become engaged in military conflict. Those who take a nation-state view stress the interaction of internal political, socioeconomic, and cultural forces. And those who take a micro view focus on the social impact of war on individuals and the groups to which they belong.

Analysis at the global level focuses on macro issues such as the distribution of resources, struggles over political philosophies, and debates about boundaries. Often it involves nations with competing political and economic systems, as was the case in World War I, World War II, and the Cold War. Some have argued that the conflict in Iraq is about bringing freedom and democracy to the Middle East, and others argue it is motivated by oil and profits.

Sociologists have devoted much effort to studying the internal decision-making process that leads to war. During the Vietnam War, Presidents Johnson and Nixon both misled Congress, painting a falsely optimistic picture of the likely outcome. Based on their intentional distortions, Congress appropriated the military funds the two administrations requested. However,

war Conflict between organizations that possess trained combat forces equipped with deadly weapons.

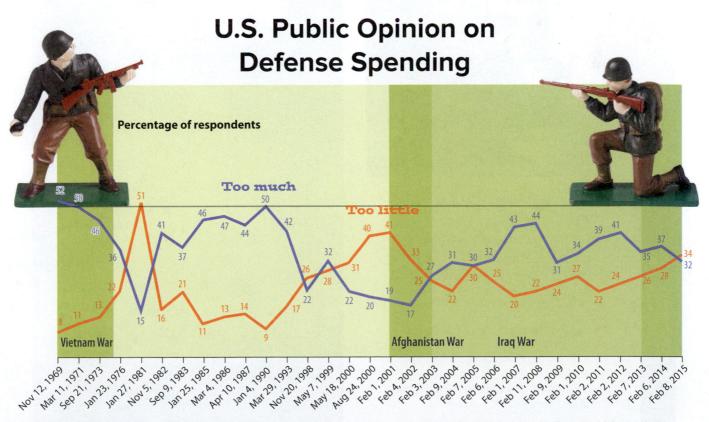

U.S. Public Opinion on Defense Spending

Percentage of respondents

Too much

Too little

Vietnam War   Afghanistan War   Iraq War

Nov 12, 1969 · Mar 11, 1971 · Sep 21, 1973 · Jan 23, 1976 · Jan 27, 1981 · Nov 5, 1982 · Sep 9, 1983 · Jan 25, 1985 · Mar 4, 1986 · Apr 10, 1987 · Jan 4, 1990 · Mar 29, 1993 · Nov 20, 1998 · May 7, 1999 · May 18, 2000 · Aug 24, 2000 · Feb 1, 2001 · Feb 4, 2002 · Feb 3, 2003 · Feb 9, 2004 · Feb 7, 2005 · Feb 6, 2006 · Feb 1, 2007 · Feb 11, 2008 · Feb 9, 2009 · Feb 1, 2010 · Feb 2, 2011 · Feb 2, 2012 · Feb 7, 2013 · Feb 6, 2014 · Feb 8, 2015

Note: Respondents replied to the question "There is much discussion as to the amount of money the government in Washington should spend for national defense and military purposes. How do you feel about this? Do you think we are spending too little, about the right amount, or too much?"

Source: Gallup 2015.   *Photos: (left and right):* © The McGraw-Hill Companies Inc./Ken Cavanagh photographer.

in 1971, *The New York Times* published a set of classified documents now known as "The Pentagon Papers," which revealed that many members of both administrations had knowingly distorted the real prospects for the war. Two years later—over Nixon's veto—Congress passed the War Powers Act, which requires the president to notify Congress of the reasons for committing combat troops to a hostile situation (Patterson 2003).

Even though government leaders make the decision to go to war, public opinion plays a significant role in its execution. By 1971 the number of U.S. soldiers killed in Vietnam had surpassed 50,000, and antiwar sentiment was strong. Wars conducted by the United States since that time have tended to follow a similar pattern. Initial support both for the importance of going to war and for military spending to support it tends to give way the longer it takes to finish the job. This proved true for the conflicts in both Iraq and Afghanistan.

terrorism The use or threat of violence against random or symbolic targets in pursuit of political aims.

A major change relating to the conduct of war involves the composition of the U.S. military. Women represent a growing presence among the troops. As of January 2015, there were 201,383 women serving on active duty and women made up 15 percent of active military personnel (Department of Defense 2015). Increasingly, women are serving not just as support personnel but also as an integral part of combat units. The first casualty of the war in Iraq, in fact, was Private First Class Lori Piestewa, a member of the Hopi tribe and a descendant of Mexican settlers in the Southwest.

At the level of interpersonal interaction, war can bring out the worst as well as the best in people. In 2004, graphic images of the abuse of Iraqi prisoners by U.S. soldiers at Iraq's Abu Ghraib prison shocked the world. For social scientists, the deterioration of the guards' behavior brought to mind psychology professor Philip Zimbardo's mock prison experiment at Stanford University in 1971, in which volunteer guards in a simulated prison acted sadistically toward volunteer prisoneers. Zimbardo concluded it was the positions of power the guards occupied relative to the inmates that led to their behavior rather than the characteristics of the individuals themselves. In July 2004 the U.S. military began using a documentary film about the experiment to train military interrogators to avoid mistreatment of prisoners (Zarembo 2004).

TERRORISM

The Boston Marathon bombings in April 2013 were yet another reminder of the ability of a small number of people with a political agenda to instill fear in the hearts and

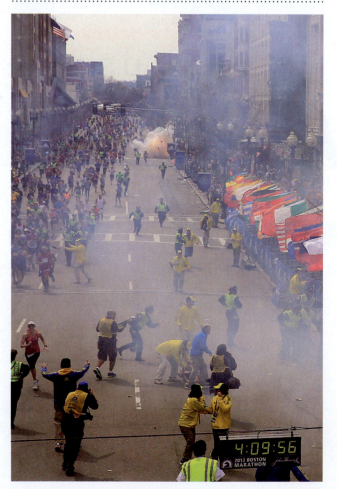

The Boston Marathon was the site of a terrorist attack in April 2013. Photo: © Photo by David L. Ryan/The Boston Globe via Getty Images.

POPSOC

When it first came out, the film *Zero Dark Thirty*, which portrayed the capture and killing of al-Qaeda leader Osama bin Laden, seemed like a lock to win an Oscar for Best Picture. Soon, however, a negative buzz emerged because of its seemingly positive portrayal of the use of torture and questions about whether it was a propaganda film put together with assistance of the U.S. military. It ultimately lost the award to *Argo.* The controversy should not be surprising. Movies with a political agenda have been around since the beginning of Hollywood. Films such as *The Birth of a Nation, This Is the Army, Dr. Strangelove, M*A*S*H,* and *Three Kings* all had political points they sought to make.

Photo: © Snap Stills/Rex Features via AP Images.

minds of millions. Acts of terror, whether perpetrated by a few or by many people, can be a powerful force. Formally defined, **terrorism** is the use or threat of violence against random or symbolic targets in pursuit of political aims. For terrorists, the end justifies the means. They believe that the status quo is oppressive and that desperate measures are essential to end the suffering of the deprived.

An essential aspect of contemporary terrorism involves use of the media. Terrorists may wish to keep secret their individual identities, but they want their political messages and goals to receive as much publicity as possible. The purpose of many acts of terrorist violence is more symbolic than strategic or tactical. These attacks represent a statement made by people who feel that the world has gone awry, that accepted political paths to problem resolution are ineffective or blocked, and that there is a larger or cosmic struggle going on, raising the stakes and so justifying the means (Juergensmeyer 2003). Whether through calls to the media, anonymous manifestos, or other means, terrorists typically admit responsibility for and defend their violent acts.

Terrorism is a global concern. In 2013, there were 17,958 deaths from terrorist attacks around the world, 82 percent of which occurred in just five countries: Iraq, Afghanistan, Pakistan, Nigeria, and Syria. There were 24 countries that experienced over 50 deaths and 102 in which there were zero (Institute for Economics and Peace 2014). Since September 11, 2001, governments around the world have renewed their efforts to fight terrorism. Even though the public generally regards increased surveillance and social control as a necessary evil, these measures have nonetheless raised governance issues. For example, some citizens in the United States and elsewhere have expressed concern that measures such as the USA PATRIOT Act of 2001 threaten civil liberties. Citizens also complain about the heightened anxiety created by the vague "terror alerts" the federal government issues from time to time. Worldwide, immigration and the processing of refugees have slowed to a crawl, separating families and preventing employers from filling job openings. As these efforts to combat political violence illustrate, the term *terrorism* is an apt one (Howard and Sawyer 2003).

> **peace** The absence of war or, more broadly, a proactive effort to develop cooperative relations among nations.

PEACE

Sociologists have considered **peace** both as the absence of war and as a proactive effort to develop cooperative relations among nations. It is important to note, however, that armed conflict involves more than just warring nations. From 1945 to the end of the 20th century, the 25 major wars that occurred between countries killed a total of

Going GLOBAL

Global Terrorist Attacks

■■■■ Highest impact of terrorism ■ Lowest impact of terrorism ■ No impact of terrorism ■ No records

Source: Institute for Economics and Peace 2014.

3.3 million people. Although this is significant, the 127 civil wars that occurred in the same time period resulted in 16 million deaths. In other words, five times as many people died as a result of conflicts *within* nations as died in wars *between* nations (Fearon and Laitin 2003).

Sociologists and other social scientists who draw on sociological theory and research have tried to identify conditions that deter war. One of their findings is that international trade may act as a deterrent to armed conflict. As countries exchange goods, people, and then cultures, they become more integrated and less likely to threaten each other's security. Viewed from this perspective, not just trade but also immigration and foreign exchange programs have a beneficial effect on international relations.

Another means of fostering peace is the activity of international charities and activist groups, or nongovernmental organizations (NGOs). The Red Cross and Red Crescent, Doctors Without Borders, and Amnesty International donate their services wherever they are needed, without regard to nationality. In the past decade or so, these NGOs have been expanding in number, size, and scope. By sharing news of local conditions and clarifying local issues, they often prevent conflicts from escalating into violence and war. Some NGOs have initiated cease-fires, reached settlements, and even ended warfare between former adversaries.

Finally, many analysts stress that nations cannot maintain their security by threatening violence. Peace, they contend, can best be maintained by developing strong mutual security agreements among potential adversaries (Etzioni 1965; Shostak 2002). Following this path involves active diplomacy and, to the extent that it involves negotiations with countries viewed as enemies, can be controversial.

From election protests to peace movements, stories such as these provide hope that people can make a difference. Even though large-scale economic trends can have negative impacts on companies, communities, and individuals, as well as shaping political outcomes, positive social change is possible. Sociological analysis helps us see the underlying processes at work in the economy and politics, and in so doing can assist us in recognizing places in those systems where opportunities for bringing about such change exist.

SOCIOLOGY IS A VERB

Playing Politics

Identify some elected officials—local, state, or federal—and interview them about their life in politics. What motivated them to run? What have they been able to accomplish? What frustrations do they face in getting things done? What would they change if they could? What advice would they give you? Keep notes of what they say, and reflect on the lessons learned about opportunities for, and obstacles to, change.

For REVIEW

I. How are economic and political power organized?

- The two major economic systems are capitalism and socialism, though in practice most economies are some mix of the two. Political systems of government include monarchy, oligarchy, dictatorship, totalitarianism, and democracy. A debate exists when looking at formal power in the United States about the degree to which there is a small, cohesive group of power elites who effectively rule or if leadership is more diverse and pluralistic, operating through democratic processes.

II. How does power operate?

- Power involves the capacity to get others to do what you want, ranging from use of force to acceptance of authority. In the case of authority, followers accept your power as legitimate, whether based on a traditional, rational-legal, or charismatic foundation.

III. How has the economy changed over time?

- From the Industrial Revolution through deindustrialization to the more recent global economic crisis, the modern economy is more dynamic and the consequences of change more far reaching both for nations and for individuals. Through political engagement people have the potential to influence the direction of that change.

SOCVIEWS on Government and Economy

Functionalist View

Power and authority are exercised in society to maintain social order for the good of the whole.

The economic system is a social institution that organizes the production, distribution, and consumption of goods and services.

The political system maintains **order** in society through internal policing and diplomatic relations with outsiders.

ORDER, SYSTEMS, ALLOCATION OF RESOURCES
KEY CONCEPTS

Conflict View

Power and authority are exercised to preserve and extend the integrity of the elites in society.

Capitalism primarily benefits the owners of the means of production; **socialism** allows workers to benefit from their own **labor power.**

The **power elite**, a small group of military, industrial, and government leaders, shape the direction of society.

COERCION, POWER ELITE, LABOR POWER
KEY CONCEPTS

Interactionist View

Power and authority are **socially constructed** through interactions with others.

Authority depends upon followers accepting the legitimacy of their leader's right to rule.

In the U.S. political system, leaders are selected by those who **vote**; the political parties try to **persuade** the voters to support their positions.

AUTHORITY, PERSUASION
KEY CONCEPTS

MAKE THE CONNECTION

After reviewing the chapter, answer the following questions:

1
How would each perspective explain the political battles in Wisconsin over rights and responsibilities?

2
How might each perspective seek to explain charismatic authority?

3
How might theorists from each perspective explain war?

4
Are you an active or an apathetic voter? What factors influence your approach? Which perspective best describes the way you participate in the political world?

Pop Quiz

1. **The systematic and widespread reduction of investment in domestic manufacturing and material production is called**
   a. deindustrialization.
   b. downsizing.
   c. postindustrialization.
   d. gentrification.

2. **What is the term used to describe outsourcing of work to foreign contractors?**
   a. exploitation
   b. offshoring
   c. alienation
   d. downsizing

3. **According to Max Weber, what is the definition of power?**
   a. The recognized set of procedures for implementing and achieving society's goals.
   b. The combination of strength and stamina.
   c. The mechanical and electrical energy that provided the foundation for the Industrial Revolution.
   d. The ability to exercise one's will over others, even if they resist.

4. **Which of the following is *not* part of the classification system of authority developed by Max Weber?**
   a. traditional authority
   b. pluralist authority
   c. legal-rational authority
   d. charismatic authority

5. **Within a capitalist economy, what does laissez-faire mean?**
   a. The means of production and distribution in a society are collectively held.
   b. People should compete freely, with minimal government intervention in the economy.
   c. A single business firm controls the market.
   d. Society depends on mechanization to produce its goods and services.

6. **Which of the following are primarily characterized by the transfers of money, goods, and services that are not reported to the government?**
   a. globalization
   b. the mixed economy
   c. laissez-faire capitalism
   d. the informal economy

7. **In which type of government do only a few individuals rule?**
   a. a monarchy
   b. a democracy
   c. a dictatorship
   d. an oligarchy

8. **According to the model proposed by C. Wright Mills, in whose hands does power rest?**
   a. the people
   b. the power elite
   c. the aristocracy
   d. representative democracy

9. **When it comes to voter turnout, where does the United States rank compared to other nations?**
   a. the first, with the highest level of turnout
   b. in the top 10 internationally
   c. in about the top third of all nations
   d. in the bottom half of all nations

10. **Which of the following terms best describes the threat of violence against random or symbolic targets in pursuit of political aims?**
    a. politics
    b. power
    c. terrorism
    d. authority

1. (a), 2. (b), 3. (d), 4. (b), 5. (b), 6. (d), 7. (d), 8. (b), 9. (d), 10. (c)

Social Class

WHAT'S TO COME

EASY STREET

Grayer is four years old. He takes lessons in French, Latin, music, swimming, ice skating, karate, and physical education—in addition to attending preschool. When he failed to get into the elite kindergarten of his mother's choice, she hired a grief counselor for him. He lives on Park Avenue in Manhattan with his mother and father, but the person with whom he spends most of his time is his nanny.

Grayer's fictional character was drawn from the real-life experiences of Emma McLaughlin and Nicola Kraus (2002), who worked as nannies to help pay their way through college. They told their stories in the book *The Nanny Diaries*, which later became a film (2007). They depict a world in which, like ours, social class matters.

It turns out that there really are people in Manhattan and elsewhere who obsess about the kindergarten program their children get into for fear that it will affect their child's long-term success. And they are willing to pay tutors a lot of money to help prepare their kids for kindergarten placement tests. Some also shell out $20,000 or more per year to enroll their kids in elite pre-kindergarten school programs to give them an additional advantage (Austin and Acuna 2012; Marks 2005; Otterman 2009; Phillips 2012; Zernike 2011).

Other families also provide their children with full-time nannies. Sima, one of the nannies in the novel, was an engineer in her home country of El Salvador. She came to the United States with her husband and children, but when he was unable to obtain a green card, her husband went back to El Salvador with the kids. Nan, the main nanny character in the book, refers to Sima as "a woman who has a higher degree than I will ever receive, in a subject I couldn't get a passing grade in, and who has been home [to see her husband and children] less than one month in the last twenty-four" (p. 173).

In her book *Just Like Family,* Tasha Blaine (2009) interviewed more than 100 nannies and found that stories of immigrant women leaving their own families for months or years at a time to raise the children of others were not uncommon. They often felt guilty about leaving their children behind only to, in essence, mother someone else's, but they did so to give their own kids a better life financially. The nannies Blaine interviewed frequently found themselves caught in between being an employee and being "like family." This ambiguous relationship often led to their being taken advantage of economically and emotionally.

As You READ >>

- **What is social class?**
- **How does social class operate?**
- **What are the consequences of social class?**

>> Life Chances

One of the lessons we learn from sociology is that place matters. Being born to a wealthy Park Avenue family in New York City confers something quite different than being born into a poor family in El Salvador. To describe the ways in which the positions we occupy shape our outcomes, Max Weber introduced the concept of **life chances** by which he meant that our likelihood for success is shaped by our access to valued material, social, and cultural resources. The college you choose, the job you have, the money you make, the car you drive, the neighborhood you live in, the health care you receive, and many other matters are shaped by the social positions you occupy.

In sociology, the significance of position and power is affirmed by including "the consequences of difference" in sociology's definition. This phrase highlights the importance sociologists place on investigating how resources are distributed, and how we justify those distributions. In this chapter and those that follow we will take a closer look at such consequences, with particular attention paid to social class, gender, race, and ethnicity.

life chances The likelihood that our success is shaped by our access to valued material, social, and cultural resources.

stratification A structured ranking of entire groups of people that perpetuates unequal economic rewards and power in a society.

slavery A system of enforced servitude in which some people are owned by others as property.

SOCTHINK

What factors have shaped your life chances? What kinds of resources have you inherited from others? What resources might you have lacked access to?

SYSTEMS OF STRATIFICATION

To better understand how our economic position shapes our likely outcomes, we need a better appreciation of the structures within which we find ourselves. Not all societies structure themselves in the same way, but difference exists within all societies. Sociologists call the social inequality that is built into the structure of society **stratification,** by which they mean the structured ranking of entire groups of people that perpetuates unequal economic rewards and power in a society. The *strata* in *stratification* refer to different layers or levels of power and influence built into the structure of society. Sociologists focus on four major systems of stratification: slavery, caste, estate, and social class.

Slavery **Slavery** is a system of enforced servitude in which some people are owned by others as property. Slaves become objects rather than subjects. Owners are free to treat them in the same way they might their horses or cattle.

The practice of slavery has varied over time. Most of the slaves in ancient Greece were prisoners of war or individuals captured and sold by pirates. Although succeeding generations could inherit slave status, it was not necessarily

© Bettmann/Corbis

... Slavery continues to be practiced around the world. Approximately 20.9 million people globally are in bondage to forced labor. Of these, 4.5 million are victims of forced sexual exploitation, 21 percent of whom are children.

Source: International Labour Office 2012. *Photo:* © Per-Anders Petterson/Getty Images.

debt bondage, forced labor, child labor and child servitude, sexual slavery, sale of children, forced marriage, and the sale of wives. In many developing countries, bonded laborers are imprisoned in lifetime employment. Though slavery is outlawed in the United States and Europe, guest workers and illegal immigrants have been forced to labor for years under terrible conditions, either to pay off debts or to avoid being turned over to immigration authorities. According to a U.S. Department of Justice report, 82 percent of the trafficking incidents it investigated involved sex trafficking, with 40 percent involving the sexual exploitation of a child (Banks and Kyckelhahn 2011).

caste A stratification system in which boundaries between strata are clear, relations between levels are regulated, and social status is ascribed.

Castes In a stratification system based on **caste,** boundaries between strata are clear, relations between levels are regulated, and social status is ascribed. The caste into which you are born remains the same until you die. It determines your opportunities throughout life, including who your friends are, what occupation you will pursue, and whom you will marry. Caste-based systems are rigid, allowing for limited and formalized interaction between castes.

The most familiar caste-based system is based primarily in India and is associated with Hinduism. In this system there are four major castes, or *varnas:* priests (*Brahman*), warriors (*Kshatriya*), merchants (*Vaishya*), and artisans/farmers (*Shudra*). Within those four major castes there are thousands of subcaste groupings. A fifth category, the *Dalit,* commonly referred to as untouchables, is considered to be so lowly and unclean as to have no place within this system of stratification. In 1950, after gaining independence from Great Britain, India adopted a new constitution that formally outlawed the caste system. In addition, economic changes tied to urbanization and the impact of technology have undercut its taken-for-granted status. Yet caste continues to play a powerful role in shaping patterns of social interaction throughout India.

permanent. A person's status might change, depending on which city-state happened to triumph in a military conflict. In effect, all citizens had the potential to become slaves or gain freedom, depending on the historical circumstances. By contrast, slavery in the United States and Latin America was an ascribed status, and slaves faced racial and legal barriers to freedom.

Today, the Universal Declaration of Human Rights, which is binding on all members of the United Nations, prohibits slavery in all its forms. According to the United Nations (2010), contemporary forms of slavery include

© Dr. Parvinder Sethi

Even though individuals can't change their caste, that doesn't mean change over time is impossible. Subcastes within India, for example, have been able to improve their overall standing by adopting the principles and practices of castes above them. This process is known as Sanskritization, after the language of ancient India in which most of the Hindu scriptures are written. Because the priestly Brahman caste represents the highest class, adopting that lifestyle, including becoming a vegetarian and giving up alcohol, became a marker of hoped-for higher status for the group, though this is most successful for groups that are already near the top (Bahadur 2008; Srinivas 1956; Staal 1963). Seeking to look and act like members of a higher stratum to gain social status is not unique to caste-based systems.

Estates The **estate system** divides power in society into three primary sectors: the church, the nobility, and the commoners. This stratification system was characteristic of medieval Europe, especially in England and France. French bishop Adalbéron de Laon gave names to these three estates in a poem to French king Robert the Pious around the year 1030. He identified them as *Oratores, Bellatores,* and *Laboratores,* or those who pray, those who fight, and those who work (Le Goff 1990). Members of the first estate included bishops, monks, priests, and nuns. The second estate was comprised of knights, lords and ladies, dukes and duchesses, and others of noble birth. Peasants and serfs were part of the third estate and their labor produced food for all. In this feudal system, the ruling monarch, usually the king, ruled over all, but, over time, representatives from each of these groups were granted some degree of voice in the political system. Vestiges of the estate system remain in England in the form of the Church of England, the House of Lords, and the House of Commons.

estate system A system of stratification that divides power in society into three primary sectors: the church, the nobility, and the commoners.

social class A system of stratification primarily based on socioeconomic status, both real and perceived.

The power in this system rested primarily on the nobles' ownership of land, though the church had substantial land holdings as well. Peasants provided the nobles with their income by paying them rents, primarily in the form of produce, in exchange for the opportunity to work the land. The nobles, with help from the knights among them, pledged to maintain order and protect the peasants from bandits and rival nobles. As in the caste system, social status was largely ascribed. The nobles inherited their titles and property, and there was little commoners could do to change their lot in life. One area that did provide some degree of opportunity was the church. By the 12th century, the priesthood emerged as a distinct category in most of Europe. In addition, opportunities for local merchants and artisans began to expand. For the first time, there were groups of people whose wealth did not depend on land ownership or agriculture. Their success ultimately contributed to the demise of feudalism and the rise of capitalism.

The estate system included those who pray, those who fight, and those who work. Photo: © The British Library/The Image Works.

Social Class In the final stratification system, **social class,** social position is determined primarily by socioeconomic status, both real and perceived. Social class can be assessed objectively and subjectively. Objective indicators primarily include education, occupation, and income. A college graduate who is a mechanical engineer earning $83,000 per year is higher than a high school graduate working as a dental assistant earning $32,000. Subjective class identification, the degree to which a person identifies with a particular social class category, also plays a role. It's entirely possible, for example, for a person who makes a lot of money to identify with the social class within which she or he was born (Rubin et al. 2014). The perceptions others have also plays a significant role because, as we learned with the Thomas theorem, perception shapes action, which, in the case of social class, may well affect the degree to which we are allowed access to valued resources. Because social class can involve multiple, sometimes contradictory, indicators, settling on a universal, all-purpose model of social classes is problematic.

Sociologists commonly use a five-class model to describe the class system in the United States, though many other models are available (Beeghley 2007; Kerbo 2011). At the top are the *upper class,* including 1–2 percent of the population who are wealthy, well-respected, and politically powerful. Just beneath them are the *upper-middle class,* which is comprised primarily of business executives, doctors, lawyers, architects, and other professionals; they make up about 15 percent of the population. The next 30–35 percent include members of the *middle class,* which is comprised of less affluent professionals, such as school teachers and nurses, along with owners of small businesses, clerical workers, and others who have decent jobs but a minimal amount of autonomy—that is, control over what they do and when they do it. The fourth group is the *working class,* whose jobs typically involve some degree of manual labor, including carpenters, plumbers, and factory workers, who make up another 30–35 percent of the population. The final group is the *underclass,* commonly referred to as "the poor," who make up 15–20 percent of the population. People in this class have limited and inconsistent access to resources, and membership includes a disproportionate number of African Americans, Hispanics, immigrants, and single mothers.

When asked to identify their social class, people in the United States struggle with how to respond. One of the difficulties comes from widespread assumption that social classes do not exist in the United States. Another is the difficulty people have in placing themselves in relationship to others. In particular, there seems to be an aversion to categorizing oneself as either rich or poor. As a result, many people, including those whose life chances are significantly different than each other, identify themselves as part of the middle class. For example, looking at income (which is one of the objective indicators of social class), when asked how much money it takes to consider someone rich, 54 percent of people who earned under $30,000 per year chose an income level of less than $100,000. Among those making $100,000 or more, only 2 percent indicated a threshold that low. At this income level, 46 percent said it would take $500,000 or more per year to be considered rich (Reeves 2015).

What Class Am I ?

- Upper Class
- Upper-Middle Class
- Middle Class
- Lower-Middle Class
- Lower Class

Note: Respondents were asked, "Which of the social classes would you say you belong in?" Their answers were then grouped into categories based on family income.

Source: Pew 2015a.

SOCIAL MOBILITY

A society's system of stratification significantly shapes one's life chances. Though the opportunity for changing position is possible in all, the likelihood of doing so varies significantly. In most cases, the fairytale story of the peasant girl who marries a prince is nothing more than that. To better understand opportunities for **social mobility,** meaning movement within or between society's strata, sociologists investigate the degree to which a society is open versus closed.

> **social mobility** Movement within or between society's strata.
>
> **open system** A society with a system of stratification that allows for social mobility between strata.
>
> **closed system** A society with a system of stratification that does not allow for social mobility between strata.
>
> **horizontal mobility** The movement of an individual from one social position to another of the same rank.
>
> **vertical mobility** The movement of an individual from one social position to another of a different rank.

Open versus Closed Stratification Systems A society with an **open system** of stratification allows for social mobility between strata. Of the stratification systems discussed earlier, class-based systems have the potential to be more open than others. In principle, capitalism seeks to identify those with the greatest ability and reward them for their efforts regardless of whether their parents were rich or poor. The possibility for mobility becomes an incentive for hard work.

A society with a **closed system** of stratification does not allow for social mobility between strata. Social positions are ascribed, so the position into which you are born is the position within which you remain throughout life. Caste systems are mostly closed with limited opportunity for movement within one's lifetime. Societies with barriers to mobility, whether based on religion, gender, race, ethnicity, class, or any other positional variables, are more closed than those without such barriers.

Types of Social Mobility

Sociologists also distinguish between mobility *within* a stratum versus movement *between* levels. For example, a bus driver who becomes a hotel clerk moves from one social position to another of approximately the same rank. Sociologists call this kind of movement **horizontal mobility.** However, if the bus driver were to become a lawyer, he or she would experience **vertical mobility**—the movement of an individual from one social position to another of a different rank (Sorokin [1927] 1959). Vertical mobility can involve moving upward or downward in a society's stratification system.

Sociologists also contrast the significance of mobility across an individual's career or lifetime versus movement

© Sean Gallup/Getty Images

that spans generations. **Intergenerational mobility** involves changes in the social position of children relative to their parents. Thus, a plumber whose father was a physician provides an example of downward intergenerational mobility. A film star whose parents were both factory workers illustrates upward intergenerational mobility. Because education contributes significantly to upward mobility, any barrier to the pursuit of advanced degrees limits intergenerational mobility (Isaacs, Sawhill, and Haskins 2008).

Intragenerational mobility, in contrast, involves changes in social position within a person's adult life. Thus, a woman who enters the paid labor force as a teacher's aide and eventually becomes superintendent of the school district experiences upward

intergenerational mobility
Changes in the social position of children relative to their parents.

intragenerational mobility
Changes in social position within a person's adult life.

Movies on SOCIAL CLASS

5

The Help
In the 1960s South, three women from different classes build an unlikely friendship.

Winter's Bone
A teen living in the Ozarks investigates her father's criminal dealings.

Water
An Indian widow attempts to escape the social restrictions of her position.

Rich Hill
Three boys and their families struggle to get by.

The Great Gatsby
Lifestyles of the rich and famous.

SOCTHINK

What is the story of social mobility in your family? To what extent have there been shifts both across and within generations? What factors, such as family connections or historical events, contributed to the social mobility that occurred?

intragenerational mobility. A man who becomes a cab driver after his accounting firm goes bankrupt undergoes downward intragenerational mobility.

In the United States one way to define the "American Dream" is as upward vertical mobility that is intragenerational. In other words, a person could experience a significant shift in social class position over the course of her or his

© BananaStock/Punchstock RF

turns out that the old saying "It's not what you know; it's who you know" has some truth to it. Position and connections make it possible for us to increase the likelihood of accomplishing our goals. Finally, *cultural* resources include our tastes, language, and way of looking at the world. They represent our knowledge of cognitive, normative, and material elements of culture that we can draw on when acting to accomplish our goals. A simple but classic example involves knowing which fork to use for the various courses of a formal dinner. But it also includes knowing how to respond when we are put on the spot, whether in a business meeting, at a rock concert, or in class. Viewing social class in terms of material, social, and cultural resources enables us to better understand the degree to which living the American Dream is possible.

SOCTHINK

Paul Fussell (1992), in his book *Class: A Guide through the American Status System,* argued that the writing on our clothes says a lot about our social class. What story do the logos, brands, and writing on your clothes tell about you? How might your clothing choices have differed had you been in a different class position?

Did You Know?

. . . Six members of the Walton family, heirs of Walmart founder Sam Walton, own more wealth than the bottom 40 percent of U.S. families combined.

Photo: © AP Photo/Paul Sakuma.

career, from a relatively low-level position to one of significant wealth and power. Though this does happen, the "American reality" is that we tend to end up in positions relatively close to where we began.

>> Social Class in the United States

The stratification system in the United States is predominantly class based. Within it, three categories of resources play a major role in shaping our life chances. *Material* resources refer to economic assets that we own or control, including money, property, and land. *Social* resources include prestige based on the position we occupy and connections based on the social networks we are a part of. It

Percentage Share of Total Income

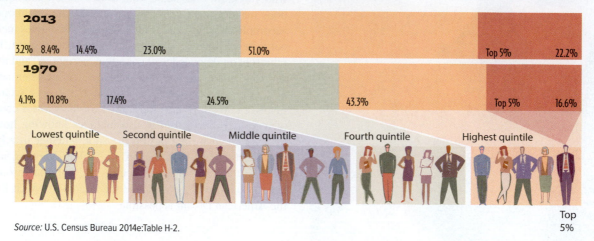

2013

3.2% 8.4% 14.4% 23.0% 51.0% Top 5% 22.2%

1970

4.1% 10.8% 17.4% 24.5% 43.3% Top 5% 16.6%

Lowest quintile Second quintile Middle quintile Fourth quintile Highest quintile

Top 5%

Source: U.S. Census Bureau 2014e:Table H-2.

income Money received over some period of time.

wealth The total value of all material assets minus debts at a single point in time.

INCOME AND WEALTH

Income and wealth provide social class with its material foundation. **Income** refers to money received over some period of time. It can come in the form of wages per hour or salary per year, but also as returns on investments, such as stock dividends or profit from the sale of property including homes. **Wealth** consists of the total value of all material assets minus debts at a single point in time. It includes savings, stocks, land, or any other material asset of value. If you were to sell everything you own and pay off all your debts, what you had left would be the value of your wealth. These material resources make our class-based lifestyles possible (Bourdieu 1986). As such, if we are to understand social classes in the United States, we need a clear picture of their distribution.

Income Income inequality is a basic characteristic of a class system. In 2013, the median household income in the United States was $51,939, approximately the same as the previous year. In other words, half of all households had higher incomes in that year, and half had lower incomes. But this fact does not fully convey the income disparities in our society. We get some sense of income inequality by contrasting the median (middle) score with the mean (arithmetic average), which in 2013 was $72,641. The mean is so much higher because some people make a lot more money than others, which draws the mean up, making it a less useful statistic for describing "average" or typical income (DeNavas-Walt and Proctor 2014).

We gain additional insight into this inequality by looking at the relative placement of households from bottom to top. One of the most common ways to present income dispersion is to line up all income-earning households from low to high and then break them into quintiles, or blocks of 20 percent. There are approximately 123 million households in the United States, so each quintile would include an equal number of about 24.6 million households. Doing so allows us to get a sense of what the average income is within each of these quintiles, along with the percentage of the total income pie that each quintile earns.

As we can see in the "Percentage Share of Total Income" and "Average Household Income by Quintile" graphs, looking at the population in this way shows a significant degree of income inequality. Focusing on the extremes, the mean income for households in the lowest quintile is $11,651, while households in the top quintile average $185,206. Those households in the top 5 percent, the ones most responsible for bringing up the arithmetic mean, average $322,343. Those in the bottom quintile earn just 3.2 percent of the nation's total income, while those in the top quintile earn 51.1 percent. In fact, the top 5 percent earns a significantly greater percent of total income than the bottom 40 percent combined (U.S. Census Bureau 2014e:Table H-2).

Even though the top quintile is taking home a larger share of the income pie, implying that the rich are getting richer, it is still possible that the incomes earned for the other groups also increased. As the saying goes, a rising tide lifts all boats. In other words, if the economy expands, the overall size of the pie gets bigger, so all can benefit. And if we compare income over time, we find some support

Average Household Income by Quintile

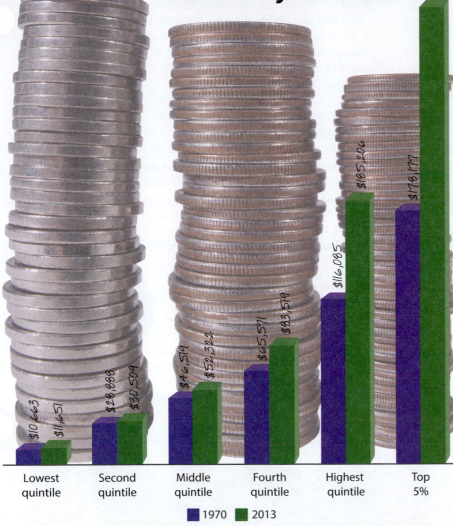

$10,663
$11,651
$28,888
$30,509
$46,519
$52,322
$65,571
$83,519
$116,085
$185,206
$178,177
$322,343

Lowest quintile	Second quintile	Middle quintile	Fourth quintile	Highest quintile	Top 5%

■ 1970 ■ 2013

Source: U.S. Census Bureau 2014e:Table H-3.   *Photo:* © Getty Images RF.

for that contention. As demonstrated in the accompanying graph, the mean household income for all five quintiles rose between 1970 and 2013, but the percentage increase varied significantly. The income for the lowest quintile increased by $988 or 9.3 percent. The income for the top quintile went up $69,121 or 59.5 percent. And the income for the top 5 percent of households rose $144,166 or 80.9 percent. Everyone is doing better, but the gap between the top and the bottom is getting larger.

As we saw in Chapter 9, Occupy Wall Street brought particular attention to the income advantages of the top 1 percent. Economists Thomas Piketty and Emmanuel Saez found that, in 2011, the average income for those in this group was $435,623. Even within this category, however, substantial income differences exist. At the top of the top, for example, the average income for the 15,837 families in the top 0.01 percent was $23.7 million. And, according to the IRS, the top 400 U.S. households had an average

income of $336 million. On the other end of the scale, 15.6 million households reported incomes under $15,000 (DeNavas-Walt and Proctor 2014); Internal Revenue Service 2015; Piketty and Saez 2013).

To provide a simple measure of the distribution of anything in a population, including income and wealth, Italian statistician Corrado Gini created the Gini index, a single number ranging between zero and one. The larger the Gini coefficient, the greater the inequality. If everyone in the population owns exactly the same wealth, or earns the same income, the Gini index equals zero. If one person owns everything and everyone else owns nothing, the Gini index equals one. The real value of the Gini index is as a comparative statistic because it allows us to see whether inequality is increasing or decreasing over time. In the United States, the Gini index for income reached a low of 0.386 in 1968. Since that time it has risen fairly steadily. In 1990 it reached 0.428, and by 2013 it reached 0.476 (U.S. Census Bureau 2014:Table H-4). This upswing indicates that income inequality has increased significantly during that time.

Wealth Wealth in the United States is even more unevenly distributed than income.

Distribution of Wealth Owned, by Percentile

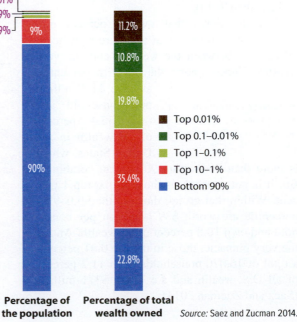

0.01%
0.09%
0.9%
9%
90%

11.2%
10.8%
19.8%
35.4%
22.8%

■ Top 0.01%
■ Top 0.1–0.01%
■ Top 1–0.1%
■ Top 10–1%
■ Bottom 90%

Percentage of the population

Percentage of total wealth owned

Source: Saez and Zucman 2014.

POVERTY

In 2013, 45.3 million people in the United States—14.5 percent of the population—were living in poverty. Based on official calculations, a family consisting of two adults and two children with a combined annual income of $23,624 or less fell below the poverty line. By contrast, a single person under the age of 65 must earn less than $12,119 annually to be officially considered poor (DeNavas-Walt and Proctor 2014).

Defining Poverty Such figures make it seem like a simple matter to define who is living in poverty: You are either above the threshold or below it. Sociologists have found, however, that our conceptions of poverty vary. For example, we can define poverty in either absolute or relative terms.

Absolute poverty refers to a minimum level of subsistence that no family should be expected to live below. According to this definition, someone who is below the

Going GLOBAL

The Poverty Rate in Households with Children, Selected Countries

The median wealth for households in 2011 was $68,828, but the mean was $338,950 (U.S. Census Bureau 2013b). The large difference between the two is a consequence of the extreme amounts of wealth held by the richest households. The top 10 percent of households own 77.2 percent of all wealth in the United States with an average worth of $2.56 million. The bottom 90 percent own the remaining 22.8 percent with a net worth of $84,000 per household (Saez and Zucman 2014).

Breaking down that top 10 percent into smaller pieces reveals that there are significant differences between the wealthy and the very wealthy. Those among the 90–99th percentile average $1.3 million per household and own 35.4 percent of all wealth in the United States, which is more than the bottom 90 percent combined. But it is not as much as those in the top 1 percent. Within that group, those in the 99.0–99.9 percentile are worth $39.7 million per household and own 10.8 percent of all wealth. And at the very pinnacle, those in the top 0.01 percent, a total of 16,070 households, own 11.2 percent of all U.S. wealth and are worth $371 million (Saez and Zucman 2014).

absolute poverty A minimum level of subsistence that no family should be expected to live below.

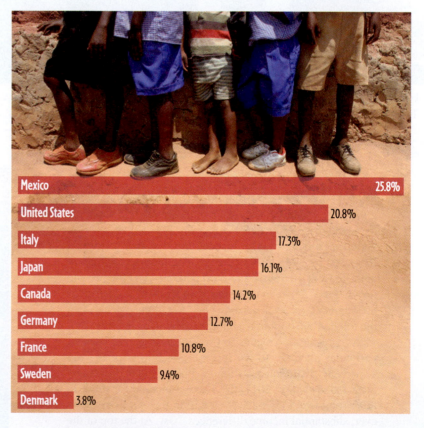

Country	Poverty Rate
Mexico	25.8%
United States	20.8%
Italy	17.3%
Japan	16.1%
Canada	14.2%
Germany	12.7%
France	10.8%
Sweden	9.4%
Denmark	3.8%

Source: OECD 2014b.   *Photo:* © Jason R Warren/E+/Getty Images.

poverty level ultimately lacks sufficient resources to survive. Many nations, including the United States, use some form of this criterion as the basis of their definition of poverty. A comparatively high proportion of children in U.S. households are poor, meaning that their families are unable to afford necessary consumer goods (food, shelter, and clothing).

In contrast, **relative poverty** is a floating standard of deprivation by which people at the bottom of a society, whatever their lifestyles, are judged to be disadvantaged in comparison with the nation as a whole. For example, people who have sufficient food, clothing, and shelter might nonetheless be considered poor if they live in a wealthy nation such as the United States, because they can't afford to buy things the culture defines as important but are not essential for survival such as a refrigerator. Similarly, someone who would be considered poor by U.S. standards might be well-off by global standards of poverty; hunger and starvation are daily realities in many regions of the world. In addition, when viewed in historical terms, someone currently defined as poor may be better off in absolute terms than a poor person in the 1930s or 1960s.

Historically, the poverty line in the United States was first calculated based on a formula established in 1964. President Lyndon B. Johnson had declared a War on Poverty, but at the time, no official measure of poverty existed. To enact an official measure, the Johnson administration turned to the work of Mollie Orshansky, a food economist at the research bureau of the Social Security Administration. Orshansky proposed combining two facts

> ### Civilization is unbearable, but it is less unbearable at the top.
>
> Timothy Leary

to establish a general poverty threshold. The first came from a study that found that families spend approximately one-third of their budget on food. The second was the estimated cost of a minimally nutritious diet established by U.S. Department of Agriculture dieticians. Orshansky combined these two pieces of information to establish the poverty threshold as three times the cost of the USDA diet. She assumed that families facing poverty would cut back on both food and nonfood expenditures at approximately the same rate so that the 3-to-1 ratio would hold (Fisher 1992, 2008; Orshansky 1965).

There has been a long-standing debate about whether this approach to defining poverty in the United States measures the true nature of poverty. For example, critics argue that the measure is too simplistic, or that the multiplier should be higher because families now spend one-fourth or one-fifth of their budget on food. Recognizing the limits of the official definition, the U.S. government started calculating a supplemental measure of poverty in the fall of 2011. This more complex measure takes into account the actual costs of food, clothing, shelter, utilities, taxes, work expenses, and out-of-pocket medical costs. In addition to income, it counts food stamps and tax credits as available resources. And it is adjusted to reflect price differences across geographic regions (U.S. Census Bureau 2010b).

relative poverty A floating standard of deprivation by which people at the bottom of a society, whatever their lifestyles, are judged to be disadvantaged in comparison with the nation as a whole.

© Dr. Parvinder

Who Are the Poor? One of the lessons we learn by analyzing those who fall below the poverty line is that our stereotypes about poverty are flawed. For example, many people in the United States believe that the vast majority of the poor are able to work but will not. Yet, of the 45.3 million people in poverty, 29.4 percent are either under age 18 or 65 years old or older. Many working-age adults who are poor do work outside the home, although often in part-time positions. In 2013, 2.7 million people who worked full-time, year-round, and 8 million of those who worked part-time, were in poverty. Of those poor adults who do not work, many are ill or disabled, or are occupied in maintaining a home. As we can see in the table "Who Are the Poor in the United States?" the likelihood of being in poverty is also shaped by factors such as age, race, ethnicity, and family type (DeNavas-Walt and Proctor 2014).

Since World War II, an increasing proportion of the poor people of the United States have been women, many of whom are divorced or never-married mothers. In 1959 female householders accounted for 23 percent of the nation's poor families; by 2013, that figure had risen to 50.9 percent (DeNavas-Walt and Proctor 2014). A major factor in this feminization of poverty has been the increase in families with women as single heads of household. In 2013, 30.6 percent of families headed by single mothers lived in poverty, compared to 15.9 percent for single-father households and 5.8 percent for married couples. Contributing to such rates are factors such as the difficulty

in finding affordable child care and sex discrimination in the labor market (DeNavas-Walt and Proctor 2014).

The type of community within which people live also plays a role. In 2013, 43.1 percent of poor people in the United States lived in big cities within metropolitan areas. These urban residents are the focus of most governmental efforts to alleviate poverty. Yet, according to many observers, the plight of the urban poor is growing worse, owing to the devastating interplay of inadequate education and limited employment prospects. Traditional employment opportunities in the industrial sector are largely closed to the unskilled poor. Past and present discrimination heightens these problems for those low-income urban residents who are Black and Hispanic (DeNavas-Walt and Proctor 2014).

Analyses of people who are poor in general reveal that they are, however, not a static social class. The overall composition of the poor changes continually; some individuals and families move above the poverty level after a year or two, while others slip below it. In a study of

SOCTHINK

Should welfare recipients be required to work? If so, should the government subsidize preschool and afterschool care for their children while they are at work?

Who Are the Poor in the United States?

	Percentage of the total U.S. population	Percentage of the poor population by category
Age		
Under 18 years old	23.5	32.4
18 to 64 years old	62.3	58.3
65 years and older	14.2	9.3
Race/Ethnicity		
Whites (non-Hispanic)	62.4	41.5
Blacks	13.0	24.4
Hispanics	17.3	28.1
Asians and Pacific Islanders	5.4	3.9
Families		
Married couples	73.5	38.1
Female householder, no husband present	18.7	50.9
Male householder, no wife present	7.8	11.0

Note: Age and race/ethnicity percentages are based on total persons. Families percentages are based on total families.

Source: DeNavas-Walt and Proctor 2014: Tables 3,4.   Photos: *(clockwise from right):* © Wild Horse Photography/Getty Images RF; © David Buffington/Getty Images RF; © Design Pics/Con Tanasiuk RF; © BananaStock/JupiterImages RF; © iStock.com/eyecrave LLC RF.

economic insecurity from ages 25 to 60, sociologist Mark Rank found that 79 percent of the U.S. population experience at least one year in which they are unemployed, receive welfare benefits, or are officially poor or near poverty. Focusing just on poverty and near poverty, 54.1 percent spend a year with an income less than 150 percent of the poverty line at some point during their prime adult working-age lives. Considering long-term welfare use, only 3.8 percent of that population received such benefits for 10 or more consecutive years (Rank, Hirschl, and Foster 2014:37).

In 1996, in a historic shift in federal policy, Congress passed the Personal Responsibility and Work Opportunity Reconciliation Act, ending the long-standing federal guarantee of assistance to every poor family that meets eligibility requirements. The law sets a lifetime limit of five years of welfare benefits and requires all able-bodied adults to work after receiving two years of

People below Poverty Level

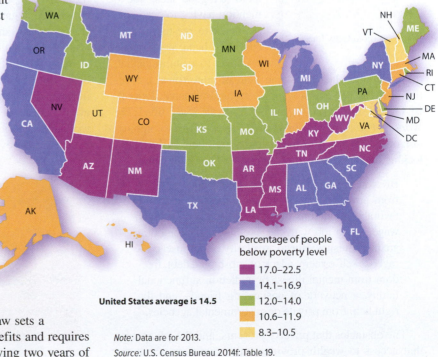

United States average is 14.5

Percentage of people below poverty level

- 17.0–22.5
- 14.1–16.9
- 12.0–14.0
- 10.6–11.9
- 8.3–10.5

Note: Data are for 2013.

Source: U.S. Census Bureau 2014f: Table 19.

benefits (although hardship exceptions are allowed). The federal government gives block grants to the states to use as they wish in assisting poor and needy residents, and it permits states to experiment with ways to move people off welfare.

Other countries vary widely in their commitment to social service programs. But most industrialized nations devote higher proportions of their expenditures to housing, Social Security, welfare, health care, and unemployment compensation than the United States does. For example, in Cuba, 96 percent of health care expenditures are paid for by the government, compared to 82 percent in the United Kingdom and 70 percent in Canada. The U.S. government pays out 45 percent of health care expenditures, ranking close to Mexico and China (World Bank 2010a).

The domino effects of a lack of economic resources can be severe. Poor people often also lack the social network connections to help them get good jobs, not to mention having to overcome the negative prestige associated with being poor. When it comes to cultural capital, they also often lack the same kind of educational credentials that can serve as a valuable cultural resource. Journalist David Shipler (2004), in his in-depth study titled *The Working Poor: Invisible in America,* referred to the combination of factors that poor people must overcome as the "interlocking deficits of poverty." As Shipler (2004:4–5) put it,

Breaking away and moving a comfortable distance from poverty seems to require a perfect lineup of favorable conditions. A set of skills, a good starting wage, and a job with the likelihood of promotion are prerequisites. But so are clarity of purpose, courageous self-esteem, a lack of substantial debt, freedom from mental illness or addiction, a functional family, a network of upstanding friends, and the right help from private or governmental agencies.

The obstacles that poverty presents, and the advantages that access to wealth provides, raise questions about the

© Bfoto/Getty Images RF

degree to which a person can succeed based on his or her abilities alone or whether the social position people inherit determines their likely outcome.

THE AMERICAN DREAM

The American Dream is as much about opportunity as it is success. The existence of substantial levels of income and wealth inequality, and the persistence of poverty, are not themselves contrary to the American Dream. In the United States, 60 percent of adults believe that people who want to get ahead can make it if they are willing to work hard. This belief does not vary significantly by income level (Pew Research Center 2014i). Even though the gap between rich and poor is wide, people in the United States are less likely to see that gap as a big problem than do people in a wide variety of other nations, including England, France, Greece, Russia, China, and Pakistan (Pew Research Center 2013i). Americans want to assume that the system is fair and that both the rich and the poor are deserving of their positions (Putnam 2015).

Meritocracy Faith in opportunity manifests itself in a commitment to meritocracy. A meritocracy is a system in which a person's social status is achieved through a combination of ability and effort. To put it in terms of stratification and social mobility, a meritocracy is an open system in which your position is earned.

The commitment to meritocracy in the United States works in tandem with the principle of equality. That value is set forth within the opening lines of the Declaration of Independence: "We hold these truths to be self-evident, that all men are created equal, that they are endowed by their Creator with certain unalienable Rights, that among these are Life, Liberty and the Pursuit of Happiness." This conviction regarding our fundamental sameness implies that everyone should have a chance for success regardless of their station in life. Our outcomes should be based on something other than having had the good fortune of being born into the right family. Differences in outcomes in terms of income, wealth, and poverty are accepted, and even valued, because they provide incentives for hard work and sacrifice, so long as everyone has an opportunity to succeed (Reeves 2015).

© ziggymaj/Getty Images RF

The desire to put the principle of meritocracy into practice was apparent early on in American history in the works of people like Benjamin Franklin and Thomas Jefferson. It provided the justification for Horace Mann's commitment to public education as the great equalizer (see Chapter 8). One of his goals was to have schools spread a common American culture through a shared curriculum. Values, including the importance of meritocracy, were reinforced. Children in 1843, for example, in their *McGuffey's Eclectic Readers,* one of the most commonly assigned textbook series in American history, read passages such as this:

> The road to wealth, to honor, to usefulness, and happiness, is open to all, and all who will, may enter upon it with the almost certain prospect of success. In this free community, there are no privileged orders. Every man finds his level. If he has talents, he will be known and estimated, and rise in the respect and confidence of society. (Quoted in Weiss 1969:33)

Similarly, in the late 1800s, the best-selling books by Horatio Alger, including titles such as *Struggling Upward, Mark the Match Boy,* and *Rough and Ready,* reinforced the rags-to-riches ideal. In *Ragged Dick,* for example, the title character is told as a boy, "You know in this free country poverty in early life is no bar to a man's advancement" (Alger [1868] 1985:55). In Alger's stories, a person's character and values trump social position as superior resources all but ensuring certain success (Reeves 2014).

Faith in the American Dream remains strong. President Barack Obama reinforced the U.S. commitment to meritocracy in his second inaugural address. In it he declared, "We are true to our creed when a little girl born into the bleakest poverty knows that she has the same chance to succeed as anybody else, because she is an American; she is free, and she is equal, not just in the eyes of God but also in our own" (Obama 2013). There is, in the United States, an almost sacred aura that surrounds the principle of meritocracy. Violation of this principle would represent a betrayal of the public trust.

Aristocracy In many ways, commitment to meritocracy was the counterpoint to the rule by the British monarchy that early American colonists rebelled against. In an aristocracy, social status is ascribed and membership in the privileged or elite ranks is inherited. Unlike the sameness principle undergirding meritocracy, this system presupposes the existence of innate differences between people. Some are born to lead while others are destined to follow. *Aristocracy* literally means "rule by the best," and, over time, that came to mean the nobility. The principle of aristocracy undergirds both the caste and estate systems of stratification. Because differences are presumed to be inherited, there are limited opportunities for social mobility.

In the United States, there are signs of growing concern about the degree to which opportunities for social mobility remain possible. The 60 percent of people who believe that "anyone can get ahead if they work hard" has declined from 74 percent in 1999, and the percentage of people who now say that "hard work and determination are no guarantee of success for most people" rose from 23 to 38 percent (Pew Research Center 2014i). Social mobility does occur, but most people do not move very far. In comparing father's and son's income, researchers found that sons of low-income fathers have almost a 60 percent chance of rising above the lowest quintile, but only a 22.5 percent chance of reaching the median and a 4.5 percent chance of breaking into the top quintile (Mishel, Bernstein, and Shierholz 2009). Similarly, as we can see in the "Wealth Mobility" graph, when looking at wealth, 36 percent of children with parents in the lowest quintile end up there themselves while only 7 percent make it to the top quintile. On the other end of the scale, 36 percent of children with parents in the top wealth quintile stay there, whereas only 11 percent drop down into the bottom quintile (Haskins 2008:8). In fact, the likelihood of ending up in the same position as your parents has been rising since about 1980 (Aaronson and Mazumder 2007).

© Corbis

SOCTHINK

The percentage of financial aid in the form of grants has gone down while the percentage of loan aid has increased. Why do you think that has occurred? What are the consequences of such a shift for social mobility?

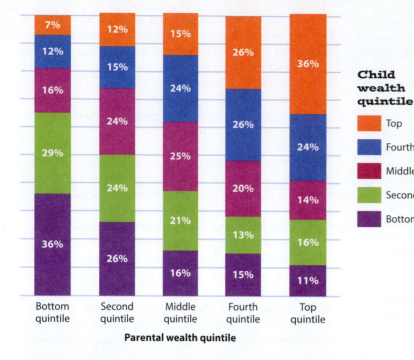

Wealth Mobility: Percentage of Children in Each Wealth Quintile Compared to Parental Wealth Quintile

Child wealth quintile
- Top
- Fourth
- Middle
- Second
- Bottom

Source: Haskins 2008.

Access to higher education plays an important role in social mobility. In 2013, 45.5 percent of high school students in the lowest income quintile enrolled in college the following fall compared to 78.5 percent of those from the highest quintile (U.S. Department of Education 2015: Table 302.30). For students from families with the lowest incomes, the cost can be prohibitive. Only 11 percent of children from the poorest families in the United States have earned college degrees, compared to 53 percent of children from the top fifth of the population. Those moderate-income students who do graduate, and even those who fail to complete their degrees, are often saddled with heavy postgraduate debt (Isaacs et al. 2008).

Political scientist Robert Putnam (2015) uses the expression "opportunity gap" to describe what appears to be a growing divide between the children of the well-to-do compared to children from working-class and poor families. Increased levels of neighborhood segregation, educational segregation, and social network segregation, including the increased likelihood of marrying a same-class spouse, he claims, all contribute to a growing class divide. Well-off parents provide their children with a whole host of advantages, including private schools, tutors, educational vacations, and specialized summer camps, making the divide even wider (Duncan and Murnane 2011; Putnam 2015). After analyzing academic achievement over time, sociologist Sean Reardon found, "The achievement gap between children from high- and low-income families is roughly 30 to 40 percent larger among children born in 2001 than among those born twenty-five years earlier" (Reardon 2011:93). Parents' level of education, occupation, and income combined play a major role in this divide between those who are college graduates and those who are not (Lareau 2011; Putnam 2015).

Likelihood of Graduating from College

Note: Test performance is for a standardized 8th-grade math test. Family status is based on parent's education, occupation, and income. College graduation rate measure is for 12 years after the test.

Source: Putnam 2015: 190.

The economic, social, and cultural advantages children at the top receive provide a cushion that protects these children should failure occur. Putnam writes, "Parental wealth is especially important for social mobility, because it can provide informal insurance that allows kids to take more risks in search of more reward" (Putnam 2015:36). Over time, as those at the top transmit increased access to resources to their children, the rungs of the mobility ladder get farther apart, making it difficult for people with limited resources to reach the next level.

Education Pays: Full-Time, Year-Round Workers Aged 25–64

Education level	Median annual earnings
Professional degree	$102,266
Doctorate degree	$92,336
Master's degree	$72,263
Bachelor's degree	$59,294
Associate's degree	$43,919
Some college, no degree	$41,128
High school grad (includes GED)	$35,755
Some high school, no degree	$27,022

Source: U.S. Census Bureau 2014a:Table 1.2.2.1.   *Photo:* © McGraw-Hill Companies, Inc./Mark Dierker, photographer.

When there's an overt commitment to meritocracy in principle, it becomes easy to minimize the degree to which inherited resources shape likely outcomes. Aristocracy in practice becomes a hidden privilege as people downplay the extent to which their advantages mattered (Hayes 2012; McNamee and Miller 2014; Young 2001). Sociologist Thomas Shapiro provides an example of just that in his interview with Joe and Briggette Barry, a middle-class couple whose parents gave them $32,000 to help them buy a house, bought them three different cars, helped pay their daughter's tuition to a private school, helped with mortgage payments when Joe was between jobs, set up a trust fund for their daughter's college education, and provided numerous other forms of assistance. Yet when asked how they acquired their assets, Briggette responded, "we worked our butts off for what we have" (Shapiro 2004:75). It is no doubt true, but underplays the difference between those who work just as hard but lack access to similar economic resources. As Shapiro points out, the effect of such denial is particularly felt in the African American community where access to wealth is significantly lower than in the White, non-Hispanic community. The same holds true for women who, as a result of unequal treatment, wage discrimination, and occupational segregation, do not receive the same opportunities for advancement as do men (see Chapters 12 and 13).

>> Sociological Perspectives on Stratification

By paying attention to the structure of the stratification system, and how resources within it are distributed, we can better understand how a society committed to the principle of meritocracy might produce the practice of aristocracy. Sociologists provide us with tools to focus our attention on key resources that enable us to discern who has power and why. As noted, three categories of resources are critical: material, social, and cultural.

MARX AND MATERIAL RESOURCES

Karl Marx focuses his attention primarily on the distribution of material resources. He argues that, throughout history, power was determined by ownership of the means of production (see Chapter 9). As a result, Marx's model of class has two basic categories: owners and non-owners. During feudal times, for example, the nobility owned the land and the peasants did not. Under capitalism, the ruling class, known as the **bourgeoisie,** own the means of production, including factories and machinery. The working class, known as the **proletariat,** do not own the means of production so must sell their labor power to the capitalist in exchange for a wage.

bourgeoisie The ruling class under capitalism due to their ownership of the means of production.

proletariat The working class under capitalism who must sell their labor power in exchange for a wage because they lack ownership of the means of production.

The logic of capitalism as a system determines how each group acts. The competition in the marketplace that is at the heart of capitalism initially pits capitalists against each other in their pursuit of profit. In their desire to gain greater market share, capitalists attempt to reduce the costs of production in general and labor costs in particular. They reduce these costs through mechanization (inventing new machines capable of taking over more of the labor), de-skilling (simplifying the work process by breaking it down into its most basic steps so that minimal knowledge

Did You Know?

The highest-paid CEO in 2013 was Charif Souki of Cheniere Energy, a company focused on the liquefaction, transportation, and exportation of natural gas. The company has yet to make a profit. The top-earning woman CEO was Martine Rothblatt at $38.2 million with United Therapeutics.

Sources: de Aennle 2014; Equilar 2014. *Photo:* © Anthony Harvey/Getty Images for The New York Times.

class consciousness The subjective awareness held by members of a class regarding their common vested interests and need for collective political action to bring about social change.

false consciousness A term used by Karl Marx to describe an attitude held by members of a class that does not accurately reflect their objective position.

is required), and offshoring (finding labor in other parts of the world capable of doing the work for less money). It's not that capitalists are personally greedier than others or have a particular desire to exploit their workers; they act based on the principles inherent in the system.

Marx argued that this downward pressure on workers' wages and working conditions is unrelenting. It ultimately leads to the development of a massive global working class of largely poor, unskilled workers competing against each other for low-wage jobs, resulting in racial, ethnic, and nationalistic conflict among the proletariat. Ironically, it is the technological innovation of capitalism that makes a better future possible. Marx praised this aspect of capitalism because it solves the problem of production like no other previous economic system. Capitalism, he writes, was "the first to show what man's activity can bring about. It has accomplished wonders far surpassing Egyptian pyramids, Roman aqueducts, and Gothic cathedrals" (Marx and Engels [1848] 1998:38). As a result, we no longer face inevitable scarcity. We can now produce enough so that no one in the world needs to go hungry.

Once this technological obstacle to providing for all our needs was solved, Marx felt that the only obstacle to an equitable society would be the capitalist system of social relations. Its emphasis on private property enabled the few at the top, the bourgeoisie, to own and control much more than they could ever hope to need or want while the majority at the bottom, the proletariat, struggled. Eventually, Marx argued, the proletariat would see that they had no real interest in the existing set of social relations. They would develop **class consciousness**—a subjective awareness of common vested interests and the need for collective political action to bring about social change. This would lead to the overthrow of capitalism in favor of a system of

more equitable distribution in the form of socialism and then communism.

A question that often arises in response to Marx's work is this: why hasn't that revolution happened? One answer is that Marx thought capitalists would work against the development of such class consciousness by shaping society's accepted values and norms. The term *dominant ideology* describes a set of cultural beliefs and practices that helps to maintain powerful social, economic, and political interests. From this perspective, one of the possible functions of meritocracy as a value is to reinforce the belief that mobility is possible even when limited opportunity exists in practice. In addition, belief in meritocracy reinforces the idea that those at the top belong there as a consequence of ability and effort and, therefore, deserve whatever riches and power they can accumulate (Fraser 2015). As a result, workers must overcome what Marx termed **false consciousness**—an attitude held by members of a class that does not accurately reflect their objective position. A worker with false consciousness may adopt an individualistic viewpoint toward capitalist exploitation ("*I* am being exploited by *my* boss"). In contrast, the class-conscious worker realizes that all workers are being exploited by the bourgeoisie and have a common stake in revolution.

Because Marx paid attention to the structure of the system itself, he was able to identify inherent tensions between social classes based on their control over material resources. Much more recently, economist Thomas Piketty did something similar in his surprise best seller *Capital in the Twenty-First Century* (2014). In this expansive historical overview of economic growth, Piketty maintains that, in the long run, the rate of return on capital, including profits, rents, interest, and dividends, is greater than overall economic growth including increased income and output. Piketty uses the formula $r > g$ to describe this relationship. One reviewer summarized it this way, "Simply having money is the best way to get more money" (Doctorow 2014). Yet, in the United States, the commitment to meritocracy makes it difficult to accept the consequences of this simple fact. Denial was possible, in part, because, for most of the 20th century, the economy grew faster than normal due to technological innovation and wealth grew more slowly as a consequence of the destructive impact of both world wars and the Great Depression. According to Piketty, that anomalous period, which helped produce a prosperous middle class in the middle of the century, has come to an end. In effect, Piketty is arguing that increasing inequality is an inevitable consequence of the structure of capitalism, and this, he says, "poses a challenge to the meritocratic model" (2014:27). What we learn from both Marx and Piketty is that control over material resources conveys substantial advantages.

WEBER AND SOCIAL RESOURCES

Max Weber accepted Marx's premise that social class plays a substantial role in shaping outcomes, but he argued that Marx's conception of power was too narrow, because

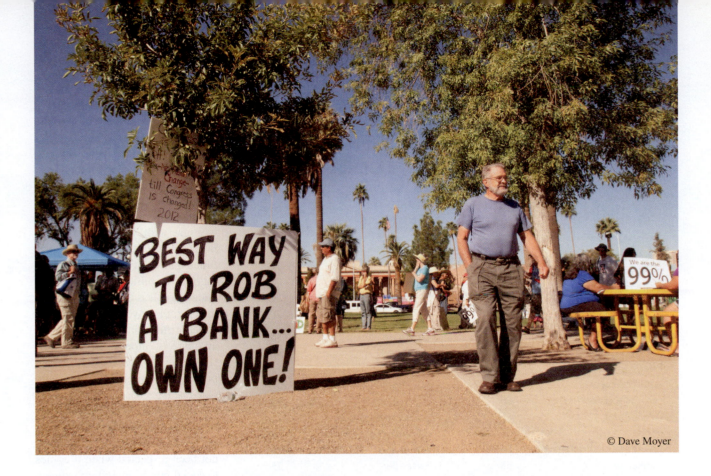

© Dave Moyer

it focused almost exclusively on ownership of the means of production. Weber argued that, in addition to material resources, social resources mattered, too. In response, he proposed a multidimensional model of stratification that included three components: class, status, and party.

Weber used the term **class** to refer to a group of people who have a similar level of economic resources. He identified two core elements of class: material resources and skill knowledge in the marketplace. In the first instance, class is about how much you own. Like Marx, this included ownership of the means of production, but Weber argued that ownership of other economic resources, including land, savings, and stocks, also defined a person's class position. And, while Marx maintained that mechanization and extreme division of labor would make skilled labor less valuable under capitalism, Weber argued that, given the complexity of modern society, knowledge would continue to be a valuable commodity in the labor market, something that employers would reward. By developing our skill knowledge—for example, by going to college—we enhance our class position.

Whereas class represents a material resource, status is a social resource. Weber used the term **status group** to refer to people who share the same perceived level of prestige. The power that your status provides depends upon how others view you, including both positive and negative estimations of honor. **Prestige** refers to the respect and admiration that a particular status holds in a society. For example, sociologists have ranked

some occupations as higher and others as lower. We see doctors and lawyers as more prestigious than librarians and social workers who are higher than janitors and maids (Davis, Smith, and Marsden 2007). But prestige in a class-based system involves

class A group of people who have a similar level of economic resources.

status group People who share the same perceived level of prestige.

prestige The respect and admiration that a particular status holds in a society.

Did You Know?

. . . According to Harris polls, the status of teachers has risen more than any other occupational category they have tracked over the past 30 years. In 2009, 54 percent of respondents identified teachers as having "very great prestige" compared with 29 percent in 1977.

Source: Harris Interactive 2009. *Photo:* © Lew Robertson/Corbis RF.

Prestige Rankings of Occupations

Occupation	Score
Physician	86
Lawyer	75
College professor	74
Architect	73
Dentist	72
Psychologist	69
Clergy	69
Pharmacist	68
Registered nurse	66
High school teacher	66
Accountant	65
Athlete	65
Elementary school teacher	64
Banker	63
Veterinarian	62
Legislator	61
Airline pilot	61
Police officer or detective	60
Actors and directors	58
Librarian	54
Firefighter	53
Social worker	52
Dental hygienist	52
Electrician	51
Funeral director	49
Farm manager	48
Mail carrier	47
Secretary	46
Insurance agent	45
Bank teller	43
Nurse's aide	42

Occupation	Score
Farmer	40
Correctional officer	40
Receptionist	39
Carpenter	39
Barber	36
Child care worker	36
Hotel clerk	32
Bus driver	32
Auto body repairer	31
Truck driver	30
Salesworker (shoes)	28
Garbage collector	28
Waiter and waitress	28
Bartender	25
Bill collector	24
Farm worker	23
Janitor	22
Maid	20
Newspaper vendor	19
Car washer	19

Note: 100 is the highest and 0 the lowest possible prestige score.

Source: J. Davis, Smith, and Marsden 2007. *Photos: (top):* © Pixtal/AGE Fotostock RF; *(bottom):* © PhotoAlto RF.

to have significant social prestige along with a low economic standing, as is the case for many clergy members who are highly regarded within their faith communities, but who often receive relatively modest incomes.

People tend to give those with high levels of socioeconomic status the benefit of the doubt and to withhold respect from those who occupy low-status positions. As we saw with white-collar crime in Chapter 6, business executives found guilty of crimes involving millions or billions of dollars frequently get less harsh punishments than people involved in common street crimes involving minimal amounts of money. In this way, status becomes a form of social power conveying advantage and disadvantage based on perceived social position. This can be particularly problematic for members of groups who historically have not been respected when it comes to social power, including women, African Americans, Hispanics, gays and lesbians, and others.

Membership in status groups also has a social networking component. The right kinds of connections can open doors for people who have them, but those who lack them may never get a chance to even knock. The networks we build through school, work, and family are not equally accessible to all and, for those who have this advantage, it is easy to underplay its significance. To them, such advantages seem like a normal, taken-for-granted component of their social lives.

The third major element in Weber's multidimensional model of stratification focuses on organizational resources. **Party** refers to the capacity to organize to accomplish some particular goal. This is what we mean when we talk of a political party, but such organization extends beyond politics to all spheres of life. As we have seen previously with Weber, bureaucracies represent the ideal form of this resource because they are organized explicitly to maximize available resources and to accomplish their goals in the most efficient manner possible. For Weber, party was a potential

socioeconomic status (SES) A measure of social class position based on a combination of education, occupation, and income.

party The capacity to organize to accomplish some particular goal.

more than just occupation. **Socioeconomic status (SES)** is a measure of social class position that combines education, occupation, and income. Class and status are not necessarily linked. It is possible

Personal Sociology

Cultural Capital

As a professor, I have seen that grades are shaped by more than just effort and inherent intellectual ability. Students with more cultural capital, including significant background educational resources, simply do not have to work as hard. Seniors in my introductory course, for example, know the rules of the game. In comparison, first-year students often have a hard time distinguishing what is essential versus what is secondary. Over time, however, most learn how to study effectively. This same principle is at work before students even arrive on campus. Students who come to college with the kinds of cultural capital that professors reward have advantages over those who lack such resources.

resource, available to any individuals or groups who would seize it. The civil rights movement in the United States provides a classic example. With minimal class or status resources as defined by the larger society, organization was critical to the success of this movement.

SOCTHINK

How might a group coordinate its class, status, and party resources to accomplish its goals? Pick a group on campus or in your community that is seeking to bring about social change, and imagine how you might advise group members using Weber's principles.

Weber maintained that, in practice, these three resources work together to shape individual and group power. People who are strong in one area can leverage that power to increase resources in the others. For example, people donate material resources to political causes in the hope that doing so will advance social and organizational interests. Those who already possess power in all three areas have advantages over those who do not.

BOURDIEU AND CULTURAL RESOURCES

Marx emphasized material resources, and Weber highlighted the significance of social resources in the form of both status and party. Sociologist Pierre Bourdieu added to these the significance of cultural resources. He introduced the concept of **cultural capital,** by which he meant our tastes, knowledge, attitudes, language, and ways of thinking that we exchange in interaction with others. Often associated with artistic or literary preferences, cultural capital goes much deeper than this because it is rooted in our perception of reality itself. For Bourdieu, because some culture is more highly valued than other culture, it represents a form of power.

Bourdieu argued that people in different social class positions possess different types of cultural capital. From NASCAR to Mozart, for example, the tastes of the working class typically differ from those of the upper class. Symphonic concerts, operas, and foreign films, for instance, are considered "high culture," whereas "pop culture," including popular movies, TV shows, and most music CDs, is considered "middle-brow" or below. People draw distinctions, for example, between watching *Masterpiece* on PBS versus *American Ninja Warrior* and listening to Placido Domingo versus Bruno Mars. Such judgments are based on a certain level of cultural elitism in which those at the top are able to define their preferences as apparently superior to those of the masses (C. Wilson 2007). The cultural capital of people who are working class, often disparaged as redneck or ghetto, is valued least of all—until it is claimed by others as their own, as was the case with jazz, blues, rock and roll, and rap (Gans 1971).

> **cultural capital** Our tastes, knowledge, attitudes, language, and ways of thinking that we exchange in interaction with others.

Even though they like to deny that it exists, Americans have a fascination with social class as explored in pop culture. This curiosity is especially apparent with the appeal of British programs such as *Downton Abbey, Masterpiece Classic, Sherlock Holmes, Doctor Who,* and *Absolutely Fabulous.* Perhaps it's just the accents, but the social class dimensions of British society are often core elements of these shows. Such programs provide a window into how social stratification is practiced differently in other societies. *Downton Abbey,* for example, portrays the lives of an aristocratic family and their servants in the early 20th century.

POPSOC

Photo: © Carnival Films for Masterpiece/PBS: Courtesy Everett Collection.

When we interact with others, we draw on the cultural capital resources we possess. Such interaction is fairly easy with others who share the same basic set of resources. When interaction occurs with others who possess a different stock of cultural capital, however, it becomes more complex. We see these kinds of difficulties when executives try to interact casually with workers on the factory floor or when we find ourselves dining in a place where we aren't quite sure what the rules are. If this were only a matter of social difference between various subcultures, it might not be a big deal. But the cultural capital of the elite is also tied to their control over economic and social resources. As a result, cultural capital can be used as a form of exclusion from jobs, organizations, and opportunities. For example, a qualified applicant may not be hired because, during the interview, he or she used inappropriate syntax or was not adequately familiar with cultural references, such as current news events or the latest in the world of golf. Employers tend to hire people they feel comfortable with, and cultural capital plays a significant role in that process (Kanter 1993).

Compounding this problem of cultural inequality is the fact that our preferences and perceptions often pass down from parent to child in the same way that material capital is inherited. Parents teach their children linguistic patterns and cultural tastes, from the use of double negatives to the appreciation of literature (Rothstein 2009). Cultural capital is also reproduced in the next generation in the context of schools, where class distinctions within the community shape the curriculum and patterns of discipline. Sociologist Jessi Streib (2011) found that, already by age four, children had adopted cultural conventions based on their social class positions. For eight months she conducted research at a diverse preschool and found that children from upper-middle-class families were more talkative and demanding of the teacher's time and attention than were working-class kids. The linguistic style of the higher-class children was more consistent with the classroom culture, and, as a result, they were more likely to get their needs met.

Social mobility from this perspective involves more than just acquiring more money and better social connections. Winning the lottery, for example, does not transform a person at the bottom of the hierarchy into one at the top, or, as Bourdieu put it, "Having a million does not in itself make one able to live like a millionaire" (1984:374). Such movement requires a social and cultural transformation as well. For mobility to happen, individuals must earn and learn a different set of knowledge and skills, as well as a whole new lifestyle: new tastes, attitudes, language, and thoughts.

MATERIAL, SOCIAL, AND CULTURAL RESOURCES

Using these sociological tools enables us to better understand how social stratification operates. We learn that we must be particularly attentive to the type of social stratification system in place and to the categories of resources that determine positions within those systems. In closed systems, position is largely determined through inheritance at birth and there is little you can do to change it. In the U.S. class-based system, some degree of mobility is possible. But it turns out that being rich or poor involves more than just having more or less money. We must be attentive to social and cultural resources as well.

> Anyone who has ever struggled with poverty knows how extremely expensive it is to be poor.
>
> James A. Baldwin

. . . **Researchers found that, by the age of three, children whose parents have professional jobs have heard 500,000 instances of praise and 80,000 of disapproval. In families receiving welfare, the ratio reverses; children have been praised 75,000 times and reprimanded 200,000 times.**

Did You Know?

Source: Hart and Risley 1995.   Photo: © Digital Vision RF.

When it comes to social order, it is easier for us, and for others, to continue along the same paths than to carve out new ones. In so doing, the status quo reproduces itself. Our social resources, including networks of relationships with family, friends, and coworkers, constrain the kinds of connections that might open up new pathways for us. Our cultural resources, including preferences, tastes, and knowledge, limit what we might imagine as possible or desirable. While some at the top look down on those at the bottom as irresponsible and short-sighted, members of the working-class may make fun of rich people's hoity-toity preference for opera and ballet and criticize their values as materialistic and selfish, lacking commitment to family and friends (MacLeod 2009).

As a result of material, social, and cultural resource differences, changing classes may involve the difficult task of changing identities, leading some to argue that the United States is more caste-like (Fussell 1992). Mobility would involve new social networks, new lifestyles, and new tastes. Complicating matters further, changing classes requires more than just changing ourselves, it also requires recognition and acceptance by others. Just as there may be interlocking deficits of poverty, there may also be interlocking advantages of wealth. One of those privileges is exclusion, denying others access to valuable social network connections. When considering the consequences of difference, implementing meritocracy and living up to the American Dream turn out to be challenging undertakings. But an understanding and appreciation for the challenges involved can empower people to take the steps necessary to succeed.

SOCIOLOGY IS A VERB

Sociological Autobiography

Write your sociological autobiography through the lens of class. How have your life chances been shaped by your access to material resources, such as your family income and wealth? By social resources—namely, your family and friendship network connections? By cultural resources—including taste, language, artistic and pop culture preferences, and educational attainment of family members? How might your life have been totally different if you had been born into another family with a different stock of resources?

For REVIEW

I. What is social class?

- Like slavery, caste, and estate, it is a stratification system in which people and groups are ranked, but it places them based primarily on economic position.

II. How does social class operate?

- Three categories of resources are key: material, including income and wealth; social, including social networks and prestige; and cultural, including tastes, education, and knowledge. Power is based on access to and control over these resources.

III. What are the consequences of social class?

- Although class-based systems are more open than the others, our life chances are shaped by our inherited class position and the material, social, and cultural resources that go with it. For most people, the social mobility that does occur, whether in terms of occupation, income, or wealth, is of a relatively short distance.

Functionalist View

All societies have some degree of stratification in order to ensure that all of society's needs are met.

In a society with a complex **division of labor**, some positions will inevitably be more important or require more skill than others.

Those with more talent and determination fill the higher-paid and more prestigious positions, whereas those who do not develop their talents take the low-ranking jobs.

DIVISION OF LABOR, SOCIAL MOBILITY
KEY CONCEPTS

Conflict View

Stratification systems perpetuate unequal economic rewards and facilitate exploitation.

Social class standing is largely an **ascribed status**.

People in power maintain and spread their interests and influence through their hold on the **dominant ideology** in a society.

Income and wealth are **distributed unequally** in U.S. society, and the gap between the rich and the poor is steadily increasing.

STRATIFICATION, INEQUALITY, DOMINANT IDEOLOGY
KEY CONCEPTS

Interactionist View

Social mobility results from interactions in which people attempt to better their place in the class system (for example, getting degrees, **networking**, acquiring cultural capital).

When we interact with others, we **exchange** our cultural capital resources, such as knowledge, tastes, attitudes, and ways of thinking.

Our social class helps determine our taste in clothes, food, music, TV shows, and many other everyday preferences.

NETWORKING, EXCHANGE
KEY CONCEPTS

MAKE THE CONNECTION

After reviewing the chapter, answer the following questions:

1
Analyze social mobility from the point of view of the three perspectives. In what way might mobility be functional? How would conflict theory explain it? What role does interaction play in getting ahead?

2
How do the conflict and the interactionist perspectives intersect in Marx's concept of "false consciousness"?

3
How would a theorist from each perspective explain the distribution of material, social, and cultural resources in society?

4
Think about your own "life chances." Which perspectives help you see factors that shaped your opportunities and outcomes?

Pop Quiz

1. **What expression did Max Weber coin to describe the fact that our likelihood for success is shaped by our access to valued material, social, and cultural resources?**
   a. *verstehen*
   b. cultural capital
   c. social mobility
   d. life chances

2. **Which of the systems of stratification included "those who pray, those who fight, and those who work"?**
   a. slavery
   b. caste
   c. estate
   d. class

3. **A plumber whose father was a physician is an example of**
   a. downward intergenerational mobility.
   b. upward intergenerational mobility.
   c. downward intragenerational mobility.
   d. upward intragenerational mobility.

4. **What term describes money received over some period of time?**
   a. wealth
   b. material resources
   c. assets
   d. income

5. **What percentage of total income in the United States does the top quintile earn?**
   a. 14.4 percent
   b. 23.0 percent
   c. 51.0 percent
   d. 77.2 percent

6. **What does absolute poverty refer to?**
   a. income below the 10th percentile as measured globally
   b. a minimum level of subsistence that no family should be expected to live without
   c. income below the 10th percentile within any society
   d. a level of deprivation by which people at the bottom of a society are judged to be disadvantaged in comparison with the nation as a whole

7. **Approximately what percentage of the U.S. population lived in poverty in 2013?**
   a. 3.2 percent
   b. 8.4 percent
   c. 14.5 percent
   d. 22.8 percent

8. **According to Karl Marx, the class that owns the means of production is the**
   a. nobility.
   b. proletariat.
   c. Brahman.
   d. bourgeoisie.

9. **Which of the following were viewed by Max Weber as distinct components of stratification?**
   a. conformity, deviance, and social control
   b. class, status, and party
   c. class, caste, and age
   d. class, prestige, and esteem

10. **According to Pierre Bourdieu, our tastes, our education, the way we talk, and the things we like all represent forms of**
    a. social capital.
    b. esteem.
    c. cultural capital.
    d. intelligence.

1. (d), 2. (c), 3. (a), 4. (d), 5. (c), 6. (b), 7. (c), 8. (d), 9. (b), 10. (c)

11

© 2011 Gallo Images/Getty Images

Global Inequality

STRUGGLING TO SURVIVE IN A WORLD OF PLENTY

In the summer of 2011 the eastern African nations of Somalia, South Sudan, Ethiopia, and Kenya were in the midst of Africa's worst famine in 60 years. More than 12 million people faced severe food shortages, and hundreds of thousands of people sought assistance in various camps established to provide humanitarian assistance. In southern and central Somalia alone it was estimated that 257,900 people died between October 2010 and April 2012, 132,900 of whom were under five years old (Checchi and Robinson 2013; Gettleman 2011). In spite of the severity of the crisis, and even though many more people were affected, donations for assistance were down substantially compared to other international crises such as the Indian Ocean tsunami in 2004, Hurricane Katrina in 2005, and the earthquake in Haiti in 2010 (Strom 2011).

Although crises such as these can raise awareness of the level of global inequality, daily struggles to find food are a long-term and ongoing problem around the world. In Haiti, for example, even before the massive 2010 earthquake, three-quarters of the population lived on less than $2 a day. Individuals such as Georges Jean Wesner would get up every day at 4:00 A.M. to walk two hours to get two small pails of rice and beans from a charity food kitchen—his only available source of food for his family. There are no available jobs from which to earn a living. Some even turn to eating patties made of mud, oil, and sugar, about which Olwich Louis Jeune, 24, says, "It's salty and it has butter, and you don't know you're eating dirt. . . . It makes your stomach quiet down" (Lacey 2008, M. Williams 2008).

Sociologically, to understand problems such as these, we must look beyond the lack of rain and the local availability of food to understand why people are dying of starvation. We must include analyses of the political and economic systems that affect the availability of resources.

As Dominique Strauss-Kahn, the former managing director of the International Monetary Fund, stated during a previous food crisis, "There is enough food to feed the world . . . the problem is that prices have risen and many people cannot afford food. So we need to get food—or the money to buy food—to those most in need" (International Monetary Fund 2008). In other words, we produce enough globally so that everyone can have enough, but we do not allocate resources in such a way that people now facing starvation can gain access to the food they need to survive.

As You READ >>

- **How did the global divide develop?**
- **How significant is global stratification?**
- **Why did the global movement for universal human rights develop?**

>> The Global Divide

Globally, we are more interdependent now than ever. We buy hoodies from Lesotho, blue jeans from Nicaragua, shoes from China, backpacks from the United States, coffee from Guatemala, pineapples from Thailand, tomatoes from Mexico, cars from South Korea, and a whole host of other products from places we may never have heard of before, much less visited. Our clothes are frequently more well traveled than we are. Yet, for the most part we have no real sense of the conditions under which the products we love are made. As we saw in Chapter 1, the people upon whom we depend are often unknown and invisible to us. Sociology provides us with tools to better understand the experiences of people around the world who make the lives we lead possible.

Throughout most of human history, providing sufficient food, clothes, and shelter was a struggle for nearly everyone. Now, thanks in part to the technological innovation brought on by the Industrial Revolution and its

© Dr. Parvinder Sethi

© Photofusion Picture Library/ Alamy

© B2M Productions/Getty Images RF

aftermath, a substantial percentage of the world's population no longer has to worry about providing for their subsistence needs. And yet, the resulting benefits of increased agricultural productivity and explosive economic growth have not been evenly distributed around the world.

We get a glimpse of the global distribution of resources, and its consequences, by looking at differences between developing and industrial nations. For example, the likelihood of dealing with the death of a child or the burden of disease is much greater for those in developing nations.

Gross National Income per Capita

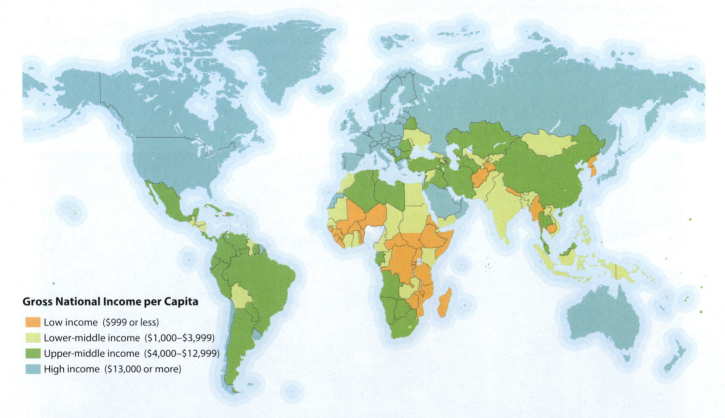

Gross National Income per Capita

- ▮ Low income ($999 or less)
- ▮ Lower-middle income ($1,000–$3,999)
- ▮ Upper-middle income ($4,000–$12,999)
- ▮ High income ($13,000 or more)

Note: All data are from 2013 with the exception of Belgium, Burkina Faso, Bosnia and Herzegovina, Lithuania, Namibia, Norway, Timor-Leste, Uzbekistan, and South Africa, which are from 2012.

Source: World Bank 2015a.

Going GLOBAL

Measuring Global Inequality

Country	HDI
Niger	0.337
Ethiopia	0.435
Afghanistan	0.468
Haiti	0.471
India	0.568
Guatemala	0.628
China	0.719
Brazil	0.744
Russia	0.778
UAE	0.827
USA	0.914
Norway	0.944

Note: The Human Development Index combines data on health, education, and income to provide a snapshot for each of 187 countries. Scores range from 0 to 1. These data are for 2013.

Source: United Nations Development Programme 2014.   *Photo:* © Ryan McVay/Getty Images RF.

People living in the industrial nations of the world, even though they comprise a much smaller share of the total population, have much higher incomes and many more exports than people living in the developing nations. They also are healthier, live longer, and have greater security due to what those nations spend on health care and the military (Sachs 2005a; Sutcliffe 2002). As we will see, the divide within countries in terms of income, wealth, poverty, and social mobility is also significant.

Average income varies significantly across the nations along a continuum from those that are the richest in economic resources to those that are the poorest. The contrast between those at the top and those at the bottom is stark. For example, in 2013, per capita gross national income (the total value of goods and services produced per citizen) in industrialized countries such as the United States, Canada, Switzerland, France, and Australia was more than $40,000. By comparison, more than

30 countries, including Malawi, Ethiopia, Nepal, Rwanda, and Afghanistan, had a per capita gross national income of less than $1,000 (World Bank 2015a).

>> Perspectives on Global Stratification

To better understand how today's global system developed, and how its various parts fit together, theorists have taken a step back to look at the world from a top-down, macro perspective. We will focus on three major areas of analysis. These include the rise of modernization, the legacy of colonialism, and the growth of multinational corporations.

THE RISE OF MODERNIZATION

The desire to understand the causes and consequences of the transition from traditional to modern society played a substantial role in the founding of sociology as a discipline. Most early sociologists presumed that societies evolved along a common path from simple to complex or from primitive to advanced. Auguste Comte, for example, proposed that sociologists should be leaders, using their scientific knowledge to guide us toward a more rational, humane, and good society. Émile Durkheim envisioned a future society with a natural balance between interdependence and individual freedom. And Karl Marx anticipated a more egalitarian society in which the problem of scarcity was solved making material and social inequality a thing of the past.

> **modernization** The far-reaching process by which nations pass from traditional forms of social organization toward those characteristic of post–Industrial Revolution societies.

SOCTHINK

Early sociologists were optimistic that positive social change was inevitable. To what extent do you think people today share this vision of the inevitable rise of the good society? How might cynicism about the possibility for change contribute to the maintenance of the status quo?

This notion that the present was superior to the past, with its petty tyrannies and irrational superstitions, and that the future would unite us all, shaped how people viewed the world throughout much of the 20th century. Many people supposed that, through **modernization,** nations would move from traditional forms of social organization toward forms characteristic of post–Industrial Revolution

THE PROGRESS OF THE CENTURY.

THE LIGHTNING STEAM PRESS.   THE ELECTRIC TELEGRAPH.   THE LOCOMOTIVE.   THE STEAMBOAT.

PUBLISHED BY CURRIER & IVES   Copyright 1876 by Currier & Ives N.Y.   125 NASSAU ST. NEW YORK

© Library of Congress

societies. Features of the latter include a complex division of labor in which work is specialized; the separation of institutions including family, economy, government, education, and religion into specialized spheres, each with their own experts; the decline of the local and the rise of a societal or global orientation; the rise of rational decision making in the public sphere and a corresponding decline in public religious authority; and the spread of both cultural diversity, as more peoples from different backgrounds come into contact with each other, and a corresponding growth in egalitarianism as a value that embraces such diversity (Bruce 2000).

colonialism The maintenance of political, social, economic, and cultural dominance over a people by a foreign power for an extended period.

According to modernization theorists, countries such as China and India are in the process of becoming modern societies. Even if the transition from traditional to modern is difficult for many, the presupposition is that people will benefit from doing so in the long term. People in the United States and Europe experienced similar displacement and poverty in the early years of the Industrial Revolution, only later to lead more comfortable lives, and the same future awaits people in developing nations (Lipset 1959).

Critics of the modernization perspective suggest that terms such as *modernization* and even *development* contain an ethnocentric bias. They maintain that there is an implicit presupposition in this model that people in such nations are more "primitive" and that modern Western culture is more advanced, more "civilized." The unstated assumption is that what "they" (people living in developing countries) really want is to become more like "us" (people in modern industrialized nations). From this perspective, "they" want "our" economic development and our cultural values, including democracy, freedom, and consumerism. Such modernization, according to critics, represents a form of cultural imperialism. Many groups around the world reject this modernization path, viewing such "development" as an attack on their way of life and a threat to their core values and norms (Césaire 1972).

THE LEGACY OF COLONIALISM

An alternative perspective to modernization maintains that the rise of modernity has less to do with an inevitable evolution along a singular path than it has to do with power and control over resources. **Colonialism** occurs when a foreign power maintains political, social, economic, and cultural domination over a people for an extended period.

POPSOC

In an analysis of more than 1,000 U.S. films, communications professor Jack Shaheen (2006, 2009, 2012) found that only 5 percent of Arab and Muslim characters were presented in a positive light. Arabs are repeatedly caricatured as Bedouin bandits, seductive belly dancers, villainous oil tycoons, or fanatical terrorists. The use of racial and ethnic stereotypes in American films and television shows is a form of symbolic power. Such portrayals reinforce the dominance of the majority groups at the expense of minorities who may lack the material, social, and cultural resources to provide alternative, more nuanced narratives to broader audiences.

Sociologist Immanuel Wallerstein (2000, 2004, 2010) views the global economic system as being divided between nations that control wealth and nations from which resources are taken. Through his **world systems analysis,** Wallerstein has described the unequal economic and political relationships in which certain industrialized nations (among them the United States, Japan, and Germany) and their global corporations dominate the core of this system. At the semiperiphery of the system are countries with marginal economic status, such as China, Ireland, and India. Wallerstein suggests that the poor developing countries of Asia, Africa, and Latin America are on the periphery of the world economic system. The key to Wallerstein's analysis is the exploitative relationship of core nations toward noncore nations. Core nations and their corporations control and exploit noncore nations' economies. Unlike other nations, they are relatively independent of outside control (Hardt and Negri 2009).

neocolonialism Continuing dependence of former colonies on foreign countries.

world systems analysis A view of the global economic system as one divided between certain industrialized nations that control wealth and developing countries that are controlled and exploited.

The division between core and periphery nations is both significant and remarkably stable. A study by the International Monetary Fund (2000) found little change over the past century for the 42 economies studied. The only changes were Japan's movement up into the group of core nations and China's movement down toward the margins of the semiperiphery nations, a decline that has perhaps been reversed in recent years owing to economic changes there.

In simple terms, it is rule by outsiders. The long reign of the British Empire over much of North America, parts of Africa, and India is an example of colonial domination. The same can be said of French rule over Algeria, Tunisia, and other parts of North Africa. Theorists from this perspective maintain that relations between the colonial nation and the colonized people are similar to those between the dominant capitalist class and the proletariat, as described by Marx (Fanon 1963).

By the 1980s such global political empires had largely disappeared. Most of the nations that were colonies before World War I had achieved political independence and established their own governments. However, for many of these countries, the transition to genuine self-rule was not yet complete. Colonial domination had established patterns of economic exploitation that continued even after nationhood was achieved—in part because the former colonies were unable to develop their own industry and technology (Acemoglu and Robinson 2012). Their dependence on more-industrialized nations, including their former colonial masters, for managerial and technical expertise, investment capital, and manufactured goods kept the former colonies in a subservient position. Such continuing dependence and foreign domination are referred to as **neocolonialism.**

World Systems Analysis at the Beginning of the 21st Century

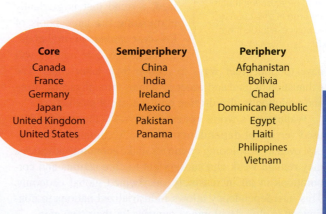

Core	Semiperiphery	Periphery
Canada	China	Afghanistan
France	India	Bolivia
Germany	Ireland	Chad
Japan	Mexico	Dominican Republic
United Kingdom	Pakistan	Egypt
United States	Panama	Haiti
		Philippines
		Vietnam

Note: Figure shows only a partial listing of countries.

SOCstudies

Big Mac Index

Global average

City	
Nairobi	
Jakarta	
Mumbai	
Mexico City	
São Paulo	
Beijing	
Shanghai	
Johannesburg	
Rome	
Madrid	
Moscow	
London	
Paris	
Frankfurt	
Sydney	
Chicago	
Toronto	
New York	
Tokyo	

0   20   40   60   80   100   120   140   160
Minutes

Note: Number of minutes it takes a worker with an average net wage to earn sufficient income to purchase a Big Mac.

Source: Aisslinger and Kutz 2012.   *Photo:* © Picturenet/Blend Images/Getty Images RF.

dependency theory An approach contending that industrialized nations continue to exploit developing countries for their own gain.

multinational corporation A commercial organization that is headquartered in one country but does business throughout the world.

Yet Wallerstein (2000, 2010) speculates that the world system as we currently understand it may soon undergo unpredictable changes. The world is becoming increasingly urbanized, a trend that is gradually eliminating the large pools of low-cost workers in rural areas. In the future, core nations will have to find other ways to reduce their labor costs. The exhaustion of land and water resources through clear-cutting and pollution is also driving up the costs of production.

Wallerstein's world systems analysis is the most widely used version of **dependency theory.** According to this theory, even as developing countries make economic advances, they remain weak and subservient to core nations and corporations in an increasingly intertwined global economy. This interdependency allows industrialized nations to continue to exploit developing countries for their own gain.

According to world systems analysis and dependency theory, a growing share of the human and natural resources of developing countries is being redistributed to the core industrialized nations. This redistribution happens in part because developing countries owe huge sums of money to industrialized nations as a result of foreign aid, loans, and trade deficits. The global debt crisis has intensified the Third World dependency rooted in colonialism, neo-colonialism, and multinational investment. International financial institutions are pressuring indebted countries to take severe measures to meet their interest payments. The result is that developing nations may be forced to devalue their currencies, freeze workers' wages, increase privatization of industry, and reduce government services and employment.

These trends are part of the larger process of *globalization*—the worldwide integration of government policies, cultures, social movements, and financial markets through trade and the exchange of ideas. Because the forces of world financial markets transcend governance by conventional nation-states, international organizations such as the World Bank and the International Monetary Fund have emerged as major players in the global economy. The function of these institutions, which are heavily funded and influenced by core nations, is to encourage trade and development and to ensure the smooth operation of international financial markets. As such, they are seen as promoters of globalization and defenders primarily of the interests of core nations. Critics call attention to a variety of related issues, including violations of workers' rights, the destruction of the environment, the loss of cultural identity, and discrimination against minority groups in periphery nations.

THE GROWTH OF MULTINATIONAL CORPORATIONS

Worldwide, corporate giants have played a key role in the rise of globalization. The term **multinational corporations** refers to commercial organizations that are headquartered in one country but do business around the world. Such private trade and lending relationships are not new; merchants have conducted business abroad for hundreds of years, trading gems, spices, garments, and other goods. Today's multinational giants are not merely buying and selling overseas; they are also producing goods all over the world (Wallerstein 1974, 2004). Through deindustrialization and outsourcing, corporate executives also have relocated production jobs around the globe.

SOCTHINK

Increasingly, we compete with workers around the world for jobs. What impact has the rise of globalization had on job prospects in your community and your country?

Going GLOBAL

Multinational Corporations Compared to Nations

Legend: ▦ Global 500 annual revenues ▮ GDP for comparable nations

Millions of dollars

Rank	Entity	Value
1	Wal-Mart Stores	$476,294
26	Norway	512,580
2	Royal Dutch Shell	$459,599
27	Venezuela	438,284
3	Sinopec Group	$457,201
28	Austria	428,322
4	China National Petroleum	$432,007
29	United Arab Emirates	402,340
5	ExxonMobil	$407,666
30	Thailand	387,252
6	BP	$396,217
31	Colombia	378,415
7	State Grid	$333,386
34	Denmark	335,878
8	Volkswagen	$261,539
42	Finland	267,329
9	Toyota Motor	$256,454
43	Greece	242,230
10	Glencore	$232,694
44	Pakistan	232,287

Note: Corporations are paired with comparably sized countries. Dollar amounts are in millions.

Sources: For corporate data, *Fortune* 2015; for GDP data, World Bank 2015b.

Increasingly, it is not just production jobs that are being relocated. Today's global factories may now have the "global office" alongside them. Multinationals based in core nations are beginning to establish reservation services and centers for processing data and insurance claims in the periphery nations. As service industries become a more important part of the international marketplace, many companies are concluding that the low costs of overseas operations more than offset the expense of transmitting information around the world.

These multinational corporations are huge, with total revenues on a par with the total value of goods and services exchanged in entire nations. Foreign sales represent an important source of profit for multinational corporations, encouraging them to expand into other countries (in many cases, the developing nations). The U.S. economy is heavily dependent on foreign commerce, much of which is conducted by multinationals. In 2014 the combined value of U.S. exports and imports of goods and services was the equivalent of 29.9 percent of total economic output as measured by gross domestic product (Bureau of Economic Analysis 2015).

Modernization Consistent with the modernization approach, some analysts believe that the relationship between the corporation and the developing country is mutually beneficial. Multinational corporations can help the developing nations of the world by bringing industries and jobs to areas where subsistence agriculture once served as the only means of survival. Multinationals also promote rapid development through the diffusion of inventions and innovations from industrial nations. The combination of skilled technology and management provided by multinationals and the relatively cheap labor available in developing nations benefits the corporation. Multinationals can take maximum advantage of technology while reducing costs and boosting profits. Through their international ties, multinationals also make the nations of the world more interdependent. These international ties may reduce the likelihood of global conflict. A country cannot afford to sever diplomatic relations or engage in warfare with a nation that is the headquarters for its main business suppliers or a key market for its exports.

Dependency Critics of multinational expansion challenge this favorable evaluation of the impact of corporations. They argue that multinationals exploit local workers to maximize profits. For example, Starbucks—the international coffee retailer based in Seattle—gets some of its coffee beans from farms in Ethiopia. It sold its "Black Apron Exclusives" coffee in a fancy black box for $26 per pound, but it paid Ethiopian workers who picked the beans 66 cents per day (Knudson 2007).

© Siqui Sanchez/The Image Bank/Getty Images

Multinational corporations have become so big that they have more economic resources than do some nations. What consequences arise from the fact that they can relocate their headquarters, offices, and production facilities anywhere in the world? How might this affect a nation's political power?

Multinational corporations wield a significant amount of economic, social, and political power, and they use it to their advantage. Jobs that used to be done in the United States or Europe get transferred to developing nations where labor costs less and health, safety, and environmental regulations are weaker. Workers in these nations, in pursuit of better access to material resources than they would otherwise have, provide a steady stream of cheap labor for these companies. If workers or governments become too demanding, companies can up and move again.

Sociologists studying the effects of foreign investment by multinationals have found that, although it initially may contribute to a host nation's wealth, such investment eventually increases economic inequality within developing nations. This finding holds for both income and ownership. The upper and middle classes benefit most from economic expansion; the lower classes are less likely to benefit. And because multinationals invest in limited economic sectors and restricted regions of a nation, only some sectors benefit. The expansion of such sectors of the host nation's economy, such as hotels and high-end restaurants, appears to retard growth in

© Tom Stoddard Archive/Getty Images

agriculture and other economic sectors. Moreover, multinational corporations often buy out or force out local entrepreneurs and companies, thereby increasing economic and cultural dependence (Kerbo 2009; Wallerstein 1979b, 2004).

Governments in developing nations are not always prepared to deal with the sudden influx of foreign capital and its effects on their economies. One particularly striking example of how unfettered capitalism can harm developing nations is found in the Democratic Republic of Congo (formerly Zaire). Congo has significant deposits of the metal columbite-tantalite—coltan, for short—which is used in the production of electronic circuit boards. Until the market for cell phones, pagers, and laptop computers heated up recently, U.S. manufacturers obtained most of their coltan from Australia. But at the height of consumer demand, they turned to miners in Congo to increase their supply.

Predictably, the escalating price of the metal—as much as $400 per kilogram at one point, or more than three times the average Congolese worker's yearly wages—attracted undesirable attention. Soon the neighboring countries of Rwanda, Uganda, and Burundi, at war with one another and desperate for resources to finance the conflict, were raiding Congo's national parks, slashing and burning to expose the coltan underneath the forest floor. In 2010 the U.S. Congress passed the Dodd-Frank Act, which included a provision requiring manufacturing companies to disclose whether they used any "conflict minerals," including coltan, cassiterite, gold, wolframite, or their derivatives, originating from the Democratic Republic of Congo or adjoining nations. According to a UN report, the result has been reforms in how business and government operate in Congo (Lezhnev 2011; Wyatt 2012).

>> Stratification Around the World

As these economic investments by multinationals suggest, at the same time the gap between rich and poor nations is widening, so too is the gap between rich and poor citizens within nations. As discussed previously, stratification in developing nations is closely related to their relatively weak and dependent position in the global economy. Local elites work hand in hand with multinational corporations and prosper from such alliances. At the same time, the economic system creates and perpetuates the exploitation of industrial and agricultural workers.

INCOME AND WEALTH

Global inequality is staggering. As the "Quintile Distribution of Income" graph displays, income differences between the haves and have-nots are substantial. In South Africa, for example, the bottom quintile earns 2.5 percent of the country's total income compared to 69.6 percent for the top quintile. Compare that to Ukraine, for example, where the bottom quintile takes home 10.2 percent of total income compared to

Quintile Distribution of Income

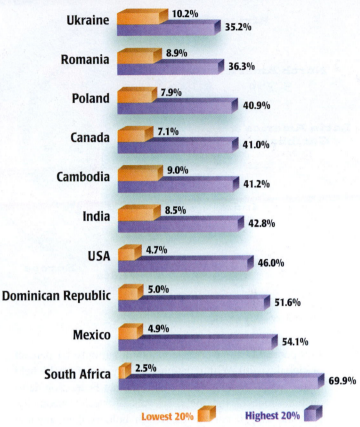

Note: Percentage of income earned by the top and bottom quintiles. Data are for the most recent year available.

Source: World Bank 2015c, 2015d.

35.2 percent for the top. Globally, countries that consistently have substantial income inequality include, among others, Seychelles, Haiti, Colombia, Brazil, Namibia, Honduras, and Rwanda (World Bank 2015c, 2015d). The lack of available, regular, well-paying jobs in such countries makes it extremely difficult for those at the bottom to provide for their needs.

The distribution for wealth is even more unequal. The top 10 percent of the world's population own 87.4 percent of global household wealth, and the top 1 percent own 48.2 percent. On the other end of the spectrum, the bottom 50 percent of the world's population combined own less than 1 percent of global wealth. Median household wealth globally is estimated to be $3,641 per adult. To make it into the top 1 percent takes $798,285. Analyzing the distribution globally, one sees that the bulk of the wealth is held by countries in North America, Europe, and the rich Asia-Pacific nations. The United States has 5.1 percent of the world's adult population but owns 31.8 percent of global household wealth. Contrast this with India, which has 16.4 percent of the world's population but only 1.4 percent of global wealth. In addition, the entire continent of Africa has

Global Wealth Distribution

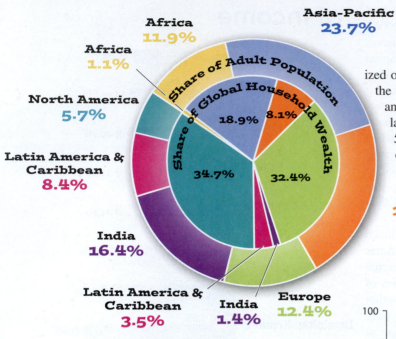

Share of Adult Population / Share of Global Household Wealth

- **Africa** 11.9%
- **Africa** 1.1%
- **North America** 5.7%
- **Latin America & Caribbean** 8.4%
- **India** 16.4%
- **Latin America & Caribbean** 3.5%
- **India** 1.4%
- **Europe** 12.4%
- **Asia-Pacific** 23.7%
- **China** 21.4%

Inner ring values: 18.9%, 8.1%, 34.7%, 32.4%

Source: Shorrocks, Davies, and Lluberas 2014: Table 2-4.

11.9 percent of the world's population but only 1.1 percent of global wealth. Within nations, the amount of wealth held by the top 10 percent varies. The Russian Federation demonstrates one of the highest levels of wealth inequality, with the top 10 percent of wealth holders there owning 84.8 percent of household wealth—significantly more than Japan, where the top 10 percent hold 48.5 percent of the wealth (Shorrocks, Davies, and Lluberas 2014).

Women in developing countries often face significant obstacles, making it difficult for them to attain economic assets. Karuna Chanana Ahmed, a sociologist from India who has studied women in developing nations, calls women "the most exploited among the oppressed" (J. Anderson and Moore 1993). Beginning at birth, women face sex discrimination. They are commonly fed less than male children, are denied educational opportunities, and often are hospitalized only when they are critically ill. In countries such as the United States, France, Colombia, Russia, Hungary, and Ireland, the proportion of the nonagricultural labor force made up by women approaches or exceeds 50 percent. In other nations the rate can be significantly lower: Yemen 11.7 percent, Iraq 12.1 percent, Pakistan 12.6 percent, Saudi Arabia 14.3 percent, Iran 15.3 percent, Syria 15.9 percent, and Egypt 19.1 percent.

Wealth Concentration

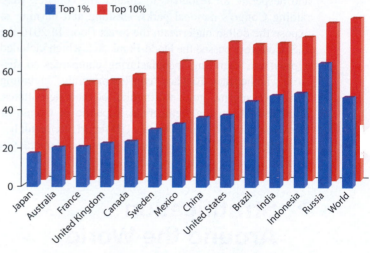

Legend: Top 1% (blue), Top 10% (red)

Countries (x-axis): Japan, Australia, France, United Kingdom, Canada, Sweden, Mexico, China, United States, Brazil, India, Indonesia, Russia, World

Note: Columns represent the percentage of the country's wealth held by the top 10 percent and top 1 percent.

Source: Shorrocks, Davies, and Lluberas 2014.

In Afghanistan, it is illegal for a wife to step out of the house without her husband's permission. In Saudi Arabia, women are prohibited from driving, walking alone in public, and socializing with men other than those in their families (Kearl 2014; Al-Shihri 2011; World Bank 2015e).

POVERTY

In developing countries, any deterioration in the economic well-being of the least well-off threatens their very survival. Using the global poverty line established by the World Bank of $1.25 per day, 1.2 billion people in the world are considered poor, and 2.7 billion people live on less than $2.50 a day. In fact, 80 percent of the world's population lives on less than $10 a day (Chen and Ravallion 2008; Shah 2010).

5 Movies on GLOBAL INEQUALITY

Kinyarwanda
Resilience and reconciliation in Rwanda.

Virunga
Civil war, poachers, oil reserves, and gorillas.

Blood Diamond
A South African mercenary and a miner race to acquire a precious diamond.

The World Before Her
Beauty boot camp in India.

A Separation
An Iranian couple's tale of love, loss, and family.

Mapping Global Poverty

Note: The size of each country shows the proportion of the world population living in poverty there.

Source: www.worldmapper.org.   *Photo:* Copyright © SASI Group (University of Sheffield) & Mark Newman (University of Michigan).

Percentage of Population Living on Less than $1.25 a Day

Country	Percentage
Egypt	1.7%
Dominican Republic	2.2%
China	11.8%
Honduras	17.9%
Pakistan	21.0%
India	32.7%
Bangladesh	43.3%
Kenya	43.4%
Rwanda	63.2%
Nigeria	68.0%
Madagascar	81.3%
Liberia	83.8%

Source: United Nations Development Programme 2014:Table 6.   *Photos:* © Image Club RF.

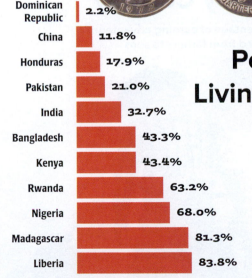

SOCTHINK

What are the major obstacles to accomplishing the Millennium Project's goals? To what extent are they economic, social, and/or cultural? Is it simply a matter of will?

Though poverty is a worldwide problem affecting billions of people, it is distributed unequally. As the "Mapping Global Poverty" map demonstrates, if we drew each country to scale based on its number of poor people, Africa and Asia would appear huge. The relatively affluent areas of North America and Europe would be quite small.

In an effort to reduce global poverty, the United Nations passed the Millennium Declaration in 2000, promising to "spare no effort to free our fellow men, women, and children from the abject and dehumanizing conditions of extreme poverty." It established 2015 as the target date for reaching specific, measurable goals to alleviate hunger and improve education, gender equality, and child mortality.

When they were first established, many of the Millennium Project goals seemed extremely optimistic. Yet, when 2015 arrived, substantial progress had been made. Three goals were met years ahead of schedule—namely, targets related to poverty, water, and slums. The goal of reducing extreme poverty by half was accomplished five years early. In developing regions, the proportion of people living on less than $1.25 a day fell from 47 percent in 1990 to 22 percent by 2010. And in China, the extreme poverty rate fell from 60 percent in 1990 to 12 percent by 2010. The target of cutting in half the proportion of people without access to improved water sources was also attained, improving circumstances for more than two billion people between 1990 and 2010. More than 200 million people living in slums experienced improvements in water access, sanitation, durable housing, or less crowded living conditions, more than doubling the 2020 target. In addition to these successes, primary education reached parity between girls and boys, and there were sizable gains in access to primary schools. Considerable progress has been made toward reducing child mortality, which fell by more than one-third, and maternal mortality, which was cut in half. People with HIV or AIDS now have greater access to medical treatment; rates of both tuberculosis and malaria have declined substantially saving millions of lives. Building on the successes of goals met, and challenged by those not met, the United Nations proposed 17 new targets, the Sustainable Development Goals, to be met by 2030 (Ford 2015; United Nations 2014a).

To accomplish the project's goals, planners estimate that industrial nations must set aside 0.7 percent of their **gross national income (GNI)**—the total value of a nation's goods and services—for aid to developing nations. In 2014, only six countries contributed at least that much: United Arab Emirates, Sweden, Luxembourg, Norway, Denmark, and the United Kingdom. Although the United States contributes more aid dollars than any other nation ($32.2 billion in 2014), when measured as a percentage of gross national income, its level of contribution of 0.19 percent is well below average when compared to that of other nations. The United Arab Emirates had the highest GNI percent rate at 1.17 percent (OECD 2015a, 2015b).

gross national income (GNI) The total value of a nation's goods and services.

SOCIAL MOBILITY

Although there is significant global inequality, perhaps sufficient social mobility exists to provide hope for those born without significant access to

Official Development Assistance

	Percentage of gross national income	Total, million U.S. dollars
United States	0.19	$32,2⬛⬛
United Kingdom	0.71	$18,078
Germany	0.41	$15,940
France	0.36	$10,298
Japan	0.19	$9,804
Sweden	1.10	$6,470
Netherlands	0.64	$5,522
Norway	0.99	$5,341
United Arab Emirates	1.17	$4,861
Australia	0.27	$4,498

Note: Money totals represent government aid contributed to promote the economic development and welfare of developing nations. Data are from 2014.
Source: OECD 2015a, 2015b.

Intergenerational Earnings Mobility by Country

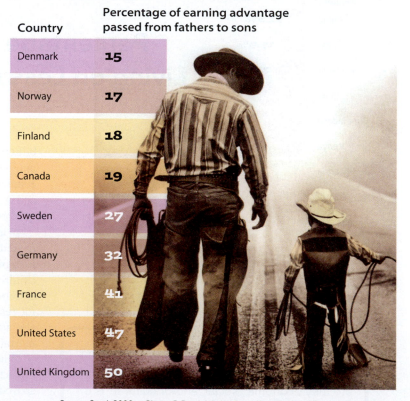

Country	Percentage of earning advantage passed from fathers to sons
Denmark	15
Norway	17
Finland	18
Canada	19
Sweden	27
Germany	32
France	41
United States	47
United Kingdom	50

Source: Corak 2006.   *Photo:* © Randolph Jay Braun/Getty Images RF.

Did You Know?

. . . Working 14 hours a day at 13 cents an hour, it would take seamstress Robina Akther of the Western Dresses factory in Dhaka, Bangladesh, 50 years to earn $16,200.

Source: Fishman 2006.   *Photo:* © Glow Images RF.

resources. As we saw in Chapter 10, mobility can and does happen in the United States, though the majority of such movement is over only short distances. Here we look at the possibility for mobility in both industrial nations and developing nations, and we consider the impact gender has on mobility.

Intergenerational Mobility Across Nations The likelihood of earning more or less than your parents varies across nations. Though Americans have more faith in their ability to get ahead than do those in other countries, their likelihood of doing so is lower than in most other industrialized nations (Isaacs 2008). As the "Intergenerational Earnings Mobility by Country" table shows, for example, when analyzing earnings, the amount of money fathers earn has a strong influence on the likely earnings of sons (Corak 2006). What this means, in contrast to the classic vision of the American Dream, is that there is less chance for intergenerational mobility in the United States than in those Scandinavian countries.

In developing nations, macrolevel social and economic changes often overshadow microlevel movement from one occupation to another. For example, there is typically a substantial wage differential between rural and urban areas, which leads to high levels of migration to the cities. Yet the urban industrial sectors of developing countries generally cannot provide sufficient employment for all those seeking work.

In large developing nations, the most socially significant mobility is the movement out of poverty. This type of mobility is difficult to measure and confirm, however, because economic trends can differ from one area of a country to another. For instance, China's rapid income growth has been accompanied by a growing disparity in income between urban and rural areas and among different regions. Similarly, in India during the economic development of the 1990s, poverty declined in urban areas but may have remained static at best in rural areas. Around the world, social mobility is also dramatically influenced by catastrophes such as crop failure and warfare (World Bank 2006).

Gender Differences and Mobility Only recently have researchers begun to investigate the effect of gender on the mobility patterns of developing nations. Many aspects of the development process—especially modernization in rural areas and the rural-to-urban migration just described—may result in modification or abandonment of traditional cultural practices and even marital systems. The effects on women's social standing and mobility are not necessarily positive. As a country develops and modernizes, women's vital role in food production deteriorates, jeopardizing both their autonomy and their material well-being. Moreover, the movement of families to the cities weakens women's ties to relatives who can provide food, financial assistance, and social support.

In the Philippines, however, women have moved to the forefront of the indigenous peoples' struggle to protect their ancestral land from exploitation by outsiders. Having established their right to its rich minerals and forests, members of indigenous groups had begun to feud among themselves over the way in which the land's resources should be developed. Aided by the United Nations Partners in Development Programme, women volunteers established the Pan-Cordillera Women's Network for Peace and Development, a coalition of women's groups dedicated to resolving local disputes. The women mapped boundaries, prepared development plans, and negotiated more than 2,000 peace pacts among community members. They have also run in elections, campaigned on issues related to social problems, and organized residents to work together for the common good (United Nations Development Programme 2000:87).

SOCIAL STRATIFICATION IN MEXICO

To get a more complete picture of these global stratification issues, it helps to look at a particular case. Here we will focus on the dynamics of stratification in Mexico, a country of 122 million people.

As we saw in Chapter 6, drug-related homicides have become a serious problem in Mexico. Although the reasons for this are historical and complex (Camp 2010a, 2010b), economic factors play a substantial role. The same is true for the hundreds of men, women, and children who die attempting to cross into the United States each year in search of opportunity. Though solid numbers are difficult to come by, the United States Border Patrol reported 307 border deaths in 2014. The two areas with the highest numbers were Rio Grande Valley with 115 and Tucson with 107 (U.S. Customs and Border Protection 2014a).

Why do Mexicans turn to drug trafficking or risk their lives crossing the dangerous desert that lies between the two countries? The answer to this question can be found primarily in the income disparity between the two nations—one an industrial giant and the other a partially developed country still recovering from a history of colonialism and neocolonialism. Since the early 20th century, there has been a close cultural, economic, and political relationship between Mexico and the United States, one in which the United States is the dominant party. According to Immanuel Wallerstein's analysis, the United States is at the core while neighboring Mexico is still on the semiperiphery of the world economic system.

Mexico's Economy If we compare Mexico's economy to that of the United States, differences in the standard of living and in life chances are quite dramatic, even though Mexico is considered a semiperiphery nation. Gross national income is a commonly used measure of an average resident's economic well-being. In 2013 the gross national income per person in the United States came to $53,470; in Mexico, it was a mere $9,940. In Mexico, 36.3 percent of adults aged 25–64 have completed high school compared to 89.3 percent in the United States. And fewer than 5.9 of every 1,000 infants in the United States die in the first year of life, compared to about 12.5 per 1,000 in Mexico (National Center for Education Statistics 2013: Table 603.10; World Bank 2015a, 2015f).

Not only is Mexico unquestionably a poor country, but the gap between its richest and poorest citizens is substantial. The top quintile earns 54.1 percent of total income while the bottom earns just 4.9 percent. The World Bank reports that 6.5 percent of Mexico's population survives on just $2 per day. The average amount of wealth per adult in Mexico is $35,234 compared to $347,845 in the United States. And in the battle for world's richest person, in 2015, America's Bill Gates edged out Mexico's Carlos Slim Helú, $79.2 billion to $77.1 billion (Dolan and Kroll 2015; Shorrocks et al. 2014; United Nations Development Programme 2014; World Bank 2015c, 2015d).

Political scientist Jorge Castañeda (1995:71), who later served as Mexico's foreign minister, called Mexico a "polarized society with enormous gaps between rich and poor, town and country, north and south, white and brown (or *criollos* and *mestizos*)." He added that the country is also divided along lines of class, race, religion, gender, and age. To better understand the nature of the stratification within Mexico, we examine race relations and the plight of Mexican Indians, the status of Mexican women, and immigration to the United States and its impact on the U.S.–Mexican borderlands.

Race Relations in Mexico: The Color Hierarchy
Mexico's indigenous Indians account for an estimated 14 percent of the nation's population. According to a United Nations report, more than 90 percent of Mexico's indigenous people (the ethnic group historically native to a region) live in extreme poverty. The literacy rate in Mexico as a whole is 92 percent, but it hovers around 50 percent among the indigenous population (Cevallos 2009; Minority Rights Group International 2007; United Nations Development Programme 2008).

The subordinate status of Mexico's Indians is but one reflection of the nation's color hierarchy, which links social class status to the appearance of racial purity. At the top of this hierarchy are the *criollos,* the 10 percent of the population who are typically White, well-educated members of the business and intellectual elites, with familial roots in Spain. In the middle is the large, impoverished *mestizo* majority, most of whom have brown skin and a mixed racial lineage as a result of intermarriage. At the bottom of the color hierarchy are the destitute, full-blooded Mexican Indian minority and a small number of Blacks, some descended from 200,000 African slaves brought to Mexico. This color hierarchy is an important part of day-to-day life—enough so that some Mexicans in the cities use hair dyes, skin lighteners, and blue or green contact lenses to appear White and European. Ironically, however, nearly all Mexicans are considered part Indian because of centuries of intermarriage (Castañeda 1995; Standish and Bell 2004).

---SOCTHINK---
How might racial categories in Mexico differ from those in the United States? Why might such differences arise?

Many observers take note of widespread denial of prejudice and discrimination against people of color in Mexico. Schoolchildren are taught that the election of Benito Juárez, a Zapotec Indian, as president of Mexico

Did You Know?

. . . The government of Mexico also has to deal with what to do about immigrants who enter that country illegally. In 2010, government authorities expelled 63,608 undocumented immigrants from Central American nations, such as Guatemala, El Salvador, and Honduras.

Source: Instituto Nacional de Migración, México 2011. Photo:© Pixtal/ age fotostock RF.

Personal Sociology

Study Abroad

Central College, where I teach, started its first international program in 1965. It was a leader in establishing study abroad programs for students. It now operates programs around the world in places such as Mérida in Mexico, Bangor in Wales, and Accra in Ghana. Central instituted these programs to provide students with a prolonged experience in another country in hopes that such exposure would enable them to go beyond being just a tourist and achieve a deeper understanding of another culture. And going abroad really does make a difference. My students are often nervous to go but come back with great stories. It is clear that the experience has changed how they understand both the world and themselves.

in the 19th century proves that all Mexicans are equal. Yet there has been a marked growth in recent decades of formal organizations and voluntary associations representing indigenous Indians (Escárcega 2008; Stavenhagen 1994; Utne 2003).

The Status of Women in Mexico Though the United Nations convened the first international conference on the status of women in Mexico in 1975, and opportunities there have improved, women still face significant obstacles. Women now constitute 38.5 percent of the labor force—an increase from 29.9 percent in 1990. Unfortunately, Mexican women are even more mired in the lowest-paying jobs than their counterparts in industrial nations, on average earning 42 percent less than men. Men are still typically viewed as heads of the household, making it difficult for women to obtain credit and technical assistance in many parts of the country and to inherit land in rural areas. As for education, the literacy rate for women in Chiapas (71 percent) and Oaxaca (73 percent), states with high levels of indigenous populations, is well below the national average (INEGI 2009; United Nations Development Programme 2008).

In recent decades, Mexican women have organized to address an array of economic, political, and health issues. For example, as far back as 1973, women in Monterrey—the nation's third-largest city—protested the continuing disruptions of the city's water supply. Through coordinated efforts, including delegations of politicians, rallies, and public demonstrations, they succeeded in improving Monterrey's water service, a major concern in developing nations. After being denied the opportunity to run for mayor in her hometown in 2007, Eufrosina Cruz organized QUIEGO (Queremos Unir Integrando por la Equidad y Género en Oaxaca, meaning "we want to come together for equity and gender in Oaxaca") to raise awareness about political rights for

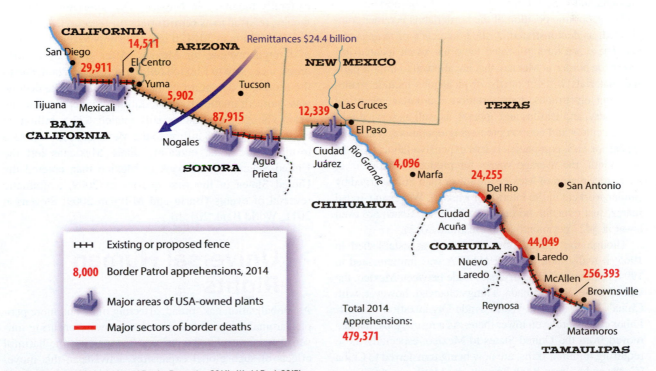

The Borderlands

Existing or proposed fence

8,000   Border Patrol apprehensions, 2014

Major areas of USA-owned plants

Major sectors of border deaths

Remittances $24.4 billion

Total 2014 Apprehensions: 479,371

Sources: Data from U.S. Customs and Border Protection 2014b; World Bank 2015h.

women in her home state and ultimately throughout Mexico (Bennett, Dávila-Poblete, and Rico 2005; Cevallos 2009).

To ensure greater political representation by women in office, Mexico passed a series of laws setting gender quotas for candidates. First established in 1996, Mexico strengthened these laws over time, now requiring that women comprise at least 40 percent of the nominees. In 2014, Mexico passed an amendment to article 41 of its Federal Constitution to cement its commitment to gender parity throughout its political system. These policy changes worked. In 1990, women accounted for 3.1 percent of seats in the Senate and 8.8 percent of seats in the Chamber of Deputies. After the 2012 election, those numbers rose to 33 percent in the Senate and 37 percent in the Chamber of Deputies. Mexico now ranks 20th among 194 nations in female representation, substantially higher than 95th for the United States (Baldez 2004; Inter-Parliamentary Union 2015; Lucio 2014; QuotaProject 2014).

The Borderlands Growing recognition of the borderlands reflects the increasingly close and complex relationship between Mexico and the United States. The term **borderlands** refers to the area of common culture along the border between Mexico and the United States. Legal and illegal emigration from Mexico to the United States, day laborers crossing the border regularly to go to work in the United States, the implementation of the North American Free Trade Agreement (NAFTA), the exchange of media across the border— all make the notion of separate Mexican and U.S. cultures obsolete in the borderlands.

borderlands The area of common culture along the border between Mexico and the United States.

remittances The monies that immigrants return to their families of origin. Also called *remesas*.

The economic position of the borderlands is rather complicated, as demonstrated by the emergence of *maquiladoras*. These are foreign-owned factories, often located just across the border in Mexico, that are allowed to import parts and materials without tariffs. Typical jobs include manufacturing electronics, transportation equipment, electrical machinery, and textiles and apparel, as well as service jobs in call centers and coupon processing operations. The chief appeal for U.S. companies is less expensive labor. At $514 per month, the average wages for production workers in the border region of Mexico are lower than $629 earned by similar workers in the interior of Mexico. Wages in Ciudad Juárez, just over the border from El Paso, Texas, are even lower at $422 per month (Hunt Institute 2015).

Though the maquiladora program was established in 1965, it really took off after NAFTA was implemented in 1994, removing most barriers to trade between Mexico, the United States, and Canada. Things changed, however, with China's entry into the World Trade Organization in 2001. Labor costs were even lower there. As a result, jobs that had moved from the United States to Mexico, especially those requiring minimal skills, are now being transferred to China (Cañas and Gilmer 2009; Sargent and Matthews 2009).

Emigration to the United States The movement of people between Mexico and the United States significantly affects both nations. In 2013, 99,385 people who were born in Mexico became naturalized U.S. citizens, twice the number from India, the second leading country. Another 135,028 gained lawful permanent resident status in the United States. However, in 2013, 424,978 individuals from Mexico were apprehended and classified as "aliens" by U.S. immigration officials, which constituted 64 percent of those apprehended (Lee and Foreman 2014; Monder and Yankay 2014; Simansky 2014).

From the Mexican point of view, the United States too often regards Mexico simply as a reserve pool of cheap labor, encouraging Mexicans to cross the border when workers are needed but discouraging and cracking down on them when they are not. Some people, then, see immigration more as a labor market issue than a law enforcement issue. Viewed from the perspective of world systems analysis and dependency theory, it is yet another example of a core industrialized nation exploiting a developing country.

SOCTHINK

How do U.S. consumers benefit from the buildup of factories along the U.S.–Mexican border? What impact might they have on U.S. workers?

Many Mexicans who have come to the United States send a portion of their earnings back across the border to family members in Mexico. This substantial flow of money, referred to as **remittances** (or *remesas*), amounted to $24.4 billion in 2014. It is second only to oil as a source of foreign revenue for Mexico. After years of growth, remittances sent to Mexico fell 3.6 percent in 2008, due to the economic downturn in the United States. The decline was more dramatic in 2009, falling 15 percent for the year. Though remittances still totaled $21.5 billion, it meant a loss of $3.8 billion to the Mexican economy. As a result of the weak economy, more Mexicans left the United States to head back to Mexico than entered the United States in the first quarter of 2009, a dramatic reversal of events (Barta and Millman 2009; Stevenson 2011; World Bank 2015h).

>> Universal Human Rights

As globalization has spread, affecting more and more peoples around the world, a movement toward ensuring universal human rights has arisen. Recognizing the harmful effects of such global expansion, activists in this movement fight to preserve and protect the interests of people

Mass grave site in Srebrenica, Bosnia-Herzegovina. Photo: © Marco Di Lauro/Getty Images.

who lack significant power or access to resources. The sheer size and economic might of multinational corporations, along with their freedom to move jobs and plants around the world without regard for the impact on national populations, encouraged the establishment of universal human rights as a countervailing source of power. The goal of human rights activists is to establish a nonnegotiable and inviolable foundation of rights that applies no matter where people are or which governments or multinational corporations are involved.

DEFINING HUMAN RIGHTS

The term **human rights** refers to universal moral rights that all people possess by virtue of being human. The most important elaboration of human rights appears in the Universal Declaration of Human Rights, adopted by the United Nations (UN) in 1948. This declaration prohibits slavery, torture, and degrading punishment; grants everyone the right to a nationality and its culture; affirms freedom of religion and the right to vote; proclaims the right to seek asylum in other countries to escape persecution; and prohibits arbitrary interference with one's privacy and the arbitrary seizure of a person's property. It also emphasizes that mothers and children are entitled to special care and assistance.

At first the United States opposed a binding obligation to the Universal Declaration of Human Rights. The government feared loss of national sovereignty—the right to rule over its people without external interference. This concern was driven in part by the existence of racial segregation

laws that were still common at the time the UN issued the Universal Declaration and that violated the human rights principles. By the early 1960s, however, the United States had begun to use the declaration to promote democracy abroad (Forsythe 1990).

> **human rights** Universal moral rights possessed by all people because they are human.

In the 1990s concerns about human rights brought the term *ethnic cleansing* into the world's vocabulary as a euphemism for forcible expulsion and murder. In the former Yugoslavia, Serbs initiated a policy intended to "cleanse" Muslims from parts of Bosnia-Herzegovina and ethnic Albanians from the province of Kosovo. Hundreds of thousands of people were killed in fighting there, while many others were uprooted from their homes. Moreover, reports surfaced of Serbian soldiers raping substantial numbers of Muslim, Croatian, and Kosovar women. Regrettably, ethnic cleansing has since spread to other parts of the world, including East Timor, Iraq, Kenya, and Sudan.

An ongoing human rights concern is the transnational crime of trafficking in humans. Each year an estimated 600,000–800,000 men, women, and children are transported across international borders for slavery or sexual exploitation. In 2000 Congress passed the Trafficking Victims Protection Act, which established minimum standards for the elimination of human trafficking. The act requires the State Department to monitor other countries' efforts to vigorously investigate, prosecute, and convict individuals who participate in trafficking—including government officials. Each year the department reports its findings, dividing countries into three groups, or tiers, depending on their level

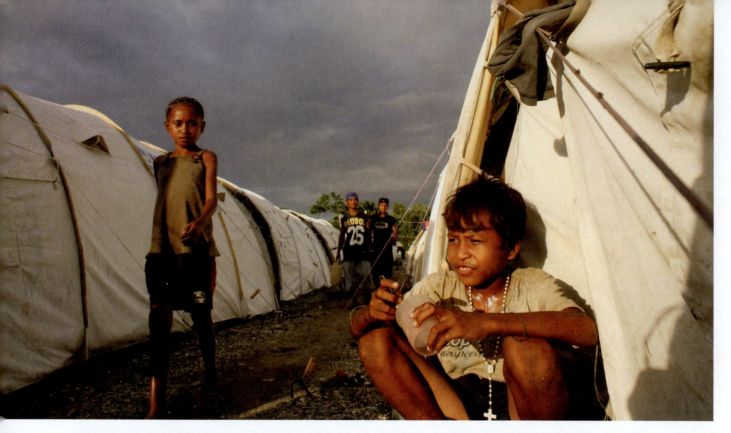

Ongoing violence in East Timor has driven children like these to seek safety in refugee camps in the country. Photo: © Paula Bronstein/Getty Images RF.

Human Trafficking Report

Tier 1 Full Compliance	Tier 2 Significant Effort	Tier 2 Watch List Some Effort, but Trafficking Remains a Concern	Tier 3 Noncompliant, No Effort
Australia	Bahamas	Angola	Algeria
Canada	Brazil	Bahrain	Cuba
Denmark	Greece	Cambodia	Iran
France	Hong Kong	China	Kuwait
Germany	India	Haiti	Libya
Israel	Japan	Jamaica	Malaysia
Italy	Mexico	Kenya	North Korea
Norway	Niger	Madagascar	Russia
Poland	Romania	Pakistan	Saudi Arabia
South Korea	Senegal	Rwanda	Syria
Spain	Turkey	Sudan	Uzbekistan
United States	Vietnam	Ukraine	Yemen

Note: Table does not include all countries; each tier lists only a sampling of nations.

Source: U.S. Department of State 2014b.

of compliance. Tier-1 countries are thought to be largely in compliance with the act. Tier-2 nations are making a significant effort to comply, while tier-2 "watch" nations are making efforts to comply, though trafficking remains a real concern. Tier-3 countries are not compliant (International Labour Office 2012; U.S. Department of State 2014b).

PRINCIPLE AND PRACTICE

When it comes to human rights, the balance between principle and practice can be problematic. In the wake of the terrorist attacks of September 11, 2001, increased police personnel and surveillance at U.S. airports and border crossings caused some observers to wonder whether human rights were not being jeopardized in the name of security. At the same time, thousands of noncitizens of Arab and south Asian descent were questioned for no other reason than their ethnic and religious backgrounds. A few were placed in custody, sometimes without access to legal assistance. And as the war on terror moved overseas, human rights concerns escalated. In 2005 then secretary-general Kofi Annan of the UN criticized the United States and Britain for equating people who were resisting the presence of foreign troops in Afghanistan and Iraq with terrorists (A. Parker 2004; Steele 2005).

What this points to is the significance of perspective even when it comes to something that appears to be a fundamental principle. Cultural insiders and outsiders can disagree about what constitutes a violation. For example, was India's caste system an inherent violation of human rights? What about the many cultures of the world that view the subordinate status of women as an essential element in their traditions? Should human rights be interpreted differently in different parts of the world?

SOCTHINK

To what extent do you think violations of human rights are excusable in a time of war? At such times, how might our perception of the balance between rights and security alter what we think of as universal?

We can consider, as an example, female genital mutilation, a practice that is common in more than 30 countries around the world but that has been condemned in Western nations as a human rights abuse. This controversial practice often involves removal of the clitoris, in the belief that its excision will inhibit a young woman's sex drive, making her chaste and thus more desirable to her future husband. Though some countries have passed laws against the practice, they have gone largely unenforced. Emigrants from countries where genital mutilation is common often insist that their daughters undergo the procedure, to protect them from Western

cultural norms that allow premarital sex (Religious Tolerance 2008). To what extent should outside nations have the power to dictate such internal laws? In this sense, the movement for universal human rights also represents a form of cultural imperialism.

In 1993 the United States opted for an absolute definition of human rights, insisting that the Universal Declaration of Human Rights set a single standard for acceptable behavior around the world. In practice, however, interpretation still plays a role. Some human rights activists have argued that the United States practices selective enforcement of human rights. Critics contend, for example, that officials in the United States are more likely to become concerned about human rights abuses when oil is at stake, as in the Middle East, or when military alliances come into play, as in Europe.

SOCTHINK

How active should the U.S. government be in addressing violations of human rights in other countries? At what point, if any, does concern for human rights turn into ethnocentrism through failure to respect the distinctive norms, values, and customs of another culture?

HUMAN RIGHTS ACTIVISM

Efforts to protect and ensure human rights seldom come from inside governments but arise out of social movements that organize to generate economic, social, and political pressure in an effort to force change. For example, in June 2008 Human Rights Watch (www.hrw.org), a premier international human rights organization, called for other African nations to impose sanctions on Zimbabwe after what they called the sham reelection of President Robert Mugabe. They monitor human rights abuses around the world, including calling U.S. officials to end abuses against prisoners in the Guantánamo Bay detention camps.

In Sudan the Save Darfur Coalition (www.savedarfur.org) fights for justice and relief for refugees who were attacked, driven off their land and out of the country, and often killed by the Janjaweed, a group of armed gunmen backed by the Sudanese government. Their cause was helped significantly with the release of the film *The Devil Came on Horseback*—translated from the Janjaweed—in which ex-marine Brian Steidle, who was hired as a human rights

> There can be no peace as long as there is grinding poverty, social injustice, inequality, oppression, environmental degradation, and as long as the weak and small continue to be trodden by the mighty and powerful.
>
> the Dalai Lama

observer by the African Union, documented genocide in Darfur with photos and video. He ultimately testified before Congress and at the UN, providing his documentation to support the genocide claims. In addition to numerous other organizational efforts, the Save Darfur Coalition also coordinated an agreement on May 28, 2008, in which presidential candidates Barack Obama, John McCain, and Hillary Clinton issued a joint statement demanding an end to the violence in Darfur. Though the Sudanese government maintains that the war is officially over, violence continues. In May 2010 Ibrahim Gambari, the head of UNAMID, the joint African Union–UN Mission in Darfur, put it this way: "Results have been mixed despite our best efforts. . . . In the area of security and the protection of civilians some progress has been made, but pockets of instability remain" (UN News Service 2010). However, on July 9, 2011, the Republic of South Sudan officially became an independent, sovereign state.

Médecins Sans Frontières (Doctors Without Borders), the world's largest independent emergency medical aid organization, won the 1999 Nobel Peace Prize for its work in countries worldwide. Founded in 1971 and based in Paris, the organization has 30,000 doctors, nurses, and other expert volunteers working around the world. In 2013 they conducted over 9 million outpatient consultations, vaccinated 2.5 million against measles, treated 1.9 million malaria cases, helped 182,234 women deliver babies, and assisted many thousands of other patients for various ailments (Doctors Without Borders 2014).

In the past few decades, awareness has been growing of lesbian and gay rights as an aspect of universal human rights. In 1994 Amnesty International published a pioneering report in which it examined abuses in Brazil, Greece, Mexico, Iran, the United States, and other countries, including cases of torture, imprisonment, and extrajudicial execution. Later in 1994 the United States issued an order that would allow lesbians and gay men to seek political asylum in the United States if they could prove they had suffered government persecution in their home countries solely because of their sexual orientation (Amnesty International 2009b; Johnston 1994). One result of this policy change was that dozens of gay men and lesbians from Mexico and other Latin American nations were granted asylum in the United States each year. As their treatment has improved in those nations, the likelihood of receiving asylum has declined (Connolly 2008).

SOCTHINK

Should other nations and the UN have the power to force the United States to change its laws to comply with human rights principles?

SOCIOLOGY IS A VERB

Global Perspectives

The world is huge, and there are so many places about which we know so little. Pick a country you are unfamiliar with, perhaps one you didn't even know existed. Find out all you can about its history, politics, economy, family structures, beliefs, and so on. If possible, contact an organization that assists immigrants from there to learn more about their experiences as first-generation immigrants here. What might you learn by trying to understand the world from their perspective?

One of the things we learn from sociology is that we are embedded in larger networks in which decisions and events that happen far away, and about which we may know little or nothing, shape our daily life experiences. And the choices we make can have substantial consequences for the lives of others. Ethnic cleansing in Sudan, human rights violations in Iraq and Afghanistan, increased surveillance in the name of counterterrorism, violence against women inside and outside the family, governmental persecution of lesbians and gay men—all of these are vivid reminders that social inequality can have life-and-death consequences. In each case, people recognized the consequences of global inequality, and individuals, groups, and nations took steps to address the problems. By developing a more fully formed sociological imagination, we can more readily see such issues and take necessary steps toward addressing them.

For REVIEW

I. How did the global divide develop?

- Theorists emphasizing modernization argue that it is part of the natural evolution of societies as they pass through the effects of the Industrial Revolution and beyond. Dependency theorists argue that it is due to a fundamental power struggle between wealthy nations at the core and developing nations at the periphery.

II. How significant is global stratification?

- Analyses of wealth, income, poverty, and social mobility demonstrate a wide gap both within and between nations.

III. Why did the global movement for universal human rights develop?

- As global inequality became more apparent, activists worked to establish a foundational set of human rights that would protect people regardless of who or where they were.

SOCVIEWS on Global Inequality

Functionalist View

Through **modernization**, nations make the transition from traditional forms of organization to postindustrial societies for the benefit of all.

Globalization involves the worldwide **integration** of government policies, cultures, social movements, and financial markets through trade and exchange of ideas.

Multinational organizations create jobs and industries in developing countries, foster innovation, and make nations of the world **interdependent**.

Conflict View

There is significant **inequality** between the rich and the poor within as well as across nations, but the scourge of poverty is most evident in Africa and Asia.

According to world system analysis, modernization can result in political, economic, and cultural **imperialism**.

The economic success of core nations depends upon the extraction of raw materials and cheap labor from periphery nations.

KEY CONCEPTS
IMPERIALISM, INEQUALITY

Interactionist View

People undergoing modernization often experience a dramatic change in the established ways of working and interacting.

Encounters with people from different cultures open us up to alternative ways of thinking and acting.

Many women in developing nations face inequality in employment opportunities, education, and health care, thus limiting their **social interaction** in the community.

KEY CONCEPTS
SOCIAL INTERACTION, ENCOUNTERS

MAKE THE CONNECTION

After reviewing the chapter, answer the following questions:

1
How might each perspective seek to better understand the situation in countries such as Haiti and Sudan?

2
How do the modernization and world systems theories fit with the functionalist and conflict perspectives?

3
How would each perspective provide insight into the situation of immigration between the United States and Mexico?

4
What ties do you have to a developing nation—perhaps as a tourist, or a second-generation immigrant, or an activist? Which perspective best fits those ties? Why?

Pop Quiz

1. Which of the following terms is used by contemporary social scientists to describe the far-reaching process by which nations pass from traditional forms of social organization toward those characteristic of post–Industrial Revolution societies?

   a. dependency

   b. globalization

   c. industrialization

   d. modernization

2. The maintenance of political, social, economic, and cultural domination over a people by a foreign power for an extended period of time is referred to as

   a. globalization.

   b. government-imposed stratification.

   c. colonialism.

   d. dependency.

3. Immanuel Wallerstein's world systems analysis focuses on

   a. the unequal access to and control of resources between core and periphery nations.

   b. the natural evolutionary development of all societies toward the modern ideal.

   c. the rise of multinational corporations.

   d. the global pattern of inequality faced by women.

4. Companies that are headquartered in one country but do business throughout the world are known as

   a. global corporations.

   b. multinational corporations.

   c. maquiladoras.

   d. international agencies.

5. Approximately how much of global household wealth is owned by households in North America?

   a. 10 percent

   b. 25 percent

   c. 35 percent

   d. 50 percent

6. Which of the following Millennium Project goals has already been accomplished?

   a. cutting levels of extreme poverty around the world in half

   b. reducing by half the proportion of people without access to improved sources of water

   c. substantially improving the lives of 100,000 people living in extreme conditions in slums around the world

   d. all of the above

7. Globally, approximately how many people subsist on less than $1.25 per day?

   a. 500 million

   b. 1.2 billion

   c. 3.2 billion

   d. 5 billion

8. Karuna Chanana Ahmed, a sociologist from India who has studied developing nations, calls which group the most exploited of oppressed people?

   a. children

   b. women

   c. elderly people

   d. poor people

9. Which of the following terms refers to the foreign-owned factories established just across the border in Mexico, where the companies that own them don't have to pay taxes or high wages, or provide insurance or benefits for their workers?

   a. *maquiladoras*

   b. *hombres*

   c. *mujeres*

   d. *remesas*

10. In what year did the United Nations adopt the Universal Declaration of Human Rights?

    a. 1865

    b. 1919

    c. 1948

    d. 1993

1. (d), 2. (c), 3. (a), 4. (b), 5. (b), 6. (d), 7. (b), 8. (b), 9. (a), 10. (c)

12

Gender and Sexuality

© Bryce Yukio Adolphson

QUOTIDIAN CRUELTIES

It was eleven thirty at night when a group of men came for Woineshet Zebene. She was in a deep sleep, but they took her from her home in the Ethiopian countryside and battered and raped her over the next two days. Afterward, it was expected that she would marry the man who led the assault. When she refused, she was again kidnapped, beaten, and raped. A court official to whom she pleaded for help advised her to "get over it" and marry her attacker. She was 13 years old. Though something like this is unlikely to happen to a typical teenage girl in the United States, sadly, halfway around the world, Woineshet's story is not uncommon.

Every day, women from all over the globe face systematic violence and discrimination. In their book *Half the Sky*, journalists Nicholas Kristof and Sheryl WuDunn (2009) tell the stories of many women and girls, including Woineshet, who are victims of such abuses. Women are particularly vulnerable to sex trafficking, gender-based violence (including honor killings and mass rape), and death or serious injury during childbirth due to inadequate medical care. For example, in Ghana, 21 percent of women report that their first sexual experience was by rape. Regarding inadequate health care, 1 in 7 women in Nigeria, 1 in 22 in sub-Saharan Africa, and 1 in 70 in India die during childbirth, compared to 1 in 4,800 in the United States.

Such practices often go unnoticed because they represent "quotidian cruelties"—the everyday practice of violence and discrimination that is largely invisible and considered inevitable or even natural. Fortunately, women around the world have successfully fought to change local attitudes and practices. In India, for example, Ruchira Gupta founded Apne Aap Women Worldwide, with its mission to end sex trafficking (www.apne-aap.org). In Pakistan, Mukhtar Mai used settlement money she received after having been gang raped to establish her School for Girls; she later expanded it to include a free legal clinic, a public library, and a women's shelter. And in Kenya, Myla Rodgers established the organization Mama Hope. In addition to helping build health clinics, poultry farms, drip irrigation gardens, and other projects, the group produced a number of viral videos designed to show African people as active, engaged, intelligent, and multidimensional. The videos portray the people of Kenya, Uganda, Tanzania, Ghana, and elsewhere not as objects to be manipulated or subjects to be studied, but as participants who, when given access to and control over even limited amounts of economic resources, have the vision and ability to transform their futures for the better.

As You READ >>

- How has our understanding of gender and sexuality shifted over time?

- How has opportunity for women in the United States changed over time?

- To what extent does gender still shape access to resources?

>> The Social Construction of Gender

When a baby is born, one of the first questions people ask is "Is it a boy or a girl?" The answer to this question represents one of our primary and most powerful statuses. From those earliest days, it shapes how others will interact with us as newborns. Later it influences the clothes we wear, the friends we choose, the kinds of games we play, the college majors we consider, the types of jobs we have, the amount of money we earn, and much more. And answering the question seems such a simple thing. Yet, from a sociological perspective, understanding what it means to be a boy or a girl—and later to become men and women—involves more than anatomy alone.

SEX AND GENDER

Historically, sociologists drew a distinction between sex and gender in order to differentiate between biology and culture. **Sex** refers to biological differences between males and females. **Gender** involves the social and cultural significance that we attach to those presumed biological differences. Over time, even this distinction has become too limiting to fully depict our experiences as humans.

Sex emphasizes the differences between males and females that occur at the cellular, hormonal, and anatomical levels. From this perspective, we assume it is easy to tell

© Rainer Elstermann/Getty Images RF

the difference between males and females. Women have XX chromosome patterns, estrogen hormones, ovaries, and a vagina; men have XY chromosomes, androgen hormones, testicles, and a penis. The presupposition is that the dividing line is clear; there is no significant biological overlap between the sexes. This model is known as a simple two-sex, or dimorphic, model, in which the line between males and females is distinct and absolute (Fausto-Sterling 2000, 2012; Richardson 2013).

The problem with such a simplistic division is that we find many exceptions to what is assumed to be the rule. Many people exhibit physical characteristics that we presume to belong to the "opposite" sex: women with facial hair, men with high voices, tall women and short men, women with narrow hips and broad shoulders, men who are slight of build or who have "breasts," women who experience "male pattern baldness," and so on. Differences go beyond these secondary sex characteristics to include people whose cellular, hormonal, and anatomical characteristics are sexually ambiguous. As geneticist Anne Fausto-Sterling (2000) points out in a critique of the simplistic male–female model, "On close inspection, absolute dimorphism disintegrates even at the level of basic biology. Chromosomes, hormones, the internal sex structures, the gonads and the external genitalia all vary more

sex The biological differences between males and females.

gender The social and cultural significance that we attach to the biological differences of sex.

After she won the gold medal in the 800-meter race at the 2009 World Championships, questions were raised about South African runner Caster Semenya's sex. She was ordered to submit to a series of psychological, gynecological, and endocrine tests and was cleared for continued competition in international track and field events (Karkazis et al. 2012). Photo: © Michael Steele/ Getty Images.

than most people realize" (p. 20). We know, for example, that both males and females have androgen and estrogen hormones and that sex hormone levels vary by individual.

Biologically, Fausto-Sterling (1993) suggests we have at least five sexes, not just two. In addition to male and female, we exhibit at least three intersexual categories. The first category includes "true hermaphrodites," who have one testis and one ovary. In other words, they are theoretically capable of producing both sperm and eggs. The second category includes "male pseudohermaphrodites." They have testes and what appear to be female genitalia, lacking a penis and ovaries. The third category includes "female pseudohermaphrodites," who have ovaries along with some male genitalia but no testes. She later suggested that even these five sexes present an overly simplistic model of the range of biological diversity, which better resembles a continuum (Fausto-Sterling 2000, 2012).

Doctors studying what have come to be known medically as disorders of sex development (DSDs) have discovered that the basic biology of sex extends well beyond the XX and XY chromosome combinations (Davis 2014; Richardson 2013). Researchers have identified more than 25 genes involved in the development of DSDs. For example, XY individuals with extra copies of the *WNT4* gene, which promotes ovarian development and suppresses testicular development, can develop a rudimentary uterus and Fallopian tubes. Individuals who are XX but with the *RSPO1* gene can develop ovotestis, a gonad incorporating both ovarian and testicular development (Ainsworth 2015). When considering the biology of sex, DSD researcher Eric Vilain, the director of the Center for

Gender-Based Biology at the University of California, Los Angeles, concludes, "Biologically, it's a spectrum" (Ainsworth 2015).

When babies are born presenting ambiguous indicators of maleness or femaleness, even though such conditions rarely pose a health threat, physicians typically perform surgery to make the baby fit more neatly into one category or the other. In recent years, ethical questions have been raised about the appropriateness of doing so, especially when the person most affected has no voice in the matter (Ainsworth 2015; Karkazis 2008). In 2013, the United Nations issued a statement condemning such nonconsensual surgeries (Méndez 2013). Increasingly, countries have adopted policies to recognize the complexity of sex. In 2011, Australia began allowing people to select a third sex category on their passports. In 2013, Germany allowed parents to leave the gender category on their child's birth certificate blank. In 2015, Thailand was in the process of revising its constitution to formally recognize a third gender category as a human right (Commonwealth of Australia 2013; Heine 2013; Park and Dhitavat 2015).

Our biological diversity calls for a more complex model of our species than the dimorphic model of sex supplies. Gender, partnered with a more comprehensive conception of sex, enables us to capture a wider range of expressions of our humanity. Social constructions of gender vary over time and across cultures suggesting that biology alone does not narrowly determine maleness and femaleness. Through socialization we typically internalize the cognitive, normative, and material culture deemed appropriate or natural for men and women within the context of our societies.

GENDER-ROLE SOCIALIZATION

Because we lack complex instincts that narrowly determine our behaviors, we construct our expressions of masculinity and femininity and reinforce those gender expressions through socialization. For example, the process of becoming boys and girls begins at birth:

> During the first six months of life, mothers tend to look at and talk to girl infants more than to boy infants, and mothers tend to respond to girls' crying more immediately than they do to boys'. In fact, these behaviors tend to be greater for girls over the first two years of life. Boys, on the other hand, receive more touching, holding, rocking, and kissing than do girls in the first few months,

SOCTHINK

Why do most women in the United States assume that shaving their legs is natural? What role does it play as a rite of passage?

Artist Nickolay Lamm used crowdfunding to release Lammily, a fashion doll matching the body proportions of an average 19-year-old American woman.   Photo: © Nickolay Lamm/Rex Features/AP Photos.

When Emily and Eleanor were little, they covered our refrigerator with pictures they drew of our family. In the pictures, the girls wore dresses while I wore pants. They had long eyelashes and I did not. They had long hair, and I had what looked like a plate on my head. I asked Eleanor, "What about the women we know with short hair and the men we know with long hair?" She replied, "Yeah, but women have long hair and men have short hair." She knew there were people who didn't fit her hair theory, but she had already come to accept an image in which the line between men and women was obvious, important, and inevitable.

but the situation is reversed by age six months. By one year, female infants are allowed and encouraged to spend significantly more time than males in touching and staying in close proximity to their mothers. The girls are encouraged to move away at later ages, but never as much as boys are. (Kimmel 2004:130)

As children grow, we continue to reinforce male–female differences through our actions. Male babies get blue blankets; females get pink ones. Boys are expected to play with trucks, blocks, and toy soldiers; girls receive dolls and kitchen goods. Boys must be masculine—active, aggressive, tough, daring, and dominant—but girls must be feminine— soft, emotional, sweet, and submissive. An examination of the ads in any parenting magazine shows that these traditional gender-role patterns remain influential in the socialization of children in the United States (Kilbourne 2010).

Gender Displays Gender socialization never ends. In all of our interactions, we receive positive and negative feedback based on our gender performance. It is not

hard to test how rigid gender-role socialization can be. Just try breaking some gender norm—say, by smoking a cigar in public if you are female, or wearing a skirt to work if you are male. Corrective feedback will likely follow. That was exactly the assignment given to sociology students at the University of Colorado and at Luther College in Iowa. Professors asked students to behave in ways that they thought violated the norms of how a man or woman should act. Over the years that this ongoing experiment has been performed, students consistently received clear signals—ranging from amusement to disgust—that their actions were inappropriate and that they should instead behave in ways defined as appropriate by dominant heterosexual gender norms (Nielsen, Walden, and Kunkel 2000).

When we interact with others, we usually display our gender clearly. When we find ourselves in situations lacking explicit gender cues, we are often unsure how to proceed. For example, sociologists Candace West and Don Zimmerman (1987) recount a meeting in a computer store where the sex of the person involved remained ambiguous:

The person who answered my questions was truly a *salesperson*. I could not categorize him/ her as a woman or a man. What did I look for? (1) Facial hair: She/he was smooth skinned, but some men have little or no facial hair. (This varies by race; Native Americans and blacks often have none.) (2) Breasts: She/he was wearing a loose shirt that hung from his/her shoulders. And,

© Art Montes De Oca/Taxi/Getty Images

as many women who suffered through a 1950s adolescence know to their shame, women are often flat-chested. (3) Shoulders: His/hers were small and round for a man, broad for a woman. (4) Hands: Long and slender fingers, knuckles a bit large for a woman, small for a man. (5) Voice: Middle range, unexpressive for a woman, not at all the exaggerated tones some gay males affect. (6) His/her treatment of me: Gave off no signs that would let me know if I were of the same or different sex as this person. There were not even any signs that he/she knew his/her sex would be difficult to categorize and I wondered about this even as I did my best to hide these questions so I would not embarrass him/her while we talked of computer paper. I left still not knowing the sex of my salesperson, and was disturbed by that unanswered question (child of my culture that I am). (pp. 133–134)

Most of the time we do not actually see the "parts" that biologically define someone as male or female; we rely instead on other indicators such as clothes and shapes to be sufficient. As sociologist Judith Lorber (1994) put it, "Clothing, paradoxically, often hides the sex but displays the gender" (p. 22). We depend on established cues (such as outfits and hairstyles) to recognize someone's sex when we interact, often taking that recognition for granted.

Women's Gender Roles Parents, schools, friends, and the mass media all socialize us to internalize dominant gender norms. The positive and negative sanctions that we experience during such interactions shape the thoughts, actions, and appearances we accept as appropriate. Women, for example, continue to face pressure to be thin, beautiful, submissive, sexy, and maternal (Pai and Schryver 2015).

Films, television programs, and magazine ads all contribute to an idealized image of feminine beauty (Brown 2015; Kilbourne 2010). As we saw in Chapter 6, this image, dubbed the "beauty myth" by Naomi Wolf (1992), is largely unattainable for most women. It contributes to millions of cosmetic procedures each year for those seeking it. And as noted in Chapter 2, even supermodels such as Cindy Crawford feel they cannot achieve their own idealized images. Part of the reason is that these images are often not real. Instead, they are altered with the assistance of computer programs such as Photoshop (Gurari, Hetts, and Strube 2006). Attaining an idealized image can be particularly problematic for those who do not match the White and heterosexual assumptions upon which it is built (Milillo 2008; Reel et al. 2008; Tate 2009).

As we increasingly recognize the impact of such artificial images, attempts have been made to offer alternative images of women in the mass media. This includes magazines that have featured images of models or celebrities without makeup or photo retouching, as in the April 2010 issue of French *Elle,* which featured unretouched images of models and actresses without makeup. Similarly, Germany's most

Gender and Jobs: On Screen and Off

Movies tend to underestimate the actual levels of occupational representation of women in the United States. There are significantly more women lawyers, doctors, and bartenders in the real world than there are in films. But even in occupations where women dominate, such as teacher, secretary, or nurse, women are still slightly unrepresented in films (Hickey 2015).

POPSOC

Note: Data for the percentage of occupational film roles held by women come from movies released since 1995. Gender percentages for actual U.S. occupations come from the Bureau of Labor Statistics.

Source: Hickey 2015.

popular women's magazine, *Brigitte,* banned professional models from its pages. In Spain, fashion designers have established a minimum body mass index (BMI) score of 18 for runway models. And Israel passed a law banning models with a BMI less than 18.5 from fashion runways and advertisements; for example, a 5-foot, 8-inch-tall model must weigh at least 119 pounds. The law also requires publications to disclose when they have digitally altered photos to make models appear thinner. In 2013, as part of its ongoing Campaign for Real Beauty, Dove ran a commercial using a portrait artist to demonstrate that women's self-descriptions were substantially less attractive than the descriptions others had of them.

Gendered messages about being a woman are about more than just beauty. They also project idealized images of "women's proper place," identifying some social status positions as more appropriate than others. Studies show that children's books reinforce such messages. One study of 5,618 children's books published throughout the 20th century found that male characters were represented twice as often as females. The disparity was greatest when portraying animal characters as males or females. Little Golden Books were more unequal than other series they studied. Starting in the 1970s they found a trend toward greater equity, though a significant imbalance remains. The preschool teacher or nurse. They may lie about their occupations when introduced to others in order to avoid negative reactions. For example, researchers interviewed a 35-year-old male nurse who reported that he would claim to be "a carpenter or something like that" when he "went clubbing," because women weren't interested in getting to know a male nurse. Subjects of the study made similar accommodations in casual exchanges with other men (Bagilhole and Cross 2006; Cross and Bagilhole 2002).

There may be a price to pay for such narrow conceptions of manhood. Boys who successfully adapt to cultural standards of masculinity may grow up to be inexpressive men who cannot share their feelings with others. They remain forceful and tough, but they are also closed and isolated. These traditional gender roles may be putting men at a disadvantage. Today girls outdo boys in high school, grabbing a disproportionate share of the leadership positions, from valedictorian to class president to yearbook editor—everything, in short, except captain of the boys' athletic teams. And their advantage continues after high school. In the 1980s, girls in the United States became more likely than boys to go to college. In 2012 women accounted for 56 percent of college students nationwide (Kena et al. 2014:58). And starting in 2005–2006, more women than men in the United States earned doctoral degrees (Aud et al. 2012:284).

Increasing numbers of men in the United States have criticized the restrictive aspects of the traditional male gender role. Australian sociologist R. W. Connell (2002, 2005) has written about **multiple masculinities,** meaning that men learn and play a full range of gender roles. These may include a nurturing-caring role, an effeminate-gay role, or their traditional role. Sociologist Michael Kimmel gave voice to this broader conception

> **multiple masculinities** The idea that men learn and play a full range of gender roles.

of what it means to be a man when he was sitting with his newborn son in the park. When a woman came up to him and said that he was expressing his "feminine side," he responded, "I'm not expressing anything of the sort, ma'am. I'm being tender and loving and nurturing toward my child. As far as I can tell, I'm expressing my *masculinity*" (Kimmel 2004:290–291).

GENDER ACROSS CULTURES

Though socialization into gender roles can narrow what we come to think of as appropriate behavior, examples such as Kimmel's suggest that what we define as appropriate does change over time. Gender expectations also differ across cultures. That gender expectations and performance vary across time and place suggests that masculinity and femininity are not strictly determined by our genes.

© Susan Church

researchers conclude, "This widespread pattern of underrepresentation of females may contribute to a sense of unimportance among girls and privilege among boys" (J. McCabe et al. 2011:221). Other studies have found similar gendered patterns. Women are often shown as helpless, passive, and in need of a male caretaker. Fathers, in a study of children's picture books, were significantly less likely to touch, hug, kiss, talk to, or feed children (D. Anderson and Hamilton 2005; Etaugh 2003; Hamilton et al. 2006).

Men's Gender Roles Conventional gender-role expectations also exist for men. For example, stay-at-home fathers are still relatively uncommon. Among married-couple families with children under 15, there are 27 times as many stay-at-home moms than stay-at-home dads. Although it is still rare for men to stay home to care for their children, there is evidence that attitudes are changing. In a nationwide survey 69 percent of respondents said that if one parent stays home with the children, it makes no difference whether that parent is the mother or the father. Only 30 percent thought that the mother should be the one to stay home (Robison 2002; U.S. Census Bureau 2012l: Table SHP-1).

While attitudes toward parenting may be changing, traditional gender-role expectations continue to have a significant impact. Men, too, receive messages from family, peers, and the media about what it means to be masculine. One of the most powerful expectations is to be tough, both physically and emotionally, in sports, at work, and even in relationships. Males who fail to conform to such gender norms face criticism and even humiliation. Boys, for example, run the risk of being called a "chicken," "sissy," or "fag" even by fathers or brothers (Katz 1999; Pascoe 2007). Such name-calling represents a form of social control that limits the likelihood of new gender norms being established.

We also see the effects of gendered expectations demonstrated by men in nontraditional occupations, such as

As we saw in the case of Woineshet Zebene at the beginning of the chapter, women face significant oppression, violence, and discrimination in nations around the globe. Whether in the form of sex trafficking, socially condoned rape, or denial of medical services, the simple fact of being a woman is enough to justify such practices in some countries. Quotidian cruelties exist in these cultures because women are not seen as fully human (Kristof and WuDunn 2009).

Other cultures take dramatically different approaches toward gender. Some assume the existence of three or four gender categories. Judith Lorber (1994) notes that "male women," biological males who live for the most part as women, and "female men," biological females who live for the most part as men, can be found in various societies. "Female men" can be found in some African and Native American societies, and in Albania, where they take on male work and family roles. "Male women" include the *berdaches,* also known as two-spirit people, of the Native Americans of the Great Plains; the *hijras* of India; and the *xanith* (Nanda 1997; Reddy 2005). Michael Kimmel (2004) describes the *xanith* of Oman in the Middle East:

> They work as skilled domestic servants, dress in men's tunics (but in pastel shades more associated with feminine colors), and sell themselves in passive homosexual relationships. They are permitted to speak with women on the street (other men are prohibited). At sex-segregated public events, they sit with the women. However, they can change their minds. (p. 65)

These gender categories are a well-accepted part of their social lives. Individuals who fill them are not simply tolerated or viewed as deviant. Two-spirit people, for example, have high status because they are thought to have special powers (Kimmel, 2004; Roscoe 1997).

Beginning with the path-breaking work of Margaret Mead ([1935] 2001) and continuing through contemporary fieldwork, scholars have shown that gender roles can

Thousands of hijras gathered for a festival near Kolkata, India.
Photo: © Salkat Paul/Pacific Press/LightRicket via Getty Images

vary greatly from one physical environment, economy, and political system to the next. Peggy Reeves Sanday's (2002, 2008) work in West Sumatra, Indonesia, for example, describes the 4-million-member Minangkabau society as one in which men and women are not competitors but partners for the common good. This society is characterized by a nurturing approach to the environment, blended with Islamic religious ethics. Women control the land through inheritance; in the event of a divorce, the ex-husband leaves with only his clothes. The larger community may be governed by men, women, or both men and women working together. Sanday's findings, together with Mead's, confirm the influential role of culture and socialization in gender-role differentiation.

REIMAGINING SEX AND GENDER

When it comes to gender, many people assume that the patterns we observe are a given, that biology, as the old saying goes, is destiny. Or, more specifically, that our sex defines our experience as men and women in obvious and predictable ways. We hear echoes of this sentiment in places such as John Gray's best-selling book, *Men Are from Mars, Women Are from Venus* (1992). This powerful analogy presents men and women as aliens from different planets, implying that the chasm between them is natural, inevitable, and difficult, if not impossible, to bridge (Carothers and Reis 2013; Hyde 2005). There are, however, signs that this assumption about the natural relationship between sex and gender is being called into question.

Moving beyond a simple, dimorphic model of sex opens the door to new opportunities for both men and women. It suggests that the line between what anthropologist Lisa Peattie and sociologist Martin Rein refer to as the natural and the artificial shifts over time. When we say something is *natural,* what we mean is that it should be accepted as given and cannot be changed. For example, when people contend that "men are more rational," or that "women are more nurturing," the assumption is that these stereotypes are determined by our biology and thus immutable. Analysis of how gender is expressed across cultures and over time suggests, however, that many such characteristics are really *artificial—* that is, they are social constructions subject to change (Peattie and Rein 1983).

Some major shifts in social life have been brought about by challenging what is considered "natural." Even into the 20th century it was thought that women's biological makeup justified their exclusion from schools, the workplace, and politics—social locations in which women's participation is now taken for granted. For example, women were once banned from colleges and universities in the United States, because it was presumed that they were biologically incapable of succeeding. At the Jefferson Medical College in Philadelphia in 1847, Professor Charles

... In an exploratory experiment controlling college students' knowledge of the professor's gender for an online course, students gave better teaching evaluations to professors the students thought were male. This was true even when the actual professor was a woman (MacNell, Driscoll, and Hunt 2014).

Did You Know?

Photo: © Asia Images/Getty Images RF.

SOCTHINK

Given that our understandings of gender vary across time and place, why are we so committed to the notion that gender differences are narrowly determined by biology?

Meigs, in a famous speech delivered to an all-male class of gynecology students, said of women, "She has a head almost too small for intellect and just big enough for love. . . . She reigns in the heart . . . the household altar is her place of worship and service" (quoted in Collins 2003:89–90). In 1874, at Harvard University, Dr. Edward Clarke, a member of its board of overseers, wrote that women were too delicate to handle the rigors of college education. The increased effort needed for thinking would sap energy from a woman's uterus and ovaries, leading these reproductive organs to shrink (Clarke 1874). In fact, Harvard did

not formally admit women to its undergraduate program until the early 1970s. When women were finally given the opportunity to attend college, a right they had to fight hard for to win, they excelled. They now have a higher overall grade point average, and they outnumber men among college graduates. What was once thought to be natural is now recognized to have been a social construction. It turns out that the problem wasn't biology; it was the socially constructed culture that denied opportunity (Chee, Pino, and Smith 2005).

On the flip side, the notion that men just aren't as nurturing as women persists. It appears to grow out of the presumption that women, because they give birth and nurse babies, are naturally better at providing love, care, and protection. Yet research demonstrates that when men have the primary responsibility for raising children, they do the same things conventionally associated with "mothering." For example, sociologist Barbara Risman conducted research on single fathers and concluded that "when males take full responsibility for child care, when they meet expectations usually confined to females, they

WOMAN MAY WEAR TROUSERS.

Attorney General of Kansas Rules There Is No Law Against It.

TOPEKA. Kan., April 28.—Gov. Stubbs received a letter yesterday from a widow at Oswego asking permission to wear men's trousers while at work at her home. It said she was supporting a large family, which necessitated outside work, and that in wearing skirts she was badly handicapped.

The letter was turned over to the Attorney General, who ruled there was no law prohibiting a woman from wearing men's trousers, especially if she were the head of the house.

Source: Published: April 29, 1910. Copyright © The New York Times.

develop intimate and affectionate relationships with their children. Despite male sex-role training, fathers respond to the nontraditional role of single parent with strategies stereotypically considered feminine" (Risman 1986:101). Similarly, researchers looking at response patterns for nearly 30,000 parents found no significant differences between North American mothers and fathers on factors including nurturance, warmth, responsiveness, encouragement, interaction, or disciplinary strictness. Thus it is not strictly biology that determines nurturing; it is the social structure and a person's position within it (Barnett and Rivers 2004; Lytton and Romney 1991; Risman and Johnson-Sumerford 1998).

Identifying some aspect of our definitions of sex and gender as artificial reveals the complex relationship between the two. Questioning our conceptions of the natural, however, is never easy, as women who have worked for the right to vote and equal opportunity in the workplace have discovered. Confronting these notions can look like an attempt to defy reality itself, but such defiance is necessary to enact significant social change.

>> Working for Change: Women's Movements

One of the lessons we learn from research on gender is that change is possible. As we saw with college education for women, past norms need not determine future practices. Change, however, seldom comes without conflict. People have fought against existing cultural assumptions about what is natural in order to advance opportunity for women in politics, the economy, and other spheres of public and private life. **Feminism** is the term for this belief in social, economic, and political equality for women.

feminism The belief in social, economic, and political equality for women.

THE FIRST WAVE

The feminist movement in the United States was born in upstate New York, in the town of Seneca Falls, in the summer of 1848. On July 19 the first women's rights convention began, attended by Elizabeth Cady Stanton, Lucretia Mott, and other pioneers in the struggle for women's rights. This first wave of feminists faced ridicule and scorn as they fought for legal and political equality for women. They were not afraid to risk controversy on behalf of their cause; in 1872, Susan B. Anthony was arrested for attempting to vote in that year's presidential election.

Ultimately, the early feminists won many victories. The pinnacle accomplishment of the first wave was the passage and ratification of the 19th Amendment to the Constitution, which granted women the right to vote in national elections beginning in 1920. After this peak, however, suffrage did not lead to other reforms related to women's social and economic position, and in the early and mid-20th century, the women's movement became a much less powerful force for social change.

THE SECOND WAVE

What is called the second wave of feminism in the United States emerged in the 1960s and came into full force in the 1970s. Betty Friedan's book *The Feminine Mystique* played a crucial part, as did two other pioneering books that argued for women's rights: Simone de Beauvoir's *The Second Sex* (1952) and Kate Millett's *Sexual Politics* (1970). Friedan was an upper-middle-class, White, suburban housewife who worked part-time as a freelance journalist in the 1950s. As part of a story she planned to write, she surveyed her college classmates about their lives. What she heard repeatedly from women like her was that they shared a sense of nameless, aching dissatisfaction that she famously labeled "the problem that has no name." Even though they were living what many considered the American Dream, something was missing. They mostly blamed themselves for this feeling of emptiness or

Did You Know?

. . . When it comes to science education in the United States, the fact that boys consistently score higher than girls on standardized tests has led many to assume that the difference is related to gender. Yet, in a broader study of 65 countries, girls were more likely to outperform boys. The countries where boys do better tend to be in western/northern Europe and the Americas. Girls outdo boys in Asia, eastern/southern Europe, and the Middle East.

Source: Fairfield and McLean 2012. *Photo:* © M. Constantini/Photoalto RF.

incompleteness, and when they sought help, doctors and psychiatrists prescribed charity work, community activities, or perhaps tranquilizers.

In *The Feminine Mystique,* Friedan argued that the problem was not with women as individuals, but with the position they occupied in American society at the time. Friedan's realization that this was not a private trouble but a public issue represents a classic case of using the sociological imagination. Women were cut off from the public sphere, and their lack of access to valued economic, social, and cultural resources—including money and power in the workplace—was the real problem. (Friedan herself attributed part of her own relative happiness to the fact that she retained dual status as both journalist and housewife.) To challenge this structural problem, women had to fight against the cultural assumption that the primary and most "natural" goal for women was to be a wife and mother in the private sphere. As Friedan put it, "We can no longer ignore that voice within women that says, 'I want something more than my husband and my children and my home' " (1963:32).

In 1966, Friedan helped found the National Organization for Women (NOW) to fight for equality for women; she served as its president until 1970. In addition to political and legal battles, one of the organization's tools was "consciousness-raising groups." Among other goals, these groups sought to elevate awareness among women regarding the degree to which they shared "the problem that has no name." This shared consciousness could then lead to collective action and the development of a new structure with enhanced opportunities. Choice was a core value at the center of these efforts. The existing system limited options for women in many areas of social life. Feminists fought to open up structural opportunity and to ensure that women could make choices about going to college, pursuing a career based on ability rather than gender expectations, getting married or staying single, having children or remaining childless, and so on.

The question of whether women should have control over their reproductive rights and their bodies has also played a significant role in this movement. In the United States, most people support a woman's right to a legal abortion, but with reservations.

Nancy Pelosi, Democrat from California, was the first female Speaker of the U.S. House of Representatives. Photo: © Scott J Ferrell/Getty Images.

© JP Laffont/Sygma/Corbis

According to a national survey, 51 percent say it should be legal in all or most cases while 43 percent argue it should be illegal in all or most cases. At opposite extremes, 19 percent say there should be no restrictions while 14 percent say abortion should never be allowed (Pew Research Center 2014j). These percentages have stayed fairly steady for the past 35 years.

As more and more women identified existing cultural practices as sexist attitudes and practices—including attitudes they themselves had accepted through socialization into traditional gender roles—they began to challenge male dominance. A sense of sisterhood, much like the class consciousness that Marx hoped would emerge in the proletariat, became evident. Individual women identified their interests with women as a whole, and they rejected the principle that their happiness depended on their acceptance of submissive and subordinate roles.

SOC THINK

What does it mean to be a feminist today?

THE THIRD WAVE

In the 1980s, partially because of second-wave successes in opening up opportunities and earning greater respect for women, a sense developed that the central goals of feminism had largely been accomplished. Some scholars argued that we had entered a postfeminist era. In the early 1990s, however, a new style of feminism arose that went beyond fighting the structural obstacles that motivated the first and second waves. It ventured into the cultural sphere to embrace a multiplicity of voices, expressions, and experiences. This third wave was part of a conceptual shift away from a singular focus on equality of persons, which it takes as a given, to a celebration of difference (Brooks 1997; Lotz 2007; Showden 2009).

standpoint theory Because our social positions shape our perceptions, a more complete understanding of social relations must incorporate the perspectives of marginalized voices.

intersectionality Gender, sexuality, race, ethnicity, and class must not be studied in isolation, because they have intermingled effects on our identity, knowledge, and outcomes.

The third wave arose in part as a generational shift; younger women were dissatisfied with the dominant image of feminism as stodgy and uptight. It also represented a shift in message toward a more varied and pluralistic understanding of what feminism is. This was evident in two early anthologies that played a pivotal role presenting the multiplicity of voices this movement represents: Rebecca Walker's *To Be Real: Telling the Truth and Changing the Face of Feminism* (1995) and Barbara Findlen's *Listen Up: Voices from the Next Feminist Generation* (1995). Previously, feminists were characterized as White, upper-middle class, and heterosexual. Third-wave feminists place greater emphasis on agency and subjectivity; are committed to personal empowerment; are more open about sexuality and sexual exploration; and celebrate diversity of gender, race, ethnicity, and class. Embracing a multiplicity of identities led to a commitment to social justice and a global perspective so that other voices have the opportunity to be heard (Baumgardner and Richards 2000; Groeneveld 2009; Lotz 2007; Zimmerman, McDermott, and Gould 2009).

There is in the third wave a bit of the postmodern idea of self-creation, according to which we can choose our identities from a buffet of possibilities and create our own realities. This fits with the notion that our sex is not

Did You Know?

... In a study of *Sports Illustrated* covers—not counting the annual swimsuit issue—women appeared on only 4.9 percent from 2000 to 2011. In fact, women were more likely to have appeared from 1954 to 1965, when they were featured on 12.6 percent of the covers.

Source: J. Weber and Carini 2013. *Photo:* © Thomas Coex/Getty Images.

narrowly determined by biology and that our expression of our gender need not be singular in nature but is open to our creativity and control. One result is a more playful or ironic element to the movement, especially when it comes to so-called girlie feminism, which seeks to reclaim things like lipstick, high heels, and more sexualized images of women as viable emblems of feminist empowerment. Critics have argued that this rhetoric of choice inappropriately minimizes the continued power of racial, sexual, and class positions in society (Munford 2007; Renegar and Sowards 2009; Showden 2009).

One of the outgrowths of this new feminist perspective was the recognition that defining others primarily by any one position may diminish the importance of the multiple positions we all occupy. To look at the social location of Hispanic women, for example, we must pay mind to both their gender and their ethnicity (as well as other factors). Two significant theoretical developments arising out of this multiple-identity approach are standpoint theory and intersectionality. **Standpoint theory** maintains that our understanding of reality is shaped by the positions we occupy and the experiences we have. Given that the views of some (based on their gender, sexuality, race, ethnicity, or class) are privileged over others, this theory emphasizes the importance of listening to the voices of those who are in some way considered outsiders. Such attention provides a deeper and richer understanding of social systems (Collins 2000; Harding 2004; Hartsock 1983; D. Smith 1987). **Intersectionality** represents a second major development. According to this approach, we cannot speak of gender or race or class or sexuality as if they exist in isolation from each other. Rather, these combine within us in ways that make it difficult to separate the effects of each. Thus research must analyze the intermingled effects of multiple social statuses on identity, knowledge, and

U.S. Attitudes About Homosexuality

80

70 **Always Wrong**

60

50

40

30

20 **Not Wrong at All**

10

0

'73 '74 '76 '77 '80 '82 '84 '85 '87 '88 '89 '90 '91 '93 '94 '96 '98 2000 02 '04 '06 '08 '10 '12 '14

Note: Responses are to the question "What about sexual relationship between two adults of the same sex—do you think it is always wrong, almost always wrong, wrong only sometimes, or wrong at all?" Data are from the General Social Survey, a regularly administered national survey of the U.S. adult population.

Sources: T. Smith 2011; T. Smith et al. 2014.   *Photos: scale:* © Comstock/Alamy RF; *plastic grooms:* © Photodisc/Getty Images RF; *bride/groom:* © Image Club RF.

expression of who we are in a way similar to gender, race, ethnicity, and class. In terms of our sexual practices, sexuality shapes what we do (or do not do) and with whom.

SEXUALITY AND IDENTITY

Sexual expression is not simply a result of biological urges and instincts. It is situated within, and an outgrowth of, existing social, cultural, and historical processes. Though alternative expressions of sexuality have a long history in the United States, their existence and practice has not always been acknowledged (Duberman, Vicinus, and Chauncy 1989; Escoffier 1997). During the 1960s, experimentation with "free love" helped open the door to more widespread recognition of such expressions. At the same time organizations arose, such as the Gay Liberation Front in 1969 and the Gay Activist Alliance in 1970, that raised awareness that alternatives existed and sought to establish the legitimacy of alternative sexualities in the public consciousness. As a result, people became more aware of the concept of **sexual orientation**—the categories of people to whom we are sexually attracted—as a form of personal and community identity. Initially, in keeping with the dimorphic model of sex, the two major subcategories included **heterosexual,** those who were sexually attracted to members of the opposite sex, and **homosexual,** those who were attracted to members of the same sex. Homosexual men were identified as gay, and homosexual women were identified as lesbian. **Bisexual** was later added to these subcategories to include those who were attracted to both men and women.

outcomes (Alimahomed 2010; Harding 2004; Shields 2008). For both standpoint theory and intersectionality, a narrative approach in research, in which we hear the voices of those who are other to us, is critical.

>> The Social Construction of Sexuality

The shifts that occur in how sex and gender are defined—as more complex than simple binary categories of male and female or masculine and feminine—also apply to sexuality. In the United States, as a consequence of the dimorphic model of sex, the dominant ideology presumed heterosexual relationships, in which the idealized norm was chastity until marriage followed by lifelong faithfulness to a single partner. This vision reached perhaps its zenith in the 1950s television portrayal of families in programs such as *Leave It To Beaver* and *Father Knows Best*. Times have changed.

Sexuality denotes our identities and activities as sexual beings. In terms of identity, our sexuality represents an

sexuality Denotes our identities and activities as sexual beings.

sexual orientation The categories of people to whom we are sexually attracted.

heterosexual A category of sexual orientation that includes those who are sexually attracted to members of the opposite sex.

homosexual A category of sexual orientation that includes those who are attracted to members of the same sex.

bisexual A category of sexual orientation that includes those who are attracted to both men and women.

Thomas Beatie was born female and underwent sexual reassignment surgery to become male. He kept his female reproductive organs in hopes of one day of becoming a parent. When his wife could not become pregnant, he conceived and gave birth to their first child in 2008.   Photo: © AP Photo/Hermann J. Knippertz.

This model of sexuality, even though it extended awareness of sexuality beyond the 1950s version, still presents the dividing lines as clear-cut and absolute. Classifying where you or others belong is presumed to be a simple matter of identifying your sexual practices and selecting the appropriate category. But people's experiences of sexuality are more complex and varied than that. For example, what about those who have had occasional homosexual experiences in their past but are now practicing heterosexuals? Or those who engage in same-sex practices but do not identify themselves as gay, lesbian, or bisexual? In an attempt to clarify just one of these definitions, historian David Halperin (2009) identified 13 different formulations of bisexuality, thus highlighting the ambiguity in drawing these lines.

Over time, in response to the limitations of this approach, a new model presented sexuality as a continuum rather than an either-or designation. A key component of this approach is the recognition of people who are **transgender**—those who appear to be biologically one sex but who identify with the gender of another—as an additional category. Such recognition highlights the socially constructed nature of sexuality as opposed to its biological element, and creates more space for alternative expressions of sexuality. This is particularly true if transgender

transgender People who appear to be biologically one sex but who identify with the gender of another.

heteronormativity A term that sociologists use to describe the cultural presupposition that heterosexuality is the appropriate standard for sexual identity and practice and that alternative sexualities are deviant, abnormal, or wrong.

is defined even more broadly, as historian Susan Stryker (2007) suggests, "as anything that disrupts or denaturalizes normative gender, and which calls our attention to the process through which normativity is produced" (p. 60). From this perspective, transgender involves transgressions of dominant gender norms in ways that enable us to recognize their existence and power (Brooks and Quina 2009; Crabtree 2009; Kinsey, Pomeroy, and Gebhardt 1953; Kinsey, Pomeroy, and Martin 1948; Waites 2009).

Though awareness of alternative forms of sexuality has increased, a cultural expectation of heterosexuality remains dominant in the United States. Sociologists use the term **heteronormativity** to describe the cultural presupposition that heterosexuality is the appropriate standard for sexual identity and practice and that alternative sexualities are deviant, abnormal, or wrong (Chambers 2007; Elia 2003). As an example of heteronormativity, a 1957 survey found that "four out of five people believed that anyone who preferred to remain single was 'sick,' 'neurotic,' or 'immoral'" (Coontz 2005:230). Additionally, homosexuality was categorized as a psychological disorder until 1972 in the American Psychiatric Association's official *Diagnostic and Statistical Manual of Mental Disorders* (*DSM*). A new edition, *DSM-5*, came out in 2013. The category "gender identity disorders," including those who are transgender and transsexual, was removed and replaced with "gender dysphoria." The intent was to minimize the stigma attached to the diagnosis while still recognizing its existence. Some argue that it is important to maintain these diagnoses, because transgender people who seek gender reassignment surgery might not get proper diagnosis and treatment without such a designation (Drescher 2010, 2011; Melby 2009; Winters 2012).

Heteronormativity is a form of ethnocentrism that generalizes a particular cultural ideal (heterosexuality) onto all other populations, thus denying legitimacy to those outside it (Chambers 2007). It can be maintained in subtle, often invisible ways during our everyday interactions. The television series *Glee* captured just such a moment in an encounter between Kurt, a gay high school student, and his father, Burt, who is generally understanding and supportive of Kurt's sexuality. Kurt was saddened at the seeming ease with which his dad talked sports with Finn, the school's

© Bobby Bank/Getty Images

star quarterback. His father tries to reassure him by saying, "Kurt, I love you. And I am sympathetic to all your stuff. But come on, buddy, we've got a deal here, right? I don't try to change you; you don't try to change me. You are my son, and a little guy talk with some other kid isn't going to change that." Kurt replies, "Guy talk? I'm a guy." It is precisely at moments such as this, when a person becomes invisible as a guy because he does not conform to the dominant gender expectations, that heteronormativity is at work.

SOCTHINK

How is heteronormativity reinforced in the current top-rated songs and television programs? Can you think of any exceptions?

Socialization plays a key role in determining our sexual identity (R. Parker 2009). Just as was the case with gender, we face significant pressure to obey dominant norms for masculinity and femininity. In her book *Dude You're a Fag,* sociologist C. J. Pascoe (2007) set out to understand how heteronormativity is reproduced. She conducted an ethnographic study of boys in a working-class high school. She found that one of the ways they reinforced existing masculinity norms was by casually using the term *fag* to call out anyone who deviates from the dominant masculine ideal. According to Pascoe, calling someone a fag was not so much an antigay act (though she admits it was that, too) as it was a means of keeping guys in line. Whereas it was possible to be a homosexual and still be masculine, being a fag represented a form of failed masculinity. The threat of being a fag hangs over boys like a specter or ghost that could possess them at any time; only eternal vigilance keeps it at bay. Pascoe argues that rejecting this role also represented a repudiation of femininity. So not only did this discourse support existing heteronormative standards, it also reinforced traditional conceptions of gender. Other researchers found similar results in a study of "hogging," in which men have sex with overweight or obese women not as a means of establishing a relationship with them but as a game to prove their masculinity to other guys (Prohaska and Gailey 2010).

Such examples point to the fact that differences in sexuality are not just matters of orientation and alternative preferences; they are connected to larger systems of power in which some statuses are privileged over others (Brickell 2009). We construct our sexual identities, making sense of who we are, within the contexts of our social structures. Within these worlds, not all paths are accepted as equally legitimate. In the United States, establishing a sexual identity as something other than heterosexual has been difficult owing to the meanings attached to such identities and the lack of broader cultural support for them. These power differences contribute to discrimination and threats of violence. According

to the FBI, for example, 20.3 percent of the 6,921 hate crime offenses reported in 2013 involved sexual orientation (U.S. Department of Justice 2014c).

SOCTHINK

How does gendered name-calling, such as joking that a guy is a fag, function to maintain clear-cut gender boundaries? What consequences does it have for gays, lesbians, or heterosexual girls?

In an effort to ensure the civil, political, and social rights of those in lesbian, gay, bisexual, and transgender (LGBT) communities around the world, a group of human rights experts gathered in Indonesia in 2006 to establish the Yogyakarta Principles (http://www.yogyakartaprinciples .org/). The principles are built on the supposition of universal human rights and seek to extend these rights to include sexual orientation and gender identity. They identify 29 basic principles including the right to equality and non-discrimination, the right to work, and the right to found a family. This movement arose in part because homosexuality remains a crime in many nations; in some it is punishable by death.

In places where there has been more openness about sexuality, increasingly, sexual preference may not necessarily be the primary mode of identification, but it exists in combination with gender, race, ethnicity, nationality, and class (Stein 2010). As alternative expressions of sexuality become more accepted and less alternative, their role as master status through which all identity is filtered may become less powerful. Instead, in keeping with the intersectionality perspective, sexuality may become but one significant piece of identity that shapes who we are and the paths we are likely to pursue (Gomez 1997).

SEXUALITY IN ACTION

While our sexuality shapes our conception of who we are, it also has consequences for what we do. In sociological terms, as suggested by the Thomas theorem (see Chapter 1), our sexual identity is shaped by our interactions with others. We then act on the basis of those perceptions. In our everyday lives, our perceptions of ourselves and our sexual practices often reinforce each other. Working out our sexuality in practice includes the types of sex acts we perform and the types of sexual relationships we establish with others.

Because such topics are generally considered to be taboo, people are often both ignorant and curious about actual sexual practices. The Kinsey Reports (*Sexual Behavior in the Human Male* [1948] and *Sexual Behavior in the Human Female* [1953]) provided the earliest in-depth research studies on people's sexual practices. Compiled by American biologist Alfred C. Kinsey and his colleagues, the reports, particularly their finding that

Alfred C. Kinsey, with the help of his team of researchers, provided unprecedented insight into people's sexual practices in the United States. Photo: © Hulton Archive/Getty Images.

Relationship Values by Gender and Sexual Identity

Importance of love

Straight women	91.15%
Lesbian women	73.09%
Bisexual women	85.74%
Straight men	81.59%
Gay men	82.14%
Bisexual men	79.02%

Importance of faithfulness

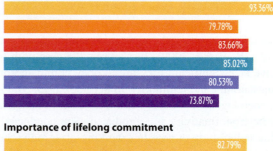

Straight women	93.36%
Lesbian women	79.78%
Bisexual women	83.66%
Straight men	85.02%
Gay men	80.53%
Bisexual men	73.87%

Importance of lifelong commitment

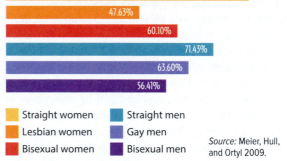

Straight women	82.79%
Lesbian women	47.63%
Bisexual women	60.10%
Straight men	71.43%
Gay men	63.60%
Bisexual men	56.41%

Straight women • Straight men
Lesbian women • Gay men
Bisexual women • Bisexual men

Source: Meier, Hull, and Ortyl 2009.

8 percent of men had been in predominantly homosexual relationships for at least three years between ages 16 and 55, were considered shocking at the time. Both volumes became best sellers. Their studies opened the door for others to conduct additional research (Bullough 1998; Laumann et al. 1994; T. Smith 2006).

The National Survey of Family Growth (NSFG) provides recent data and includes detailed information on actual sexual practices. It is conducted by the National Center for Health Statistics (NCHS) and the Centers for Disease Control and Prevention (CDC), and is based on a national sample of more than 13,000 respondents (Chandra, et al. 2011). Summarizing the results of heterosexual relationship patterns, the NSFG researchers report:

> Among adults aged 25–44, about 98% of women and 97% of men ever had vaginal intercourse, 89% of women and 90% of men ever had oral sex with an opposite-sex partner, and 36% of women and 44% of men ever had anal sex with an opposite-sex partner. (p. 1)

They also investigated the numbers of opposite-sex partners that people aged 25–44 have had in their lifetime, finding that, among women, 32 percent report they have had 1 or 2 male partners, 36 percent say 3 to 6, and 10 percent report they have had 15 or more. For men the numbers are 19 percent with 1 or 2 partners, 29 percent say 3 to 6, and 28 percent report 15 or more. The median number of partners was 3.6 for women and 6.1 for men. Among married couples, 3.9 percent of married men and

2.2 percent of married women reported more than one opposite-sex partner in the previous 12 months. Among those cohabitating, 15 percent of men and 13 percent of women reported more than one opposite-sex partner within the previous year (Chandra et al. 2011).

One contentious question in such studies is the percentage of homosexuals in the U.S. population. A commonly used figure (derived from the Kinsey Reports) estimates that approximately 10 percent of the population is homosexual. The NSFG study distinguished between having had same-sex experiences and identifying with particular sexual orientations. The researchers found that, among men aged 25–44, 5.7 percent have had same-sex sexual contact in their lifetime. Among women of the same age, 12.9 percent have had same-sex sexual contact in their lifetime. Likelihoods of engaging in same-sex sexual behavior varied by educational attainment. Men with higher levels of education were somewhat *more* likely to have engaged in such behaviors compared to other men. Women with a bachelor's degree or higher were *less* likely to have

Sexuality Self-Identification, Ages 18–44

	Men	Women
Heterosexual	95.6	93.6
Homosexual	1.8	1.2
Bisexual	1.2	3.9
Something else	0.2	0.4
No response	1.2	0.8

Note: Percentage is in response to the question "Do you think of yourself as a heterosexual, homosexual, bisexual, or something else?"

Source: Chandra et al. 2013.

© 2010 Jason LaVeris/FilmMagic/Getty Images

engaged in such behaviors compared to other women (Chandra, Copen, and Mosher 2013).

Simply having had same-sex experiences does not necessarily result in a same-sex identity. The NSFG researchers asked, "Do you think of yourself as a heterosexual, homosexual, bisexual, or something else?" As the "Sexuality Self-Identification" table indicates, 96 percent of men and 94 percent of women identify themselves as heterosexual. The numbers of people who identify as homosexual and bisexual are lower than the numbers of those who have engaged in such practices. Overall, the percentage of men and women aged 18–44 who identify themselves as either homosexual or bisexual is less than 4 percent. This finding is consistent with other recent national studies on sexual behavior in the United States (Chandra et al. 2013; Gates 2010; Indiana University Center for Sexual Health Promotion 2010).

The age at which people have their first sexual experiences has historically been an additional interest of researchers. In terms of opposite-sex experiences, the percentage of teens who have had sexual intercourse rises with each subsequent year. At age 15, 23 percent of girls and 21 percent of boys have had vaginal sexual intercourse; by age 17, it is 44 percent for both girls and boys; among 18- to 19-year-olds, it is 62 percent for females and 66 percent for males. Of those aged 15–17, approximately 6.7 percent of girls and 9.8 percent of boys had engaged in oral sex but had not had vaginal intercourse (Chandra et al. 2011).

One of the concerns about those who have sex at a young age is sexual coercion. In fact, among girls who had their first sexual intercourse before age 14, 18 percent said that they really didn't want it to happen at the time. Another 52 percent had mixed feelings about whether they wanted sex or not. For boys who were the same age, 8.9 percent didn't want it to happen and 34 percent had mixed feelings. Put another way, among those who had sex before age 20, 41 percent of females and 63 percent of males really wanted it to happen at the time (Martinez, Copen, and Abma 2011:Table 9).

When it comes to same-sex experiences among those who are younger, females have a higher likelihood of having had same-sex contact. Among those aged 15–19, 11 percent of women and 2.5 percent of men report having had some form of sexual contact with a member of the same sex. Of those aged 20–24, 15.8 percent of women and 5.6 percent of men report such contact. When it comes to self-identification, women aged 18–19 are the most likely to identify as something other than heterosexual, with 5.8 percent selecting bisexual and 1.9 percent choosing homosexual. By contrast, men of the same age report at 1.1 percent and 1.6 percent, respectively (Chandra et al. 2011).

One of the most significant developments in the history of human sexuality was the invention of the birth control pill. It was approved for use in the United States in 1960 and helped spark the sexual revolution. Together with other modern forms of birth control, the pill made it possible to engage in sex without significant risk of getting pregnant.

© NYC Department of Health and Mental Hygiene/AP

rate is 84 percent, Japan's is 44 percent, and India's is 48 percent. Compare these countries with Africa, where the overall rate is 26 percent (though there is substantial variation between countries). Some African nations have extremely low rates (for example, Somalia at 1.2 percent, Chad at 1.6 percent, and Guinea at 3.3 percent). Others have rates higher than the global average (for example, Zimbabwe at 57 percent, Egypt at 58 percent, and South Africa at 59 percent). Just as was the case for women in the United States, greater control over fertility by women internationally increases their opportunities for self-determination. It also increases the likelihood of extending basic human rights and protections to women in countries around the world (Inglehart, Norris, and Welzel 2002; Kristof and WuDunn 2009; United Nations 2013b).

SOCTHINK

How might economic, social, and cultural factors influence a society's pattern of birth control use? How might these factors influence a society's attitudes about gender?

SOCTHINK

Why are young women the most likely category to both engage in same-sex practices and embrace alternative sexual identities?

>> Gender and Inequality

Although the work of early sociologists such as Harriet Martineau, Charlotte Perkins Gilman, and Ida B. Wells-Barnett highlighted the significance of gender inequality, in the 1950s sociologists Talcott Parsons and Robert Bales (1955) argued that families need both an instrumental and an expressive leader. The **instrumental leader** is the person in the family who bears responsibility for completion of tasks, focuses on distant goals, and manages the external relationship between the family and other social institutions. The **expressive leader** is the person in

instrumental leader The person in the family who bears responsibility for the completion of tasks, focuses on distant goals, and manages the external relationship between one's family and other social institutions.

expressive leader The person in the family who bears responsibility for the maintenance of harmony and internal emotional affairs.

It gave women greater control over their sexuality and their careers by allowing them to control their fertility. Effective birth control also resulted in debates about how sex should be viewed, whether primarily for procreation (that is, having babies) or recreation (for pleasure, love, and commitment) or both. Religious groups, including the Roman Catholic Church, continue to struggle with these issues (Benagiano and Mori 2009).

Internationally, birth control practices vary significantly from country to country. The overall global average for use of modern forms of birth control—condoms, the pill, and sterilization—is 57 percent among women aged 15–49 who are married or in a union. For Europe as a whole, 59 percent of people use a modern form of birth control. The rate jumps to 74 percent in the countries of northern Europe (such as Norway and the United Kingdom) and 67 percent in western Europe (including France and Germany). In Asia, China's

Trends in U.S. Women's Participation in the Paid Labor Force

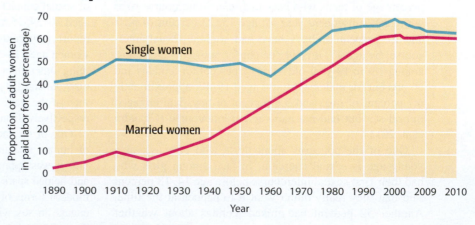

Source: U.S. Census Bureau 1975, 2011h:Table 597.

© Thomas Northcut/Digital Vision/Getty Images RF

the family who bears responsibility for the maintenance of harmony and internal emotional affairs. According to their theory, women's interest in expressive goals frees men for instrumental tasks, and vice versa. Women become naturally anchored in the family as wives, mothers, and household managers; men become anchored in the occupational world outside the home.

As a result of insights from feminist theorists and findings from further research, sociologists now argue that such separate abilities are not innate but are instead social constructs. The key sociological task is to analyze how gender expectations are created and maintained—for example, through gender-role socialization—and then to investigate the consequences of such constructs.

SEXISM AND DISCRIMINATION

Sociologists are interested in understanding the "consequences of difference," that is, the impact the social structures we build have on the distribution of valued resources. When it comes to gender, sociologists investigate the degree of sexism that exists within social systems. **Sexism** is the ideology that claims one sex is superior to the other. The term generally refers to male prejudice and discrimination against women. It is not enough, however, to understand gender inequality only by looking at the attitudes and practices of individuals, such as sexist remarks and acts of aggression. We must analyze it as a characteristic of the social system itself. Sociologists refer to such patterns of treatment that, as part of a society's normal operations, systematically deny a group access to resources and opportunities as **institutional discrimination.**

All the major institutions in the United States—including the government, the armed forces, large corporations, the media, universities, and the medical establishment—are controlled by men. Analysis of patterns of distribution allow for some assessment of the degree to which institutional sexism exists.

> **sexism** The ideology that claims one sex is superior to the other.
>
> **institutional discrimination** A pattern of treatment that systematically denies a group access to resources and opportunities as part of society's normal operations.

WOMEN IN THE UNITED STATES

More than 35 years ago, the U.S. Commission on Civil Rights (2009) concluded that the phrase in the Declaration of Independence proclaiming that "all men are created equal" had been taken literally for too long. It found that women in the United States experienced a

Women's Representation in U.S. Occupations

Underrepresented		Overrepresented	
Occupation	Percentage female	Occupation	Percentage female
Firefighters	3.5	High school teachers	56.7
Aircraft pilots	5.5	Cashiers	71.7
Mechanical engineer	7.2	File clerks	80.1
Civil engineers	12.1	Social workers	80.3
Police officers	13.4	Elementary Teachers	81.0
Clergy	15.5	Librarians	84.1
Printers	18.1	Tellers	84.3
Chefs and head cooks	20.0	Registered nurses	90.1
Computer programmers	23.0	Receptionists	92.2
Architects	25.0	Word processors and typists	94.1
Lawyers	33.1	Childcare workers	94.8
Physicians	35.5	Dental hygienists	98.3

Note: Women constitute 47 percent of the entire labor force. These data are for 2013. The elementary teacher category includes middle school teachers.

Source: Bureau of Labor Statistics 2014e: Table 11.   *Photo:* © JupiterImage, Creatas Image/Getty Images RF.

Gender Wage Gap by Age

Women's median weekly earnings as a percentage of men's

Age (years)	
16–19	89.7%
20–24	89.8%
25–34	89.4%
35–44	80.2%
45–54	76.6%
55–64	77.1
65+	73.7%

Note: Wage gap is women's median weekly earnings as a percentage of men's. Overall weekly earnings wage gap is 82.1 percent.

Source: Bureau of Labor Statistics 2014f:Table 1.   *Photo:* © Corbis RF.

consistent pattern of inequality. Looking at the workplace, income, housework, politics, and more, we can see that its concern is still valid.

Labor Force Participation The labor market has opened up significantly since Betty Friedan published *The Feminine Mystique* in 1963. Today, millions of women—married or single, with or without children, pregnant or recently having given birth—are in the labor force. Overall, 57.2 percent of adult women in the United States were in the labor force in 2013, compared to 43.3 percent in 1970. By contrast, in 2013, 69.7 percent of adult men in the United States were in the labor force, compared to 79.7 percent in 1970. Among women with children under age 6, 39 percent were in the labor force in 1975 compared to 64.7 percent in 2013 (Bureau of Labor Statistics 2014e: Tables 2 and 7).

Still, women entering the job market find their options restricted in important ways. As is evident in the "Women's Representation in U.S. Occupations" table, significant occupational gender segregation exists. For example, in 2013, women accounted for 98 percent of all dental hygienists and 84 percent of all librarians. Entering such sex-typed occupations often places women in "service" roles that parallel the traditional gender-role standard (Bureau of Labor Statistics 2014e: Table 11).

Women are underrepresented in occupations historically defined as "men's jobs," which often offer much greater financial rewards and prestige than women's jobs. For example, in 2013, women accounted for 47 percent of the paid labor force of the United States, yet they constituted only 5.5 percent of aircraft pilots, 12.1 percent of civil engineers, 13.4 percent of all police officers, and 35.5 percent of physicians. Sixty-nine percent of professional women are in health care or education (Bureau of Labor Statistics 2014e).

Income Today we claim to value "equal pay for equal work," meaning that someone's sex (along with race, ethnicity, or age) shouldn't matter in determining what the person earns; the only characteristic that should matter is job performance. But in practice, women do not earn as much on average as men, even in the same occupations. When comparing individuals who worked full-time, year-round in 2013, the median income for men was $50,033, and the median for women was $39,157 (DeNavas-Walt and Proctor 2014). In other words, women earned 78 cents for every dollar that men earned overall.

Taking occupational segregation into account does not explain away the wage gap. Women are often more concentrated in occupations with lower average wages than men (child care worker or receptionist versus physician or civil engineer). In 2013, out of 141 specific jobs for which there were sufficient data, there were only three in which women earned more on average than men: bakers, wholesale and retail buyers, and computer occupations (all others). Significant wage gaps exist within occupations across the board. For example, wage gaps persist in the three occupations for which women receive the highest

Did You Know?

. . . In 1965 mothers spent an average of 31.9 hours per week on housework compared to 4.4 hours for fathers. In 2011, the number of hours for mothers fell to 17.8, while the number for fathers rose to 9.8.

Source: Parker and Wang 2013.   *Photo:* © Comstock Images/Getty Images RF.

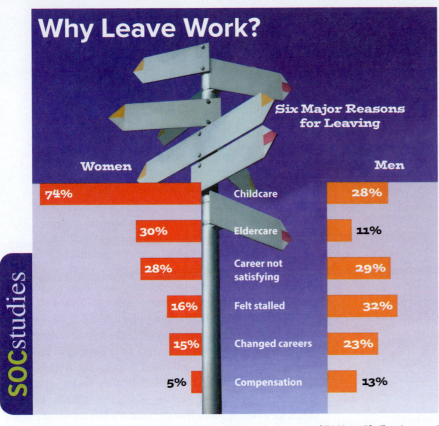

Why Leave Work?

Six Major Reasons for Leaving

Women		Men
74%	Childcare	28%
30%	Eldercare	11%
28%	Career not satisfying	29%
16%	Felt stalled	32%
15%	Changed careers	23%
5%	Compensation	13%

Note: Reasons cited as major factors in voluntarily leaving their jobs in a survey of "highly qualified" workers, aged 28–55, defined as those with a graduate degree, a professional degree, or a bachelor's degree with honors.

Source: Hewlett, Foster, Sherbin, Shiller, and Sumberg 2010.   *Photo:* © narvikk/Getty Images RF.

SOCstudies

average pay: pharmacist (86 percent of men's earnings), lawyer (79 percent), and chief executive (80 percent). Of course, in some occupations the wage gap is significantly wider, including insurance agent (71 percent), marketing and sales manager (68 percent), and physician/surgeon (72 percent) (Bureau of Labor Statistics 2014e:Table 18).

Even in occupations where women are more likely to be concentrated, they still earn less on average than do men in the same field. Examples include social worker (84 percent), elementary or middle school teacher (91 percent), and registered nurse (88 percent). Being a man in a predominantly female occupation seems to be an asset, while the reverse does not appear to be true (Bureau of Labor Statistics 2014e:Table 2).

The Glass Ceiling As we saw with Sheryl Sandberg (see Chapter 1), the higher you look up the corporate ladder, the fewer women you see. These positions tend to have higher pay and greater power, yet women have often been passed over when it came to these jobs. The term **glass ceiling** refers to the invisible barrier that blocks the promotion of qualified individuals in a work environment because of the individual's gender, race, or ethnicity. In 1995, the federal government's Glass Ceiling Commission (1995) offered the first comprehensive study of the barriers in hiring decisions. It concluded that prejudice

against women and minority group candidates plays a substantial role in hiring outcomes. It also concluded that the supply of qualified top-level candidates is limited by the cumulative effects of similar practices throughout the career path, limiting access to the training and experiences necessary to be considered for top-level jobs.

In recent years, corporations have made a concerted effort to increase their executive-level diversity, but they still have a long way to go if their goal is balanced representation between men and women. In 2013, only 4 percent of the chief executive officers (CEOs) and 10 percent of chief financial officers (CFOs) at S&P 1500 companies were women. Only 15 percent of their board of director positions are occupied by women, and 22 percent of the companies had no female board members at all. To put it another way, men hold 85 percent of the seats on these boards, a source of a significant amount of power and influence (Ernst and Young 2013). There are countries around the world that seem to do a better job of including women in these positions but none approach gender equality. In Norway, 36 percent of the board members in firms on their stock index are women. In both Finland and France it is 30 percent, Sweden comes in at 29 percent, and the United Kingdom has 23 percent. Some other countries do worse, including India at 9.5 percent and Japan with 3.1 percent (Catalyst 2015).

Home and Work Today, many women face the challenge of trying to juggle work and family. Who does the housework when women become productive wage earners? In dual-income families, fathers do an average of 9.4 hours of housework per week compared to 15.7 hours for women. Even in households where she works and he does not, wives still do more housework (K. Parker and Wang 2013).

Sociologist Arlie Hochschild (1989, 1990, 2005) has used the phrase **second shift** to describe the double burden—work outside the home followed by child care and housework—that many women face and few men share equitably. On the basis of interviews with and observations of 52 couples over an eight-year period, Hochschild reported that the wives (and not their husbands) drive home from the office while planning domestic schedules and playdates

glass ceiling An invisible barrier that blocks the promotion of a qualified individual in a work environment because of the individual's gender, race, or ethnicity.

second shift The double burden—work outside the home followed by child care and housework—that many women face and few men share equitably.

for children—and then begin their second shift. Drawing on national studies, she concluded that women spend 15 fewer hours each week in leisure activities than their husbands. In a year, these women work an extra month of 24-hour days because of the second shift; over a dozen years, they work an extra year of 24-hour days.

Movies 5 ON GENDER AND SEXUALITY

The Kids Are All Right
Two children of a lesbian couple look for their biological father.

Beginners
A young man's father comes out of the closet at age 75.

Jennifer's Body
A feminist take on horror films.

Fight Club
An outsized exploration of modern masculinity.

Transamerica
A male-to-female transsexual travels the country with her son.

Young Women and Men Voters (18–29) in Presidential Elections

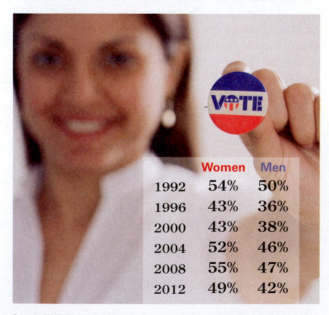

	Women	Men
1992	54%	50%
1996	43%	36%
2000	43%	38%
2004	52%	46%
2008	55%	47%
2012	49%	42%

Source: CIRCLE 2013b.   *Photo:* © Tetra Images/Getty Images RF.

Hochschild found that the married couples she studied were fraying at the edges, and so were their careers and their marriages. With such reports in mind, many feminists have advocated greater governmental and corporate support for child care, more-flexible family leave policies, and other reforms designed to ease the burden on the nation's families (Mann, Sullivan, and Gershuny 2011; Moen and Roehling 2005).

Politics Turning to political involvement, after years of struggle, women won the right to vote with the passage of the 19th Amendment in 1920. Looking at voter participation rates, we can see that they have taken advantage of that opportunity. In fact, a higher percentage of women turn out to vote than do men. This has been true in every presidential election since 1980. In the 2012 election, the turnout rate for 18- to 29-year-old women was 7 percentage points higher than that for men (CIRCLE 2013b).

When it comes to holding elected office, however, we find the same kind of underrepresentation in positions of power by women as is evident in the workplace. Even though women make up slightly more than half of the population, they make up a significantly smaller proportion of elected officials. In 2015, for example, only 6 of the nation's 50 states had a female governor (New Hampshire, New Mexico, Oklahoma, Oregon, Rhode Island, and South Carolina).

Women have made slow but steady progress in certain political arenas. In 1981, out of 535 members of Congress, only 21 were women: 19 in the House of Representatives and 2 in the Senate. By 2015, a record 104 percent of the members of Congress were women: 84 in the House and 20 in the Senate. Yet even when Nancy Pelosi served as Speaker of the House from 2007 to 2011—the first woman ever to serve in that role—the membership and leadership of Congress remained overwhelmingly male. Since 1789, 12,174 men have served as members of Congress compared to only 307 women—a mere 2.5 percent of the total (Center for American Women and Politics 2015a, 2015b).

At the Supreme Court, Sandra Day O'Connor became the nation's first female justice in 1981 (and retired in 2006). She was joined by Ruth Bader Ginsberg in 1993. In August 2009, Sonia Sotomayor became the third woman and first Hispanic on the Court. In August 2010 Elena Kagan was sworn in to the Court, making it the first time three women have ever served as justices on the Court at the same time. In the executive branch, no woman has ever been elected either president or vice president of the United States, although Hillary Clinton challenged that barrier in 2016.

Violence Against Women As the story of Woineshet Zebene at the beginning of this chapter suggests, violence against women is a global problem. The full extent of such violence, both in the United States and abroad, is unknown because such crimes often go unreported and unrecognized. Globally, the World Health Organization estimates that 35.6 percent of women have been victims of sexual or physical violence by an intimate partner. Rates vary significantly by region including 65.6 percent in central sub-Saharan Africa and 41.7 percent in South Asia to 16.3 percent in East Asia and 19.3 percent in western Europe (World Health Organization 2013b).

Violence against women in the United States remains a significant problem. According to the National Crime Victimization Survey (see Chapter 6), there were 300,170 rapes and sexual assaults in 2013. Overall, only 34.8 percent of these rapes and sexual assaults were reported to police (Truman and Langton 2014). Other studies suggest that the likelihood of reporting such acts to police may be significantly lower.

Research shows that women and girls of all ages are subject to acts of violence. Among high school girls, 13 percent had been hit, slapped, or physically hurt on purpose

Bineta Diop, founder of Femmes Africa Solidarité, which focuses on women-led peace building, was one of Time magazine's 100 Most Influential People in the World in 2011.   Photo: © Elisabetta Villa/Getty Images.

Going GLOBAL

Gender Inequality in Industrial Nations

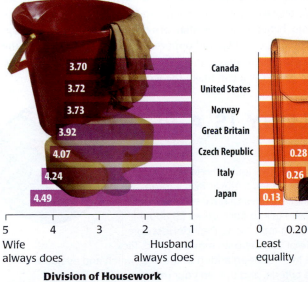

Country	Division of Housework	Empowerment
Canada	3.70	0.81
United States	3.72	0.68
Norway	3.73	1.00
Great Britain	3.92	0.46
Czech Republic	4.07	0.28
Italy	4.24	0.26
Japan	4.49	0.13

Division of Housework scale: 5 (Wife always does) 4 3 2 1 (Husband always does)

Empowerment scale: 0 (Least equality) 0.20 0.40 0.60 0.80 1.00 (Most equality)

Division of Housework
(includes laundry, grocery shopping, dinner preparation, and care for sick family members)

Empowerment
(includes the proportions of women in parliament, in management, and in professional/technical positions)

Striking differences exist in women's empowerment—that is, the percentage of women in leadership positions—from one country to the next (right). Yet there is much less difference in the division of housework, even in the same countries (left).

Source: Adapted from Fuwa 2004:757.   Photos: bucket: © Ingram Publishing/Alamy RF; briefcase: © Leonold Nyshko/Getty Images RF.

by their boyfriend or girlfriend in the previous year, and 14.4 percent had been physically forced to have sexual intercourse when they did not want to (Centers for Disease Control and Prevention 2014c:Table 21). In a survey of college women, 19 percent experienced either an attempted or completed sexual assault while in college. Overall, 3.4 percent of college women had been forcibly raped and 8.5 percent had been raped while incapacitated—drunk, passed out, drugged, or asleep. Among college women who were victims of a forced sexual assault, only 13 percent reported it to police or campus security, though 69 percent disclosed the incident to a family member or friend (Krebs et al. 2007). In a national survey of adult women in the United States, researchers found that 18 percent had been raped at some point in their lifetime. Only 16 percent of these women had reported it to law enforcement officials (Kilpatrick et al. 2007). And in the most extreme form of violence, 2,340 women were murdered by their intimate partners in 2007 (Catalano et al. 2009).

The likelihood of violence against women is shaped in part by cultural attitudes about women, along with the relative power women possess in society. As Kristof and WuDunn (2009) put it, "People get away with enslaving village girls for the same reason that people got away with enslaving blacks two hundred years ago: The victims are perceived as discounted humans" (p. 24).

Increased education and opportunity for women, they suggest, leads to a curtailing of violence. In the United States, the fight for self-determination by women has had a substantial effect on opportunity for women in politics, the workplace, and relationships.

WOMEN AROUND THE WORLD

Globally, women grow half the world's food, but they rarely own land. They constitute one-third of the world's paid labor force but frequently hold the lowest-paying jobs. Women workers often toil long hours for low pay, contributing significantly to their families' incomes, and still bear the responsibility for the majority of unpaid labor in society (OECD 2011; Quisumbing, Meinzen-Dick, and Bassett 2008; UNCTAD 2009).

Opportunities for women vary significantly around the world. In an attempt to quantify the degree of global gender inequality, the World Economic Forum releases an annual report ranking nations in four areas: the economy, education, health, and politics. The resulting Gender Gap Index score for each country ranges from 0 to 1. In 2014 only five countries—Iceland, Finland, Norway, Sweden, and Denmark—scored above 0.8. The United States ranked 20th, with a score of 0.75, behind nations such as the Philippines, the United Kingdom, South Africa, and Nicaragua. Ten nations, including Yemen, Pakistan, Chad, and Syria, scored below 0.6. Considering each of the four indicators, there were 26 nations that received scores of 1.0 on educational attainment and 35 that had reached virtual equality in health and survival with scores of 0.9796. Scores for economic participation and opportunity were lower with only Burundi scoring above 0.85, and those for political empowerment were the lowest of the four with only Iceland above 0.65. Countries in the Middle East and in Africa had the lowest average rankings, primarily because of their low scores on economic and political indicators (Hausmann et al. 2014).

Although people in most nations agree that women should have equal rights, significant variation exists. For example, in Egypt, 45 percent of men agree, compared to 76 percent of women, a gap of 31 percent. In Nigeria the gap is 21 percent, and in Kenya it is 20. Similar gaps exist in Egypt, Pakistan, and Jordan regarding whether a woman should be able to work outside the home. On the question of education, in Egypt, Pakistan, and India, at least 50 percent believe that a university education is more important for a boy than for a girl (Pew Research Center 2010f).

Globally, when it comes to housework and child care, women spend 2.5 more hours per day doing unpaid labor than do men, according to a study of 29 countries. In some nations, including Mexico, the average is as high as 5 hours more per day (OECD 2011). Sociologist Makiko Fuwa (2004) found that countries that placed greater emphasis on empowerment for women tended to have more balanced housework loads between men and women.

Change is possible. In an effort to address some of the structural inequality that exists, legislators in Norway established minimum quotas for the number of female members of boards of directors for companies. As the architects of the plan put it, "Instead of assuming what people *can't* do at work, provide opportunities for employees to prove what they can do." Norway now has the highest average percentage of female board members of any nation (Norwegian Ministry of Children and Equality 2009).

Sociology often confronts us with things that can make us uncomfortable, such as gender inequality. The point of doing so is a more complete understanding of what we do and why we do it. Such knowledge can lead us to new and better practices that provide greater understanding, fairness, equality, and opportunity. Through practicing the sociological imagination, as Betty Friedan did in the case of gender, we can make the world a better place.

SOCIOLOGY IS A VERB

The Bechdel Test

According to the Bechdel Test, developed by cartoonist Alison Bechdel, a movie fails if three criteria are not met: (1) It has to have at least two women in it, (2) who talk to each other, (3) about something besides a man. Go to BechdelTest.com to see how some of your favorite movies faired. Pick out a movie that has not been added to the site; watch and evaluate it according to the criteria, and upload your results.

For REVIEW

I. **How has our understanding of gender and sexuality shifted over time?**
   - The presumption that gender and sexuality are narrowly determined by our biology has given way to an understanding of both as socially constructed, complex, and multidimensional.

II. **How has opportunity for women in the United States changed over time?**
   - In the 1950s women's primary roles were wife and mother. Since that time, largely because of the efforts of the second wave of the women's movement, their labor force participation and income have risen significantly.

III. **To what extent does gender still shape access to resources?**
   - Women continue to be paid less than men in the same occupations, tend to be segregated into a narrower range of female-dominated occupations, bear greater responsibility for housework, and are underrepresented as elected officials.

SOCVIEWS on Gender and Sexuality

Functionalist View

Gender roles establish the proper behavior, attitudes, and activities expected of men and women for a stable society.

Shifts in sexuality are a consequence of changes in what modern societies need, especially in terms of reproduction, to maintain social order.

Families need both an **instrumental leader** and an **expressive leader**; historically, women's natural gravitation to expressive goals freed men for instrumental tasks, and vice versa.

GENDER ROLES, INSTRUMENTAL LEADER, EXPRESSIVE LEADER
KEY CONCEPTS

Conflict View

The presumption that gender is determined by nature results in a belief that biology is destiny, an ideology that reinforces the existing system of gender inequality.

Heteronormativity is a form of power that limits alternative expressions of sexuality and contributes to discrimination.

Even after the feminist movements produced substantial changes, women still face significant **discrimination** in wages, occupations, and politics.

KEY CONCEPTS
IDEOLOGY, DISCRIMINATION, SEXISM

Interactionist View

Our conceptions of gender and sexuality are not determined by biology but, rather, are the consequences of historical, social, and cultural practices over time.

Male–female differences and heterosexual preferences get reinforced through **everyday interaction,** such as giving trucks to boys and dolls to girls.

The negative responses people have when gender and sexuality norms are broken—reinforce existing dominant roles.

KEY CONCEPTS
SOCIAL CONSTRUCTION, GENDER NORMS, ROLES

MAKE THE CONNECTION

After reviewing the chapter, answer the following questions:

1
How would each of the perspectives seek to explain the experiences of women around the world, such as Woineshet Zebene, who face significant violence and discrimination?

2
How would each of the three perspectives look at the supposition that differences between men and women are "natural" and always have been?

3
How would the macro approaches of the conflict and functionalist perspectives study gender and sexuality differently than the micro approach of the interactionist perspective?

4
How does each perspective contribute to your understanding of your own gender-role socialization?

Pop Quiz

1. **What term do sociologists use to describe the biological differences between males and females?**
   a. gender
   b. sexism
   c. anatomy
   d. sex

2. **What term does geneticist Anne Fausto-Sterling use to describe those who have biological characteristics typically associated with both males and females?**
   a. sex
   b. gender
   c. intersexual
   d. gender displays

3. **When college students conducted an experiment in which they violated expected gender norms, they demonstrated the power of**
   a. gender-role socialization.
   b. biological determinism.
   c. instrumental leadership.
   d. the glass ceiling.

4. **What is the expression used when claiming that gender for men is not narrowly limited to traditional conceptions of masculinity?**
   a. intersexual
   b. gender modification
   c. sex
   d. multiple masculinities

5. **What do groups such as the *berdaches, hijras,* and *xanith* reveal about the nature of sex and gender?**
   a. All societies share the same dimorphic, male–female model of sex.
   b. The number of sex and gender categories varies across cultures.
   c. Socialization plays a significant role in modern societies, but a more limited role in traditional societies.
   d. Sex categories vary across cultures, but expressions of gender are universal.

6. **The primary accomplishment of the first wave of the women's movement was**
   a. making women citizens.
   b. gaining the right to an abortion.
   c. earning the right to nondiscrimination in the workplace.
   d. winning the right to vote.

7. **What term describes the categories of people to whom we are sexually attracted?**
   a. heteronormativity
   b. sexual orientation
   c. sexuality
   d. sexual displays

8. **According to early sociologists Talcott Parsons and Robert Bales, which type of leader bears responsibility for completion of tasks, focuses on more-distant goals, and manages the external relationship between the family and other social institutions?**
   a. expressive
   b. charismatic
   c. instrumental
   d. traditional

9. **Overall, when comparing full-time, year-round workers, how much do women earn compared to every dollar men earn?**
   a. 42 cents
   b. 63 cents
   c. 78 cents
   d. 92 cents

10. **The expression "second shift" refers to**
    a. doing the emotional work of maintaining family relationships.
    b. maintaining the household including housework in addition to a job outside the home.
    c. having a work shift ranging approximately between 4:00 P.M. and midnight.
    d. doing paid labor at the workplace.

1. (d), 2. (c), 3. (a), 4. (d), 5. (b), 6. (d), 7. (b), 8. (c), 9. (c), 10. (b)

13

Race and Ethnicity

© Kim Kim Foster/The State/MCT/Getty Images

#BLACKLIVESMATTER

On August 9, 2014, in Ferguson, Missouri, Michael Brown was stopped by Officer Darren Wilson because Brown matched the just-broadcast description of a suspect who stole cigarillos from a nearby convenience store. A confrontation ensued. By the time it was over, Wilson had fired 12 shots and Brown, who was unarmed, lay dead in the street. Eyewitness accounts of the encounter conflicted, some arguing Brown turned at one point and raised his hands in surrender. Wilson claimed that Brown reached for what might have been a weapon and charged at him. Huge protests broke out in the days that followed, and "Hand's up, don't shoot!" became a rallying cry.

Michael Brown's case was but one of a series of high-profile incidents involving police officers killing African American males. On July 17, 2014, in New York City, Eric Garner, 43, was put into a choke hold by Officer Daniel Pantaleo, a maneuver prohibited by NYPD policy, and brought to the ground. The whole encounter was caught on video and Garner can be heard repeatedly saying, "I can't breathe. I can't breathe." He died of cardiac arrest on the way to the hospital.

On November 22, 2014, Tamir Rice, 12, was playing around in a Cleveland, Ohio, park with a toy Airsoft pistol he'd just received from a friend. Police were called and when Officer Timothy Loehmann arrived on the scene, he jumped out of his squad car and, within two seconds, fired shots at Rice, killing him. Loehmann claimed to have asked Rice three times to put up his hands and that Rice failed to do so.

On April 4, 2015, in North Charleston, South Carolina, Walter Scott, 50, was pulled over for a broken taillight. During the stop, Scott jumped out of his car and took off running. When Officer Michael Slager caught up to Scott, a struggle ensued during which, according to the officer, Scott tried to grab his Taser. Scott, who was unarmed, then ran again, a retreat filmed on a bystander's cell phone, and Slager fired eight times, hitting Scott in the back, killing him.

When it comes to the consequences of difference, one of the lessons we learn, over and over again, is that African American men too often pay with their lives.

As You READ >>

- How do sociologists define race and ethnicity?
- What are prejudice and discrimination, and how do they operate?
- What are the consequences of race and ethnicity for opportunity?

>> Racial and Ethnic Groups

Race has been a vexing issue in the United States since its founding, and even before that. The establishment of the first permanent English settlement in the Americas at Jamestown in 1607 began a long-running rocky relationship between the European settlers and the already present Native Americans. The settlement would likely not have survived had it not been for the assistance it received, especially in the form of food, from the 25,000-member Powhatan tribe, including Pocahontas, the daughter of Chief Powhatan (Price 2003). To make money, the settlers turned toward planting tobacco—a skill taught them by the Powhatans—which resulted in their seizing more and more land, leading to a cycle of violence. In the Massacre of 1622, members of the Powhatan tribe attacked Jamestown, killing 347 English settlers. The settlers then used this attack to justify going on the offensive, setting the stage over the next centuries of back-and-forth encounters across the continent between Native Americans and European settlers (Woolley 2007).

Concurrently, African slaves were brought to Point Comfort, near Jamestown, in 1619. The Africans were purchased from Captain John Colyn Jope, a Calvinist minister and ship commander, in exchange for food "at the best and easyest rate they could [obtain]" (Sluiter 1997:396). Jope had seized the Africans from the *São João Bautista*, a Portuguese slave ship that was headed from Luanda, Angola, to Vera Cruz, one of the main ports of entry for African slaves in what is now Mexico (Hashaw 2007; Sluiter 1997). In all likelihood, the Africans were relatively recent captives from the area around Luanda (Thornton 1998). Jamestown's labor-intensive tobacco economy required many workers, and indentured servants—who worked for some established period of time to pay off their passage to the New World—made up a majority of the workforce. It is likely that at least some of these African slaves were treated as indentured servants who later gained their freedom while others may have been enslaved for life (Hashaw 2007; Wood 1997).

These two examples point toward the perseverance of racial conflict throughout American history, the ramifications of which continue into the present. Sociologists, in their quest to describe and explain the consequences of difference, explore issues of race and ethnicity over time and across cultures. To better understand how they do so, we must first clarify what we mean by these two related concepts. **Race** refers to biological differences between humans, defined as socially significant and presumed to divide the population into genetically distinct subgroups. **Ethnicity** refers to the cultural differences between humans, defined as socially significant and presumed to divide the population into socially distinct subgroups. Racial differences typically include variations in skin color, facial

race Biological differences between humans, defined as socially significant and presumed to divide the population into genetically distinct subgroups.

ethnicity The cultural differences between humans, defined as socially significant and presumed to divide the population into socially distinct subgroups.

Did You Know?
. . . In 2012, 49 percent of U.S. public school students were members of a racial or ethnic minority. This represents an increase from 35.2 percent in 1995.

Source: National Center for Education Statistics 2014:Table 203.50. *Photo:* © Image Source, all rights reserved RF.

Racial and Ethnic Groups in the United States

Classification	Number in Thousands	Percentage of Total Population
Racial Groups		
Whites (non-Hispanic)	197,392	62.4%
Blacks/African Americans	38,808	12.3
Asian Americans	15,841	5.0
Chinese	3,782	1.2
Asian Indians	3,189	1.0
Filipinos	2,665	0.8
Vietnamese	1,693	0.5
Koreans	1,446	0.5
Japanese	794	0.3
Native Hawaiian/Pacific Islanders	482	0.2
American Indians, Alaska Natives	2,059	0.7
Ethnic Groups		
White (single or mixed, non-Hispanic)		
Germans	46,163	14.6
Irish	33,348	10.5
English	24,484	7.7
Italians	17,235	5.5
Poles	9,383	3.0
Scottish and Scotch-Irish	8,287	2.6
French	8,229	2.6
Hispanics (or Latinos)	53,986	17.1
Mexican Americans	34,586	10.9
Puerto Ricans	5,138	1.6
Cubans	2,013	0.6
Salvadorans	1,975	0.6
Guatemalans	1,303	2.4
Dominicans	1,258	0.4
Total (all groups)	**316,129**	

Source: U.S. Census Bureau 2014g: Table S0201.

© Jeff Greenberg/Alamy

features, hair texture and color, and the like, while ethnic differences manifest themselves through varieties of customs, languages, food preferences, and so on. A relevant third term, **minority groups,** refers to a subordinate group whose members, even if they represent a numeric majority, lack access to and control over valued resources in society.

RACE

Historically in the United States, it was presumed that racial categorization was a simple matter: Race was biologically determined in straightforward ways, and the dividing lines between groups were clear. It was also assumed that, for the most part, a person's parents would both be of the same race, so identifying a child's racial makeup was also a simple matter. Of course there were times when people from different racial groups had children. In the 19th century, potential ambiguity was resolved in the United States by establishing the "one-drop rule." In that case, if a person had any ancestors who were Black, no matter how many generations back, the person was labeled Black, even if he or she appeared to be White.

We now know that such simplistic attempts to define race in narrowly biological terms say more about society than biology. Modern scientific research proves that no clear biological dividing lines exist between racial groups. That doesn't mean that biological variation attributed to racial difference doesn't exist; it certainly does. The key is whether or not such differences justify the division of the human population into distinct races.

When it comes to genetic variation, the biological differences within what we think of as racial groups are actually greater than the differences between those groups. Genetic researchers Luca Cavalli-Sforza, Paolo Menozzi, and Alberto Piazza (1994), for example, point out that people from northeast China are genetically closer to Europeans, Eskimos, and North American Indians than they are to people from south China (p. 84). In fact, the overall degree of human genetic variation is quite small when compared with genetic variation among other large mammals—due primarily to the fact that communities of human beings have always interacted and reproduced, even across great distances (Greenwood 2013; MacEachern 2003:20). To put it in simple terms, humans have always been sleeping with people from the next tribe over.

Scientists working on the Human Genome Project (HGP) have mapped all the genes of human beings, providing us with the most detailed description of our biological makeup available. They concluded that race as we understand it does not exist. Around the globe, we simply share too many genes. Craig Venter (2000), one of the project's lead scientists, declared in his presentation of the HGP results that "the concept of race has no genetic or scientific basis," and in a later interview, he said, "Race is a social concept, not a scientific one" (quoted in Angier 2000). The researchers found that apparent differences, such as in skin color, represent different combinations, in greater or lesser degrees, of the same shared genes.

Social Construction of Race To understand race, we must move beyond biology to understand the ways in which we socially construct racial categories. If we look cross-culturally, we see that different groups define racial categories in different ways at different times. Each society defines which physical differences are important while ignoring other characteristics that could serve as a basis for social differentiation. In the United States, we see differences in both skin color and hair color, yet people learn that differences in skin color have a dramatic social and political meaning whereas differences in hair color do not.

When observing skin color, many people in the United States tend to lump others rather casually into the traditional categories of "Black," "White," and "Asian." More-subtle differences in skin color often go unnoticed. In many nations of Central America and South America, by contrast, people recognize skin color gradients on a continuum from light to dark. Brazil has approximately 40 color groupings, and in other countries people may be described as "Mestizo Honduran," "Mulatto Colombian," or "African Panamanian." What can seem "obvious" in one cultural context may not seem so in another.

We develop our understanding of racial categories through the process of what sociologists Michael Omi and Howard Winant (1994) have called **racial formation**—a sociohistorical process in which racial categories are created, inhibited, transformed, and destroyed. Omi and Winant argue that race is neither fundamentally biological nor an illusion that can simply be ignored. To understand race, one must pay careful attention to the social, economic, and political forces that have established it as a basic distinction among human beings. Historically, those in positions of power have categorized whole groups of people as fundamentally distinct from each other (for example, when the one-drop rule was instituted) and then used their control over resources to treat people differently based on those distinctions. The result is a social structure that reinforces presumed racial differences and justifies unequal treatment on the basis of race. The creation of a reservation system for Native Americans in the late 1800s is one example of racial formation. Federal officials combined what were distinctive tribes into a single racial group, which we refer to today as Native Americans.

Given that our understanding of race was rooted in particular historical circumstances, it has shifted over time as those circumstances changed. For example, the massive

Did You Know?

. . . In the 2010 Census, the number of Americans who checked both "Black" and "White" as their race rose 134 percent compared to the 2000 Census. Barack Obama was not one of them. He self-identified as Black.

Source: Cohn 2011.   *Photo:* © Patrick Kelley/USGS.

influx of immigrants in the 19th century, from places such as Ireland, Germany, China, Italy, and eastern Europe, complicated the supposed simplicity of the Black–White divide. These immigrant groups were often judged to be biologically beneath White citizens. For instance, both the Irish and the Italians were regarded as members of another race inferior to Whites. Many African Americans of the time regarded being Irish as lower socially than being Black. Over time, both the Irish and the Italians came to be seen as two White ethnic groups. This was accomplished in part by positioning themselves as distinct from African Americans in order to identify more closely with the White majority (Guglielmo 2003; Ignatiev 1995; Roediger 2005).

minority group A subordinate group whose members, even if they represent a numeric majority, lack access to, and control over, valued resources in society

racial formation A sociohistorical process in which racial categories are created, inhibited, transformed, and destroyed.

© Steve Granitz/WireImage/Getty Images

Even though these differences are socially constructed, their consequences are no less real. Race is often used to justify unequal access to economic, social, and cultural resources based on the assumption that such inequality is somehow "natural." This can happen through the use of **stereotypes,** for example, which are unreliable generalizations about all members of a group that do not recognize individual differences within the group. Anthropologist Ashley Montagu (1997), who was at the forefront of the movement to use scientific evidence to demonstrate the socially constructed nature of race, suggested that "the very word (*race*) is racist; that the idea of 'race,' implying the existence of significant biologically determined mental differences rendering some populations inferior to others, is wholly false" (p. 35).

stereotype An unreliable generalization about all members of a group that does not recognize individual differences within the group.

Multiple Identities As the number of people who consider themselves biracial or multiracial grows, the limits of our racial categories become increasingly apparent. Prominent figures have helped bring this trend into the limelight. Golfer Tiger Woods provides a classic example. Woods created his own racial category, referring to himself as "Cablinasian," a combination of his Caucasian, Black, American Indian, and Asian (Chinese and Thai) ancestry. Other examples include President Barack Obama, who had a Black father originally from Kenya and a White mother originally from Kansas, and Academy Award–winning actress Halle Berry, who had an African American father and a White, British-born mother.

In recognition of the growing diversity of the U.S. population, and the growing numbers of interracial marriages, for the first time in 2000 and again in 2010 the U.S. Census allowed people to select more than one category when identifying their race. People can now choose from five major race categories—White, Black, Asian, Native American, and Native Hawaiian or Other Pacific Islander—in addition to "Some other race." Considering all the combinations people might select, a total of 57 race categories are now possible (Humes et al. 2011).

In the 2010 Census more than 9 million people in the United States, 2.9 percent overall, reported that they were of two or more races. Of these, 20.4 percent chose both Black and White, the most frequent combination. Within racial categories, more than half of those who chose Native Hawaiian or Other Pacific Islander also selected another race, whereas those who self-identified as White were least likely to do so (Humes et al. 2011).

This expansion of possible racial categories is part of the Census Bureau's ongoing effort to provide a snapshot of race as it is understood at various points in U.S. history. As the "U.S. Race Categories, 1790–2010" table demonstrates, racial categories used by the Census Bureau have shifted over time. The most recent expansion to allow multiracial identification is a direct consequence of the limitations of using fewer categories to reflect an increasingly diverse society. To get an accurate count, the Census Bureau needs categories that are mutually exclusive, meaning that each individual fits in one place and one place only. To do so, it must expand the number of available options beyond the three- or five-race models that historically seemed, by common sense, to be sufficient.

Puerto Rican Day Parade, New York City. Photo: © Stephen Chernin/Getty Images.

ETHNICITY

An ethnic group is set apart from others explicitly because of its national origin or cultural patterns. Distinctive characteristics can include language, diet, sports, and religious beliefs, along with various traditions, norms, and values. Among the ethnic groups in the United States are peoples with a Spanish-speaking background, referred to collectively as Latinos or Hispanics, such as Puerto Ricans, Mexican Americans, and Cuban Americans. Other ethnic groups in this country include Jewish, Irish, Italian, and Norwegian Americans.

The distinction between race and ethnicity is not always clear-cut. While the conventional approach views race as biological and ethnicity as cultural, racial groups express their identity in cultural ways (including language, norms, values, diet, and so on). Alternatively, ethnic groups may self-identify as a race. The Census Bureau runs into this difficulty in its attempt to catalog each. It treats race and ethnicity as separate items, but in its ethnicity question, the only category recognized is "Hispanic, Latino, or Spanish origin." This situation creates difficulties for groups that see themselves as a distinct ethnicity and find the race options inadequate to describe who they are. In such circumstances, many people choose "Some other race" and then write in an ethnicity or nationality (such as Mexican, Iranian, or Saudi Arabian) as their race. In the 2010 Census, of those who selected "other," 97 percent also selected Hispanic as their ethnicity. In fact, 41 percent of those who self-identified as Hispanic also selected "Some other race" (Humes et al. 2011; U.S. Commission on Civil Rights 2009:4).

The Census has continued to try to make these categories clear. In an attempt to clarify confusion about the relationship between race and ethnicity, the 2010 Census included the line "For this census, Hispanic origins are not races" (U.S. Census Bureau 2010c). In preparation for the 2020 Census, in keeping with the way people self-identify using elements of both biological ancestry and cultural heritage,

U.S. Race Categories, 1790–2010

Year	Race Categories
1790	Free white males Free white females All other free persons Slaves
1890	White Black Mulatto Chinese Indian
1940	White Negro Indian Chinese, Japanese, Filipino, Hindu, Korean Other
1990	White Black or Negro American Indian Eskimo Aleut Asian or Pacific Islander, Chinese, Filipino, Hawaiian, Korean, Vietnamese, Japanese, Asian Indian, Samoan, Guamanian, other Asian or Pacific Islander Other race
2010	White Black, African American, or Negro American Indian or Alaska Native (print name of tribe) Asian: Asian Indian, Chinese, Filipino, Japanese, Korean, Vietnamese, Other Asian Native Hawaiian, Guamanian or Chamorro, Samoan, or Other Pacific Islander Some other race (print race)

Sources: Nobles 2000:1739; U.S. Census Bureau 2010c.   *Photo:* © Ryan McVay/Getty Images RF.

Did You Know?

. . . Of the Muslims in the United States, **65 percent are foreign born.** Of those who were born here, **about one-half are African American.** Approximately **one-fourth of all U.S. Muslims are third generation.**

Photo: © AP Photo/Bob Child.

officials are considering collapsing race and ethnicity into a single question, effectively making Hispanic into a racial category (Krogstad and Cohn 2014). To address the limitations of the ethnicity question, the Census also studied the possibility of expanding it to include additional options (for example, German, French, Italian) to more fully reflect people's self-identified ethnic origin (U.S. Commission on Civil Rights 2009). As currently practiced, the Census further complicates things by including some ethnic nationalities as examples within racial categories (for example, Japanese and Chinese as examples in the Asian category) but does not do so for others (for instance, White or Black). Such examples highlight the fact that race and ethnicity are more complex in practice than the commonsense models we may believe.

prejudice A preconceived and unjustified judgment of individuals, whether positive or negative, based on their membership in a particular group.

racism The belief that one race is supreme and all others are innately inferior.

>> Prejudice and Discrimination

The social significance we attach to biological and cultural differences can have life and death consequences. Defining descendants from Africa as less than fully human enabled the justification of slavery as an institution in the United States for nearly its first 100 years. In keeping with the Thomas theorem (see Chapter 1), we need to be particularly attentive to those things we perceive to be true because our perceptions shape our actions. When it comes to race and ethnicity, perception in the form of prejudice is often linked to discrimination, a type of action.

PREJUDICE

Prejudice is a preconceived and unjustified judgment of individuals, whether positive or negative, based on their membership in a particular group. Defining characteristics frequently include race and ethnicity, but prejudice may also be based on gender, disability, age, or other statuses. Frequently, prejudice results from *ethnocentrism*—the tendency to assume that one's own culture and way of life represent the norm or are superior to all others. Ethnocentric people judge other cultures by the standards of their own group without taking into account the perspectives and experiences of others. This often leads to prejudice against cultures they view as inferior.

One important and widespread ideology that reinforces prejudice is **racism**—the belief that one race is supreme and all others are innately inferior. Such beliefs may exist even if they are not explicitly stated as part of a society's dominant values. Over the past three generations, nationwide surveys have consistently shown growing support

Before passage of the Civil Rights Act in 1964, segregation of public accommodations was the norm throughout the South.
Photo: © Bruce Roberts/Science Source.

Hate Crime Offenses

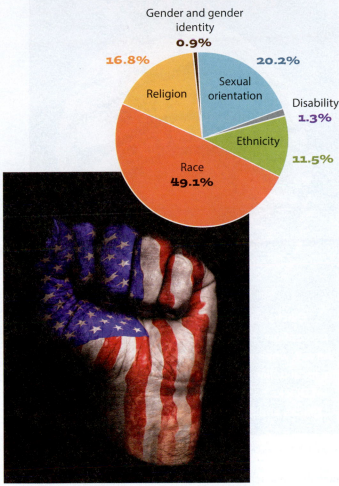

Gender and gender identity
0.9%

Sexual orientation
20.2%

Religion
16.8%

Disability
1.3%

Ethnicity
11.5%

Race
49.1%

Source: U.S. Department of Justice 2014c:Table 1.
Photo: © Duncan Walker/Getty Images RF.

among Whites for integration, interracial dating, and the election of minority group members to public office—including even the presidency of the United States. Nevertheless, there are persistent patterns of unequal treatment. People claim not to be prejudiced, affirming principles such as equal opportunity, yet many fail to put these ideals into practice.

Some sociologists suggest that **color-blind racism,** which uses the principle of race neutrality to perpetuate a racially unequal status quo, is at work (Bonilla-Silva 2010). In such cases, commitment to the principle of equality actually serves to perpetuate inequality. In a system where inequality based on race and ethnicity is built into the structure of society, unwillingness to address these issues explicitly in those terms serves to perpetuate the status quo. Although the practice might seem counter to the principle of equality, some nations have established quotas in political representation

and hiring to force the social structure to provide greater opportunity, a practice that is controversial in the United States.

DISCRIMINATION

Prejudice often leads to **discrimination,** the practice of denying equal access to opportunities and resources on the basis of group membership rather than merit or rights. As is the case with prejudice, discrimination may be based on membership in a racial or ethnic group, but can also be determined by sex, age, disability, and other statuses. Prejudice concerns what we think; discrimination involves what we do.

Interpersonal Discrimination When discrimination is practiced, it is experienced on an interpersonal level. It occurs when a particular individual in a position of relative power acts to deny someone something of value, for example a job, a promotion, an opportunity to volunteer, or a seat on a bus. Though often rooted in prejudice, the two are not always linked. A prejudiced company president who is White, for example, might choose—despite her or his prejudices—to hire a Guatemalan American because that person is the most qualified. That would be prejudice without discrimination. On the other hand, a White corporate president with a completely respectful view of Guatemalan Americans might refuse to hire them for executive posts out of fear that biased clients would take their business elsewhere. In that case, the president's action would constitute discrimination without prejudice.

> **color-blind racism** The use of race-neutral principles to perpetuate a racially unequal status quo.

> **discrimination** The practice of denying equal access to opportunities and resources on the basis of group membership rather than merit or rights.

To better track the scope of overt racist acts in the United States, Congress passed the Hate Crime Statistics

Members of the Ku Klux Klan, masked in white robes and hoods, used nighttime cross-burnings to instill terror. Photo: © William Campbell/Sygma/Corbis.

Act in 1990. A **hate crime** is a criminal offense committed because of the offender's bias against an individual based on race, religion, ethnicity, national origin, or sexual orientation. The act was amended in 2009 to also include gender and gender identity. In 2013, 6,933 hate crime offenses were reported to authorities. Overall, 60.6 percent of those crimes involved racial or ethnic bias (Department of Justice 2014c:Table 1). Offenses include crimes against individuals (including murder, rape, and assault) and crimes against property (such as vandalism, theft, and arson).

hate crime A criminal offense committed because of the offender's bias against an individual based on race, gender, religion, ethnicity, national origin, or sexual orientation.

racial profiling Any police-initiated action based on race, ethnicity, or national origin rather than on a person's behavior.

In sociologist Devah Pager's experiments investigating racial discrimination in hiring (see Chapter 2), a White job applicant with a prison record received slightly more callbacks than a Black applicant with no criminal record. Repeated experiments have produced similar results (Pager 2003, 2007; Pager and Western 2012). Over time, the cumulative impact of such differential behavior contributes to significant differences in access to critical resources.

Racial Profiling Another form of discrimination involves **racial profiling,** which is any arbitrary action initiated by an authority based on race, ethnicity, or national origin rather than on a person's behavior. Generally, racial profiling occurs when law enforcement officers, including customs officials, airport security, and police, assume that people who fit a certain description are likely to engage in illegal activities. For example, whether in the form of Driving While Black (see Chapter 6) or, as we saw at the beginning of this chapter, the possible life-and-death consequences of an encounter with police that goes bad, African American males live in fear that police officers are out to get them. Researchers investigating arrests for marijuana use found that, even when controlling for factors such as prior arrests, prior hard drug use, prior property crimes, prior assault, prior gun carrying, and

neighborhood reputation, African Americans were still substantially more likely to be arrested. As the researchers put it, "the racial disparity in drug arrests between blacks and whites cannot be explained by race differences in the *extent* of drug offending or the *nature* of drug offending. In fact, in this sample, African-Americans (and Hispanics) were no more, and often less, likely to be involved in drug offending than whites" (Mitchell and Caudy 2015:22). The strength of this relationship between race and arrest increased with age, peaking for suspects in their twenties.

After Michael Brown was killed in Ferguson, the U.S. Justice Department conducted an investigation of the police department there. In an analysis of traffic stops, 85 percent of the stops, 90 percent of the citations, and 93 percent of the arrests involved African Americans, even though

Federal troops were needed to support the Supreme Court decision that led to the integration of schools in the 1950s.   Photo: © Bettmann/Corbis.

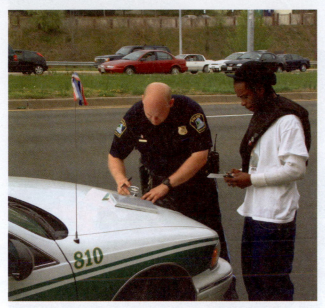

© Tom Carter/PhotoEdit

Institutional Discrimination Persistent patterns of inequality suggest that discrimination is practiced not only by individuals in one-to-one encounters but also by institutions in their daily operations. Social scientists are particularly concerned with the ways in which structural factors, such as employment, housing, health care, and government operations, maintain the social significance of race and ethnicity. As we saw with gender in Chapter 12, *institutional discrimination* refers to the denial of opportunities and equal rights to individuals and groups that results from the normal operations of a society. This kind of discrimination consistently affects certain racial and ethnic groups more than others.

A telltale sign of institutional discrimination is the ongoing presence of racial and ethnic income inequality. As we saw with the gender wage gap (see Chapter 12), a person's ascribed social status frequently predicts his or her income level. As the "Median Income by Race, Ethnicity,

Blacks represent only 67 percent of the population. During vehicle stops, Black drivers in Ferguson were more than twice as likely to be searched, but 26 percent less likely to have contraband. Based on the study, United States Attorney General Eric Holder concluded, "Our investigation showed that Ferguson police officers routinely violate the Fourth Amendment in stopping people without reasonable suspicion, arresting them without probable cause, and using unreasonable force against them" (U.S. Department of Justice 2015a, 2015b).

The protests following the deaths of Michael Brown and others sought to give voice to the persistent pattern of racial profiling experienced by African Americans in the United States. In an analysis of FBI records of 1,217 deadly police shootings from 2010 to 2012, researchers found that 15- to 19-year-old Black males were killed at a much higher rate than White males of the same age, 31.17 per million compared to 1.47 per million (Gabrielson, Grochowski Jones and Sagara 2014). Of the 426 individuals killed by police during an arrest in 2012, 31 percent were African American, and of those not attacking police while killed, 39 percent were Black (Lind 2015). Unfortunately, these FBI records are not complete—local police department reporting of these details is voluntary—and the actual number of deadly police shootings is likely double (Banks et al. 2015).

In instances where someone dies in an encounter with police, concern exists, especially in the African American community, that the officer's actions do not receive sufficient scrutiny. Out of more than 12,000 death incidents since 2005, 54 officers have been charged after shooting and killing a suspect. Of these cases, two-thirds of the victims were African American, almost always unarmed, and 80 percent of the officers were White. Eleven of the officers were convicted, 21 were set free, and 19 were still pending. Of officers convicted in connection to these deaths, the average sentence was four years (Kindy and Kelly 2015).

Median Income by Race, Ethnicity, and Gender

Median income

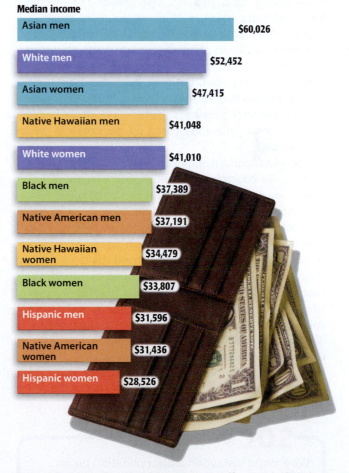

Asian men	$60,026
White men	$52,452
Asian women	$47,415
Native Hawaiian men	$41,048
White women	$41,010
Black men	$37,389
Native American men	$37,191
Native Hawaiian women	$34,479
Black women	$33,807
Hispanic men	$31,596
Native American women	$31,436
Hispanic women	$28,526

Note: Includes only people working full-time, year-round, 16 years and older in the United States. White refers to non-Hispanic Whites.

Source: U.S. Census Bureau 2014g:Table S0201. *Photo:* © Comstock Images/ Jupiter Images RF.

© Francis Miller/Time Life Pictures/Getty Images

and Gender" graph demonstrates, a clear difference exists when taking race, income, and gender into account. Those who are Asian or White make more money, on average, than those from other racial and ethnic groups. A variety of factors, including educational attainment, occupation, and seniority, likely explain some of those gaps. At the very least, however, the income differences point to the fact that the lived experience of individuals—the opportunities presented to them and obstacles they face—varies significantly based on the group to which they belong.

The glass ceiling that limits women's access to top-level positions in business and politics (see Chapter 12) also affects opportunity for members of racial and ethnic minority groups. In 2012, Whites held 86.7 percent of all board of director seats at Fortune 500 companies, African Americans held 7.4 percent, Asian/Pacific Islanders held 2.6 percent, and Hispanics held 3.3 percent. At the level of board chair, the percentages are even more unequal with 95.3 percent being held by men, along with a handful of women, who are White. When looking at the Fortune 100 firms, only small increases in boardroom representation have occurred since 2004 (Catalyst et al. 2013). This is in spite of the fact that research suggests that companies with more diverse boards are more profitable than those that remain more homogeneous (Virtcom 2009).

SOCTHINK

Why might institutional discrimination be an even greater concern than interpersonal discrimination?

Attempts have been made to eradicate or compensate for discrimination in the United States. The 1960s saw the passage of many pioneering civil rights laws, including the landmark 1964 Civil Rights Act, which prohibits discrimination in public accommodations and publicly owned facilities on the basis of race, color, creed, national origin, and gender. In two important rulings in 1987, the Supreme Court held that federal prohibitions against racial discrimination protect members of all ethnic minorities—including Hispanics, Jews, and Arab Americans—even though they may be considered White.

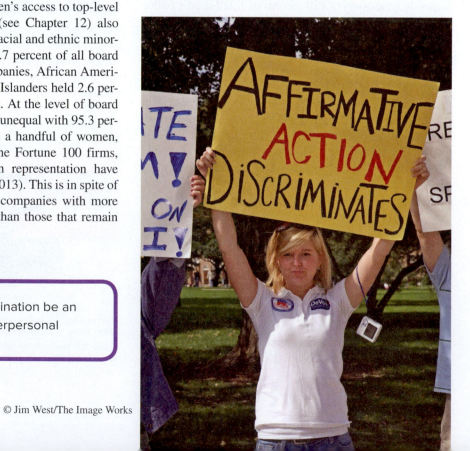

© Jim West/The Image Works

For more than 40 years, government, schools, and industry have instituted affirmative action programs to overcome past discrimination. **Affirmative action** refers to positive efforts to recruit minority group members or women for jobs, promotions, and educational opportunities. Many people resent these programs, arguing that advancing one group's cause merely shifts the discrimination to another group. By giving priority to African Americans in admissions, for example, schools may deny more academically qualified White candidates. In many parts of the country and many sectors of the economy, affirmative action is being rolled back, even though it was never fully implemented.

Discriminatory practices continue to pervade nearly all areas of life in the United States. In part, that is because various individuals and groups actually benefit from racial and ethnic discrimination in terms of money, status, and influence. Discrimination permits members of the majority to enhance their wealth, power, and prestige at the expense of others. Less qualified people get jobs and promotions simply because they are members of the dominant group. Such individuals and groups will not surrender these advantages easily.

>> Sociological Perspectives on Race and Ethnicity

Sociologists seek to understand and explain why prejudice and discrimination develop and persist and what might be done to address them. As we have seen, often such negative characteristics exist because they serve certain interests. Here we look at how prejudice and discrimination contribute to the maintenance of the existing social order by reinforcing the dominant culture.

SOCIAL ORDER AND INEQUALITY

From the functionalist perspective in sociology, if something in society persists over long periods of time, it must contribute to social order in some positive way. If true, one possible conclusion about prejudice and discrimination is that they help us build and maintain a stronger sense of social identity and integration, even if it is at the expense of others. Just as responses to crime help unify society in opposition to the criminal (see Chapter 6), pointing to the racial or ethnic "other" can help unify "us" against "them," even though the consequences can be devastating for those against whom prejudice and discrimination are practiced.

When prejudice and discrimination become built into the institutional structure of society, they help preserve the existing system of inequality. **Exploitation theory,** for example, argues that such practices are a basic part of the capitalist economic system (Blauner 1972; Cox 1948; Hunter 2000). Racism keeps minorities in low-paying jobs,

thereby supplying the capitalist ruling class with a pool of cheap labor. Moreover, by forcing racial minorities to accept low wages, capitalists can restrict the wages of all members of the proletariat.

Perceptions of Discrimination

Black respondents

Hispanic respondents

White respondents

How often do Blacks face discrimination when . . . ?

Applying to a college or university

Applying for a job

Renting an apartment or buying a house

Eating at a restaurant or shopping in a retail store

Almost always/frequently

Not often/hardly ever

Source: Pew Research Center 2007:30.

SOCstudies

affirmative action Positive efforts to recruit minority group members or women for jobs, promotions, and educational opportunities.

exploitation theory A belief that views racial subordination in the United States as a manifestation of the class system inherent in capitalism.

SOC THINK

What are the cost and benefits of establishing hiring quotas based on race, ethnicity, or gender to ensure greater opportunity?

Business owners can always replace workers from the dominant group who demand higher wages with minorities who have no choice but to accept low-paying jobs. This increases the likelihood that working-class members of the majority group will develop racist attitudes toward working-class members of minority groups, whom they view as threats to their jobs. As a result, they direct their hostilities not toward the capitalists but toward other workers, thereby not challenging the structure of the existing system.

Maintaining these practices, however, comes at significant cost to society. For example, a society that practices discrimination fails to use the resources of all individuals. Discrimination limits the search for talent and leadership to the dominant group. Discrimination also aggravates social problems such as poverty, delinquency, and crime. Such effects require the investment of a good deal of time and money in which the primary goal is to maintain barriers to the full participation of all members (Rose 1951).

contact hypothesis The theory that in cooperative circumstances interracial contact between people of equal status will reduce prejudice.

genocide The deliberate, systematic killing of an entire people or nation.

Challenging prejudice and discrimination, however, involves questioning taken-for-granted views of the world in which people have invested their faith and trust. Women in the 1950s in the United States had to do just that. They challenged the idea that it was "natural" for women to stay at home and have babies rather than get an education and enter the paid labor force. During the same time, workers in the civil rights movement faced a similar challenge in confronting social attitudes that represented barriers to the full participation of African Americans in U.S. society.

THE CONTACT HYPOTHESIS

At its heart, racism is about division, separating the human population into us versus them. As society becomes more global and interdependent, more people from diverse cultural backgrounds have increased opportunities to interact with others unlike them on a daily basis. When people interact with others as people, rather than as stereotypes or distant others, the possibility arises for prejudice and discrimination to decrease.

The **contact hypothesis** states that in cooperative circumstances, interracial contact between people of equal status will cause them to become less prejudiced and to abandon old stereotypes. People begin to see one another as individuals and to discard the broad generalizations characteristic of stereotyping. Note the phrases "equal status" and "cooperative circumstances." When workers from different racial or ethnic groups compete with each other for valued resources, rather than cooperate toward shared goals, hostilities can actually increase, highlighting the significance of power and position when it comes to the issue of racism (Allport 1979; Fine 2008).

As Latinos and other minorities slowly gain access to better-paying and higher-responsibility jobs, the contact hypothesis may take on even greater significance. The trend in our society is toward increasing contact between individuals from dominant and subordinate groups. That may be one way of eliminating—or at least reducing—racial and ethnic stereotyping and prejudice. Another may be the establishment of interracial coalitions, an idea suggested by sociologist William Julius Wilson (1999). To work, such coalitions would obviously need to provide an equal role for all members.

PATTERNS OF INTERGROUP RELATIONS

The possibility of equal status, however, is shaped by how societies handle racial and ethnic differences. Some societies are more open to diverse groups maintaining their cultural traditions. Others pressure groups to abandon their beliefs and practices in favor of those of the dominant society. We will focus on six characteristic patterns of intergroup relations: genocide, expulsion, amalgamation, assimilation, segregation, and pluralism. Each pattern defines the dominant group's actions and the minority group's responses. The first two are relatively rare, though their consequences are extreme; the final four are more common.

Genocide The most devastating pattern of intergroup relations is **genocide**—the deliberate, systematic killing of an entire people or nation. This is precisely what happened

Civil rights activist Rosa Parks being fingerprinted upon her arrest in 1955 for her act of civil disobedience in refusing to give up her seat on a bus to a White man.   Photo: © AP Photo/Gene Herrick.

Movies

on RACE AND ETHNICITY

5

Selma
Marching to Montgomery for voting rights.

District 9
A sci-fi movie takes on segregation.

Fruitvale Station
The death and life of a young, African American father.

Real Women Have Curves
Hispanic American women adapt to life in the United States.

The Overnights
A 21st-century Grapes of Wrath–style migration to North Dakota.

when Turkish authorities killed 1 million Armenians beginning in 1915. The term is most commonly associated with Nazi Germany's extermination of 6 million European Jews, along with gays, lesbians, and the Romani people ("Gypsies"), during World War II. The term also describes the United States' policies toward Native Americans in the 19th century. In 1800 the Native American (or American Indian) population of the United States was about 600,000;

POPSOC

As part of their annual study of the top 100 films, researchers at USC's Annenberg School for Communication and Journalism found that, out of the 3,932 speaking roles they identified, 74.1 percent were White. The percentage of Black characters, at 14.1, closely approximated their proportion of the U.S. population, but Hispanics, at 4.9 percent, were significantly underrepresented in these films.

Source: Smith, Choueiti, and Pieper 2014. *Photo:* Atsush Nishjima/© Paramount Pictures/Courtesy Everett Collection.

by 1850 warfare with the U.S. cavalry, disease, and forced relocation to inhospitable environments had reduced it to 250,000.

Expulsion Another extreme response is **expulsion**—the systematic removal of a group of people from society. In 1979 Vietnam expelled nearly 1 million ethnic Chinese, partly as a result of centuries of hostility between Vietnam and neighboring China. Similarly, Serbian forces began a program of "ethnic cleansing" in 1991, in the newly independent states of Bosnia and Herzegovina. Throughout the former Yugoslavia, the Serbs drove more than 1 million Croats and Muslims from their homes. Some they tortured and killed; others they abused and terrorized, in an attempt to "purify" the land (Cigar 1995; Petrovic 1994). More recently, the government of Sudan has pushed people off their land and out of the country in Darfur (Steidle 2007).

Amalgamation When a majority group and a minority group combine to form a new group, **amalgamation** results. This often occurs through intermarriage over several generations. This pattern can be expressed as $A + B + C \rightarrow D$, where A, B, and C represent different groups in a society, and D signifies the end result, a unique cultural-racial group unlike any of the initial groups (Newman 1973).

The belief in the United States as a "melting pot" became compelling in the early 20th century, particularly since that image suggested that the nation had an almost divine mission to amalgamate various groups into one people. In actuality, however, many residents were not willing to include Native Americans, Jews, Blacks, Asians, and Irish Roman Catholics in the melting pot. Therefore, this pattern does not adequately describe dominant-subordinate relations in the United States.

Assimilation In India, many Hindus complain about Indian citizens who emulate the traditions and customs of the British. In France, people of Arab and African origin, many of them Muslim, complain they are treated as second-class citizens—a charge that provoked riots in 2005. In Australia, Aborigines who have become part of the dominant society refuse to acknowledge their darker-skinned grandparents on the street. All these cases are examples of the effects of **assimilation**—the process through which a person forsakes his or her own cultural tradition to become part of a different culture. Generally, it is practiced by minority group members who want to conform to the standards

expulsion The systematic removal of a group of people from society.

amalgamation The process through which a majority group and a minority group combine to form a new group.

assimilation The process through which a person forsakes his or her own cultural tradition to become part of a different culture.

of the dominant group. Assimilation can be described as a pattern in which $A + B + C \rightarrow A$. The majority, A, dominates in such a way that members of minorities B and C imitate it and attempt to become indistinguishable from it (Newman 1973).

Assimilation can strike at the very roots of a person's identity. In the United States, some immigrants have changed their ethnic-sounding family names to names that better fit into the dominant White Protestant culture. Jennifer Anastassakis, for example, changed her name to Jennifer Aniston, Ralph Lipschitz became Ralph Lauren, Natalie Portman switched from Natalie Hershlag, and the Academy Award–winning British actress Helen Mirren gave up her birth name of Ilyena Vasilievna Mironova. Name changes, switches in religious affiliation, and the dropping of native languages can obscure one's roots and heritage. Especially across generations, assimilation can lead to the virtual death of a culture in that family's history. It is not uncommon for grandchildren

segregation The physical separation of two groups of people in terms of residence, workplace, and social events; often imposed on a minority group by a dominant group.

apartheid A former policy of the South African government, designed to maintain the separation of Blacks and other non-Whites from the dominant Whites.

of immigrants who have not learned the language or the cultural traditions of their ancestors to regret this loss.

Segregation Separate schools, separate seating on buses and in restaurants, separate washrooms, even separate drinking fountains—these were all part of the lives of African Americans in the South when segregation ruled early in the 20th century. **Segregation** refers to the physical separation of two groups of people in terms of residence, workplace, and social events. Generally, a dominant group imposes this pattern on a minority group. Segregation is rarely complete, however. Intergroup contact inevitably occurs, even in the most segregated societies.

From 1948 (when it received its independence) to 1990, the Republic of South Africa severely restricted the movement of Blacks and other non-Whites by means of a wide-ranging system of segregation known as **apartheid.** Apartheid even included the creation of separate homelands where Blacks were expected to live. However, decades of local resistance to apartheid, combined with international pressure, led to marked political changes in the 1990s. In 1994 a prominent Black activist, Nelson Mandela, became South Africa's president in the first election in which Blacks (the majority of the nation's population) were allowed to vote. Mandela had spent almost 28 years in South African prisons for his anti-apartheid activities. His election was widely viewed as the final blow to South Africa's oppressive policy of segregation.

Former South African President Nelson Mandela oversaw that country's transition from a segregated society. Photo: © Daniel Berehulak/Getty Images.

© David McNew/Getty Images

Long-entrenched social patterns are difficult to change, however. A recent analysis of living patterns in U.S. metropolitan areas shows that, despite federal laws that forbid housing discrimination, residential segregation is still the norm. Even though 65 percent of Americans say they prefer to live in a racially diverse community, across the nation, neighborhoods remain divided along both racial and ethnic lines. The average White person lives in an area that is at least 83 percent White, whereas the average African American lives in a neighborhood that is mostly Black. The typical Latino lives in an area that is 42 percent Hispanic. The five most segregated U.S. metropolitan areas when it comes to measuring Black–White residential patterns were Milwaukee, Wisconsin; New York City; Chicago, Illinois; Detroit, Michigan; and Cleveland, Ohio (Bolt, Ozuekren, and Phillips 2010; Frey 2011; Taylor and Morin 2008).

Pluralism In a pluralistic society, a subordinate group does not have to forsake its lifestyle and traditions. **Pluralism** is based on mutual respect for one another's cultures among the various groups in a society. This pattern allows a minority group to express its own culture and still participate without prejudice in the larger society. Earlier, we described amalgamation as A + B + C → D, and assimilation as A + B + C → A. Using this same approach, we can conceive of pluralism as A + B + C → A + B + C; that is, all the groups coexist in the same society (Newman 1973).

In the United States, pluralism is more of an ideal than a reality. There are distinct instances of pluralism—the ethnic neighborhoods in major cities, such as Koreatown, Little Tokyo, Andersonville (Swedish Americans), and Spanish Harlem—yet there are also limits to cultural freedom. To survive, a society must promote a certain consensus among its members regarding basic ideals, values, and beliefs. Thus, if a Romanian immigrant to the United States wants to move up the occupational ladder, he or she cannot avoid learning English.

> **pluralism** Mutual respect for one another's cultures among the various groups in a society, which allows minorities to express their own cultures without experiencing prejudice.

Switzerland exemplifies the modern pluralistic state. There the absence of both a national language and a dominant religious faith leads to a tolerance for cultural diversity. In addition, various political devices safeguard the interests of ethnic groups in a way that has no parallel in the United States. By contrast, Great Britain has had difficulty achieving cultural pluralism in a multiracial society. East Indians, Pakistanis, and Blacks from the Caribbean and Africa experience prejudice and discrimination within the dominant White society there. Some British advocate cutting off all Asian and Black immigration, and a few even call for expulsion of those non-Whites currently living in Britain.

PRIVILEGE

One often-overlooked aspect of discrimination is the privileges that dominant groups enjoy at the expense of others. For instance, we tend to focus more on the difficulty women have balancing career and family than on the ease with which men avoid household chores and advance in the workplace. Similarly, we concentrate more on discrimination against racial and ethnic minorities than on the advantages members of the White majority enjoy. Indeed, most White people rarely think about their "Whiteness," taking their status for granted. However, sociologists and other social scientists are becoming increasingly interested in what it means to be "White," because White privilege is the other side of the proverbial coin of racial discrimination (Painter 2010).

Feminist scholar Peggy McIntosh (1988) became interested in White privilege after noticing that most men would not acknowledge the privileges attached to being male—even if they would agree that being female had its disadvantages. She wondered whether White people suffer from a similar blind spot regarding their own racial privilege. Intrigued, McIntosh began to list all the ways in which she benefited from her Whiteness. She soon realized that the list of unspoken advantages was long and significant.

McIntosh found that as a White person, she rarely needed to step out of her comfort zone, no matter where she went. If she wished to, she could spend most of her time with people of her own race. She could find a good place to live in a pleasant neighborhood, buy the foods she liked to eat from almost any grocery store, and get her hair styled in almost any salon. She could attend a public meeting without feeling that she did not belong or that she was different from everyone else.

McIntosh discovered, too, that her skin color opened doors for her. She could cash checks and use credit cards without suspicion, and she could browse through stores without being shadowed by security guards. She could be seated without difficulty in a restaurant. If she asked to see the manager, she could assume he or she would be of her own race. If she needed help from a doctor or a lawyer, she could get it.

McIntosh also realized that her Whiteness made the job of parenting easier. She did not need to worry about protecting her children from people who didn't like them because of their race. She could be sure that their books would show pictures of people who looked like them and that their history texts would describe White people's achievements. She knew that the television programs they watched would include White characters.

Finally, McIntosh had to admit that others did not constantly evaluate her in racial terms. When she appeared in public, she didn't need to worry that her clothing or behavior might reflect poorly on White people. If she was recognized for an achievement, it was seen as her own accomplishment, not that of an entire race. And no one ever assumed that the personal opinions she voiced should be those of all White people. Because McIntosh blended in with the people around her, she wasn't always onstage.

> Whites of course have the privilege of not caring, of being colorblind. Nobody else does.

Ursula K. Le Guin

SOCTHINK

McIntosh recommends that we all step back and consider unearned advantages we inherit owing to the positions we may occupy. What would be on your list? What disadvantages might you inherit?

These are not all the privileges White people take for granted as a result of their membership in the dominant racial group in the United States. As Devah Pager's study showed, White job seekers enjoy a tremendous advantage over equally well-qualified—even better-qualified—Blacks. Whiteness *does* carry privileges—to a much greater extent than most people who are White realize.

>> Race and Ethnicity in the United States

Few societies have a more diverse population than the United States. The nation is truly a multiracial, multiethnic society and is becoming more so. According to results from the 2010 Census, 92 percent of the population growth in the United States over the previous decade was due to increased numbers of racial and ethnic minorities, with Hispanics accounting for 56 percent overall (Passel, Cohn, and Lopez 2011).

RACIAL GROUPS

The three largest racial minorities in the United States are African Americans, Native Americans, and Asian Americans.

African Americans "I am an invisible man," wrote Black author Ralph Ellison in his novel *Invisible Man* (1952:3). "I am a man of substance, of flesh and bone, fiber and liquids—and I might even be said to possess a mind. I am invisible, understand, simply because people refuse to see me." Today, many African Americans still feel invisible. African Americans make up 13 percent of the total U.S. population but are over-represented as a portion of the population of people who are officially poor making up 24.4 percent of that group. Overall, 27.2 percent of African Americans were in poverty compared to 9.6 percent of non-Hispanic Whites (DeNavas-Walt and Proctor 2014).

Contemporary institutional discrimination and individual prejudice against African Americans are rooted

Racial and Ethnic Groups in the United States, 1790–2050 (Projected)

1790

African Americans **19%**

White **81%**

1880

12%

88%

1970

11%

Hispanic **5%**

All others **2%**

White non-Hispanic **83%**

2013

17%

12%

Asian **5%**

3%

62%

2050 (projected)

27%

13%

8%

5%

47%

Note: U.S. Census categories vary over time.

Sources: Gibson and Jung 2002: Table 1; U.S. Census Bureau 2014g: Table S0201, 2014h: Table 11. *Photo:* © Ken Usami/Getty Images RF.

situation because they could not own property legally and could not pass on the benefits of their labor to their children. In spite of generations of slavery with its long-term economic consequences, African Americans never received slave reparations to compensate for the historical injustices of forced servitude (Williams and Collins 2004).

The end of the Civil War did not bring genuine freedom and equality for Blacks. Whites were able to maintain their dominance formally through legalized segregation and informally by means of vigilante terror and violence. The southern states passed "Jim Crow" laws to enforce official segregation, and the Supreme Court in the case

Poverty Rates by Race and Ethnicity

Black	**27.2%**
Hispanic, any race	**23.5%**
Asian	**10.5%**
White, non-Hispanic	**9.6%**

Source: DeNavas-Walt and Proctor 2014: Table 3.

in the history of slavery in the United States. Many other subordinate groups had little wealth and income, but as sociologist W. E. B. Du Bois (1909) and others have noted, enslaved Blacks were in an even more oppressive of *Plessy v. Ferguson* upheld them as constitutional in 1896. In addition, Blacks faced the danger of lynching campaigns, often led by the Ku Klux Klan, during the late 1800s and early 1900s (Franklin and Moss 2000).

During the 1950s and 1960s, a vast civil rights movement emerged, with many competing factions and strategies for change. The Southern Christian Leadership Conference (SCLC), founded by Dr. Martin Luther King Jr., used nonviolent civil disobedience to oppose segregation. The National Association for the Advancement of Colored People (NAACP) favored use of the courts to press for equality for African Americans. Many younger Black leaders, most notably Malcolm X, turned toward an ideology of Black power. Proponents of **Black power** rejected the goal of assimilation into White middle-class society. They defended the beauty and dignity of Black and African cultures and supported the creation of Black-controlled political and economic institutions (Ture and Hamilton 1992).

Black power A political philosophy, promoted by many younger Blacks in the 1960s, that supported the creation of Black-controlled political and economic institutions.

Despite numerous courageous actions to achieve Black civil rights, Black and White citizens are still separate, still unequal. The median household income for African American households is $34,598, compared to $58,270 for non-Hispanic Whites. The majority of Black children from middle-income families end up earning less than their parents, whereas 68 percent of children in middle-income White families earn more. And in part because of unequal access to health care, the life expectancy of African Americans is shorter than that of Whites (DeNavas-Walt and Proctor 2014; Isaacs 2008).

Substantial variation exists in the types of occupations African Americans occupy. Overall, African Americans make up 11.2 percent of persons employed in the labor force. Using this number as a baseline, it is possible to highlight jobs in which African Americans are over- and underrepresented. For example, African Americans comprise only 1.8 percent of artists, 1.6 percent of architects, 2.9 percent of CEOs, 4.7 percent of dentists, and 6.4 percent of physicians.

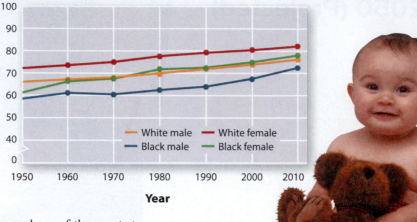

Life Expectancy by Race and Sex, 1950–2010

Life expectancy at birth

- White male
- White female
- Black male
- Black female

Year

Source: National Center for Health Statistics 2013:Table 18.   *Photo:* © Getty Images RF.

By contrast, they constitute 21.9 percent of social workers, 21.6 percent of postal clerks, 24.7 percent of taxi drivers, 34.5 percent of barbers, and 36.4 percent of nurses' aides (Bureau of Labor Statistics 2014g: Table 11).

In politics, though African Americans remain underrepresented, progress in the number of elected officials has improved over time. Between 1969 and 2015, the number of African Americans in Congress rose from 6 to a record of 46, and the election of Barack Obama as president represents a major breakthrough in the glass ceiling. However, African Americans still make up only 8.6 percent of Congress. Such lack of progress is especially distressing in view of sociologist W. E. B. Du Bois's observation over a century ago that Blacks could not expect to achieve equal social and economic opportunity without first gaining political rights (Manning 2015).

Native Americans Today 2.5 million Native Americans represent a diverse array of cultures distinguishable by language, family organization, religion, and livelihood.

Did You Know?

. . . With the release of *The Princess and the Frog* in 2009, Princess Tiana became Disney's first African American princess in a feature film. At the same time, Disney was criticized for drawing on racial stereotypes of 1920s New Orleans in the film.

Photo: © Walt Disney Co./Courtesy Everett Collection.

Major Asian American Groups in the United States

Korean **9.1%**

Japanese **5.0%**

Vietnamese **10.7%**

Other Asian **14.3%**

Chinese **23.9%**

Asian Indian **20.1%**

Filipino **16.8%**

Source: U.S. Census Bureau 2014g:Table S0201.

The outsiders who came to the United States—European settlers and their descendants—came to know these native peoples' forebears as "American Indians." By the time the Bureau of Indian Affairs (BIA) was organized as part of the War Department in 1824, Indian–White relations had featured three centuries of hostility that had led to the virtual elimination of native peoples. During the 19th century, many bloody wars wiped out a significant part of the nation's Indian population. By the end of the century, schools for Indians—operated by the BIA or by church missions—prohibited the practice of Native American cultures. Yet at the same time, such schools did little to make the children effective competitors in White society (Humes et al. 2011).

Life remains difficult for members of the 562 tribal groups in the United States, whether they live in urban areas or on reservations. For example, median household income for American Indians is $36,641 compared to $57,684 for non-Hispanic White households (U.S. Census Bureau 2014g: Table S0201). In addition, one Native American teenager in six has attempted suicide—a rate four times higher than the rate for other teenagers. Over time, some Native Americans have chosen to assimilate and abandon all vestiges of their tribal cultures to escape certain forms of prejudice. However, by the 1990s, an increasing number of people in the United States were

openly claiming a Native American identity. Since 1960 the federal government's count of Native Americans has quadrupled. According to the 2010 Census, the Native American population increased 18 percent during the 2000s. Demographers believe that more and more Native Americans who previously concealed their identity are no longer trying to pass as White (Grieco and Cassidy 2001; Humes et al. 2011).

The introduction of gambling on Indian reservations has transformed the lives of some Native Americans. Native Americans got into the gaming industry in 1988, when Congress passed the Indian Gambling Regulatory Act. The law stipulates that states must negotiate agreements with tribes interested in commercial gaming; they cannot prevent tribes from engaging in gambling operations even if state law prohibits such ventures. The income from these lucrative operations is not evenly distributed, however. About two-thirds of recognized Indian tribes are not involved in gambling ventures. And those tribes that earn substantial revenues from gambling constitute only a small fraction of Native Americans (J. Taylor and Kalt 2005).

Asian Americans Asian Americans are a diverse group, one of the fastest-growing segments of the U.S. population. Among the many groups of Americans of Asian descent are Vietnamese Americans, Chinese Americans, Japanese Americans, and Korean Americans.

Asian Americans are often held up as a **model** or **ideal minority** group, supposedly because they have succeeded economically, socially, and educationally despite past prejudice and discrimination. Yet this representation minimizes the degree of diversity among Asian Americans. For example, 80 percent of Vietnamese children in the United States speak a language other than English at home, and 25 percent of them speak English with difficulty. Contrast this with Filipino children, 34 percent of whom speak another language at home and 8 percent of whom have difficulty with English. Educational attainment also varies significantly between groups. The likelihood of having completed at least a bachelor's degree among 25- to 29-year-olds ranges from 80 percent for those of Asian Indian descent and 70 percent for Chinese to 45 percent for Vietnamese and 36 percent for Other Asian nationalities. Poverty rates also vary. The rate for Filipino children is 5 percent, and for Asian Indians it is 7.5 percent. Among Vietnamese children, in contrast, it is 15.2, and for those of Other Asian nationalities it is 19.9 percent (Aud, Fox, and KewalRamani 2010).

Examples such as these highlight the limitations of viewing people of Asian descent in the United States as a singular group. But even given high overall levels of attainment in education and income, those of Asian descent can still face a glass ceiling. For example, in 2010 only 2.1 percent of board of directors seats at Fortune

> **model or ideal minority**
> A subordinate group whose members supposedly have succeeded economically, socially, and educationally despite past prejudice and discrimination.

500 companies were held by persons of Asian or Pacific Islander descent (Catalyst 2011a).

Vietnamese Americans Each Asian American group has its own history and culture. Vietnamese Americans, for instance, came to the United States primarily during and after the Vietnam War—especially after the U.S. withdrawal from the region in 1975—and currently number 1.7 million and their median household income is $57,441 (U.S. Census Bureau 2014g:Table S0201). Assisted by local agencies, refugees from communist Vietnam settled throughout the United States, tens of thousands of them in small towns. Over time, Vietnamese Americans have gravitated toward the larger urban areas, establishing ethnic enclaves featuring Vietnamese restaurants and grocery stores.

> One day our descendants will think it incredible that we paid so much attention to things like the amount of melanin in our skin or the shape of our eyes or our gender instead of the unique identities of each of us as complex human beings.
>
> ———
>
> Franklin Thomas

In 1995 the United States resumed normal diplomatic relations with Vietnam. Gradually, the *Viet Kieu*, or Vietnamese living abroad, began to return to their old country to visit, but usually not to take up permanent residence. Today, more than 40 years after the end of the Vietnam War, sharp differences of opinion remain among Vietnamese Americans, especially the older ones, concerning the war and the present government of Vietnam (Pfeifer 2008).

Chinese Americans Unlike African slaves and Native Americans, the Chinese were initially encouraged to immigrate to the United States. From 1850 to 1880, thousands of Chinese came to America, lured by job opportunities created by the discovery of gold, including the building of the transcontinental railroad. However, as employment possibilities decreased and

The Image of Diversity

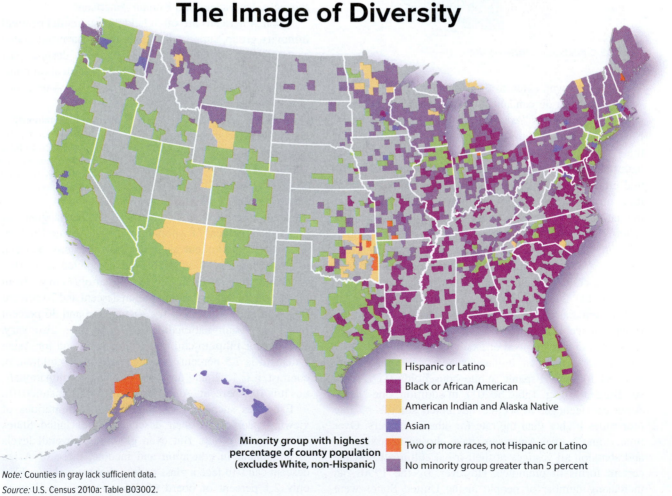

Minority group with highest percentage of county population (excludes White, non-Hispanic)

- Hispanic or Latino
- Black or African American
- American Indian and Alaska Native
- Asian
- Two or more races, not Hispanic or Latino
- No minority group greater than 5 percent

Note: Counties in gray lack sufficient data.

Source: U.S. Census 2010a: Table B03002.

competition for jobs grew, the Chinese became the target of a bitter campaign to limit their numbers and restrict their rights. Chinese laborers were exploited, then discarded.

In 1882 Congress enacted the Chinese Exclusion Act, which prevented Chinese immigration and even forbade Chinese in the United States to send for their families. As a result, the Chinese population declined steadily until after World War II. More recently, the descendants of the 19th-century immigrants have been joined by a new influx from Hong Kong and Taiwan. These groups may contrast sharply in their degree of assimilation, desire to live in Chinatowns, and feelings about this country's relations with the communist People's Republic of China.

Currently, 3.8 million Chinese Americans live in the United States with an average income of $68,149 (U.S. Census Bureau 2014g: Table S0201). Some Chinese Americans have entered lucrative occupations, yet many immigrants struggle to survive under living and working conditions that belie the model minority stereotype. In major U.S. cities, including New York and San Francisco, Chinatown districts contain illegal sweatshops in which recent immigrants—many of them Chinese women—work for minimal wages. Even in legal factories in the garment industry, hours are long and rewards are limited (Greenhouse 2008; Louie 2001; Shi 2008; Shipler 2004).

Japanese Americans Approximately 794,000 Japanese Americans live in the United States with a median household income of $70,756 (U.S. Census Bureau 2014g: Table S0201). As a people, they are relatively recent arrivals. In 1880 only 148 Japanese lived in the United States, but by 1920 there were more than 110,000. Japanese immigrants—called the *Issei,* or first generation—were usually males seeking employment opportunities. Many Whites saw them (along with Chinese immigrants) as a "yellow peril" and subjected them to prejudice and discrimination.

In 1941 the attack on Hawaii's Pearl Harbor by Japan had severe repercussions for Japanese Americans. The federal government decreed that all Japanese Americans on the West Coast had to leave their homes and report to "evacuation camps." Japanese Americans became, in effect, scapegoats for the anger that other people in the United States felt concerning Japan's role in World War II. By August 1943, 113,000 Japanese Americans had been forced into hastily built camps. In striking contrast, only a few German Americans and Italian Americans were sent to such camps (Neiwert 2005).

This mass detention was costly for Japanese Americans. The Federal Reserve Board estimates their total income and property losses at nearly half a billion dollars. Moreover, the psychological effect on these citizens—including the humiliation of being labeled "disloyal"—was immeasurable. Eventually, children born in the United States to the *Issei,* called *Nisei,* were allowed to enlist in the army and serve in Europe in a segregated combat unit. Others resettled in the East and Midwest to work in factories.

In 1983 a federal commission recommended government payments to all surviving Japanese Americans who had been held in detention camps. The commission reported that the detention was motivated by "race prejudice, war hysteria, and a failure of political leadership." It added that "no documented acts of espionage, sabotage, or fifth-column activity were shown to have been committed" by Japanese Americans. In 1988 President Ronald Reagan signed the Civil Liberties Act, which required the federal government to issue individual apologies for all violations of Japanese Americans' constitutional rights and established a $1.6 billion trust fund to pay reparations to the approximately 82,250 surviving Japanese Americans who had been detained (U.S. Department of Justice 1999). Each person who applied and was eligible received $20,000 with payments starting in 1990.

Korean Americans Just under 1.5 million Korean Americans live in the United States with an average household income of $58,004 (U.S. Census Bureau 2014g:Table S0201). Today's Korean American community is the result of three waves of immigration. The initial wave arrived between 1903 and 1910, when Korean laborers migrated to Hawaii. The second wave followed the end of the Korean War in 1953; most of those immigrants were wives of U.S. servicemen and war orphans. The third wave, continuing to the present, has reflected the admissions priorities established by the 1965 Immigration Act. These well-educated immigrants arrive in the United States with professional skills, though they often must settle, at least initially, for positions of lower responsibility than those they held in Korea.

In the early 1990s, the apparent friction between Korean Americans and another minority racial group, African Americans, attracted nationwide attention. In New York City, Los Angeles, and Chicago, Korean American merchants confronted Blacks who were allegedly threatening them or robbing their stores. Black neighborhoods responded with hostility to what they perceived as the disrespect and arrogance of Korean American entrepreneurs. In South Central Los Angeles, the only places to buy groceries, liquor, and gas were owned by Korean immigrants, who had largely replaced White businesspeople. African Americans were well aware of the dominant role that Korean Americans

> A fully functional multiracial society cannot be achieved without a sense of history and open, honest dialogue.
>
> Cornel West

played in their local retail markets. During the 1992 riots in South Central, small businesses owned by Koreans were a particular target. More than 1,800 Korean businesses were looted or burned during the riots (Kim 1999).

Conflict between the two groups was dramatized in Spike Lee's movie classic *Do the Right Thing*. The situation stems from Korean Americans' position as the latest immigrant group to cater to the needs of inner-city populations abandoned by those who have moved up the economic ladder. This type of friction is not new; generations of Jewish, Italian, and Arab merchants have encountered similar hostility from another oppressed minority that to outsiders might seem an unlikely source.

Arab Americans Arab Americans are immigrants and their descendants who hail from the 22 nations of the Arab world. As defined by the League of Arab States, these are the nations of North Africa and what is commonly known as the Middle East. Not all residents of those countries are Arab; for example, the Kurds of northern Iraq are not Arab. And some Arab Americans may have immigrated to the United States from non-Arab countries such as Great Britain or France, where their families have lived for generations.

The Arabic language is the single most unifying force among Arabs, although not all Arabs, and certainly not all Arab Americans, can read and speak Arabic. Moreover, the language has evolved over the centuries so that people in different parts of the Arab world speak different dialects. The fact that the Muslim holy book, the Qur'an, was originally written in Arabic gives the language special importance to Muslims.

Estimates of the size of the Arab American community differ widely. According to the U.S. Census, 1.8 million

people of Arab ancestry now reside in the United States with a median household income of $51,634 (U.S. Census Bureau 2014g:Table S0201). Iraq, Egypt, Lebanon, and Jordan were the top four Arab countries of origin for the foreign-born population in the United States (U.S. Census Bureau 2014g:Table B05006). As with other racial and ethnic groups, the Arab American population is concentrated in certain areas of the United States. Their rising numbers have led to the development of Arab retail centers in several cities, including Dearborn and Detroit, Michigan; Los Angeles; Chicago; New York City; and Washington, D.C. (David 2008).

As a group, Arab Americans are extremely diverse. Many families have lived in the United States for several generations; others are foreign born. Despite the stereotype, most Arab Americans are *not* Muslim, and not all practice religion. The majority of Arab Americans are Christian. Nor can Arab Americans be characterized as having a specific family type, gender role, or occupational pattern (Arab American Institute 2008; David 2004).

ETHNIC GROUPS

Many different ethnic groups have come together in the United States resulting in a shifting mosaic of cultures. Three major groupings include Hispanics (Latinos), Jews, and White ethnics.

Hispanics At 54 million, Hispanics make up the largest minority group in the United States, an increase from 35.3 million in 2000. The fastest-growing subgroups are those who come from the Central American nations of El Salvador, Honduras, and Guatemala (Humes et al. 2011). The majority of the overall Hispanic population increase is due not to immigration, however, but to higher birthrates within the Hispanic population (K. Johnson and Lichter 2010).

Though the growth in the Hispanic population has been a national phenomenon, more than half resides in California, Texas, and Florida. Major urban areas have also experienced substantial expansion. Hispanics now outnumber African Americans in 8 of the 10 largest U.S. cities. Even Chicago and Philadelphia, the two exceptions, are among the cities with the largest Hispanic populations (see "U.S. Cities with Highest Number of Hispanics" graph). In these cities, the proportion of the Latino population varies from 29 percent for New York City to 81 percent in El Paso, Texas (Ennis, Ríos-Vargas, and Albert 2011; U.S. Census Bureau 2010a:Table DP-5).

The various Latino groups share a heritage of Spanish language and culture, which can cause serious problems in their assimilation. An intelligent student whose first language is Spanish may be presumed to be slow or even unruly by English-speaking schoolchildren, and frequently by English-speaking teachers as well. The labeling of Latino children as underachievers, as learning disabled, or as emotionally disturbed can act as a self-fulfilling prophecy for some children. Bilingual education aims at easing

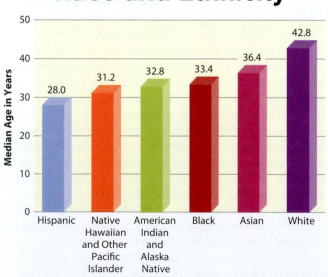

Age Variation by Race and Ethnicity

Note: The five racial group categories reported here do not include Hispanics.

Source: U.S. Census Bureau 2014g: Table S0201.

U.S. Cities with Highest Numbers of Hispanics

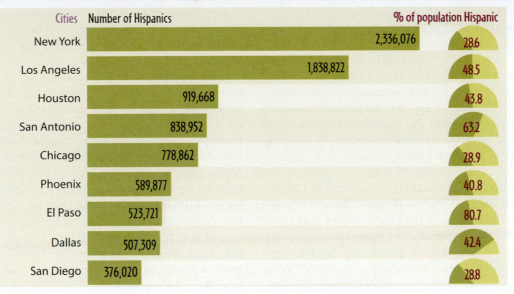

Cities	Number of Hispanics	% of population Hispanic
New York	2,336,076	28.6
Los Angeles	1,838,822	48.5
Houston	919,668	43.8
San Antonio	838,952	63.2
Chicago	778,862	28.9
Phoenix	589,877	40.8
El Paso	523,721	80.7
Dallas	507,309	42.4
San Diego	376,020	28.8

Source: Ennis et al. 2011.

Major Hispanic Groups in the United States

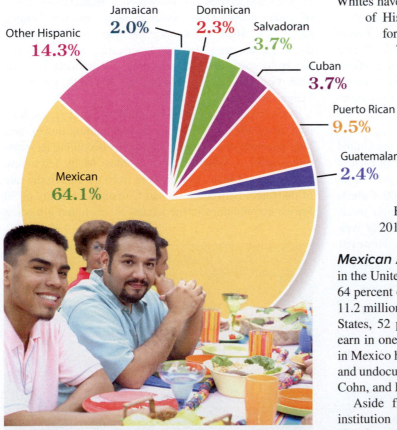

Other Hispanic **14.3%**

Jamaican **2.0%**

Dominican **2.3%**

Salvadoran **3.7%**

Cuban **3.7%**

Puerto Rican **9.5%**

Guatemalan **2.4%**

Mexican **64.1%**

Source: U.S. Census Bureau 2014g:Table S0201. *Photo:* © PhotoDisc/Getty Images RF.

the educational difficulties experienced by Hispanic children and others whose first language is not English.

The educational challenges facing Latinos is reflected in the fact that 72 percent of Hispanics aged 25–29 have completed high school, compared to 94 percent for non-Hispanic Whites. At the college level, 39 percent of Whites have a bachelor's degree, whereas only 13 percent of Hispanics have the same. The average income for Hispanic households is $41,508, which is 72 percent as much as non-Hispanic White households. Educational attainment of Hispanics is, however, on the rise. Dropout rates for Latino youths fell dramatically from 32.4 percent in 1990 to 11.7 percent in 2013. And, among the 2012 high school graduating class, the percentage of Hispanics who went directly to college exceeded the rate for non-Hispanic Whites for the first time (Fry and Taylor 2013; National Center for Education Statistics 2014; U.S. Census Bureau 2014g:Table S0201).

Mexican Americans The largest Hispanic population in the United States is Mexican American. Approximately 64 percent of them were born in the United States. Of the 11.2 million unauthorized immigrants living in the United States, 52 percent are from Mexico. The opportunity to earn in one hour what it would take an entire day to earn in Mexico has drawn millions of immigrants, documented and undocumented, north (Brown and Patten 2014; Passel, Cohn, and Rohel 2014).

Aside from the family, the most important social institution in the Mexican American community is the church—specifically, the Roman Catholic Church. This strong identification with the Catholic faith has reinforced the already formidable barriers between Mexican Americans and their predominantly White and Protestant neighbors in the Southwest. At the same time, the Catholic Church helps many immigrants develop a sense of identity and assists their assimilation into the dominant culture of the United States. The complexity of the Mexican American community is underscored by the fact that Protestant churches—especially those that endorse expressive, open worship—have attracted increasing numbers of Mexican Americans (Pew Research Center 2014k).

anti-Semitism Anti-Jewish prejudice.

Puerto Ricans The second-largest segment of Latinos in the United States is Puerto Ricans. Since 1917 residents of Puerto Rico have held the status of American citizens; many have migrated to New York and other eastern cities. Puerto Ricans have experienced serious poverty both in the United States and on the island. With a median household income of $39,660, those who live in the continental United States earn 68.8 percent of what non-Hispanic White households earn (U.S. Census Bureau 2014g:Table S0201).

Politically, Puerto Ricans in the United States have not been as successful as Mexican Americans in organizing for their rights. For many mainland Puerto Ricans—as for many residents of the island—the paramount political issue is the destiny of Puerto Rico itself. Should it continue in its present commonwealth status, petition for admission to the United States as the 51st state, or attempt to become an independent nation? This question has divided Puerto Rico for decades and remains a central issue in Puerto Rican elections. In a 1998 referendum, for example, voters supported a "none of the above" option, effectively favoring continuation of the commonwealth status over statehood or independence.

Cuban Americans Cuban immigration to the United States dates back as far as 1831, but it began in earnest following Fidel Castro's seizure of power in the Cuban revolution of 1959. The first wave of 200,000 Cubans included many professionals with relatively high levels of schooling; these men and women were largely welcomed as refugees from communist tyranny. However, more recent waves of immigrants have aroused growing concern, partly because they were less likely to be skilled professionals. After Castro's revolution, the United States severed formal relations with Cuba, preventing all trade and banning travel. In recent years that stance softened. In April 2009, President Obama signed a bill easing both economic and travel restrictions. In January 2015, the Obama administration began a series of talks with Cuba intended to officially normalize relations.

Jewish Americans The Jewish population in the United States exceeds 6 million and comprises approximately 2.1 percent of the total U.S. population. They play a prominent role in the worldwide Jewish community because the United States has the world's largest concentration of Jews. Like the Japanese, many Jewish immigrants came to this country and became white-collar professionals in spite of prejudice and discrimination (Sheskin and Dashefsky 2013).

Anti-Semitism—that is, anti-Jewish prejudice—has often been vicious in the United States, although rarely so widespread and never so formalized as in Europe. In many cases, Jews have been used as scapegoats for other people's failures. Given such attitudes, Jews continue to face discrimination. Despite high levels of education and professional training, they are still conspicuously absent from the top management of large corporations (except for the few firms founded by Jews). Until the late 1960s, many prestigious universities maintained restrictive quotas that limited Jewish enrollment. Private social clubs and fraternal groups frequently limit membership to gentiles (non-Jews), a practice upheld by the Supreme Court in the 1964 case *Bell v. Maryland*.

The Anti-Defamation League (ADL) of B'nai B'rith funds an annual tally of reported anti-Semitic incidents. Although the number has fluctuated, the 1994 tabulation reached the highest level in the 20 years the ADL had been recording them. In 2014, the total reported incidents of harassment, threats, vandalism, and assaults came to 912, which represented a 21 percent increase over 2013, but a significant decrease from 1757 in 2005. Some incidents were inspired and carried out by neo-Nazi skinheads—groups of young people who champion racist and anti-Semitic ideologies. Such threatening behavior only intensifies the fears of many Jewish Americans, who remember the Holocaust—the extermination of 6 million Jews by Nazi Germany during World War II (Anti-Defamation League 2015).

As is true for other minorities in the United States, Jewish Americans face the choice of maintaining ties to their long religious and cultural heritage or becoming as indistinguishable as possible from gentiles. Many Jews have tended to assimilate, as is evident from the rise in the rate of marriages between Jews and Christians. A study of 50 Jewish communities in the United States found a median

© Ingram Publishing RF

intermarriage rate of 33 percent. Many people in the Jewish community worry that intermarriage will lead to a rapid decline in those who identify themselves as "Jewish." Yet, when asked which was the greater threat to Jewish life in the United States—intermarriage or anti-Semitism—only 33 percent of respondents chose intermarriage; 62 percent selected anti-Semitism (American Jewish Committee 2005; Sheskin and Dashefsky 2007).

White Ethnics Overall, 62.4 percent of the U.S. population is composed of non-Hispanic Whites. The nation's White ethnic population includes about 46 million people who claim at least partial German ancestry, 33 million Irish Americans, 17 million Italian Americans, and 9 million Polish Americans, as well as immigrants from other European nations. Some of these people continue to live in close-knit ethnic neighborhoods, whereas others have largely assimilated and left the "old ways" behind (Hixson, Hepler, and Kim 2011; U.S. Census Bureau 2014g:Table S0201).

Many White ethnics today identify only sporadically with their heritage. **Symbolic ethnicity** refers to an ethnic identity that emphasizes concerns such as ethnic food or political issues rather than on deeper ties to one's ethnic heritage. It is reflected in the occasional family trip to an ethnic bakery, the celebration of a ceremonial event such as St. Joseph's Day among Italian Americans, or concern about the future of Northern Ireland among Irish Americans. Except in cases in which new immigration reinforces old traditions, symbolic ethnicity tends to decline with each passing generation (Anagnostou 2009a, 2009b; Gans 2009; Waters 2009).

Whites increasingly feel excluded and even threatened by efforts to embrace multiculturalism and expand diversity (Plaut, Garnett, Buffardi, and Sanchez-Banks 2011). According to a national survey, Whites now perceive the level of anti-White bias to be greater than bias against Blacks. Greater numbers of Whites now believe that opportunity for Blacks comes at the expense of Whites (Norton and Sommers 2011).

Communities throughout the United States celebrate their ethnic heritage with local festivals such as Cinco de Mayo, Octoberfest, and Tulip Time. Photo: © Cyndi Atkins.

In many respects, the plight of White ethnics involves the same basic issues as that of other subordinate people in the United States. How ethnic can people be—how much can they deviate from an essentially White, Anglo-Saxon, Protestant norm—before society responds to their desire to be different? The United States does seem to reward people for assimilating. Yet, as we have seen, assimilation is no easy process. In the years to come, more and more people will face the challenge of fitting in, not only in the United States, but also around the world as the flow of immigrants from one country to another continues to increase.

> **symbolic ethnicity** An ethnic identity that emphasizes concerns such as ethnic food or political issues rather than deeper ties to one's ethnic heritage.

>> Immigration

According to a United Nations report, there are 232 million international immigrants in the world (United Nations 2013c). This includes 38.5 million foreign-born individuals in the United States. Of these, 53 percent are from Latin America, 28 percent from Asia, 13 percent from Europe, and 4 percent from Africa (U.S. Census Bureau 2014g:Table DP-2). The constantly increasing numbers of immigrants and the pressure they put on employment opportunities and welfare capabilities in the countries they enter raise difficult questions for many of the world's economic powers. Who should be allowed in? At what point should immigration be curtailed (Bloemraad, Korteweg, and Yurdakul 2008)?

Going GLOBAL

World Immigration Since 1500

Source: Allen 2008.

IMMIGRATION TRENDS

The migration of people is not uniform across time or space. At certain times, war or famine may precipitate large movements of people, either temporarily or permanently. Temporary dislocations occur when people wait until it is safe to return to their home areas. However, more and more migrants who cannot eke out an adequate living in their home nations are making permanent moves to developed nations. The major migration streams flow into North America, the oil-rich areas of the Middle East, and the industrial economies of western Europe and Asia. Currently, seven of the world's wealthiest nations (including Germany, France, the United Kingdom, and the United States) shelter about one-third of the world's migrant population but less than one-fifth of the world's total population. As long as disparities in job opportunities exist among countries, there is little reason to expect this international trend to reverse.

Even though the sending nation loses a significant source of labor and talent due to emigration, the process does contribute to its economy. For example, it reduces the size of the population that an economy with limited resources has a difficult time supporting, and it leads to an economic infusion in the form of remittances—monies that immigrants send back to their home nations. Worldwide, immigrants send more than $583 billion a year back home to their relatives—an amount that represents a major source of income for developing nations. In 2014, over $131 billion was sent from the United States to other countries in the form of remittances. The single largest recipient was Mexico with $24.4 billion, followed by China with $16.3 billion, and India at $11.2 billion (World Bank 2015h).

Immigrants continue to face obstacles owing to their relative lack of resources. Immigrant women, for example, face all the challenges that immigrant men do, plus some additional ones. Typically, they bear the responsibility for obtaining services for their families, particularly their children. Women are often left to navigate the bureaucratic tangle of schools, city services, and health care, as well as the unfamiliar stores and markets they must shop at to feed their families. Women who need special medical services or are victims of domestic violence are often reluctant to seek outside help. Finally, because many new immigrants view the United States as a dangerous place to raise a family, women must be especially watchful over their children's lives (Hondagneu-Sotelo 2003).

One consequence of global immigration has been the emergence of transnationals—people or families who move across borders multiple times in search of better jobs and education. The industrial tycoons of the early 20th century, whose power outmatched that of many nation-states, were among the world's first transnationals. Today, however, millions of people, many of very modest means, move back and forth between countries much as commuters do between city and suburbs. More and more of these people have dual citizenship. Rather than being shaped by allegiance to one country, their identity is rooted in their struggle to

Going GLOBAL

Legal Migration to the United States, 1820–2010

Millions of immigrants

1820s	1840s	1860s	1880s	1900s	1920s	1940s	1960s	1980s	2000s
0.1						0.5			
	0.6					1.0			
		1.7							
			2.3				2.5		
	2.6		2.8				3.2		
				3.7			4.2		
			5.2		4.1				
					5.7			6.2	
								9.8	10.3
				8.8					

Europe and Canada

All Others

Source: Homeland Security; 2012.   *Photo:* © iStock.com/pixhook RF.

SOCTHINK

Birthrates in the United States, as in many industrialized nations, are low. Populations in many states face natural decrease and will shrink without immigration to compensate for those low birthrates. Given this, why does immigration still cause such tension among many communities in the United States? Might this change as people in such states realize they need those immigrants?

survive—and in some instances prosper—by transcending international borders (Croucher 2004; Sassen 2005).

IMMIGRATION POLICIES

Countries that have long been a destination for immigrants, such as the United States, usually have policies to determine who has preference to enter. Often, clear racial and ethnic biases are built into these policies. In the 1920s U.S. policy gave preference to people from western Europe while making it difficult for residents of southern and eastern Europe, Asia, and Africa to enter the country. During the late 1930s and early 1940s, the federal government refused to loosen restrictive immigration quotas in order to allow Jewish refugees to escape the terror of Nazi Germany. In line with this policy, the SS *St. Louis,* with more than 900 Jewish refugees on board, was denied permission to dock in the United States in 1939. The ship was forced to sail back to Europe, where at least a few hundred of its passengers later died at the hands of the Nazis (Morse 1967; G. Thomas and Witts 1974).

Since the 1960s U.S. policy has encouraged the immigration of relatives of U.S. residents and of people who have desirable skills. This policy has significantly altered the pattern of sending nations. Previously, Europeans dominated, but for the past 40 years, immigrants have come primarily from Latin America and Asia. Thus, an ever-growing proportion of the U.S. population will be Asian or Hispanic. To a large extent, fear and resentment of racial and ethnic diversity is a key factor in opposition to immigration. In many nations, people are concerned that the new arrivals do not reflect and will not embrace their own cultural and racial heritage. Others fear that immigrants represent an economic threat, because they increase the supply of available workers. In 1986 Congress approved the Immigration Reform and Control Act which, for the first time, outlawed the hiring of undocumented immigrants and subjected employers to fines and even imprisonment if they violated the law.

Under the George W. Bush administration, numerous high-profile workplace raids occurred to send a very public message that they were serious about cracking down on illegal immigration. Since the election of Barack Obama, the number of such raids has declined, although the number of people exported has gone up (Simanski 2014). Workplace raids have been replaced by what are sometimes called "silent raids," in which the Immigration Customs and Enforcement (ICE) agency focuses instead on inspecting employers' hiring paperwork to see whether their workers have the legal documentation necessary for employment. In doing this, ICE targets sectors that have historically hired immigrant undocumented laborers such as the garment industry, fast-food chains, and agricultural companies. The effect is that these workers lose their jobs. After one such raid, the clothing maker American Apparel laid off 1,500 workers, approximately a quarter of its workforce. The goal of this approach is to shut down the supply of jobs for workers who lack legal documentation, thus discouraging illegal immigration. Companies who employ these workers, however, are not entirely pleased, because it means that they will have to pay more to attract applicants to these difficult and often tedious jobs (Jordan 2011).

Battles over immigration continue. Immigrants have staged massive marches to pressure Congress to speed the naturalization process and develop ways for illegal immigrants to gain legal residency. Opponents of illegal immigration have called for more resources with which to track down and deport illegal immigrants and close up the U.S.–Mexican border. Numerous states, including Georgia, Alabama, and Texas, are also considering legislation patterned after the 2010 Arizona statute. Despite this widespread public dissatisfaction with the nation's immigration policy, little progress has been made. Congress has had difficulty reaching a bipartisan compromise that pleases both sides.

Race and ethnicity in the United States pose a challenge to the principle that everyone is created equal. The vast majority of people in the United States have rejected outright racism in which people adhere to beliefs asserting the inherent superiority of their race or ethnic group over others. But inequality in practice continues to be a significant issue, with substantial differences in access to material, social, and cultural resources based on racial and ethnic background. This inequality of opportunity becomes especially problematic when built into the structure of society itself in the form of institutional discrimination. Sociology enables us to better see and understand such patterns so that we might make more informed decisions about what to do about them.

SOCIOLOGY IS A VERB

Privilege

As an experiment in personal sociology, and in the spirit of Peggy McIntosh's work on privilege, make a list of the unearned advantages and disadvantages that flow out of your racial and ethnic heritage. Doing so can make us more aware of both the opportunities and obstacles that are not a consequence of our individual effort or merit. How and why might such a list be more challenging for some groups than others?

For REVIEW

I. How do sociologists define race and ethnicity?

- Race is defined by the social significance that groups attach to external physical characteristics. Ethnicity is rooted in cultural and national traditions that define a population. Sociologists emphasize the significance of culture and its consequences for both.

II. What are prejudice and discrimination, and how do they operate?

- Prejudice involves attitudes and beliefs whereas discrimination involves actions. In both cases, they represent a negative response to a group of people that denies them full equality as persons. Institutional discrimination is built into the structure of society itself, systematically denying some groups access to key resources.

III. What are the consequences of race and ethnicity for opportunity?

- Racial and ethnic groups in the United States—including African Americans, Native Americans, Asian Americans, Hispanic Americans, Jewish Americans, and White ethnic Americans—face differing levels of opportunity based on their relative position in society. Groups within each of these categories continue to face significant structural inequality.

Functionalist View

Historically, race and ethnicity have contributed to **social integration** and **identity** by providing clear boundaries between groups.

Amalgamation, assimilation, and pluralism function to bring **order** to society. Immigration is functional for the host nation if it gains needed workers and for the sending nation when remittances are sent back.

INTEGRATION, IDENTITY, ORDER
KEY CONCEPTS

Conflict View

Prejudice, discrimination, ethnocentrism, stereotyping, racism, and hate crimes are all manifestations of perceived **superiority** of a dominant group over subordinate minority groups.

Institutional discrimination denies opportunities and equal rights to individuals and groups as part of the normal operations of society.

Exploitation theory holds that prejudice and discrimination help preserve inequality in the economic system as a whole.

KEY CONCEPTS
DISCRIMINATION, EXPLOITATION, RACISM

Interactionist View

According to the **contact hypothesis**, interracial contact between people in cooperative circumstances will lessen prejudice and stereotyping.

Racial **profiling** occurs when arbitrary actions are taken by authorities based on a person's perceived racial or ethnic identity.

Being White in the United States represents an often unacknowledged form of privilege in everyday encounters.

KEY CONCEPTS
CONTACT, INTERACTION

MAKE THE CONNECTION
After reviewing the chapter, answer the following questions:

1
How would each perspective approach the issue of African American deaths at the hands of police?

2
How would each perspective explain stereotyping?

3
How do the functionalist and conflict perspectives intersect in both color-blind racism and affirmative action?

4
Using the interactionist perspective, describe an example of interracial contact you have experienced along with its consequences.

Pop Quiz

1. **How do sociologists define race?**
   a. genetic differences between categories of humans based on clear chromosomal markers that specify a person's race
   b. the biological differences between humans, defined as socially significant and presumed to divide the population into genetically distinct subgroups
   c. the cultural differences between humans, defined as socially significant and presumed to divide the population into socially distinct subgroups
   d. levels of melatonin, which shape skin color and divide the human population into distinct groups

2. **According to the findings of the Human Genome Project, race**
   a. determines intellectual ability.
   b. is a biological, not a social, concept.
   c. explains significant social outcomes.
   d. has no genetic or scientific basis.

3. **Starting with the 2000 U.S. Census, there were a total of _____ possible race combinations you could choose from to identify yourself.**
   a. 3
   b. 6
   c. 27
   d. 57

4. **Suppose that a White employer refuses to hire a Vietnamese American and selects an inferior White applicant. This decision is an act of**
   a. prejudice.
   b. ethnocentrism.
   c. discrimination.
   d. stigmatization.

5. **Working together as computer programmers for an electronics firm, a Hispanic woman and a Jewish man overcome their initial prejudices and come to appreciate each other's strengths and talents. This scenario is an example of**
   a. the contact hypothesis.
   b. a self-fulfilling prophecy.
   c. amalgamation.
   d. reverse discrimination.

6. **Intermarriage over several generations, resulting in various groups combining to form a new group, would be an example of**
   a. pluralism.
   b. assimilation.
   c. segregation.
   d. amalgamation.

7. **The term that Peggy McIntosh uses to describe the unearned advantages that those in the majority take for granted is**
   a. privilege.
   b. discrimination.
   c. racism.
   d. institutional discrimination.

8. **Jennifer Anastassakis changed her name to Jennifer Aniston. Her action was an example of**
   a. expulsion.
   b. assimilation.
   c. segregation.
   d. pluralism.

9. **Which of the following is the largest overall minority group in the United States?**
   a. African Americans
   b. Asian Americans
   c. Latinos
   d. Arab Americans

10. **Which of the following approaches to immigration enforcement has become most common in the Obama administration?**
    a. high-profile workplace raids
    b. relaxed enforcement reducing the number of deportations
    c. targeting of community organizations that provide services to immigrants
    d. silent raids focusing on employers and documentation

1. (b), 2. (d), 3. (d), 4. (c), 5. (a), 6. (d), 7. (a), 8. (b), 9. (c), 10. (d)

14

Population, Health, and Environment

DEEP WATERS

On April 20, 2010, an explosion at the Deepwater Horizon oil-drilling platform approximately 40 miles off the coast of Louisiana in the Gulf of Mexico marked the beginning of an environmental catastrophe. Workers had just completed a series of pressure tests to ensure the well's integrity when methane gas entered the drill column and erupted out of the well. The blowout protector, designed to automatically seal the well in such cases, failed. Eleven members of the 126-person crew aboard the oil rig were killed in the resulting explosion. At the wellhead on the Gulf floor, as many as 4.2 million barrels of oil, the equivalent of nearly 6,000 Olympic-sized swimming pools, escaped into the water.

A year earlier, as part of the oil-drilling approval process, BP, the corporation that owns the rights to the well, filed an exploration plan with the Minerals Management Service (MMS), an agency of the U.S. Department of the Interior. In that report, BP repeatedly minimized both the likelihood of an accident and any possible impact should one occur, reporting that, "in the event of an unanticipated blowout resulting in an oil spill, it is unlikely to have an impact" (BP Exploration & Production Inc. 2009). BP maintained that any effects would likely be "sublethal" to fish, marine mammals, turtles, and birds. It also argued that the well's distance from shore would ensure minimal impact on beaches, wildlife refuges, and wilderness areas in the event of an oil spill. And the corporation expressed confidence in its ability to contain, recover, and remove any spill. Having filed this report, BP received an exemption from the MMS, freeing it from conducting a detailed environmental impact analysis.

After conducting nearly a yearlong investigation, the United States Coast Guard (2011) released a report finding that a convergence of factors, including flawed technology, inadequate maintenance, systemic failures in the company's safety management system, and lax government oversight, brought about this disastrous result. Five years after the disaster, legal settlements regarding the amount of damages owed to various parties had been reached and BP (2015) claimed to have spent $28 billion to cover cleanup and settlement costs, but the total fine BP faced from the U.S. government had not yet been decided. Just as the natural environment consists of an interdependent web of relationships, so also does the social environment. We must develop a more complete understanding of both to avoid catastrophic outcomes like this one in the future.

As You READ >>

- **What role do population dynamics play in shaping our lives?**
- **What does sociology contribute to something as seemingly biological as health?**
- **What environmental lessons do we learn from sociology?**

One of the advantages of the sociological imagination is that it provides us with a better understanding of the big picture of society and where we fit in it. It does so by contextualizing our beliefs and practices within a larger social framework, one that is often invisible to us. We have already seen this at work with regard to various components of social structure, including family, religion, education, economy, and politics. In sociology, place matters. This is no less true when it comes to the topics of population, health, and environment. Approaching these issues in a way that takes into account a big-picture perspective allows us to see how our individual outcomes are shaped by the positions we occupy.

>> Population

Today there are more than 7.2 billion people on Earth, a number that goes up by 210,562 each day and 146 every minute (U.S. Census Bureau 2015i). Every single one of us must live off the limited resources the planet provides. To better understand our life chances, as well as those of others, we must take into account the direction that population trends are heading. **Demography**—the statistical study of population dynamics—is the discipline committed to studying such patterns. It focuses on how populations change over time, with particular attention to whether or not they are growing, shrinking, or staying the same. It also includes analysis of the composition of those populations—particularly age and sex with special emphasis on the degree to which a group's makeup influences its likelihood for population change. For example, if the population is young, there is more potential for women to bear children, increasing the possibility for future population growth.

In their analysis, demographers begin by specifying the population to be studied. They might select a city, county, state, or, most often, a nation—though they could choose any group with a specified population boundary. They then gather data about that group over some specified period of time, usually per year, to see how many new members join and how many existing members leave. New arrivals come via birth and immigration, while departures occur through death and emigration. Demographers can then use their results to show how a population changes from one point in time to another or to contrast differences between populations.

BIRTH

Births are the primary means by which a population replaces its members from one generation to the next. Yet the likelihood of each of our births was shaped by

demography The statistical study of population dynamics.

World Population Clock, 2015

	Births	Deaths	Population Increase
Year	134,034,782	57,179,795	76,854,987
Day	367,219	156,657	210,562
Minute	255	109	146

Source: U.S. Census Bureau 2015i.   *Photo:* © Digital Vision/Getty Images RF.

population dynamics above and beyond the desires of our biological parents. The rate at which women give birth varies significantly over time and place. To better understand these patterns—whether studying England in the Middle Ages, the United States in the late 19th century, or Afghanistan today—demographers analyze trends in **fertility,** the number of children born in a given period of time. The two primary measures they use to do so are the crude birthrate and the total fertility rate.

A population's **crude birthrate** refers to the number of live births per 1,000 people in the population in a given year. It is described as crude because it provides a simple measure, without taking additional factors into consideration, thus allowing for straightforward comparisons between populations. In the United States, for example, the crude birthrate dropped from 23.7 in 1960 to 15.7 in 1985 to 12.5 in 2013, suggesting the long-term possibility of declining population size. Contrast this with the 2013 rates in a variety of other nations, such as Niger at 49.7, Afghanistan at 34.1, China at 12.1, and Germany at 8.5 and a global rate of 19.2 (World Bank 2015i). One variable in isolation, however, is not sufficient to understand the full scope of population change.

A second indicator is a population's **total fertility rate,** which measures the average number of children a woman would have during her lifetime given current birthrates and assuming she survives through her childbearing years. This indicator is, in some ways, easier to understand because we may already be familiar with the notion that "the average family has 2.5 children." To provide a more precise count, rather than tying the indicator to particular family situations that are subject to change, this benchmark measures it per woman regardless of her family status. Doing so provides a more universally comparable statistic. In the United States in 1960, the average number of children a woman had in her lifetime was 3.65. The rate fell to 1.74 in 1976 before rising again to 1.87 in 2013. This rate varies widely by country, with Niger at 7.6, Afghanistan at 4.9, India at 3.27, and Bosnia and Herzegovina at 1.28 in 2013. (World Bank 2015j).

To sustain a population over time—apart from the addition of immigrants who join from the outside—the total fertility rate must fall no lower than approximately 2.1, which is known as the **replacement fertility rate.** This is considered the minimum number of children a woman would need to average in her lifetime to reproduce the population in the next generation. The reason for this number is fairly simple. Because men can't have babies, the average woman must have at least two children so that two parents are replaced in the next generation by two children. The number is boosted a bit to account for the fact that not all females survive through their childbearing years and because the ratio between males and females is not exactly 50/50. The global total fertility rate fell from 4.98 in 1960 to the point where the average woman now has 2.46 children in her lifetime. This decline suggests a slowing in the overall population growth rate and, if trends continue, the possibility of zero population growth, or even global population decline, at some point in the future (World Bank 2015j).

Total Fertility Rates

Average number of births per woman*

*If the woman survives to the end of her childbearing years.

Source: Google 2015a.

DEATH

Just as new arrivals occur through birth, departures occur through death. And just as with birth, demographers use a simple measure of mortality to allow for comparisons between populations. The **crude death rate** is a measure of the number of deaths per 1,000 people in a population in a given year. In the United States the crude death rate fell from 9.5 in 1960 to 8.2 in 2013. That rate compares with a high of 17.2 in Sierra Leone and a low of 1.03 in United Arab Emirates (World Bank 2015k). Overall, this measure is more difficult to interpret, because it is influenced by the age composition of the population. For example, in a society in which the population is on average older, the death rate may be higher, even though people are living longer. Because of this, demographers often turn to two additional measures: infant mortality and life expectancy.

A population's **infant mortality rate** measures the number of deaths in infants less than one year old per 1,000 live births per year. It is considered a major indicator of the overall well-being of a population, because it is a reflection of available health care, economic opportunity, and inequality.

fertility The number of children born in a given period of time.

crude birthrate The number of live births per 1,000 people in the population in a given year.

total fertility rate The average number of children a woman would have during her lifetime given current birthrates and assuming she survives through her childbearing years.

replacement fertility rate The minimum number of children a woman would need to average in her lifetime to reproduce the population in the next generation.

crude death rate The number of deaths per 1,000 people in a population in a given year.

infant mortality rate The number of deaths in infants less than one year old per 1,000 live births per year.

The fact that the numbers vary substantially also suggests that actions can be taken to improve the likelihood that a baby survives infancy. The rate in the United States in 1960 was 25.9. It fell to 10.7 by 1985 and then to 5.9 in 2013 owing to improved prenatal care and medical innovations. Internationally the global rate fell from 121.3 in 1960 to 33.6 in 2013. Sierra Leone had the top rate at 107.2, followed by Angola (101.6), Central African Republic (96.1), and Somalia (89.8). At the other end of the scale, Iceland and Luxembourg tied for the lowest rate at 1.6; Finland and Japan were next at 2.1 (World Bank 2015f).

The mortality statistic that is perhaps easiest for us to identify with is **life expectancy,** the projected number of years a person can expect to live based on his or her year of birth. It represents an often unwelcome reminder that factors beyond our individual control influence our life chances. For example, a baby born in Sierra Leone in 2013 has an average life expectancy of 45.6 years, but one born in Japan at the same time can anticipate living until the age of 83.3. The global average in 2013 was 71 years. Again, such differences point to the sociological fact that place matters. The same is true of time. In the United States life expectancy has increased from 69.8 in 1960 to 78.8 in 2013, owing to such factors as advances in health care, reductions in smoking rates, and increases in exercise and fitness (World Bank 2015l). As life expectancy expands, population size typically increases, because the number of people departing in any given year goes down.

MIGRATION

In addition to birth and death, arrivals and departures occur through **migration,** the movement of people from one population group to another. **Immigration** occurs when someone joins a population group of which they were not previously a member. **Emigration** occurs when a member of a population leaves that group. In other words, an immigrant is someone who arrives, and an emigrant is someone who departs.

Reasons for joining or leaving a population group can be varied. Sometimes an immigrant joins a new group because of the opportunities that doing so provides. This might include new job opportunities, connections with families, freedom of religious expression, or other factors that make migration appealing. Such influences are known as *pull* factors, because they serve as a sort of magnet attracting the immigrant to the new place. Other times people leave locations, because they seek to get away from unappealing features in their home country including violence, oppression, and lack of jobs. These are known as *push* factors, because they encourage the emigrant to leave.

life expectancy The projected number of years a person can expect to live based on his or her year of birth.

migration The movement of people from one population group to another.

immigration When individuals join a population group of which they were not previously a member.

emigration When members of a population leave that group.

SOCTHINK

What factors may have influenced those in your family to migrate (whether recently or generations ago)? What roles did push and pull play?

As we saw in Chapter 13, immigration is a global phenomenon. From 1950 to 2010, 92 million people departed what the United Nations classifies as less-developed regions, including various nations in Asia, Latin America and the Caribbean, and Africa and migrated to more developed regions (see the "Global Migration, 1950–2010" graph). The nation that saw the greatest net number of departures during that period was Mexico with 13.8 million, followed by Bangladesh with 12.1 million and China with 8.9 million. If we control for the effect of population size, countries among those with the lowest net migration rates from 2005 to 2010, meaning they were most likely to lose people, included Samoa, Zimbabwe, and El Salvador, whereas those with the highest rates of joiners included Qatar, United Arab Emirates, and Bahrain. The single most common destination location, receiving the greatest net number of migrants from 1950 to 2010, was the United States, with 43.4 million (United Nations 2011a, 2011b).

In the United States, 12.5 percent of the population is foreign born, of which one-half arrived from Latin America

Life Expectancy

The average number of years a newborn is expected to live*

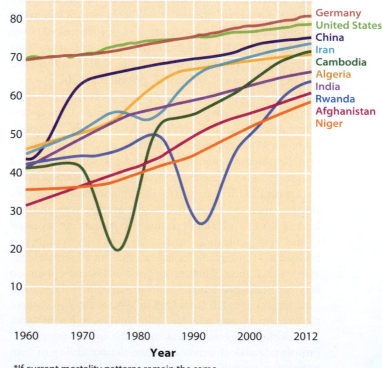

*If current mortality patterns remain the same.
Source: Google 2015b.

Global Migration, 1950–2010

Source: United Nations 2011a.

laws. In 2013, a total of 662,483 individuals were apprehended by U.S. immigration officials, two-thirds of them by U.S. Border Patrol and the remainder by Immigration and Customs Enforcement (ICE) agents. Of that total, 424,978 came from Mexico and 73,208 from Guatemala (Simanski 2014).

and more than one-quarter came from Asia (see the accompanying "U.S. Foreign-Born Population" graph). As indicated in Chapter 13, Mexico leads the way as the source country, accounting for approximately 30 percent, followed by China at 5.2 percent, Philippines at 4.5, and India at 4.3. California is the most common destination for these immigrants, with 26 percent of the foreign-born population living there. New York, Texas, and Florida are also common destinations, each accounting for approximately 10 percent of the foreign-born population (Grieco and Trevelyan 2010).

Immigrants in the United States are classified into four major categories by the Department of Homeland Security (Homeland Security 2012). Lawful permanent residents are those who have been granted lawful permanent residence in the United States. Sometimes referred to as having received their "Green Card," they can legally get a job, attend public schools or colleges, and even join the military. In 2013 there were 990,553 such recipients, two-thirds of whom were family-sponsored immigrants, meaning they were direct relatives of U.S. citizens (Monger and Yankay 2014). Naturalization, the second category, includes foreign citizens or nationals who become U.S. citizens. In 2013 there were 779,929 new naturalized citizens, 36 percent of whom came from Asia (Lee and Foreman 2014). The third category consists of those who have been granted formal refuge in the United States owing to persecution, or its imminent threat, in their home country. In 2013, 69,909 people living outside the country were granted refugee status enabling admission into the United States, and another 25,199 were granted asylum status. The three top countries from which refugees came were Iraq, Burma, and Bhutan. The leading sources of asylees were China, Egypt, and Ethiopia (Martin and Yankay 2014). The final category includes people entering the United States in violation of U.S. immigration

By combining data on births, deaths, and migration, it is possible to create a single indicator that provides a more complete picture of population dynamics. One such measure is a population's **growth rate,** which represents the overall percentage change in a population per year. It is important to consider this overall rate in conjunction with the other measures, because the internal population dynamics at any given time can vary. For example, birthrates and death rates might both rise or fall over a given time period, or one might go up while the other goes down, and migration rates can be similarly variable. The growth rate measure provides a snapshot of whether the population as a whole is growing or shrinking.

Globally, the world's population increases each year, because the overall birthrate rate exceeds the overall death rate. From 2005 to 2010, the world's population grew an average of 1.2 percent per year. This rate represents a decline from the 2.07 percent annual increase during the late 1960s, but it is still significantly higher than the projected annual rate of 0.1 percent by the year 2100. In other words, even though the population will continue to rise by several billion over the next several decades, projections show a substantial decline in the rate of the overall population increase (United Nations 2013d). This prediction of a leveling off of total population after generations of growth is consistent with the population model known as the demographic transition.

growth rate The overall percentage change in a population per year.

DEMOGRAPHIC TRANSITION

The most defining characteristic of population dynamics in the past 100 years or so is its explosive growth. Throughout most of human history, global population levels were relatively stable. The world's total population 2,000 years ago was approximately 300 million people. It took 1,500 years for it to reach the 500-million mark and another 300 years to surpass 1 billion in 1804. At that point population growth began accelerating rapidly (see the accompanying "World Population Growth" graph). From 1927 to 2012 the population grew from 2 billion to 7 billion and is projected to top the 10-billion mark in 2062 (United Nations 1999, 2013e).

Perhaps the best-known attempt to come to terms with the population explosion was offered early on by English economist Thomas Malthus (1766–1834). In 1798 he

U.S. Foreign-Born Population

Other regions **2.7%**

Africa **3.9%**

Europe **12.7%**

Asia **27.7%**

Latin America **53.1%**

Foreign **12.5%**

Native **87.5%**

Source: Grieco and Trevelyan 2010.

published the first edition of his book *An Essay on the Principle of Population,* in which he argued that there are natural limits to the number of people the environment can sustain. He claimed that, even though total food production expands to provide for a growing population, it does so at an arithmetic rate $(1 \rightarrow 2 \rightarrow 3 \rightarrow 4 \rightarrow 5)$. The problem is that population grows at a geometric rate $(1 \rightarrow 2 \rightarrow 4 \rightarrow 8 \rightarrow 16)$. Ultimately, population will grow so fast there won't be sufficient land to provide enough food for everyone. Crises would inevitably occur—including

demographic transition As societies transform from preindustrial to postindustrial, their population size shifts from small but stable with high birthrates and death rates, through a period of significant population growth, to large but stable, when both birth and death rates are low.

poverty, famine, disease, and war—and people would die as a result, reducing the population size to a more sustainable level. For Malthus, history is a never-ending struggle over resources in which people attempt to escape want, a battle that those who control resources are more likely to win. As a result, the burden of this misery falls more heavily on the poor. Though he did argue that people could and should exercise moral restraint to rein in population growth by delaying marriage and practicing celibacy, ultimately, Malthus's emphasis was on control of population through the increased mortality rates that result from crises over resources (Malthus 1878).

An alternative, and somewhat less dismal, model of population change is known as the **demographic transition.** According to this model, as societies transform from preindustrial to postindustrial, their population size shifts from small but stable, with high birthrates and death rates, through a period of significant population growth, to large but stable, when both birthrates and death rates are low (Notestein 1945; Thompson 1929, 1948). Unlike

World Population (billions)

World Population Growth

2016

2062: 10 billion — 10

2040: 9 billion

2024: 8 billion — 8

2012: 7 billion

1999: 6 billion — 6

1987: 5 billion

1974: 4 billion — 4

1959: 3 billion

1927: 2 billion — 2

1804: 1 billion

Year: 0 — 50 — 1000 — 1500 — 2000

Year

Source: United Nations 1999, 2013e.

Malthus, theorists here do not see elevated death rates through disease and war as inevitable checks on population growth. Instead, they argue that a natural decline in fertility rates occurs owing to technological, social, and economic changes. In basic terms, they portray the transition of a population with large families but short life spans to one with small families and long life spans as virtually inevitable (Bongaarts 2009; Kirk 1996; Myrskylä, Kohler, and Billari 2009). This transition has four primary stages.

Stage 1: Preindustrial Society This is the stage humans occupied throughout most of our history. As is evident in the accompanying "World Population Growth" graph, global population size was steady for a very long time. In terms of demographic factors, nations at this stage are characterized by high fertility rates and high death rates. The economies of such nations are primarily agricultural, and more children means more workers to produce the food necessary for survival. Because infant and child mortality rates are high in this stage, having more children ensures that some will make it to adulthood. Life expectancy in such nations tends to be short. To provide a visual representation of this distribution, demographers use population pyramids to show the ratio of the population by both age groupings (usually in 5-year increments) and sex. As the accompanying graph for Afghanistan demonstrates, pyramids for nations at this stage tend to have a wide base, indicating a large percentage of children in the population, and to narrow quickly at the top, showing the relatively small percentage of those who are elderly.

Stage 2: Early Industrial Society In this stage, death rates fall while birthrates remain high. More babies survive infancy and additional children make it to adulthood. Because there are more young adults, and the birthrate stays high, even more babies are born. On top of that, overall life expectancy increases. The result is a population explosion. This occurs as a consequence of innovations taking place in the society. Advances in technology lead to increased food supplies, cleaner water, improved sanitation, and better medical care. Developments in agricultural technology and techniques, such as crop rotation, are particularly important. In population pyramid terms, the base widens as the total number of children grows and the top both expands and gets taller owing to more people living longer. Historically, nations that entered this phase early on in the Industrial Revolution, such as the United States or Germany, saw slower population growth rates during this stage than have more recent developing nations. Gaining access to existing advances in medical technology often plays a critical role for developing nations, because it can dramatically decrease death rates(Bongaarts 2009).

Stage 3: Late Industrial Society Over time, fertility rates also begin to drop. People start to realize that, with mortality rates falling, having many children is no longer necessary to ensure that some survive into adulthood. Additionally, as the economy transitions away from

Afghanistan Population Pyramid

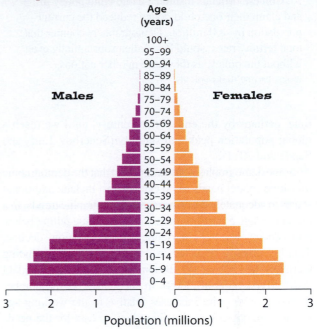

Source: United Nations 2013f.

agriculture, children are no longer needed as workers to assist in food production. In fact, especially with the establishment of child labor laws, children can become a liability rather than an asset. They are no longer primarily producers who contribute, becoming instead consumers whose needs must be met. Advances in contraception technology facilitate this choice to have fewer children. One effect of declining fertility rates is increased opportunity for women. As they spend less time bearing children, women are freed up to play expanded roles in the public spheres of politics and the economy. Because the adult population is relatively young, without an overwhelming number of children or elderly people to support, the economy often thrives, creating what is sometimes referred to as a demographic dividend (Bongaarts 2009).

Stage 4: Postindustrial Society Eventually the demographic transition is complete and population size becomes stable once again. This occurs because birthrates and death rates both reach low levels. Globally this takes a long time, but within a country the amount of time can vary: longer in early industrializing nations but less time for more recent developing nations. Total fertility rates reached replacement levels in Europe and North America by 1980 and are anticipated to do so in Asia and Latin America by 2020 (Bongaarts 2009). As a result of these changes, the population pyramid develops sides that are more vertical before they angle in to its pinnacle (see the accompanying "Global Population Pyramid" graph). According to this theory, as these trends spread it is just a matter of

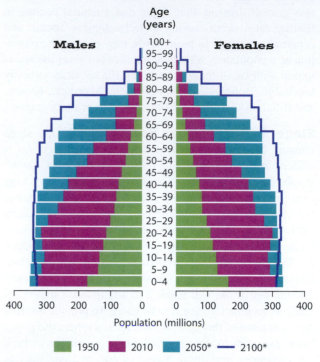
Global Population Pyramid

time, perhaps by the end of this century, until we reach a global population peak and stability (Scherbov, Lutz, and Sanderson 2011).

Some demographers have suggested that the demographic transition model needs to be extended to include additional stages to adequately describe recent demographic trends. In a possible Stage 5, fertility rates would continue falling below replacement levels, contributing to population decline. This has already occurred in numerous nations, including Germany and China (D. Bloom et al. 2010; Hvistendahl 2010; Myrskylä et al. 2009). In such cases, as the number of people who retire increases relative to the working-age population, questions arise about how to care for the needs of an aging population. In the United States ongoing political struggles over health care are driven, to some extent, by concerns about the ability to pay for increased Medicare costs caused by the demographic surge in retirees in the coming years (OASDI 2011). Some countries, such as Japan, have begun taking steps to boost fertility by establishing programs, such as extended paid maternity leave and subsidized day care, that encourage people to have more children (Suzuki 2009).

In recent years, some of these nations with below-replacement birthrates have experienced a fertility rebound, a possible Stage 6 of the demographic transition model. Demographers suggest that this is most likely to occur in countries with the highest scores on the United Nations Human Development Index (HDI). As we saw in Chapter 11, this index ranges from 0 to 1 and is based on three societal dimensions, including health, education, and income. Countries with an HDI score of greater than 0.86, such as the United States and Norway, are most likely to experience this rebound (Myrskylä et al. 2009). Parents in such countries can worry less about having sufficient individual and collective resources to provide for the needs of their children.

Anorexia is not a new disease, though it is discussed much more openly today. Victoria Beckham is one of several celebrities who have spoken publicly about struggling with an eating disorder. Photo: © WireImage/Getty Images.

*Numbers for 2050 and 2100 are projections based on existing birthrate and death rate trends.

Source: United Nations 2013f.

Studying population dynamics is important, because the world into which we are born is not of our own choosing, yet it shapes our life chances. When we were born, how long we live, and our likelihood for migration are all part of larger social trends. Understanding the nature and direction of these patterns can empower us to create new pathways in hopes of a better future. Such informed innovation has contributed to advances in health care, education, and environmental protection, substantially improving the life chances of people all around the world.

>> Sociological Perspectives on Health and Illness

To understand health, we cannot focus on biology alone. We must consider relationships, contexts, and the significance and impact of culture and society. Whether we are considered "healthy" or "ill" is not our decision alone to make. Family, friends, coworkers, physicians, and others all shape how we perceive the state of our health. A sociological understanding must take into

SOC THINK

What factors do you think might explain the fertility rebound in countries with high HDI scores?

account how society defines health and illness, what the consequences of such definitions are, and how social position and access to resources shape health outcomes.

CULTURE, SOCIETY, AND HEALTH

Our conceptions of what it means to be healthy vary over time and across cultures. In an attempt to provide a more universally applicable definition, the World Health Organization (WHO), in the preamble to its constitution, defined health as a "state of complete physical, mental, and social well-being, and not merely the absence of disease and infirmity" (World Health Organization 1948). Based on this absolute standard, most of us are probably not fully healthy most of the time. In practice, people fall somewhere along a continuum between this ideal at one extreme and death on the other.

Where we live influences where along that continuum we might fall. For example, the care we receive and the risks we face vary based upon whether we live in the city or the country. In rural areas, people may have to travel many miles to see a doctor or specialist. And in cities, urban dwellers face stresses, threats, and environmental risks different from those that people living in the country face. Another variable is cultural attitudes toward health care treatments. For example, in Japan, organ transplants are rare. The Japanese do not generally favor harvesting organs from brain-dead donors. As a result, they forgo the benefits that such transplants provide.

Researchers have shown that diseases, too, are rooted in the shared meanings of particular cultures. The term **culture-bound syndrome** refers to a disease or illness that cannot be understood apart from some specific social context. This means that there is something particular about the culture—how it is organized, what it believes, what is expected of members—that contributes to that malady (Burns 2013; Romans et al. 2012; Wedge 2012).

In the United States, a culture-bound syndrome known as anorexia nervosa has received significant attention in recent decades. First described in England in the 1860s, this condition is characterized by an intense fear of becoming obese and a distorted image of one's body. Those who suffer from anorexia nervosa (primarily young women in their teens or 20s) lose weight drastically through self-induced semistarvation. Anorexia nervosa is best understood in the context of Western culture, which typically views the slim, youthful individual as healthy and beautiful, and the fat person as ugly and lacking in self-discipline.

Throughout most of the 20th century, U.S. researchers dealt with the concept of culture-bound syndromes only in cross-cultural studies. However, increases in immigration, especially after the Immigration and Nationality Act of 1965 opened the doors to more immigrants, along with efforts by the medical establishment to reach out to immigrant communities, have led to a belated recognition that not everyone views medicine in the same way. Medical practitioners are now being trained to recognize cultural beliefs that are related to medicine. For example, people from Central America may consider pain a consequence of the imbalance of nature, and Muslim women are particularly concerned about personal modesty. Health care professionals are increasingly incorporating such knowledge into their practices.

ILLNESS AND SOCIAL ORDER

From a functionalist perspective, social order is paramount and illness represents a threat to the normal processes of society. To maintain order, we place social pressure on people to continue to perform their normal roles even when they feel sick. As a result, we debate about what it means to be "sick enough" to be considered truly ill. At what point, for example, do we stay home from school or work due to illness, and who gets to decide? All of us have likely faced this dilemma, sometimes dragging ourselves out of bed and going anyway because we felt we needed to be there, whether for the sake of ourselves or for others.

When people cross the line into illness, they take on what sociologists call the **sick role,** a form of legitimate deviance in which the person who becomes ill has a corresponding set of rights and responsibilities associated with that status. A

culture-bound syndrome A disease or illness that cannot be understood apart from some specific social context.

sick role A form of legitimate deviance in which the person who becomes ill has a corresponding set of rights and responsibilities associated with that status.

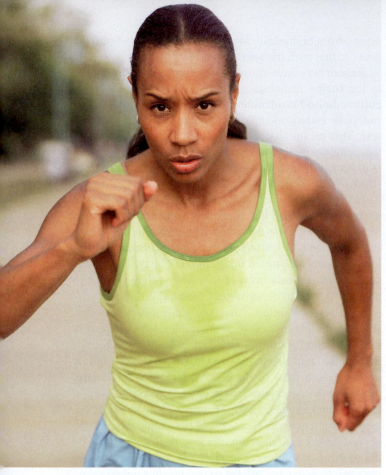

© LWA/Dann Tardif/Blend Images RF

sick person can violate the norms that regularly guide their everyday actions, whether as student, parent, or employee. They have a right to expect that others will not blame them for failure to conduct their usual responsibilities and that they will be given space and time to recover. That does not mean they are exempt from social obligations. Those who are deemed legitimately sick have a responsibility to get better as soon as possible, which includes seeking competent

medicalization The process of redefining new areas of social life as the legitimate domain for medical expertise by converting them into treatable medical conditions.

professional care. Failure to do so can result in negative sanctions (Parsons 1951, 1975). In fact, especially in the context of competitive work environments, we often look down on those who seem to get sick too easily or frequently, suspecting that they are either lazy or weak. Such attitudes present significant difficulties for those facing chronic health problems.

SOCTHINK

What factors shape your likelihood of doing all you can to avoid "being sick"? How might the power others have over you influence your actions? What positions do they occupy relative to you?

Health Care Fortunes

While working on revisions for this chapter, my retina detached and I went blind in one eye. Fortunately, I had access to experts, especially my retina specialist Dr. Heilskov, all of whom provided me with the best possible advice and care. Three operations later, my sight has largely been restored. And, (again) fortunately, I had health insurance to help pay those sizable medical bills. Had I been in the position of the majority of the world's population—lacking access to such care and coverage—I would have remained blind in that eye for life. To me, this ordeal affirmed one of the most basic lessons of sociology: Our life chances are shaped by the social positions we occupy.

Physicians and nurses have the power to label people as healthy or sick and, thus, to function as gatekeepers for the sick role. For example, instructors often require students to get a note from a health care professional to verify a claim of illness as a legitimate excuse for missing a paper or an exam. The ill person becomes dependent on the doctor or nurse, because physicians and nurses control the resources that patients need, whether it be a note for a professor or a prescription for medication. We look to such professionals to solve our health care needs, trusting that they have sufficient expertise and experience to diagnose and treat our problems.

POWER, RESOURCES, AND HEALTH

The faith we place in physicians to heal what ails us has helped them attain significant levels of prestige and power. Over time, the jurisdiction over which medical professionals have authority has expanded. Theorists use the phrase "medicalization of society," taking this extension of medical legitimacy into new realms (Conrad 2007; Zola 1972, 1983).

The Medicalization of Society The process of **medicalization** involves redefining new areas of social life as the legitimate domain for medical expertise by converting them into treatable medical conditions. This includes aspects we used to take for granted as involving natural human processes, such as childbirth, aging, menopause, sex, diet, mental health, addictions, sexuality, and even parenting and childhood (Cacchioni and Tiefer 2012; Chavigny 2014; Fainzang 2013; Francis 2012; Shaw 2013). We accept, and even encourage, the expansion of the boundaries of medicine because we hope that these experts can provide factual and effective cures to complex human problems, as they have to various infectious diseases.

This transference of authority to medical professionals is not without consequences. The presumed expertise of these specialists—and the specialized discourse that goes with it—makes it more difficult for common people to join in the discussion and exert their influence, even though their lives may be significantly affected by decisions the experts make. In addition, the natural science orientation of this model makes it more difficult to view these issues as also being shaped by social, cultural, or psychological factors (Caplan 1989; J. Davis 2006; Starr 1982).

As medical professionals expand their authority, they also engage in boundary maintenance to ensure that only those with appropriate knowledge and training are certified to practice medicine. One of the effects historically was to place some practitioners, such as chiropractors and nurse-midwives, outside the domain of legitimate medicine. Despite the fact that midwives first brought professionalism to child delivery, they have been portrayed by doctors as having invaded the "legitimate" field of obstetrics, in both the United States and Mexico. Nurse-midwives have sought licensing as a way to achieve professional respectability, but physicians continue to exert power to ensure that midwifery remains a subordinate occupation (Scharnberg 2007; Shaw 2013).

Inequities in Health Care Another serious concern regarding power and resources in the context of contemporary medicine involves the glaring inequities that exist in health care. Around the world, poor areas tend to be underserved because medical services concentrate where the wealth is.

© Blend Images/Getty Images RF

The United States, for example, has 24.2 physicians per 10,000 people, whereas other nations, such as Afghanistan (2.3), Chad (0.4), and Malawi (0.2) have much lower rates (World Health Organization 2014a).

> **brain drain** The immigration to the United States and other industrialized nations of skilled workers, professionals, and technicians who are needed in their home countries.

The supply of health care in poorer countries is further reduced by what is referred to as **brain drain**—the immigration to the United States and other industrialized nations of skilled workers, professionals, and technicians who are needed in their home countries. As part of this brain drain, physicians, nurses, and other health care professionals have come to the United States from developing countries such as India, Pakistan, and various African states. Their emigration represents yet another way in which the world's core industrialized nations enhance their quality of life at the expense of developing countries (List 2009).

Such inequities in health care have clear life-and-death consequences. For example, as we saw earlier, there are dramatic differences in infant mortality rates between developing countries such as Afghanistan, Sierra Leone, and Pakistan and industrialized nations such as Iceland, Japan, and Australia. Such differences in infant mortality reflect unequal distribution of health care resources based on the wealth or poverty of various nations as seen, for example, in prenatal nutrition, delivery procedures, and infant screening measures. An additional way that developing countries suffer the consequences of health care inequality is in reduced life expectancy. Average life expectancy in sub-Saharan African nations is 54 compared to 80 in European Union nations. By comparison, in the United States it is nearly 79 years (World Bank 2015f, 2015l).

Labeling and Power Sometimes the power to label and the power to oppress go hand in hand. A historical example illustrates perhaps the ultimate extreme in labeling social behavior as a sickness. As enslavement of Africans in the United States came under increasing attack in the 19th century, medical

5 Movies on HEALTH AND MEDICINE

The Diving Bell and the Butterfly
A man suddenly becomes completely paralyzed.

Contagion
Don't breathe or you could be next.

Living in Emergency
Volunteers for Doctors Without Borders provide medical care under extreme conditions.

Silver Linings Playbook
Two patients try to come to terms with their maladies.

Life, Above All
A 12-year-old girl uncovers her community's unspoken struggle with AIDS.

authorities provided new rationalizations for the oppressive practice. Noted physicians published articles stating that the skin color of Africans deviated from "healthy" white skin coloring because Africans suffered from congenital leprosy. Moreover, physicians classified the continuing efforts of enslaved Africans to escape from their White masters as an example of the "disease" of drapetomania (or "crazy runaways"). In 1851 the prestigious *New Orleans Medical and Surgical Journal* suggested that the remedy for this "disease" was to treat slaves kindly, as one might treat children. Apparently, these medical authorities would not entertain the view that it was healthy and sane to flee slavery or join in a slave revolt (Szasz 1971).

Globally, the power of one particular label—"HIV positive"—has become quite evident. This label often functions as a master status that overshadows all other aspects of a person's life. Once someone is told that he or she has tested positive for HIV, the virus associated with AIDS, that person is forced to confront immediate and difficult questions: Should I tell my family members? My sex partners? My friends? My coworkers? My employer? How will these people respond? People's intense fear of the disease has led to prejudice and discrimination—even social ostracism—against those who have (or are suspected of having) AIDS. A person who has AIDS must deal not only with the serious medical consequences of the disease, but also with the distressing social consequences associated with the label.

Although the numbers of new cases and deaths have recently shown evidence of decline, approximately 1.19 million people in the United States were living with AIDS as of 2013 (Centers for Disease Control and Prevention 2015a). Globally, an estimated 35 million people are now infected with HIV. There were 2.1 million new cases in 2013, which represents a 38 percent decline in new HIV infections compared to 2001. Of people with HIV,

Going GLOBAL

Infant Mortality Rates in Selected Countries

Infant deaths per 1,000 live births

Sierra Leone 107.2

Somalia 89.8

Pakistan 69

Haiti 54.7

India 41.4

World 33.6

Mexico 12.5

United States 5.9

Canada 4.6

Australia 3.4

Japan 2.1

Luxembourg 1.6

Source: World Bank 2015f.

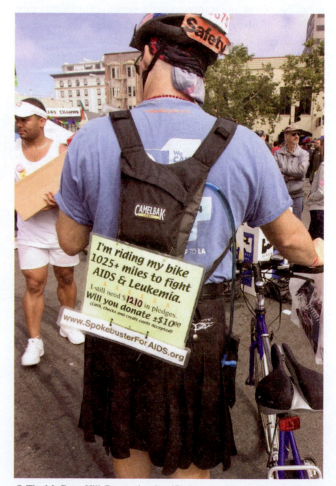

© The McGraw-Hill Companies, Inc./Christopher Kerrigan, photographer

Going GLOBAL

HIV/AIDS Cases

Eastern Europe/Central Asia
1.3 million
91,000

East Asia
880,000
41,000

North America
1.3 million
20,000

Western/Central Europe
860,000
7,600

Caribbean
250,000
11,000

North Africa/Middle East
260,000
17,000

Sub-Saharan Africa
25.0 million

South/Southeast Asia
3.9 million
220,000

Central & South America
1.5 million
52,000

People living with HIV
Deaths from AIDS in 2012
100,000 people

1.2 million

Oceania (Australia/New Zealand)
51,000
1,200

Note: Total number of adults and children living with HIV, 35.3 million; total number of estimated adult and child deaths during 2012, 1.6 million.

Source: UNAIDS 2013.

22 million are not receiving any life-saving medical treatment for the disease and 19 million don't even know they are infected (UNAIDS 2014).

In the United States, because those in high-risk groups—gay men and IV drug users—were comparatively powerless, and labeled as such, policy makers were slow to respond to the AIDS crisis. Over time and with increased education and advocacy, however, the response has improved, and today people with HIV or AIDS who receive appropriate medical treatment are living longer than they did in the past. The high cost of drug treatment programs has generated intensive worldwide pressure on the major pharmaceutical companies to lower the prices to patients in developing nations, especially in sub-Saharan Africa. Bowing to this pressure, several of the companies have agreed to make the combination therapies available at cost. As a result, the accessibility of HIV treatment has increased steadily, though inequalities remain. By the end of 2013, almost 12.9 million patients were receiving antiretroviral therapy. Of those living with HIV, 37 percent now receive these treatments compared to only 10 percent in 2006. Estimates are that, since 1995, retroviral therapy has averted 7.6 million deaths around the world (UNAIDS 2014).

According to labeling theorists, we can view a variety of life experiences as illnesses or not. Recently, the medical community has recognized premenstrual syndrome, posttraumatic disorders, and hyperactivity as medical disorders. Probably the most noteworthy medical example of labeling is the case of homosexuality. For years, psychiatrists classified being gay or lesbian not as a lifestyle but as a mental disorder subject to treatment. This official sanction by the psychiatry profession became an early target of the growing gay and lesbian rights movement in the United States. In 1974 members of the American Psychiatric Association voted to drop homosexuality from the standard manual on mental disorders (Conrad 2007).

NEGOTIATING CURES

In practice, we seek to strike a balance between the authority of the physician and the agency of the patient. Physicians use cues to reinforce their prestige and power. According to medical sociologist Brenda Beagan (2001, 2003), the technical language students learn in medical school becomes the basis for the script they follow as novice physicians. The familiar white coat and stethoscope is their costume—one that helps them appear confident and professional at the same time that it identifies them as doctors to patients and other staff members. Beagan found that many medical students struggle to project the appearance of competence they think their role demands, but over time most become accustomed to expecting respect and deference.

social epidemiology The study of the role social factors play in the development and distribution of disease throughout the population.

prevalence The total number of cases of a specific disorder that exist at a given time.

incidence The number of new cases of a specific disorder that occur within a given population during a stated period.

morbidity rate The incidence of disease in a given population.

mortality rate The incidence of death in a given population.

Patients, however, are not passive. Active involvement in health care can have positive or negative consequences. Sometimes, patients play an active role in health care by failing to follow a physician's advice. For example, some patients stop taking medications long before they should. Some decrease or increase the dosage on purpose (because they think they know better what they need), and others never even fill their prescriptions. Such noncompliance results in part from the prevalence of self-medication in our society; many people are accustomed to self-diagnosis and self-treatment.

Patients' active involvement in their health care can have very positive consequences. Some patients consult books, magazines, and websites about preventive health care techniques, attempt to maintain a healthful and nutritious diet, carefully monitor any side effects of medication, and adjust the dosage based on perceived side effects. Recognizing this change, pharmaceutical firms are advertising their prescription drugs directly to potential customers. For their part, medical professionals are understandably suspicious of these new sources of information. Studies, including one published in the *Journal of the American Medical Association,* found that health information on the Internet can be incomplete and inaccurate, even on the best sites. Nevertheless, there is little doubt that Internet research is transforming patient–physician encounters (Adams and de Bont 2007; Arora et al. 2008; Berland 2001).

>> Social Epidemiology

By looking at patterns of health and illness throughout society, we can better understand which factors are at work in shaping health outcomes. **Social epidemiology** investigates the role social factors play in the development and distribution of disease throughout the population. The social positions we occupy shape our chances for a healthy life.

Analysis of biological factors alone is insufficient. We must also consider the impact factors such as social class, ethnicity, race, and gender have on our overall health. Statuses such as these influence our access to material, social, and cultural resources. Having enough money to afford health insurance or to purchase foods for a healthy diet; having social connections that open doors in times of crisis or concern; having knowledge about where to get medical information, what to ask the doctor, and what foods to consume are all examples of how our social position shapes our health care outcomes. And yet we tend to minimize the consequences of such differences when considering health care solutions.

To describe how widespread a disease is and how fast it is spreading, social epidemiologists report on rates of prevalence and incidence. **Prevalence** refers to the total number of cases of a specific disorder that exist at a given time. **Incidence** refers to the number of new cases of a specific disorder that occur within a given population during a specified period of time, usually a year. Staying with the AIDS example, the 35 million people globally living with HIV is an example of prevalence. Incidence refers to the 2.1 million new cases in 2013 (UNAIDS 2014).

To better understand and measure the prevalence and incidence of disease within and between cultures, researchers rely on rates to provide standardized measures. **Morbidity rates,** for example, measure the incidence of disease in a given population. This is distinct from the **mortality rate,** which refers to the incidence of death in a given population. As we shall see, social class, race, ethnicity, gender, and age can all affect a population's morbidity rates (Barr 2008).

SOCIAL CLASS

Social class is clearly associated with differences in morbidity and mortality rates. Studies in the United States and other countries have consistently shown that people in the lower classes have higher rates of mortality and disability than those in higher classes. One study concluded that Americans with 12 years or less of schooling could expect to die seven years sooner than those with more than 12 years of schooling (Meara, Richards, and Cutler 2008; Pear 2008).

A number of factors appear to influence the effect class has on health. Crowded living conditions, substandard housing, poor diet, and stress all contribute to the ill health of many low-income people in the United States. In certain instances, poor education may lead to a lack of awareness of measures necessary to maintain good health. Financial strains are certainly a major factor in the health problems of less affluent people.

People who are poor—many of whom belong to racial and ethnic minorities—are less able than others to afford quality medical care (see the accompanying "People without Health Insurance" graph). Not surprisingly, those with high incomes are significantly more likely to have health insurance, either because they can afford it or because they have jobs

©Jean-Marc Giboux/Getty Images

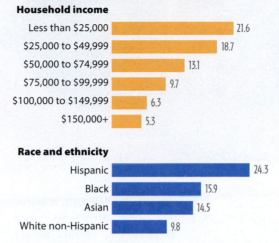

Did You Know?

... In research looking at how social class operates, sociologist Annette Lareau (2003) found that middle-class parents and children were more likely to engage with physicians, asking questions and questioning diagnoses. Working-class patients were more deferential to the doctor's authority.

Photo: © RubberBall Productions RF.

People without Health Insurance

Household income

Less than $25,000	21.6
$25,000 to $49,999	18.7
$50,000 to $74,999	13.1
$75,000 to $99,999	9.7
$100,000 to $149,999	6.3
$150,000+	5.3

Race and ethnicity

Hispanic	24.3
Black	15.9
Asian	14.5
White non-Hispanic	9.8

Note: Numbers represent the percentage of people without health insurance for the full calendar year.
Source: J. Smith and Medalia 2014.

that provide it. The middle class has been particularly hard hit by the decision of companies to eliminate employer-provided coverage (the most common form of health insurance). Such rates declined steadily from 2000 to 2010 (DeNavas-Walt et al. 2012; E. Gould 2008).

The ultimate price to pay for a lack of health insurance is the increased risk of early death. Uninsured women who develop breast cancer tend to be diagnosed later—when treatment is less effective—than insured women. Uninsured men who develop high blood pressure are more likely than others to forgo screenings and medication, a decision that jeopardizes their health. According to a 2009 Harvard Medical School study, approximately 45,000 deaths per year are associated with lack of health insurance (Wilper et al. 2009).

What is particularly troubling about social class differences is that they appear to be cumulative. Little or no health care in childhood or young adulthood is likely to mean more illness later in life. The longer that low income presents a barrier to adequate health care, the more chronic and difficult to treat illness becomes (Prus 2007).

Karl Marx would have argued, and some contemporary sociologists agree, that capitalist societies such as the United States care more about maximizing profits than they do about the health and safety of industrial workers. As a result, government

> ### It is a lot harder to keep people well than it is to just get them over a sickness.
>
> ———————
>
> DeForest Clinton Jarvis

agencies do not take forceful action to regulate conditions in the workplace, and workers suffer many preventable job-related injuries and illnesses. As we will see later in this chapter, research also shows that the lower classes are more vulnerable to environmental pollution, another consequence of capitalist production, than are the affluent, not only where they work but where they live as well.

RACE AND ETHNICITY

The health profiles of many racial and ethnic minorities reflect the social inequality evident in U.S. society. The poor economic and environmental conditions of groups such as African Americans, Hispanics, and Native Americans are manifested in high morbidity and mortality

Infant Mortality Rates in the United States

Race and ethnicity	Infant deaths per 1,000 live births
Black, non-Hispanic	11.5
American Indian or Alaska Native	8.3
Hispanic	5.3
White, non-Hispanic	5.2
Asian or Pacific Islander	4.3

Note: Rates represent the number of infant deaths per 1,000 live births.
Source: Mathews and MacDorman 2013.

© Fancy Photography/Veer RF

curanderismo Latino folk medicine, a form of holistic health care and healing.

explain the higher rates of hypertension found among African Americans (and Hispanics) compared to Whites. Hypertension—twice as common in Blacks as in Whites—is believed to be a critical factor in Blacks' high mortality rates from heart disease, kidney disease, and stroke (Fiscella and Holt 2008).

Mexican Americans and many other Latinos adhere to cultural beliefs that make them less likely to use the established medical system. They may interpret their illnesses according to traditional Latino folk medicine, or *curanderismo*—a form of holistic health care and healing. *Curanderismo* influences how one approaches health care and even how one defines illness. Although most Hispanics use folk healers, or *curanderos,* infrequently, perhaps 20 percent rely on home remedies. Some define such illnesses as *susto* (fright sickness) and *atague* (fighting attack) according to folk beliefs. Because these complaints often have biological bases, sensitive medical practitioners need to deal with them carefully to diagnose and treat illnesses accurately (Tafur, Crowe, and Torres 2009).

Also affecting Latino morbidity rates is the fact that Latinos are much more likely to wait to seek treatment. Partly because of a lack of health insurance, they seek treatment for pressing medical problems at clinics and emergency rooms rather than receiving regular preventive care through a family physician. Such delays in treatments increase the severity of the consequences of illness and disease (Durden and Hummer 2006).

rates for these groups. It is true that some afflictions, such as sickle-cell anemia among Blacks, are influenced by genetics, but in most instances, environmental factors contribute to the differential rates of disease and death.

As noted earlier, infant mortality is regarded as a primary indicator of health care. There is a significant gap in the United States between the infant mortality rates of African Americans and Whites. On average, the rate of infant death is more than twice as high among Blacks. Non-Hispanic African Americans account for 14.7 percent of all live births in the nation but 27.5 percent of infant deaths. Low birth weight among African Americans plays a major part in that difference (Mathews and MacDorman 2013).

Considering mortality rates, Blacks have higher death rates from heart disease, pneumonia, diabetes, and cancer than do Whites. The death rate from stroke is twice as high among African Americans. Such epidemiological findings are related to the social class effects noted previously—the fact that average income for African Americans is lower than that for Whites. The effect of these factors can be seen in terms of life expectancy. According to statistics from the Centers for Disease Control and Prevention, overall life expectancy in the United States is 78.7 years, but for Whites it is 79 years compared to 75.3 years for Blacks. This gap is lower than the high of 7.1 years in 1989 (National Center for Health Statistics 2014: Table 18).

The medical establishment is not exempt from institutional discrimination. There is evidence that minorities receive inferior care even when they are insured. Despite having access to care, Blacks, Latinos, and American Indians are treated unequally as a result of differences in the quality of various health care plans. Furthermore, national clinical studies have shown that even allowing for differences in income and insurance coverage, racial and ethnic minorities are less likely than other groups to receive both standard health care and life-saving treatment (Dressler, Oths, and Gravlee 2005; A. Green et al. 2007).

Having to deal with the effects of racism may itself contribute to the medical problems of Blacks. The stress that results from racial prejudice and discrimination helps

GENDER

Men and women do differ in their overall health. For example, women live longer than men. Girls born in 2009 can

Smoking Rates by Gender

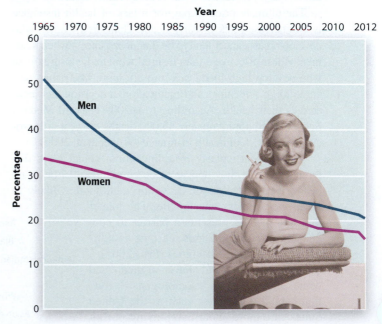

Source: National Center for Health Statistics 2014: Table 56.

Photo: © Photo by Victor Keppler/George Eastman House/Getty Images.

anticipate an average life expectancy of 81.1 years, compared to 76.3 for boys. The good news for men is that, though life expectancy continues to rise for both men and women, rates have been rising even faster for men. As a result, the life expectancy gap between men and women has declined from 7.6 years for those born in 1970 to 4.8 years in 2011 (National Center for Health Statistics 2014: Table 18).

Greater longevity for women appears to be tied to lifestyle differences between men and women that grow out of gendered norms. Historically, women's lower rate of cigarette smoking (reducing their risk of heart disease, lung cancer, and emphysema), lower consumption of alcohol (reducing the risk of auto accidents and cirrhosis of the liver), and lower rate of employment in dangerous occupations explain about one-third of their greater longevity than men. Researchers argue that women are much more likely than men to seek treatment, to be diagnosed as having a disease, and thus to have their illnesses reflected in the data examined by epidemiologists (National Center for Health Statistics 2014). Changes in lifestyle do matter. The declining gap in smoking rates between men and women accounts for some of the reduction in the difference in life expectancy between men and women.

With everything from birth to beauty being treated in an increasingly medical context, women have been particularly vulnerable to the medicalization of society. Ironically, even given the increased power of the medical establishment in women's lives, medical researchers have often excluded them from clinical studies. Female physicians and researchers charge that sexism lies at the heart of such research practices and insist there is a desperate need for studies of female subjects (Pinnow et al. 2009; Rieker and Bird 2000).

AGE

Health is the overriding concern of older adults. Most older people in the United States report having at least one chronic illness, but only some of those conditions are potentially life threatening or require medical care. The quality of life among older people is of particular concern in the face of potentially escalating health problems. A substantial number of older people in the United States are troubled by arthritis and other chronic diseases, and many have visual or hearing impairments that can interfere with the performance of everyday tasks (Hootman et al. 2006; National Center for Health Statistics 2014).

Older people are also especially vulnerable to certain mental health problems. Alzheimer's disease, the leading cause of dementia in the United States, afflicts an estimated 5.1 million of people aged 65 years and older. That

Availability of Physicians by State

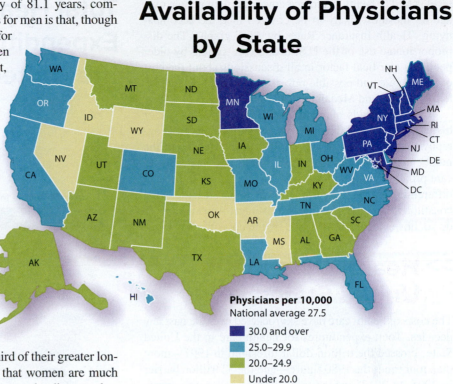

Physicians per 10,000
National average 27.5

- ■ 30.0 and over
- ■ 25.0–29.9
- ■ 20.0–24.9
- ■ Under 20.0

Source: National Center for Health Statistics 2014: Table 101.

number is projected to grow to 13.8 million as the U.S. population ages (Alzheimer's Association 2015).

Because of their increased health risks, the rate at which older people in the United States (aged 75 and older) use health services is more than three times greater than that for younger people (aged 15–24). This heightened use

Health Insurance Rates by Age

Source: J. Smith and Medalia 2014:Table 2.

level is tied to health insurance coverage, with people over age 65 the most likely to be covered (see the accompanying "Health Insurance Rates by Age" graph). The disproportionate use of the U.S. health care system by older people is a critical factor in all discussions about the cost of health care and possible reforms of the health care system (J. Smith and Medalia 2014: Table 2).

A person's odds of good health are shaped by her or his class, race and ethnicity, gender, and age. Even geography matters, as there are significant differences in the number of physicians from one state to the next. Health care professionals and program advisers need to take such differential effects into account when considering what constitutes equitable health care coverage. Any attempts to do so, however, are constrained by the cost of health care.

>> Health Care in the United States

The costs of health care have skyrocketed over the past few decades. Total expenditures for health care in the United States crossed the trillion-dollar threshold in 1997—more than four times the 1980 figure—and the $2 trillion barrier in 2005. In 2013, expenditures worked out to an average of $9,255 per person. The United States devotes a greater proportion of its total spending to health care, 17.6 percent as measured by GDP, than does any other country in the world. Contrast the U.S. rate with rates in countries such as France (11.6), Canada (10.9), Japan (10.0), Sweden (9.5), or the United Kingdom (9.4). Health care in the United States has become a major economic concern (Centers for Medicare and Medicaid Services 2014a, 2014b; World Health Organization 2014a).

A HISTORICAL VIEW

Today, state licensing and medical degrees confer a widely recognized level of authority on medical professionals. This was not always the case. The "popular health movement" of the 1830s and 1840s emphasized preventive care and what is termed "self-help." It voiced strong criticism of "doctoring" as a paid occupation. New medical philosophies or sects established their own medical schools and challenged the authority and methods of traditional doctors. By the 1840s most states had repealed medical licensing laws, and the health care field was largely unregulated (Porter 1998, 2004).

In response, through the leadership of the American Medical Association (AMA), founded in 1848, "regular" doctors marginalized lay practitioners, sectarian doctors, and female physicians in general. They institutionalized their authority through standardized programs of education and licensing. Only those who successfully completed AMA programs gained legitimate authority as medical practitioners.

© Jules Frazier/Getty Images RF

Total Health Care Expenditures in the United States

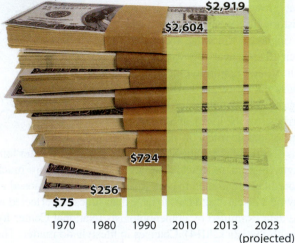

Total expenditure in billions of dollars

$5,159
$2,919
$2,604
$724
$256
$75

1970 1980 1990 2010 2013 2023 (projected)

Source: Centers for Medicare and Medicaid Services 2014a, 2014b.
Photo: © Comstock Images/Alamy RF.

The authority of the physician no longer depended on lay attitudes or on the person occupying the sick role; increasingly, it was built into the structure of the medical profession and the health care system.

As the institutionalization of health care proceeded, the medical profession gained control over both the market for its services and the various organizational hierarchies that govern medical practice, financing, and policy making. By the 1920s physicians controlled hospital technology, the division of labor of health personnel, and indirectly, other professional practices such as nursing and pharmaceutical services (Coser 1984; Starr 1982; Whorton 2002).

THE ROLE OF GOVERNMENT

Not until the 20th century did health care receive federal aid in conjunction with the expansion of medicine as a social institution. The first significant government involvement was the 1946 Hill-Burton Act, which provided subsidies for building and improving hospitals, especially in rural areas. An even more important development was the enactment in 1965 of two wide-ranging government assistance programs: Medicare, which is essentially a compulsory health insurance plan for the elderly, and Medicaid, which is a noncontributory federal and state insurance plan for the poor. These programs greatly expanded federal involvement in health care financing for needy men, women, and children.

While health care costs were rising, a growing portion of the U.S. population (42 million in 2013) remained uninsured. An inability to afford coverage was a major factor. In 1993 the Clinton administration proposed health care reform designed to provide universal coverage, but the legislation failed to pass. Throughout the George W. Bush administration, the United States remained the only wealthy, industrialized nation that did not provide some form of universal coverage (J. Smith and Medalia 2014).

By 2009 there was widespread political agreement that the existing system, with its projected escalating costs, was not sustainable. The Obama administration pledged to enact reform that would both contain costs and expand coverage. Though there was general consensus regarding these aims, there were significant disagreements on how best to accomplish them. Some supported a single-payer system in which the government is the primary source of health care funding. Others continued to support market-based reforms that minimize government involvement. A significant intervening position focused on whether or not the government should provide a "public option," allowing people to choose a government-funded plan among many private company plans.

In March 2010 Congress passed, and President Obama signed into law, the Patient Protection and Affordable Care Act and the Health Care and Education Reconciliation Act. Key provisions include:

- Young adults may stay on their parents' health care plans until age 26.
- Coverage for checkups and other preventive care does not require co-pays.
- Annual caps and lifetime limits on the cost of benefits patients can receive were eliminated.
- People with preexisting conditions cannot be denied coverage, and companies are no longer able to cut employees from a plan when they get sick.

- Most Americans are required to purchase some form of health insurance.
- Tax credits for the purchase of insurance are available for individuals and families between 100 and 400 percent of the poverty level.
- Companies with more than 50 employees are required to provide an employer-sponsored health plan that provides a mandated level of minimal coverage.
- Small businesses are eligible to receive tax credits to assist them in providing coverage.
- State-based insurance exchanges offer a choice of plans for small businesses and people who lack employer-supplied coverage.
- Insurance companies are required to provide greater transparency regarding spending on overhead costs.

The acts passed Congress with virtually no bipartisan support. Republicans continued to prefer market-based solutions arguing that free-market capitalism would lead to greater efficiency and cost control. With the implementation of the Affordable Care Act in 2014, the uninsured rate fell from 17.1 percent at the end of 2013 to 11.9 percent at the beginning of 2015 (Levy 2015).

> **holistic medicine** Therapies in which the health care practitioner considers the person's physical, mental, emotional, and spiritual characteristics.

POPSOC

Our perception of doctors and health care is shaped by the media. For a long time, *E.R.* was the king of the hospital heap on television. In recent years, *Grey's Anatomy*, *Nurse Jackie*, and *House* took off. If such programs were our only source of information about backstage life among doctors and nurses, what would we conclude about the nature of health care in the United States?

COMPLEMENTARY AND ALTERNATIVE MEDICINE

In modern forms of health care, people rely on physicians and hospitals for the treatment of illness. Yet a significant proportion of adults in the United States attempt to maintain good health or respond to illness through the use of alternative health care techniques. For example, in recent decades, interest has been growing in holistic medical principles, first developed in China. **Holistic medicine** refers to therapies in which the health care practitioner considers the person's physical, mental, emotional, and spiritual characteristics. The individual is regarded as a totality rather than a collection of interrelated organ systems. Treatment methods include massage, chiropractic medicine, acupuncture, respiratory exercises, and the use of herbs as remedies. Nutrition, exercise, and visualization may also be used to treat ailments (Barnes, Bloom, and Nahin 2008; Stratton and McGivern-Snofsky 2008).

President Barack Obama signs the Affordable Care Act into law.
Photo: © Chip Somodevilla/Getty Images.

Rising Medicare Expenses

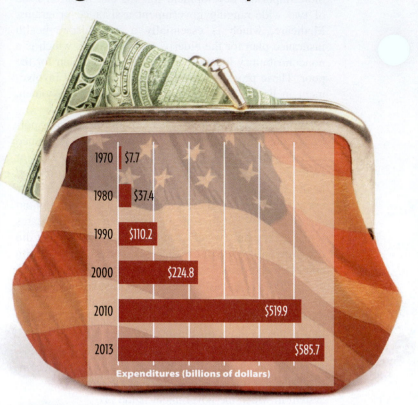

Year	Expenditures (billions of dollars)
1970	$7.7
1980	$37.4
1990	$110.2
2000	$224.8
2010	$519.9
2013	$585.7

Source: Centers for Medicare and Medicaid Services 2014a:Table 3.   Photo: © Grigory Bibikov/Getty Images RF.

The medical establishment—professional organizations, research hospitals, and medical schools—continues to zealously protect its authority. However, a major breakthrough occurred in 1992 when the federal government's National Institutes of Health (NIH)—the nation's major funding source for biomedical research—opened the National Center for Complementary and Alternative Medicine and empowered it to accept grant requests. A 2007 NIH-sponsored national study found that 38.3 percent of adults in the United States had used some form of complementary or alternative medicine within the previous year. Examples of practices include use of natural products (such as echinacea or omega-3 fatty acids), deep breathing, meditation, chiropractic treatment, massage, yoga, diet-based therapies (including vegetarian, macrobiotic, and Atkins), homeopathic treatment, and acupuncture. When private or communal prayer was included as part of the NIH-sponsored 2002 study, the number rose to 62.1 percent (Barnes et al. 2004, 2008).

On the international level, the WHO has begun to monitor the use of alternative medicine around the world. According to the WHO, 80 percent of people in some African and Asian countries use alternative medicine, from herbal treatments to the services of a faith healer. In most countries, these treatments are largely unregulated, even though some of them can be fatal. For example, kava kava, an herbal tea used in the Pacific Islands to relieve anxiety, can be toxic to the liver in concentrated form. Other alternative treatments have been found to be effective in the treatment of serious diseases, such as malaria and sickle-cell anemia. The WHO's goal is to compile a list of such practices, as well as to encourage the development of universal training programs and ethical standards for practitioners of alternative medicine (World Health Organization 2005, 2008a).

Sociological analysis of health and illness suggests that if we are to understand sickness we must look beyond biology. Society and culture, family and friends, the medical profession, and social position all help shape medical outcomes. Given the increasing costs of health care, and the fact that different groups experience different outcomes, this issue becomes one of equality and fairness. Lives are at stake. It is precisely such concerns that drive debates about the expansion of health care coverage as a social right.

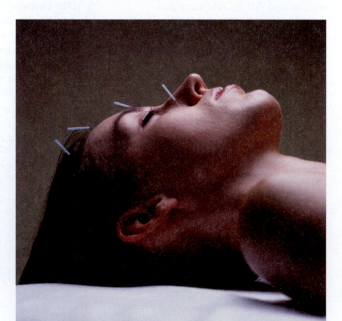

© Anthony Saint James/Getty Images RF

>> Sociological Perspectives on the Environment

Humans' interdependent relationships with one another also extend to the natural environment. The choices we make are constrained by available natural resources. Through technology we modify nature to suit our needs and throughout history humans have demonstrated an astonishing ability to do so, but not without consequences. The benefits of the Industrial Revolution came with costs such as air pollution, water pollution, and global climate change. We have entered an era of what some are calling the Anthropocene, a geological epoch in which human actions, even at a micro level, have global environmental consequences (Sample 2014).

HUMAN ECOLOGY

Human ecology is an area of study that is concerned with interrelationships between people and their environment. As biologist and environmentalist Barry Commoner (1971:39) put it during the early stages of the modern environmental movement, "Everything is connected to everything else." Human ecologists focus on how the physical environment shapes people's lives and on how people influence the surrounding environment.

In an application of the human ecological perspective, sociologists and environmentalists have identified several relationships between the environment and people. Among them are the following:

- *The environment provides the resources essential for life.* These include air, water, and materials used to create shelter, transportation, and needed products. If human societies exhaust these resources—for example, by polluting the water supply or cutting down rain forests—the consequences could be dire.
- *The environment serves as a waste repository.* More so than other living species, humans produce a huge quantity and variety of waste products—bottles, cans, boxes, paper, sewage, garbage, and so on. Various types of pollution have become more common because human societies are generating more wastes than the environment can safely absorb.
- *The environment "houses" our species.* It is our home, our living space, the place where we reside, work, and play. At times we take this truism for granted, but not when day-to-day living conditions become unpleasant and problematic. If our air is polluted, if our tap water turns brown, or if toxic chemicals seep into our neighborhood, we remember why it is vital to live in a healthful environment.

There is no shortage of illustrations of the interconnectedness of humans and the environment. For example, scientific research has linked pollutants in the environment to

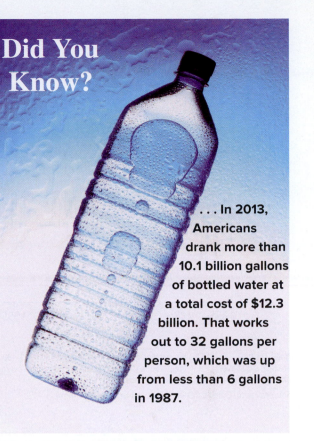

Did You Know?

. . . In 2013, Americans drank more than 10.1 billion gallons of bottled water at a total cost of $12.3 billion. That works out to 32 gallons per person, which was up from less than 6 gallons in 1987.

Source: Rodwan 2014.   *Photo:* © Digital Vision Ltd/Getty Images RF.

people's health and behavior. The increasing prevalence of asthma, lead poisoning, and cancer has been tied to human alterations to the environment. Similarly, the rise in melanoma (skin cancer) diagnoses has been linked to global climate change. And ecological changes in our food and diet have been related to childhood obesity and diabetes.

> **human ecology** The area of study concerned with the interrelationships between people and their environment.

With its view that "everything is connected to everything else," human ecology stresses the trade-offs inherent in every decision that alters the environment. In facing the environmental challenges of the 21st century, government policy makers and environmentalists must determine how they can fulfill humans' pressing needs for food, clothing, and shelter while preserving the environment as a source of resources, a waste repository, and a home.

POWER, RESOURCES, AND THE ENVIRONMENT

Analyzing environmental issues from a world systems approach allows us to better understand the global consequences of differential access to resources. This approach highlights the difference in relative power between core nations, which control wealth and so dominate the global economy, and developing countries, which lack control and whose resources are exploited. This process only

Global Temperature, 1850–2015

Temperature variation (°C) vs. Year

Note: The base line (0° C) is the average global air temperature from 1961–1990. Temperatures beneath that line are below that average and temperatures above that line are above that average. The hottest years on record have all occurred within the past two decades.

Source of data: Climatic Research Unit, University of East Anglia.

There is, in fact, a certain amount of ethnocentrism involved when people in industrialized countries insist that those developing nations change their practices to save the planet. In calling for the poverty-stricken and "food-hungry" populations of the world to sacrifice, they should also consider the lifestyle consequences for the "energy-hungry" nations. The industrialized nations of North America and Europe account for only 12 percent of the world's population but are responsible for 60 percent of worldwide consumption. The money their residents spend on ocean cruises each year could provide clean drinking water for everyone on the planet. Ice cream expenditures in Europe alone could be used to immunize every child in the world. The global consumer represents a serious environmental threat, but it is often difficult to look in the mirror and blame ourselves because our individual contribution to the problem seems so small. Collectively, however, the choices we make have a significant global impact (Diamond 2008; Gardner, Assadourian, and Sarin 2004).

The rise in global consumption is tied to a capitalist system that depends upon growth for its survival. Capitalism creates a "treadmill of production" (Baer 2008; Schnaiberg 1994). Cutting back on consumption means cutting back on purchases, which leads to reduced production and the loss

intensifies the destruction of natural resources in poorer regions of the world. Less affluent nations are being forced to exploit their mineral deposits, forests, and fisheries in order to meet their debt obligations. People in developing nations often end up turning to the only means of survival available to them, including plowing mountain slopes, burning sections of tropical forests, and overgrazing grasslands (Palm et al. 2005; Pollini 2009).

Brazil exemplifies this interplay between economic troubles and environmental destruction. Each year more than 4.3 million acres of rain forest are cleared for crops and livestock. The elimination of the rain forest affects worldwide weather patterns, heightening the gradual warming of the earth. These socio-economic patterns, with their harmful environmental consequences, are evident not only in Central and South America, but also in many regions of Africa and Asia (INPE 2010).

Although destruction of the rain forest has long been a concern, only in the past few decades have policy makers begun to listen to the indigenous peoples who live in these areas. Preservation of the rain forests may make sense at the global level, but for many local peoples, it limits their ability to cultivate crops or graze cattle. Even though it harms the global environment, they feel they have no choice but to take advantage of their available resources. In 2008 native peoples from Brazil to the Congo to Indonesia convened to make the case that wealthier countries should compensate them for conservation of the tropical rain forests (Barrionuevo 2008).

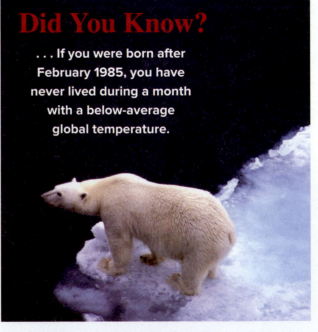

Did You Know?

. . . If you were born after February 1985, you have never lived during a month with a below-average global temperature.

Source: NOAA 2014.   *Photo:* © Paul Miles/Axiom Photographic Agency/Getty Images.

of profits and jobs. This treadmill necessitates creating an increasing demand for products, obtaining natural resources at minimal cost, and manufacturing products as quickly and cheaply as possible—no matter what the long-term environmental consequences.

ENVIRONMENTAL JUSTICE

In autumn 1982 nearly 500 African Americans participated in a six-week protest against a hazardous waste landfill containing cancer-causing chemicals in Warren County, North Carolina. Their protests and legal actions continued until 2002, when decontamination of the site finally began. This 20-year battle can be seen as yet another "not-in-my-backyard" (NIMBY) event in which people desire the benefits of growth but want someone else to pay for its negative effects. In any event, the Warren County struggle is viewed as a transformative moment in contemporary environmentalism: the beginning of the environmental justice movement (Bullard 2000; McGurty 2007; North Carolina Department of Environment and Natural Resources 2008).

Environmental justice is a legal strategy based on claims that racial minorities are subjected disproportionately to environmental hazards. Some observers have heralded environmental justice as the "new civil rights of the 21st century" (Kokmen 2008:42). Since the advent of the environmental justice movement, activists and scholars have identified other environmental disparities that break along racial and social class lines. In general, poor people and people of color are much more likely than others to be victimized by the everyday consequences of economic development, including air pollution from expressways and incinerators (Sandler and Pezzullo 2007).

Sociologists Paul Mohai and Robin Saha (2007) examined more than 600 hazardous waste treatment, storage, and disposal facilities in the United States. They found that non-Whites and Latinos make up 43 percent of the people who live within one mile of these dangerous sites. There are two possible explanations for this finding. One is that racial and ethnic minorities possess less political power than others, so they cannot prevent toxic sites from being located in their backyards. The other is that they end up settling near the sites after they are constructed, because economics and the forces of discrimination push them into the least desirable living areas.

> ## Suburbia is where the developer bulldozes out the trees, then names the streets after them.
>
> Bill Vaughn

Following reports from the Environmental Protection Agency (EPA) and other organizations documenting the discriminatory location of hazardous waste sites, President Bill Clinton issued an executive order in 1994 requiring all federal agencies to ensure that low-income and minority communities have access to better information about their environment, as well as an opportunity to participate in shaping government policies that affect their health. Initial efforts to implement the policy, along with increased activity by the environmental justice movement, aroused widespread opposition because of the delays the policy imposes in establishing new industrial sites. Some observers question the wisdom of an order that slows economic development in areas that are in dire need of employment opportunities. Others counter that such businesses employ few unskilled or less skilled workers and only make the environment less livable (Stretesky 2006; D. Taylor 2000).

> **environmental justice** A legal strategy based on claims that racial minorities are subjected disproportionately to environmental hazards.

Meanwhile, the poor and oppressed continue to bear the brunt of environmental pollution. In the 1990s the federal government, unable to find a disposal site for spent nuclear fuel, turned to tribal reservations. Agents eventually persuaded a tiny band of Goshute Indians in Skull Valley, Utah, to accept more than 44,000 barrels of the highly radioactive substance, which will remain dangerous for an

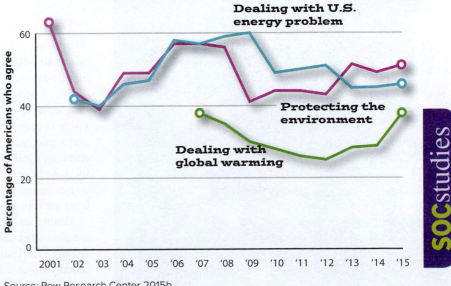

Should Environmental Issues Be Top Priorities of Congress?

Source: Pew Research Center 2015b.

estimated 10,000 years. The government dropped the plan only after opposition from surrounding towns and cities, whose residents objected to the movement of the material through their communities. This was not the first time the government had attempted to persuade the impoverished tribe to accept environmentally objectionable installations. The military's nerve-gas storage facility resides on or near the reservation, along with the Intermountain Power Project, which generates coal-fired electrical power for consumers in California (Eureka County 2006; Foy 2006).

>> Environmental Problems

The environmental problems caused by development have effects far beyond the places where they are created. Witness Muhammad Ali, a Bangladeshi man who has had to flee floodwaters five times in the last decade. Scientists believe that global warming is to blame both for worsening monsoons and for the raging waters of the Iamuna River, swollen by abnormally high glacier melt from the Himalayas. Every time the river floods, Ali tears down his house, made of tin and bamboo, and moves to higher ground. But he is running out of land

© Bill Kearney

Movies on THE ENVIRONMENT

Sun Come Up
The Carteret Islands in the South Pacific are being swallowed up by the ocean.

An Inconvenient Truth
The truth about global warming.

Food, Inc.
The effects of the food manufacturing industry on the environment.

Chasing Ice
A climate change skeptic's doubts melt through the lens of his camera.

WALL-E
A robot in the year 2700 discovers his destiny.

5

to move to. "Where we are standing, in five days it will be gone," he says. "Our future thinking is that if this problem is not taken care of, we will be swept away" (Goering 2007).

Public opinion polls show growing concerns about climate change after years of decline (Pew Resource Center 2015b). And yet, in 2015, the percentage of people who considered themselves to be either active participants in, or sympathetic to, the environmental movement declined to 57 percent from 71 percent in 2000. In 2015, 42 percent said the effects of global warming are generally exaggerated, though the 35 percent who said it was generally underestimated represented an increase from 25 percent in 2010 (Gallup 2015a).

AIR POLLUTION

Worldwide, 3.7 million premature deaths occurred in 2012 due to air pollution. Of these, 88 percent lived in low- and middle-income countries (World Health Organization 2014b). Unfortunately, in cities around the world, residents have come to accept polluted air as normal. Urban air pollution is caused primarily by emissions from automobiles and secondarily by emissions from electric power plants and heavy industries. Air pollution not only limits visibility, but also can lead to health problems as uncomfortable as eye irritation and as deadly as lung cancer. Such problems are especially severe in developing countries.

People are capable of changing their behavior, but they are also often unwilling to make such changes permanent. During the 1984 Olympics in Los Angeles, authorities asked residents to carpool and stagger their work hours to relieve traffic congestion and improve the quality of

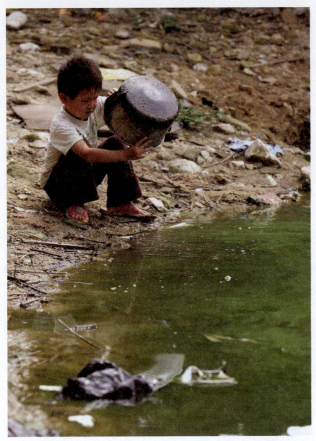
© China Photos/Getty Images

environment, including the impact on birds, fish, mammals, and their habitats. The impact of the spill on various species has been substantial. For example, in the two years following its occurrence, 675 dolphins were stranded in the northern Gulf of Mexico compared to an annual average of 74 before the spill, deep-water corals experienced significant stress, the nitrogen cycle for microorganisms was inhibited, and 102 species of birds were harmed (Cornwall 2015; National Geographic 2012).

This incident is one among many water-based accidents that have resulted in significant environmental harm. When the oil tanker *Exxon Valdez* ran aground in Prince William Sound, Alaska, in 1989, its cargo of 11 million gallons of crude oil spilled into the sound and washed onto the shore, contaminating 1,285 miles of shoreline. Altogether, about 11,000 people joined in a massive cleanup effort that cost more than $2 billion. Globally, oil spills occur regularly. In 2002 the oil tanker *Prestige* spilled twice as much fuel as the *Valdez,* greatly damaging coastal areas in Spain and France (ITOPF 2006).

Less dramatic than large-scale accidents or disasters, but more common in many parts of the world, are problems with the basic water supply. Worldwide, more than 748 million people lack safe and adequate drinking water, and 2.5 billion lack access to improved sanitation facilities—a problem that further threatens the quality of water supplies. The health costs of unsafe water are enormous (World Health Organization 2014c, 2014d).

Given such water shortages, it should not come as a surprise that water is now a highly contested commodity in many parts of the world. In the United States, competition over water is intense, especially in booming Las Vegas and the Southwest. In the Middle East, the immense political challenges posed by ethnic and religious conflict are often complicated by battles over

the air athletes would breathe. These changes resulted in a remarkable 12 percent drop in ozone levels. After the Olympics ended, however, people reverted to their normal behavior, and the ozone levels climbed once again. Similarly, China took drastic action to ensure that Beijing's high levels of air pollution did not mar the 2008 Olympic Games. Construction work in the city ceased, polluting factories and power plants closed down, and workers swept roads and sprayed them with water several times a day. This temporary solution, however, has not solved China's ongoing pollution problem (*The Economist* 2008b).

WATER POLLUTION

Throughout the United States, waste materials dumped by industries and local governments have polluted streams, rivers, and lakes. Consequently, many bodies of water have become unsafe for fishing and swimming, let alone drinking. Around the world, pollution of the oceans is an issue of growing concern. The Deepwater Horizon spill in the Gulf of Mexico represents the ripple effects that such accidents can have on the

How Serious Is Global Warming?

Percentage (y-axis, 0 to 60)

2001 '02 '03 '04 '05 '06 '07 '08 '09 '10 '11 '12 '13 '14 '15 (x-axis)

— Generally exaggerated   — Generally underestimated

Note: Respondents were also given the option of selecting "Generally correct."

Source: Gallup 2015b.

Going GLOBAL

CO_2 Emissions per Capita

Country	CO_2 Emissions per Capita
Kuwait	31.32
United States	17.56
Canada	14.68
Russian Federation	12.23
Japan	9.14
United Kingdom	7.86
China	6.19
World	4.88
Mexico	3.76
India	1.67
Guatemala	0.78
Haiti	0.21
Malawi	0.08

0.00 5.00 10.00 15.00 20.00 25.00 30.00 35.00
CO_2 Emissions per Capita

Note: Annual emissions per capita measured in metric tons.
Source: World Bank 2015m.

water. There, competing nations accuse each other of taking unfair advantage of existing water supplies, and water tanks are a likely target for both military forces and terrorists (Carmichael 2007).

GLOBAL CLIMATE CHANGE

The scientific evidence for global climate change is clear, consistent, and compelling, yet public opinion polls show that people remain skeptical. Global warming, the term most frequently associated with climate change, refers to the significant rise in the earth's surface temperatures that occurs when industrial gases such as carbon dioxide turn the planet's atmosphere into a virtual greenhouse. Even one additional degree of warmth in the planet's average temperature increases the likelihood of wildfires, shrinking rivers and lakes, desert expansion, and torrential downpours, including typhoons and hurricanes. Despite the potential catastrophic risks, 48 percent of Americans believe that the seriousness of global warming is generally exaggerated (Newport 2010).

Scientists now track carbon dioxide emissions around the world and can map the current and projected contribution each country makes (see the accompanying "CO_2 Emissions per Capita" graph). Such analyses show the sizable and growing contribution made by the United States (Lymas 2008). For some politicians, however, the problem seems too abstract and distant. Others recognize that effective solutions demand a difficult-to-manage multinational response, and they fear that their nation may bear too much of the cost. The Kyoto Protocol, established in 1997 and enacted in 2005, was intended to provide a unified response in which the nations of the world would take collective responsibility to reduce global emissions of greenhouse gases. As of 2015, 191 countries had ratified the accord, but the United States was not one of them. Opponents of the Kyoto Protocol argue that doing so would place the nation at a disadvantage in the global marketplace (Energy Information Administration 2008; United Nations Framework Convention on Climate Change 2015b).

We can again draw on world systems analysis when it comes to seeing who pays the highest price for global climate changes. Historically, core nations have been the major emitters of greenhouse gases. Today, much manufacturing has moved to semiperiphery and periphery nations, where greenhouse gas emissions are escalating. Ironically, many of those who are now calling for a reduction in the human activity that contributes to global climate change are located in core nations, which have contributed disproportionately to the problem. We want our hamburgers, but we decry the destruction of the rain forests to create grazing land for cattle. We want inexpensive clothes and toys, but we condemn developing countries for depending on coal-fired power plants, the number of which are expected to increase 46 percent by 2030. The challenge of global climate change, then, is closely tied to global inequality (M. Jenkins 2008; Leonard 2010; Roberts, Grines, and Manale 2003).

Threatened and Endangered Species

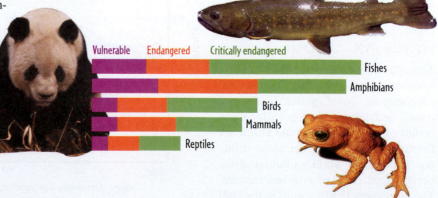

Source: IUCN 2011.

Photos: (panda): © Fuse/Getty Images RF; *(fish):* Bart Bammet/USFWS; *(toad):* Courtesy USFWS, Charles H. Smith.

In addition to the environmental costs of supporting global population increase, technological advances also contribute to environmental concerns. At least since the Industrial Revolution and the invention of the steam engine, the automobile, coal-burning power plants, and more, the environmental effects of technological innovation have been extreme. Biologist and environmentalist Barry Commoner argued that additional contributors to the problem include plastics, detergents, synthetic fibers, pesticides, herbicides, and chemical fertilizers. We appreciate the lifestyles that such innovations allow us to experience, but we pay a significant price for their benefits (Commoner 1971, 1990; Ehrlich 1968).

THE GLOBAL RESPONSE

Globalization can be both good and bad for the environment. On the negative side, it can create a race to the bottom as polluting companies relocate to countries with less stringent environmental standards. Also of concern is that

Perceptions of Global Climate Change

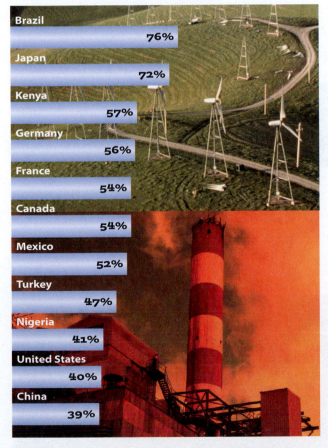

Brazil 76%

Japan 72%

Kenya 57%

Germany 56%

France 54%

Canada 54%

Mexico 52%

Turkey 47%

Nigeria 41%

United States 40%

China 39%

Note: Percentage of people citing climate change as a major threat to their country.

Source: Pew Research Center 2013j. *Photos: (top):* © Kim Steele/Getty Images RF; *(bottom):* © Stockbyte/PunchStock RF.

© Brand X Images/Jupiter RF

globalization allows multinationals to exploit the resources of developing countries for short-term profit. From Mexico to China, the industrialization that often accompanies globalization has increased pollution of all types.

Yet globalization can have a positive impact as well. As barriers to the international movement of goods, services, and people fall, multinational corporations have an incentive to carefully consider the cost of natural resources. As the establishment of the Kyoto Protocol demonstrated, countries around the world can come together on a global level to take action that makes a significant difference. Collectively, the nations met their emissions goal by the target year of 2012, and in December of that year they agreed to the Doha Amendment to the Kyoto Protocol which established a new set of goals to be met by 2020. Globally, however, CO_2 emissions continued to rise primarily due to increases from China and other developing nations (Clark 2012; (United Nations Framework Convention on Climate Change 2015a).

Overusing or wasting resources makes little sense, especially when they are in danger of depletion (Kwong 2005). Perhaps, as Émile Durkheim might have argued long ago, by recognizing our mutual interdependence, we will take the steps necessary to bring about positive social change.

There are signs that individuals, countries, and corporations are beginning to do just that. For example, individuals are taking greater responsibility for their global impact by recycling and switching to fluorescent light bulbs (Morales 2010). Increasing numbers of corporations are "going green" and even finding profits in doing so. Sociology helps us better see the ways we are interconnected by highlighting the significance of the system as a whole, as well as raising awareness about the inequalities that are a consequence of the global system we have constructed. Such analysis can prepare us to more effectively respond to the global challenges we face.

SOCIOLOGY IS A VERB

Health and Environment

Conduct a mini-survey of 10 friends, family members, and/or classmates. How concerned are they about global climate change? How concerned are they about health care? What do they think are the major issues in each? What are the obstacles to positive change in each? Record their responses. How did answers vary depending upon how old they are, how much education they have, whether they are male or female, or other possible variables?

© Corbis RF

For REVIEW

I. What role do population dynamics play in shaping our lives?

- Population dynamics provide a context within which we are born, live, move, and even die, and population trends vary significantly across time and between nations, shaping our life chances.

II. What does sociology contribute to something as seemingly biological as health?

- Our understanding of what counts as health and illness is shaped by the society to which we belong. Similarly, our social position and control over resources shape our likelihood of exposure to illness and our access to health care.

III. What environmental lessons do we learn from sociology?

- The natural environment represents our human home, within which all social interaction occurs, and the way we organize our social relations influences the effects we have on the environment. Countries that control a larger amount of resources have a bigger impact and therefore bear a greater responsibility for those effects.

SOCVIEWS on Population, Health, and Environment

Functionalist View

Over time, population levels naturally reach a balance that maximizes social order.

Health care is a social institution that provides for our health and welfare and thus preserves **social order**.

As we become more socially, economically, and environmentally **interdependent**, new, more global conscious, norms and values arise.

SOCIAL ORDER, INTERCONNECTEDNESS
KEY CONCEPTS

Conflict View

Popula- tion crises are driven more by battles over resources than by natural processes.

Core nations **exploit** the natural resources of developing nations on the periphery without taking responsibility for the consequences.

Poor people and minorities suffer disproportionately from **inequities** in health care and exposure to environmental hazards, such as toxic waste and air and water pollution.

KEY CONCEPTS
CONTROL, INEQUALITY, EXPLOITATION

Interactionist View

Changes in population trends show the importance of the choices we make in shaping society.

Patients can play an **active role** in their health both by seeking out a physician's services and by choosing whether or not to follow a doctor's orders.

The degree to which we think significant environmental problems exist is a consequence of **socialization** by family, friends, teachers, television, and so on.

KEY CONCEPTS
ACTIVITY, INTERACTION

MAKE THE CONNECTION

After reviewing the chapter, answer the following questions:

1
How would each perspective approach the study of the Deep Horizon oil spill in the Gulf of Mexico?

2
How would each of the perspectives approach the demographic transition model, and how would their insights differ?

3
What insights would we gain from each perspective regarding the current state of health care in the United States, including recent health care reform efforts?

4
Look at your experience with the medical world from an interactionist perspective. What were your interactions with the doctors and nurses like? Have you taken an active role or a passive role as a patient?

Pop Quiz

1. **How is the total fertility rate defined?**
   a. number of children born over a given period of time
   b. number of live births per 1,000 people in the population in a given year
   c. average number of children a woman would have during her lifetime given current birthrates and assuming she survives through her childbearing years
   d. minimum number of children a woman would need to average in her lifetime to reproduce the population in the next generation

2. **What term is used when people leave a population group to which they had belonged?**
   a. immigration
   b. replacement
   c. emigration
   d. transition

3. **What was the relationship between birthrates and death rates throughout most of human history as described by the demographic transition model?**
   a. Both were low.
   b. Death rates were low; birthrates were high.
   c. Birthrates were low; death rates were high.
   d. Both were high.

4. **A disease that cannot be understood apart from its specific social context is an example of**
   a. human ecology.
   b. culture-bound syndrome.
   c. the sick role.
   d. holistic medicine.

5. **Which of the following represents a form of legitimate deviance in which the person who becomes ill has a corresponding set of rights and responsibilities associated with that status?**
   a. medicalization
   b. the sick role
   c. brain drain
   d. social epidemiology

6. **In the area of social epidemiology, what does prevalence refer to?**
   a. the rate at which key indicators change over time
   b. the total number of cases of a specific disorder that exist at a given period of time
   c. the likelihood that a disease or illness will be labeled as such in a given cultural context
   d. the number of new cases of a specific disorder that occur within a given population during a stated period

7. **The age group that is most likely to be covered by some form of health insurance is**
   a. under 18.
   b. 18–34.
   c. 35–64.
   d. 65 and older.

8. **Compared to other nations around the world, how much does the United States spend on health care (as measured by GDP)?**
   a. near the bottom
   b. about in the middle or median
   c. at about the 75th percentile
   d. more than virtually all other nations

9. **What is the term used for the geological epoch in which human actions affect the environment on a global scale?**
   a. Jurassic
   b. Homocene
   c. demographic
   d. Anthropocene

10. **What is the international treaty that sought to reduce global emissions of greenhouse gases?**
    a. Valdez Treaty
    b. Kyoto Protocol
    c. Port Huron Statement
    d. Gore Accord

1. (c), 2. (c), 3. (d), 4. (b), 5. (b), 6. (b), 7. (d), 8. (d), 9. (d), 10. (b)

Social Change

CHANGING THE WORLD
ONE CAMPUS AT A TIME

In the summer of 1964, college students traveled to Mississippi to change the world. As volunteers in Freedom Summer, their goal was to make a difference in the lives of African Americans who had been systematically denied the right to vote, quality education, and legal and political representation. The volunteers—mostly upper-middle-class White students from northern colleges—registered Black voters, established Freedom Schools, and provided legal advice and medical assistance. By the end of the summer, they had registered 17,000 voters and taught 3,000 children. In 1964, 6.7 percent of voting-age African Americans in Mississippi were registered, but by 1967, 66.5 percent were registered (Colby 1986; McAdam 1988).

From April 18 to May 8, 2001, students at Harvard University occupied Massachusetts Hall, the location of the president's and provost's offices, as part of their Living Wage Campaign. The city of Cambridge, where Harvard is located, had passed a living-wage ordinance ensuring a minimum wage of $10 per hour, adjustable for inflation. Students argued that a school with a multibillion-dollar endowment could do better than the $6.50 many employees were receiving. After numerous attempts at negotiation, students decided to make a statement. During the sit-in, students organized daily pickets and rallies involving thousands of people. After three weeks, the administration agreed to establish a committee to implement living-wage principles (Progressive Student Labor Movement 2008).

Concerns about global climate change have given rise to increased student activism throughout the United States. Students at Swarthmore occupied that school's investment offices; students at Mary Washington staged a 21 day sit in outside the president's office; students at Yale were cited for trespassing and fined $92 for their sit-in; and students at Harvard blockaded the entrances to their main administration building. Consciousness-raising efforts such as these appear to be working. In 2012, Unity College became the first college in America to divest its endowment from fossil fuel holdings. It has since been joined by 26 other schools. As one student protester put it, "We are Generation Climate, because our generation will inherit the burden of the climate crisis, and . . . now is the time to take collective action to change history" (Gordon 2015).

Society is the product of our collective action. By acting the same, we reproduce the status quo. By acting differently, as college students have demonstrated over and over again, we have the power to change the world.

As You READ >>

- How and why does social change happen?
- What factors shape the success of a social movement?
- What does it mean to practice sociology?

>> Global Social Change

We are at a truly dramatic era in history in terms of global social change. Within the past few decades, we have witnessed the computer revolution and the explosion of Internet connectivity; the collapse of communism; major regime changes and severe economic disruptions in Africa, the Middle East, and eastern Europe; the spread of AIDS; the first verification of the cloning of a complex animal, Dolly the sheep; and the first major terrorist attack on U.S. soil. Today we continue to face global challenges including international terrorism, ongoing domino effects of a global economic meltdown, and climate change, along with other threats.

One of the most significant transformations so far in the 21st century was the emergence of the Arab Spring. This term refers to the substantial political upheaval that occurred in a number of northern African and Arabian Peninsula nations from 2010 through 2012. To supporters, these changes represented the beginning of new life, although it was a death that helped trigger them.

The protests started in Tunisia on December 18, 2010, after Mohamed Bouazizi, a 26-year-old street vendor whose vegetable cart had been confiscated by local police and who had grown tired of years of humiliation and corruption, set himself on fire as a form of both protest and resignation. He died 18 days later. Bouazizi's act became a symbol of the frustration felt by many others in the region.

Facilitated by text messaging and social networking sites, word spread quickly, helping spawn huge protests in Tunisia, which sparked rallies in numerous countries including Egypt (where Tahrir Square became a rallying place), Libya, Yemen, Syria, Bahrain, and others. Many of those who participated were young, well educated, and technologically savvy. They sought economic and political reforms, greater opportunities for self-determination, and hope for a better life. As a result of the protests, in addition to many other consequences, Tunisian President Zine El Abidine Ben Ali was ousted after 23 years in power. Egyptian President Hosni Mubarak, who had been in power for nearly 30 years, resigned. Libyan leader Colonel Muammar el-Qaddafi, who ruled for 42 years, was overthrown and killed, and Yemeni President Ali Abdullah Saleh stepped down after 33 years in power (Gelvin 2012; Noueihed and Warren 2012; Raghavan 2011; Shenker et al. 2011).

Part of what makes the Arab Spring movement significant is that it represented the overthrow of entrenched and repressive political regimes and the promise of greater empowerment and opportunity in the hands of the people. Those in positions of power are frequently able to use their control over valued

Did You Know?

". . . When the first call for protesters for Occupy Wall Street went out, organizers made an explicit reference to Arab Spring protests in Egypt. They wrote, 'Are you ready for a Tahrir moment'? On Sept 17, protesters flood into lower Manhattan, set up tents, kitchens, peaceful barricades and occupy Wall Street."

Photo: © AP Photo/Abdeljalil Bounhar.

resources to reinforce the status quo, yet these protests demonstrate the power of agency and engaged social action. In time, some of these nations, such as Bahrain, Lebanon, and Egypt, experienced a backlash, including harsh reprisals and authoritarian rule, that came to be known as Arab Winter (Amnesty International 2011; Byman 2011; Fisher 2012).

Sociology helps us understand such shifts by paying attention both to large-scale, or macro, shifts that alter the basic landscape of society and the relationships among groups, and to the small-scale, or micro, changes in social interaction within which decisions are made that can alter the course of history. We construct society through our everyday actions. As such, we have the power to change society by altering the choices we make. Of course, some people, because of their control over valued resources, have more power than do others. Sociology can better focus our attention so that we might understand which direction change might follow.

social change Significant alteration over time in behavior patterns and culture, including norms and values.

>> Sociological Perspectives on Social Change

As humans, we are creative beings. We continually innovate and experiment, developing new technologies, ideas, and ways of doing things. Each innovation represents an example of **social change,** which involves significant alteration over time in behavior patterns and culture. Social change can occur so slowly as to be almost undetectable to those it affects, but it can also happen with breathtaking rapidity.

The United States: A Changing Nation

Population	1850	1940	1950	2013
Total in millions	23.3	132.1	180.7	316.1
Percentage under age 15	41%	25%	31%	19%
Education	**1850**	**1940**	**1960**	**2013**
Percentage aged 25+ who have not completed high school	88%	75%	59%	12%
Percentage aged 19–24 enrolled in higher education	<1%	8%	24%	39%
Labor Force Participation	**1850**	**1940**	**1960**	**2015**
Men working in their 20s	94%	86%	86%	79%
Women working in their 20s	22%	51%	74%	70%
Health	**1850**	**1940**	**1960**	**2011**
Physicians per 100,000 population	176	133	150	274
Life expectancy at birth, in years	38	63	70	79
Technology	**1870**	**1940**	**1960**	**2013**
Copyrights issued	5,600	176,997	243,926	577,000
Patents issued	12,137	42,238	47,170	302,948
Family	**1890**	**1940**	**1960**	**2012**
Men median age at first marriage	26	24	23	29
Women median age at first marriage	22	22	20	27
Birthrate for women aged 20–24 per 1,000	168.4	135.6	258.1	83.1

SOCstudies

Note: Data are comparable, although definitions vary somewhat across time. Education rate for 1850 is for those over age 70. Earliest birthrate is from 1905.

Sources: Bureau of Labor Statistics 2015e; Carter et al. 2006: vol.1: 28–29, 401–402, 440, 541, 685, 697, 709, vol. 2: 441–442, vol. 3: 422–425, 427–428; National Center for Education Statistics 2014: Tables 104.10, 302.60; National Center for Health Statistics 2014a:Tables 3, 18, 101; U.S. Census Bureau 2010f: Table 80, 2015a:Table MS-2; U.S. Copyright Office 2013; U.S. Patent and Trademark Office 2015.   *Photo:* © Nisian Hughes/Getty Images.

In the past century or so, for example, the U.S. population has more than doubled, the percentage of people finishing high school and attending college has skyrocketed, women have entered the paid labor force in significant numbers, life expectancy has risen, technological innovation has exploded, men and women have been marrying later, and family size has shrunk. In our global, interdependent world, there is no reason to suspect that such changes will cease, and many future changes will be difficult to predict.

Explaining social change is clearly a challenge in the diverse and complex world we inhabit. Nevertheless, sociologists have sought to analyze, interpret, and explain social change. In some instances, they have examined historical events to arrive at a better understanding of contemporary changes. We look at change from three perspectives so that we might better identify issues we should include when considering how and why change happens.

> All change is not growth, as all movement is not forward.
>
> Ellen Glasgow

THE EVOLUTION OF SOCIETIES

One of the defining features of modern societies is the degree to which they are characterized by seemingly constant change. Sociology developed as a discipline to come to terms with that change. Early sociologists using the functionalist perspective refashioned Charles Darwin's evolutionary model of nature to explain adaptation in society. According to their **social evolution** theory, societies progress from simple to complex over time. From this perspective, traditional societies contain within them the essential building blocks that serve as the foundation for all societies. Analysis of "primitive" societies would reveal the indispensable tasks, or functions, that must be addressed if society is to survive. As societies become more "civilized," even though complexity increases, those core functions still need to be fulfilled. They believed that gaining a rational understanding of the laws of society would enhance our capacity to control and direct social change.

During the 1840s, Auguste Comte, one of sociology's founders, posited the Law of Three Stages to describe social change over time. During the theological stage, people base their knowledge and decision making on religious principles. To explain why things happen, people turn toward the direct involvement in our daily lives of supernatural or divine beings—gods, demons, and the like. During this stage, according to Comte, people are irrational and superstitious. In the metaphysical stage, worship of concrete, active beings gives way to the belief that abstract forces guide what happens in the world. This perspective assumes that there is an underlying logic built within the universe. Knowledge is advanced by studying the fundamental essence of things. In Comte's positive stage, knowledge is built on facts revealed using the scientific method. Natural and social scientists seek to uncover the underlying laws that govern the universe. Empirical investigation trumps philosophical reflection, and researchers adhere to the principle of "show me, don't tell me." During this stage, according to Comte, people are rational, guided by logic and reason, making progress not only possible, but inevitable.

This evolutionary analogy tends to reinforce the notion that those who adapt to changed circumstances are inherently superior. Since Comte's time, sociologists have largely rejected the idea that all societies follow a singular path from simple to complex. Social change can happen in different ways and at different paces not only *between* societies, but also *within* societies. Within the United States, for example, many small towns are still rooted in an agricultural economy which is reflected in their local culture, and in many developing nations, cell phone service has become a normal part of everyday life. Most sociologists have also rejected the ethnocentric notion that traditional societies are primitive and that modern societies are civilized. Traditional societies, in their adaptation to their environments, exhibit significant levels of sophistication and innovation.

SOCTHINK

Why would early theorists have thought of traditional societies as "primitive"? How is this a reflection of the evolutionary theoretical paradigm they adopted?

EQUILIBRIUM AND SOCIAL ORDER

Another functionalist approach to studying social change portrays societies as naturally tending toward stability or social order. Sociologist Talcott Parsons, for example, maintained that even seemingly significant social outbreaks, such as protests and riots, are but temporary disruptions along the pathway to enhanced social stability. According to his **equilibrium model,** society's natural tendency is toward social order with change in one part of society counterbalanced by adjustments in others.

Parsons (1966) maintained that four processes of social change are inevitable. The first, differentiation, refers to the increasing complexity of social organization. We see this in

> **social evolution** A theory of social change that holds that societies progress from simple to complex over time.
>
> **equilibrium model** The theory that society's natural tendency is toward social order with change in one part of society counterbalanced by adjustments in others.

5 Movies ON SOCIAL MOVEMENTS AND SOCIAL CHANGE

Citizenfour
A whistleblower stands up to the U.S. government.

Syriana
An oil company colludes with the U.S. government.

The Square
Egypt in the midst of Arab Spring.

Beasts of the Southern Wild
When you're small, you gotta fix what you can.

Freedom Riders
Young activists challenge segregation in the American South.

the form of job specialization as is evident in bureaucratic systems. The transition from a healer—a single person who handles all of your health care needs—to a series of positions, including physician, anesthetist, nurse, and pharmacist, is an illustration of differentiation in the field of medicine. This second process is accompanied by adaptive upgrading, in which social institutions become more specialized in their purposes. The division of physicians into obstetricians, internists, surgeons, and so forth is an example of adaptive upgrading.

The third process Parsons identified is the inclusion of groups that were previously excluded because of their gender, race, ethnicity, and social class. In the past two decades or so, medical schools have practiced inclusion by admitting increasing numbers of women and African Americans. Finally, Parsons contended that societies experience value generalization—the development of new values that legitimate a broader range of activities. The acceptance of preventive and alternative medicine is an example of value generalization: society has broadened its view of health care. All four processes identified by Parsons stress consensus—societal agreement on the nature of social organization and values (Gerhardt 2002).

SOCTHINK

Why might the equilibrium model have a difficult time addressing such issues as inequality and poverty as social problems to be solved?

One of the sources of potential strain that can lead to such social adaptation involves technological innovation. As we saw in Chapter 3, sociologist William F. Ogburn (1922) distinguished between material and nonmaterial aspects of culture. Material culture includes inventions, artifacts, and technology; nonmaterial culture encompasses ideas, norms, communications, and social organization. Ogburn pointed out that technology often changes faster than do the ideas and values with which we make sense of such change. Thus, the nonmaterial culture, including values and norms, typically must respond to changes in the material culture. Ogburn introduced the term *cultural lag* to refer to the period of adjustment when the nonmaterial culture is still struggling to adapt to new material conditions. One example is the Internet, which spread quickly but now raises serious questions about personal privacy.

Parsons and other theorists would argue that those parts of society that persist, even including crime, terrorism, and poverty, do so because they contribute to social stability. Critics note, however, that his approach virtually disregards the use of coercion by the powerful to maintain the illusion of a stable, well-integrated society (Gouldner 1960). From the conflict perspective, control over resources plays a significant role in the structure of society and the maintenance of social order.

RESOURCES, POWER, AND CHANGE

Karl Marx, who utilized the conflict approach, accepted the evolutionary argument that societies develop along a particular path. History, according to Marx, proceeds through a series of stages, and during each stage, those who control the means of production exploit an entire class of people. Thus, ancient society exploited slaves, the estate system of feudalism exploited serfs, and modern capitalist society exploits the working class. Change happens when a revolution in social relations occurs leading

© AP Photo/Alex Brandon

to the next stage. Ultimately, once the problem of production is solved (see Chapter 9), human society would move toward the final stage of development: a classless communist society, or "community of free individuals," as Marx described it in 1867 in *Das Kapital* (Marx [1867] 2000:478).

Marx argued that conflict is a normal and desirable aspect of social change. In fact, change must be encouraged if social inequality is to be eliminated. In his view, people are not restricted to a passive role in responding to inevitable cycles or changes in the material culture. Rather, Marxist theory offers a tool for those who wish to seize control of the historical process and gain their freedom from injustice. Efforts to promote social change are, however, likely to meet with resistance.

Certain individuals and groups have a stake in maintaining the existing state of affairs. Social economist Thorstein Veblen (1857–1929) coined the term **vested interests** to refer to those people or groups who will suffer in the event of social change. For example, historically the American Medical Association (AMA) has taken strong stands against national health insurance and the professionalization of midwifery. National health insurance was seen as a threat to physicians' income and authority, and a rise in the status of midwives could threaten the preeminent position of doctors as deliverers of babies. In general, those with a disproportionate share of society's wealth, status, and power, such as members of the AMA, have a vested interest in preserving the status quo (Furedi 2006; Scelfo 2008; Veblen 1919).

Economic factors play an important role in resistance to social change. For example, it can be expensive for manufacturers to meet mandated standards for the safety of products and workers and for the protection of the environment. In the pursuit of both profit and survival, many firms seek to avoid the costs of meeting strict safety and environmental standards. If they have sufficient power in society, they can effectively pass the costs of such practices on to others who must bear the consequences. To battle against such influence requires countervailing sources of power. Government regulations, for example, force all companies to bear the common burden of such costs, and labor unions can present the unified power of workers as a group.

Communities, too, protect their vested interests, often in the name of "protecting property values." The abbreviation NIMBY stands for "not in my backyard," a cry often heard when people protest landfills, prisons, nuclear power facilities, and even bike trails and group homes for people with developmental disabilities. The targeted community may not challenge the need for the facility, but may simply insist that it be located elsewhere. The NIMBY attitude has become so common that it is almost impossible for policy makers to find acceptable locations for facilities such as hazardous waste dumps. Unfortunately, it is often those with the fewest resources who end up on the losing end of such battles (Lambert 2009; Schelly and Stretesky 2009).

In today's world, change is inevitable. From sociology we learn that we need to watch for the ways in which change evolves out of existing practices. We also must be aware of the ways in which societies perpetuate existing social order by seeking an acceptable level of balance between stability and change. Finally, we recognize the role that power and control over resources plays in shaping what changes do or do not occur. In all these cases, because of the ways it both enables and constrains, we must be aware of the role that technology plays in affecting the nature and direction of social change.

> **vested interests** Those people or groups who will suffer in the event of social change and who have a stake in maintaining the status quo.

>> Technology and the Future

As discussed in Chapter 3, technology is a form of culture in which humans modify the natural environment to meet our wants and needs. Technological advances—the telephone, the automobile, the airplane, the television, the atomic bomb, and more recently, the computer, digital media, and the cellular phone—have brought striking changes to our culture, our patterns of socialization, our social institutions, and our day-to-day social interactions. Technological innovations are, in fact, emerging and being accepted with remarkable speed.

In the past generation alone, industrial countries have seen a major shift in consumer technologies. We no longer buy electronic devices to last for 10 years. Increasingly, we buy them with the expectation that within 2 years or less, we will need to upgrade to an entirely new

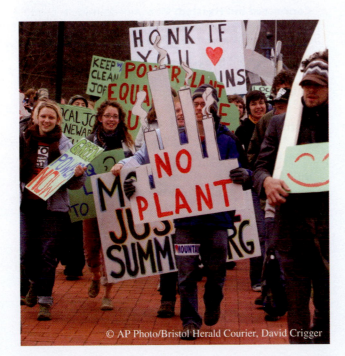

© AP Photo/Bristol Herald Courier, David Crigger

© Oliver Lantzendorffer/Getty Images RF

Adopting Technology

technology, whether it be a smartphone or a home computer. These technologies have both positive and negative consequences. They enable us to communicate with almost anyone, almost anywhere, at almost any time. Yet they also facilitate outsourcing and globalization, resulting in the loss of local jobs and the decline of communities.

COMPUTER TECHNOLOGY

Driven in part by the spread of mobile phones around the world, Internet access has gone global. While the revolutions in transportation and communication have brought us together since the Industrial Revolution, the Internet provides a potential for immediate global connection that previously was virtually and physically impossible. In 2015, the Internet reached 3 billion users, or 42.3 percent of the world's population (Internet World Stats 2015a).

The Internet evolved from a computer system built in 1962 by the U.S. Defense Department to enable scholars and military researchers to continue their government work, even if part of the nation's communications system were destroyed by nuclear attack. For years, it was difficult to gain access to the Internet without holding a position at a university or a government research laboratory. Today, however, virtually anyone with sufficient resources can reach the Internet with a wireless-enabled computer or a smartphone. People buy and sell cars, trade stocks, auction off items, research new medical remedies, vote, connect with friends, and coordinate social movements, to mention just a few of the thousands of possibilities (Shirky 2008).

If we look at global Internet use, the regions with the greatest number of users are Asia and Europe. Asia alone represents more than 1 billion users. However, in terms of access, a larger proportion of the population in North America—87.7 percent—can connect to the Internet than in any other continent. Even though Asia has the greatest number of users, only 34.7 percent of the population there has Internet access. Another sign of

Omnivores: 8% of American adults constitute the most active participants in the information society, consuming information goods and services at a high rate and using them as a platform for participation and self-expression.

The Connectors: 7% of the adult population surround themselves with technology and use it to connect with people and digital content. They get a lot out of their mobile devices and participate actively in online life.

Lackluster Veterans: 8% of American adults make up a group who are not at all passionate about their abundance of modern information and communication technologies (ICTs). Few like the intrusiveness their gadgets add to their lives and not many see ICTs adding to their personal productivity.

Productivity Enhancers: 9% of American adults happily get a lot of things done with information technology, both at home and at work.

Mobile Centrics: 10% of the general population are strongly attached to their cell phones and take advantage of a range of mobile applications.

Connected but Hassled: 9% of American adults fit into this group. They have invested in a lot of technology, but the connectivity is a hassle for them.

Inexperienced Experimenters: 8% of adults have less ICT on hand than others. They feel competent in dealing with technology, and might do more with it if they had more.

Light but Satisfied: 15% of adults have the basics of information technology, use it infrequently, and do not consider it to be an important part of their lives.

Indifferents: 11% of adults have a fair amount of technology on hand, but it does not play a central role in their daily lives.

Off the Net: 15% of the population, mainly older Americans, are off the modern information network.

Note: From a Pew Internet and American Life Project Survey conducted in April 2006.

Source: Horrigan 2007:vii.   *Photo:* © Ryan Mc Vay/Getty Images RF.

Internet Use and Penetration by World Region

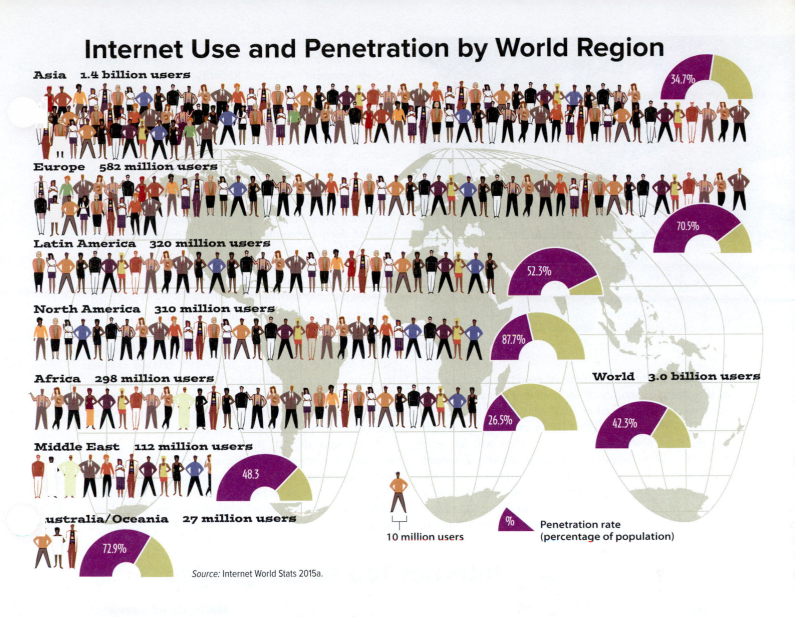

Asia   1.4 billion users

34.7%

Europe   582 million users

70.5%

Latin America   320 million users

52.3%

North America   310 million users

87.7%

Africa   298 million users

26.5%

World   3.0 billion users

42.3%

Middle East   112 million users

48.3

Australia/Oceania   27 million users

72.9%

10 million users

% Penetration rate (percentage of population)

Source: Internet World Stats 2015a.

the global nature of this expansion has been the increase in languages used on the Internet. While English continues to lead, the number of Chinese-speaking users increased 1,910 percent between 2000 and 2013, and Arabic speakers increased 5,297 percent, compared to 469 percent for English speakers (Internet World Stats 2015a, 2015b).

Unfortunately, a digital divide persists, and not everyone can get onto the information highway, especially not the less affluent. Moreover, this pattern of inequality is global. In Africa, for example, only 26.5 percent of the population has access to the Internet. The core nations that Immanuel Wallerstein described in his world systems analysis have a virtual monopoly on information technology; the peripheral nations of Asia, Africa, and Latin America depend on the core nations both for technology and for the information it provides. For example, North America, Europe, and a few industrialized nations in other regions possess almost all the world's Internet hosts—computers that are connected directly to the worldwide network.

PRIVACY AND CENSORSHIP IN A GLOBAL VILLAGE

In addition to the digital divide, sociologists have also raised concerns about threats to privacy and the possibility of censorship. Recent advances have made it increasingly easy for business firms, government agencies, and even criminals to retrieve and store information about everything from our buying habits to our Web-surfing patterns. In public places, at work, and on the Internet, surveillance devices now track our every move, be it a keystroke or an ATM withdrawal. As technology spreads, so does the exposure to risk. In 2006, for example, the theft of a laptop computer from the home of an employee of the Veterans Administration compromised the names, Social Security numbers, and dates of birth of up to 26.5 million veterans. In 2013, 40 million credit cards from the retail store Target were compromised.

The problem extends beyond threats such as identity theft and illegal acts by individuals. Increasingly, questions are being raised about the questionable use of technology

© Elmer Martinez/AFP/Getty Images

vigilant in protecting their right to privacy (Liang and Lu 2010; Moyer 2010). In June 2013, it was revealed that the U.S. government's National Security Agency (NSA) was regularly and indiscriminately collecting phone records from millions of Verizon users (Greenwald 2013). The information allowed it to track who called whom, when, where, and for how long. In addition, through its PRISM program, the NSA was tapping into user data from Google, Facebook, and other sites, allowing it access to emails, chats, and other online activities (Greenwald and MacAskill 2013).

In the United States, legislation regulating the surveillance of electronic communications has not always upheld citizens' right to privacy. In 1986 the federal government passed the Electronic Communications Privacy Act, which outlawed the surveillance of telephone calls except with the permission of both the U.S. attorney general and a federal judge. Telegrams, faxes, and email did not receive the same degree of protection, however. In 2001, one month after the terrorist attacks of September 11, Congress passed the USA PATRIOT Act, which relaxed existing legal checks on surveillance by law enforcement officers. Federal agencies are now freer to gather data electronically, including credit card receipts and banking records (Etzioni 2007; Singel 2008; Zetter 2009).

In the early days of Internet expansion, many people were quite concerned about sharing any personal information online for fear that someone might use it against them. Now, with the advent of Facebook, Instagram, Twitter, and a whole host of other social networking sites, many Internet users see no such risk. People regularly share their

by those in legitimate positions of power as a routine part of their jobs. In short, new technologies threaten not just our privacy but our freedom from surveillance and censorship (O'Harrow 2005). There is, for example, the danger that the most powerful groups in a society will use technology to violate the privacy of the less powerful. Indeed, officials in China have attempted to censor online discussion groups and web postings that criticize the government. Civil liberties advocates remind us that the same abuses can occur in the United States if citizens are not

Internet Top 10 Languages

Millions of users

Language	Users
English	565
Chinese	510
Spanish	165
Japanese	99
Portuguese	83
German	75
Arabic	65
French	60
Russian	60
Korean	39
Rest of world languages	351

Source: Internet World Stats 2015b.

thoughts, feelings, and actions with others, including total strangers. But Facebook's frequent privacy setting changes and selling of customers' personal information raised red flags for many, and others have learned the hard way that schools and employers can use this information to make decisions about discipline and hiring (Finder 2006; Relerford et al. 2008; Solove 2008).

BIOTECHNOLOGY AND THE GENE POOL

Another field in which technological advances have spurred global social change is biotechnology. Sex selection of fetuses, genetically engineered organisms, the cloning of animals—these have been among the significant yet controversial scientific advances in the field of biotechnology in recent years. No phase of life now seems exempt from therapeutic or medical intervention. In fact, sociologists view many aspects of biotechnology as an extension of the recent trend toward the medicalization of society. Through genetic manipulation, the medical profession is expanding its turf still further (Clarke et al. 2003).

One area of genetic modification that has raised concern involves genetically modified (GM) food. This issue arose in Europe but has since spread to other parts of the world, including the United States. The idea behind the technology is to increase food production and make agriculture more efficient and economical. But critics use the term *frankenfood* (as in Frankenstein) to refer to everything from breakfast cereals made from genetically engineered grains to "fresh" GM tomatoes. Members of the

© Photodisc/PunchStock RF

antibiotech movement object to tampering with nature and are concerned about the possible health effects of GM food. Supporters of GM food include not just biotech companies but also those who see the technology as a way to help feed the growing populations of Africa and Asia (Bouis 2007; Schurman 2004).

Even as the genetic modification of plants continues to be a concern, the debate about the genetic manipulation of animals escalated in 1997 when scientists in Scotland announced that they had cloned a sheep, which they named Dolly. After many unsuccessful attempts, they were finally able to replace the genetic material of a sheep's egg with DNA from an adult sheep, creating a lamb that was a clone of the adult. Shortly thereafter, Japanese researchers successfully cloned cows. Since then many other species have been successfully cloned (see the "Cloning Milestones" timeline); it is now even possible to get your pet cat or dog cloned, and scientists have begun work on cloning the extinct woolly mammoth with a goal of giving birth to a mammoth baby by 2016 (Grossman 2012). Such accomplishments point to the possibility that in the near future, scientists may be able to clone human beings.

Manipulation that goes even further than cloning involves potentially altering species through genetic engineering. Fish and plant genes have already been mixed to create frost-resistant potato and tomato crops. More recently, human genes have been implanted in pigs to provide humanlike kidneys for organ transplants. Geneticists working with mouse fetuses have managed to disable genes that carry an undesirable trait and replace them with genes carrying a desirable trait. And in April 2015

Cloning Milestones

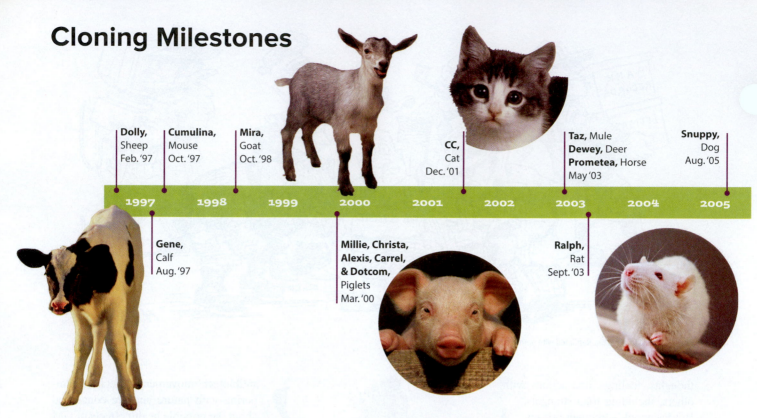

Dolly, Sheep Feb. '97

Cumulina, Mouse Oct. '97

Mira, Goat Oct. '98

CC, Cat Dec. '01

Taz, Mule
Dewey, Deer
Prometea, Horse May '03

Snuppy, Dog Aug. '05

1997 1998 1999 2000 2001 2002 2003 2004 2005

Gene, Calf Aug. '97

Millie, Christa, Alexis, Carrel, & Dotcom, Piglets Mar. '00

Ralph, Rat Sept. '03

Photos: (calf): © Fuse/Getty Images RFF; *(goat):* © G.K. & Vikki Hart/Getty Images RF; *(cat):* © Photodisc/Getty Images RF; *(pig):* © Image Source/PunchStock RF; *(rat):* © Eric Lorentzen-Newberg/Getty Images RF.

scientists announced that they had succeeded in genetically modifying human embryos. The Chinese scientists targeted a gene responsible for a potentially fatal blood disorder and they used nonviable embryos that could not have resulted in live births. These modified genes are heritable. If they were to be implanted in a baby that was born

SOCTHINK

If you could modify your children's genes to protect them from genetic diseases, would you do it? How about enhancing their abilities such as eyesight, strength, or intelligence?

and grew to have children of his or her own, he or she could pass on these genes to the next generation, the possible consequences of which are unknown (Cyranoski and Reardon 2015). Such advances raise ethical concerns related to applying such engineering to humans to eliminate disease or infirmities or to enhance physical abilities such as sight or strength (Avise 2004). This concern is shared by most Americans, 84 percent of whom say cloning humans is morally wrong; 62 percent say the same about cloning animals (Gallup 2011b). Even William F. Ogburn could not have anticipated the extent of such scientific developments when he first proposed the problem of cultural lag in the 1920s.

Five Questions to Ask When Adopting New Technology

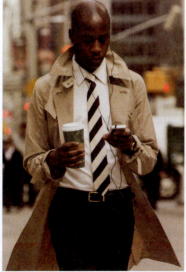

- What is the problem for which this technology is the solution?
- Whose problem is it?
- What new problems might be created because we solve the problem?
- Which people and institutions might be most seriously harmed?
- Which people and institutions might acquire special economic and political power?

Source: Postman 1988.   *Photo:* © Jose Luis Pelaez Inc./Getty Images RF.

RESISTANCE TO TECHNOLOGY

Given such consequences, it should come as no surprise that, through the ages, there have been those who questioned

Personal Sociology

Technology and Society

I confess to having mixed emotions about new technology. I love my iPhone and couldn't resist the appeal of the iPad. Yet I worry about the consequences such technologies have on my relationships with others. We are quick to adopt the latest gadgets, but what about the effects of abandoning old norms? I'm sure all of us have encountered that earbud-wearing cell-phone talker who barely seems to notice we exist. Technologies such as Facebook do enable us to maintain connections with distant friends and family. But what happens to our relationships with the people right next to us when our attention is diverted to status updates and text messages?

---

whether such technological innovation equals progress. Inventions that grew out of the Industrial Revolution, for example, led to strong resistance in some countries. In England, beginning in 1811, masked craft workers took extreme measures: They mounted nighttime raids on factories and destroyed some of the new machinery. The government hunted these rebels, known as **Luddites,** and ultimately banished or hanged them. In a similar effort in France, angry workers threw their wooden shoes (sabots) into factory machinery to destroy it, giving rise to the term *sabotage*. Although the resistance of the Luddites and the French workers was short-lived and unsuccessful, they have come to symbolize resistance to technology.

It would be a mistake, however, to simply dismiss the actions of the Luddites and French workers as anti-technology or irrational. Their primary concern was with the impact such technology had on their employment, their communities, and their way of life. They recognized that it would undercut taken-for-granted norms and values and fought against such threats. While it is easy to write such groups and individuals off as being against progress—or even as technophobes that fear change—their bigger concern is the impact adoption of technologies has on society. The Amish, for example, are often dismissed as backward, when, in fact, they are quite rational and deliberative about adopting technology. They carefully weigh the benefits new technologies would provide against the potential costs adoption would have on family and community life. They do not assume that, simply because something makes work easier or faster, it is necessarily better. For the Amish, working together in community is more highly valued than working more quickly in isolation (Hostetler 1993; Hurst and McConnell 2010).

Sociologist Jacques Ellul (1964, 1980, 1990) argued that the key factor to consider when analyzing our modern technological society is not simply the *technology,* by which he meant the physical tools we create as we modify our material environment, but what he referred to more generally as *technique.* By this he meant our systemic commitment to maximizing efficiency and increasing productivity in all areas of human endeavor. Success, whether in business, education, or love, is increasingly measured in quantitative terms. That which cannot be measured is suspect. For example, we see evidence of this at work in the No Child Left Behind education reforms. Performance on particular kinds of tests, in a narrow range of subjects, is becoming the primary indicator of learning. Although living in a technique-focused system has the advantage of technical progress, we lose something human in the process—art, beauty, and qualitative, as opposed to quantitative, values. Ellul's concerns echo those of Max Weber about the dehumanizing consequences of bureaucracy.

> **Luddites** Rebellious craft workers in 19th-century England who destroyed new factory machinery as part of their resistance to the Industrial Revolution.

Most of us today automatically adopt the latest technologies without taking time to step back and ask what consequences they might have for social order and meaning. Communications professor Neil Postman (1988, 1993, 1999) argues that, instead of passively accepting technological innovations, we should critically examine whether or not we really need them and investigate what consequences adoption might have on ourselves, our relationships, and our society (see Postman's "Five Questions" figure). In a sense, Postman is calling us to recognize ways in which our choices are influenced by the technological system within which we live. Doing so enables us to resist unconscious acceptance and exercise greater freedom in the choices that we make.

Did You Know?

. . . In 1916 Margaret Sanger opened a family planning and birth control clinic. Nine days later, it was raided by police, and she served 30 days in jail as a result. She was undeterred and continued working to dispense birth control information.

Photo: Library of Congress, Prints and Photographs Division [LC-USZ62-29808].

>> Social Movements

We do have the power to resist change even when it seems inevitable. More than that, we also have the power to bring about positive social change. Although factors such as the physical environment, population, technology, and social inequality serve as sources of change, it is the collective effort of individuals organized in social movements that ultimately leads to change. Sociologists use the term **social movements** to refer to organized collective activities to bring about or resist fundamental change in an existing group or society. Herbert Blumer (1955:19) recognized the special importance of social movements when he defined them as "collective enterprises to establish a new order of life."

In many nations, including the United States, social movements have had a dramatic impact on the course of history and the evolution of the social structure. Consider the actions of abolitionists, suffragists, civil rights workers, and anti–Vietnam War activists. Members of each social movement stepped outside traditional channels for bringing about social change, yet they had a noticeable influence on public policy. In the Arab Spring protests, equally dramatic collective efforts helped topple repressive regimes in a largely peaceful manner, in nations that many observers had thought were "immune" to such social change.

Social movements change how we think and act. Even if they initially fail to accomplish their explicit goals, social movements can influence cultural attitudes and expectations in ways that open people up to future change. Initially, people viewed the ideas of Margaret Sanger and other early advocates of birth control as radical, yet contraceptives are now widely available in the United States. Similarly, protests—whether against the practices of multinational corporations, same-sex marriage, the unethical treatment of animals, environmental destruction, or war—challenge us to question our taken-for-granted understandings of what is happening and why. This holds true even if we never formally participate ourselves or do not fully subscribe to all the beliefs and practices of the protestors.

At least since the work of Karl Marx, sociologists have studied how and why social movements emerge. Obviously, one factor is that people become discontented with the way things are. To explain how this develops and is transformed into action, sociologists rely on two primary explanations: relative deprivation and resource mobilization.

social movement An organized collective activity to bring about or resist fundamental change in an existing group or society.

relative deprivation The conscious feeling of a negative discrepancy between legitimate expectations and present actualities.

> I cannot say whether things will get better if we change; what I can say is they must change if they are to get better.
>
> Georg Christoph Lichtenberg

RELATIVE DEPRIVATION

Those members of a society who feel most frustrated with and disgruntled by social and economic conditions are not necessarily the worst off in an objective sense. Social scientists have long recognized that what is most significant is how people perceive their situation. As Marx pointed out, although the misery of the workers was important to their perception of their oppressed state, so was their position in relation to the capitalist ruling class (McLellan 2000).

The term **relative deprivation** refers to the conscious feeling of a negative discrepancy between legitimate expectations and present actualities. In other words, things aren't as good as one hoped they would be. Such a state may be characterized by scarcity rather than a complete lack of necessities. A relatively deprived person is dissatisfied because he or she feels downtrodden relative to some appropriate reference group. Thus, blue-collar workers who live in two-family houses on small plots of land—though hardly destitute—may nevertheless feel deprived in comparison to corporate managers and professionals who live in lavish homes in exclusive suburbs (Stewart 2006).

In addition to the feeling of relative deprivation, however, two other elements must be present before discontent will be channeled into a social movement. First, people must feel that they have a right to their goals, that they deserve better than what they have. For example, the struggle against European colonialism in Africa intensified when growing numbers of Africans decided that it was legitimate for them to have political and economic independence. Second, the disadvantaged group must perceive that its goals cannot be attained through conventional means. This belief may or may not be correct. In any case, the group will not mobilize into a social movement unless there is a shared perception that members can end their relative deprivation only through collective action (Walker and Smith 2002).

Critics of this approach have noted that people don't need to feel deprived to be moved to act. In addition, this approach fails to explain why certain feelings of deprivation are transformed into social movements, whereas in other, similar situations, no collective effort is made to reshape society. Consequently, in recent years, sociologists

SOCTHINK

Are there any issues on your campus or in your community that people persistently complain about? If so, what factors might inhibit them from organizing to bring about social change?

have paid increasing attention to the forces needed to bring about the emergence of social movements (Finkel and Rule 1987; Ratner 2004).

RESOURCE MOBILIZATION APPROACH

It takes more than desire to start a social movement. It helps to have money, political influence, access to the media, and personnel. The term **resource mobilization** refers to the ways in which a social movement utilizes such resources. The success of a movement for change will depend in good part on what resources it has and how effectively it mobilizes them (Balch 2006; J. Jenkins 2004; Ling 2006).

Sociologist Anthony Oberschall (1973:199) has argued that to sustain social protest or resistance, there must be an "organizational base and continuity of leadership." As people become part of a social movement, norms develop to guide their behavior. Members of the movement may be expected to attend regular meetings of organizations, pay dues, recruit new adherents, and boycott "enemy" products or speakers. In forming a distinct identity, an emerging social movement may give rise to special language or new words for familiar terms. In recent years, social movements have been responsible for new terms of

self-reference such as *Blacks* and *African Americans* (to replace *Negroes*), *senior citizens* (to replace *old folks*), *gays* (to replace *homosexuals*), and *people with disabilities* (to replace *the handicapped*).

Leadership is a central factor in the mobilization of the discontented into social movements. Often, a movement will be led by a charismatic figure, such as occurred in the civil rights movement with Dr. Martin Luther King Jr. Charisma alone, however, may not be enough. If a group is to succeed, coordinated action is essential. As they grow, such organizations may find they need to take advantage of the efficiency that bureaucratic structures provide. This can result in their taking on some of the characteristics of the groups they were organized to protest. For example, leaders might dominate the decision-making process without directly consulting followers. The bureaucratization of social movements is not inevitable, however. More-radical movements that advocate major structural change in society and embrace mass actions tend not to be hierarchical or bureaucratic (Fitzgerald and Rodgers 2000; Michels [1915] 1949). Innovations in social networking technologies, including Facebook and Twitter, facilitate the organization of mass protests, as was evidenced in the 2011 Arab Spring uprisings and in cell phone videos that captured apparent brutality on the part of police officers directed against African American males in 2015.

One of the tasks such movements face is to raise consciousness among those who would be inclined to support the movement but who may lack the language or the sense of solidarity with others to mount a systematic critique of the existing system. Marx, for example, recognized the importance of recruitment when he called on workers to become aware of their oppressed status and to develop a class consciousness. Like theorists of the resource mobilization approach, Marx held that a social movement would require leaders to sharpen the awareness of the oppressed. They would need to help workers to overcome feelings of *false consciousness*—attitudes that do not reflect workers' objective position—in order to organize a revolutionary movement (see Chapter 10).

> **resource mobilization** The ways in which a social movement utilizes such resources as money, political influence, access to the media, and personnel.

GENDER AND SOCIAL MOVEMENTS

Betty Friedan's publication of *The Feminine Mystique* in 1963 gave voice to a sense (that many women had at the time) that something was wrong, but they did not know that others felt the same way. The book alone, however, was not enough. One of the challenges faced by women's liberation activists of the late 1960s and early 1970s was to convince women that they were being deprived of their rights and of socially valued resources. Consciousness-raising groups represented a critical tool used by women's liberation activists in the 1960s and 1970s. In these groups, women gathered to discuss topics relevant to their experience in the home, at work, in politics, and more.

© Mario Tama/Getty Images

new social movement An organized collective activity that addresses values and social identities, as well as improvements in the quality of life.

This helped create a popular base that contributed to significant political and social change (Morgan 2009; Sarachild 1978).

Sociologists point out that gender continues to be an important element in understanding social movements. In our male-dominated society, women continue to find themselves cut off from leadership positions in social movement organizations. Though women often serve disproportionately as volunteers in these movements, their contributions are not always recognized, nor are their voices as easily heard as men's. Gender bias causes the real extent of their influence to be overlooked. Indeed, traditional examination of the sociopolitical system tends to focus on such male-dominated corridors of power as legislatures and corporate boardrooms, to the neglect of more female-dominated domains such as households, community-based groups, and faith-based networks. But efforts to influence family values, child rearing, relationships between parents and schools, and spiritual values are clearly significant to a culture and society (Ferree and Merrill 2000; Kuumba 2001; V. Taylor 1999, 2004).

Before the June 2009 presidential election in Iran, women's social movement organizations foresaw an opportunity for change and organized to take advantage of it. Almost 40 equal rights groups combined to form an organization called the "Coalition of Women's Movements to Advocate Electoral Demands." Noushin Ahmadi Khorasani (2009), a key leader of the women's rights movement in Iran, described the opportunity this way: "We could grasp this relatively short and transient moment with both hands, with hope and motivation (and looking forward to tomorrow) in order to voice our demands." During the government crackdown on the protests that followed the election, women continued to fight for change. Perhaps the most visible symbol of their fight was Neda Agha-Soltan, a protestor who was shot and bled to death in the street. The violent image was caught on video and

quickly spread around the world (Gheytanchi 2009; Ravitz 2009). Women continue to play a substantial role in social movements, as demonstrated by their leadership in many of the democratic uprisings during the 2011 Arab Spring protests (Ghitis 2011).

NEW SOCIAL MOVEMENTS

Beginning in the late 1960s, European social scientists observed a change in both the composition and the targets of emerging social movements. Previously, traditional social movements had focused on economic issues, often led by labor unions or by people who shared the same occupation. However, many social movements that have become active in recent decades—including the second and third waves of feminism, the peace movement, and the environmental movement—do not have the social class roots typical of the labor movements in the United States and Europe over the past century (Carty and Onyett 2006).

The term **new social movements** refers to organized collective activities that address values and social identities, as well as improvements in the quality of life. These movements may be involved in developing collective identities. Many have complex agendas that go beyond a single issue and even cross national boundaries. Educated, middle-class people are significantly represented in some of these new social movements, such as the women's movement and the movement for lesbian and gay rights (Tilly 1993, 2004).

New social movements generally do not view government as their ally in the struggle for a better society. They typically do not seek to overthrow the government, but they may criticize, protest, or harass public officials. Researchers have found that members of new social movements call into question the legitimacy of arguments made by established authorities. Even scientific or technical claims, they argue, do not simply represent objective facts, but often serve specific interests. This characteristic is especially evident in the environmental and anti-nuclear-power movements, whose activists present their own experts to counter those of government or big business (Clammer 2009; Jamison 2006; Rootes 2007).

SOCTHINK

Online sites such as changemakers.net serve as information clearinghouses and networking hubs for social activists. How might the existence of such resources shape social activism both positively and negatively?

The environmental movement is one of many new social movements with a worldwide focus. In their efforts to reduce air and water pollution, curtail global climate change, and protect endangered animal species, environmental activists have realized that strong regulatory measures within a single country are not sufficient. Similarly, labor union leaders and human rights advocates cannot adequately address exploitative sweatshop conditions in a developing country if a multinational corporation can simply move the factory to another country, where workers earn even less. Whereas traditional views of social movements tended to emphasize resource mobilization on a local level, new social movement theory offers a broader, global perspective on social and political activism (Obach 2004).

>> Sociology Is a Verb

Ultimately, social change happens because we begin to act in new ways. It involves our stepping off expected paths and, in doing so, creating new sets of norms. Although external changes in our technological and environmental contexts do influence social change, it still takes people willing to do things differently to bring about such shifts.

Sociology is a tool that helps open up new pathways for us. By enabling us to see things we might have missed before, it helps us view ourselves and the world around us differently. Sociology allows us to recognize how the distribution of social, cultural, and material resources gives advantage to some and disadvantage to others. It helps us understand whether the things we do are consistent with what we claim to believe. It can inform our conversation of whether we are headed where we want to go. It does these things by getting us to pay attention to the world around us in a new way.

We need to move from thinking of sociology as only something we learn about to thinking of sociology as something we *do*. In our daily lives, sociology can help us better understand our own individual actions and the actions of those around us. In the context of our larger society and the world, it also enables us to better appreciate the forces at work shaping outcomes—knowledge that we can then use to act in ways that make the world a better place. In both our personal and public lives, we need to practice sociology in the same way that doctors practice medicine.

PERSONAL SOCIOLOGY

Sociology can help us in our everyday lives to better understand our beliefs and actions and to make more informed choices. We learn from sociology that we are in society and society is in us. Self and society are not two separate things. Being an individual necessitates understanding the importance of place, of position, of connection, and of interaction. Though we like to believe that any choice is available to us, in reality, our options are limited.

Practicing sociology means asking uncomfortable questions and not settling for easy answers. It means taking into account the significance of both the individual and society, of both action and structure, of both freedom and constraint. It means recognizing the significance of power and the impact that access to material, social, and cultural resources has

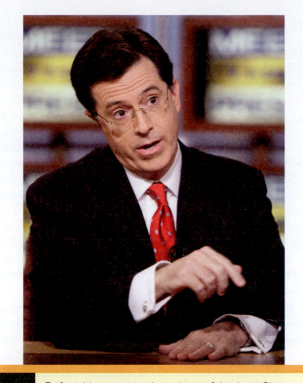

Before his current role as host of the *Late Show* on CBS, Stephen Colbert worked for several years as a sarcastic correspondent on *The Daily Show* on Comedy Central, but he became famous for spoofing TV talking heads on his show, *The Colbert Report*. He was quite serious, however, when he gave advice in a 2006 commencement speech at Knox College. He challenged students not to give in to cynicism, telling them, "Cynicism masquerades as wisdom, but it is the farthest thing from it. Because cynics don't learn anything. Because cynicism is a self-imposed blindness, a rejection of the world because we are afraid it will hurt us or disappoint us. Cynics always say 'no.' But saying 'yes' begins things. Saying 'yes' is how things grow. Saying 'yes' leads to knowledge. 'Yes' is for young people. So for as long as you have the strength to, say 'yes.'"

Photo: © Alex Wong/Getty Images.

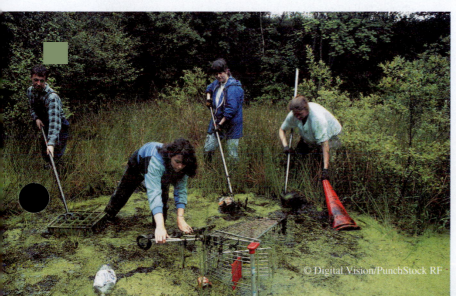

© Digital Vision/PunchStock RF

on the choices available to us. In short, as we saw in Chapter 1, doing *personal sociology* means recognizing the impact our individual position has on who we are and how we think and act, and taking responsibility for the impacts our actions have on others.

From the beginning, sociologists wanted to understand our constraints so that we might be able to change them. As sociologist Pierre Bourdieu (1998b) put it, "To those who always tax the sociologist with determinism and pessimism, I will only say that if people became fully aware of them, conscious action aimed at controlling the structural mechanisms that engender moral failure would be possible" (p. 56). In other words, we need to be honest with ourselves about the degree to which society limits our choices so that we might be empowered to make choices that are more informed and therefore more effective in helping us attain our goals.

> **public sociology** The process of bringing the insights gained through sociological observation and analysis into the public sphere, thereby seeking to bring about positive social change.

As individuals, we need to learn to see the degree to which we follow visible and invisible rules. We need to ask whether our current paths represent the values, norms, and goals that we really want to follow. As we have seen, the shows we watch, the things we buy, our likelihood for suicide, our chances of facing a wage gap, our perception of reality, our very selves—all are shaped by the positions we occupy. Understanding these influences empowers us to change.

PUBLIC SOCIOLOGY: TOOLS FOR CHANGE

Beyond providing a more informed understanding of why we as individuals act and think the way we do, sociology calls on us to look beyond ourselves to the world around

> Another world is not only possible, she is on her way. On a quiet day, I can hear her breathing.
>
> Arundhati Roy

us and ask, What might we do to make the world a better place? Since the discipline was founded, sociologists have sought to understand and explain social processes for the purpose of shaping the future of society. **Public sociology** involves bringing the insights gained through sociological observation and analysis into the public sphere, thereby seeking to bring about positive social change. As Michael Burawoy, former president of the American Sociological Association, put it, public sociology seeks to speak to a wide audience, aiming to "enrich public debate about moral and political issues by infusing them with sociological theory and research" (Burawoy 2004:1603).

Because we construct the existing social structures through our collective and recurring actions, we bear responsibility for their consequences. Existing systems—the structure and culture we create—are not inevitable. We can choose to change them; we can act differently, as the accompanying table "Citizen Activities in a Democratic Society" suggests. It can be difficult to step off the "paths of least resistance" that support the existing system (A. Johnson 1997), and the consequences for action and belief that run counter to the status quo can be severe. But we can do so.

What we cannot do is absolve ourselves of responsibility for the systems we end up with. In fact, to not act differently is to support the existing system of inequality. As sociologist Scott Schaffer (2004) points out, we can no longer ignore practices that violate our basic beliefs, trying to wash our hands of responsibility:

> Our hands are already dirty; the question I leave here is whether our hands will be dirtied through action intended to bring concrete, actual, enacted freedom into the world, or through our choice to preserve ourselves at the cost of all others in the here and now and in the future. (pp. 271–272)

Our cynicism and resignation only reinforce systems of oppression and violence. To not act to bring about positive change still represents a choice, and we bear responsibility either way.

By helping us to see why we think and act as we do, by helping us clarify the relationship between belief and practice, and by helping us better understand the consequences of difference, personal and public sociology can encourage discussion that can lead to a better future. We can use the tools of sociology to allow ourselves to enter into

Citizen Activities in a Democratic Society

PRIVATE LIFE	CIVIC LIFE	
Individual activity	**Civic engagement activities**	
	Nonpolitical activities	Political participation
Family School Work	Recycling Fellowship meetings Service activities	Voting Attending political meetings Political campaigning
Functions Cultivates personal relationships, serves individual needs—e.g., getting an education, earning a living	Provides community services and acts as a training ground for political participation	Fulfills demands of democratic citizenship

conversations in which we share our stories with others (both positive and negative), clarifying places where we agree and disagree, and opening ourselves up to our blind spots. We often want to avoid uncomfortable conflict, opting instead for polite discourse, but to fail to be more genuinely engaged in our cultural and structural differences virtually ensures a lack of progress toward implementing our core principles (Schaffer 2004).

PRACTICING SOCIOLOGY

Change comes because people continue not only to believe that it is possible but also to act on their hopes and dreams. As ethnographer Studs Terkel (2003) put it, "In all epochs, there were at first doubts and the fear of stepping forth and speaking out, but the attribute that spurred the warriors on was hope. And then *act*" (p. xviii).

We can change the world for the better. We can do so by becoming more informed about ourselves and others and then acting on that knowledge. Here are some possibilities for action:

- *Practice personal sociology.* Become more conscious of the factors that shape your beliefs and actions.
- *Become more aware of privilege.* Identify the advantages you have, especially relative to the rest of the world; you likely have sufficient food, clothes, and shelter; you can read this; you can plan for the future; and so on.
- *Become more informed.* We have access to more information about our world now than ever. Seek it out; find out what's going on.

Did You Know?

. . . Martin Luther King Jr. graduated with a BA in sociology from Morehouse College in Atlanta, Georgia, in 1948.

Photo: © Popperfoto/Getty Images.

- *Interpret what you learn.* Analyze the information you receive. Remember that data never speak for themselves; they aren't just facts but are embedded in networks and systems that have their own interests.
- *Vote.* Elected leaders in a democracy, whether local, state, or national, are chosen by voters. It may not seem like your individual vote is significant, but the simple fact is that all those votes still add up to a winner. And even if your candidate cannot win, you can still make a statement; for example, if you don't think any of the candidates would make a good choice, write in someone who would.
- *Participate in local politics.* Think of politics as a contact sport: Go to rallies, protests, school board meetings, city council meetings, and more. You might be surprised how much of a difference a single voice can make, especially on the local level.
- *Run for office.* Don't assume that such positions of leadership are only for others who are somehow better or more informed than you. We need more people to believe that they can lead so that we get more diversity in our leaders.
- *Volunteer.* There are local organizations in every community seeking to bring about positive social change. You might contact a local school to see if you can read to kids, work at a homeless shelter, or help build houses with Habitat for Humanity.
- *Join.* There are many organizations that provide long-term outreach opportunities, such as AmeriCorps, the Peace Corps, and the American Red Cross, in which you provide assistance to people with varieties of needs, in communities near and far.
- *Organize.* Work to bring about the world you envision; there are undoubtedly others out there who share your views. Find them and work with them, both inside and outside existing institutions, to bring about change.
- *Fight for change.* Regardless of where you are, whether in your relationships, your family, your workplace, your community, or elsewhere, work to bring about positive social change. We have the power to change the world; we can't do so in a vacuum, but if sociologists are at all correct about the social construction of reality, things could be otherwise.

As Comte wrote at sociology's very founding, "Science leads to foresight, and foresight leads to action" (quoted in Bourdieu 1998b:55). It is only by seeing those things that limit us that we can move toward freedom.

We learn a lesson from sociology that is reminiscent of the one Ebenezer Scrooge learns in Charles Dickens's *A Christmas Carol*, written in 1843. Scrooge, a miserly businessman, thinks only of himself, caring little if anything for others, including his employee, his family, and the poor. But on Christmas Eve, he is visited by three

At its core, Scrooge's resolution represents what we are called to do by the sociological imagination. Just as history and biography intersect, so also do we need to understand that the past, created by the actions of ourselves and those who came before us, has shaped who we are now. As American novelist and essayist James Baldwin ([1965] 1985) wrote, "The great force of history comes from the fact that we carry it within us, are unconsciously controlled by it in many ways, and history is literally *present* in all that we do" (p. 410). Further, our present actions shape the future directions of both our lives and the lives of others in the worlds around us and of those yet to come. Like Scrooge, we can reject the myth of the isolated individual and affirm the significance of relationships and companionship (to return to one of the root word meanings of sociology). By simultaneously holding the past, present, and future together in our minds, we can act to make the world a better place to live.

Sociology is more than just a noun. Sociology is a verb. It is something we do, not something we possess. Our overreliance on individualistic models, and our failure to appreciate the impact of social forces, presents a distorted picture of our freedom. An appreciation of the relationship between self and society and of the consequences of difference allows us to make more informed choices and to shape the future. It allows us to provide answers to the questions "Why do we think the way we think?" and "Why do we act the way we act?" Sociology shouldn't be something confined to college classrooms. It shouldn't be left only to professionals. We are all sociologists now, and there is work to be done.

ghosts: the Ghost of Christmas Past, the Ghost of Christmas Present, and the Ghost of Christmas Yet to Come. After each of these spirits shows him visions of their time, Scrooge repents, promising to live "an altered life" in which he will reaffirm relationships and reconnect to those around him. What is particularly interesting sociologically is the way he phrases his promise: "I will live in the Past, the Present, and the Future! The Spirits of all Three shall strive within me."

SOCIOLOGY IS A VERB

Sociology as a Way of Life

Sociology is a rich and complex discipline with so much more than can possibly be covered in an introductory course. Consider exploring what else is out there and take another sociology course in an area that sparks your interest. Even if you don't, try to engage your sociological imagination every day. Investigate. Learn. Vote. Organize. Run for office. Fight for change. Practice sociology. Make a difference.

I. How and why does social change happen?

- Social change evolves out of past social practices; it represents a response by those in society to maintain social order by seeking an acceptable level of balance between stability and change; and it is influenced by the distribution of power and control over resources, which shapes what changes do or do not occur. Technological innovation has played a powerful role causing social change.

II. What factors shape the success of a social movement?

- There needs to be a sense of relative deprivation in which people have a sense that injustice exists that can and should be challenged. In addition, people must have the capacity to mobilize resources to bring about the change they seek.

III. What does it mean to practice sociology?

- Personal sociology involves better understanding the influence social factors have on our thoughts and actions and using this information to our advantage. Public sociology means taking responsibility for the collective impacts our individual actions have in shaping society and opportunity and working for positive social change.

© Digital Vision/Getty Images RF

SOCVIEWS on Social Change

Functionalist View

Social change is a way for society to make adjustments in order to return to a state of **stability** or balance.

The four processes of social change identified by Parsons—differentiation, adaptive upgrading, inclusion, and value generalization—stress **consensus** in society.

Social movements and protests enable us to see the dysfunctions of the existing system, and thus facilitate positive social change.

EQUILIBRIUM, CONSENSUS, STABILITY
KEY CONCEPTS

Conflict View

Groups in society that **control** valued resources can either inhibit or facilitate social change more effectively than other groups.

Though new technology can provide tools that facilitate greater freedom, those in positions of power can use it to exert greater control and surveillance.

Social change should be encouraged as a way of eliminating **inequality** and correcting social **injustice**.

CONTROL, SURVEILLANCE, VESTED INTERESTS
KEY CONCEPTS

Interactionist View

Every individual has the power to change society through the everyday **choices** he or she makes and **actions** he or she takes (i.e., words we use, relationships we build, voting, volunteering, organizing for change).

Technological innovations in communication allow us to **connect** and interact with people around the world but may also cut us off from those right next to us.

Social movements consist of the **collective activities** of individuals in search of change.

ACTION, ORGANIZATION, CONNECTION
KEY CONCEPTS

MAKE THE CONNECTION

After reviewing the chapter, answer the following questions:

1
How would each perspective explain the activism of college students described in the opening vignette?

2
Why does "culture lag" occur? Why might the interactionist perspective be particularly helpful to explain it?

3
According to each perspective, what effects have new communication technologies (for example, the Internet, cell phones, and so on) had on our interactions, relationships, and communities?

4
How would drawing an insight from each perspective enable you to more effectively bring about social change?

Pop Quiz

1. **According to the definition, what is social change?**
   a. tumultuous, revolutionary alterations that lead to changes in leadership
   b. a significant alteration over time in behavior patterns and culture
   c. regular alterations in a consistent social frame of reference
   d. subtle alterations in any social system

2. **Nineteenth-century theories of social change reflect the pioneering work in biological evolution done by**
   a. Albert Einstein.
   b. Harriet Martineau.
   c. Francis Crick.
   d. Charles Darwin.

3. **According to Talcott Parsons's equilibrium model, during which process do social institutions become more specialized in their purposes?**
   a. differentiation
   b. adaptive upgrading
   c. inclusion
   d. value generalization

4. **Which of the following did William F. Ogburn use to describe the period of maladjustment during which the nonmaterial culture is still struggling to adapt to new material conditions?**
   a. economic shift
   b. political turmoil
   c. social change
   d. culture lag

5. **What term did sociologist Jacques Ellul use to describe our systematic commitment to maximizing efficiency and increasing human productivity in all areas of human life?**
   a. technology
   b. management
   c. technique
   d. kaizen

6. **You are a student and do not own a car. All your close friends who are attending your college or university have vehicles of their own. You feel downtrodden and dissatisfied. You are experiencing**
   a. relative deprivation.
   b. resource mobilization.
   c. false consciousness.
   d. depression.

7. **It takes more than desire to start a social movement; it helps to have money, political influence, access to the media, and workers. The ways in which a social movement uses such things are referred to collectively as**
   a. relative deprivation.
   b. false consciousness.
   c. resource mobilization.
   d. economic independence.

8. **Karl Marx held that leaders of social movements must help workers overcome feelings of**
   a. class consciousness.
   b. false consciousness.
   c. socialist consciousness.
   d. surplus value.

9. **Organized collective activities that promote autonomy and self-determination, as well as improvements in the quality of life, are referred to as**
   a. new social movements.
   b. social revolutions.
   c. resource mobilizations.
   d. crazes.

10. **Recognizing the impact our individual position has on who we are and how we think and act and taking responsibility for the effects our actions have on others is known as**
    a. resource mobilization.
    b. false consciousness.
    c. public sociology.
    d. personal sociology.

1. (b), 2. (d), 3. (b), 4. (d), 5. (c), 6. (a), 7. (c), 8. (b), 9. (a), 10. (d)

A

Absolute poverty   A minimum level of subsistence that no family should be expected to live below.   *230*

Achieved status   A social position that is within our power to change.   *98*

Activity theory   A theory of aging that suggests that those elderly people who remain active and socially involved will have an improved quality of life.   *88*

Adoption   The socially recognized and affirmed transfer of the legal rights, responsibilities, and privileges of parenthood.   *155*

Affirmative action   Positive efforts to recruit minority group members or women for jobs, promotions, and educational opportunities.   *307*

Ageism   Prejudice and discrimination based on a person's age.   *89*

Agency   The freedom individuals have to choose and to act.   *5*

Agrarian society   The most technologically advanced form of preindustrial society. Members are engaged primarily in the production of food, but they increase their crop yields through technological innovations such as the plow.   *115*

Alienation   Loss of control over our creative human capacity to produce, separation from the products we make, and isolation from our fellow producers.   *109*

Amalgamation   The process through which a majority group and a minority group combine to form a new group.   *309*

Anomie   A weak sense of social solidarity due to a lack of agreed-upon rules to guide behavior.   *12*

Anticipatory socialization   Processes of socialization in which a person "rehearses" for future positions, occupations, and social relationships.   *83*

Anti-Semitism   Anti-Jewish prejudice.   *320*

Apartheid   A former policy of the South African government, designed to maintain the separation of Blacks and other non-Whites from the dominant Whites.   *310*

Applied sociology   The use of the discipline of sociology with the specific intent of yielding practical applications for human behavior and organizations.   *18*

Argot   Specialized language used by members of a group or subculture.   *59*

Ascribed status   A social position assigned to a person by society without regard for the person's unique talents or characteristics.   *97*

Assimilation   The process through which a person forsakes his

or her own cultural tradition to become part of a different culture.   *309*

Authority   Power that is recognized as legitimate by the people over whom it is exercised.   *200*

B

Bilateral descent   A kinship system in which both sides of a person's family are regarded as equally important.   *146*

Bisexual   A category of sexual orientation that includes those who are attracted to both men and women.   *281*

Black power   A political philosophy, promoted by many younger Blacks in the 1960s, that supported the creation of Black-controlled political and economic institutions.   *314*

Borderlands   The area of common culture along the border between Mexico and the United States.   *262*

Bourgeoisie   The ruling class under capitalism due to their ownership of the means of production.   *237*

Brain drain   The immigration to the United States and other industrialized nations of skilled workers, professionals, and technicians who are needed in their home countries.   *337*

Bureaucracy   A formal organization built upon the principle of maximum efficiency.   *109*

Bureaucratization   The process by which a group, organization, or social movement increasingly relies on technical-rational decision making in the pursuit of efficiency.   *111*

C

Capitalism   An economic system in which owners of private property compete in the marketplace in pursuit of profit.   *202*

Caste   A stratification system in which boundaries between strata are clear, relations between levels are regulated, and social status is ascribed.   *223*

Causal logic   A relationship exists between variables in which change in one brings about change in the other.   *26*

Charismatic authority   Power made legitimate by a leader's exceptional personal or emotional appeal to his or her followers.   *201*

Class   A group of people who have a similar level of economic resources.   *239*

Class consciousness   The subjective awareness held by members of a class regarding their common vested interests and need for collective political action to bring about social change.   *238*

Clinical sociology   The use of the discipline of sociology with the specific intent of altering social relationships or restructuring social institutions.   *18*

Closed system   A society with a system of stratification that does not allow for social mobility between strata.   *225*

Coalition   A temporary or permanent alliance geared toward a common goal.   *103*

Code of ethics   The standards of acceptable behavior developed by and for members of a profession.   *38*

Cognitive culture   Our mental and symbolic representations of reality.   *51*

Cognitive theory of development   The theory that children's thought progresses through four stages of development.   *74*

Cohabitation   The practice of a man and a woman living together in a sexual relationship without being married.   *159*

Colonialism   The maintenance of political, social, economic, and cultural dominance over a people by a foreign power for an extended period.   *250*

Color-blind racism   The use of race-neutral principles to perpetuate a racially unequal status quo.   *303*

Conflict perspective   A sociological approach that assumes that social behavior is best understood in terms of tension between groups over power or the allocation of resources, including housing, money, access to services, and political representation.   *16*

Conformity   Abiding by the norms of our peers even though they have no direct authority over us.   *122*

Contact hypothesis   The theory that in cooperative circumstances interracial contact between people of equal status will reduce prejudice.   *308*

Content analysis   The systematic coding and objective recording of data, guided by some rationale.   *37*

Control group   The subjects in an experiment who are not introduced to the independent variable by the researcher.   *34*

Control theory   A view of conformity and deviance that suggests that our connection to members of society leads us to systematically conform to society's norms.   *127*

Control variable   A factor that is held constant to test the relative impact of an independent variable.   *30*

Correlation   A relationship between two variables in which a change in one coincides with a change in the other.   *27*

Correspondence principle   Schools' reproduction of the existing class structure through socializing students to embrace their social class position.   *174*

Counterculture   A subculture that deliberately opposes certain aspects of the larger culture.   *60*

Credentialism   An increase in the lowest level of education required to enter a field.   *174*

Crime   A violation of criminal law for which some governmental authority applies formal penalties.   *129*

Crude birthrate   The number of live births per 1,000 people in the population in a given year.   *329*

Crude death rate   The number of deaths per 1,000 people in a population in a given year.   *329*

Cultural capital   Our tastes, knowledge, attitudes, language, and ways of thinking that we exchange in interaction with others.   *241*

Cultural lag   A period of adjustment when the nonmaterial culture is still struggling to adapt to new material conditions.   *50*

Cultural relativism   The viewing of people's behavior from the perspective of their own culture.   *62*

Cultural transmission   A school of criminology that argues that criminal behavior is learned through social interactions.   *136*

Cultural universal   A common practice or belief shared by all societies.   *46*

Culture   Everything humans create in establishing our relationships to nature and with each other.   *45*

Culture shock   The feelings of disorientation, uncertainty, and even fear that people experience when they encounter unfamiliar cultural practices.   *61*

Culture-bound syndrome   A disease or illness that cannot be understood apart from some specific social context.   *335*

Curanderismo   Latino folk medicine, a form of holistic health care and healing.   *342*

D

Degradation ceremony   An aspect of the socialization process within some total institutions, in which people are subjected to humiliating rituals.   *85*

Deindustrialization   The systematic and widespread reduction of investment in domestic manufacturing and material production.   *197*

Democracy   In a literal sense, government by the people.   *207*

Demographic transition   As societies transform from preindustrial to postindustrial, their population size shifts from small but stable with high birthrates and death rates, through a period of significant population growth, to large but stable, when both birthrates and death rates are low.   *332*

Demography   The statistical study of population dynamics.   *328*

Denomination   A large, organized religion that is not officially linked to the state or government.   *185*

Dependency theory   An approach that contends that industrialized nations continue to exploit developing countries for their own gain.   *252*

Dependent variable   The variable in a causal relationship that is subject to the influence of another variable.   *26*

Deviance   Behavior that violates the standards of conduct or expectations of a group or society.   *127*

Dictatorship   A government in which one person has nearly total power to make and enforce laws.   *206*

Differential association A theory of deviance that holds that violation of rules results from exposure to attitudes favorable to criminal acts. *136*

Differential justice Differences in the way social control is exercised over different groups. *139*

Diffusion The process by which a cultural item spreads from group to group or society to society. *49*

Discovery The process of uncovering or revealing an existing aspect of reality. *48*

Discrimination The practice of denying equal access to opportunities and resources on the basis of group membership rather than merit or rights. *303*

Disengagement theory A theory of aging that suggests that society and the aging individual mutually sever many of their relationships. *87*

Dominant ideology A set of cultural beliefs and practices that legitimates existing powerful social, economic, and political interests. *58*

Downsizing Organizational restructuring to reduce the size of a company's workforce. *198*

Dramaturgical approach A view of social interaction in which people are seen as actors on a stage, attempting to put on a successful performance. *72*

Dyad The most basic building block of a social network, it consists of two nodes and the relationship between them. *103*

E

Ecclesia A religious organization that claims to include most or all members of a society and is recognized as the national or official religion. *184*

Economy A social institution dedicated to the production, distribution, and consumption of goods and services. *197*

Education A social institution dedicated to the formal process of transmitting culture from teachers to students. *168*

Egalitarian family An authority pattern in which spouses are regarded as equals. *150*

Elite model A view of society as being ruled by a small group of individuals who share a common set of political and economic interests. *211*

Emigration When members of a population leave that group. *330*

Endogamy The restriction of mate selection to people within the same group. *152*

Environmental justice A legal strategy based on claims that racial minorities are subjected disproportionately to environmental hazards. *349*

Equilibrium model The theory that society's natural tendency is toward social order with change in one part of society counterbalanced by adjustments in others. *361*

Established sect A religious group that is the outgrowth of a sect, yet remains isolated from society. *185*

Estate system A system of stratification that divides power in society into three primary sectors: the church, the nobility, and the commoners. *224*

Ethnicity The cultural differences between humans, defined as socially significant and presumed to divide the population into socially distinct subgroups. *297*

Ethnocentrism The tendency to assume that one's own culture and way of life represent what's normal or are superior to all others. *61*

Ethnography The study of an entire social setting through extended systematic observation. *33*

Exogamy The requirement that people select a mate outside certain groups. *152*

Experiment An artificially created situation that allows a researcher to manipulate variables. *34*

Experimental group The subjects in an experiment who are exposed to an independent variable introduced by a researcher. *34*

Exploitation theory A belief that views racial subordination in the United States as a manifestation of the class system inherent in capitalism. *307*

Expressive leader The person in the family who bears responsibility for the maintenance of harmony and internal emotional affairs. *286*

Expulsion The systematic removal of a group of people from society. *309*

Extended family A family in which relatives—such as grandparents, aunts, or uncles—live in the same household as parents and their children. *147*

F

Face-work The efforts people make to maintain a proper image and avoid public embarrassment. *73*

False consciousness A term used by Karl Marx to describe an attitude held by members of a class that does not accurately reflect their objective position. *238*

Familism Placing the interests of the family before those of the individual. *155*

Feminism The belief in social, economic, and political equality for women. *278*

Fertility The number of children born in a given period of time. *329*

Folkways Norms governing everyday behavior, whose violation raises comparatively little concern. *55*

Force The actual or threatened use of coercion to impose one's will on others. *200*

Formal norm A norm that generally has been written down and that specifies strict punishments for violators. *56*

Formal social control Social control that is carried out by authorized agents, such as police officers, judges, school administrators, and employers. *125*

Functionalist definition of families   A definition of families that focuses on how families provide for the physical, social, and emotional needs of individuals and of society as a whole.   *149*

Functionalist perspective   A sociological approach that emphasizes the way in which the parts of a society are structured to maintain its stability.   *16*

Fundamentalism   Rigid adherence to core religious doctrines, often accompanied by a literal application of scripture or historical beliefs to today's world.   *182*

G

Gemeinschaft   A close-knit community, often found in rural areas, in which strong personal bonds unite members.   *113*

Gender   The social and cultural significance that we attach to the biological differences of sex.   *271*

Gender roles   Expectations regarding the proper behavior, attitudes, and activities of males and females.   *76*

Generalized other   The attitudes, viewpoints, and expectations of society as a whole that a child takes into account in his or her behavior.   *72*

Genocide   The deliberate, systematic killing of an entire people or nation.   *308*

Gerontology   The study of the sociological and psychological aspects of aging and the problems of aging adults.   *87*

Gesellschaft   A community, often urban, that is large and impersonal, with little commitment to the group or consensus on values.   *113*

Glass ceiling   An invisible barrier that blocks the promotion of a qualified individual in a work environment because of the individual's gender, race, or ethnicity.   *289*

Globalization   The worldwide integration of government policies, cultures, social movements, and financial markets through trade and the exchange of ideas.   *19*

Goal displacement   Overzealous conformity to official regulations of a bureaucracy.   *110*

Gross national income (GNI)   The total value of a nation's goods and services.   *258*

Group   Two or more people, united by a shared sense of identity or purpose, who interact with each other over time in ways that distinguish them from outsiders.   *101*

Growth rate   The overall percentage change in a population per year.   *331*

H

Hate crime   A criminal offense committed because of the offender's bias against an individual based on race, religion, ethnicity, national origin, or sexual orientation.   *304*

Hawthorne effect   The unintended influence that observers of experiments can have on their subjects.   *35*

Health   As defined by the World Health Organization, a state of complete physical, mental, and social well-being, not merely the absence of disease and infirmity.   *335*

Heteronormativity   A term that sociologists use to describe the cultural presupposition that heterosexuality is the appropriate standard for sexual identity and practice and that alternative sexualities are deviant, abnormal, or wrong.   *282*

Heterosexual   A category of sexual orientation that includes those who are sexually attracted to members of the opposite sex.   *281*

Hidden curriculum   Teaching students to submit to authority and accept society's dominant ideology.   *174*

Holistic medicine   Therapies in which the health care practitioner considers the person's physical, mental, emotional, and spiritual characteristics.   *345*

Homogamy   The conscious or unconscious tendency to select a mate with personal characteristics and interests similar to one's own.   *153*

Homophily   Our tendency to establish close social network relationships with others who share our same knowledge, beliefs, practices, and characteristics.   *105*

Homosexual   A category of sexual orientation that includes those who are attracted to members of the same sex.   *281*

Horizontal mobility   The movement of an individual from one social position to another of the same rank.   *225*

Horticultural society   A preindustrial society in which people plant seeds and crops rather than merely subsist on available foods.   *115*

Hospice care   Treatment of terminally ill individuals in their own homes, or in special hospital units or other facilities, with the goal of helping them die comfortably, without pain.   *90*

Human ecology   The area of study concerned with the interrelationships between people and their environment.   *347*

Human relations approach   An approach to the study of formal organizations that emphasizes the role of people, communication, and participation in a bureaucracy and tends to focus on the informal structure of the organization.   *113*

Human rights   Universal moral rights possessed by all people because they are human.   *263*

Hunting-and-gathering society   A preindustrial society in which people rely on whatever foods and fibers are readily available in order to survive.   *114*

Hypothesis   A testable statement about the relationship between two or more variables.   *26*

I

I   The acting self that exists in relation to the Me.   *70*

Ideal type   An abstract model of the essential characteristics of a phenomenon.   *109*

Immigration   When individuals join a population group of which they were not previously a member.   *330*

Impression management The altering of the presentation of the self in order to create distinctive appearances and satisfy particular audiences. *72*

Incest taboo The prohibition of sexual relationships between certain culturally specified relatives. *152*

Incidence The number of new cases of a specific disorder that occur within a given population during a stated period. *340*

Income Money received over some period of time. *228*

Independent variable The variable in a causal relationship that causes or influences a change in a second variable. *26*

Index crimes The eight types of crime reported annually by the FBI in the *Uniform Crime Reports:* murder, forcible rape, robbery, aggravated assault, burglary, larceny-theft, motor vehicle theft, and arson. *130*

Industrial society A society that depends on mechanization to produce its goods and services. *115*

Infant mortality rate The number of deaths of infants under one year old per 1,000 live births in a given year. *329*

Informal economy Transfers of money, goods, or services that are not reported to the government. *205*

Informal norm A norm that is generally understood but not precisely recorded. *56*

Informal social control Social control that is carried out casually by ordinary people through such means as laughter, smiles, and ridicule. *124*

In-group A category of people who share a common identity and sense of belonging. *102*

Innovation The process of introducing a new idea or object to a culture through discovery or invention. *48*

Institutional discrimination A pattern of treatment that systematically denies a group access to resources and opportunities as part of society's normal operations. *287*

Instrumental leader The person in the family who bears responsibility for the completion of tasks, focuses on distant goals, and manages the external relationship between one's family and other social institutions. *286*

Interactionist perspective A sociological approach that generalizes about everyday forms of social interaction in order to explain society as a whole. *16*

Intergenerational mobility Changes in the social position of children relative to their parents. *226*

Intersectionality Gender, sexuality, race, ethnicity, and class must not be studied in isolation, because they have intermingled effects on our identity, knowledge, and outcomes. *280*

Interview A face-to-face or telephone questioning of a respondent to obtain desired information. *32*

Intragenerational mobility Changes in social position within a person's adult life. *226*

Invention The combination of existing cultural artifacts to create something new. *48*

Iron law of oligarchy The principle that all organizations, even democratic ones, tend to develop into bureaucracies ruled by an elite few. *112*

K

Kinship The state of being related to others. *146*

L

Labeling theory An approach to deviance that attempts to explain why certain people are viewed as deviants while others engaged in the same behavior are not. *138*

Laissez-faire The principle that people should be able to compete freely, without government interference, in the capitalist marketplace. *202*

Language A system of shared symbols; it includes speech, written characters, numerals, symbols, and nonverbal gestures and expressions. *51*

Laws Formal norms enforced by the state. *56*

Liberation theology Use of a church, primarily Roman Catholic, in a political effort to eliminate poverty, discrimination, and other forms of injustice from a secular society. *191*

Life chances The likelihood that our success is shaped by our access to valued material, social, and cultural resources. *222*

Life course approach A research orientation in which sociologists and other social scientists look closely at the social factors that influence people throughout their lives, from birth to death. *83*

Life expectancy The projected number of years a person can expect to live based on his or her year of birth. *330*

Looking-glass self A theory that we become who we are based on how we think others see us. *70*

Luddites Rebellious craft workers in 19th-century England who destroyed new factory machinery as part of their resistance to the Industrial Revolution. *369*

M

Macrosociology Sociological investigation that concentrates on large-scale phenomena or entire civilizations. *13*

Master status A status that dominates others and thereby determines a person's general position in society. *98*

Material culture Our physical modification of the natural environment to suit our purposes. *50*

Matriarchy A society in which women dominate in family decision making. *150*

Matrilineal descent A kinship system in which only the mother's relatives are significant. *146*

McDonaldization The process by which the principles of efficiency, calculability, predictability, and control shape

organization and decision making, in the United States and around the world. *111*

Me The socialized self that plans actions and judges performances based on the standards we have learned from others. *70*

Mean A number calculated by adding a series of values and then dividing by the number of values. *33*

Mechanical solidarity Social cohesion based on shared experiences, knowledge, and skills in which things function more or less the way they always have, with minimal change. *114*

Median The midpoint, or number that divides a series of values into two groups of equal numbers of values. *33*

Medicalization The process of redefining new areas of social life as the legitimate domain for medical expertise by converting them into treatable medical conditions. *336*

Microsociology Sociological investigation that stresses the study of small groups and the analysis of our everyday experiences and interactions. *13*

Midlife crisis A stressful period of self-evaluation that begins at about age 40. *85*

Migration The movement of people from one population group to another. *330*

Minority group A subordinate group whose members, even if they represent a numeric majority, lack access to, and control over, valued resources in society. *298*

Mixed economy An economic system that combines elements of both capitalism and socialism. *204*

Mode The single most common value in a series of scores. *33*

Model or ideal minority A subordinate group whose members supposedly have succeeded economically, socially, and educationally despite past prejudice and discrimination. *315*

Modernization The far-reaching process by which nations pass from traditional forms of social organization toward those characteristic of post–Industrial Revolution societies. *249*

Monarchy A form of government headed by a single member of a royal family, usually a king, queen, or some other hereditary ruler. *206*

Monogamy A form of marriage in which one woman and one man are married only to each other. *147*

Monopoly Control of a market by a single business firm. *202*

Morbidity rate The incidence of disease in a given population. *340*

Mores Norms deemed highly necessary to the welfare of a society. *55*

Mortality rate The incidence of death in a given population. *340*

Multinational corporation A commercial organization that is headquartered in one country but does business throughout the world. *252*

Multiple masculinities The idea that men learn and play a full range of gender roles. *272*

N

Natural science The study of the physical features of nature and the ways in which they interact and change. *7*

Neocolonialism Continuing dependence of former colonies on foreign countries. *251*

New religious movement (NRM) or cult A small, alternative faith community that represents either a new religion or a major innovation in an existing faith. *186*

New social movement An organized collective activity that addresses values and social identities, as well as improvements in the quality of life. *372*

Nonmaterial culture Ways of using material objects, as well as customs, ideas, expressions, beliefs, knowledge, philosophies, governments, and patterns of communication. *50*

Nonverbal communication The use of gestures, facial expressions, and other visual images to communicate. *53*

Norm An established standard of behavior maintained by a society. *55*

Normative culture Consists of the ways we establish, abide by, and enforce principles of conduct. *55*

Nuclear family A married couple and their unmarried children living together. *147*

O

Obedience Doing what a person in a position of authority over you says you should. *123*

Observation A research technique in which an investigator collects information through direct participation and/or by closely watching a group or community. *33*

Offshoring Outsourcing of work to foreign contractors. *198*

Oligarchy A form of government in which a few individuals rule. *206*

Open system A society with a system of stratification that allows for social mobility between strata. *225*

Operational definition Transformation of an abstract concept into indicators that are observable and measurable. *26*

Organic solidarity Social cohesion based on mutual interdependence in the context of extreme division of labor. *114*

Organized crime The work of a group that regulates relations among criminal enterprises involved in illegal activities, including prostitution, gambling, and the smuggling and sale of illegal drugs. *132*

Out-group A category of people who do not belong or do not fit in. *102*

P

Party The capacity to organize to accomplish some particular goal. *240*

Patriarchy A society in which men dominate in family decision making. *150*

Patrilineal descent A kinship system in which only the father's relatives are significant. *146*

Peace The absence of war, or, more broadly, a proactive effort to develop cooperative relations among nations. *217*

Personal sociology The practice of recognizing the impact our individual position has on who we are and how we think and act, and of taking responsibility for the impacts our actions have on others. *16*

Pluralism Mutual respect for one another's cultures among the various groups in a society, which allows minorities to express their own cultures without experiencing prejudice. *311*

Pluralist model A view of society in which many competing groups within the community have access to government so that no single group is dominant. *209*

Political system The social institution that is founded on a recognized set of procedures for implementing and achieving society's goals. *206*

Politics The competition between individuals or groups over the allocation of valued resources. *206*

Polyandry A form of polygamy in which a woman may have more than one husband at the same time. *147*

Polygamy A form of marriage in which an individual may have several husbands or wives simultaneously. *147*

Polygyny A form of polygamy in which a man may have more than one wife at the same time. *147*

Postindustrial society A society whose economic system is engaged primarily in the processing and control of information. *115*

Postmodern society A technologically sophisticated, pluralistic, interconnected, globalized society. *116*

Power The ability to exercise one's will over others even if they resist. *200*

Power elite A small group of military, industrial, and government leaders who control the fate of the United States. *211*

Prejudice A preconceived and unjustified judgment of individuals, whether positive or negative, based on their membership in a particular group. *302*

Prestige The respect and admiration that a particular status holds in society. *239*

Prevalence The total number of cases of a specific disorder that exist at a given time. *340*

Primary group A small group characterized by intimate, face-to-face association and cooperation. *101*

Private troubles Problems we face in our immediate relationships with particular individuals in our personal lives. *3*

Profane The ordinary and commonplace elements of life, as distinguished from the sacred. *180*

Proletariat The working class under capitalism who must sell their labor power in exchange for a wage because they lack ownership of the means of production. *237*

Protestant ethic Max Weber's term for the disciplined commitment to worldly labor driven by a desire to bring glory to God, shared by followers of Martin Luther and John Calvin. *190*

Public issues Problems we face as a consequence of the positions we occupy within the larger social structure. *3*

Public sociology The process of bringing the insights gained through sociological observation and analysis into the public sphere, thereby seeking to bring about positive social change. *374*

Q

Qualitative research Research that relies on what is seen in field or naturalistic settings more than on statistical data. *33*

Quantitative research Research that collects and reports data primarily in numerical form. *32*

Questionnaire A printed, written, or computerized form used to obtain information from a respondent. *32*

R

Race Biological differences between humans, defined as socially significant and presumed to divide the population into genetically distinct subgroups. *297*

Racial formation A sociohistorical process in which racial categories are created, inhibited, transformed, and destroyed. *299*

Racial profiling Any police-initiated action based on race, ethnicity, or national origin rather than on a person's behavior. *304*

Racism The belief that one race is supreme and all others are innately inferior. *302*

Random sample A sample for which every member of an entire population has the same chance of being selected. *28*

Rational-legal authority Authority based on formally agreed-upon and accepted rules, principles, and procedures of conduct that are established in order to accomplish goals in the most efficient manner possible. *201*

Reference group Any group that individuals use as a standard for evaluating themselves and their own behavior. *102*

Relative deprivation The conscious feeling of a negative discrepancy between legitimate expectations and present actualities. *370*

Relative poverty A floating standard of deprivation by which people at the bottom of a society, whatever their lifestyles, are judged to be disadvantaged in comparison with the nation as a whole. *231*

Reliability   The extent to which a measure produces consistent results. *29*

Religion   A social institution dedicated to establishing a shared sense of identity, encouraging social integration, and offering believers a sense of meaning and purpose. *180*

Religious belief   A statement to which members of a particular religion adhere. *182*

Religious experience   The feeling or perception of being in direct contact with the ultimate reality, such as a divine being, or of being overcome with religious emotion. *183*

Religious ritual   A practice required or expected of members of a faith. *183*

Remittances   The monies that immigrants return to their families of origin. Also known as *remesas*. *262*

Replacement fertility rate   The minimum number of children a woman would need to average in her lifetime to reproduce the population in the next generation. *329*

Representative democracy   A system of government in which citizens elect political leaders to make decisions on behalf of the people. *207*

Research design   A detailed plan or method for obtaining data scientifically. *30*

Resocialization   The process of discarding former behavior patterns and accepting new ones as part of a transition in one's life. *84*

Resource mobilization   The ways in which a social movement utilizes such resources as money, political influence, access to the media, and personnel. *371*

Rite of passage   A ritual marking the symbolic transition from one social position to another dramatizing and validating changes in a person's status. *82*

Role conflict   The situation that occurs when incompatible expectations arise from two or more social statuses held by the same person. *99*

Role exit   The process of disengagement from a role that is central to one's self-identity in order to establish a new role and identity. *100*

Role strain   The difficulty that arises when the same social status imposes conflicting demands and expectations. *99*

Role taking   The process of mentally assuming the perspective of another and responding from that imagined viewpoint. *71*

S

Sacred   Elements beyond everyday life that inspire respect, awe, and even fear. *180*

Sample   A selection from a larger population that is statistically representative of that population. *28*

Sanction   A penalty or reward for conduct concerning a social norm. *58*

Sandwich generation   The generation of adults who simultaneously try to meet the competing needs of their parents and their children. *85*

Sapir-Whorf hypothesis   The structure and vocabulary of language shapes our perception of reality and therefore also our actions. *52*

Science   The body of knowledge obtained by methods based on systematic observation. *7*

Scientific management approach   Theory of management that measures all aspects of the work process to eliminate any inefficiencies. *112*

Scientific method   A systematic, organized series of steps that ensure maximum objectivity and consistency in researching a problem. *24*

Secondary analysis   A variety of research techniques that make use of previously collected and publicly accessible information and data. *36*

Secondary group   A formal, impersonal group in which there is little social intimacy or mutual understanding. *102*

Second shift   The double burden—work outside the home followed by child care and housework—that many women face and few men share equitably. *289*

Sect   A relatively small religious group that has broken away from some other religious organization to renew what it considers the original vision of the faith. *185*

Secularization   Religion's diminishing influence in the public sphere, especially in politics and the economy. *186*

Segregation   The physical separation of two groups of people in terms of residence, workplace, and social events; often imposed on a minority group by a dominant group. *310*

Self   Our sense of who we are, distinct from others, and shaped by the unique combination of our social interactions. *70*

Serial monogamy   A form of marriage in which a person may have several spouses in his or her lifetime, but only one spouse at a time. *147*

Sex   The biological differences between males and females. *271*

Sexism   The ideology that claims one sex is superior to the other. *287*

Sexual orientation   The categories of people to whom we are sexually attracted. *281*

Sexuality   Denotes our identities and activities as sexual beings. *281*

Sick role   A form of legitimate deviance in which the person who becomes ill has a corresponding set of rights and responsibilities associated with that status. *335*

Significant other   An individual who is most important in the development of the self, such as a parent, friend, or teacher. *71*

Single-parent family   A family in which only one parent is present to care for the children. *156*

Slavery   A system of enforced servitude in which some people are owned by others as property.   *222*

Social change   Significant alteration over time in behavior patterns and culture, including norms and values.   *360*

Social class   A system of stratification primarily based on socioeconomic status, both real and perceived.   *224*

Social control   The techniques and strategies for preventing deviant human behavior in any society.   *122*

Social disorganization theory   The theory that attributes increases in crime and deviance to the absence or breakdown of communal relationships and social institutions, such as the family, school, church, and local government.   *137*

Social epidemiology   The study of the role social factors play in the development and distribution of disease throughout the population.   *340*

Social evolution   A theory of social change that holds that societies progress from simple to complex over time.   *361*

Social inequality   A condition in which members of society have different amounts of wealth, prestige, or power.   *6*

Social institution   An integrated and persistent social network dedicated to ensuring that society's core needs are met.   *106*

Social interaction   A reciprocal exchange in which two or more people read, react, and respond to each other.   *95*

Social mobility   Movement within or between society's strata.   *225*

Social movement   An organized collective activity to bring about or resist fundamental change in an existing group or society.   *370*

Social network   A web of relationships through which people interact both directly and indirectly to accomplish formal and informal goals.   *103*

Social role   A set of expected behaviors for people who occupy a given social status.   *98*

Social science   The study of the social features of humans and the ways in which they interact and change.   *7*

Social structure   The underlying framework of society consisting of the positions people occupy and the relationships between them.   *96*

Socialism   An economic system under which the means of production and distribution are collectively owned.   *203*

Socialization   The lifelong process through which people learn the attitudes, values, and behaviors appropriate for members of a particular culture.   *68*

Societal-reaction approach   Another name for *labeling theory*.   *138*

Society   The structure of relationships within which culture is created and shared through regularized patterns of social interaction.   *46*

Sociobiology   The systematic study of how biology affects human social behavior.   *47*

Socioeconomic status (SES)   A measure of social class position based on a combination of education, occupation, and income.   *240*

Sociological imagination   Our recognition of the interdependent relationship between who we are as individuals and the social forces that shape our lives.   *3*

Sociology   The systematic study of the relationship between the individual and society and of the consequences of difference.   *2*

Standpoint theory   Because our social positions shape our perceptions, a more complete understanding of social relations must incorporate the perspectives of marginalized voices.   *280*

Status   The social positions we occupy relative to others.   *97*

Status group   People who share the same perceived level of prestige.   *239*

Stereotype   An unreliable generalization about all members of a group that does not recognize individual differences within the group.   *300*

Stigma   Labeling individuals or members of a group as less than whole persons due to some attribute that marks them as different in the eyes of others.   *128*

Strain theory of deviance   Robert Merton's theory of deviance as an adaptation of socially prescribed goals or of the means governing their attainment, or both.   *135*

Stratification   A structured ranking of entire groups of people that perpetuates unequal economic rewards and power in a society.   *222*

Subculture   A segment of society that shares a distinctive pattern of mores, folkways, and values that differs from the pattern of the larger society.   *59*

Substantive definition of the family   A definition of the family based on blood, meaning shared genetic heritage, and law, meaning social recognition and affirmation of the bond including both marriage and adoption.   *145*

Survey   A study, generally in the form of an interview or questionnaire, that provides researchers with information about how people think and act.   *31*

Symbol   A gesture, object, or word that forms the basis of human communication.   *71*

Symbolic ethnicity   An ethnic identity that emphasizes concerns such as ethnic food or political issues rather than deeper ties to one's ethnic heritage.   *321*

T

Teacher-expectancy effect   The impact that a teacher's expectations about a student's performance may have on the student's actual achievements.   *173*

Technology   A form of culture in which humans modify the natural environment to meet particular wants and needs.   *50*

Terrorism   The use or threat of violence against random or symbolic targets in pursuit of political aims.   *217*

Theory   In sociology a set of statements that seeks to explain problems, actions, or behavior.   *8*

Total fertility rate   The average number of children a woman would have during her lifetime given current birthrates and assuming she survives through her childbearing years.   *329*

Total institution   An institution that regulates all aspects of a person's life under a single authority, such as a prison, the military, a mental hospital, or a convent.   *84*

Totalitarianism   Virtually complete government control and surveillance over all aspects of a society's social and political life.   *206*

Tracking   The practice of placing students in specific curriculum groups on the basis of their test scores and other criteria.   *173*

Traditional authority   Legitimate power conferred by custom and accepted practice.   *200*

Transgender   People who appear to be biologically one sex but who identify with the gender of another.   *282*

Transnational crime   Crime that occurs across multiple national borders.   *133*

Triad   Within a social network, it consists of three nodes and the direct and indirect relationships between them.   *103*

V

Validity   The degree to which a measure or scale truly reflects the phenomenon under study.   *29*

Value   A collective conception of what is considered good, desirable, and proper—or bad, undesirable, and improper—in a culture.   *53*

Value neutrality   Max Weber's term for objectivity of sociologists in the interpretation of data.   *39*

Variable   A measurable trait or characteristic that is subject to change under different conditions.   *25*

Vertical mobility   The movement of an individual from one social position to another of a different rank.   *225*

Vested interests   Those people or groups who will suffer in the event of social change and who have a stake in maintaining the status quo.   *363*

Victimization survey   A questionnaire or interview given to a sample of the population to determine whether people have been victims of crime.   *130*

Victimless crime   A term used by sociologists to describe the willing exchange among adults of widely desired, but illegal, goods and services.   *132*

W

War   Conflict between organizations that possess trained combat forces equipped with deadly weapons.   *215*

Wealth   The total value of all material assets minus debts at a single point in time.   *228*

White-collar crime   Illegal acts committed by affluent, "respectable" individuals in the course of business activities.   *131*

World systems analysis   A view of the global economic system as one divided between certain industrialized nations that control wealth and developing countries that are controlled and exploited.   *251*

A

Aaronson, Daniel, and Bhashkar Mazumder. 2007. "Intergenerational Economic Mobility in the U.S., 1940 to 2000." FRB Chicago Working Paper No. WP 2005–12, revised February 2007. Federal Reserve Bank of Chicago. Accessed June 21, 2008 (http://ssrn.com/abstract5869435).

Abercrombie, Nicholas, Stephen Hill, and Bryan S. Turner. 1980. *The Dominant Ideology Thesis.* London: George Allen and Unwin.

———. 1990. *Dominant Ideologies.* Cambridge, MA: Unwin Hyman.

———. 2006. *The Penguin Dictionary of Sociology,* 5th ed. New York: Penguin Books.

Aberle, David E., A. K. Cohen, A. K. Davis, M. J. Leng Jr., and F. N. Sutton. 1950. "The Functional Prerequisites of a Society." *Ethics* 60 (January): 100–111.

Acemoglu, Daron, and James A. Robinson. 2012. *Why Nations Fail: The Origins of Power, Prosperity, and Poverty.* New York: Crown Business.

Adair-Toteff, Christopher. 2005. "Max Weber's Charisma." *Journal of Classical Sociology* 5 (2): 189–204.

Adams, Jimi. 2007. "Stained Glass Makes the Ceiling Visible: Organizational Opposition to Women in Congregational Leadership." *Gender and Society* 21 (February): 80–115.

Adams, Samantha, and Antoinette de Bont. 2007. "Information Rx: Prescribing Good Consumerism and Responsible Citizenship." *Health Care Analysis* 15 (4): 273–290.

Addams, Jane. 1910. *Twenty Years at Hull-House.* New York: Macmillan.

———. 1930. *The Second Twenty Years at Hull-House.* New York: Macmillan.

Adler, Patricia A., and Peter Adler. 1985. "From Idealism to Pragmatic Detachment: The Academic Performance of College Athletes." *Sociology of Education* 58 (October): 241–250.

———. 1996. "Preadolescent Clique Stratification and the Hierarchy of Identity." *Sociological Inquiry* 66 (2): 111–142.

———. 2012. "Tales from the Field: Reflections on Four Decades of Ethnography." *Qualitative Sociology Review* 7 (1): 10–32.

Adler, Patricia A., Steve J. Kless, and Peter Adler. 1992. "Socialization to Gender Roles: Popularity Among Elementary School Boys and Girls." *Sociology of Education* 65 (July): 169–187.

Administration for Children and Families. 2015. "Head Start Program Facts: Fiscal Year 2014." Washington, DC: U.S. Department of Health and Human Services. Accessed March 10, 2015 (http://eclkc.ohs.acf.hhs.gov/hslc/data/factsheets/docs/hs-program-fact-sheet-2014.pdf).

Ainsworth, Claire. 2015. "Sex Redefined." *Nature* 518: 288–291.

Aisslinger, Marcel, and Rebecca Kutz. 2012. "Overview." *Prices and Earnings: Edition 2012,* CIO Wealth Management Research, September 7–12. Accessed June 4, 2013 (www.ubs.com/global/en/wealth_management/wealth_management_research/prices_earnings.html).

Alger, Horatio Jr. [1868] 1985. *Ragged Dick and Struggling Upward.* New York: Penguin Books.

Alimahomed, Sabrina. 2010. "Thinking Outside the Rainbow: Women of Color Redefining Queer Politics and Identity." *Social Identities* 16 (2): 151–168.

Allen, John L. 2008. *Student Atlas of World Politics,* 8th ed. New York: McGraw-Hill.

Alliance for Board Diversity. 2013. *Missing Pieces: Women and Minorities on* Fortune *500 Boards.* 2012 Alliance for Board Diversity (ABD) Census. Catalyst, the Proust Group, the Executive Leadership Council, the Hispanic Association on Corporate Responsibility, and Leadership Education for Asian Pacifics, Inc., August 15. Accessed April 27, 2015 (http://theabd.org/2012_ABD%20Missing_Pieces_Final_8_15_13.pdf).

Allport, Gordon W. 1979. *The Nature of Prejudice,* 25th anniversary ed. Reading, MA: Addison-Wesley.

Al-Shihri, Abdullah. 2011. "Saudi Woman Held by Police—for Driving." *The Independent,* May 22. Accessed June 12, 2011 (www.independent.co.uk/news/world/middle-east/saudi-woman-held-by-police-ndash-for-driving-2287650.html).

Alzheimer's Association. 2015. "2015 Alzheimer's Disease Facts and Figures." Accessed May 2, 2015 (www.alz.org/facts/overview.asp).

Amato, Paul R., and Alan Booth. 1997. *A Generation at Risk.* Cambridge, MA: Harvard University Press.

American Jewish Committee. 2005. "2005 Annual Survey of American Jewish Opinion." Accessed June 3, 2010 (www.ajc.org/site/apps/nlnet/content3.aspx?c5ijIT12PHKoG&b5846741&ct51740283).

American Society of Plastic Surgeons. 2014. "2013 Plastic Surgery Statistics Report." ASPS National Clearing House of Plastic Surgery Procedural Statistics. Arlington Heights, IL: ASPS. Accessed February 19, 2015 (www.plasticsurgery.org/Documents/news-resources/statistics/2013-statistics/plastic-surgery-statistics-full-report-2013.pdf).

American Sociological Association. 1999. *Code of Ethics and Policies and Procedures of the ASA Committee on Professional Ethics.* Washington, DC: American Sociological Association. Accessed May 1, 2013 (www.asanet.org/images/asa/docs/pdf/CodeofEthics.pdf).

Amnesty International. 1994. *Breaking the Silence: Human Rights Violations Based on Sexual Orientation.* New York: Amnesty International.

———. 2009b. "Sexual Orientation and Gender Identity." Accessed June 15, 2009 (www.amnesty.org/en/sexual-orientation-and-gender-identity).

———. 2011. "Annual Report 2011: The State of the World's Human Rights." Accessed May 28, 2012 (www.amnesty.org/en/annual-report/2011).

———. 2015. *Amnesty International Report 2014/15: The State of the World's Human Rights.* London: Amnesty International, Ltd. Accessed April 15, 2015 (www.amnesty.org/en/documents/pol10/0001/2015/en/).

Anagnostou, Yiorgos. 2009a. "A Critique of Symbolic Ethnicity: The Ideology of Choice?" *Ethnicities* 9 (1): 94–122.

———. 2009b. "About Facts and Fictions: Reply to Herbert Gans and Mary Waters." *Ethnicities* 9 (1).

Anderson, David, and Mykol C. Hamilton. 2005. "Gender Role Stereotyping of Parents in Children's Picture Books: The Invisible Father." *Sex Roles* 52: 145–151.

Anderson, John Ward, and Molly Moore. 1993. "Born Oppressed: Women in the Developing World Face Cradle-to-Grave Discrimination, Poverty." *The Washington Post,* February 14, p. A1.

Anderson, Terry H. 2007. *The Sixties,* 3rd ed. Englewood Cliffs, NJ: Prentice Hall.

Angier, Natalie. 2000. "Do Races Differ? Not Really, Genes Show." *The New York Times,* August 22, p. F6. Accessed June 30, 2008 (http://query.nytimes.com/gst/fullpage.html?res59E07E7DF1E3EF931A1575BC0A9669C8B63&scp52&sq5natalie1angier&st5nyt).

Anti-Defamation League. 2015. "2014 Audit of Anti-Semitic Incidents." Accessed April 29, 2015 (www.adl.org/anti-semitism/united-states/c/2014-audit-of-anti-semitic-incidents.html).

Arab American Institute. 2008. "Arab Americans: Demographics." Accessed July 1, 2008 (www.aaiusa.org/arab-americans/22/demographics).

Arora, Neeraj K., Bradford W. Hesse, Barbara K. Rimer, K. Viswanath, Marla L. Clayman, and Robert T. Croyle. 2008. "Frustrated and Confused: The American Public Rates Its Cancer-Related Information-Seeking Experiences." *Journal of General Internal Medicine* 23 (3): 223–228.

Association of Theological Schools. 2015. "ATS Data Tables 2014-2015." The Commission on Accrediting, Association of Theological Schools in the United States and Canada, Pittsburgh. Accessed March 10, 2015 (www.ats.edu/uploads/resources/institutional-data/annual-data-tables/2014-2015-annual-data-tables.pdf).

Atchley, Robert C. 1976. *The Sociology of Retirement.* New York: Wiley.

Aud, Susan, Mary Ann Fox, and Angelina KewalRamani. 2010. "Status and Trends in the Education of Racial and Ethnic Groups." National Center for Education Statistics, U.S. Department of Education, Washington, DC, NCES 2010-015. Accessed June 20, 2011 (http://nces.ed.gov/pubsearch/pubsinfo.asp?pubid52010015).

Aud, Susan, William Hussar, Grace Kena, Erin Roth, Eileen Manning, Xiaolei Wang, and Jijun Zhang. 2012. *The Condition of Education 2012.* NCES Report 2012-045. National Center for Education Statistics, U.S. Department of Education, Washington, DC, May 24. Accessed May 25, 2012 (http://nces.ed.gov/pubs2012/2012045.pdf).

Austin, Christina, and Kirsten Acuna. 2012. "Check Out the Elite Schools Where Celebrities Send Their Kids." *Business Insider,* September 27. Accessed June 2, 2013 (www.businessinsider.com/where-celebrity-kids-go-to-school-2012-9).

Avise, John C. 2004. *The Hope, Hype, and Reality of Genetic Engineering: Remarkable Stories from Agriculture, Industry, Medicine, and the Environment.* New York: Oxford University Press.

B

Backhaus, Peter. 2013. "The Japanese Traffic Light Blues: Stop on Red, Go on What?" *The Japan Times,* February 25. Accessed January 19, 2015 (www.japantimes.co.jp/life/2013/02/25/language/the-japanese-traffic-light-blues-stop-on-red-go-on-what/#.VMgFdC6fnjY).

Badoo. 2011. "Three Quarters of European Princes Marry Commoners." Badoo Trading Limited, April 26. Accessed May 30, 2011 (http://corp.badoo.com/entry/press/23/).

Baer, Hans. 2008. "Global Warming as a By-product of the Capitalist Treadmill of Production and Consumption—the Need for an Alternative Global System." *Australian Journal of Anthropology* 19 (1): 58–62.

Bagilhole, Barbara, and Simon Cross. 2006. " 'It Never Struck Me as Female': Investigating Men's Entry into Female-Dominated Occupations." *Journal of Gender Studies* 15 (1): 35–48.

Bahadur, Amar. 2008. "Sanskritization and Caste Opposition: A Shift from Ritual to Political-Economic Power." *Himalayan Journal of Sociology and Anthropology* 3: 1–10.

Bahr, Peter Riley. 2008. "*Cooling Out* in the Community College: What Is the Effect of Academic Advising on Students' Chances of Success?" *Research in Higher Education* 49: 704–732.

Baio, Andy. 2015. "Pirating the 2015 Oscars: HD Edition." *The Message,* January 22. Accessed February 19, 2015 (https://medium.com/message/pirating-the-2015-oscars-hd-edition-6c78e0cb471d).

Balch, Robert W. 2006. "The Rise and Fall of Aryan Nations: A Resource Mobilization Perspective." *Journal of Political & Military Sociology* 34 (1): 81–113.

Baldez, Lisa. 2004. "Elected Bodies: The Gender Quota Law for Legislative Candidates in Mexico." *Legislative Studies Quarterly* 29: 231–258.

Baldwin, James. [1965] 1985. "White Man's Guilt." Pp. 409–414 in *The Price of the Ticket: Collected Nonfiction, 1948–1985.* New York: St. Martin's Press.

Balfour, Gillian. 2006. "Re-imagining a Feminist Criminology." *Canadian Journal of Criminology & Criminal Justice* 48 (5): 735–752.

Banks, Duren, Lance Couzens, Caroline Blanton, and Devon Cribb. 2015. "Arrest-Related Deaths Program Assessment: Technical Report." U.S. Department of Justice, Office of Justice Programs, NCJ 248543, March. Accessed April 27, 2015 (www.bjs.gov/content/pub/pdf/ardpatr.pdf).

Banks, Duren, and Tracey Kyckelhahn. 2011. "Characteristics of Suspected Human Trafficking Incidents, 2008–2010." NCJ 233732, April. Bureau of Justice Statistics, Office of Justice Programs, U.S. Department of Justice. Accessed June 8, 2011 (http://bjs.ojp.usdoj.gov/content/pub/pdf/cshti0810.pdf).

Banks, Pauline, and Maggie Lawrence. 2006. "The Disability Discrimination Act, a Necessary, but Not Sufficient Safeguard for People with Progressive Conditions in the Workplace? The Experiences of Younger People with Parkinson's Disease." *Disability and Rehabilitation* 28 (1): 13–24.

Barna Group. 2001. "Religious Beliefs Vary Widely by Denomination." Ventura, CA: The Barna Group. Accessed June 1, 2009 (www.barna.org/barna-update/article/5-barna-update/53-religious-beliefs-vary-widely-by-denomination).

Barnes, Patricia M., Barbara Bloom, and Richard L. Nahin. 2008. "Complementary and Alternative Medicine Use Among Adults and Children: United States, 2007." *National Health Statistics Reports* 12. Hyattsville, MD: National Center for Health Statistics. Accessed May 20, 2010 (http://nccam.nih.gov/news/2008/nhsr12.pdf).

Barnes, Patricia M., Eve Powell-Griner, Kim McFann, and Richard L. Nahin. 2004. "Complementary and Alternative Medicine Use Among Adults, United States, 2002." Advance data from *Vital and Health Statistics* 343. Hyattsville, MD: National Center for Health Statistics. Accessed July 5, 2008 (http://nccam.nih.gov/news/cam-survey_fs1.htm).

Barnett, Rosalind, and Caryl Rivers. 2004. *Same Difference: How Gender Myths Are Hurting Our Relationships, Our Children, and Our Jobs.* New York: Basic Books.

Barr, Donald A. 2008. *Health Disparities in the United States: Social Class, Race, Ethnicity, and Health.* Baltimore, MD: Johns Hopkins University Press.

Barrett, David B., Todd M. Johnson, and Peter F. Crossing. 2011. "The 2010 Annual Megacensus of Religions." Pp. 508–509 in *Time Almanac 2011.* Chicago: Encyclopædia Britannica.

Barrionuevo, Alexei. 2008. "Amazon's 'Forest Peoples' Seek a P in Striking Global Climate Agreements." *The New York Time* April 6, p. 6.

Barta, Patrick, and Joel Millman. 2009. "The Great U-Turn." *The Wall Street Journal,* June 6. Accessed June 15, 2009 (http://online.wsj.com/article_email/SB124424701106590613-lMyQjAxMDI5N-DA0NzIwNDc3Wj.html).

Basinger, Jeanine. 2012. *I Do and I Don't: A History of Marriage in the Movies.* New York: Knopf.

Baudrillard, Jean. [1981] 1994. *Simulacra and Simulation.* Ann Arbor: University of Michigan Press.

Baumgardner, Jennifer, and Amy Richards. 2000. *Manifesta: Young Women, Feminism and the Future.* New York: Farrar, Straus and Giroux.

Beagan, Brenda. 2003. "Teaching Social and Cultural Awareness to Medical Students: 'It's All Very Nice to Talk About It in Theory, but Ultimately It Makes No Difference.' " *Academic Medicine* 78 (6): 605–614.

Beagan, Brenda L. 2001. " 'Even If I Don't Know What I'm Doing I Can Make It Look Like I Know What I'm Doing': Becoming a Doctor in the 1990s." *Canadian Review of Sociology and Anthropology* 38: 275–292.

Bearman, Peter S., James Moody, and Katherine Stovel. 2004. "Chains of Affection: The Structure of Adolescent Romantic and Sexual Networks." *American Journal of Sociology* 110 (July): 44–91.

Beauvoir, Simone de. 1952. *The Second Sex.* New York: Knopf.

Becker, Howard S. 1963. *The Outsiders: Studies in the Sociology of Deviance.* New York: Free Press.

———, ed. 1964. *The Other Side: Perspectives on Deviance.* New York: Free Press.

Beeghley, Leonard. 2007. *The Structure of Social Stratification in the United States,* 5th ed. Boston: Allyn & Bacon.

Bell, Daniel. 1953. "Crime as an American Way of Life." *Antioch Review* 13 (Summer): 131–154.

————. 1999. *The Coming of Post-industrial Society: A Venture in Social Forecasting.* With new foreword. New York: Basic Books.

————. 2001. *Liberation Theology After the End of History: The Refusal to Cease Suffering.* New York: Routledge.

Benagiano, Giuseppe, and Maurizio Mori. 2009. "The Origins of Human Sexuality: Procreation or Recreation?" *Reproductive BioMedicine Online* 18 (S1): 50–59.

Benhorin, Shira, and Susan D. McMahon. 2008. "Exposure to Violence and Aggression: Protective Roles of Social Support Among Urban African American Youth." *Journal of Community Psychology* 36 (6): 723–743.

Bennett, Drake. 2010. "This Will Be on the Midterm. You Feel Me? Why So Many Colleges Are Teaching *The Wire.*" *Slate,* March 24. Accessed April 9, 2010 (www.slate.com/id/2245788/).

Bennett, V., S. Dávila-Poblete, and M. N. Rico, eds. 2005. *Opposing Currents: The Politics of Water and Gender in Latin America.* Pittsburgh, PA: University of Pittsburgh Press.

Berenson, Alex, and Diana B. Henriques. 2008. "Look at Wall St. Wizard Finds Magic Had Skeptics." *The New York Times,* December 12. Accessed May 21, 2009 (www.nytimes.com /2008/12/13/business/13fraud.html).

Bergen, Raquel Kennedy. 2006. *Marital Rape: New Research and Directions.* Harrisburg, PA: VAW Net.

Berger, Peter. 1969. *The Sacred Canopy: Elements of a Sociological Theory of Religion.* Garden City, NY: Anchor Books.

Berger, Peter, and Thomas Luckmann. 1966. *The Social Construction of Reality.* New York: Doubleday.

Berland, Gretchen K. 2001. "Health Information on the Internet: Accessibility, Quality, and Readability in English and Spanish." *Journal of the American Medical Association* 285 (March 23): 2612–2621.

Berlin, Brent, and Paul Kay. 1991. *Basic Color Terms: Their Universality and Evolution.* Berkeley: University of California Press.

Bernburg, Jón Gunnar, Marvin D. Krohn, and Craig Rivera. 2006. "Official Labeling, Criminal Embeddedness, and Subsequent Delinquency: A Longitudinal Test of Labeling Theory." *Journal of Research in Crime & Delinquency* 43 (1): 67–88.

Bhatia, Aatish. 2012. "The Crayola-fication of the World: How We Gave Colors Names, and It Messed with Our Brains (Part I)." *Wired,* June 5. Accessed January 19, 2015 (www.wired. com/2012/06/the-crayola-fication-of-the-world-how-we-gave-colors-names-and-it-messed-with-our-brains-part-i/).

Bhrolcháin, Máire Ní. 2001. "'Divorce Effects' and Causality in the Social Sciences." *European Sociological Review* 17 (1): 33–57.

Bianchi, Suzanne M., John P. Robinson, and Melissa A. Milkie. 2006. *Changing Rhythms of American Family Life.* New York: Sage.

Bisi, Simonetta. 2002. "Female Criminality and Gender Difference." *International Review of Sociology* 12 (1): 23–43.

Black, Donald. 1995. "The Epistemology of Pure Sociology." *Law and Social Inquiry* 20 (Summer): 829–870.

Blaine, Tasha. 2009. *Just Like Family: Inside the Lives of Nannies, the Parents They Work for, and the Children They Love.* Boston: Houghton Mifflin Harcourt.

Blair, J. Pete, and Katherine W. Schweit. 2014. "A Study of Active Shooter Incidents, 2000–2013." Texas State University and Federal Bureau of Investigation, U.S. Department of Justice, Washington DC. Accessed February 19, 2015 (www.fbi.gov/news/stories/2014/september/fbi-releases-study-on-active-shooter-incidents/pdfs/a-study-of-active-shooter-incidents-in-the-u.s.-between-2000-and-2013).

Blass, Thomas. 1999. "The Milgram Paradigm After 35 Years: Some Things We Now Know About Obedience to Authority." *Journal of Applied Psychology* 29: 955–978.

Blauner, Robert. 1972. *Racial Oppression in America.* New York: Harper and Row.

Bligh, Michelle C., and Jeffrey C. Kohles. 2009. "The Enduring Allure of Charisma: How Barack Obama Won the Historic 2008 Presidential Election." *Leadership Quarterly* 20 (3): 483–492.

Bloemraad, Irene, Anna Korteweg, and Gökçe Yurdakul. 2008. "Citizenship and Immigration: Multiculturalism, Assimilation, and Challenges to the Nation-State." *Annual Review of Sociology* 34: 153–179.

Bloom, David E., David Canning, Günther Fink, and Jocelyn E. Finlay. 2010. "The Cost of Low Fertility in Europe." *European Journal of Population* 26: 141–158.

Blumer, Herbert. 1955. "Collective Behavior." Pp. 165–198 in *Principles of Sociology,* 2nd ed., ed. Alfred McClung Lee. New York: Barnes and Noble.

Boaz, Rachel Floersheim. 1987. "Early Withdrawal from the Labor Force." *Research on Aging* 9 (December): 530–547.

Bolt, Gideon, A. Sule Ozuekren, and Deborah Phillips. 2010. "Linking Integration and Residential Segregation." *Journal of Ethnic & Migration Studies* 36 (2): 169–186.

Bongaarts, John. 2009. "Human Population Growth and the Demographic Transition." *Philosophical Transactions of the Royal Society, Series B, Biological Sciences* 364: 2985–2990.

Bonilla-Silva, Eduardo. 2010. *Racism Without Racists: Color-Blind Racism and the Persistence of Racial Inequality in America,* 3rd ed. Lanham, MD: Rowman & Littlefield.

Booth, Alan, and Paul R. Amato. 2001. "Parental Predivorce Relations and Offspring Postdivorce Well-Being." *Journal of Marriage and the Family* 62: 197–212.

Bouis, Howarth E. 2007. "The Potential of Genetically Modified Food Crops to Improve Human Nutrition in Developing Countries." *Journal of Development Studies* 43 (1): 79–96.

Bourdieu, Pierre. 1962. *The Algerians.* Preface by Raymond Aron. Boston: Beacon Press.

————. 1984. *Distinction: A Social Critique of the Judgment of Taste.* Cambridge, MA: Harvard University Press.

————. 1986. "The Forms of Capital." Pp. 241–258 in *Handbook of Theory and Research for the Sociology of Education,* ed. J. G. Richardson. New York: Greenwood Press.

————. 1998a. *Acts of Resistance: Against the Tyranny of the Market.* New York: New Press.

————. 1998b. *On Television.* New York: New Press.

Bowles, Samuel, and Herbert Gintis. 1976. *Schooling in Capitalistic America: Educational Reforms and the Contradictions of Economic Life.* New York: Basic Books.

BP. 2015. "Gulf of Mexico: Environmental Recovery and Restoration—Five Year Report." March. Accessed April 30, 2015 (www.bp.com/content/dam/bp/pdf/gulf-of-mexico/BP_Gulf_Five _Year_Report.pdf).

BP Exploration & Production Inc. 2009. *Initial Exploration Plan: Mississippi Canyon Block 252.* OCS-G 32306, February. Accessed May 19, 2010 (www.gomr.mms.gov/PI/PDFImages/ PLANS/29/29977.pdf).

Brand, Jennie E., and Yu Xie. 2010. "Who Benefits Most from College? Evidence for Negative Selection in Heterogeneous Economic Returns to Higher Education." *American Sociological Review* 75 (2): 273–302.

Brandon, Emily. 2012. "The New Ideal Retirement Age: 67." Planning to Retire, Money, *U.S. News & World Report*, May 8. Accessed May 22, 2012 (http://money.usnews.com/money/blogs/ planning-to-retire/2012/05/08/the-new-ideal-retirement-age-67).

Brannigan, Augustine, and William Zwerman. 2001. "The Real 'Hawthorne Effect.'" *Society* 38 (January/February): 55–60.

Brewer, Rose M., and Nancy A. Heitzeg. 2008. "The Racialization of Criminal Punishment." *American Behavioral Scientist* 51 (January): 625–644.

Brickell, Chris. 2009. "Sexuality and the Dimensions of Power." *Sexuality & Culture* 13 (2): 57–74.

Brooks, Ann. 1997. *Postfeminisms: Feminism, Cultural Theory, and Cultural Forms.* New York: Routledge.

Brooks, Kelly D., and Kathryn Quina. 2009. "Women's Sexual Identity Patterns: Differences Among Lesbians, Bisexuals, and Unlabeled Women." *Journal of Homosexuality* 56 (8): 1030–1045.

Brown, Anna, and Eileen Patten. 2014. "Statistical Portrait of Hispanics in the United States, 2012." Pew Research

Center's Hispanic Trends Project, Washington, DC, April 29. Accessed April 28, 2015 (www.pewhispanic.org/2014/04/29/statistical-portrait-of-hispanics-in-the-united-states-2012/).

Brown, Harriet. 2015. *Body of Truth: How Science, History, and Culture Drive Our Obsession with Weight—and What We Can Do About It.* Boston: Da Capo Press.

Brown, Meta, Andrew Haughwout, Donghoon Lee, Maricar Mabutas, and Wilbert van der Klaauw. 2012. "Grading Student Loans." Federal Reserve Bank of New York, March 5. Accessed May 22, 2012 (http://libertystreeteconomics.newyorkfed.org/2012/03/grading-student-loans.html).

Brown, Robert McAfee. 1980. *Gustavo Gutierrez.* Atlanta: John Knox.

Brownfield, David, Ann Marie Sorenson, and Kevin M. Thompson. 2001. "Gang Membership, Race, and Social Class: A Test of the Group Hazard and Master Status Hypotheses." *Deviant Behavior* 22 (1): 73–89.

Bruce, Steve. 2000. *Choice and Religion: A Critique of Rational Choice Theory.* New York: Oxford University Press.

Bryant, Ben. 2013. "Duke and Duchess of Cambridge Break with Tradition to Choose Friends as Prince George's Godparents." *The Telegraph,* October 13. Accessed February 26, 2015 (www.telegraph.co.uk/news/uknews/prince-george/10375662/Duke-and-Duchess-of-Cambridge-break-with-tradition-to-choose-friends-as-Prince-Georges-godparents.html).

Buffett, Warren E. 2010. "Pretty Good for Government Work." The New York Times, November 16. Accessed June 3, 2015 (www.nytimes.com/2010/11/17/opinion/17buffett.html).

Bullard, Robert. 2000. *Dumping in Dixie: Race, Class, and Environmental Quality,* 3rd ed. Boulder, CO: Westview Press.

Bulle, Wolfgang F. 1987. *Crossing Cultures? Southeast Asian Mainland.* Atlanta: Centers for Disease Control and Prevention.

Bullough, Vern L. 1998. "Alfred Kinsey and the Kinsey Report: Historical Overview and Lasting Contributions." *Journal of Sex Research* 35 (2): 127–131.

Burawoy, Michael. 2004. "Public Sociologies: Contradictions, Dilemmas, and Possibilities." *Social Forces* 82: 1603–1618.

Bureau of Economic Analysis. 2015. "Gross Domestic Product: Fourth Quarter and Annual 2014 (Advance Estimate)." U.S. Department of Commerce, Washington, DC, BEA 15-04, January 30. Accessed April 11, 2015 (www.bea.gov/newsreleases/national/gdp/2015/pdf/gdp4q14_adv.pdf).

Bureau of Labor Statistics. 2010b. "Civilian Labor Force, 2019–2050." Employment Projections, Labor Force (Demographic) Data. Accessed April 20, 2010 (www/bls.gov/emp/ep_data_labor_force.htm).

———. 2013b. "Employment Characteristics of Families—2012." U.S. Department of Labor, USDL-13-0730. Accessed May 28, 2013 (www.bls.gov/news.release/pdf/famee.pdf).

———. 2013d. "2013 Employment & Earnings Online: Household Survey Data." U.S. Department of Labor. Accessed May 31, 2013 (http://bls.gov/opub/ee/2013/cps/annual.htm).

———. 2013e. "The Employment Situation—April 2013." U.S. Department of Labor, USDL-13-0785, May 1. Accessed June 1, 2013 (www.bls.gov/news.release/pdf/empsit.pdf).

———. 2014a. "Employment Characteristics of Families—2013." U.S. Department of Labor, USDL-14-0658, April 25. Accessed February 26, 2015 (www.bls.gov/news.release/pdf/famee.pdf).

———. 2014b. "College Enrollment and Work Activity of 2013 High School Graduates." U.S. Department of Labor, 14-0657. Accessed March 10, 2015 (www.bls.gov/news.release/pdf/hsgec.pdf).

———. 2014c. "Women in the Labor Force: A Databook." U.S. Department of Labor, U.S. Bureau of Labor Statistics, Report 1049, May. Accessed March 18, 2015 (www.bls.gov/cps/wlf-databook-2013.pdf).

———. 2014d. "Labor Force Characteristics by Race and Ethnicity, 2013." U.S. Department of Labor, U.S. Bureau of Labor Statistics, August. Accessed March 18, 2015 (www.bls.gov/opub/reports/cps/race_ethnicity_2013.pdf).

———. 2014e. "Women in the Labor Force: A Databook." U.S. Department of Labor, U.S. Bureau of Labor Statistics, Report 1052, December. Accessed April 21, 2015 (www.bls.gov/opub/reports/cps/women-in-the-labor-force-a-databook-2014.pdf).

———. 2014f. "Highlights of Women's Earnings in 2013." U.S. Department of Labor, U.S. Bureau of Labor Statistics, Report 1051, December. Accessed April 21, 2015 (www.bls.gov/opub/reports/cps/highlights-of-womens-earnings-in-2013.pdf).

———. 2014g. "Annual Average Household Data." 2014 Employment & Earnings Online, Household Survey Data. Accessed April 28, 2015 (www.bls.gov/opub/ee/2014/cps/annual.htm).

———. 2015a. "Unemployment: Rates for States." Local Area Unemployment Statistics. Washington, DC: U.S. Department of Labor. Accessed January 7, 2015 (www.bls.gov/web/laus/laumstrk.htm).

———. 2015b. "Unemployment: Rates & Levels—Labor Force Statistics Including the National Unemployment Rate." Current Population Survey, Databases, Tables & Calculators by Subject. Washington, DC: U.S. Department of Labor. Accessed January 7, 2015 (www.bls.gov/data/#unemployment).

———. 2015c. "2015 Employment & Earnings Online: Household Survey Data." U.S. Department of Labor. Accessed March 10, 2015 (www.bls.gov/opub/ee/2015/cps/annual.htm).

———. 2015d. "Consumer Expenditures in 2013." BLS Reports, Report 1053, February. Accessed March 26, 2015 (www.bls.gov/cex/csxann13.pdf).

———. 2015e. "Employment: Labor Force Statistics." Current Population Survey, Databases, Tables & Calculators by Subject. Washington, DC: U.S. Department of Labor. Accessed May 4, 2015 (www.bls.gov/data/#employment).

Burger, Jerry M. 2009. "Replicating Milgram: Would People Still Obey Today?" *American Psychologist* 64: 1–11.

Burgoon, Judee K., Laura K. Guerrero, and Kory Floyd. 2010. *Nonverbal Communication.* New York: Allyn & Bacon.

Burke, Moira, Carlos Greg Diuk, and Adrien Friggeri. 2015. "Cupid in Your Network." Facebook Research. Accessed May 6, 2015 (https://research.facebook.com/blog/448802398605370/cupid-in-your-network/).

Burns, Corrinne. 2013. "Are Mental Illnesses Such as PMS and Depression Culturally Determined?" *The Guardian*, May 20. Accessed June 7, 2013 (www.guardian.co.uk/science/blog/2013/may/20/mental-illnesses-depression-pms-culturally-determined?CMP=twt_fd).

Burns, Crosby, Kimberly Barton, and Sophia Kerby. 2012. "The State of Diversity in Today's Workforce." Center for American Progress, Washington, DC, July. Accessed June 1, 2013 (www.americanprogress.org/wp-content/uploads/issues/2012/07/pdf/diversity_brief.pdf).

Butler, Robert N. 1990. "A Disease Called Ageism." *Journal of American Geriatrics Society* 38 (February): 178–180.

Bynum, Daniel. 2011. "After the Hope of the Arab Spring, the Chill of an Arab Winter." *The Washington Post,* December 1. Accessed May 4, 2015 (www.washingtonpost.com/opinions/after-the-hope-of-the-arab-spring-the-chill-of-an-arab-winter/2011/11/28/gIQABGqHIO_story.html).

C

Cacchioni, Thea, and Leonore Tiefer. 2012. "Why Medicalization? Introduction to the Special Issue on the Medicalization of Sex." *Journal of Sex Research* 49: 307–310.

Cacioppo, John T., Stephanie Cacioppo, Gian C. Gonzaga, Elizabeth L. Ogburn, and Tyler J. VanderWeele. 2013. "Marital Satisfaction and Break-Ups Differ Across On-Line and Off-Line Meeting Venues." *PNAS* 110: 10135–10140.

Cai, Yong. 2010. "China's Below-Replacement Fertility: Government Policy or Socioeconomic Development?" *Population and Development Review* 36: 419–440.

Call, V. R., and J. D. Teachman. 1991. "Military Service and Stability in the Family Life Course." *Military Psychology* 3: 233–250.

Camp, Roderic Ai. 2010a. *The Metamorphosis of Leadership in a Democratic Mexico*. New York: Oxford University Press.

———. 2010b. "Armed Forces and Drugs: Public Perceptions and Institutional Challenges." Pp. 291–325 in *Shared Responsibility: U.S.–Mexico Policy Options for Confronting Organized Crime*, ed. Eric L. Olson, David A. Shirk, and Andrew Selee. San Diego: University of San Diego Trans-Border Institute.

Cañas, Jesus, and Robert W. Gilmer. 2009. "The Maquiladora's Changing Geography." Federal Reserve Bank of Dallas, *Southwest Economy:* Second Quarter. Accessed June 14, 2009 (http://dallasfed.org/research/swe/2009/swe0902c.cfm).

Caplan, Ronald L. 1989. "The Commodification of American Health Care." *Social Science and Medicine* 28 (11): 1139–1148.

Caplow, Theodore, and Louis Hicks. 2002. *Systems of War and Peace*, 2nd ed. Lanham, MD: University Press of America.

Carmichael, Mary. 2007. "Troubled Waters." *Newsweek* 149 (June 4): 52–56.

Carothers, Bobbi J., and Harry T. Reis. 2013. "Men and Women Are from Earth: Examining the Latent Structure of Gender." *Journal of Personality and Social Psychology* 104 (2): 385–407.

Carr, Nicholas. 2010. *The Shallows: What the Internet Is Doing to Our Brains*. New York: Norton.

———. 2014. *The Glass Cage: Automation and Us*. New York: Norton.

Carson, Rachel. 1962. *Silent Spring*. Boston: Houghton Mifflin.

Carter, Susan B., Scott Sigmund Gartner, Michael R. Haines, Alan L. Olmstead, Richard Sutch, and Gavin Wright. 2006. *Historical Statistics of the United States: Earliest Times to the Present, Millennial Edition*. 5 vols. Cambridge, UK: Cambridge University Press.

Carty, Victoria, and Jake Onyett. 2006. "Protest, Cyberactivism and New Social Movements: The Reemergence of the Peace Movement Post 9/11." *Social Movement Studies* 5 (3): 229–249.

Castañeda, Jorge G. 1995. "Ferocious Differences." *Atlantic Monthly* 276 (July): 68–69, 71–76.

Castells, Manuel. 1997. *The Power of Identity*. Vol. 1 of *The Information Age: Economy, Society and Culture*. London: Blackwell.

———. 1998. *End of Millennium*. Vol. 3 of *The Information Age: Economy, Society and Culture*. London: Blackwell.

———. 2000. *The Information Age: Economy, Society and Culture* (3 vols.), 2nd ed. Oxford and Malden, MA: Blackwell.

Catalano, Shannan, Erica Smith, Howard Snyder, and Michael Rand. 2009. "Female Victims of Violence." Bureau of Justice Statistics, Selected Findings, September, NCJ 228356. Accessed June 2, 2010 (http://bjs.ojp.usdoj.gov/content/pub/pdf/fvv.pdf).

Catalyst. 2011a. "2011 Catalyst Census: *Fortune* 500 Women Board Directors." Catalyst, the Prout Group, the Executive Leadership Council, the Hispanic Association on Corporate Responsibility, and Leadership Education for Asian Pacifics, Inc. Accessed May 26, 2012 (www.catalyst.org/file/533/2011_fortune_500_census_wbd.pdf).

———. 2015. *2014 Catalyst Census: Women Board Directors*. New York: Catalyst.

Cavalli-Sforza, L. Luca, Paolo Menozzi, and Alberto Piazza. 1994. *The History and Geography of Human Genes*. Princeton, NJ: Princeton University Press.

Cavanagh, Sean. 2012. "Complex Policy Options Abound Amid International Comparisons." *Education Week* 31 (16): 6–10.

CDC. 2014. "Detailed Tables for *Deaths: Final Data for 2013.*" Centers for Disease Control and Prevention, *National Vital Statistics Report* 64 (2). Accessed February 19, 2015 (www.cdc.gov/nchs/data/nvsr/nvsr64/nvsr64_02.pdf).

Center for American Women and Politics. 2015a. "Facts on Women Officeholders, Candidates and Voters." Eagleton Institute of Politics, Rutgers University, New Brunswick, NJ. Accessed April 21, 2015 (www.cawp.rutgers.edu/fast_facts/index.php).

———. 2015b. "Historical Information About Women in Congress." Eagleton Institute of Politics, Rutgers University, New Brunswick, NJ. Accessed April 21, 2015 (www.cawp.rutgers.edu/fast_facts/levels_of_office/Congress-HistoricalInfo.php).

Centers for Disease Control and Prevention. 2008. "Youth Risk Behavior Surveillance—United States, 2007." Surveillance Summaries, June 6. *Morbidity and Mortality Weekly Report* 57 (SS-4). Accessed June 1, 2010 (www.cdc.gov/mmwr/PDF/ss/ss5704.pdf).

———. 2012. "National Marriage and Divorce Rate Trends." National Center for Health Statistics, Atlanta, GA. Accessed May 29, 2013 (www.cdc.gov/nchs/nvss/marriage_divorce_tables.htm).

———. 2014a. "Deaths: Final Data for 2012." *National Vital Statistics Reports* 60 (9). Hyattsville, MD: National Center for Health Statistics. Accessed January 7, 2015 (www.cdc.gov/nchs/data/nvsr/nvsr63_09.pdf).

———. 2014b. "Marriage Rates by State: 1990, 1995, and 1999–2012." National Center for Health Statistics, Atlanta, GA. Accessed February 26, 2015 (www.cdc.gov/nchs/data/dvs/state_marriage_rates_90_95_and_99-12.pdf).

———. 2014c. "Youth Risk Behavior Surveillance—United States, 2013." Surveillance Summaries, June 13. *Morbidity and Mortality Weekly Report* 63(4). Accessed April 21, 2015 (www.cdc.gov/mmwr/pdf/ss/ss6304.pdf).

———. 2015a. "Diagnoses of HIV Infection in the United States and Dependent Areas, 2013." *HIV Surveillance Report, 2013,* 25 (February). Accessed May 1, 2015 (www.cdc.gov/hiv/pdf/g-l/hiv_surveillance_report_vol_25.pdf).

Centers for Medicare and Medicaid Services. 2014a. "National Health Expenditure Data: Historical." Department of Health and Human Services. Accessed May 2, 2015 (www.cms.gov/Research-Statistics-Data-and-Systems/Statistics-Trends-and-Reports/NationalHealthExpendData/NationalHealthAccountsHistorical.html).

———. 2014b. "National Health Expenditure Data: Projected." Department of Health and Human Services. Accessed May 2, 2015 (www.cms.gov/Research-Statistics-Data-and-Systems/Statistics-Trends-and-Reports/NationalHealthExpendData/NationalHealthAccountsProjected.html).

Césaire, Aimé. 1972. *Discourse on Colonialism*. New York: Monthly Review Press.

Cevallos, Diego. 2009. "Indigenous Woman Fights for Rights." *Inter Press Service,* April 1. Accessed June 15, 2009 (www.ips.org/mdg3/mexico-indigenous-woman-on-the-offensive/#more-21).

Chalabi, Mona, and Andrew Flowers. 2014. "Dear Mona, What's the Most Popular Name in America?" Hope the Numbers Help, FiveThirtyEight Life, November 20. Accessed January 10, 2015 (http://fivethirtyeight.com/features/whats-the-most-common-name-in-america/).

Chambers, Samuel. 2007. " 'An Incalculable Effect': Subversions of Heteronormativity." *Political Studies* 55 (3): 656–679.

Chambliss, William. 1973. "The Saints and the Roughnecks." *Society* 11 (November/December): 24–31.

Chandra, Anjani, Casey E. Copen, and William D. Mosher. 2013. "Sexual Behavior, Sexual Attraction, and Sexual Identity in the United States: Data from the 2006–2010 National Survey of Family Growth." *International Handbook on the Demography of Sexuality, International Handbooks of Population* 5: 45–66.

Chandra, Anjani, William D. Mosher, Casey Copen, and Catlainn Sionean. 2011. "Sexual Behavior, Sexual Attraction, and Sexual Identity in the United States: Data from the 2006–2008 National Survey of Family Growth." National Center for Health Statistics. *National Health Statistics Reports* 36, March 3. Accessed August 9, 2011 (www.cdc.gov/nchs/data/nhsr/nhsr036.pdf).

Chavigny, Katherine A. 2014. " 'An Army of Reformed Drunkards and Clergymen': The Medicalization of Habitual Drunkenness, 1857–1910." *Journal of the History of Medicine & Allied Sciences* 69: 383–425.

Checchi, Francesco, and W. Courtland Robinson. 2013. "Mortality Among Populations of Southern and Central Somalia Affected by Severe Food Insecurity and Famine During 2010–2012." A Study Commissioned by the United Nations Food and

Agriculture Organization's Food Security and Nutrition Analysis Unit and the Famine Early Warning Systems Network, May 2. Accessed April 2, 2015 (www.fews.net/sites/default/files/documents/reports/Somalia_Mortality_Estimates_Final_Report_1May2013_upload.pdf).

Chee, Kyong Hee, Nathan W. Pino, and William L. Smith. 2005. "Gender Differences in the Academic Ethic and Academic Achievement." *College Student Journal* 39 (3): 604–618.

Chen, Shaohua, and Martin Ravallion. 2008. "The Developing World Is Poorer Than We Thought, but No Less Successful in the Fight Against Poverty." Policy Research Working Paper 4703, World Bank Development Research Group, August 2008. Accessed June 13, 2009 (www.wds.worldbank.org/external/default/WDSContent-Server/IW3P/IB/2008/08/26/000158349_20080826113239/Rendered/PDF/WPS4703.pdf).

Cheng, Shu-Ju Ada. 2003. "Rethinking the Globalization of Domestic Service." *Gender and Society* 17 (2): 166–186.

Cherlin, Andrew. 2008. *Public and Private Families: An Introduction,* 5th ed. New York: McGraw-Hill.

———. 2009. *The Marriage-Go-Round: The State of Marriage and the Family in America Today.* New York: Knopf.

Chesney-Lind, Meda. 1989. "Girls' Crime and Women's Place: Toward a Feminist Model of Female Delinquency." *Crime and Delinquency* 35: 5–29.

Chesney-Lind, Meda, and Lisa Pasko. 2004. *The Female Offender: Girls, Women, and Crime,* 2nd ed. Thousand Oaks, CA: Sage.

Christakis, Nicholas A., and James H. Fowler. 2010. "Social Network Sensors for Early Detection of Contagious Outbreaks." *PLoS ONE* 5: e12948. Accessed February 11, 2015 (http://nrs.harvard.edu/urn-3:HUL.InstRepos:8852307).

Christian, Joseph. 2009. "Coffee Culture: A Symbol of Middle-Class Lifestyle." *China Daily,* November 3. Accessed April 1, 2010 (www.chinadaily.com.cn/cndy/2009–11/03/content_8903174.htm).

Chu, Henry. 2011. "Britain Celebrates the Royal Wedding." *Los Angeles Times,* April 29. Accessed May 30, 2011 (http://articles.latimes.com/2011/apr/29/world/la-fg-royal-wedding-20110430).

Chua, Amy. 2011. *The Battle Hymn of the Tiger Mother.* New York: Penguin Press.

Chun, Helen, Maria I. Tavarez, Grace E. Dann, and Michael P. Anastario. 2011. "Interviewer Gender and Self-Reported Sexual Behavior and Mental Health Among Male Military Personnel." *International Journal of Public Health* 56 (2): 225–229.

Cigar, Norman. 1995. *Genocide in Bosnia: The Policy of "Ethnic Cleansing."* College Station: Texas A&M University Press.

CIRCLE. 2013a. "The Youth Vote in 2012." The Center for Information & Research on Civic Learning & Engagement, Medford, MA, May 10. Accessed June 2, 2013 (www.civicyouth.org/wp-content/uploads/2013/05/CIRCLE_2013FS_outhVoting-2012FINAL.pdf).

———. 2013b. "Voter Turnout Among Young Women and Men in the 2012 Presidential Election." The Center for Information & Research on Civic Learning & Engagement, Medford, MA, May 10. Accessed June 5, 2013 (www.civicyouth.org/wp-content/uploads/2013/05/fs_gender_13_final.pdf).

Clammer, John. 2009. "Sociology and Beyond: Towards a Deep Sociology." *Asian Journal of Social Science* 37 (3): 332–346.

Clark, Burton. 1960. "The 'Cooling-Out' Function in Higher Education." *American Journal of Sociology* 65: 569–576.

———. 1980. "The 'Cooling-Out' Function Revisited." *New Directions for Community Colleges* 32: 15–31.

Clark, Duncan. 2012. "Has the Kyoto Protocol Made Any Difference to Carbon Emissions?" *The Guardian,* November 26. Accessed May 3, 2015 (www.theguardian.com/environment/blog/2012/nov/26/kyoto-protocol-carbon-emissions).

Clark, Jonathan R., Robert S. Huckman, and Bradley R. Staats. 2013. "Learning from Customers: Individual and Organizational Effects in Outsourced Radiological Services." *Organization Science* 24: 1539–1557.

Clarke, Adele E., Janet K. Shim, Laura Maro, Jennifer Ruth Fosket, and Jennifer R. Fishman. 2003. "Bio Medicalization: Technoscientific Transformations of Health, Illness, and U.S. Biomedicine." *American Sociological Review* 68 (April): 161–194.

Clarke, Edward H. 1874. *Sex in Education; or, A Fair Chance for the Girls.* Boston: James R. Osgood.

Clemons, Steve. 2011. "GOP an Oligarchy or Democracy? It Matters." *The Atlantic,* July 6. Accessed July 22, 2011 (www.theatlantic.com/national/archive/2011/07/gop-an-oligarchy-or-democracy-it-matters/241506/).

Clinard, Marshall B., and Robert F. Miller. 1998. *Sociology of Deviant Behavior,* 10th ed. Fort Worth, TX: Harcourt Brace.

Cline, Krista Marie Clark. 2010. "Psychological Effects of Dog Ownership: Role Strain, Role Enhancement, and Depression." *The Journal of Social Psychology* 150: 117–131.

Cohn, D'Vera. 2011. "Multi-Race and the 2010 Census." Pew Research Center, April 6. Accessed June 18, 2011 (http://pewresearch.org/pubs/1953/multi-race-2010-census-obama).

Colby, David C. 1986. "The Voting Rights Act and Black Registration in Mississippi." *Publius* 16 (Fall): 123–137.

Coleman, James William. 2006. *The Criminal Elite: Understanding White-Collar Crime,* 6th ed. New York: Worth.

Collins, Gail. 2003. *America's Women.* New York: HarperCollins.

Collins, Patricia Hill. 2000. *Black Feminist Thought,* 2nd ed. New York: Routledge.

Commoner, Barry. 1971. *The Closing Circle.* New York: Knopf.

———. 1990. *Making Peace with the Planet.* New York: Pantheon Books.

Commonwealth of Australia. 2013. "Australian Government Guidelines on the Recognition of Sex and Gender." July. Accessed April 19, 2015 (www.ag.gov.au/Publications/Documents/AustralianGovernmentGuidelinesontheRecognitionofSexandGender/AustralianGovernmentGuidelinesontheRecognitionofSexand-Gender.PDF).

Connell, R. W. 2002. *Gender.* Cambridge, UK: Polity Press.

———. 2005. *Masculinities,* 2nd ed. Berkeley: University of California Press.

Connolly, Ceci. 2008. "As Latin Nations Treat Gays Better, Asylum Is Elusive." *The Washington Post,* August 12. Accessed May 28, 2010 (www.washingtonpost.com/wp-dyn/content/article/2008/08/11/AR2008081102038.html).

Conrad, Peter. 2007. *The Medicalization of Society: On the Transformation of Human Conditions into Treatable Disorders.* Baltimore, MD: Johns Hopkins University Press.

Cooley, Charles H. 1902. *Human Nature and the Social Order.* New York: Scribner.

Coontz, Stephanie. 1992. *The Way We Never Were: American Families and the Nostalgia Trap.* New York: Basic Books.

———. 2005. *Marriage, a History: From Obedience to Intimacy or How Love Conquered Marriage.* New York: Viking.

———. 2006. "A Pop Quiz on Marriage." *The New York Times,* February 19, p. 12.

———. 2008. "The Future of Marriage." *Cato Unbound,* January 14. Accessed August 2, 2010 (www.cato-unbound.org/2008/01/14/stephanie-coontz/the-future-of-marriage).

———. 2011. *A Strange Stirring: The Feminine Mystique and American Women at the Dawn of the 1960s.* New York: Basic Books.

Cooper, Bruce S., and John Sureau. 2007. "The Politics of Homeschooling: New Developments, New Challenges." *Educational Policy* 21 (January and March): 110–131.

Cooper, K., S. Day, A. Green, and H. Ward. 2007. "Maids, Migrants and Occupational Health in the London Sex Industry. *Anthropology and Medicine* 14 (April): 41–53.

Corak, Miles. 2006. "Do Poor Children Become Poor Adults? Lessons from a Cross Country Comparison of Generational Earnings Mobility." Institute for the Study of Labor (IZA) Discussion Paper No. 1993, March. Accessed June 24, 2008 (http://papers.ssrn.com/sol3/papers.cfm?abstract_id5889034).

Cornwall, Warren. 2015. "*Deepwater Horizon:* After the Oil." *Science* April 3. 22–29.

Coser, Rose Laub. 1984. "American Medicine's Ambiguous Progress." *Contemporary Sociology* 13 (January): 9–13.

Côté, James E. 2000. *Arrested Adulthood: The Changing Nature of Identity and Maturity in the Late World.* New York: New York University.

Cox, Oliver C. 1948. *Caste, Class, and Race: A Study in Social Dynamics.* Detroit, MI: Wayne State University Press.

Crabtree, Catherine. 2009. "Rethinking Sexual Identity." *Existential Analysis* 20 (2): 248–261.

Crouch, Simon R., Elizabeth Waters, Ruth McNair, Jennifer Power, and Elise Davis. 2014. "Parent-Reported Measures of Child Health and Well-Being in Same-Sex Parent Families: A Cross-Sectional Survey." *BMC Public Health* 14: 636.

Croucher, Sheila L. 2004. *Globalization and Belonging: The Politics of Identity in a Changing World.* Lanham, MD: Rowman & Littlefield.

CTIA. 2014. "Background on CTIA's Semi-Annual Wireless Industry Survey." CTIA—the Wireless Association. Accessed January 23, 2015 (www.ctia.org/docs/default-source/Facts-Stats/ctia_survey _ye_2013_graphics-final.pdf?sfvrsn=2).

Cullen, Lisa Takevchi. 2007. "Till Work Do Us Part." *Time,* October 8, pp. 63–64.

Cumming, Elaine, and William E. Henry. 1961. *Growing Old: The Process of Disengagement.* New York: Basic Books.

Currie, Elliott. 1985. *Confronting Crime: An American Challenge.* New York: Pantheon Books.

———. 1998. *Crime and Punishment in America.* New York: Metropolitan Books.

Curtiss, Susan. 1977. *Genie: A Psycholinguistic Study of a Modern Day "Wild Child."* New York: Academic Press.

Cusack, Carole M., and Justine Digance. 2009. "The Melbourne Cup: Australian Identity and Secular Pilgrimage." *Sport in Society* 12 (7): 876–889.

Cyranoski, David, and Sara Reardon. 2015. "Chinese Scientists Genetically Modify Human Embryos." *Nature,* April 22. Accessed May 5, 2015 (www.nature.com/news/chinese-scientists -genetically-modify-human-embryos-1.17378).

D

Dahl, Robert A. 1961. *Who Governs?* New Haven, CT: Yale University Press.

Daisey, Mike. 2002. *21 Dog Years: Doing Time @ Amazon.com.* New York: Free Press.

Dao, James. 1995. "New York's Highest Court Rules Unmarried Couples Can Adopt." *New York Times,* November 3, pp. A1, B2.

Darwin, Charles. 1859. *On the Origin of Species.* London: John Murray.

David, Gary. 2004. "Scholarship on Arab Americans Distorted Past 9/11." *Al Jadid* (Winter/Spring): 26–27.

———. 2008. "Arab Americans." Pp. 84–87 in *Encyclopedia of Race, Ethnicity, and Society,* vol. 1, ed. Richard T. Schaefer. Thousand Oaks, CA: Sage.

Davidson, Adam. 2014. "It's Official: The Boomerang Kids Won't Leave." *The New York Times,* June 20. Accessed February 26, 2015 (www.nytimes.com/2014/06/22/magazine/its-official-the -boomerang-kids-wont-leave.html).

Davis, Darren W., and Brian D. Silver. 2003. "Stereotype Threat and Race of Interviewer Effects in a Survey on Political Knowledge." *American Journal of Political Science* 47(1): 33–45.

Davis, Georgiann. 2014. "The Power in a Name: Diagnostic Terminology and Diverse Experiences." *Psychology & Sexuality* 5: 15–27.

Davis, Gerald. 2003. *America's Corporate Banks Are Separated by Just Four Handshakes.* Accessed August 2, 2010 (www.ns.umich .edu/index.html?Releases/2002/Dec02/chr121002).

———. 2004. "American Cronyism: How Executive Networks Inflated the Corporate Bubble." *Contexts* (Summer): 34–40.

Davis, James A., Tom W. Smith, and Peter V. Marsden. 2007. *General Social Surveys, 1972–2006: Cumulative Codebook.* Chicago: National Opinion Research Center.

Davis, Joseph E. 2006. "How Medicalization Lost Its Way." *Society* 43 (6): 51–56.

Davis, Kingsley, and Wilbert E. Moore. 1945. "Some Principles of Stratification." *American Sociological Review* 10 (April): 242–249.

Dawson, Lorne. 2009. "Church-Sect-Cult: Constructing Typologies of Religious Groups." Pp. 525–544 in *The Oxford Handbook of the Sociology of Religion,* ed. Peter B. Clarke. New York: Oxford University Press.

de Aennle, Conrad. 2014. "More Security, Still Spectacular: C.E.O. Pay Still Huge, as Boards Show Independence." *The New York Times,* June 7. Accessed March 29, 2015 (www.nytimes .com/2014/06/08/business/average-total-pay-for-most-highly-paid- executives.html).

Death Penalty Information Center. 2013. "Facts About the Death Penalty." Washington, DC, May 16. Accessed May 24, 2013 (www. deathpenaltyinfo.org/documents/FactSheet.pdf).

———. 2015. "Facts About the Death Penalty." Washington, DC, February 11. Accessed February 19, 2015 (www.deathpenaltyinfo .org/documents/FactSheet.pdf).

Deflem, Mathieu. 2005. "'Wild Beasts Without Nationality': The Uncertain Origins of Interpol, 1898–1910." Pp. 275–285 in *Handbook of Transnational Crime and Justice,* ed. Philip Rerchel. Thousand Oaks, CA: Sage.

———. 2008. *Sociology of Law: Visions of a Scholarly Tradition.* Cambridge, UK: Cambridge University Press.

DeGregory, Lane. 2008. "The Girl in the Window." *The St. Petersburg Times,* July 31. Accessed May 14, 2013 (www.tampabay.com/ features/humaninterest/the-girl-in-the-window/750838).

———. 2011. "Three Years Later, 'The Girl in the Window' Learns to Connect." *Tampa Bay Times,* August 19. Accessed May 14, 2013 (www.tampabay.com/features/humaninterest/three-years -later-the-girl-in-the-window-learns-to-connect/1186860).

Delwiche, Theodore R. 2014. "Harvard Makes Admissions Offers to 5.9 Percent of Applicants to the Class of 2018." *The Harvard Crimson,* March 27. Accessed March 10, 2015 (www.thecrimson .com/article/2014/3/27/regular-admissions-class-2018/).

DeNavas-Walt, Carmen, and Bernadette D. Proctor. 2014. "Income and Poverty in the United States: 2013." *Current Population Reports,* P60-249. Washington, DC: U.S. Government Printing Office. Accessed January 7, 2015 (www.census.gov/content/dam/ Census/library/publications/2014/demo/p60-249.pdf).

DeNavas-Walt, Carmen, Bernadette D. Proctor, and Jessica C. Smith. 2012. "Income, Poverty, and Health Insurance Coverage in the United States: 2011." *Current Population Reports,* P60-243. Washington, DC: U.S. Government Printing Office. Accessed May 1, 2013 (www.census.gov/prod/2012pubs/p60-243.pdf).

Denzin, Norman K. 2009. *The Research Act: A Theoretical Introduction to Sociological Methods.* Piscataway, NJ: Transaction.

Department of Defense. 2015. "Active Duty Military Personnel by Service by Rank/Grade: January 2015 (Women Only)." DoD Personnel, Workforce Reports & Publications. Accessed March 18, 2015 (https://www.dmdc.osd.mil/appj/dwp/dwp_reports.jsp).

Devitt, James. 1999. *Framing Gender on the Campaign Trail: Women's Executive Leadership and the Press.* New York: Women's Leadership Conference.

Diamond, Jared. 2008. "What's Your Consumption Factor?" *The New York Times,* January 2. Accessed May 21, 2010 (www.nytimes .com/2008/01/02/opinion/02diamond.html).

Dickens, Charles. 1843. *A Christmas Carol.* London: Chapman and Hall. Accessed July 7, 2008 (www.gutenberg.org/ dirs/4/46/46-h/46-h.htm).

Doctorow, Cory. 2014. "Thomas Piketty's Capital in the 21st Century." *BoingBoing,* June 24. Accessed June 8, 2015 (http://boingboing .net/2014/06/24/thomas-pikettys-capital-in-t.html).

Doctors Without Borders. 2014. *U.S. Annual Report 2013.* New York, September 17. Accessed April 16, 2015 (www.doctorswithoutborders .org/our-work/publications/annual-reports/us-reports).

Dolan, Kerry A., and Luisa Kroll. 2015. "Inside the Forbes Billionaires List: Facts and Figures." *Forbes,* March 2. Accessed

April 15, 2015 (www.forbes.com/sites/kerryadolan/2015/03/02/inside-the-2015-forbes-billionaires-list-facts-and-figures/).

Domhoff, G. William. 1978. *Who Really Rules? New Haven and Community Power Reexamined.* New Brunswick, NJ: Transaction.

———. 2006. *Who Rules America?* 5th ed. New York: McGraw-Hill.

———. 2009. "The Power Elite and Their Challengers: The Role of Nonprofits in American Social Conflict." *American Behavioral Scientist* 52 (7): 955–973.

Doress, Irwin, and Jack Nusan Porter. 1977. *Kids in Cults: Why They Join, Why They Stay, Why They Leave.* Brookline, MA: Reconciliation Associates.

Dotinga, Randy. 2014. "When Parents Need Care, Daughters Carry the Burden." *CBS News*, August 19. Accessed February 2, 2015 (www.cbsnews.com/news/when-parents-need-care-daughters-carry-the-burden-study-says/).

Drescher, Jack. 2010. "Queer Diagnoses: Parallels and Contrasts in the History of Homosexuality, Gender Variance, and the *Diagnostic and Statistical Manual.*" *Archives of Sexual Behavior* 39 (2): 427–460.

———. 2011. "The Removal of Homosexuality from the DSM: Its Impact on Today's Marriage Equality Debate." *Journal of Gay & Lesbian Mental Health* 16 (2): 124–135.

Dressler, William W., Kathryn S. Oths, and Clarence C. Gravlee. 2005. "Race and Ethnicity in Public Health Research: Models to Explain Health Disparities." Pp. 231–252 in *Annual Review of Anthropology 2005,* ed. William H. Durham. Palo Alto, CA: Annual Reviews.

Duberman, Martin Bauml, Martha Vicinus, and George Chauncey Jr., eds. 1989. *Hidden from History: Reclaiming the Gay and Lesbian Past.* New York: New American Library.

Du Bois, W. E. B. [1903] 1994. *The Souls of Black Folk.* New York: Dover.

———. [1909] 1970. *The Negro American Family.* Cambridge, MA: MIT Press.

Duggan, Maeve, Nicole B. Ellison, Cliff Lampe, Amanda Lenhart, and Mary Madden. 2015. "Social Media Update 2014." Pew Research Center, January 9. Accessed February 2, 2015 (www.pewinternet.org/files/2015/01/PI_SocialMedia-Update20144.pdf).

Duncan, Greg J., and Richard J Murnane. 2011. "Introduction: The American Dream, Then and Now." Pp. 3–23 in *Whither Opportunity?: Rising Inequality, Schools, and Children's Life Chances*, ed. Greg J. Duncan and Richard J. Murnane. New York: Russell Sage Foundation.

Duneier, Mitchell. 1994a. "On the Job, but Behind the Scenes." *Chicago Tribune,* December 26, pp. 1, 24.

———. 1994b. "Battling for Control." *Chicago Tribune,* December 28, pp. 1, 8.

———. 1999. *Sidewalk.* New York: Farrar, Straus and Giroux.

Duong, Thi Hoa, Ulla-Britt Jansson, and Ann-Lena Hellström. 2013. "Vietnamese Mothers' Experiences with Potty Training Procedure for Children from Birth to 2 Years of Age." *Journal of Pediatric Urology* 9: 808–814.

Durden, T. Elizabeth, and Robert A. Hummer. 2006. "Access to Health-Care Among Working-Age Hispanic Adults in the United States." *Social Science Quarterly* 87 (December): 1319–1343.

Durkheim, Émile. [1887] 1972. "Religion and Ritual." Pp. 219–238 in *Émile Durkheim: Selected Writings,* ed. A. Giddens. Cambridge, UK: Cambridge University Press.

———. [1893] 1933. *Division of Labor in Society,* trans. George Simpson. New York: Free Press.

———. [1895] 1964. *The Rules of Sociological Method,* trans. Sarah A. Solovay and John H. Mueller. New York: Free Press.

———. [1895] 1982. *The Rules of Sociological Method and Selected Texts on Sociology and Its Method,* trans. W. D. Halls. New York: Free Press.

———. [1897] 1951. *Suicide,* trans. John A. Spaulding and George Simpson. New York: Free Press.

E

Eagan, Kevin, Jennifer B. Lozano, Sylvia Hurtado, and Matthew H. Case. 2013. *The American Freshman: National Norms Fall 2013.* Los Angeles: Higher Education Research Institute, UCLA. Accessed January 19, 2015 (www.heri.ucla.edu/tfsPublications.php).

Ebaugh, Helen Rose Fuchs. 1988. *Becoming an Ex: The Process of Role Exit.* Chicago: University of Chicago Press.

Eckert, Penelope, and Sally McConnell-Ginet. 2003. *Language and Gender.* New York: Cambridge University Press.

The Economist. 2008a. "Maharishi Mahesh Yogi." February 16: 95.

———. 2008b. "A Ravenous Dragon: A Special Report on China's Quest for Resources." March 15: 1–22.

Edin, Kathryn, and Maria Kefalas. 2005. *Promises I Can Keep: Why Poor Women Put Motherhood Before Marriage.* Berkeley: University of California Press.

EEOC. 2014. "Age Discrimination Employment Act (Includes Concurrent Charges with Title VII, ADA and EPA) FY 1997–FY 2014." U.S. Equal Employment Opportunity Commission. Accessed February 2, 2015 (www.eeoc.gov/eeoc/statistics/enforcement/adea.cfm).

eHarmony. 2014. "Who We Are." Accessed February 26, 2014 (www.eharmony.com/about/eharmony/).

Ehrlich, Paul R. 1968. *The Population Bomb.* New York: Ballantine Books.

Elgin, Suzette Haden. 1984. *Native Tongue.* New York: Feminist Press.

———. 1988. *A First Dictionary and Grammar of Láadan,* 2nd ed. Madison, WI: Society for the Furtherance and Study of Fantasy and Science Fiction.

Elia, John P. 2003. "Queering Relationships: Toward a Paradigmatic Shift." *Journal of Homosexuality* 45 (2–4): 61–86.

Elish, Jill. 2010. "Failed College Dreams Don't Spell Depression, Study Finds." *Florida State News,* March 19. Accessed April 19, 2010 (www.fsu.edu/news/2010/03/19/failed.dreams/).

Elliott, Michael. 2005. "Hopelessly Devoted: Being a Fan Is Like Having Your Own Personal Time Machine." *Time,* June 20, p. 76.

Ellison, Brandy. 2008. "Tracking." Pp. 301–304 in *Encyclopedia of Race, Ethnicity, and Society,* vol. 2, ed. Richard T. Schaefer. Thousand Oaks, CA: Sage.

Ellison, Ralph. 1952. *Invisible Man.* New York: Random House.

Ellul, Jacques. 1964. *The Technological Society.* New York: Knopf.

———. 1980. *The Technological System.* New York: Continuum.

———. 1990. *The Technological Bluff.* Grand Rapids, MI: Eerdmans.

El Nasser, Haya, and Paul Overberg. 2011. "Fewer Couples Embrace Marriage; More Live Together." *USA Today,* May 26. Accessed June 1, 2011 (www.usatoday.com/news/nation/census/2011–05-26-census-unmarried-couples_n.htm).

Emerson, Michael O., David Hartman, Karen Cook, and Douglas Massey. 2006. "The Rise of Religious Fundamentalism." *Annual Review of Sociology* 32: 127–144.

Energy Information Administration. 2008. "Emissions of Greenhouse Gases in the United States 2007." Office of Integrated Analysis and Forecasting, U.S. Department of Energy, Washington, DC. Accessed June 28, 2009 (www.eia.doe.gov/oiaf/1605/ggrpt/pdf/0573(2007).pdf).

Engels, Friedrich. [1884] 1959. "The Origin of the Family, Private Property, and the State." Pp. 392–394 in *Marx and Engels: Basic Writings on Politics and Philosophy,* ed. Lewis Feuer. Garden City, NY: Anchor Books.

Ennis, Sharon R., Merarys Ríos-Vargas, and Nora G. Albert. 2011. "The Hispanic Population: 2010." 2010 Census Briefs, C2010BR-04, May. Accessed June 20, 2011 (www.census.gov/prod/cen2010/briefs/c2010br-04.pdf).

Eom, Young-Ho, and Hang-Hyun Jo. 2014. "Generalized Friendship Paradox in Complex Networks: The Case of Scientific Collaboration." *Scientific Reports* 4: 4603. Accessed February 11, 2015 (www.nature.com/srep/2014/140408/srep04603/pdf/srep04603.pdf).

Equilar. 2014. "200 Highest-Paid CEO Pay Ranking Released." Press release, Redwood City, CA, June 8. Accessed March 29, 2015 (www.equilar.com/press-room/press-releases/266-equilar-200-highest-paid-ceo-pay-ranking-released).

Ernst and Young. 2015. "Diversity Drives Diversity: From the Boardroom to the C-Suite." Accessed April 21, 2015 (www.ey.com/Publication/vwLUAssets/EY-Diversity-drives-diversity/%24FILE/EY-Diversity-drives-diversity.pdf).

Escárcega, Sylvia. 2008. "Mexico." Pp. 898–902 in *Encyclopedia of Race, Ethnicity, and Society,* vol. 2, ed. Richard T. Schaefer. Thousand Oaks, CA: Sage.

Escoffier, Jeffrey. 1997. "Homosexuality and the Sociological Imagination: The 1950s and 1960s." Pp. 248–261 in *A Queer World: The Center for Lesbian and Gay Studies Reader,* ed. Martin Duberman. New York: New York University Press.

Etaugh, Claire. 2003. "Witches, Mothers and Others: Females in Children's Books." *Hilltopics* (Winter): 10–13.

Etzioni, Amitai. 1965. *Political Unification.* New York: Holt, Rinehart and Winston.

———. 2007. "Are New Technologies the Enemy of Privacy?" *Knowledge, Technology & Policy* 20 (2): 115–119.

Eureka County. 2006. "EPA Hears Testimony on Proposed Radiation Rule." *Nuclear Waste Office Newsletter* 11 (Winter). Eureka County Yucca Mountain Information Office.

F

Fainzang, Sylvie. 2013. "The Other Side of Medicalization: Self-Medicalization and Self-Medication." *Culture, Medicine, & Psychiatry* 37: 488–504.

Fairfield, Hannah, and Alan McLean. 2012. "Girls Lead in Science Exam, but Not in the United States." *The New York Times,* February 4. Accessed June 5, 2013 (www.nytimes.com/interactive/2013/02/04/science/girls-lead-in-science-exam-but-not-in-the-united-states.html).

Fanon, Frantz. 1963. *The Wretched of the Earth*. New York: Grove.

Farley, Melissa, and Victor Malarek. 2008. "The Myth of the Victimless Crime." *The New York Times,* March 12. Accessed May 20, 2009 (www.nytimes.com/2008/03/12/opinion/12farley.html).

Farr, Grant M. 1999. *Modern Iran.* New York: McGraw-Hill.

Fausto-Sterling, Anne. 1993. "The Five Sexes: Why Male and Female Are Not Enough." *The Sciences* (July/August): 18–23.

———. 2000. "The Five Sexes, Revisited." *The Sciences* (July/August): 18–23.

———. 2012. *Sex/Gender: Biology in a Social World.* New York: Routledge.

Fearon, James D., and David D. Laitin. 2003. "Ethnicity, Insurgency, and Civil War." *American Political Science Review* 97 (March): 75–90.

Federal Bureau of Investigation. 2012. "Organized Crime." Accessed April 24, 2012 (www.fbi.gov/about-us/investigate/organizedcrime).

Feld, Scott L. 1991. "Why Your Friends Have More Friends Than You Do." *American Journal of Sociology* 96: 1464–1477.

Felson, David, and Akis Kalaitzidis. 2005. "A Historical Overview of Transnational Crime." Pp. 3–19 in *Handbook of Transnational Crime and Justice,* ed. Philip Reichel. Thousand Oaks, CA: Sage.

Ferree, Myra Marx, and David A. Merrill. 2000. "Hot Movements, Cold Cognition: Thinking About Social Movements in Gendered Frames." *Contemporary Society* 29 (May): 454–462.

File, Thom. 2013. "The Diversifying Electorate—Voting Rates by Race and Hispanic Origin in 2012 (and Other Recent Elections)." Current Population Survey, U.S. Census Bureau, P20–568. Accessed June 1, 2013 (www.census.gov/prod/2013pubs/p20-568.pdf).

Finder, Alan. 2006. "For Some, Online Persona Undermines a Résumé." *The New York Times,* June 11. Accessed June 30, 2009 (www.nytimes.com/2006/06/11/us/11recruit.html).

Findlen, Barbara, ed. 1995. *Listen Up: Voices from the Next Feminist Generation.* Seattle, WA: Seal Press.

Fine, Gary C. 2008. "Robbers Cave." Pp. 1163–1164 in *Encyclopedia of Race, Ethnicity, and Society,* vol. 3, ed. Richard T. Schaefer. Thousand Oaks, CA: Sage.

Finkel, Steven E., and James B. Rule. 1987. "Relative Deprivation and Related Psychological Theories of Civil Violence: A Critical Review." *Research in Social Movements* 9: 47–69.

Fiscella, Kevin, and Kathleen Holt. 2008. "Racial Disparity in Hypertension Control: Tallying the Death Toll." *Annals of Family Medicine* 6: 497–502.

Fischer, Eric. 2011. "Race and Ethnicity 2010." Accessed April 28, 2015 (https://www.flickr.com/photos/walkingsf/sets/72157626354149574/).

Fisher, Gordon M. 1992. "The Development and History of the Poverty Thresholds." *Social Security Bulletin* 55 (4): 3–14. Accessed April 25, 2010 (www.ssa.gov/history/fisheronpoverty.html).

———. 2008. "Remembering Mollie Orshansky—the Developer of the Poverty Thresholds." *Social Security Bulletin* 68 (3): 79–83. Accessed April 25, 2010 (www.ssa.gov/policy/docs/ssb/v68n3/v68n3p79.pdf).

Fisher, Max. 2012. "The Middle East Didn't Really Get Any Freer in 2011." *The Atlantic,* January 19. Accessed May 28, 2012 (www.theatlantic.com/international/archive/2012/01/the-middle-east-didnt-really-get-any-freer-in-2011/251653/).

Fishman, Charles. 2006. *The Wal-Mart Effect: How the World's Most Powerful Company Really Works—and How It's Transforming the American Economy.* New York: Penguin Books.

Fitzgerald, Kathleen J., and Diane M. Rodgers. 2000. "Radical Social Movement Organization: A Theoretical Model." *Sociological Quarterly* 41 (4): 573–592.

Force, W. R. 2011. "Another Two Cents on England (and Crawley): Masculinity, Culture, and Tucson." Sociology Lens, The Society Pages, April 26. Accessed March 10, 2012 (http://thesocietypages.org/sociologylens/2011/04/26/another-two-cents-on-england-and-crawley-masculinity-culture-and-tucson/).

Ford, Liz. 2015. "Sustainable Development Goals: All You Need to Know." *The Guardian,* January 19. Accessed April 14, 2015 (www.theguardian.com/global-development/2015/jan/19/sustainable-development-goals-united-nations).

Forsythe, David P. 1990. "Human Rights in U.S. Foreign Policy: Retrospect and Prospect." *Political Science Quarterly* 105 (3): 435–454.

Fortune. 2015. "Global 500 2014." *Fortune.* Accessed April 11, 2015 (http://fortune.com/global500/).

Fowler, James H., and Nicholas A. Christakis. 2008. "Dynamic Spread of Happiness in a Large Social Network: Longitudinal Analysis over 20 Years in the Framingham Heart Study." *British Medical Journal* 337: 1–9.

Foy, Paul. 2006. "Interior Rejects Goshute Nuclear Waste Stockpile." *Indian Country Today* 20 (September 18): 1.

Francis, Ara. 2012. "Stigma in an Era of Medicalization and Anxious Parenting: How Proximity and Culpability Shape Middle-Class Parents' Experiences of Disgrace." *Sociology of Health & Illness* 34: 927–942.

Franklin, John Hope, and Alfred A. Moss. 2000. *From Slavery to Freedom: A History of African Americans,* 8th ed. Upper Saddle River, NJ: Prentice Hall.

Fraser, Steve. 2015. *The Age of Acquiescence: The Life and Death of American Resistance to Organized Wealth and Power.* New York: Little, Brown.

French, Howard W. 2000. "The Pretenders." *The New York Times Magazine,* December 3, pp. 86–88.

Freudenburg, William R. 2005. "Seeing Science, Courting Conclusions: Reexamining the Intersection of Science, Corporate Cash, and the Law." *Sociological Forum* 20 (March): 3–33.

Frey, William H. 2011. "White-Black Segregation." Brookings Institution and University of Michigan Social Science Data Analysis Network's Analysis of 2010 Census Data, CensusScope. Accessed April 28, 2015 (www.censusscope.org/2010Census/index.php).

Friedan, Betty. 1963. *The Feminine Mystique.* New York: Dell.

Friend, Christian, Andrea Hunter, and Anne Fletcher. 2011. "Parental Racial Socialization and the Academic Achievement of African American Children: A Cultural-Ecological Approach." *Journal of African American Studies* 15: 40–57.

Friman, H. Richard. 2004. "The Great Escape? Globalization, Immigrant Entrepreneurship and the Criminal Economy." *Review of International Political Economy* 11 (1): 98–131.

Fry, Richard, and D'Vera Cohn. 2010. "Women, Men and the New Economics of Marriage." A Social & Demographic Trends Report, Pew Research Center, January 19. Accessed June 2, 2011 (http://pewsocialtrends.org/files/2010/11/new-economics-of -marriage.pdf).

———. 2011. "Living Together: The Economics of Cohabitation." A Social & Demographic Trends Report, Pew Research Center, June 27. Accessed May 8, 2012 (www.pewsocialtrends.org/files/2011/06/ pew-social-trends-cohabitation-06-2011.pdf).

Fry, Richard, and Jeffrey S. Passel. 2014. "In Post-Recesson Era, Young Adults Drive Continuing Rise in Multi-Generational Living." Washington, DC: Pew Research Center's Social and Demographic Trends project, July 17. Accessed February 26, 2015 (www.pewsocialtrends.org/files/2014/07/ST-2014-07-17-multigen -households-report.pdf).

Fry, Richard, and Paul Taylor. 2013. "Hispanic High School Graduates Pass Whites in Rate of College Enrollment." Pew Research Hispanic Center, May 9. Accessed June 6, 2013 (www.pewhispanic.org/files/2013/05/PHC_college _enrollment_2013-05.pdf).

Furedi, Frank. 2006. "The End of Professional Dominance." *Society* 43 (6): 14–18.

Furstenberg, Frank F., Jr. 2010 "On a New Schedule: Transitions to Adulthood and Family Change." *The Future of Children* 20 (1): 67–87.

Fussell, Elizabeth. 2006. "Leaving New Orleans: Social Stratification, Networks, and Hurricane Evacuation." Understanding Katrina: Perspectives from the Social Sciences, Social Science Research Council, Brooklyn, NY. Accessed June 10, 2009 (http: //understandingkatrina.ssrc.org/Fussell).

Fussell, Paul. 1992. *Class: A Guide Through the American Status System.* New York: Touchstone.

Fuwa, Makiko. 2004. "Macro-Level Gender Inequality and the Division of Household Labor in 22 Countries." *American Sociological Review* 69 (December): 751–767.

G

Gabler, Neal. 2006. *Walt Disney: The Triumph of the American Imagination.* New York: Knopf.

Gabrielson, Ryan, Ryann Grochowski Jones, and Eric Sagara. 2014. "Deadly Force, in Black and White." *ProPublica,* October 10. Accessed April 26, 2015 (www.propublica.org/article/ deadly-force-in-black-and-white).

Gallup. 2008c. "Religion." Accessed March 14, 2008 (www. gallup.com).

———. 2011b. "Doctor-Assisted Suicide Is Moral Issue Dividing Americans Most." Washington, DC: Gallup, Inc. Accessed August 12, 2011 (www.gallup.com/poll/147842/Doctor-Assisted-Suicide-Moral-Issue-Dividing-Americans.aspx).

———. 2015a. "Environment." Washington, DC: Gallup, Inc. Accessed May 3, 2015 (www.gallup.com/poll/1615/Environment. aspx).

———. 2015b. "Military and National Defense." Washington, DC: Gallup, Inc. Accessed March 18, 2015 (www.gallup.com/ poll/1666/military-national-defense.aspx).

Gans, Herbert. 1971. "The Uses of Poverty: The Poor Pay All." *Social Policy,* July/August, pp. 20–24.

———. 2009. "Reflections on Symbolic Ethnicity: A Response to Y. Anagnostou." *Ethnicities* 9 (1): 123–130.

Gao, George. 2015. "How Do Americans Stand Out from the Rest of the World?" Pew Research Center, March 12. Accessed May 28, 2015 (www.pewresearch.org/fact-tank/2015/03/12/ how-do-americans-stand-out-from-the-rest-of-the-world/).

Gardner, Gary, Erik Assadourian, and Radhika Sarin. 2004. "The State of Consumption Today." Pp. 3–21 in *State of the World 2004,* ed. Brian Halweil and Lisa Mastny. New York: Norton.

Garfinkel, Harold. 1956. "Conditions of Successful Degradation Ceremonies." *American Journal of Sociology* 61 (March): 420–424.

Garrett, Ruth Irene. 2003. *Crossing Over: One Woman's Escape from Amish Life.* New York: HarperOne.

Gates, Gary J. 2010. "Sexual Minorities in the 2008 General Social Survey: Coming out and Demographic Characteristics." The Williams Institute, UCLA, October. Accessed August 9, 2011 (www3. law.ucla.edu/williamsinstitute/pdf/Sexual-Minorities-2008-GSS .pdf).

Gates, Gary J., and Frank Newport. 2012. "Special Report: 3.4% of U.S. Adults Identify as LGBT." Gallup, Inc., October 18. Accessed February 11, 2015 (www.gallup.com/poll/158066/special-report-adults-identify-lgbt.aspx).

Gaviria, Marcela, and Martin Smith. 2009. "The Madoff Affair." *PBS Frontline,* May 12. Accessed May 21, 2009 (www.pbs.org/wgbh /pages/frontline/madoff).

Gelvin, James L. 2012. *The Arab Uprisings: What Everyone Needs to Know.* New York: Oxford University Press.

Gentleman, Amelia. 2007. "Police Ignore Serial Killings in Delhi Slum, Exposing Unequal Justice for India's Poor." *The New York Times,* January 7, p. 8.

Gerhardt, Uta. 2002. *Talcott Parsons: An Intellectual Biography.* New York: Cambridge University Press.

Gettleman, Jeffrey. 2011. "Somalis Waste Away as Insurgents Block Escape from Famine." *The New York Times,* August 1. Accessed August 8, 2011 (www.nytimes.com/2011/08/02/world/ africa/02somalia.html).

Gheytanchi, Elham. 2009. "Iranian Women Lead the Protests." *San Francisco Chronicle,* June 29. Accessed June 30, 2009 (www. sfgate.com/cgi-bin/article.cgi?f5/c/a/2009/06/29/ED8618EMUC .DTL).

Ghitis, Frida. 2011. "Women of Arab Spring Still Fighting for Liberation." *Salt Lake Star Tribune,* June 21. Accessed August 12, 2011 (www.startribune.com/opinion/otherviews/124292204.html).

Gibson, Campbell, and Kay Jung. 2002. "Historical Census Statistics on Population Totals by Race, 1790 to 1990, and by Hispanic Origin, 1970 to 1990, for the United States, Regions, Divisions, and States." Population Division, U.S. Census Bureau, Washington, DC, September, Working Paper Series No. 56. Accessed May 17, 2010 (www.census.gov/population/www /documentation/twps0056/twps0056.html).

Ginder, Scott, A., Janice E. Kelly-Reid, and Farrah B. Mann. 2014. *Enrollment in Postsecondary Institutions, Fall 2011; Financial Statistics, Fiscal Year 2011; and Graduation Rates, Selected Cohorts, 2003–08.* U.S. Department of Education, NCES 2012-174rev. Washington, DC: National Center for Education Statistics. Accessed May 30, 2013 (http://nces.ed.gov/ pubs2012/2012174rev.pdf).

Gitlin, Todd. 1993. *The Sixties: Years of Hope, Days of Rage.* New York: Bantam Books.

Glass Ceiling Commission. 1995. "Good for Business: Making Full Use of the Nation's Human Capital—the Environmental Scan." A Fact-Finding Report of the Federal Glass Ceiling Commission, Washington, DC. Accessed June 19, 2011 (www.dol.gov/oasam/ programs/history/reich/reports/ceiling.pdf).

Glassner, Barry. 2010. "Still Fearful." *Chronicle of Higher Education* 56 (January 22): B11–B12.

Glaze, Lauren E., and Danielle Kaeble. 2014. "Correctional Populations in the United States, 2013." Bureau of Justice Statistics Bulletin, December, NCJ 248479. Accessed February 19, 2015 (www.bjs.gov/content/pub/pdf/cpus13.pdf).

Goering, Laurie. 2007. "The First Refugees of Global Warming." *Chicago Tribune,* May 2, pp. 1, 25.

Goffman, Alice. 2014a. *On the Run: Fugitive Life in an American City.* Chicago: University of Chicago Press.

—————.2014b. "Surveillance City: The War on Drugs in Urban Neighborhoods." The 2014 Nathan Levin Lecture on Public Policy, Public Policy Forums, the Center for New York City Affairs, New School, New York City, June 18, 2014. Accessed January 10, 2015 (http://blogs.newschool.edu/cnyca/2014/05/21/surveillance-city-the-war-on-drugs-in-urban-neighborhoods/).

Goffman, Erving. 1959. *The Presentation of Self in Everyday Life.* New York: Doubleday.

—————. 1961. *Asylums: Essays on the Social Situation of Mental Patients and Other Inmates.* Garden City, NY: Doubleday.

—————. 1963. *Stigma: Notes on Management of Spoiled Identity.* Englewood Cliffs, NJ: Prentice Hall.

—————. 1979. *Gender Advertisements.* Cambridge, MA: Harvard University Press.

Goldstein, Melvyn C., and Cynthia M. Beall. 1981. "Modernization and Aging in the Third and Fourth World: Views from the Rural Hinterland in Nepal." *Human Organization* 40 (Spring): 48–55.

Gomez, Jewelle L. 1997. "The Event of Becoming." Pp. 17–23 in *A Queer World: The Center for Lesbian and Gay Studies Reader,* ed. Martin Duberman. New York: New York University Press.

Goodwin, Paula Y., William D. Mosher, and Anjani Chandra. 2010. "Marriage and Cohabitation in the United States: A Statistical Portrait Based on Cycle 6 (2002) of the National Survey of Family Growth." *Vital and Health Statistics* 23 (28). National Center for Health Statistics, Washington, DC.

Google. 2015a. "Fertility Rate." World Bank Development Indicators, Public Data Visualization Program. Accessed May April 30, 2015 (www.google.com/publicdata/explore?ds=d5bncppjof8f9_&ctype=l&strail=false&bcs=d&nselm=h&met_y=sp_dyn_tfrt_in&scale_y=lin&ind_y=false&rdim=country&idim=country:NER:AFG:RWA:KHM:IND:DZA:USA:IRN:CHN:DEU&ifdim=country&hl=en&dl=en&ind=false).

—————.2015b. "Life Expectancy." World Bank Development Indicators, Public Data Visualization Program. Accessed April 30, 2015 (www.google.com/publicdata/explore?ds=d5bncppjof8f9_&ctype=l&strail=false&bcs=d&nselm=h&met_y=sp_dyn_le00_in&scale_y=lin&ind_y=false&rdim=country&idim=country:AFG:KHM:CHN:DEU:IND:IRN:DZA:USA:NER:RWA&ifdim=country&hl=en&dl=en&ind=false).

Gottfredson, Michael, and Travis Hirschi. 1990. *A General Theory of Crime.* Palo Alto, CA: Stanford University Press.

Gordon, Brian. 2015. "UMaine Students Rally for Climate Change Action." *University of Southern Maine Free Press,* April 20. Accessed May 4, 2015 (http://usmfreepress.org/2015/04/20/umaine-students-rally-for-climate-change-action/).

Gould, Elise. 2008. "The Erosion of Employer-Sponsored Health Insurance: Declines Continue for the Seventh Year Running." EPI Briefing Paper No. 223, October 9. Washington, DC: Economic Policy Institute. Accessed June 26, 2009 (http://epi.3cdn.net/d1b4356d96c21c91d1_ilm6b5dua.pdf).

Gouldner, Alvin. 1960. "The Norm of Reciprocity." *American Sociological Review* 25 (April): 161–177.

—————. 1970. *The Coming Crisis of Western Sociology.* New York: Basic Books.

Gramsci, Antonio. 1929. *Selections from the Prison Notebooks,* ed. and trans. Quintin Hoare and Geoffrey Nowell Smith. London: Lawrence and Wishort.

Granovetter, Mark S. 1973. "The Strength of Weak Ties." *American Journal of Sociology* 78: 1360–1380.

Gray, John. 1992. *Men Are from Mars, Women Are from Venus: A Practical Guide for Improving Communication and Getting What You Want in Your Relationships.* New York: HarperCollins.

Green, Alexander R., Dana R. Carney, Daniel J. Pallin, Long H. Ngo, Kristal L. Raymond, Lisa I. Iezzoni, and Mahzarin R. Banaji. 2007. "Implicit Bias Among Physicians and Its Prediction of Thrombolysis Decisions for Black and White Patients." *Journal of General Internal Medicine* 9 (September): 1231–1238.

Greenhouse, Steven. 2008. "Queens Factory Is Found to Owe Workers $5.3 Million." *The New York Times,* July 23. Accessed June 20, 2009 (http://cityroom.blogs.nytimes.com/2008/07/23/a-queens-sweatshop-found-to-owe-workers-53-million/).

Greenwald, Glenn. 2013. "NSA Collecting Phone Records of Millions of Verizon Customers Daily." *The Guardian,* June 5. Accessed June 7, 2013 (www.guardian.co.uk/world/2013/jun/06/nsa-phone-records-verizon-court-order).

Greenwald, Glenn, and Ewen MacAskill. 2013. "NSA PRISM Program Taps in to User Data of Facebook, Yahoo and Others." *The Guardian,* June 6. Accessed June 7, 2013 (www.guardian.co.uk/world/2013/jun/06/us-tech-giants-nsa-data).

Greenwood, Veronique. 2013. "We Are All Princes, Paupers, and Part of the Human Family." Nautilus, May 17. Accessed June 6, 2013 (http://nautil.us/blog/we-are-all-princes-paupers-and-part-of-the-human-family).

Grieco, Elizabeth M., and Rachel C. Cassidy. 2001. "Overview of Race and Hispanic Origin." *Current Population Reports,* Ser. CENBR/01–1. Washington, DC: U.S. Government Printing Office.

Grieco, Elizabeth M., and Edward N. Trevelyan. 2010. "Place of Birth of the Foreign-Born Population: 2009." American Community Survey Briefs, ACSBR/09-15, October. Accessed June 26, 2011 (www.census.gov/prod/2010pubs/acsbr09-15.pdf).

Groeneveld, Elizabeth. 2009. " 'Be a Feminist or Just Dress Like One': BUST, Fashion and Feminism as Lifestyle." *Journal of Gender Studies* 18 (2): 179–190.

Gross, Jane. 2005. "Forget the Career. My Parents Need Me at Home." *The New York Times,* November 24, pp. A1, A20.

Grossman, Samantha. 2012. "The Woolly Mammoth's Return? Scientists Plan to Clone Extinct Creature." *Time,* NewsFeed, March 14. Accessed May 29, 2012 (http://newsfeed.time.com/2012/03/14/the-woolly-mammoths-return-scientists-plan-to-clone-extinct-creature/).

Guglielmo, Jennifer. 2003. "White Lies, Dark Truths." Pp. 1–14 in *Are Italians White? How Race Is Made in America,* ed. Jennifer Guglielmo and Salvatore Salerno. New York: Routledge.

Gurari, Inbal, John Hetts, and Michael Strube. 2006. "Beauty in the 'I' of the Beholder: Effects of Idealized Media Portrayals on Implicit Self-Image." *Basic & Applied Social Psychology* 28 (3): 273–282.

Gutiérrez, Gustavo. 1990. "Theology and the Social Sciences." Pp. 214–225 in *Liberation Theology at the Crossroads: Democracy or Revolution?* ed. Paul E. Sigmund. New York: Oxford University Press.

H

Halper, Mark. 2013. "Hooking China on Coffee." *SmartPlanet*, May 3. Accessed May 7, 2013 (www.smartplanet.com/blog/bulletin/hooking-china-on-coffee/18742).

Halperin, David M. 2009. "Thirteen Ways of Looking at a Bisexual." *Journal of Bisexuality* 9 (3/4): 451–455.

Hamilton, Mykol C., David Anderson, Michelle Broaddus, and Kate Young. 2006. "Gender Stereotyping and Underrepresentation of Female Characters in 200 Popular Children's Books: A Twenty-first Century Update." *Sex Roles* 55 (11/12): 757–765.

Hampton, Keith, Lee Rainie, Weixu Lu, Inyoung Shing, and Kristen Purcell. 2015. "Social Media and the Cost of Caring." Pew Research Center, January 15. Accessed January 2, 2015 (www.pewinternet.org/2015/01/15/social-media-and-stress/).

Hampton, Keith N., Lauren F. Sessions, Eun Ja Her, and Lee Rainie. 2009. "Social Isolation and New Technology: How the Internet and Mobile Phones Impact Americans' Social Networks." Pew Internet and American Life Project, November. Accessed May 23, 2011 (www.pewinternet.org/Reports/2009/18--Social-Isolation-and-New-Technology.aspx).

Harding, Sandra. 2004. "Introduction: Standpoint Theory as a Site of Political, Philosophic, and Scientific Debate." Pp. 1–16 in *The Feminist Standpoint Theory Reader: Intellectual and Political Controversies,* ed. Sandra Harding. New York: Routledge.

Harding, Sandra, ed. 2003. *The Feminist Standpoint Theory Reader: Intellectual and Political Controversies.* New York: Routledge.

Hardt, Michael, and Antonio Negri. 2009. *Commonwealth.* Cambridge, MA: Belknap Press.

Harlow, Harry F. 1971. *Learning to Love.* New York: Ballantine Books.

Harrington, Michael. 1962. *The Other America: Poverty in the United States.* Baltimore: Penguin Books.

———. 1980. "The New Class and the Left." Pp. 123–138 in *The New Class,* ed. B. Bruce Briggs. New Brunswick, NJ: Transaction.

Harris Interactive. 2009. "Firefighters, Scientists and Doctors Seen as Most Prestigious Occupations." The Harris Poll #86, August 4. Accessed June 9, 2011 (www.harrisinteractive.com/vault/Harris-Interactive-Poll-Research-Pres-Occupations-2009-08.pdf).

Hart, Betty, and Todd R. Risley. 1995. *Meaningful Differences in the Everyday Experience of Young American Children.* Baltimore, MD: Paul H. Brookes.

Hart, Zachary P., Vernon D. Miller, and John R. Johnson. 2003. "Socialization, Resocialization and Communication Relationships in the Context of an Organizational Change." *Communication Studies* 54 (4): 483–495.

Hartsock, Nancy C. M. 1983. "The Feminist Standpoint: Developing the Ground for a Specifically Feminist Historical Materialism." Pp. 283–310 in *Discovering Reality: Feminist Perspectives in Epistemology, Methodology, and Philosophy of Science,* ed. Sandra Harding and Merrill B. Hintikka. Dordrecht, The Netherlands: Reidel.

Hashaw, Tim. 2007. *The Birth of Black America: The First African Americans and the Pursuit of Freedom at Jamestown.* New York: Carroll & Graf.

Haskins, Ron. 2008. "Wealth and Economic Mobility." Chap. 4 in *Getting Ahead or Losing Ground: Economic Mobility in America.* Washington, DC: Pew Charitable Trusts. Accessed August 2, 2010 (http://economicmobility.org/assets/pdfs/EMP_Wealthand EconomicMobility_ChapterIV.pdf).

Haslam, Nick, Steve Loughnan, and Gina Perry. 2014. "Meta-Milgram: An Empirical Synthesis of the Obedience Experiments." *PLoS ONE* 9 (4): e93927. Accessed February 19, 2015 (http://journals.plos.org/plosone/article?id=10.1371/journal.pone.0093927).

Hausmann, Ricardo, Laura D. Tyson, Yasmina Bekhouche, and Saadia Zahdi. 2014. *The Global Gender Gap Report 2014.* Geneva: World Economic Forum. Accessed April 22, 2015 (www3.weforum.org/docs/GGGR14/GGGR_CompleteReport_2014.pdf).

Haviland, William A., Harald E. L. Prins, Dana Walrath, and Bunny McBride. 2005. *Cultural Anthropology: The Human Challenge,* 11th ed. Belmont, CA: Wadsworth.

Hayden, H. Thomas. 2004. "What Happened at Abu Ghraib." Accessed September 19, 2011 (www.military.com/NewContent/0,1 3190,Hayden_090704,00.html).

Hayes, Christopher. 2012. *Twilight of the Elites: America After Meritocracy.* New York: Crown.

He, Wan, Manisha Sengupta, Victoria A. Velkoff, and Kimberly A. DeBarros. 2005. "651 in the United States: 2005." *Current Population Reports,* P23–209. Washington, DC: U.S. Government Printing Office.

Heine, Friederike. 2013. "M, F or Blank: 'Third Gender' Official in Germany from November." Spiegel Online International August 16. Accessed April 19, 2015 (www.spiegel.de/international/germany/third-gender-option-to-become-available-on-german-birth-certificates-a-916940.html).

Heinle, Kimberly, Octavio Rodríguez Ferreira, and David A. Shirk. 2014. *Drug Violence in Mexico: Data and Analysis Through 2013.* Justice in Mexico Project, Special Report, April. Accessed May 6, 2015 (https://justiceinmexico.files.wordpress.com/2014/04/140415-dvm-2014-releasered1.pdf).

Helliwell, John, Richard Layard, and Jeffrey Sachs. 2013. *World Happiness Report 2013.* New York: UN Sustainable Development Solutions Network. Accessed January 7, 2015 (http://unsdsn.org/wp-content/uploads/2014/02/WorldHappinessReport2013_online.pdf).

Helms, Sarah W., Sophia Choukas-Bradley, Laura Widman, Matteo Giletta, Geoffrey L. Cohen, and Mitchell J. Prinstein. 2014. "Adolescents Misperceive and Are Influenced by High-Status Peers' Health Risk, Deviant, and Adaptive Behavior." *Developmental Psychology* 50: 2697–2714.

Henderson, Anita. 2003. "What's in a Slur?" *American Speech* 78 (1): 52–74.

Henriques, Diana B., and Jack Healy. 2009. "Madoff Goes to Jail After Guilty Pleas." *The New York Times,* March 12. Accessed May 21, 2009 (www.nytimes.com/2009/03/13/business/13madoff.html).

Herman, Charlie. 2010. "Amid Rising Demand, Price of Coffee Beans Soars." NPR, November 25. Accessed May 20, 2011 (www.npr.org/2010/11/25/131594733/price-of-coffee-beans-on-the-rise).

Hertz, Rosanna. 2006. *Single by Chance. Mothers by Choice.* New York: Oxford University Press.

Hetherington, E. Mavis, and John Kelly. 2002. *For Better or for Worse: Divorce Reconsidered.* New York: Norton.

Hewlett, Sylvia Ann, Diana Foster, Laura Sherbin, Peggy Shiller, and Karen Sumberg. 2010. *Off-Ramps and On-Ramps Revisited.* New York: Center for Work-Life Policy.

Hickey, Walt. 2015. "Government Data Agrees: Hollywood Is Even More Sexist Than the Real Workforce." Datalab March 12. Accessed April 18, 2015 (http://fivethirtyeight.com/datalab/government-jobs-data-agrees-hollywood-is-even-more-sexist-than-the-real-workforce/).

Higgins, George E., Richard Tewksbury, and Elizabeth Mustaine. 2007. "Sports Fan Binge Drinking: An Examination Using Low Self-Control and Peer Association." *Sociological Spectrum* 27 (4): 389–404.

Hirschi, Travis. 1969. *Causes of Delinquency.* Berkeley: University of California Press.

Hirschman, Charles, and Irina Voloshin. 2007. "The Structure of Teenage Employment: Social Background and the Jobs Held by High School Seniors." *Research in Social Stratification and Mobility* 25: 189–203.

Hixson, Lindsay, Bradford B. Hepler, and Myoung Ouk Kim. 2011. "The White Population: 2010." 2010 Census Briefs, Report C2010BR-05, September. Accessed May 27, 2012 (www.census.gov/prod/cen2010/briefs/c2010br-05.pdf).

Hochschild, Arlie Russell. 1989. *The Second Shift: Working Parents and the Revolution at Home.* New York: Viking Press.

———. 1990. "The Second Shift: Employed Women Are Putting in Another Day of Work at Home." *Utne Reader* 38 (March/April): 66–73.

———. 1997. *The Time Bind: When Work Becomes Home and Home Becomes Work.* New York: Henry Holt.

———. 2005. *The Commercialization of Intimate Life: Notes from Home and Work.* Berkeley: University of California Press.

Holmes, Mary. 2006. "Love Lives at a Distance: Distance Relationships over the Lifecourse." *Sociological Research Online* 11 (3).

Homeland Security. 2011. *2010 Yearbook of Immigration Statistics.* Office of Immigration Statistics. U.S. Department of Homeland Security, Washington, DC. Accessed May 18, 2012 (http://www.dhs.gov/files/statistics/publications/yearbook.shtm).

———. 2012. *2011 Yearbook of Immigration Statistics.* Office of Immigration Statistics. U.S. Department of Homeland Security, Washington, DC. Accessed June 6, 2013 (www.dhs.gov/sites/default/files/publications/immigration-statistics/yearbook/2011/ois_yb_2011.pdf).

Home School Legal Defense Association. 2005. "State Laws" and "Academic Statistics on Homeschooling." Accessed August 2, 2010 (www.hslda.org).

Hondagneu-Sotelo, Pierrette, ed. 2003. *Gender and U.S. Immigration: Contemporary Trends.* Berkeley: University of California Press.

Hootman, J., J. Bolen, C. Helmick, and G. Langmaid. 2006. "Prevalence of Doctor-Diagnosed Arthritis and Arthritis-Attributable Activity Limitation—United States, 2003–2005." *Morbidity and Mortality Weekly Report* 55 (40): 1089–1092.

Horrigan, John B. 2007. *A Typology of Information and Communication Technology Users.* Washington, DC: Pew Internet and American Life Project.

Hostetler, John A. 1993. *Amish Society,* 4th ed. Baltimore, MD: Johns Hopkins University Press.

Howard, Russell D., and Reid L. Sawyer. 2003. *Terrorism and Counterterrorism: Understanding the New Security Environment.* Guilford, CT: McGraw-Hill/Dushkin.

Huang, Gary. 1988. "Daily Addressing Ritual: A Cross-Cultural Study." Paper presented at the annual meeting of the American Sociological Association, Atlanta, GA.

Hughes, Everett. 1945. "Dilemmas and Contradictions of Status." *American Journal of Sociology* 50 (March): 353–359.

Human Rights Campaign. 2009. "Maps of State Laws & Policies." Accessed May 27, 2009 (www.hrc.org/about_us/state_laws.asp).
———. 2015. "Marriage Center." Human Rights Campaign, Washington, DC. Accessed February 26, 2015 (www.hrc.org/marriage-center).

Humes, Karen R., Nicholas A. Jones, and Roberto R. Ramirez. 2011. "Overview of Race and Hispanic Origin: 2010." 2010 Census Briefs, C2010BR-02, March. Accessed April 25, 2015 (www.census.gov/prod/cen2010/briefs/c2010br-02.pdf).

Hunter, Herbert M., ed. 2000. *The Sociology of Oliver C. Cox: New Perspectives: Research in Race and Ethnic Relations,* vol. 2. Stamford, CT: JAI Press.

Hunt Institute. 2015. "Paso del Norte Economic Indicator Review." Hunt Institute for Global Competitiveness, University of Texas at El Paso, Spring. Accessed April 16, 2015 (http://d31hzlhk6di2h5.cloudfront.net/20150413/d0/5b/25/92/6bd1e2c334d8287995ff50 36/PASO_DEL_NORTE_ECONOMIC_INDICATOR_REVIEW .pdf).

Hurst, Charles E., and David L. McConnell. 2010. *An Amish Paradox: Diversity and Change in the World's Largest Amish Community.* Baltimore, MD: Johns Hopkins University Press.

Hussar, William J., and Tabitha M. Bailey. 2014. *Projections of Education Statistics to 2022.* NCES 2014-051. National Center for Education Statistics, Institute of Education Sciences, U.S. Department of Education, Washington, DC. Accessed March 10, 2015 (http://nces.ed.gov/pubs2014/2014051.pdf).

Hvistendahl, Mara. 2010. "Has China Outgrown the One-Child Policy?" *Science* 329 (September 17): 1458–1461.

Hyde, Janet Shibley. 2005. "The Gender Similarities Hypothesis." *American Psychologist* 60 (6): 581–592.

I

Ignatiev, Noel. 1995. *How the Irish Became White.* New York: Routledge.

Illinois State Board of Education. 2015a. "eReportcard Public Site." Division of Student Assessment. Accessed March 10, 2015 (http://webprod.isbe.net/ereportcard/publicsite/getSearchCriteria.aspx).
———. 2015b. "Illinois Report Card 2013–2014." Springfield, IL. Accessed March 10, 2015 (http://illinoisreportcard.com/Default.aspx).

Indiana University Center for Sexual Health Promotion. 2010. "Special Issue: Findings from the National Survey of Sexual Health and Behavior (NSSHB)." *Journal of Sexual Medicine* 7 (Supplement 5).

INEGI. 2009. "Mujeres y Hombres en México 2005. Anexo estadístico." Instituto Nacional de Estadística y Geografía. Accessed June 14, 2009 (www.inegi.org.mx/inegi/contenidos/espanol/bvinegi/productos/integracion/sociodemografico/mujeresyhombres/2005/anexo_2005.xls).

Inglehart, Ronald, Pippa Norris, and Christian Welzel. 2002. "Gender Equality and Democracy." *Comparative Sociology* 1 (3/4): 321–346.

Innocence Project. 2015. "DNA Exonerations Nation Wide." Accessed February 19, 2015 (www.innocenceproject.org/free-innocent/improve-the-law/fact-sheets/dna-exonerations-nationwide).

INPE. 2010. "Specific Data of PRODES/INPE Confirms the Range of the Amazon Deforestation." Instituto Nacional de Pesquisas Espaciais, April 29. Accessed May 21, 2010 (www.inpe.br/ingles/news/news_dest117.php).

Institute for Economics and Peace. 2014. *Global Terrorism Index 2014: Measuring and Understanding the Impact of Terrorism.* Sydney: Institute for Economics and Peace. Accessed March 18, 2015 (www.visionofhumanity.org/sites/default/files/Global%20 Terrorism%20Index%20Report%202014_0.pdf).

Institute of International Education. 2014. "Open Doors 2014: Fast Facts." New York City: Institute of International Education, Inc. Accessed March 10, 2015 (www.iie.org/en/Research-and-Publications/Open-Doors/Data/Fast-Facts).

Instituto Nacional de Migración, México. 2011. "Extranjeros Alojados y Devueltos, Cuadro 3.2.1 (xls)." Boletín Estadístico, 2010. Gobierno Federal, México. Accessed June 13, 2011 (www.inm.gob.mx/index.php/page/Boletin_Estadistico_2010).

Internal Revenue Service. 2015. "The 400 Individual Income Tax Returns Reporting the Largest Adjusted Gross Incomes Each Year, 1992–2009." IRS Statistical Information Services, Washington, DC. Accessed March 25, 2015 (www.irs.gov/pub/irs-soi/12intop400.pdf).

International Centre for Prison Studies. 2015. "Highest to Lowest—Prison Population Total." School of Law, Birkbeck, University of London. Accessed February 19, 2015 (www.prisonstudies.org/highest-to-lowest/prison-population-total?field_region_taxonomy_tid=All).

International Institute for Democracy and Electoral Assistance. 2015. "Voter Turnout Database." International IDEA, Stockholm, Sweden. Accessed March 18, 2015 (www.idea.int/vt/viewdata.cfm).

International Labour Office. 2012. "ILO Global Estimate of Forced Labour: Results and Methodology." Special Action Programme to Combat Forced Labour, Geneva. Accessed June 2, 2013 (www.ilo.org/wcmsp5/groups/public/@ed_norm/@declaration/documents/publication/wcms_182004.pdf).

International Monetary Fund. 2000. *World Economic Outlook: Asset Prices and the Business Cycle.* Washington, DC: IMF.
———. 2008. "IMF Helping Countries Respond to Food Price Crisis." *IMF Survey Magazine: In the News,* June 3. Washington, DC: IMF. Accessed August 2, 2010 (www.imf.org/external/pubs/ft/survey/so/2008/NEW060308A.htm).

International Telecommunications Union. 2015. "Explore Key ICT Statistics." ITU's ICT Eye. Accessed February 2, 2015 (www.itu.int/net4/itu-d/icteye/).

Internet World Stats. 2015b. "Internet World Users by Language: Top 10 Languages." Accessed June 22, 2015 (www.internetworldstats.com/stats7.htm).

Inter-Parliamentary Union. 2011. "Women in Parliament in 2011: The Year in Perspective." Geneva, Switzerland. Accessed May 24, 2012 (www.ipu.org/pdf/publications/wmnpersp11-e.pdf).
———. 2015. "Women in National Parliaments: Situation as of 1st January 2015." Geneva, Switzerland. Accessed March 18, 2015 (www.ipu.org/wmn-e/classif.htm).

Isaacs, Julia B. 2007a. *Economic Mobility of Families Across Generations.* Washington, DC: Economic Mobility Project, Pew Charitable Trusts.
———. 2008. "Economic Mobility of Black and White Families." *Economic Mobility Project,* Pew Charitable Trusts, November. Accessed June 21, 2009 (www.brookings.edu/reports/2008/~/media/Files/rc/reports/2008/02_economic_mobility_sawhill/02 _economic_mobility_sawhill_ch6.pdf).

Isaacs, Julia B., Isabel V. Sawhill, and Ron Haskins. 2008. *Getting Ahead or Losing Ground: Economic Mobility in America.* Washington, DC: Pew Charitable Trusts.

Ipsos MORI. 2014. "Perceptions Are Not Reality: Things the World Gets Wrong." Ipsos MORI Perils of Perception Survey, London, October 29. Accessed January 10, 2015 (www.ipsos-mori.com/researchpublications/researcharchive/3466/Perceptions-are-not-reality-10-things-the-world-gets-wrong.aspx).

Irdeto. 2015a. "And the Winner for the Most Pirated Motion Picture Is . . . ," Irdeto Technology, Eagan, MN, February 19. Accessed February 19, 2015 (http://irdeto.com/news-and-events/and-the-winner-for-the-most-pirated-motion-picture-is-.html).

———. 2015b. "Irdeto Piracy and Business Intelligence Quick Read Report: 2015 Academy Award® Nominated Films," Irdeto Technology, Eagan, MN, February 19. Accessed February 19, 2015 (www.irdeto.com/documents/pr_quickread_oscars_piracy_and_BI_feb2015.pdf).

ITOPF. 2006. "Statistics: International Tanker Owners Pollution Federation Limited." Accessed May 2, 2007 (www.itopf.com/stats.html).

IUCN. 2011. "Table 2: Changes in Numbers of Species in the Threatened Categories (CR, EN, VU) from 1996 to 2011 for the Major Taxonomic Groups on the Red List." IUCN Red List of Threatened Species, Version 2011.1. Cambridge, UK: International Union for Conservation of Nature and Natural Resources. Accessed June 30, 2011 (www.iucnredlist.org/documents/summarystatistics/2011_1_RL_Stats_Table_2.pdf).

J

Jacobs, David, Zhenchao Qian, Jason T. Carmichael, and Stephanie L. Kent. 2007. "Who Survives on Death Row? An Individual and Contextual Analysis." *American Sociological Review* 72 (August): 610–632.

James, Susan Donaldson. 2007. "Students Use Civil Rights Tactics to Combat Global Warming." *ABC News,* January 19. Accessed June 20, 2015 (http://abcnews.go.com/Technology/GlobalWarming/Story?id=2805553).

———. 2008. "Wild Child Speechless After Tortured Life: Abandoned by Doctors and Mother, Abused in Foster Care, 'Genie' Regressed." *ABC News Online,* May 7. Accessed June 20, 2015 (http://abcnews.go.com/Health/story?id=4804490).

Jamison, Andrew. 2006. "Social Movements and Science: Cultural Appropriations of Cognitive Praxis." *Science as Culture* 15 (1): 45–59.

Jayson, Sharon. 2012a. "Young Parents, Older Adults Change Face of Cohabitation." *USA Today,* October 17. Accessed May 29, 2013 (www.usatoday.com/story/news/nation/2012/10/17/cohabitation-divorced-families-parents/1623117/).

———. 2012b. "Living Together Not Just for the Young, New Data Show." *USA Today,* October 17. Accessed May 29, 2013 (www.usatoday.com/story/news/nation/2012/10/17/older-couples-cohabitation/1630681/).

Jenkins, J. Craig. 2004. "Social Movements: Resource Mobilization Theory." Pp. 14368–14371 in *International Encyclopedia of the Social and Behavioral Sciences,* ed. Neil J. Smelser and Paul B. Baltes. New York: Elsevier.

Jenkins, Matt. 2008. "A Really Inconvenient Truth." *Miller-McCure* 1 (March/April): 38–41.

Jenness, Valerie, David A. Smith, and Judith Stepan-Norris. 2006. "Pioneer Public Sociologist C. Wright Mills, 50 Years Later." *Contemporary Sociology* 35 (6): 7–8.

Jindra, Michael. 1994. "Star Trek Fandom as a Religious Phenomenon." *Sociology of Religion* 55 (1): 27–51.

Johnson, Allan G. 1997. *The Forest and the Trees: Sociology as Life, Practice, and Promise.* Philadelphia: Temple University Press.

Johnson, Chris. 2012. "Exit Poll: Gay Voters Made Up 5 Percent of 2012 Electorate." *Washington Blade,* November 7. Accessed May 29, 2013 (www.washingtonblade.com/2012/11/07/exit-poll-gay-voters-made-up-5-percent-of-2012-electorate/).

Johnson, Kenneth M., and Daniel T. Lichter. 2010. "Growing Diversity Among America's Children and Youth: Spatial and Temporal Dimensions." *Population and Development Review* 36(1): 151–176.

Johnston, David Cay. 1994. "Ruling Backs Homosexuals on Asylum." *The New York Times,* June 12, pp. D1, D6.

Jones, David D. 2011. "Oligarchy in the Making: Is Our Democracy Doomed?" July 17. Accessed July 22, 2011 (www.phillyburbs.com/news/local/courier_times_news/opinion/guest/oligarchy-in-the-making-is-our-democracy-doomed/article_b1cf7f12-0b30-5ff6-81c6-547a8727eee2.html).

Jones, Madeline. 2012. "Plus Size Bodies, What Is Wrong with Them Anyway?" *PLUS Model Magazine*, January 8. Accessed May 27, 2012 (www.plus-model-mag.com/2012/01/plus-size-bodies-what-is-wrong-with-them-anyway/).

Jordan, Miriam. 2011. "More 'Silent Raids' over Immigration." *The Wall Street Journal,* June 16. Accessed June 21, 2011 (http://online.wsj.com/article/SB10001424052702304186404576387843087137216.html).

Josephson Institute of Ethics. 2012. "2012 Report Card on the Ethics of American Youth." Josephson Institute, Center for Youth Ethics, Los Angeles, November 20. Accessed May 8, 2013 (http://charactercounts.org/pdf/reportcard/2012/ReportCard-2012-DataTables-HonestyIntegrityCheating.pdf).

Jost, Kenneth. 2008. "Women in Politics." *CQ Researcher* 18 (March 21).

Juergensmeyer, Mark. 2003. *Terror in the Mind of God: The Global Rise of Religious Violence,* 3rd ed. Berkeley: University of California Press.

K

Kalev, Alexandria, Frank Dobbin, and Erin Kelly. 2006. "Best Practices or Best Guesses? Assessing the Efficacy of Corporate Affirmative Action and Diversity Policies." *American Sociological Review* 71: 589–617.

Kalish, Richard A. 1985. *Death, Grief, and Caring Relationships,* 2nd ed. Monterey, CA: Brooks/Cole.

Kalita, S. Mitra. 2006. "On the Other End of the Line." *The Washington Post National Weekly Edition,* January 9, pp. 20–21.

Kalmijn, Matthijs. 1998. "Intermarriage and Homogamy: Causes, Patterns, Trends." *Annual Review of Sociology* 24: 395–412.

Kamp, Marianne. 2008. *The New Woman in Uzbekistan.* Seattle: University of Washington Press.

Kanter, Rosabeth Moss. 1993. *Men and Women of the Corporation.* New York: Basic Books.

Karkazis, Katrina. 2008. *Fixing Sex: Intersex, Medical Authority, and Lived Experience.* Durham, NC: Duke University Press.

Karkazis, Katrina, Rebecca Jordan-Youn, Georgiann Davis, and Silvia Camporesi. 2012. "Out of Bounds? A Critique of the New Policies of Hyperandrogenism in Elite Female Athletes." *American Journal of Bioethics* 12: 3–16.

Karney, Benjamin R., and John S. Crown. 2007. "Families Under Stress: An Assessment of Data, Theory, and Research on Marriage and Divorce in the Military." Santa Monica, CA: RAND Corporation.

Katz, Jason. 1999. *Tough Guise: Violence, Media, and the Crisis in Masculinity.* Video. Directed by Sut Jhally. Northampton, MA: Media Education Foundation.

Kay, Katty, and Claire Shipman. 2014. "The Confidence Gap." *The Atlantic,* May. Accessed January 7, 2013 (www.theatlantic.com/features/archive/2014/04/the-confidence-gap/359815/).

Kearl, Holly. 2014. "Women Drivers in Afghanistan Must Brave the Traffic and the Stares." *The Washington Post,* October 12. Accessed April 13, 2015 (www.washingtonpost.com/blogs/she-the-people/wp/2014/10/13/women-drivers-in-afghanistan-must-brave-the-traffic-and-the-stares/).

Kena, Grace, Susan Aud, Frank Johnson, Xiaolei Wang, Jijun Zhang, Amy Rathbun, Sidney Wilkinson-Flicker, and Paul Kristapovich. 2014. *The Condition of Education 2014.* NCES 2014-083. U.S. Department of Education, National Center for Education Statistics. Washington, DC. Accessed April 19, 2015 (http://nces.ed.gov/pubs2014/2014083.pdf).

Kentor, Jeffrey, and Yong Suk Jang. 2004. "Yes, There Is a (Growing) Transnational Business Community." *International Sociology* 19 (September): 355–368.

Kerbo, Harold R. 2009. *Social Stratification and Inequality: Class Conflict in Historical, Comparative, and Global Perspective,* 7th ed. New York: McGraw-Hill.

———. 2011. *Social Stratification and Inequality: Class Conflict in Historical, Comparative, and Global Perspective,* 8th ed. New York: McGraw-Hill.

Keynes, John Maynard. 1930a. "Economic Possibilities for Our Grandchildren I." *The Nation and Athenaeum* 48(2): 36–37.

———. 1930b. "Economic Possibilities for Our Grandchildren II." *The Nation and Athenaeum* 48(3): 96–98.

Khorasani, Noushin Ahmadi. 2009. "How Social Movements Can Change Iran." *The Mark,* June 11. Accessed June 30, 2009 (www.themarknews.com/articles/290-how-social-movements -can-change-iran).

Kiatpongsan, Sorapop, and Michael I. Norton. 2014. "How Much (More) Should CEOs Make? A Universal Desire for More Equal Pay." *Perspectives on Psychological Science* 9: 587–593. Accessed January 7, 2015 (www.hbs.edu/faculty/Publication%20Files/ kiatpongsan%20norton%202014_f02b004a-c2de-4358-9811 -ea273d372af7.pdf).

Kilbourne, Jean. 2010. *Killing Us Softly 4: Advertising's Image of Women.* Video. Produced and directed by Sut Jhally. Northampton, MA: Media Education Foundation.

Kiley, Jocelyn. 2014. "61% of Young Republicans Favor Same-Sex Marriage." Pew Research Center, March 10. Accessed February 11, 2015 (www.pewresearch.org/fact-tank/2014/03/10/61-of -young-republicans-favor-same-sex-marriage/).

Kilpatrick, Dean G., Heidi S. Resnick, Kenneth J. Ruggiero, Lauren M. Conoscenti, and Jenna McCauley. 2007. "Drug-Facilitated, Incapacitated, and Forcible Rape: A National Study." National Institute of Justice Grant No. 2005-Wg-BX-0006. Accessed June 1, 2010 (www.ncjrs.gov/pdffiles1/nij/grants/219181.pdf).

Kim, Kwang Chung. 1999. *Koreans in the Hood: Conflict with African Americans.* Baltimore, MD: Johns Hopkins University Press.

Kim, Su Yeong, Yijie Wang, Diana Orozco-Lapray, Yishan Shen, and Mohammed Murtuza. 2013. "Does 'Tiger Parenting' Exist? Parenting Profiles of Chinese Americans and Adolescent Developmental Outcomes." *Asian American Journal of Psychology* 4: 7–18.

Kimmel, Michael. 2004. *The Gendered Society,* 2nd ed. New York: Oxford University Press.

Kindy, Kimberly, and Kimbriell Kelly. 2015. "Thousands Dead, Few Prosecuted." *The Washington Post,* April 11. Accessed April 26, 2015 (www.washingtonpost.com/sf/investigative/2015/04/11/ thousands-dead-few-prosecuted/).

Kinsey, Alfred C., Wardell B. Pomeroy, and Clyde E. Martin. 1948. *Sexual Behavior in the Human Male.* Philadelphia: Saunders.

Kinsey, Alfred C., Wardell B. Pomeroy, and Paul H. Gebhard. 1953. *Sexual Behavior in the Human Female.* Philadelphia: Saunders.

Kinsey, Alfred C., Wardell B. Pomeroy, and Clyde E. Martin. 1948. *Sexual Behavior in the Human Male.* Philadelphia: Saunders.

Kirk, Dudley. 1996. "Demographic Transition Theory." *Population Studies* 50: 361–387.

Kitchener, Richard F. 1991. "Jean Piaget: The Unknown Sociologist." *British Journal of Sociology* 42 (September): 421–442.

Kleinknecht, William. 1996. *The New Ethnic Mobs: The Changing Face of Organized Crime in America.* New York: Free Press.

Kliewer, Wendy, and Terri N. Sullivan. 2009. "Community Violence Exposure, Threat Appraisal, and Adjustment in Adolescents." *Journal of Clinical Child & Adolescent Psychology* 37 (4): 860–873.

Kline, Susan L., and Shuangyue Zhang. 2009. "The Role of Relational Communication Characteristics and Filial Piety in Mate Preferences: Cross-Cultural Comparisons of Chinese and US College Students." *Journal of Comparative Family Studies* 40 (3): 325–353.

Klinenberg, Eric. 2002. *Heat Wave: A Social Autopsy of Disaster in Chicago.* Chicago: University of Chicago Press.

Knudson, Tom. 2006. "Promises and Poverty: Starbucks Calls Its Coffee Worker-Friendly—but in Ethiopia, a Day's Pay Is a Dollar."
Sacramento Bee, September 23. Accessed June 12, 2009 (www. sacbee.com/502/story/393917.html).

———. 2007. "Investigative Report: Promises and Poverty." *Sacramento Bee,* September 23. Accessed August 6, 2009 (www. sacbee.com/502/story/393917.html).

Kochhar, Rakesh, and Richard Fry. 2014. "Wealth Inequality Has Widened Along Racial, Ethnic Lines Since End of Great Recession." Pew Research Center, Fact Tank: News in the Numbers, December 12. Accessed January 7, 2015 (www.pewresearch .org/fact-tank/2014/12/12/racial-wealth-gaps-great-recession/).

Koerner, Brendan I. 2003. "What Does a 'Thumbs Up' Mean in Iraq?" *Slate,* March 28. Accessed May 3, 2009 (www.slate.com/ id/2080812).

Kohn, Sally. 2014. "Stop Denying the Gender Pay Gap Exists. Even Jennifer Lawrence Was Shortchanged." *The Washington Post,* December 17. Accessed January 7, 2015 (www.washingtonpost .com/posteverything/wp/2014/12/17/stop-denying-the-gender-pay -gap-exists-even-jennifer-lawrence-was-shortchanged/).

Kokmen, Leyla. 2008. "Environmental Justice for All." *Utne Reader,* March/April, pp. 42–46.

Kooti, Farshad, Hathan O. Hodas, and Kristina Lerman. 2014. "Network Weirdness: Exploring the Origins of Network Paradoxes." *arXiv*: 1403.7242. Accessed February 11, 2015 (http://arxiv.org/ abs/1403.7242).

Kosmin, Barry A., and Ariela Keysar. 2009. *American Religious Identification Survey: ARIS 2008 Summary Report.* Hartford, CT: Trinity College. Accessed June 1, 2009 (http://b27.cc.trincoll .edu/weblogs/AmericanReligionSurvey-ARIS/reports/ARIS _Report_2008.pdf).

Kottak, Conrad. 2004. *Anthropology: The Explanation of Human Diversity.* New York: McGraw-Hill.

Kozol, Jonathan. 1991. *Savage Inequalities: Children in America's Schools.* New York: Crown.

———. 2005. *The Shame of the Nation: The Restoration of Apartheid Schooling in America.* New York: Crown.

———. 2012. *Fire in the Ashes: Twenty-Five Years Among the Poorest Children in America.* New York: Crown.

Kraybill, Donald. 2001. *The Riddle of Amish Culture,* rev. ed. Baltimore, MD: Johns Hopkins University Press.

Kraybill, Donald B., Karen M. Johnson-Weiner, and Steven M. Nolt. 2013. *The Amish.* Baltimore, MD: Johns Hopkins University Press.

Krebs, Christopher P., Christine H. Lindquist, Tara D. Warner, Bonnie S. Fisher, and Sandra L. Martin. 2007. "The Campus Sexual Assault (CSA) Study, Final Report." National Institute of Justice Grant No. 2004-WG-BX-0010. Accessed June 1, 2010 (www.ncjrs .gov.pdffiles1/nij/grants/221153.pdf).

Kreider, Rose M. 2010. "Increase in Opposite-Sex Cohabiting Couples from 2009 to 2010 in the Annual Social and Economic Supplement (ASEC) to the Current Population Survey (CPS)." Housing and Household Economic Statistics Division Working Paper. Washington, DC: U.S. Bureau of the Census. Accessed June 1, 2011 (www. census.gov/population/www/socdemo/Inc-Opp-sex-2009-to-2010 .pdf).

Kreider, Rose M., and Renee Ellis. 2011. "Number, Timing, and Duration of Marriages and Divorces: 2009." *Current Population Reports,* P70–125. Washington, DC: U.S. Census Bureau. Accessed September 19, 2011 (www.census.gov/prod/2011pubs/ p70–125.pdf).

Kristof, Nicholas D., and Sheryl WuDunn. 2009. *Half the Sky: Turning Oppression into Opportunity for Women Worldwide.* New York: Knopf.

Krogstad, Jens Manual, and D'Vera Cohn. 2014. "U.S. Census Looking at Big Changes in How It Asks About Race and Ethnicity." Pew Research Center, Fact Tank, March 14. Accessed April 26, 2015 (www.pewresearch.org/fact-tank/2014/03/14/ u-s-census-looking-at-big-changes-in-how-it-asks-about-race-and -ethnicity/).

Kruttschnitt, Candace, and Kristin Carbone-Lopez. 2006. "Moving Beyond the Stereotypes: Women's Subjective Accounts of Their Violent Crime." *Criminology* 44 (2): 321–352.

Kübler-Ross, Elisabeth. 1969. *On Death and Dying*. New York: Macmillan.

Kuhl, Patricia K. 2004. "Early Language Acquisition: Cracking the Speech Code." *Nature Reviews Neuroscience* 5: 831–843.

Kuumba, M. Bahati. 2001. *Gender and Social Movements*. Lanham, MD: AltaMira Press.

Kwong, Jo. 2005. "Globalization's Effects on the Environment." *Society* 42 (January/February): 21–28.

L

Lacey, Marc. 2008. "Hunger in Haiti Increasing Rapidly." *International Herald Tribune*, April 17. Accessed August 12, 2008 (www.iht.com/articles/2008/04/17/news/Haiti.php).

Ladner, Joyce. 1973. *The Death of White Sociology*. New York: Random Books.

Laidlaw, Ken, DaHua Wang, Claudia Coelho, and Mick Power. 2010. "Attitudes to Ageing and Expectations for Filial Piety Across Chinese and British Cultures: A Pilot Exploratory Evaluation." *Aging & Mental Health* 14 (3): 283–292.

Lambert, Emily. 2009. "Nimby Wars." *Forbes*, February 16: 98–101. Accessed June 29, 2009 (www.forbes.com/forbes/2009/0216/098.html).

Lareau, Annette. 2003. *Unequal Childhoods: Class, Race, and Family Life*. Berkeley: University of California Press.

———. 2011. *Unequal Childhoods: Class, Race, and Family Life, 2nd ed., with an update a decade later*. Berkeley: University of California Press.

Larson, Edward J. 2006. *Summer for the Gods: The Scopes Trial and America's Continuing Debate over Science and Religion*. New York: Basic Books.

Laughlin, Lynda. 2013. "Who's Minding the Kids? Child Care Arrangements: Spring 2011." U.S. Census Bureau, *Household Economic Studies*, pp. 70–135, April. Accessed May 20, 2013 (www.census.gov/prod/2013pubs/p70-135.pdf).

Laumann, Edward O., John H. Gagnon, Robert T. Michael, and Stuart Michaels. 1994. *The Social Organization of Sexuality: Sexual Practices in the United States*. Chicago: University of Chicago Press.

Lawless, John. 2005. "Nigel Newton: Is There Life After Harry? You Can Bet Your Hogwarts There Is." *The Independent*, July 3. Accessed February 2, 2015 (www.independent.co.uk/news/people/profiles/nigel-newton-is-there-life-after-harry-you-can-bet-your-hogwarts-there-is-296317.html).

Le Bon, Gustav. 1895. *The Crowd: A Study of the Popular Mind*. New York: Macmillan.

Lee, Helena. 2013. "The Babies Who Nap in Sub-Zero Temperatures." *BBC News Magazine*, February 21. Accessed February 2, 2015 (www.bbc.com/news/magazine-21537988).

Lee, James, and Katie Foreman. 2014. "U.S. Naturalizations: 2013." Annual Flow Report, Homeland Security, May. Accessed April 16, 2015 (www.dhs.gov/sites/default/files/publications/ois_natz_fr_2013.pdf).

Lefevre, Romana. 2011. *Rude Hand Gestures of the World: A Guide to Offending Without Words*. San Francisco: Chronicle Books.

Le Goff, Jacques. 1990. "Introduction: Medieval Man." Pp. 1–35 in *Medieval Callings*, ed. Jacques Le Goff. Chicago: University of Chicago Press.

Lencioni, Patrick. 2006. *Silos, Politics, and Turf Wars: A Leadership Fable About Destroying the Barriers That Turn Colleagues into Competitors*. San Francisco: Jossey-Bass.

Lengermann, Patricia Madoo, and Jill Niebrugge-Brantley. 1998. *The Women Founders: Sociology and Social Theory, 1830–1930*. Boston: McGraw-Hill.

Leonard, Annie. 2010. *The Story of Stuff: How Our Obsession with Stuff Is Trashing the Planet, Our Communities, and Our Health—and a Vision for Change*. New York: Free Press.

Levanon, Gad, Vivian Chen, and Ben Chang. 2012. "Feeling the Pain: Wage Growth in the United States During and After the Great Recession." Executive Action Series, The Conference Board, New York, April.

Levine, Kenneth J., and Cynthia A. Hoffner. 2006. "Adolescents' Conceptions of Work: What Is Learned from Different Sources During Anticipatory Socialization?" *Journal of Adolescent Research* 21 (6): 647–669.

Levy, Jenna. 2015. "In U.S., Uninsured Rate Dips to 11.9% in First Quarter." Gallup Healthways Well-Being Index, April 13.

Lewis, Michael. 2003. *Moneyball: The Art of Winning an Unfair Game*. New York: Norton.

Lewis, M. Paul, Gary F. Simons, and Charles D. Fennig, eds. 2015. *Ethnologue: Languages of the World*, 18th ed. Dallas, TX: SIL International. Accessed April 3, 2015 (www.ethnologue.com).

Lezhnev, Sasha. 2011. "New U.N. Report: U.S. Conflict Minerals Law Having Impact in Congo." *Enough*, June 16. Accessed August 8, 2011 (www.enoughproject.org/blogs/new-un-report-us-conflict-minerals-law-having-impact-congo).

Liang, Bin, and Hong Lu. 2010. "Internet Development, Censorship, and Cyber Crimes in China." *Journal of Contemporary Criminal Justice* 26 (1): 103–120.

Lierow, Diane. 2011. *Dani's Story: A Journey from Neglect to Love*. Hoboken, NJ: Wiley.

Lind, Dara. 2015. "The FBI Is Trying to Get Better Data on Police Killings. Here's What We Know Now." *Vox*, April 26. Accessed April 26, 2015 (www.vox.com/2014/8/21/6051043/how-many-people-killed-police-statistics-homicide-official-black).

Ling, Peter. 2006. "Social Capital, Resource Mobilization and Origins of the Civil Rights Movement." *Journal of Historical Sociology* 19 (2): 202–214.

Link, Bruce G., and Jo C. Phelan. 2001. "Conceptualizing Stigma." *Annual Review of Sociology* 27: 363–385.

Lino, Mark. 2014. *Expenditures on Children by Families, 2013*. Center for Nutrition Policy and Promotion, Miscellaneous Publication No. 1528-2013. U.S. Department of Agriculture, Washington, DC. Accessed February 26, 2015 (www.cnpp.usda.gov/sites/default/files/expenditures_on_children_by_families/crc2013.pdf).

Lipset, Seymour Martin. 1959. "Some Social Requisites of Democracy: Economic Development and Political Legitimacy." *American Political Science Review* 53: 69–105.

Liptak, Adam. 2008a. "Damages Cut Against Exxon in *Valdez* Case." *The New York Times*, June 26. Accessed April 3, 2015 (www.nytimes.com/2008/06/26/washington/26punitive.html).

———. 2008b. "From One Footnote, a Debate over the Tangles of Law, Science, and Money." *The New York Times*, June 26. Accessed April 3, 2015 (www.nytimes.com/2008/11/25/washington/25bar.html).

List, Justin M. 2009. "Justice and the Reversal of the Healthcare Worker 'Brain-Drain.'" *American Journal of Bioethics* 9 (3): 10–12.

Lofquist, Daphne, Terry Lugaila, Martin O'Connell, and Sarah Feliz. 2012. "Households and Families: 2010." 2010 Census Brief, C2010BR-14, April. Washington, DC: U.S. Census Bureau. Accessed May 8, 2012 (www.census.gov/prod/cen2010/briefs/c2010br-14.pdf).

Lopata, Helena Znaniecki. 1971. *Occupation: Housewife*. New York: Oxford University Press.

Lorber, Judith. 1994. *Paradoxes of Gender*. New Haven, CT: Yale University Press.

Lotz, Amanda D. 2007. "Theorising the Intermezzo: The Contributions of Postfeminism and Third Wave Feminism." Pp. 71–85 in *Third Wave Feminism: A Critical Exploration*, expanded 2nd ed., ed. Stacy Gillis, Gillian Howie, and Rebecca Munford. New York: Palgrave Macmillan.

Louie, Miriam Ching Yoon. 2001. *Sweatshop Warriors: Immigrant Women Workers Take on the Global Factory*. Cambridge, MA: South End Press.

Lovell, Joel, and Ryan Pfluger. 2014. "The Tale of Two Schools." *The New York Times Magazine*, May 4. Accessed March 10, 2015 (www.nytimes.com/interactive/2014/05/04/magazine/tale-of-two-schools.html).

Loxcel Geomatics. 2015. "How Many Starbucks Are There?" January 19. Accessed January 22, 2015 (www.loxcel.com/sbux-faq.html).

Lucal, Betsy. 2010. "Better Informed, Still Skeptical: Response to Machalek and Martin." *Teaching Sociology* 38 (1): 46–49.

Lucio, José Miguel Cabrales. 2014. "Gender and Constitutionalism in Mexico: From Quotas to Parity?" ConstitutionNet, April 28. Accessed April 16, 2015 (www.constitutionnet.org/news/gender-and-constitutionalism-mexico-quotas-parity).

Lukács, Georg. 1923. *History and Class Consciousness.* London: Merlin.

Lumpe, Lora. 2003. "Taking Aim at the Global Gun Trade." *Amnesty Now* (Winter): 10–13.

Lundquist, Jennifer Hickes. 2006. "Choosing Single Motherhood." *Contexts* 5 (Fall): 64–67.

Lyall, Sarah. 2002. "For Europeans, Love, Yes; Marriage, Maybe." *The New York Times,* March 24, pp. 1–8.

Lymas, Mark. 2008. *Six Degrees: Our Future on a Hotter Planet.* Washington, DC: National Geographic.

Lynn, Barry C. 2003. "Trading with a Low-Wage Tiger." *The American Prospect* 14 (February): 10–12.

Lytton, Hugh, and David M. Romney. 1991. "Parents' Differential Socialization of Boys and Girls: A Meta-analysis." *Psychological Bulletin* 109 (2): 267–296.

M

MacEachern, Scott. 2003. "The Concept of Race in Anthropology." Pp. 10–35 in *Race and Ethnicity: An Anthropological Focus on the United States and the World,* ed. R. Scupin. Upper Saddle River, NJ: Prentice Hall.

MacFarquhar, Neil. 2008. "Resolute or Fearful, Many Muslims Turn to Home Schooling." *The New York Times,* March 26, p. A1.

Machalek, Richard, and Michael W. Martin. 2010. "Evolution, Biology, and Society: A Conversation for the 21st-Century Classroom." *Teaching Sociology* 38 (1): 35–45.

MacLeod, Jay. 2009. *Ain't No Makin' It: Aspirations and Attainment in a Low-Income Neighborhood,* 3rd ed. Boulder, CO: Westview Press.

MacNell, Lillian, Adam Driscoll, and Andrea N. Hunt. 2014. "What's in a Name: Exposing Gender Bias in Student Ratings of Teachers." *Innovative Higher Education,* December.

Madden, Mary, Amanda Lenhart, Sandra Cortesi, Urs Gasser, Maeve Duggan, Aaron Smith, and Meredith Beaton. 2013. "Teens, Social Media, and Privacy." Pew Research Center, Internet & American Life Project, May 21. Accessed May 22, 2013 (www.pewinternet.org/~/media//Files/Reports/2013/PIP_TeensSocialMediaandPrivacy_FINAL.pdf).

Madden, Mary, Amanda Lenhart, Maeve Duggan, Sandra Cortesi, and Urs Gasser. 2013. "Teens and Technology 2013." Pew Research Center, Internet and American Life Project, March 13. Accessed May 20, 2013 (www.pewinternet.org/~/media//Files/Reports/2013/PIP_TeensandTechnology2013.pdf).

Maher, Timothy M. 2008. "Police Chiefs' Views on Police Sexual Misconduct." *Police Practice & Research* 9 (3): 239–250.

Malacrida, Claudia. 2005. "Discipline and Dehumanization in a Total Institution: Institutional Survivors' Descriptions of Time-Out Rooms." *Disability & Society* 20 (5): 523–537.

Malcolm X, with Alex Haley. 1964. *The Autobiography of Malcolm X.* New York: Grove.

Malthus, Thomas R. 1878. *An Essay on the Principle of Population: Or, A View of Its Past and Present Effects on Human Happiness, with an Inquiry into Our Prospects Respecting the Future Removal or Mitigation of the Evils Which It Occasions,* 8th ed. London: Reeves and Turner.

Mann, Horace. [1848] 1957. "Report No. 12 of the Massachusetts School Board." Pp. 79–97 in *The Republic and the School: Horace Mann on the Education of Free Men,* ed. L. A. Cremin. New York: Teachers College.

Mann, Yee Kan, Oriel Sullivan, and Jonathan Gershuny. 2011. "Gender Convergence in Domestic Work: Discerning the Effects of Interactional and Institutional Barriers from Large-Scale Data." *Sociology* 45 (2): 234–251.

Manning, Jennifer E. 2015. "Membership of the 114th Congress: A Profile." A Congressional Research Service Report for Congress, R43869, Washington, DC, January 22. Accessed March 18, 2015 (http://fas.org/sgp/crs/misc/R43869.pdf).

Mann Yee Kan, Oriel Sullivan, and Jonathan Gershuny. 2011. "Gender Convergence in Domestic Work: Discerning the Effects of Interactional and Institutional Barriers from Large-Scale Data." *Sociology* 45 (2): 234–251.

Mapel, Tim. 2007. "The Adjustment Process of Ex-Buddhist Monks to Life After the Monastery." *Journal of Religion & Health* 46 (1): 19–34.

Marks, Andrew. 2005. "Cracking the Kindergarten Code." *New York,* 38 (42): 58-63. Accessed June 2, 2013 (http://nymag.com/nymetro/urban/education/features/15141/).

Marshall, T. H. 1950. *Citizenship and Social Class and Other Essays.* Cambridge, UK: Cambridge University Press.

Martin, Daniel C., and James E. Yankay. 2013. "Refugees and Asylees: 2013." Annual Flow Report, Homeland Security, August. Accessed April 30, 2015 (www.dhs.gov/sites/default/files/publications/ois_rfa_fr_2013.pdf).

Martineau, Harriet. [1837] 1962. *Society in America.* Edited, abridged, with an introductory essay by Seymour Martin Lipset. Garden City, NY: Doubleday.

————. [1838] 1989. *How to Observe Morals and Manners.* Philadelphia: Leal and Blanchard. Sesquicentennial ed., ed. M. R. Hill. New York: Transaction.

Martinez, Gladys, Casey Copen, and Joyce C. Abma. 2011. "Teenagers in the United States: Sexual Activity, Contraceptive Use, and Childbearing, 2006–2010." National Survey of Family Growth, National Center for Health Statistics. *Vital and Health Statistics* 23 (31). Accessed May 26, 2012 (www.cdc.gov/nchs/data/series/sr_23/sr23_031.pdf).

Marx, Karl. [1845] 2000. "German Ideology." Pp. 175–208 in *Karl Marx: Selected Writings,* 2nd ed., ed. David McLellan. New York: Oxford University Press.

————. [1867] 2000. "Capital." Pp. 452–546 in *Karl Marx: Selected Writings,* 2nd ed., ed. David McLellan. New York: Oxford University Press.

Marx, Karl, and Friedrich Engels. [1847] 1955. *Selected Works in Two Volumes.* Moscow: Foreign Languages Publishing House.

————. [1848] 1998. *The Communist Manifesto: A Modern Edition.* New York: Verso.

Mathews, T. J., and Marian F. MacDorman. 2013. "Infant Mortality Statistics from the 2010 Period Linked Birth/Infant Death Data Set." *National Vital Statistics Reports* 62: December 18. Accessed May 2, 2015 (www.cdc.gov/nchs/data/nvsr/nvsr62/nvsr62_08.pdf).

Mathisen, James A. 2006. "Sport." Pp. 285–303 in *Handbook of Religion and Social Institutions,* ed. Helen Rose Ebaugh. New York: Springer.

Mayo, Elton. 1933. *The Human Problems of an Industrial Civilization.* London: Macmillan.

McAdam, Doug. 1988. *Freedom Summer.* New York: Oxford University Press.

McCabe, Donald L., Kenneth D. Butterfield, and Linda Klebe Treviño. 2006. "Academic Dishonesty in Graduate Business Programs: Prevalence, Causes, and Proposed Action." *Academy of Management Learning & Education* 5 (3): 294–305.

McCabe, Janice, Emily Fairchild, Liz Grauerholz, Bernice A. Pescosolido, and Daniel Tope. 2011. "Gender in Twentieth-Century Children's Books: Patterns of Disparity in Titles and Central Characters." *Gender & Society* 25 (2): 197–226.

McConnell-Ginet, Sally. 2011. *Gender, Sexuality, and Meaning: Linguistic Practice and Politics.* New York: Oxford University Press.

McDonald, Michael. 2009. "Election of a Century?" United States Elections Project. Accessed June 2, 2009 (http://elections.gmu.edu/Election_of_a_Century.html).

McDowell, David J., and Ross D. Parke. 2009. "Parental Correlates of Children's Peer Relations: An Empirical Test of a Tripartite Model." *Developmental Psychology* 45 (1): 224–235.

McGurty, Eileen. 2007. *Transforming Environmentalism: Warren County, PCBs, and the Origins of Environmental Justice.* Piscataway, NJ: Rutgers University Press.

McIntosh, Peggy. 1988. "White Privilege and Male Privilege: A Personal Account of Coming to See Correspondence Through Work and Women's Studies." Working Paper No. 189, Wellesley College Center for Research on Women, Wellesley, MA.

McKown, Clark, and Rhona S. Weinstein. 2008. "Teacher Expectations, Classroom Context, and the Achievement Gap." *Journal of School Psychology* 46 (3): 235–261.

McLaughlin, Emma, and Nicola Kraus. 2002. *The Nanny Diaries: A Novel.* New York: St. Martin's Press.

McLellan, David, ed. 2000. *Karl Marx, Selected Writings,* rev. ed. New York: Oxford University Press.

McNamee, Stephen J., and Robert K. Miller Jr. 2014. *The Meritocracy Myth,* 3rd ed. Lanham, MD: Rowman & Littlefield.

McPherson, Miller, Lynn Smith-Lovin, and James M. Cook. 2001. "Birds of a Feather: Homophily in Social Networks." *Annual Review of Sociology* 27: 415–222.

Mead, George H. 1934. *Mind, Self and Society,* ed. Charles W. Morris. Chicago: University of Chicago Press.

———. 1964a. *On Social Psychology,* ed. Anselm Strauss. Chicago: University of Chicago Press.

———. 1964b. "The Genesis of the Self and Social Control." Pp. 267–293 in *Selected Writings: George Herbert Mead,* ed. Andrew J. Reck. Indianapolis: Bobbs-Merrill.

Mead, Margaret. [1935] 2001. *Sex and Temperament in Three Primitive Societies.* New York: Perennial, HarperCollins.

Meara, Ellen R., Seth Richards, and David M. Cutler. 2008. "The Gap Gets Bigger: Changes in Mortality and Life Expectancy, by Education, 1981–2000." *Health Affairs* 27 (2): 350–360.

Mehl, Matthias R., Simine Vazire, Nairán Ramírez-Esparza, Richard B. Slatcher, and James W. Pennebaker. 2007. "Are Women Really More Talkative Than Men?" *Science* 317 (July 6): 82.

Meier, Robert F., and Gilbert Geis. 1997. *Victimless Crime? Prostitution, Drugs, Homosexuality, Abortion.* Los Angeles: Roxbury Books.

Méndez, Juan E. "Report of the Special Rapporteur on Torture and Other Cruel, Inhuman or Degrading Treatment or Punishment." United Nations, Human Rights Council, Twenty-Second Session, February. Accessed April 19, 2015 (http://daccess-dds-ny.un.org/doc/UNDOC/GEN/G13/105/77/PDF/G1310577.pdf).

Melby, Todd. 2009. "Creating the DSM-V." *Contemporary Sexuality* 43 (3): 1, 4–6.

Merton, Robert. 1948. "The Bearing of Empirical Research upon the Development of Social Theory." *American Sociological Review* 13 (October): 505–515.

———. 1968. *Social Theory and Social Structure.* New York: Free Press.

Merton, Robert K., and Alice S. Kitt. 1950. "Contributions to the Theory of Reference Group Behavior." Pp. 40–105 in *Continuities in Social Research: Studies in the Scope and Methods of the American Soldier,* ed. Robert K. Merton and Paul L. Lazarsfeld. New York: Free Press.

Michels, Robert. [1915] 1949. *Political Parties.* Glencoe, IL: Free Press.

Mika, Mike. 2013. "Why I Hacked Donkey Kong for My Daughter." *Wired,* March 11. Accessed May 20, 2013 (www.wired.com/gamelife/2013/03/donkey-kong-pauline-hack/).

Milgram, Stanley. 1963. "Behavioral Study of Obedience." *Journal of Abnormal and Social Psychology* 67 (October): 371–378.

———. 1975. *Obedience to Authority: An Experimental View.* New York: Harper & Row.

Milillo, Diana. 2008. "Sexuality Sells: A Content Analysis of Lesbian and Heterosexual Women's Bodies in Magazine Advertisements." *Journal of Lesbian Studies* 12 (4): 381–392.

Millett, Kate. 1970. *Sexual Politics.* Garden City, NY: Doubleday.

Mills, C. Wright. [1956] 2000. *The Power Elite.* New edition with afterword by Alan Wolfe. New York: Oxford University Press.

———. [1959] 2009. *The Sociological Imagination.* New York: Oxford University Press.

Milner, Murray Jr. 2006. *Freaks, Geeks, and Cool Kids: American Teenagers, Schools, and the Culture of Consumption.* New York: Routledge.

Minority Rights Group International. 2007. "World Directory of Minorities and Indigenous Peoples—Mexico: Overview." Geneva: United Nations High Commissioner for Refugees. Accessed June 14, 2009 (www.unhcr.org/refworld/docid/4954ce409a.html).

Mishel, Lawrence, Jared Bernstein, and Heide Shierholz. 2009. *The State of Working America 2008/2009.* Ithaca, NY: ILR Press.

Mitchell, Ojmarrh, and Michael S. Caudy. 2015. "Examining Racial Disparities in Drug Arrests." *Justice Quarterly* 32: 288–313.

Mizruchi, Mark S. 1996. "What Do Interlocks Do? An Analysis, Critique, and Assessment of Research on Interlocking Directorates." Pp. 271–298 in *Annual Review of Sociology,* ed. John Hagan and Karen Cook. Palo Alto, CA: Annual Reviews.

Moen, Phyllis, and Patricia Roehling. 2005. *The Career Mystique: Cracks in the American Dream.* Lanham, MD: Rowman & Littlefield.

Mohai, Paul, and Robin Saha. 2007. "Racial Inequality in the Distribution of Hazardous Waste: A National-Level Reassessment." *Social Problems* 54 (3): 343–370.

Monaghan, Peter. 2012. "'Our Storehouse of Knowledge About Social Movements . . . Is Going to Be Left Bare.'" *The Chronicle of Higher Education,* February 19. Accessed March 14, 2012 (http://chronicle.com/article/5-Minutes-With-a-Sociologist/130849/).

Monger, Randall, and James Yankay. 2014. "U.S. Lawful Permanent Residents: 2013." Annual Flow Report, Homeland Security, May. Accessed April 16, 2015 (www.dhs.gov/sites/default/files/publications/ois_lpr_fr_2013.pdf).

Montagu, Ashley, 1997. *Man's Most Dangerous Myth: The Fallacy of Race,* 6th ed., abridged student ed. Walnut Creek, CA: AltaMira Press.

Monte, Lindsay M., and Renee R. Ellis. 2014. "Fertility of Women in the United States: June 2012." *Current Population Reports,* P20-575, U.S. Census Bureau, Washington, DC. Accessed February 26, 2015 (www.census.gov/content/dam/Census/library/publications/2014/demo/p20-575.pdf).

Moore, Molly. 2006. "Romance, but Not Marriage." *The Washington Post National Weekly Edition,* November 27, p. 18.

Moore, Robert B. 1976. *Racism in the English Language: A Lesson Plan and Study Essay.* New York: The Racism and Sexism Resource Center for Educators.

Moore, Wilbert E. 1968. "Occupational Socialization." Pp. 861–883 in *Handbook of Socialization Theory and Research,* ed. David A. Goslin. Chicago: Rand McNally.

Morales, Lymari. 2010. "Green Behaviors Common in U.S., but Not Increasing." Washington, DC: Gallup, Inc., April 9. Accessed May 21, 2010 (www.gallup.com/poll/127292/Green-Behaviors-Common-Not-Increasing.aspx).

Morgan, Sue. 2009. "Theorising Feminist History: A Thirty-Year Retrospective." *Women's History Review* 18 (3): 381–407.

Morse, Arthur D. 1967. *While Six Million Died: A Chronicle of American Apathy.* New York: Ace.

Morselli, Carlo, Pierre Tremblay, and Bill McCarthy. 2006. "Mentors and Criminal Achievement." *Criminology* 44 (1): 17–43.

Mortimer, Jeylan T., and Michael J. Shanahan, eds. 2006. *Handbook of the Life Course.* New York: Springer Science and Business Media.

Moss, Michael, and Ford Fessenden. 2002. "New Tools for Domestic Spying, and Qualms." *The New York Times,* December 10, pp. A1, A18.

Moyer, Michael. 2010. "Internet Ideology War." *Scientific American* 302 (4): 14–16.

Mullins, Justin. 2014. "Can Facebook Make You Sad?" *BBC,* February 6. Accessed February 11, 2015 (www.bbc.com/future/story/20140206-is-facebook-bad-for-you).

Munford, Rebecca. 2007. "'Wake Up and Smell the Lipgloss': Gender, Generation, and the (A)Politics of Girl Power." Pp. 266–279 in *Third Wave Feminism: A Critical Exploration,* expanded 2nd ed., ed. Stacy Gillis, Gillian Howie, and Rebecca Munford. New York: Palgrave Macmillan.

Murdock, George P. 1945. "The Common Denominator of Cultures." Pp. 123–142 in *The Science of Man in the World Crisis,* ed. Ralph Linton. New York: Columbia University Press.

———. 1949. *Social Structure.* New York: Macmillan.

———. 1957. "World Ethnographic Sample." *American Anthropologist* 59 (August): 664–687.

Myrskylä, Mikko, Hans-Peter Kohler, and Francesco C. Billari. 2009. "Advances in Development Reverse Fertility Declines." *Nature* 460 (August 6): 741–743.

N

NAEP. 2015. "2013 Mathematics Assessment." NAEP Data Explorer, U.S. Department of Education, Institute of Education Sciences, National Center for Education Statistics, National Assessment of Educational Progress (NAEP). Accessed March 10, 2015 (http://nces.ed.gov/nationsreportcard/naepdata/dataset.aspx).

Nanda, Serena. 1997. "The Hijras of India." Pp. 82–86 in *A Queer World: The Center for Lesbian and Gay Studies Reader,* ed. Martin Duberman. New York: New York University Press.

Naples, Nancy. 2003. *Feminism and Method: Ethnography, Discourse Analysis, and Activist Research.* New York: Routledge.

Narrative 4. 2015. "What We Do." New York, NY. Accessed March 10, 2015 (www.narrative4.com/mission-vision/).

National Cancer Institute. 2008. *The Role of the Media in Promoting and Reducing Tobacco Use.* Tobacco Control Monograph No. 19. National Institutes of Health, National Cancer Institute, NIH Pub. No. 07-6242. Bethesda, MD: U.S. Department of Health and Human Services.

National Center for Education Statistics. 2013. "List of 2013 Digest Tables." Institute of Education Services, U.S. Department of Education, Washington, DC. Accessed April 2, 2015 (http://nces.ed.gov/programs/digest/2013menu_tables.asp).

———. 2014. "List of 2014 Digest Tables." Institute of Education Services, U.S. Department of Education, Washington, DC. Accessed April 2, 2015 (http://nces.ed.gov/programs/digest/2014menu_tables.asp).

National Center for Health Statistics. 2010. *Health, United States, 2010: With Special Feature on Death and Dying.* Hyattsville, MD. Accessed June 20, 2011 (www.cdc.gov/nchs/data/hus/hus10.pdf).

———. 2013. *Health, United States, 2012: With Special Feature on Emergency Care.* Hyattsville, MD. Accessed June 6, 2013 (www.cdc.gov/nchs/data/hus/hus12.pdf).

———. 2014. *Health, United States, 2013: With Special Feature on Prescription Drugs.* Hyattsville, MD. Accessed February 2, 2015 (www.cdc.gov/nchs/hus.htm).

National Conference of State Legislatures. 2015. "State Medical Marijuana Laws." January 29. Accessed February 19 (www.ncsl.org/research/health/state-medical-marijuana-laws.aspx).

National Education Association. 2014. "Rankings & Estimates: Rankings of the States 2013 and Estimates of School Statistics 2014." National Education Association, NEA Research, March. Accessed March 10, 2015 (www.nea.org/assets/docs/NEA-Rankings-and-Estimates-2013-2014.pdf).

National Geographic. 2012. "Gulf Spill Pictures: Ten New Studies Show Impact on Coast. *National Geographic,* April. Accessed May 28, 2012 (http://news.nationalgeographic.com/news/energy/2012/04/pictures/120420-gulf-oil-spill-impact-studies/).

National Institute of Justice. 2007. "Transnational Organized Crime." U.S. Department of Justice. Accessed May 20, 2009 (www.ojp.usdoj.gov/nij/topics/crime/transnational-organized-crime/welcome.htm).

NCAA. 2014. "Student Athlete Participation 1981/82–2013/14: NCAA Sports Sponsorship and Participation Rates Report." Indianapolis, IN: The National Collegiate Athletic Association. Accessed March 10, 2015 (www.ncaapublications.com/productdownloads/PR1314.pdf).

Neiwert, David A. 2005. *Strawberry Days: How Internment Destroyed the Japanese Community.* New York: Palgrave Macmillan.

Newman, William M. 1973. *American Pluralism: A Study of Minority Groups and Social Theory.* New York: Harper & Row.

Newport, Frank. 2010. "Americans' Global Warming Concerns Continue to Drop." Washington, DC: Gallup, Inc., March 11. Accessed May 21, 2010 (www.gallup.com/poll/126560/Americans-Global-Warming-Concerns-Continue-Drop.aspx).

The New York Times. 2006. "Questions Couples Should Ask (or Wish They Had) Before Marrying." *The New York Times,* December 17. Accessed August 6, 2009 (www.nytimes.com/2006/12/17/fashion/weddings/17FIELDBOX.html).

NFHS. 2014. "2013–14 High School Athletics Participation Survey." National Federation of State High School Associations, Indianapolis, IN. Accessed March 10, 2015 (www.nfhs.org/Participation Statics/PDF/2013-14_Participation_Survey_PDF.pdf).

NHPCO. 2014. "NHPCO's Facts and Figures: Hospice Care in America." National Hospice and Palliative Care Organization, October. Accessed February 2, 2015 (www.nhpco.org/sites/default/files/public/Statistics_Research/2014_Facts_Figures.pdf).

Nielsen, Joyce McCarl, Glenda Walden, and Charlotte A. Kunkel. 2000. "Gendered Heteronormativity: Empirical Illustrations in Everyday Life." *Sociological Quarterly* 41 (2): 283–296.

———. 2012. "State of the Media: U.S. Digital Consumer Report—Q3–Q4 2011." Accessed April 5, 2012 (www.nielsen.com/content/dam/corporate/us/en/reports-downloads/2012-Reports/Digital-Consumer-Report-Q4-2012.pdf).

Nielsen. 2013a. "State of the Media: The Cross-Platform Report—Quarter 3, 2012." Accessed May 20, 2013 (www.nielsen.com/content/dam/corporate/us/en/reports-downloads/2013%20Reports/Nielsen-Cross-Platform-Report-Q3-2012.pdf).

NOAA. 2014. "Global Analysis for July 2014." *State of the Climate,* National Climatic Data Center. Accessed May 2, 2015 (www.ncdc.noaa.gov/sotc/global/201407).

Nobles, Melissa. 2000. "History Counts: A Comparative Analysis of Racial/Color Categorization in U.S. and Brazilian Censuses." *American Journal of Public Health* 90: 1738–1745.

Nofziger, Stacey, and Hye-Ryeon Lee. 2006. "Differential Associations and Daily Smoking of Adolescents: The Importance of Same-Sex Models." *Youth & Society* 37 (4): 453–478.

Nolan, Patrick, and Gerhard Lenski. 2006. *Human Societies: An Introduction to Macrosociology,* 10th ed. Boulder, CO: Paradigm.

North Carolina Department of Environment and Natural Resources. 2008. "Warren County PCB Landfill Fact Sheet." Accessed April 9, 2008 (www.wastenotnc.org/WarrenCo_Fact_Sheet.htm).

Norton, Michael I., and Francesca Gino. 2013. "Rituals Alleviate Grieving for Loved Ones, Lovers, and Lotteries." *Journal of Experimental Psychology: General* (forthcoming). Accessed May 31, 2013 (http://francescagino.com/pdfs/norton_gino_jesp_2013.pdf).

Norton, Michael I., and Dan Ariely. 2011. "Building a Better America—One Wealth Quintile at a Time." *Perspectives on Psychological Science* 6 (1): 9–12. Accessed June 3, 2013 (www.people.hbs.edu/mnorton/norton%20ariely.pdf).

Norton, Michael I., and Samuel R. Sommers. 2011. "Whites See Racism as a Zero-Sum Game That They Are Now Losing." *Perspectives on Psychological Science* 6 (3): 215–218.

Norwegian Ministry of Children and Equality. 2009. "Women in Norwegian Politics." Norway, the Official Site in the United States. Accessed June 18, 2009 (www.norway.org/policy/gender/politics/politics.htm).

Notestein, Frank. 1945. "Population: The Long View." Pp. 36–57 in *Food for the World,* ed. Theodore W. Schultz. Chicago: University of Chicago Press.

Noueihed, Lin, and Alex Warren. 2012. *The Battle for the Arab Spring: Revolution, Counter-Revolution and the Making of a New Era.* New Haven, CT: Yale University Press.

O

Oakes, Jeannie. 2008. "Keeping Track: Structuring Equality and Inequality in an Era of Accountability." *Teachers College Record* 110 (3): 700–712.

OASDI. 2011. "The 2011 Annual Report of the Board of Trustees of the Federal Old-Age and Survivors Insurance and Federal Disability Insurance Trust Funds." Social Security Administration, 66–327, May 13. Washington, DC: U.S. Government Printing Office. Accessed June 29, 2011 (www.ssa.gov/oact/TR/2011/).

Obach, Brian K. 2004. *Labor and the Environmental Movement: The Quest for Common Ground.* Cambridge, MA: MIT Press.

Obama, Barack. 2013. "Inaugural Address by President Barack Obama." The White House, Office of the Press Secretary, Washington, DC, January 21. Accessed March 28, 2015 (https://www.whitehouse.gov/the-press-office/2013/01/21/inaugural-address-president-barack-obama).

Oberschall, Anthony. 1973. *Social Conflict and Social Movements.* Englewood Cliffs, NJ: Prentice Hall.

O'Brien, Valerie. 2012. "The Benefits and Challenges of Kinship Care." *Child Care in Practice* 18: 127–146.

OECD. 2011. *Society at a Glance 2011—OECD Social Indicators.* Paris: Organisation for Economic Co-operation and Development. Accessed June 9, 2011 (www.oecd.org/els/social/indicators/SAG).

———. 2014a. *Education at a Glance 2014: OECD Indicators.* Paris: OECD. Accessed May 29, 2013 (www.oecd.org/edu/Education-at-a-Glance-2014.pdf).

———. 2014b. "Rising Inequality: Youth and Poor Fall Further Behind." Income Inequality Update, Directorate for Employment, Labour, and Social Affairs, Statistics Directorate, June. Accessed March 26, 2015 (www.oecd.org/els/soc/OECD2014-Income-Inequality-Update.pdf).

———. 2015a. "Net ODA (Total, % of Gross National Income, 2000–2014)." Paris: Organisation for Economic Co-operation and Development. Accessed April 15, 2015 (https://data.oecd.org/oda/net-oda.htm).

———. 2015b. "Net ODA (Total, Million US Dollars, 2000–2014)." Paris: Organisation for Economic Co-operation and Development. Accessed April 15, 2015 (https://data.oecd.org/oda/net-oda.htm).

Ogburn, William F. 1922. *Social Change with Respect to Culture and Original Nature.* New York: Huebsch (reprinted 1966, New York: Dell).

Ogburn, William F., and Clark Tibbits. 1934. "The Family and Its Functions." Pp. 661–708 in *Recent Social Trends in the United States,* ed. Research Committee on Social Trends. New York: McGraw-Hill.

O'Harrow, Robert Jr. 2005. "Mining Personal Data." *The Washington Post National Weekly Edition* (February 6), pp. 8–10.

Okrent, Arika. 2009. *In the Land of Invented Languages: Esperanto Rock Stars, Klin   Poets, Loglan Lovers, and the Mad Dreamers Who Tried to B   Perfect Language.* New York: Spiegel and Grau.

Okun, Arthur. 1975. *Equality and Efficiency: The Big Tradeoff.* Washington, DC: Brookings Institution.

Olofsson, Parvin Tavakol, Peter Aspelin, Lott Bergstrand, and Lennart Blomqvist. 2014. "Patients' Experience of Outsourcing and Care Related to Magnetic Resonance Examinations." *Upsala Journal of Medical Sciences* 119: 343–349.

Omi, Michael, and Howard Winant. 1994. *Racial Formation in the United States: From the 1960s to the 1990s,* 2nd ed. New York: Routledge.

The Oprah Winfrey Show. 2006. "Failing Grade." What Bill and Melinda Gates Want You to Know, April 11. Accessed March 10, 2015 (www.oprah.com/world/Failing-Grade).

Orshansky, Mollie. 1965. "Counting the Poor: Another Look at the Poverty Profile." *Social Security Bulletin* 28 (1): 3–29.

Ortman, Jennifer M., Victoria A. Velkoff, and Howard Hogan. 2014. "An Aging Nation: The Older Population in the United States." *Current Population Reports* P25-1140, May. Accessed February 2, 2015 (www.census.gov/prod/2014pubs/p25-1140.pdf).

Otterman, Sharon. 2009. "Tips for the Admissions Test . . . to Kindergarten." *The New York Times,* November 20. Accessed June 2, 2013 (www.nytimes.com/2009/11/21/nyregion/21testprep.html).

P

Packer, George. 2013. *The Unwinding: An Inner History of the New America.* New York: Farrar, Straus and Giroux.

Padian, Kevin. 2007. "The Case of Creation." *Nature* 448 (July 19): 253–254.

Pager, Devah. 2003. "The Mark of a Criminal Record." *American Journal of Sociology* 108 (March): 937–975.

———. 2007 *Marked: Race, Crime, and Finding Work in an Era of Mass Incarceration.* Chicago: University of Chicago Press.

Pager, Devah, and Bruce Western. 2012. "Identifying Discrimination at Work: The Use of Field Experiments." *Journal of Social Issues* 68: 221–237.

Pager, Devah, Bruce Western, and Bart Bonikowski. 2009. "Discrimination in a Low Wage Labor Market: A Field Experiment." *American Sociological Review* 74: 777–799.

Pager, Devah, Bruce Western, and Naomi Sugie. 2009. "Sequencing Disadvantage: Barriers to Employment Facing Young Black and White Men with Criminal Records." *Annals of the American Academy of Political and Social Sciences* 623: 195–213.

Pai, Seeta, and Kelly Schryver. 2015. *Children, Teens, Media, and Body Image: A Common Sense Media Research Brief.* San Francisco: Common Sense Media. Accessed April 19, 2015 (www.commonsensemedia.org/file/csm-body-image-report-012615-interactivepdf/download).

Painter, Nell Irvin. 2010. *The History of White People.* New York: Norton.

Palm, Cheryl, Stephen A. Vosti, Pedro A. Sanchez, and Polly J. Ericksen, eds. 2005. *Slash-and-Burn Agriculture: The Search for Alternatives.* New York: Columbia University Press.

Panagopoulos, Costas. 2009. "Polls and Elections: Preelection Poll Accuracy in the 2008 General Elections." *Presidential Studies Quarterly* 39 (4): 896–907.

Panagopoulos, Costas, and Benjamin Farrer. 2014. "*Polls and Elections*: Preelection Poll Accuracy and Bias in the 2012 General Elections." *Presidential Studies Quarterly* 44: 352–363.

Park, Kristin. 2005. "Choosing Childlessness: Weber's Typology of Action and Motives of the Voluntarily Childless." *Sociological Inquiry,* August, pp. 372–402.

Park, Robert E. 1922. *The Immigrant Press and Its Control.* New York: Harper.

Parker, Alison. 2004. "Inalienable Rights: Can Human-Rights Law Help to End U.S. Mistreatment of Noncitizens?" *American Prospect,* October, pp. A11–A13.

Parker, Kim, and Eileen Patten. 2013. "The Sandwich Generation: Rising Financial Burdens for Middle-Aged Americans." Pew Research Center, January 30. Accessed February 2, 2015 (www.pewsocialtrends.org/2013/01/30/the-sandwich-generation/).

Parker, Kim, and Wendy Wang. 2013. "Modern Parenthood: Roles of Moms and Dads Converge as They Balance Work and Family." Pew Research Center, Washington, DC, March 14. Accessed June 6, 2013 (www.pewsocialtrends.org/files/2013/03/FINAL_modern_parenthood_03-2013.pdf).

Parker, Richard. 2009. "Sexuality, Culture and Society: Shifting Paradigms in Sexuality Research." *Culture, Health & Sexuality* 11 (3): 251–266.

Parry, Marc. 2013. "The American Police State: A Sociologist Interrogates the Criminal-Justice System and Tries to Stay Out of the Spotlight." *The Chronicle of Higher Education* November 18. Accessed January 10, 2015 (http://chronicle.com/article/The-American-Police-State/142965/).

Parsons, Talcott. 1951. *The Social System.* New York: Free Press.

———. 1966. *Societies: Evolutionary and Comparative Perspectives.* Englewood Cliffs, NJ: Prentice Hall.

————. 1975. "The Sick Role and the Role of the Physician Reconsidered." *Milbank Medical Fund Quarterly Health and Society* 53 (Summer): 257–278.

Parsons, Talcott, and Robert Bales. 1955. *Family, Socialization and Interaction Process.* Glencoe, IL: Free Press.

Pascoe, C. J. 2007. *Dude You're a Fag: Masculinity and Sexuality in High School.* Berkeley: University of California Press.

Passel, Jeffrey S., D'Vera Cohn, and Mark Hugo Lopez. 2011. "Hispanics Account for More than Half of Nation's Growth in Past Decade." Pew Hispanic Center, A Pew Research Center Project, March 24. Accessed June 20, 2011 (http://pewhispanic.org/reports/report.php?ReportID5140).

Passel, Jeffrey S., D'Vera Cohn, and Molly Rohel. 2014. "Unauthorized Immigrants in the U.S., 2012." Pew Research Center's Hispanic Trends Project, Washington, DC, November 18. Accessed April 28, 2015 (www.pewhispanic.org/interactives/unauthorized-immigrants-2012/map/mexican-share/).

Patten, Eileen, and Kim Parker. 2012. "A Gender Reversal on Career Aspirations: Young Women Now Top Young Men in Valuing a High-Paying Career." A Social & Demographic Trends Report, Pew Research Center, April 19. Accessed May 2, 2012 (www.pewsocialtrends.org/2012/04/19/a-gender-reversal-on-career-aspirations/).

Patterson, Thomas E. 2003. *We the People,* 5th ed. New York: McGraw-Hill.

Paxton, Pamela, Sheri Kunovich, and Melanie M. Hughes. 2007. "Gender in Politics." Pp. 263–285 in *Annual Review of Sociology 2007.* Palo Alto, CA: Annual Reviews.

Pear, Robert. 2008. "Gap in Life Expectancy Widens for the Nation." *The New York Times,* March 23. Accessed June 26, 2009 (www.nytimes.com/2008/03/23/us/23health.html).

Pearson, Allison. 2011. "Citizen Kate." *Newsweek,* April 3. Accessed May 30, 2011 (www.newsweek.com/2011/04/03/citizen-kate.html).

Peattie, Lisa, and Martin Rein. 1983. *Women's Claims: A Study in the Political Economy.* New York: Oxford University Press.

Peek, Lori. 2005. "Becoming Muslim: The Development of a Religious Identity." *Sociology of Religion* 66: 215–242.

Perrow, Charles. 1986. *Complex Organizations,* 3rd ed. New York: Random House.

Pershing, Jana L. 2003. "Why Women Don't Report Sexual Harassment: A Case Study of an Elite Military Institution." *Gender Issues* 21 (4): 3–30.

Peters, Sharon. 2009. "Puppy Love: More Pets Partake in Even Formal Weddings." *USA Today,* June 26. Accessed February 26, 2015 (http://usatoday30.usatoday.com/life/lifestyle/2009-06-23-pet-weddings_N.htm).

Petrovic, Drazen. 1994. "Ethnic Cleansing—an Attempt at Methodology." *EJIL* 5: 1–19.

Pew Charitable Trusts. 2012. "A Year or More: The High Cost of Long-Term Unemployment—Addendum." Pew Fiscal Analysis Initiative, May 2. Accessed May 22, 2012 (www.pewtrusts.org/uploadedFiles/wwwpewtrustsorg/Reports/Fiscal_Analysis/Addendum_Long-Term_Unemployment_May2012.pdf).

Pew Research Center. 2006. "More Americans Discussing—and Planning—End-of-Life Treatment." Pew Research Center for the People & the Press, Washington, DC, January 5. Accessed June 18, 2009 (http://people-press.org/reports/pdf/266.pdf).

————. 2007. "Optimism About Black Progress Declines: Blacks See Growing Values Gap Between Poor and Middle Class." Washington, DC: Pew Research Center. Accessed July 1, 2008 (http://pewsocialtrends.org/assets/pdf/Race.pdf).

————. 2008a. "U.S. Religious Landscape Survey." Pew Forum on Religion in Public Life. Washington, DC: Pew Research Center. Accessed June 14, 2008 (http://religions.pewforum.org/pdf/report-religious-landscape-study-full.pdf).

————. 2009a. "The Stronger Sex—Spiritually Speaking." Pew Forum on Religion & Public Life, February 26. Accessed April 19, 2010 (http://pewforum.org/docs/?DocID5403).

————. 2009b. "End of Communism Cheered but Now with More Reservations: Two Decades After the Wall's Fall." Pew Global Attitudes Project, November 2. Accessed April 23, 2010 (http://pewglobal.org/reports/pdf/267.pdf).

————. 2010c. "Trust in Government Database: 1958–2010." Accessed April 23, 2010 (http://people-press.org/trust/trust-database.xls).

————. 2010f. "Gender Equality Universally Embraced, but Inequalities Acknowledged." Global Attitudes Project, July 1. Accessed June 15, 2011 (http://pewglobal.org/files/pdf/Pew-Global-Attitudes-2010-Gender-Report.pdf).

————. 2010g. "The Return of the Multi-Generational Family Household." Washington, DC: Pew Research Center's Social and Demographic Trends project, March 18. Accessed February 26, 2015 (www.pewsocialtrends.org/files/2010/10/752-multi-generational-families.pdf).

————. 2011e. "Obama Leadership Image Takes a Hit, GOP Ratings Decline." The Pew Research Center for the People & the Press Report, August 25. Accessed May 24, 2012 (www.people-press.org/files/legacy-pdf/8-25-11%20Political%20Release.pdf).

————. 2012a. "More Support for Gun Rights, Gay Marriage Than in 2008, 2004." The Pew Research Center for the People & the Press, April 25. Accessed May 8, 2012 (www.people-press.org/files/legacy-pdf/4-25-12%20Social%20Issues.pdf).

————. 2012b. "Young, Underemployed and Optimistic: Coming of Age, Slowly, in a Tough Economy." A Social & Demographic Trends Report, February 9. Accessed May 22, 2012 (www.pewsocialtrends.org/files/2012/02/young-underemployed-and-optimistic.pdf).

————. 2012e. "In Changing News Landscape, Even Television Is Vulnerable: Trends in News Consumption—1991–2012." The Pew Research Center for the People & the Press, September 27. Accessed May 20, 2013 (www.people-press.org/files/legacy-pdf/2012%20News%20Consumption%20Report.pdf).

————. 2012f. "Views of Law Enforcement, Racial Progress and News Coverage of Race." Pew Research Center for the People & the Press, March 30. Accessed June 6, 2013 (www.people-press.org/2012/03/30/blacks-view-of-law-enforcement-racial-progress-and-news-coverage-of-race/).

————. 2012g. "Social Networking Popular Across Globe: Arab Publics Most Likely to Express Political Views Online." Global Attitudes Project, December 12. Accessed May 21, 2013 (www.pewglobal.org/files/2012/12/Pew-Global-Attitudes-Project-Technology-Report-FINAL-December-12-2012.pdf).

————. 2012i. "The Global Religious Landscape: A Report on the Size and Distribution of the World's Major Religious Groups as of 2010." The Pew Forum on Religion & Public Life, December. Accessed May 28, 2015 (www.pewforum.org/files/2014/01/global-religion-full.pdf).

————. 2013a. "Deficit Reduction Rises on Public's Agenda for Obama's Second Term." The Pew Research Center for the People & the Press, January 24. Accessed May 23, 2013 (www.people-press.org/files/legacy-pdf/01-24-13%20Prioritie%20Release.pdf).

————. 2013b. "Gun Homicide Rate Down 49% Since 1993 Peak; Public Unaware." Social & Demographic Trends Project, May 7. Accessed May 23, 2013 (www.pewsocialtrends.org/files/2013/05/firearms_final_05-2013.pdf).

————. 2013e. "U.S. Christians' Views on the Return of Christ." The Pew Forum on Religion & Public Life, March 26. Accessed May 31, 2013 (www.pewforum.org/Christian/US-Christians-Views-on-the-Return-of-Christ.aspx).

————. 2013h. "Party Identification." Accessed March 18, 2015 (www.pewresearch.org/data-trend/political-attitudes/party-identification/).

————. 2013i. "The U.S.'s High Income Gap Is Met with Relatively Low Public Concern." Fact Tank, News in the Numbers, December 6. Accessed March 28, 2015 (www.pewresearch.org/fact-tank/2013/12/06/the-u-s-s-high-income-gap-is-met-with-relatively-low-public-concern/).

————. 2013j. "Climate Change and Financial Instability Seen as Top Global Threats." Global Attitudes & Trends, June 24.

Accessed May 3, 2015 (www.pewglobal.org/files/2013/06/Pew-Research-Center-Global-Attitudes-Project-Global-Threats-Report-FINAL-June-24-20131.pdf).

———. 2014a. "Emerging and Developing Economies Much More Optimistic Than Rich Countries About the Future." Global Attitudes Project, October 9. Accessed January 22, 2015 (www.pewglobal.org/files/2014/10/Pew-Research-Center-Inequality-Report-FINAL-October-17-2014.pdf).

———. 2014b. "Emerging Nations Embrace Internet Mobile Technology." February 13. Accessed February 2, 2015 (www.pewglobal.org/files/2014/02/Pew-Research-Center-Global-Attitudes-Project-Technology-Report-FINAL-February-13-20147.pdf).

———. 2014c. "Global Opposition to U.S. Surveillance and Drones, but Limited Harm to America's Image." Global Attitudes Project, July 14. Accessed February 11, 2015 (www.pewglobal.org/files/2014/07/2014-07-14-Balance-of-Power.pdf).

———. 2014d. "As Midterms Near, GOP Leads on Key Issues, Democrats Have a More Positive Image." The Pew Research Center for the People & the Press, October 23. Accessed February 19, 2015 (www.people-press.org/files/2014/10/10-23-14-Political-release.pdf).

———. 2014e. "The Rising Cost of Not Going to College." Washington, DC: Social & Demographic Trends project, February 11. Accessed February 26, 2015 (www.pewsocialtrends.org/files/2014/02/SDT-higher-ed-FINAL-02-11-2014.pdf).

———. 2014f. "Changing Attitudes on Gay Marriage. Religion & Public Life," September 24. Accessed February 26, 2015 (www.pewforum.org/2014/09/24/graphics-slideshow-changing-attitudes-on-gay-marriage/).

———. 2014g. "The Rising Cost of Not Going to College." Social & Demographic Trends, February 11. Accessed March 10, 2015 (www.pewsocialtrends.org/files/2014/02/SDT-higher-ed-FINAL-02-11-2014.pdf).

———.2014h. "Beyond Red vs. Blue: The Political Typology." U.S. Politics & Policy, June 26. Accessed March 18, 2015 (www.people-press.org/2014/06/26/the-political-typology-beyond-red-vs-blue/).

———. 2014i. "Most See Inequality Growing, but Partisans Differ over Solutions." U.S. Politics & Policy, January 23. Accessed March 26, 2015 (www.people-press.org/files/legacy-pdf/1-23-14%20Poverty_Inequality%20Release.pdf).

———. 2014j. "Political Polarization in the American Public: How Increasing Ideological Uniformity and Partisan Antipathy Affect Politics, Compromise, and Everyday Life." U.S. Politics & Policy, June 12. Accessed April 20, 2015 (www.people-press.org/files/2014/06/6-12-2014-Political-Polarization-Release.pdf).

———. 2014k. "The Shifting Religious Identity of Latinos in the United States." Religion & Public Life, May 7. Accessed April 28, 2015 (www.pewforum.org/files/2014/05/Latinos-Religion-07-22-full-report.pdf).

———. 2015a. "Most Say Government Policies Since Recession Have Done Little to Help Middle Class, Poor." U.S. Politics & Policy project, March 4. Accessed March 22, 2015 (www.people-press.org/files/2015/03/03-04-15-Economy-release.pdf).

———. 2015b. "Public's Policy Priorities Reflect Changing Conditions at Home and Abroad." U.S. Politics & Policy, January 15. Accessed May 2, 2015 (www.people-press.org/files/2015/01/01-15-15-Policy-Priorities-Release.pdf).

Pfeifer, Mark. 2008. "Vietnamese Americans." Pp. 1365–1368 in *Encyclopedia of Race, Ethnicity, and Society,* vol. 3, ed. Richard T. Schaefer. Thousand Oaks, CA: Sage.

Phillips, Anna M. 2012. "After Number of Gifted Soars, a Fight for Kindergarten Slots." *The New York Times,* April 13. Accessed June 2, 2013 (www.nytimes.com/2012/04/14/nyregion/as-ranks-of-gifted-soar-in-ny-fight-brews-for-kindergarten-slots.html).

Piaget, Jean. 1954. *The Construction of Reality in the Child,* trans. Margaret Cook. New York: Basic Books.

Piketty, Thomas. 2014. *Capital in the Twenty-First Century.* Cambridge, MA: Belknap Press of Harvard University.

Piketty, Thomas, and Emmanuel Saez. 2013. "Tables and Figures Updated to 2011 in Excel Format, January 2013 for Income Inequality in the United States, 1913–1998." *The Quarterly Journal of Economics*, February 2003. Accessed June 3, 2013 (http://elsa.berkeley.edu/~sacz/TabFig2011prcl.xls).

Pinderhughes, Dianne. 1987. *Race and Ethnicity in Chicago Politics: A Reexamination of Pluralist Theory.* Urbana: University of Illinois Press.

Pinnow, Ellen, Pellavi Sharma, Ameeta Parekh, Natalie Gevorkian, and Kathleen Uhl. 2009. "Increasing Participation of Women in Early Phase Clinical Trials Approved by the FDA." *Women's Health Issues* 19 (2): 89–92.

Planty, M., W. Hussar, T. Snyder, G. Kena, A. Kewal-Ramani, J. Kemp, K. Bianco, and R. Dinkes. 2009. *The Condition of Education 2009.* NCES 2009-081. Washington, DC: National Center for Education Statistics, Institute of Education Sciences, U.S. Department of Education. Accessed May 29, 2009 (http://nces.ed.gov/pubs2009/2009081.pdf).

Planty, M., W. Hussar, T. Snyder, S. Provasnik, G. Kena, R. Dinkes, A. Kewal-Ramani, and J. Kemp. 2008. *The Condition of Education 2008.* NCES 2008-031. Washington, DC: National Center for Education Statistics, Institute of Education Sciences, U.S. Department of Education. Accessed June 14, 2008 (http://nces.ed.gov/pubs2008/2008031.pdf).

Plaut, Victoria C., Flannery G. Garnett, Laura E. Buffardi, and Jeffrey Sanchez-Burks. 2011. "'What About Me?' Perceptions of Exclusion and Whites' Reactions to Multiculturalism." *Journal of Personality and Social Psychology* 101(2): 337–353.

Pollini, Jacques. 2009. "Agroforestry and the Search for Alternatives to Slash-and-Burn Cultivation: From Technological Optimism to a Political Economy of Deforestation." *Agriculture, Ecosystems & Environment* 133 (1/2): 48–60.

Pollster.com. 2015. "Party Identification." Accessed March 18, 2015 (http://elections.huffingtonpost.com/pollster/party-identification).

Population Reference Bureau. 2014. *2014 World Population Data Sheet.* Washington, DC: Population Reference Bureau. Accessed February 2, 2015 (www.prb.org/pdf14/2014-world-population-data-sheet_eng.pdf).

Porter, Roy. 1998. *The Greatest Benefit to Mankind: A Medical History of Humanity.* New York: HarperCollins.

———. 2004. *Blood and Guts: A Short History of Medicine.* New York: Norton.

Postman, Neil. 1988. "Questioning the Media." Video. The January Series, January 12. Grand Rapids, MI: Calvin College.

———. 1993. *Technopoly: The Surrender of Culture to Technology.* New York: Vintage Books.

———. 1999. *Building a Bridge to the 18th Century: How the Past Can Improve Our Future.* New York: Knopf.

Potts, John. 2009. *A History of Charisma.* New York: Palgrave Macmillan.

Price, David A. 2003. *Love and Hate in Jamestown: John Smith, Pocahontas, and the Heart of a New Nation.* New York: Knopf.

Prior, Karen Swallow. 2013. "The Case for Getting Married Young." *The Atlantic,* March 22. Accessed February 26, 2015 (www.theatlantic.com/sexes/archive/2013/03/the-case-for-getting-married-young/274293/).

Progressive Student Labor Movement. 2008. "A Brief History of the Living Wage Debate at Harvard." Accessed July 7 (www.hcs.harvard.edu/~pslm/livingwage/timeline.html).

Prohaska, Ariane, and Jeannine Gailey. 2010. "Achieving Masculinity Through Sexual Predation: The Case of Hogging." *Journal of Gender Studies* 19 (1): 13–25.

Project on Student Debt. 2014. "Student Debt and the Class of 2013." The Institute for College Access and Success, Oakland, CA, November. Accessed March 17, 2015 (http://projectonstudentdebt.org/files/pub/classof2013.pdf).

Provasnik, S., and Planty, M. 2008. *Community Colleges: Special Supplement to the Condition of Education 2008.* NCES 2008-033. Washington, DC: National Center for Education Statistics, Institute of Education Sciences, U.S. Department of Education. Accessed May 31, 2009 (http://nces.ed.gov/pubs2008/2008033.pdf).

Prus, Steven G. 2007. "Age, SES, and Health: A Population-Level Analysis of Health Irregularities over the Lifecourse." *Sociology of Health and Illness* 29 (March): 275–296.

Pryor, John H., Sylvia Hurtado, Victor B. Saenz, José Luis Santos, and William S. Korn. 2007. *The American Freshman: Forty-Year Trends.* Los Angeles: Higher Education Research Institute, UCLA.

Putnam, Robert D. 2015. *Our Kids: The American Dream in Crisis.* New York: Simon & Schuster.

Putnam, Robert D., and David E. Campbell. 2012. *American Grace: How Religion Divides and Unites Us.* New York: Simon & Schuster.

Q

Quinney, Richard. 1970. *The Social Reality of Crime.* Boston: Little, Brown.

———. 1974. *Criminal Justice in America.* Boston: Little, Brown.

———. 1979. *Criminology,* 2nd ed. Boston: Little, Brown.

———. 1980. *Class, State and Crime,* 2nd ed. New York: Longman.

Quinnipiac. 2014. "Iraq—Getting In Was Wrong; Getting Out Was Right, U.S. Voters Tell Quinnipiac University National Poll; 92 Percent Back Background Checks for All Gun Buys." Quinnipiac University Poll, July 3. Accessed February 19, 2015 (www.quinnipiac.edu/images/polling/us/us07032014_ulps31.pdf).

Quisumbing, Agnes, Ruth Meinzen-Dick, and Lucy Bassett. 2008. "Helping Women Respond to the Global Food Price Crisis." *IFPRI Policy Brief,* 7, October. Accessed June 18, 2009 (www.ifpri.org/pubs/bp/bp007.pdf).

QuotaProject. 2012. "Global Database of Quotas for Women." International IDEA, Stockholm University and Inter-Parliamentary Union. Accessed May 24, 2012 (www.quotaproject.org/system.cfm).

———. 2014. "Mexico." Global Database of Quotas for Women. Accessed April 16, 2015 (www.quotaproject.org/uid/countryview.cfm?CountryCode=MX).

R

Raghavan, Sudarsan. 2011. "Inspired by Tunisia and Egypt, Yemenis Join in Anti-government Protests." *The Washington Post,* January 27. Accessed May 28, 2012 (www.washingtonpost.com/wp-dyn/content/article/2011/01/27/AR2011012702081.html).

Rand, Robert. 2006. *Tamerlane's Children: Dispatches from Contemporary Uzbekistan.* Oxford: Oneworld.

Rank, Mark Robert, Thomas A. Hirschl, and Kirk A. Foster. 2014. *Chasing the American Dream: Understanding What Shapes Our Fortunes.* New York: Oxford University Press.

Ratner, Carl. 2004. "A Cultural Critique of Psychological Explanations of Terrorism." *Cross-Cultural Psychology Bulletin* 38 (1/2): 18–24.

Ravitz, Jessica. 2009. "Neda: Latest Iconic Image to Inspire." *CNN,* June 24. Accessed June 30, 2009 (www.cnn.com/2009/WORLD/meast/06/24/neda.iconic.images/).

Ray, Julie, and Rajesh Srinivasan. 2010a. "Afghans More Skeptical of U.S. Leadership, Troops in 2009." Washington, DC: Gallup, Inc. Accessed March 28, 2010 (www.gallup.com/poll/125537/Afghans-Skeptical-Leadership-Troops-2009.aspx).

———. 2010b. "Taliban Increasingly Unpopular in Pakistan." Washington, DC: Gallup, Inc. Accessed March 28, 2010 (www.gallup.com/poll/126602/Taliban-Increasingly-Unpopular-Pakistan.aspx).

Rayner, Gordon. 2011. "Royal Wedding: Kate Middleton Will Be 'Oldest Bride.'" *The Telegraph,* November 16. Accessed May 31, 2011 (www.telegraph.co.uk/news/uknews/theroyalfamily/8136788/Royal-wedding-Kate-Middleton-will-be-oldest-bride.html).

Reardon, Sean F. 2011. "The Widening Academic Achievement Gap Between the Rich and the Poor: New Evidence and Possible Explanations." Pp. 91–115 in *Whither Opportunity?: Rising Inequality, Schools, and Children's Life Chances*, ed. Greg J. Duncan and Richard J. Murnane. New York: Russell Sage Foundation.

Reddy, Gayatri. 2005. *With Respect to Sex: Negotiating Hijra Identity in South India.* Chicago: University of Chicago Press.

Reel, Justine J., Sonya SooHoo, Julia Franklin Summerhays, and Diane Gill. 2008. "Age Before Beauty: An Exploration of Body Image in African-American and Caucasian Adult Women." *Journal of Gender Studies* 17 (4): 321–330.

Reeves, Richard V. 2014. *Saving Horatio Alger: Equality, Opportunity, and the American Dream.* New York: Brookings Institution.

———. 2015. "Wealth, Inequality, and the 'Me? I'm Not Rich!' Problem." *The Wall Street Journal*, February 27. Accessed March 22, 2015 (http://blogs.wsj.com/washwire/2015/02/27/wealth-inequality-and-the-me-im-not-rich-problem/).

Reid, Luc. 2006. *Talk the Talk: The Slang of 65 American Subcultures.* Cincinnati, OH: Writer's Digest Books.

Reinharz, Shulamit. 1992. *Feminist Methods in Social Research.* New York: Oxford University Press.

Reitman, Meredith. 2006. "Uncovering the White Place: Whitewashing at Work." *Social & Cultural Geography* 7 (2): 267–282.

Reitzes, Donald C., and Elizabeth J. Mutran. 2004. "The Transition to Retirement: Stages and Factors That Influence Retirement Adjustment." *International Journal of Aging & Human Development* 59 (1): 63–84.

Relerford, Patrice, Chao Xiong, Michael Rand, and Curt Brown. 2008. "42 Students Questioned, 13 Disciplined." *Minneapolis Star-Tribune,* January 10. Accessed June 30, 2009 (www.startribune.com/local/west/13663951.html).

Religious Tolerance. 2008. "Female Genital Mutilation (FGM): Informational Materials." Accessed March 1, 2008 (www.religioustolerance.org).

Renegar, Valerie R., and Stacey K. Sowards. 2009. "Contradiction as Agency: Self-Determination, Transcendence, and Counter-imagination in Third Wave Feminism." *Hypatia* 24 (2): 1–20.

Reynolds, John R., and Chardie L. Baird. 2010. "Is There a Downside to Shooting for the Stars? Unrealized Educational Expectations and Symptoms of Depression." *American Sociological Review* 75 (1): 151–172.

Richardson, Sarah S. 2013. *Sex Itself: The Search for Male and Female in the Human Genome.* Chicago: University of Chicago Press.

Richtel, Matt. 2006. "The Long-Distance Journey of a Fast-Food Order." *The New York Times,* April 11. Accessed May 13, 2009 (www.nytimes.com/2006/04/11/technology/11fast.html).

Rideout, Victoria J., Ulla G. Foehr, and Donald F. Roberts. 2010. *Generation M2: Media in the Lives of 8–18-Year-Olds.* Kaiser Family Foundation Study, Menlo Park, CA, January. Accessed April 30, 2010 (www.kff.org/entmedia/8010.cfm).

Rieker, Patricia R., and Chloe E. Bird. 2000. "Sociological Explanations of Gender Differences in Mental and Physical Health." Pp. 98–113 in *Handbook of Medical Sociology,* ed. Chloe Bird, Peter Conrad, and Allan Fremont. New York: Prentice Hall.

Risman, Barbara J. 1986. "Can Men 'Mother'? Life as a Single Father." *Family Relations* 35 (1): 95–102.

Risman, Barbara J., and Danette Johnson-Sumerford. 1998. "'Doing It Fairly: A Study of Postgender Marriages." *Journal of Marriage and Family* 60 (1): 23–40.

Ritzer, George. 2008. *The McDonaldization of Society 5.* Thousand Oaks, CA: Sage.

Roberson, Debi, Ian Davies, and Jules Davidoff. 2000. "Color Categories Are Not Universal: Replications and New Evidence from Stone Age Culture." *Journal of Experimental Psychology* 129 (3): 369–398.

Roberts, J. Timmons, Peter E. Grines, and Jodie L. Manale. 2003. "Social Roots of Global Environmental Change: A World-Systems Analysis of Carbon Dioxide Emissions." *Journal of World-Systems Research* 9 (Summer): 277–315.

Roberts, Sharon E., and James E. Côté. 2014. "The Identity Issues Inventory: Identity Stage Resolution in the Prolonged Transition to Adulthood." *Journal of Adult Development* 21: 225–238.

Robison, Jennifer. 2002. "Should Mothers Work?" Gallup, Inc., August 27. Accessed June 17, 2009 (www.gallup.com/poll/6676/Should-Mothers-Work.aspx).

References

Rodriguez, Richard. 2002. *Brown: The Last Discovery of America.* New York: Penguin Books.

Rodwan, John, Jr. 2014. "Bottled Water 2013: Sustaining Vitality." *Bottled Water Reporter* 54 (July/August): 12–22.

Roediger, David R. 2005. *Working Toward Whiteness: How America's Immigrants Became White.* New York: Basic Books.

Romans, Sarah, Rose Clarkson, Gillian Einstein, Michele Petrovic, and Donna Stewart. 2012. "Mood and the Menstrual Cycle: A Review of Prospective Data Studies." *Gender Medicine* 9 (5): 361–384.

Rootes, Christopher. 2007. "Acting Locally: The Character, Contexts and Significance of Local Environmental Mobilisations." *Environmental Politics* 16 (5): 722–741.

Roscoe, Will. 1997. "Gender Diversity in Native North America: Notes Toward a Unified Analysis." Pp. 65–81 in *A Queer World: The Center for Lesbian and Gay Studies Reader,* ed. Martin Duberman. New York: New York University Press.

Rose, Arnold. 1951. *The Roots of Prejudice.* Paris: UNESCO.

Rosen, William. 2010. *The Most Powerful Idea in the World: A Story of Steam, Industry, and Invention.* New York: Random House.

Rosenfeld, Michael J., and Reuben J. Thomas. 2012. "Searching for a Mate: The Rise of the Internet as a Social Intermediary." *American Sociological Review* 77: 523–547.

Rosenthal, Robert, and Lenore Jacobson. 1968. *Pygmalion in the Classroom.* New York: Henry Holt.

Rosin, Hanna. 2014. "The Overprotected Kid." *The Atlantic,* April. Accessed February 2, 2015 (www.theatlantic.com/features/archive/2014/03/hey-parents-leave-those-kids-alone/358631/).

Rossi, Alice S. 1968. "Transition to Parenthood." *Journal of Marriage and Family* 30 (February): 26–39.

———. 1984. "Gender and Parenthood." *American Sociological Review* 49 (February): 1–19.

Rossi Del Corso, Annalisa, and Margherita Lanz. 2013. "Felt Obligation and the Family Cycle: A Study on Intergenerational Relationships." *International Journal of Psychology* 48: 1196–1200.

Rothstein, Richard. 2009. "Equalizing Opportunity: Dramatic Differences in Children's Home Life and Health Mean That Schools Can't Do It Alone." *American Educator* 33 (2): 4–7, 45–46. Accessed April 26, 2010 (http://archive.aft.org/pubs-reports/american_educator/issues/summer2009/equalizingopportunity.pdf).

Rotman, David. 2013. "How Technology Is Destroying Jobs." *MIT Technology Review,* June 12. Accessed March 17, 2015 (www.technologyreview.com/featuredstory/515926/how-technology-is-destroying-jobs/).

Rowland, Christopher, ed. 2007. *The Cambridge Companion to Liberation Theology,* 2nd ed. New York: Cambridge University Press.

Rubie-Davies, Christine M. 2010. "Teacher Expectations and Perceptions of Student Attributes: Is There a Relationship?" *British Journal of Educational Psychology* 80 (1): 121–135.

Rubin, Alissa J. 2003. "Pat-Down on the Way to Prayer." *Los Angeles Times,* November 25, pp. A1, A5.

Rubin, Mark, Nida Denson, Sue Kilpatrick, Kelly E. Matthews, Tom Stehlik, and David Zyngier. 2014. " 'I Am Working Class': Subjective Self-Definition as a Missing Measure of Social Class and Socioeconomic Status in Higher Education Research." *Educational Researcher* 43: 196–200.

Rutter, Michael. 2010. "Gene Environment Interplay." *Depression and Anxiety* 27: 1–4.

Rutter, Michael, Terrie E. Moffitt, and Avshalom Caspi. 2006. "Gene-Environment Interplay and Psychopathology: Multiple Varieties but Real Effects." *Journal of Child Psychology and Psychiatry* 47 (3/4): 226–261.

Rymer, Russ. 1993. *Genie: An Abused Child's Flight from Science.* New York: HarperCollins.

S

Saad, Lydia. 2004. "Divorce Doesn't Last." *Gallup Poll Tuesday Briefing,* March 30 (www.gallup.com).

Sachs, Jeffrey D. 2005a. *The End of Poverty: Economic Possibilities for Our Time.* New York: Penguin Books.

Sacks, Peter. 2007. *Tearing Down the Gates: Confronting the Class Divide in American Education.* Berkeley: University of California Press.

Saez, Emmanuel. 2012. "Striking It Richer: The Evolution of Top Incomes in the United States (updated with 2009 and 2010 estimates)." Center for Equitable Growth, March 2. Accessed May 22, 2012 (http://elsa.berkeley.edu/~saez/saez-UStopincomes-2010.pdf).

Saez, Emmanuel, and Gabriel Zucman. 2014. "Wealth Inequality in the United States Since 1913: Evidence from Capitalized Income Tax Data." National Bureau of Economic Research, Working Paper 20625, October. Accessed June 8, 2015 (www.nber.org/papers/w20625).

Salganik, Matthew J., Peter Sheridan Dodds, and Duncan J. Watts. 2006. "Experimental Study of Inequality and Unpredictability in an Artificial Cultural Market." *Science* 311: 854–856.

Sample, Ian. 2014. "Anthropocene: Is This the New Epoch of Humans?" *The Guardian,* October 16. Accessed May 2, 2015 (www.theguardian.com/science/2014/oct/16/-sp-scientists-gather-talks-rename-human-age-anthropocene-holocene).

Sanday, Peggy Reeves. 2002. *Women at the Center: Life in a Modern Matriarchy.* Ithaca, NY: Cornell University Press.

———. 2008. Homepage. Accessed March 15 (www.sas.upenn.edu/~psanday).

Sandler, Ronald, and Phaedra C. Pezzullo, eds. 2007. *Environmental Justice and Environmentalism: The Social Justice Challenge to the Environmental Movement.* Cambridge, MA: MIT Press.

Sarachild, Kathie. 1978. "Consciousness-Raising: A Radical Weapon." Pp. 144–150 in *Feminist Revolution.* New York: Random House. Accessed June 30, 2009 (http://scriptorium.lib.duke.edu/wlm/fem/sarachild.html).

Sargent, James D., and Todd F. Heatherton. 2009. "Comparison of Trends for Adolescent Smoking and Smoking in Movies, 1990–2007." *Journal of the American Medical Association* 301: 2211–2213.

Sargent, John, and Linda Matthews. 2009. "China Versus Mexico in the Global EPZ Industry: Maquiladoras, FDI Quality, and Plant Mortality." *World Development* 37 (6): 1069–1082.

Sarkeesian, Anita. 2013. "Damsel in Distress (Part 1) Tropes vs Women." *Feminist Frequency: Conversations with Pop Culture,* March 7. Accessed May 20, 2013 (www.feministfrequency.com/2013/03/damsel-in-distress-part-1/).

Sassen, Saskia. 2005. "New Global Classes: Implications for Politics." Pp. 143–170 in *The New Egalitarianism,* ed. Anthony Giddens and Patrick Diamond. Cambridge, UK: Polity Press.

Sawhill, Isabel V. 2006. "Teenage Sex, Pregnancy, and Nonmarital Births." *Gender Issues* 23 (4): 48–59.

Scarce, Rik. 1994. "(No) Trial (but) Tribulations: When Courts and Ethnography Conflict." *Journal of Contemporary Ethnography* 23 (July): 123–149.

———. 1995. "Scholarly Ethics and Courtroom Antics: Where Researchers Stand in the Eyes of the Law." *American Sociologist* 26 (Spring): 87–112.

———. 2005a. "A Law to Protect Scholars." *Chronicle of Higher Education,* August 12, p. 324.

———. 2005b. *Contempt of Court: A Scholar's Battle for Free Speech from Behind Bars.* Lanham, MD: AltaMira Press.

Scelfo, Julie. 2008. "Baby, You're Home." *The New York Times,* November 12. Accessed June 29, 2009 (www.nytimes.com/2008/11/13/garden/13birth.html).

Schachtman, Tom. 2006. *Rumspringa: To Be or Not to Be Amish.* New York: North Point Press.

Schaefer, Richard T. 1998a. "Differential Racial Mortality and the 1995 Chicago Heat Wave." Paper presented at the annual meeting of the American Sociological Association, August, San Francisco.

Schaefer, Richard T., and William W. Zellner. 2007. *Extraordinary Groups,* 8th ed. New York: Worth.

Schaffer, Scott. 2004. *Resisting Ethics.* New York: Palgrave Macmillan.

Scharnberg, Kirsten. 2007. "Black Market for Midwives Defies Bans." *Chicago Tribune,* November 25, pp. 1, 10.

Schelly, David, and Paul B. Stretesky. 2009. "An Analysis of the 'Path of Least Resistance' Argument in Three Environmental Justice Success Cases." *Society & Natural Resources* 22 (4): 369–380.

Scherbov, Sergei, Wolfgang Lutz, and Warren C. Sanderson. 2011. "The Uncertain Timing of Reaching 7 Billion and Peak Population." International Institute for Applied Systems Analysis, Interim Report IR-11-002, February 21. Accessed June 29, 2011 (www.iiasa.ac.at/Admin/PUB/Documents/IR-11-002.pdf).

Schmeeckle, Maria. 2007. "Gender Dynamics in Stepfamilies: Adult Stepchildren's Views." *Journal of Marriage and Family* 69 (February): 174–189.

Schmeeckle, Maria, Roseann Giarrusso, Du Feng, and Vern L. Bengtson. 2006. "What Makes Someone Family? Adult Children's Perceptions of Current and Former Stepparents." *Journal of Marriage and Family* 68 (August): 595–610.

Schnaiberg, Allan. 1994. *Environment and Society: The Enduring Conflict.* New York: St. Martin's Press.

Schur, Edwin M. 1965. *Crimes Without Victims: Deviant Behavior and Public Policy.* Englewood Cliffs, NJ: Prentice Hall.

———. 1985. "'Crimes Without Victims: A 20-Year Reassessment." Paper presented at the annual meeting of the Society for the Study of Social Problems.

Schurman, Rachel. 2004. "Fighting 'Frankenfoods': Industry Opportunity Structures and the Efficacy of the Anti-biotech Movement in Western Europe." *Social Problems* 51 (2): 243–268.

Schwartz, Pepper. 2006. *Finding Your Perfect Match.* New York: Perigee Books.

Scott, Greg. 2005. "Public Symposium: HIV/AIDS, Injection Drug Use and Men Who Have Sex with Men." Pp. 38–39 in *Scholarship with a Mission,* ed. Susanna Pagliaro. Chicago: De Paul University.

Sennett, Richard. 2012. *Together: The Rituals, Pleasures, and Politics of Co-operation.* New Haven, CT: Yale University Press.

Shah, Anup. 2010. "Poverty Facts and Stats." *Global Issues,* March 22. April 28, 2010 (www.globalissues.org/article/26/poverty-facts-and-stats).

Shaheen, Jack. 2006. *Reel Bad Arabs: How Hollywood Vilifies a People.* Video. Directed by Sut Jhally. 50 minutes. Northampton, MA: Media Education Foundation.

———. 2009. *Reel Bad Arabs: How Hollywood Vilifies a People,* 2nd ed. New York: Olive Branch Press.

———. 2012. "The Making of the 'Green Menace.'" *The Nation,* July 2–9: 15–17.

Shapiro, Thomas M. 2004. *The Hidden Cost of Being African American: How Wealth Perpetuates Inequality.* New York: Oxford University Press.

Sharp, Gwen. 2011. "Two News Stories About Gabrielle Giffords' Shooting . . . and Husband." *Sociological Images,* January 9. Accessed March 10, 2012 (http://thesocietypages.org/socimages/2011/01/09/two-news-stories-about-gabrielle-giffords-shooting-and-husband/).

Shaw, Clifford R., and Henry D. McKay. 1969. *Juvenile Delinquency and Urban Areas.* Chicago: University of Chicago Press.

Shaw, Jessica C. 2013. "The Medicalization of Birth and Midwifery as Resistance." *Health Care for Women International* 34: 522–536.

Shenk, David. 2010. *The Genius in All of Us: Why Everything You've Been Told About Genetics, Talent, and IQ Is Wrong.* New York: Doubleday.

Shenker, Jack, Angelique Chrisafis, Lauren Williams, Tom Finn, Giles Tremlett, and Martin Chulov. 2011. "Young Arabs Who Can't Wait to Throw Off Shackles of Tradition." *The Guardian,* February 14. Accessed May 28, 2012 (www.guardian.co.uk/world/2011/feb/14/young-arabs-throw-off-shackles-tradition).

Sheskin, Arnold, and Ira M. Dashefsky. 2013. "Jewish Population in the United States, 2013." Pp. 201–277 in *The American Jewish Yearbook, 2013*, ed. Sheskin and Dashefsky. Dordrecht, The Netherlands: Springer.

Sheskin, Ira M., and Arnold Dashefsky. 2007. "Jewish Population of the United States, 2006." In *American Jewish Year Book 2006,* ed. David Singer and Lawrence Grossman. New York: American Jewish Committee.

Shi, Yu. 2008. "Chinese Immigrant Women Workers: Everyday Forms of Resistance and 'Coagulate Politics.'" *Communication and Critical/Cultural Studies* 5 (4): 363–382.

Shields, Stephanie A. 2008. "Gender: An Intersectionality Perspective." *Sex Roles* 59 (5/6): 301–311.

Al-Shihri, Abdullah. 2011. "Saudi Woman Held by Police—for Driving." *The Independent*, May 22. Accessed June 12, 2011 (www.independent.co.uk/news/world/middle-east/saudi-woman-held-by-police-ndash-for-driving-2287650.html).

Shipler, David K. 2004. *The Working Poor: Invisible in America.* New York: Knopf.

Shirky, Clay. 2008. *Here Comes Everybody: The Power of Organizing Without Organizations.* New York: Penguin Books.

Shorrocks, Anthony, Jim Davies, and Rodrigo Lluberas. 2014. *Global Wealth Databook 2014.* Zurich: Credit Suisse Research Institute. Accessed April 13, 2015 (https://publications.credit-suisse.com/tasks/render/file/?fileID=5521F296-D460-2B88-081889DB12817E02).

Short, James E. 2013a. *How Much Information? 2013 Report on American Consumers.* San Diego: Global Information Industry Center. Accessed February 2, 2015 (http://classic.marshall.usc.edu/assets/161/25995.pdf).

———. 2013b. *How Much Media? 2013: Report on American Consumers.* Institute for Communications Technology Management, USC Marshall School of Business, October. Accessed February 11, 2015 (www.marshall.usc.edu/faculty/centers/ctm/research/how-much-media).

Shostak, Arthur B. 2002. "Clinical Sociology and the Art of Peace Promotion: Earning a World Without War." Pp. 325–345 in *Using Sociology: An Introduction from the Applied and Clinical Perspectives,* ed. Roger A. Straus. Lanham, MD: Rowman & Littlefield.

Showden, Carisa R. 2009. "What's Political About the New Feminisms?" *Frontiers: A Journal of Women Studies* 30 (2): 166–198.

Silver, Ira. 1996. "Role Transitions, Objects, and Identity." *Symbolic Interaction* 10 (1): 1–20.

Silver, Nate. 2013. "How Opinion on Same-Sex Marriage Is Changing, and What It Means." *The New York Times,* March 26. Accessed May 29, 2013 (http://fivethirtyeight.blogs.nytimes.com/2013/03/26/how-opinion-on-same-sex-marriage-is-changing-and-what-it-means/).

Simanski, John F. 2014. "Immigrant Enforcement Actions: 2013." Annual Flow Report, Homeland Security, September. Accessed April 29, 2015 (www.dhs.gov/sites/default/files/publications/ois_enforcement_ar_2013.pdf).

Simmons, Robin. 2009. "Entry to Employment: Discourses of Inclusion and Employability in Work-Based Learning for Young People." *Journal of Education & Work* 22 (2): 137–151.

Simmons, Tavia, and Martin O'Connell. 2003. "Married-Couple and Unmarried-Partner Households: 2000." *Census 2000 Special Reports,* CENBR-5. Washington, DC: U.S. Government Printing Office.

Singel, Ryan. 2008. "FBI Tried to Cover Patriot Act Abuses with Flawed, Retroactive Subpoenas, Audit Finds." *Wired,* March 13. Accessed June 30, 2009 (www.wired.com/threatlevel/2008/03/fbi-tried-to-co).

Slater, Lauren. 2012. *The $60,000 Dog: My Life with Animals.* Boston: Beacon Press.

Sluiter, Engel. 1997. "New Light on the '20. and Odd Negroes' Arriving in Virginia, August 1619." *The William and Mary Quarterly* 54: 395–398.

Small Arms Survey. 2011. "Estimating Civilian Owned Firearms." Graduate Institute of International and Development Studies, Geneva, Switzerland, *Research Note* 9 (September). Accessed May 23, 2013 (www.smallarmssurvey.org/fileadmin/docs/H-Research_Notes/SAS-Research-Note-9.pdf).

Smiley, Tavis, and Cornel West. 2012. "America's New Working Poor." *Salon,* May 1. Accessed May 22, 2012 (http://www.salon.com/2012/05/01/working_in_poverty/).

Smith, Aaron. 2013. "Civic Engagement in the Digital Age." Internet & American Life Project, April 25. Accessed May 22, 2013 (www.pewinternet.org/~/media//Files/Reports/2013/PIP_CivicEngagementintheDigitalAge.pdf).

Smith, Adam. [1776] 2003. *The Wealth of Nations.* New York: Bantam Classics.

Smith, Aaron, and Janna Anderson. 2014. "AI, Robotics, and the Future of Jobs." Pew Research Center, Internet, Science & Tech, August 6. Accessed March 18, 2015 (www.pewinternet.org/files/2014/08/Future-of-AI-Robotics-and-Jobs.pdf).

Smith, Courtenay, and Alison Caporimo. 2013. "Reader's Digest Trust Poll: The 100 Most Trusted People in America." *Reader's Digest,* June. Accessed March 18, 2015 (www.rd.com/slideshows/readers-digest-trust-poll-the-100-most-trusted-people-in-america/).

Smith, Dorothy E. 1987. *The Everyday World as Problematic: A Feminist Sociology.* Boston: Northeastern University Press.

Smith, Erica L., and Alexia Cooper. 2013. "Homicide in the U.S. Known to Law Enforcement, 2011." Bureau of Justice Statistics, December, NCJ 24035. Accessed February 19, 2015 (www.bjs.gov/content/pub/pdf/hus11.pdf).

Smith, Jessica C., and Carla Medalia. 2014. "Health Insurance Coverage in the United States: 2013." *Current Population Reports,* P60-250. Washington, DC: U.S. Government Printing Office. Accessed May 2, 2015 (www.census.gov/content/dam/Census/library/publications/2014/demo/p60-250.pdf).

Smith, Stacy L., Marc Choueiti, and Katherine Pieper. 2014. "Race/Ethnicity in 600 Popular Films: Examining On Screen Portrayals and Behind the Camera Diversity." Media, Diversity, & Social Change Initiative, Annenberg School of Communication & Journalism, August 4. Accessed April 28, 2015 (http://annenberg.usc.edu/sitecore/shell/Applications/Content%20Manager/~/media/MDSCI/Racial%20Inequality%20in%20Film%202007-2013%20Final.ashx).

Smith, Adam. [1776] 2003. *The Wealth of Nations.* New York: Bantam Classics.

Smith, Dorothy E. 1987. *The Everyday World as Problematic: A Feminist Sociology.* Boston: Northeastern University Press.

Smith, Tom W. 2004. "Coming of Age in Twenty-first Century America: Public Attitudes Towards the Importance and Timing of Transitions to Adulthood." *Ageing International* 29 (2): 136–148.

———. 2006. "American Sexual Behavior: Trends, Socio-Demographic Differences, and Risk Behavior." National Opinion Research Center, University of Chicago, GSS Topical Report No. 25. Updated March, 2006. Accessed May 12, 2010 (www.norc.org/NR/rdonlyres/2663F09F-2E74-436E-AC81-6FFBF288E183/0/AmericanSexualBehavior2006.pdf).

———. 2011. "Public Attitudes toward Homosexuality." NORC/University of Chicago, September 2011. Accessed May 26, 2012 (www.norc.org/PDFs/2011%20GSS%20Reports/GSS_Public%20Attitudes%20Toward%20Homosexuality_Sept2011.pdf).

Smith, Tom W., Peter Marsden, Michael Hout, and Jibum Kim. 2014. *General Social Surveys, 1972–2012.* Chicago: National Opinion Research Center.

Social Security Administration. 2014a. *Fast Facts & Figures About Social Security, 2014.* Office of Retirement and Disability Policy, Office of Research, Evaluation, and Statistics, Washington, DC, SSA Publication No. 13-11785, September. Accessed February 2, 2015 (www.ssa.gov/policy/docs/chartbooks/fast_facts/2014/fast_facts14.pdf).

———. 2014b. "Top 10 Baby Names for 2013: Baby Name Data." Accessed January 10, 2015 (www.ssa.gov/oact/babynames/index.html).

Soderstrom, Melanie. 2007. "Beyond Babytalk: Re-evaluating the Nature and Content of Speech Input to Preverbal Infants." *Developmental Review* 27: 501–532.

Solove, Daniel J. 2008. "Do Social Networks Bring the End of Privacy?" *Scientific American* 299 (September): 100–106. Accessed June 30, 2009 (www.scientificamerican.com/article.cfm?id5do-social-networks-bring).

Sorokin, Pitirim A. [1927] 1959. *Social and Cultural Mobility.* New York: Free Press.

Spalter-Roth, Roberta, and Nicole Van Vooren. 2008a. "What Are They Doing with a Bachelor's Degree in Sociology?" American Sociological Association Department of Research and Development. Washington, DC: ASA. Accessed March 25, 2010 (www.asanet.org/images/research/docs/pdf/What%20Are%20They%20Doing%20with%20BA%20in%20Soc.pdf).

———. 2008b. "Pathways to Job Satisfaction." American Sociological Association Department of Research and Development. Washington, DC: ASA. Accessed March 25, 2010 (www.asanet.org/images/research/docs/pdf/Pathways%20to%20Job%20Satisfaction.pdf).

———. 2009. "Idealists vs. Careerists: Graduate School Choices of Sociology Majors." American Sociological Association Department of Research and Development. Washington, DC: ASA. Accessed March 25, 2010 (www.asanet.org/images/research/docs/pdf/Idealist%20vs%20Careerisst.pdf).

———. 2010. "Mixed Success: Four Years of Experiences of 2005 Sociology Graduates." American Sociological Association Department of Research and Development. Washington, DC: American Sociological Association. Accessed May 5, 2011 (www.asanet.org/research/BBMixedSuccessBrief.pdf).

Spalter-Roth, Roberta, Nicole Van Vooren, Michael Kisielewski, and Mary S. Senter. 2012. "Recruiting Sociology Majors: What Are the Effects of the Great Recession?" American Sociological Association, Department of Research & Development, November. Accessed April 26, 2013 (www.asanet.org/documents/research/pdfs/Bachelors_and_Beyond_2012_Brief2_Recruiting .pdf).

Sprague, Joey. 2005. *Feminist Methodologies for Critical Research: Bridging Differences.* Lanham, MD: AltaMira Press.

Squire, Peverill. 1988. "Why the 1936 *Literary Digest* Poll Failed." *Public Opinion Quarterly* 52: 125–133.

Srinivas, M. N. 1956. "A Note on Sanskritization and Westernization." *The Far Eastern Quarterly* 15: 481–496.

Staal, J. F. 1963. "Sanskrit and Sanskritization." *Journal of Asian Studies* 22: 261–275.

Stack, Carol. 1974. *All Our Kin: Strategies for Survival in a Black Community.* New York: Harper & Row.

Stafford, Laura. 2010. "Geographic Distance and Communication During Courtship." *Communication Research* 37 (2): 275–297.

Standish, Peter, and Steven Bell. 2004. *Culture and Customs of Mexico.* Santa Barbara, CA: Greenwood Press.

Stark, Rodney, and William Sims Bainbridge. 1979. "Of Churches, Sects, and Cults: Preliminary Concepts for a Theory of Religious Movements." *Journal for the Scientific Study of Religion* 18 (June): 117–131.

———. 1985. *The Future of Religion.* Berkeley: University of California Press.

Starr, Paul. 1982. *The Social Transformation of American Medicine.* New York: Basic Books.

Stavenhagen, Rodolfo. 1994. "The Indian Resurgence in Mexico." *Cultural Survival Quarterly* (Summer/Fall): 77–80.

Steele, Jonathan. 2005. "Annan Attacks Britain and U.S. over Erosion of Human Rights." *Guardian Weekly,* March 16, p. 1.

Steidle, Brian. 2007. *The Devil Came on Horseback: Bearing Witness to the Genocide in Darfur.* New York: PublicAffairs.

Stein, Arlene. 2010. "The Incredible Shrinking Lesbian World and Other Queer Conundra." *Sexualities* 13 (1): 21–32.

Stenning, Derrick J. 1958. "Household Viability Among the Pastoral Fulani." Pp. 92–119 in *The Developmental Cycle in Domestic Groups,* ed. John R. Goody. Cambridge, UK: Cambridge University Press.

Sterbenz, Christina. 2014. "Marriage Rates Are Near Their Lowest Levels in History—Here's Why." *Business Insider,* May 7. Accessed February 26, 2015 (www.businessinsider.com/causes-of-low-marriage-rates-2014-5).

Stevenson, Mark. 2011. "Money Sent Home by Mexican Migrants Holds Steady." *Chron,* February 1. Accessed June 13, 2011 (www.chron.com/disp/story.mpl/business/7408082.html).

Stewart, Quincy Thomas. 2006. "Reinvigorating Relative Deprivation: A New Measure for a Classic Concept." *Social Science Research* 35 (3): 779–802.

Stewart, Susan D. 2007. *Brave New Stepfamilies: Diverse Paths Toward Stepfamily Living.* Thousand Oaks, CA: Sage.

Stitt, Carmen, and Dale Kunkel. 2008. "Food Advertising During Children's Television Programming on Broadcast and Cable Channels." *Health Communication* 23: 573–584.

Stoeckel, Luke E., Lori S. Palley, Randy L. Gollub, Steven M. Niemi, and Anne Eden Evins. 2014. "Patterns of Brain Activation When Mothers View Their Own Child and Dog: An fMRI Study." *PLos ONE* 9 (10): e107205. Accessed February 26, 2015 (http://journals.plos.org/plosone/article?id=10.1371/journal.pone.0107205).

Stone, Charley, Carl Van Horn, and Cliff Zukin. 2012. "Chasing the American Dream: Recent College Graduates and the Great Recession." WorkTrends: Americans' Attitudes About Work, Employers, and Government, John J. Heldrich Center for Workforce Development, Rutgers University, May 2012. Accessed May 22, 2012 (www.heldrich.rutgers.edu/sites/default/files/content/Chasing_American_Dream_Report.pdf).

Stratton, Terry D., and Jennifer L. McGivern-Snofsky. 2008. "Toward a Sociological Understanding of Complementary and Alternative Medicine Use." *Journal of Alternative and Complementary Medicine* 14 (6): 777–783.

Strauss, Gary. 2002. " 'Good Old Boys' Network Still Rules Corporate Boards." *USA Today,* November 1, pp. B1, B2.

Streib, Jessi. 2011. "Class Reproduction by Four Year Olds." *Qualitative Sociology* 34 (2): 337–352.

Stretesky, Paul B. 2006. "Corporate Self-Policing and the Environment." *Criminology* 44 (3): 671.

Strogatz, Steven. 2012. "Friends You Can Count On." *The New York Times,* September 17. Accessed February 11, 2015 (http://opinionator.blogs.nytimes.com/2012/09/17/friends-you-can-count-on/).

Strom, Stephanie. 2011. "Off Media Radar, Famine Garners Few Donations." *The New York Times,* August 1. Accessed August 8, 2011 (www.nytimes.com/2011/08/02/world/africa/02donate.html).

Stryker, Susan. 2007. "Transgender Feminism: Queering the Woman Question." Pp. 59–70 in *Third Wave Feminism: A Critical Exploration,* expanded 2nd ed., ed. Stacy Gillis, Gillian Howie, and Rebecca Munford. New York: Palgrave Macmillan.

Sullivan, Kevin. 2006. "In War-Torn Congo, Going Wireless to Reach Home." *The Washington Post,* July 9. Accessed May 6, 2009 (www.washingtonpost.com/wp-dyn/content/article/2006/07/08/AR2006070801063.html).

Sumner, William G. 1906. *Folkways.* New York: Ginn.

Sun, Yongmin, and Yuanzhang Li. 2008. "Stable Postdivorce Family Structures During Late Adolescence and Socioeconomic Consequences in Adulthood." *Journal of Marriage and Family* 70 (1): 129–143.

Sutcliffe, Bob. 2002. *100 Ways of Seeing an Unequal World.* London: Zed Books.

Sutherland, Edwin H. 1940. "White-Collar Criminality." *American Sociological Review* 5 (February): 1–11.

———. 1949. *White Collar Crime.* New York: Dryden.

———. 1983. *White Collar Crime: The Uncut Version.* New Haven, CT: Yale University Press.

Sutherland, Edwin H., Donald R. Cressey, and David F. Luckenbill. 1992. *Principles of Criminology,* 11th ed. New York: Rowman & Littlefield.

Suzuki, Toru. 2009. "Fertility Decline and Governmental Interventions in Eastern Asian Advanced Countries." *Japanese Journal of Population* 7 (1): 47–56.

Swatos, William H., Jr. 2011. "Encyclopedia of Religion and Society." Hartford Institute for Religion Research, Hartford Seminary, Hartford, Connecticut. Accessed June 6, 2011 (http://hirr.hartsem.edu/ency/).

Swatos, William H., Jr., ed. 1998. *Encyclopedia of Religion and Society.* Lanham, MD: AltaMira Press.

Swidler, Ann. 1986. "Culture in Action: Symbols and Strategies." *American Sociological Review* 51 (April): 273–286.

Szasz, Thomas S. 1971. "The Same Slave: An Historical Note on the Use of Medical Diagnosis as Justificatory Rhetoric." *American Journal of Psychotherapy* 25 (April): 228–239.

T

Tafur, Maritza Montiel, Terry K. Crowe, and Eliseo Torres. 2009. "A Review of Curanderismo and Healing Practices Among Mexicans and Mexican Americans." *Occupational Therapy International* 16 (1): 82–88.

Tasker, Fiona. 2005. "Lesbian Mothers, Gay Fathers, and Their Children: A Review." *Journal of Developmental and Behavioral Pediatrics* 26: 224–240.

Tate, Shirley Anne. 2009. *Black Beauty: Aesthetics, Stylization, Politics.* Burlington, VT: Ashgate.

Taylor, Dorceta E. 2000. "The Rise of the Environmental Justice Paradigm."*American Behavioral Scientist* 43 (January): 508–580.

Taylor, Frederick Winslow. 1911. *The Principles of Scientific Management.* New York: Harper & Brothers.

Taylor, Jonathan B., and Joseph P. Kalt. 2005. *American Indians on Reservations: A Data Book of Socioeconomic Change Between the 1990 and 2000 Censuses.* Cambridge, MA: Harvard Project on American Indian Development.

Taylor, Paul. 2011. "Is College Worth It? College Presidents, Public Assess Value, Quality and Mission of Higher Education." A Pew Research Center Social & Demographic Trends Report, May 16. Accessed May 22, 2012 (www.pewsocialtrends.org/files/2011/05/higher-ed-report.pdf).

Taylor, Paul, and Richard Morin. 2008. "Americans Say They Like Diverse Communities; Election, Census Trends Suggest Otherwise." Pew Research Center Report, December 2. Accessed May 17, 2010 (http://pewsocialtrends.org/assets/pdf/diverse-political-communities.pdf).

Taylor, Paul, Rich Morin, Kim Parker, D'Vera Cohn, and Wendy Wang. 2009. *Growing Old in America: Expectations vs. Reality.* Pew Research Center Social & Demographic Trends Project, January. Accessed April 5, 2010 (http://pewsocialtrends.org/assets/pdf/Getting-Old-in-America.pdf).

Taylor, Verta. 1999. "Gender and Social Movements: Gender Processes in Women's Self-Help Movements." *Gender and Society* 13: 8–33.

———. 2004. "Social Movements and Gender." Pp. 14348–14352 in *International Encyclopedia of the Social and Behavioral Sciences,* ed. Neil J. Smelser and Paul B. Baltes. New York: Elsevier.

Tejada-Vera, Betzaida, and Paul D. Sutton. 2009. "Births, Marriages, Divorces, and Deaths: Provisional Data for 2008." *National Vital Statistics Reports* 57 (19). Hyattsville, MD: National Center for Health Statistics. Accessed April 11, 2010 (www.cdc.gov/nchs/data/nvsr/nvsr57/nvsr57_19.pdf).

———. 2010. "Births, Marriages, Divorces, and Deaths: Provisional Data for 2009." *National Vital Statistics Reports* 58 (25). Hyattsville, MD: National Center for Health Statistics. Accessed May 28, 2011 (www.cdc.gov/nchs/data/nvsr/nvsr58/nvsr58_25.pdf).

Terkel, Studs. 2003. *Hope Dies Last: Keeping the Faith in Difficult Times.* New York: New Press.

Terry, Sara. 2000. "Whose Family? The Revolt of the Child-Free." *Christian Science Monitor,* August 29, pp. 1, 4.

Tertilt, Michèle. 2005. "Polygyny, Fertility, and Savings." *Journal of Political Economy* 113 (6): 1341–1370.

Thomas, Gordon, and Max Morgan Witts. 1974. *Voyage of the Damned.* Greenwich, CT: Fawcett Crest.

Thomas, William I., and Dorothy Swain Thomas. 1928. *The Child in America: Behavior Problems and Programs.* New York: Knopf.

Thompson, Warren S. 1929. "Population." *American Journal of Sociology* 34 (6): 959–975.

———. 1948. *Plenty of People: The World's Population Pressures, Problems and Policies and How They Concern Us,* rev. ed. New York: Ronald Press.

Thomson, Elizabeth, and Eva Bernhardt. 2010. "Education, Values, and Cohabitation in Sweden." *Marriage & Family Review* 46 (1/2): 1–21.

Thornton, John. 1998. "The African Experience of the '20. and Odd Negroes' Arriving in Virginia in 1619." *The William and Mary Quarterly* 55: 421–434.

Tierney, John. 2003. "Iraqi Family Ties Complicate American Efforts for Change." *The New York Times,* September 28, pp. A1, A22.

Tilly, Charles. 1993. *Popular Contention in Great Britain 1758–1834.* Cambridge, MA: Harvard University Press.

———. 2004. *Social Movements, 1768–2004.* Boulder, CO: Paradigm.

Tolbert, Kathryn. 2000. "In Japan, Traveling Alone Begins at Age 6." *The Washington Post National Weekly Edition* 17, May 15, p. 17.

Tonkinson, Robert. 1978. *The Mardudjara Aborigines.* New York: Henry Holt.

Tönnies, Ferdinand. [1887] 1988. *Community and Society.* New Brunswick, NJ: Transaction.

Toossi, Mitra. 2004. "Labor Force Projections to 2012: The Graying of the U.S. Workforce." *Monthly Labor Review,* February: 37–57.

———. 2013. "Labor Force Projections to 2022: The Labor Force Participation Rate Continues to Fall." *Monthly Labor Review,* Bureau of Labor Statistics, U.S. Department of Labor, December. Accessed February 2, 2015 (www.bls.gov/opub/mlr/2013/article/labor-force-projections-to-2022-the-labor-force-participation-rate-continues-to-fall.htm).

Truman, Jennifer L., and Lynn Langton. 2014. "Criminal Victimization, 2013: National Crime Victimization Survey." *Bureau of Justice Statistics Bulletin,* October, NCJ 247648. Accessed February 19, 2015 (www.bjs.gov/content/pub/pdf/cv13.pdf).

Tucker, Erika. 2013. "The Royal Baby: How Will and Kate Are Breaking with Tradition." *Global News,* July 23. Accessed February 26, 2015 (http://globalnews.ca/news/736296/the-royal-baby-how-will-and-kate-are-breaking-with-tradition/).

Tully, Shawn. 2012. "The 2011 Fortune 500: The Big Boys Rack Up Record-Setting Profits." *CNNMoney,* May 7. Accessed May 22, 2012 (www.dailyfinance.com/2012/05/07/the-2011-fortune-500-the-big-boys-rack-up-record-setting-profit/).

Ture, Kwame, and Charles Hamilton. 1992. *Black Power: The Politics of Liberation,* rev. ed. New York: Vintage Books.

Turkle, Sherry. 2011. *Alone Together: Why We Expect More from Technology and Less from Each Other.* New York: Basic Books.

Twitchell, James B. 2000. "The Stone Age." Pp. 44–48 in *Do Americans Shop Too Much?,* ed. Juliet Schor. Boston: Beacon Press.

U

UNAIDS. 2013. "2013 Global Fact Sheet." Joint United Nations Programme on HIV/AIDS (UNAIDS). Accessed May 1, 2015 (www.unaids.org/sites/default/files/en/media/unaids/contentassets/documents/epidemiology/2013/gr2013/20130923_FactSheet_Global_en.pdf).

———. 2014. *The Gap Report.* Joint United Nations Programme on HIV/AIDS (UNAIDS), September. Accessed May 1, 2015 (www.unaids.org/sites/default/files/media_asset/UNAIDS_Gap_report_en.pdf).

UNCTAD. 2009. "Mainstreaming Gender in Trade Policy." United Nations Conference on Trade and Development, March 10–11, Geneva. Accessed June 18, 2009 (www.unctad.org/Templates/WebFlyer.asp?intItemID54760&lang51).

United Nations. 1999. "The World at Six Billion." Population Division, Department of Economic and Social Affairs, United Nations Secretariat, October. Accessed June 28, 2011 (www.un.org/esa/population/publications/sixbillion/sixbillion.htm).

———. 2010. *The Millennium Development Goals Report: 2010.* New York: United Nations. Accessed June 12, 2011 (www.un.org/millenniumgoals/reports.shtml).

———. 2011a. "Net Number of Migrants (Both Sexes Combined) by Major Area, Region and Country, 1950–2100 (Thousands)." *World Population Prospects: The 2010 Revision.* Department of Economic and Social Affairs, Population Division. Accessed June 27, 2011 (http://esa.un.org/unpd/wpp/Excel-Data/migration.htm).

———. 2011b. "Net Migration Rate by Major Area, Region and Country, 1950–2100 (per 1,000 Population)." *World Population Prospects: The 2010 Revision.* Department of Economic and Social Affairs, Population Division. Accessed June 27, 2011 (http://esa.un.org/unpd/wpp/Excel-Data/migration.htm).

———. 2013a. "World Marriage Data 2012." Department of Economic and Social Affairs, Population Division, Fertility and Family Planning Section. Accessed May 28, 2013 (www.un.org/esa/population/publications/WMD2012/MainFrame.html).

———. 2013b. "World Contraceptive Patterns 2013." Department of Economic and Social Affairs, Population Division, October. Accessed April 21, 2015 (www.un.org/en/development/desa/population/publications/family/contraceptive-wallchart-2013.shtml).

———.2013c. *International Migration Report 2013.* Department of Economic and Social Affairs, Population Division, December. Accessed April 29, 2015 (www.un.org/en/development/desa/population/publications/pdf/migration/migrationreport2013/Full_Document_final.pdf).

———. 2013d. "Population Growth Rate." *World Population Prospects: The 2012 Revision.* Population Division, Department of Economic and Social Affairs. Accessed April 30, 2015 (http://esa.un.org/wpp/Excel-Data/population.htm).

———. 2013e. "Total Population—Both Sexes." *World Population Prospects: The 2012 Revision.* Population Division, Department of Economic and Social Affairs. Accessed April 30, 2015 (http://esa.un.org/wpp/Excel-Data/population.htm).

———. 2013f. "Population by Age Groups." *World Population Prospects: The 2012 Revision.* Population Division, Department of Economic and Social Affairs. Accessed April 30, 2015 (http://esa.un.org/wpp/Excel-Data/population.htm).

———. 2014a. *The Millennium Development Goals Report 2014.* New York: United Nations. Accessed April 14, 2015 (www.un.org/millenniumgoals/2014%20MDG%20report/MDG%202014%20English%20web.pdf).

United Nations Development Programme. 2000. *Poverty Report 2000: Overcoming Human Poverty.* Washington, DC: UNDP.

———. 2008. *Human Development Indices: A Statistical Update 2008.* New York: UNDP. Accessed June 7, 2009 (http://hdr.undp.org/en/media/HDI_2008_EN_Complete.pdf).

———. 2014. *Human Development Report 2014: Sustaining Human Progress.* New York: UNDP. Accessed April 11, 2015 (http://hdr.undp.org/en/2014-report).

United Nations Framework Convention on Climate Change. 2015a. "Kyoto Protocol." Accessed May 3, 2015 (http://unfccc.int/kyoto_protocol/items/2830.php).

———. 2015b. "Status of Ratification of the Kyoto Protocol." Accessed May 3, 2015 (http://unfccc.int/kyoto_protocol/status_of_ratification/items/2613.php).

UN News Service. 2010. "Darfur: Security Council Warned of 'Significant Challenges' to Peace Process." UN News Centre, May 20. Accessed May 28, 2010 (www.un.org/apps/news/story.asp?NewsID534761&Cr5&Crl5).

United States Coast Guard. 2011. "Report of Investigation into the Circumstances Surrounding the Explosion, Fire, Sinking and Loss of Eleven Crew Members Aboard the Mobile Offshore Drilling Unit Deepwater Horizon in the Gulf of Mexico April 20–22, 2010." MISLE Activity Number: 3721503. Accessed June 30, 2011 (www.uscg.mil/history/docs/USCGDeepwaterHorizon3721503.pdf).

UNODC. 2010. *The Globalization of Crime: A Transnational Organized Crime Threat Assessment.* Vienna: United Nations Office on Drugs and Crime. Accessed April 24, 2012 (www.unodc.org/documents/data-and-analysis/tocta/TOCTA_Report_2010_low_res.pdf).

———. 2014. *Global Study on Homicide 2013: Trends, Contexts, Data.* United Nations Office on Drugs and Crime, 14.IV.1.

Accessed February 19, 2015 (www.unodc.org/documents/gsh/pdfs/2014_GLOBAL_HOMICIDE_BOOK_web.pdf).

U.S. Census Bureau. 1975. *Historical Statistics of the United States, Colonial Times to 1970.* Washington, DC: U.S. Government Printing Office.

———. 2010a. "2010 National Population Projections: Tables and Charts." Accessed June 20, 2015 (http://factfinder.census.gov/faces/nav/jsf/pages/index.xhtml).

———. 2010b. "Observations from the Interagency Technical Working Group on Developing a Supplemental Poverty Measure." Accessed April 25, 2010 (www.census.gov/hhes/www/poverty/SPM_TWGObservations.pdf).

———. 2010c. "The Questions on the Form." Accessed May 16, 2010 (http://2010.census.gov/2010census/pdf/2010_Questionnaire_Info.pdf).

———. 2010f. "Historical Income Tables—Households." Accessed June 9, 2011 (www.census.gov/hhes/www/income/data/historical/household/index.html).

———. 2011a. *Statistical Abstract of the United States: 2012* (131st Edition). Washington, DC: U.S. Government Printing Office. Accessed April 5, 2012 (www.census.gov/compendia/statab/).

———. 2012a. "Current Population Survey (CPS)—Definitions." Washington, DC: U.S. Census Bureau. Accessed May 2, 2012 (www.census.gov/cps/about/cpsdef.html).

———. 2012l. "Families and Living Arrangements: Living Arrangements of Adults." Washington, DC: U.S. Census Bureau. Accessed May 28, 2013 (www.census.gov/hhes/families/data/adults.html).

———. 2012o. "Voting and Registration in the Election of November 2012—Detailed Tables." Accessed June 2, 2013 (www.census.gov/hhes/www/socdemo/voting/publications/p20/2012/tables.html).

———. 2012q. "Selected Population Profile in the United States—2011 American Community Survey 1-Year Estimates." American FactFinder. Accessed June 6, 2013 (http://factfinder2.census.gov/faces/nav/jsf/pages/searchresults.xhtml).

———. 2013b. "Detailed Tables on Wealth and Asset Ownership: 2011." Accessed June 3, 2013 (www.census.gov/people/wealth/data/dtables.html).

———. 2013d. "Services (Main)." Accessed March 17, 2015 (www.census.gov/econ/services.html).

———. 2014a. "Table PINC-03. Educational Attainment—People 25 Years Old and Over, by Total Money Earnings in 2013, Work Experience in 2013, Age, Race, Hispanic Origin, and Sex." Annual Social and Economic Supplement. Washington, DC: U.S. Census Bureau. Accessed January 10, 2015. (www.census.gov/hhes/www/cpstables/032014/perinc/pinc03_000.htm).

———. 2014b. "2013 Poverty Table of Contents." Current Population Survey, Annual Social and Economic Supplement. Accessed February 2, 2015 (www.census.gov/hhes/www/cpstables/032014/pov/toc.htm).

———. 2014c. "Same Sex Couples Main." Washington, DC: U.S. Census Bureau. Accessed February 26, 2015 (www.census.gov/hhes/samesex/).

———. 2014d. "ACS Demographic and Housing Estimates: 2013 American Community Survey 1-Year Estimates." American FactFinder. Accessed March 18, 2015 (http://factfinder.census.gov/faces/tableservices/jsf/pages/productview.xhtml?pid=ACS_13_1YR_DP05&prodType=table).

———. 2014e. "Historical Income Tables—Households." Accessed March 22, 2015 (www.census.gov/hhes/www/income/data/historical/household/).

———. 2014f. "Historical Poverty Tables—People." Accessed March 26, 2015 (www.census.gov/hhes/www/poverty/data/historical/people.html).

———. 2014g. "Selected Population Profile in the United States—2013 American Community Survey 1-Year Estimates." American FactFinder. Accessed April 23, 2015 (http://factfinder.census.gov/faces/nav/jsf/pages/searchresults.xhtml).

———. 2014h. "2014 National Population Projections: Summary Tables." Accessed April 28, 2015 (www.census.gov/population/projections/data/national/2014/summarytables.html).

———. 2015a. "Families and Living Arrangements: Marital Status." Washington, DC: U.S. Census Bureau. Accessed February 26, 2015 (www.census.gov/hhes/families/data/marital.html).

———. 2015b. "Families and Living Arrangements: Households." Washington, DC: U.S. Census Bureau. Accessed February 26, 2015 (www.census.gov/hhes/families/data/households.html).

———. 2015c. "Families and Living Arrangements: Families." Washington, DC: U.S. Census Bureau. Accessed February 26, 2015 (www.census.gov/hhes/families/data/families.html).

———. 2015d. "Families and Living Arrangements: Family Groups." Washington, DC: U.S. Census Bureau. Accessed February 26, 2015 (www.census.gov/hhes/families/data/cps2014FG.html).

———. 2015e. "Families and Living Arrangements: Children." Washington, DC: U.S. Census Bureau. Accessed February 26, 2015 (www.census.gov/hhes/families/data/cps2014C.html).

———. 2015f. "Families and Living Arrangements: Living Arrangements of Children." Washington, DC: U.S. Census Bureau. Accessed February 26, 2015 (www.census.gov/hhes/families/data/children.html).

———. 2015g. "Families and Living Arrangements: Living Arrangements of Adults." Washington, DC: U.S. Census Bureau. Accessed February 26, 2015 (www.census.gov/hhes/families/data/adults.html).

———. 2015h. "Educational Attainment: CPS Historical Time Series Tables." Washington, DC: U.S. Census Bureau. Accessed March 10, 2015 (www.census.gov/hhes/socdemo/education/data/cps/historical/index.html).

———. 2015i. "World Vital Events per Time Unit: 2015." World Vital Events, International Data Base. Accessed April 30, 2015 (www.census.gov/population/international/data/idb/worldvitalevents.php).

U.S. Commission on Civil Rights. 1976. *A Guide to Federal Laws and Regulations Prohibiting Sex Discrimination.* Washington, DC: U.S. Government Printing Office.

———. 2009. "Racial Categorization in the 2010 Census: A Briefing Before the United States Commission on Civil Rights Held in Washington, DC, April 7, 2006." Briefing Report. Accessed May 16, 2010 (www.usccr.gov/pubs/RC2010Web_Version.pdf).

U.S. Copyright Office. 2013. "Fiscal 2013 Annual Report." Library of Congress, Washington, D.C. Accessed May 4, 2015 (http://copyright.gov/reports/annual/2013/ar2013.pdf).

U.S. Customs Border and Border Protection. 2014a. "U.S. Border Patrol Fiscal Year Southwest Border Sector Deaths (FY 1998–FY 2014)." Accessed April 16, 2015 (www.cbp.gov/sites/default/files/documents/BP%20Southwest%20Border%20Sector%20Deaths%20FY1998%20-%20FY2014_0.pdf).

———. 2014b. "U.S. Border Patrol Fiscal Year Southwest Border Sector Apprehensions (FY 1960–FY 2014)." Accessed April 16, 2015 (www.cbp.gov/sites/default/files/documents/BP%20Southwest%20Border%20Sector%20Apps%20FY1960%20-%20FY2014_0.pdf).

U.S. Department of Agriculture. 2014. "Real Per Capita GDP (2010 Dollars) Historical." International Macroeconomic Data Set, Economic Research Service, Washington, DC. Accessed March 18, 2015 (http://ers.usda.gov/data-products/international-macroeconomic-data-set.aspx).

U.S. Department of Education. 2013. "Digest of Education Statistics: Advance Release of Selected 2012 Digest Tables." National Center for Education Statistics, Institute of Education Sciences. Accessed May 30, 2013 (http://nces.ed.gov/programs/digest/2012menu_tables.asp).

———. 2014. "List of 2013 Digest Tables." Washington, DC: Institute of Education Services, U.S. Department of Education. Accessed March 10, 2015 (http://nces.ed.gov/programs/digest/2013menu_tables.asp).

———. 2015. "List of 2014 Digest Tables." Washington, DC: Institute of Education Services, U.S. Department of Education. Accessed March 10, 2015 (http://nces.ed.gov/programs/digest/2014menu_tables.asp).

U.S. Department of Health and Human Services. 2014. "The AFCARS Report." Administration for Children and Families, Administration on Children, Youth and Families, Children's Bureau, July, No. 21. Accessed February 26, 2015 (www.acf.hhs.gov/sites/default/files/cb/afcarsreport21.pdf).

U.S. Department of Justice. 1999. "Ten-Year Program to Compensate Japanese Americans Interned During World War II Closes Its Doors." Press release No. 059, February 19. Accessed June 3, 2010 (www.justice.gov/opa/pr/1999/February/059cr.htm).

———. 2014a. "Offenses Known to Law Enforcement." *Crime in the United States, 2013*. Washington, DC: U.S. Department of Justice, Federal Bureau of Investigation. February 19, 2015 (www.fbi.gov/about-us/cjis/ucr/crime-in-the-u.s/2013/crime-in-the-u.s.-2013/offenses-known-to-law-enforcement/offenses-known-to-law-enforcement).

———. 2014b. "2013 Crime Clock Statistics." *Crime in the United States, 2013*. Washington, DC: U.S. Department of Justice, Federal Bureau of Investigation. Accessed February 19, 2015 (www.fbi.gov/about-us/cjis/ucr/crime-in-the-u.s/2013/crime-in-the-u.s.-2013/offenses-known-to-law-enforcement/crime-clock).

———. 2014c. "Hate Crime Statistics 2013." *Crime in the United States, 2013*. Washington, DC: U.S. Department of Justice, Federal Bureau of Investigation. Accessed April 20, 2015 (www.fbi.gov/about-us/cjis/ucr/hate-crime/2013).

———. 2015a. "Justice Department Announces Findings of Two Civil Rights Investigations in Ferguson, Missouri." Office of Public Affairs, March 4. Accessed April 26, 2015 (www.justice.gov/opa/pr/justice-department-announces-findings-two-civil-rights-investigations-ferguson-missouri).

———. 2015b. *Investigation of the Ferguson Police Department*. Civil Rights Division, March 4. Accessed April 27, 2015 (www.justice.gov/sites/default/files/opa/press-releases/attachments/2015/03/04/ferguson_police_department_report.pdf).

U.S. Department of State. 2014a. "FY 2013 Annual Report on Intercountry Adoption." U.S. Department of State, Washington, DC, March. Accessed February 26, 2015 (http://travel.state.gov/content/dam/aa/pdfs/fy2013_annual_report.pdf).

———. 2014b. *Trafficking in Persons Report: June 2014*. Washington, DC. Accessed April 16, 2015 (www.state.gov/j/tip/rls/tiprpt/2014/).

U.S. Patent and Trademark Office. 2015. "U.S. Patent Statistics Chart: Calendar Years 1963–2014." Patent Technology Monitoring Team. Accessed May 4, 2015 (www.uspto.gov/web/offices/ac/ido/oeip/taf/us_stat.htm).

Utne, Leif. 2003. "We Are All Zapatistas." *Utne Reader,* November/December, pp. 36–37.

V

van den Bergh, Linda, Eddie Denessen, Lisette Hornstra, Marinus Voeten, and Rob W. Holland. 2010. "The Implicit Prejudiced Attitudes of Teachers: Relations to Teacher Expectations and the Ethnic Achievement Gap." *American Educational Research Journal,* January. doi: 10.3102/0002831209353594.

Van Dijk, Jan, John van Kesteren, and Paul Smit. 2007. *Criminal Victimisation in International Perspective, Key Findings from the 2004–2005 ICVS and EU ICS.* The Hague: Boom Legal. Accessed May 20, 2009 (http://rechten.uvt.nl/icvs/pdffiles/ICVS2004_05.pdf).

Vanderstraeten, Raf. 2007. "Professions in Organizations, Professional Work in Education." *British Journal of Sociology of Education* 28 (5): 621–635.

Veblen, Thorstein. [1899] 1964. *Theory of the Leisure Class.* New York: Macmillan.

———. 1919. *The Vested Interests and the State of the Industrial Arts.* New York: Huebsch.

Venkatesh, Sudhir. 2006. *Off the Books: The Underground Economy of the Urban Poor.* Cambridge, MA: Harvard University Press.

Venter, Craig. 2000. "Remarks at the Human Genome Announcement, at the White House." Accessed June 30, 2008 (www.celera.com/celera/pr_1056647999).

Virtcom. 2009. "Board Diversification Strategy: Realizing Competitive Advantage and Shareholder Value." A Whitepaper by Virtcom Consulting, prepared for CalPERS. Accessed June 22, 2009 (www.calpers-governance.org/docs-sof/marketinitiatives/initiatives/board-diversity-white-paper.pdf).

Vogt, W. Paul, Dianne C. Gardner, and Lynne M. Haeffele. 2012. *When to Use What Research Design.* New York: Guilford Press.

Vowell, Paul R., and Jieming Chen. 2004. "Predicting Academic Misconduct: A Comparative Test of Four Sociological Explanations." *Sociological Inquiry* 74 (2): 226–249.

W

Waites, Matthew. 2009. "Critique of 'Sexual Orientation' and 'Gender Identity' in Human Rights Discourse: Global Queer Politics Beyond the Yogyakarta Principles." *Contemporary Politics* 15 (1): 137–156.

Waldman, Amy. 2004a. "India Takes Economic Spotlight, and Critics Are Unkind." *The New York Times,* March 7, p. 3.

———. 2004b. "Low-Tech or High, Jobs Are Scarce in India's Boom." *The New York Times,* May 6, p. A3.

———. 2004c. "What India's Upset Vote Reveals: The High Tech Is Skin Deep." *The New York Times,* May 15, p. A5.

Walker, Iain, and Heather J. Smith, eds. 2002. *Relative Deprivation: Specification, Development, and Integration.* New York: Cambridge University Press.

Walker, Rebecca. 1995. *To Be Real: Telling the Truth and Changing the Face of Feminism.* Berkeley: University of California Press.

Wallerstein, Immanuel. 1974. *The Modern World System.* New York: Academic Press.

———. 1979b. *The End of the World as We Know It: Social Science for the Twenty-first Century.* Minneapolis: University of Minnesota Press.

———. 2000. *The Essential Wallerstein.* New York: New Press.

———. 2004. *World-Systems Analysis: An Introduction.* Durham, NC: Duke University Press.

———. 2010. "Structural Crises." *New Left Review* 62 (March/April): 133–142.

Wallerstein, Judith S., Julia M. Lewis, and Sandra Blakeslee. 2000. *The Unexpected Legacy of Divorce: A 25-Year Landmark Study.* New York: Basic Books.

Wallis, Claudia. 2008. "How to Make Great Teachers." *Time,* February 25, pp. 28–34.

Walmart. 2014. "Walmart 2014 Annual Report." Bentonville, AR: Wal-Mart Stores, Inc. Accessed March 17, 2015 (http://cdn.corporate.walmart.com/66/e5/9ff9a87445949173fde56316ac5f/2014-annual-report.pdf).

Walpole, Marybeth. 2007. "Economically and Educationally Challenged Students in Higher Education: Access to Outcomes." *ASHE Higher Education Report* 33 (3).

Walsh, Froma. 2009a. "Human Animal Bonds I: The Relational Significance of Companion Animals." *Family Process* 48: 462–480.

———. 2009b. "Human Animal Bonds II: The Role of Pets in Family Systems and Family Therapy." *Family Process* 48: 481–499.

Wang, Wendy. 2012. "The Rise of Intermarriage: Rates, Characteristics Vary by Race and Gender." A Social & Demographic Trends Report, Pew Research Center, February 16. Accessed May 8, 2012 (www.pewsocialtrends.org/files/2012/02/SDT-Intermarriage-II.pdf).

Wang, Wendy, and Kim Parker. 2014. "Record Share of Americans Have Never Married." Pew Research Center, Social & Demographic Trends, November 20. Accessed February 26, 2015 (www.pewsocialtrends.org/files/2014/09/2014-09-24_Never-Married-Americans.pdf).

Warner, R. Stephen. 2005. *A Church of Our Own: Disestablishment and Diversity in American Religion.* New Brunswick, NJ: Rutgers University Press.

———. 2007. "The Role of Religion in the Process of Segmented Assimilation." *Annals of the American Academy of Political and Social Science* 612 (1): 100–115.

Warren, Patricia, Donald Tomaskovic-Devey, William Smith, Matthew Zingraff, and Marcinda Mason. 2006. "Driving While Black: Bias Processes and Racial Disparity in Police Stops." *Criminology* 44 (3): 709–738.

The Washington Post. 2014. "Wide Support for Striking ISIS, but Weak Approval for Obama." September 9. Accessed January 7, 2015 (www.washingtonpost.com/page/2010-2019/WashingtonPost/2014/09/09/National-Politics/Polling/release_361.xml).

Waters, Mary C. 2009. "Social Science and Ethnic Options." *Ethnicities* 9 (1): 130–135.

Watts, Duncan J. 2007. "Is Justin Timberlake a Product of Cumulative Advantage?" *The New York Times*, April 15. Accessed February 2, 2015 (www.nytimes.com/2007/04/15/magazine/15wwlnidealab.t.html).

———. 2011. *Everything Is Obvious: Once You Know the Answer.* New York: Crown Business.

Weber, Jonetta D., and Robert M. Carini. 2013. "Where Are the Female Athletes in *Sports Illustrated*? A Content Analysis of Covers (2000–2011)." *International Review for the Sociology of Sport* 48 (2): 196–203.

Weber, Max. [1913–1922] 1947. *The Theory of Social and Economic Organization,* trans. A. Henderson and T. Parsons. New York: Free Press.

———. [1904] 1949. *Methodology of the Social Sciences,* trans. Edward A. Shils and Henry A. Finch. Glencoe, IL: Free Press.

———. [1904] 2009. *The Protestant Ethic and the Spirit of Capitalism,* trans. Talcott Parsons. New York: Scribner.

———. [1916] 1958a. "Class, Status, Party." Pp. 180–195 in *From Max Weber: Essays in Sociology,* ed. H. H. Gerth and C. Wright Mills. New York: Oxford University Press.

———. [1916] 1958b. *The Religion of India: The Sociology of Hinduism and Buddhism.* New York: Free Press.

———. [1921] 1958c. "Bureaucracy." Pp. 196–244 in *From Max Weber: Essays in Sociology,* ed. H. H. Gerth and C. Wright Mills. New York: Oxford University Press.

———. [1922] 1958d. "The Social Psychology of the World Religions." Pp. 267–301 in *From Max Weber: Essays in Sociology,* ed. H. H. Gerth and C. Wright Mills. New York: Oxford University Press.

Wechsler, Henry, J. E. Lee, M. Kuo, M. Seibring, T. F. Nelson, and H. Lee. 2002. "Trends in College Binge Drinking During a Period of Increased Prevention Efforts: Findings from Four Harvard School of Public Health College Alcohol Surveys: 1993–2001." *Journal of American College Health* 50 (5): 203–217.

Wechsler, Henry, and Toben F. Nelson. 2008. "What We Have Learned from the Harvard School of Public Health College Alcohol Study: Focusing Attention on College Student Alcohol Consumption and the Environmental Conditions that Promote It." *Journal of Studies on Alcohol and Drugs* 69 (4): 481–490.

Wedge, Marilyn. 2012. "Why French Kids Don't Have ADHD." *Psychology Today*, March 8. Accessed June 7, 2013 (www.psychologytoday.com/blog/suffer-the-children/201203/why-french-kids-dont-have-adhd).

Weiss, Michael J. 2000. *The Clustered World: How We Live, What We Buy, and What It All Means About Who We Are.* Boston: Little, Brown.

Weiss, Richard. 1969. *The American Myth of Success.* New York: Basic Books.

Wells-Barnett, Ida B. [1928] 1970. *Crusade for Justice: The Autobiography of Ida B. Wells,* ed. Alfreda M. Duster. Chicago: University of Chicago Press.

Werner, Carrie A. 2011. "The Older Population: 2010." 2010 Census Briefs C2010BR-09. Washington, DC: U.S. Government Printing Office. Accessed April 6, 2012 (www.census.gov/prod/cen2010/briefs/c2010br-09.pdf).

West, Candace, and Don H. Zimmerman. 1987. "Doing Gender." *Gender and Society* 1 (June): 125–151.

Wethington, Elaine. 2000. "Expecting Stress: Americans and the 'Midlife Crisis.'" *Motivation & Emotion* 24 (2): 85–103.

Whorton, James C. 2002. *Nature Cures: The History of Alternative Medicine in America.* New York: Oxford University Press.

Wickman, Peter M. 1991. "Deviance." Pp. 85–87 in *Encyclopedic Dictionary of Sociology,* 4th ed., ed. Dushkin Publishing Group. Guilford, CT: Dushkin.

Wierzbicka, Anna. 2008. "Why There Are No 'Colour Universals' in Language and Thought." *Journal of the Royal Anthropological Institute* 14 (2): 407–425.

Wilford, John Noble. 1997. "New Clues Show Where People Made the Great Leap to Agriculture." *The New York Times,* November 18, pp. B9, B12.

Williams, Alicia, John Fries, Jean Koppen, and Robert Prisuta. 2010. *Connecting and Giving: A Report on How Midlife and Older Americans Spend Their Time, Make Connections and Build Communities.* Washington, DC: AARP.

Williams, David R., and Chiquita Collins. 2004. "Reparations." *American Behavioral Scientist* 47 (March): 977–1000.

Williams, Kristine N., and Carol A. B. Warren. 2009. "Communication in Assisted Living." *Journal of Aging Studies* 23 (1): 24–36.

Williams, Mike. 2008. "Rising Cost of Food Devastates Haiti." *Atlanta Journal Constitution,* June 17. Accessed August 12 (www.ajc.com/news/content/news/stories/2008/06/16/haiti_food_crisis.html).

Williams, Robin M., Jr. 1970. *American Society,* 3rd ed. New York: Knopf.

Wills, Jeremiah B., and Barbara J. Risman. 2006. "The Visibility of Feminist Thought in Family Studies." *Journal of Marriage and Family* 68 (August): 690–700.

Wilper, Andrew P., Steffie Woolhandler, Karen E. Lasser, Danny McCormick, David H. Bor, and David U. Himmelstein. 2009. "Health Insurance and Mortality in U.S. Adults." *American Journal of Public Health* 99 (12): 2289–2295.

Wilson, Carl. 2007. *Let's Talk About Love: A Journey to the End of Taste.* New York: Continuum.

Wilson, William Julius. 1999. *The Bridge over the Racial Divide: Rising Inequality and Coalition Politics.* Berkeley: University of California Press.

Winter, Katy. 2013. "Why Kate and William Won't Have a Royal Nanny Waiting for Them When They Take Baby Cambridge Home from Hospital." *Daily Mail* July 22. Accessed February 26, 2015 (www.dailymail.co.uk/femail/article-2373721/Royal-baby-Why-Kate-Middleton-Prince-William-WONT-Royal-nanny.html).

Winters, Kelley. 2012. "An Update on Gender Diagnoses, as the DSM-5 Goes to Press." GID Reform Weblog, December 5. Accessed June 5, 2013 (http://gidreform.wordpress.com/2012/12/05/an-update-on-gender-diagnoses-as-the-dsm-5-goes-to-press/).

Wirth, Louis. 1931. "Clinical Sociology." *American Journal of Sociology* 37 (July): 49–60.

Wolf, Naomi. 1992. *The Beauty Myth: How Images of Beauty Are Used Against Women.* New York: Anchor.

Woolley, Benjamin. 2007. *Savage Kingdom: Virginia and the Founding of English America.* New York: HarperPress.

Word, David L., Charles D. Coleman, Robert Nunziator, and Robert Kominski. 2007. "Demographic Aspects of Surnames from Census 2000." Accessed January 2, 2008 (www.census.gov/genealogy/www/surnames.pdf).

World Bank. 2003. *World Development Report 2003: Sustainable Development in a Dynamic World.* Washington, DC: World Bank.

———. 2006. "India, Inclusive Growth and Service Delivery: Building on India's Success." Development Policy Review, Report No. 34580-IN. Accessed June 13, 2009 (http://siteresources.worldbank.org/SOUTHASIAEXT/Resources/DPR_FullReport.pdf).

————. 2010a. "Health Expenditure, Public (% of Total Health Expenditure): 2007." *World Development Indicators.* Accessed April 25, 2010 (http://data.worldbank.org/indicator/SH.XPD.PUBL).

————. 2013e. "Income Share Held by Highest 20%." *World Development Indicators.* Accessed May 18, 2012 (http://data.worldbank.org/indicator/SI.DST.05TH.20).

————. 2015a. "GNI per Capita, Atlas Method (Current US$)." *World Development Indicators.* Accessed April 11, 2015 (http://data.worldbank.org/indicator/NY.GNP.PCAP.CD).

————. 2015b. "GDP (Current US$)." *World Development Indicators.* Accessed April 11, 2015 (http://data.worldbank.org/indicator/NY.GDP.MKTP.CD).

————. 2015c. "Income Share Held by Highest 20%." *World Development Indicators.* Accessed April 13, 2015 (http://data.worldbank.org/indicator/SI.DST.05TH.20).

————. 2015d. "Income Share Held by Lowest 20%." *World Development Indicators.* Accessed April 13, 2015 (http://data.worldbank.org/indicator/SI.DST.FRST.20).

————.2015e. "Share of Women Employed in the Nonagricultural Sector (% of Total Nonagricultural Employment)." *World Development Indicators.* Accessed April 13, 2015 (http://data.worldbank.org/indicator/SL.EMP.INSV.FE.ZS).

————. 2015f. "Mortality Rate, Infant (per 1,000 Live Births)." *World Development Indicators.* Accessed April 15, 2015 (http://data.worldbank.org/indicator/SP.DYN.IMRT.IN).

————. 2015g. "Labor Force, Female (% of Total Labor Force)." *World Development Indicators.* Accessed April 15, 2015 (http://data.worldbank.org/indicator/SL.TLF.TOTL.FE.ZS).

————.2015h. "Bilateral Remittance Matrix, 2014." Migration & Remittances Data. Accessed April 16, 2015 (http://econ.worldbank.org/WBSITE/EXTERNAL/EXTDEC/EXTDECPROSPECTS/0,,contentMDK:22759429~pagePK:64165401~piPK:64165026~theSitePK:476883,00.html).

————. 2015i. "Birth Rate, Crude (per 1,000 People)." *World Development Indicators,* Databank. Accessed April 30, 2015 (http://data.worldbank.org/indicator/SP.DYN.CBRT.IN).

————.2015j. "Fertility Rate, Total (Births per Woman)." *World Development Indicators,* Databank. Accessed April 30, 2015 (http://data.worldbank.org/indicator/SP.DYN.TFRT.IN).

————. 2015k. "Death Rate, Crude (per 1,000 People)." *World Development Indicators,* Databank. Accessed April 30, 2015 (http://data.worldbank.org/indicator/SP.DYN.CDRT.IN).

————. 2015l. "Life Expectancy at Birth, Total (Years)." *World Development Indicators,* Databank. Accessed April 30, 2015 (http://data.worldbank.org/indicator/SP.DYN.LE00.IN).

————. 2015m. "CO_2 Emissions (Metric Tons per Capita)." *World Development Indicators,* Databank. Accessed May 3, 2015 (http://data.worldbank.org/indicator/EN.ATM.CO2E.PC).

World Health Organization. 1948. "Preamble to the Constitution of the World Health Organization." Adopted by the International Health Conference, New York, June 19–July 22, 1946; entered into force on April 7, 1948. Accessed June 30, 2011 (http://whqlibdoc.who.int/hist/official_records/constitution.pdf).

————. 2005. *WHO Global Atlas of Traditional, Complementary, and Alternative Medicine.* Geneva: WHO Press.

————. 2008a. "Traditional Medicine." Fact Sheet No. 134, December. Accessed May 21, 2010 (www.who.int/mediacentre/factsheets/fs134/en/print.html).

————. 2013b. *Global and Regional Estimates of Violence Against Women: Prevalence and Health Effects of Intimate Partner Violence and Non-Partner Sexual Violence.* Geneva: World Health Organization. Accessed April 21, 2015 (http://apps.who.int/iris/bitstream/10665/85239/1/9789241564625_eng.pdf).

————. 2014a. *World Health Statistics, 2014.* Geneva: WHO Press. Accessed April 30, 2015 (www.who.int/gho/publications/world_health_statistics/2014/en/).

————. 2014b. "Ambient (Outdoor) Air Quality and Health." Media Centre, Fact Sheet No. 313, March. Accessed May 3, 2015 (www.who.int/mediacentre/factsheets/fs313/en/).

————.2014c. "Water." Media Centre, Fact Sheet No. 391, March. Accessed May 3, 2015 (www.who.int/mediacentre/factsheets/fs391/en/).

————. 2014d. "Sanitation." Media Centre, Fact Sheet No. 392, March. Accessed May 3, 2015 (www.who.int/mediacentre/factsheets/fs392/en/).

World Meterological Organization. 2014. "WMO Statement on the Status of the Global Climate in 2013." WMO-No. 1130, Geneva, Switzerland. Accessed May 2, 2015 (http://library.wmo.int/opac/index.php?lvl=notice_display&id=15957#.VUVEHJPLvjZ).

World Values Survey. 2015. "World Values Survey Wave 6: 2010-2014." Online Data Analysis Tool. Accessed March 10, 2015 (www.worldvaluessurvey.org/WVSOnline.jsp).

Wyatt, Edward. 2012. "Use of 'Conflict Minerals' Gets More Scrutiny from U.S." *The New York Times,* March 19. Accessed May 18, 2012 (www.nytimes.com/2012/03/20/business/use-of-conflict-minerals-gets-more-scrutiny.html).

Y

Yinger, J. Milton. 1970. *The Scientific Study of Religion.* New York: Macmillan.

Yogyakartaprinciples.org. 2007. *The Yogyakarta Principles: Principles on the Application of International Human Rights Law in Relation to Sexual Orientation and Gender Identity.* Accessed May 11, 2010 (www.yogyakartaprinciples.org/principles_en.pdf).

Young, Michael. 2001. "Down with Meritocracy." *The Guardian,* June 28. Accessed March 29, 2015 (www.theguardian.com/politics/2001/jun/29/comment).

Z

Zarembo, Alan. 2004. "A Theater of Inquiry and Evil." *Los Angeles Times,* July 15, pp. A1, A24, A25.

Zeitzen, Miriam Koktvedgaard. 2008. *Polygamy: A Cross-Cultural Perspective.* New York: Berg.

Zernike, Kate. 2011. "Fast-Tracking to Kindergarten?" *The New York Times,* May 13. Accessed June 2, 2013 (www.nytimes.com/2011/05/15/fashion/with-kumon-fast-tracking-to-kindergarten.html).

Zetter, Kim. 2009. "FBI Use of Patriot Act Authority Increased Dramatically in 2008." *Wired,* May 19. Accessed June 30, 2009 (www.wired.com/threatlevel/2009/05/fbi-use-of-patriot-act-authority-increased-dramatically-in-2008).

Zimbardo, Philip G. 2007. *The Lucifer Effect: Understanding How Good People Turn Evil.* New York: Random House.

Zimmerman, Amber Lynn, M. Joan McDermott, and Christina M. Gould. 2009. "The Local Is Global: Third Wave Feminism, Peace, and Social Justice." *Contemporary Justice Review* 12 (1): 77–90.

Zola, Irving K. 1972. "Medicine as an Institution of Social Control." *Sociological Review* 20 (November): 487–504.

————. 1983. *Socio-Medical Inquiries.* Philadelphia: Temple University Press.

Zuckerman, Ezra W., and John T. Jost. 2001. "What Makes You Think You're So Popular?: Self Evaluation Maintenance and the Subjective Side of the 'Freindship Paradox.'" *Social Psychology Quarterly* 64: 201–223.

Zweigenhaft, Richard L., and G. William Domhoff. 2006. *Diversity in the Power Elite: How It Happened, Why It Matters,* 2nd ed. New York: Rowman & Littlefield.